EVERYONE HA[D] TO SAY ABOUT LUCILLE B[ALL] & AND DESI ARNAZ

HERE'S HOW THEY WERE "REVIEWED"
BY SOME OF THEIR CONTEMPORARIES,
AND HOW THEY VIEWED THEMSELVES.

"Lucille Ball and Desi Arnaz were known around the world as Lucy and Ricky Ricardo. The public confused these two television characters as a real-life couple. I had a filing with Lucille myself in the late 1930s, and I think she wanted to marry me."

"I knew Arnaz very well, too. Let me tell you, those two had a tempestuous marriage from Day One. Lucille accused Desi of cheating, but she did, too, although she denied everything. During the eight-year run of I Love Lucy, it was hell. Often, they were not speaking to each other except on camera."

—Milton Berle

"Lucille Ball looked like a two-dollar whore who had been badly beaten up by her pimp. She had a black eye, her hair was hanging down in her face, and her skin-tight dress was coming apart at the seams."

—Desi Arnaz, *remembering his first glimpse of Lucille.*
She was dressed for her role in Dance, Girl, Dance

"Lucille wasn't the kind of girl you could take home to meet mother."

—Monroe Greenthal, *publicist*

"When Lucille broke off our engagement, I tried to get my diamond ring back. She refused to give it to me. I gave her a black eye."

—Broderick Crawford

"Love! I was always falling in love."

—Lucille Ball

"Desi Arnaz was a lech! Anything female from thirteen to thirty, he'd go after."

—Actor Roger C. Carmel

"Desi didn't know the difference between sex and love. To put it bluntly, love was a good fuck. Desi could get that anywhere—and did."

—Fred Ball

"The world was my oyster. What I wanted, I had only to ask for it."

—Desi Arnaz

"I don't take out other broads. I take out hookers."

—Desi Arnaz

"Your wife is your wife. Your fooling around can in no way affect your love for her. Your marriage is sacred, and a few peccadilloes mean nothing."

—Desi Arnaz

"I brought laughter to millions. But privately, I cried a lot."

—Lucille Ball

"Desi once told me that he would always love Lucy—but Lucille Ball was another thing."

—William Frawley

"Lucille was not the type of gal to throw herself at a man. But if a guy put the make on her, and he was good-looking enough, chances are he had a damn good chance of getting somewhere."

—Kay Vaughn, a friend

"I hate failure and that divorce from Desi Arnaz was the number one failure in my life. My divorce from him was the worst period of my life. Desi or I have never been the same since, mentally or physically."

—Lucille Ball

"My mother and father had one of those historical marriages, like Napoléon and Josephine, Richard Burton and Elizabeth Taylor—destined to be trouble but destined for them to never find anyone as passionate or fabulous."

—Lucie Arnaz

"We had our daughter, our son, and two people could not have been in love or happier than we were. Then the shit hit the fan."

—Desi Arnaz

"In addition to Desi Arnaz, I got to suck off some of the most beautiful men of my era—Tyrone Power, John Payne, George Montgomery, Scott Brady, and Gary Cooper. Do I have regrets? I sure do. I didn't get to make it with Lex Barker, Johnny Weissmuller, Sterling Hayden, Steve Cochran, John Derek, Errol Flynn, and Robert Taylor."

—Cesar Romero

"I guess I'll have to learn to love the bitch."

—Vivian Vance on Lucille Ball

"Desi was like Dr. Jekyll and Mr. Hyde. He drank and gambled, and he went out with other women….and in a few cases men as well in his early days trying to break into show biz. It was always the same—booze, broads, and Cesar Romero. Desi's nature is destructive. When he builds something, the bigger he builds it, the more he wants to tear it down. That's the scenario of his life."

—Lucille Ball

"George Sanders is a polished seducer. Desi has more passion, but George has more boudoir flair. He knows how to flatter a woman and make her feel she is the Czarina of Russia. Too bad he's married to that ghastly Hungarian bombshell, Zsa Zsa Gabor."

—Lucille Ball

"I spent hot nights evoking Old Havana with the uncut salami of Desi Arnaz. He told me that since he had a redhead at home, he preferred well-stacked blondes when he committed adultery. The first time he took me out on a date at the racetrack at Del Mar, he told me he had something in common with a race horse. Even a blonde bimbo could figure that one out."

—Liz Renay, Hollywood's leading
"Star Fucker"

"When I appeared on her Lucy *show, I came to loathe Ball. Tonight, as I write this, I merely pity her. After that episode I did with her, I made a vow never to see her again. She can thank her lucky stars that I wasn't drinking back then. I might have killed her."*

—Richard Burton

"I loathed William Frawley, and the feeling was mutual. Whenever I received a new script, I raced through it, praying that there wouldn't be a scene where we had to be in bed together."

—Vivian Vance

"Vivian Vance is one of the finest gals to come out of Kansas. But I often wish she'd go back there."

—William Frawley

"After appearing on that stupid Lucy *show, I decided that Ball is a bigger bitch than me."*

—Joan Crawford

"The secret of staying young is to live honestly, eat slowly, and lie about your age."

—Lucille Ball

"Desi was a boozer, a philanderer, and a gambler who lost most of his millions. Technically, their marriage lasted two decades. Maybe five years of that were spent away from each other. I thought he was a dirty little Spic, not worthy of my daughter. She should have married William Holden."

—DeDe Ball

"I am a real ham. I love an audience. I work better with an audience. I am dead, in fact, without one."

—Lucille Ball

"How I Love Lucy *was born: We decided that instead of divorce lawyers profiting from our mistakes, we'd profit from them."*

—Lucille Ball

"I'm sometimes scared of everything that has happened to us. We didn't think that Desilu Productions would grow so big. We merely wanted to be together and have two children."

—Lucille Ball

"I will never do another TV series. I couldn't top I Love Lucy, and I'd be foolish to try. In this business, you have to know when to get off."

—Lucille Ball

"Women's Lib? Oh I'm afraid it doesn't interest me one bit. I've been so liberated it hurts."

—Lucille Ball

WHAT IS BLOOD MOON PRODUCTIONS?

"Blood Moon, in case you don't know, is a small publishing house on Staten Island that cranks out Hollywood gossip books, about two or three a year, usually of five-, six-, or 700-page length, chocked with stories and pictures about people who used to consume the imaginations of the American public, back when we actually had a public imagination. That is, when people were really interested in each other, rather than in Apple 'devices.' In other words, back when we had vices, not devices."

—The Huffington Post

Lucille Ball & Desi Arnaz
They Weren't Lucy and Ricky Ricardo

Volume One (1911-1960)
of a Two-Part Biography

by Darwin Porter and Danforth Prince

LUCILLE BALL AND DESI ARNAZ
THEY WEREN'T LUCY AND RICKY RICARDO
VOLUME ONE (1911-1960)
OF A TWO-PART BIOGRAPHY

by Darwin Porter and Danforth Prince

www.BloodMoonProductions.com

ISBN 978-1-936003-71-6

Covers and Book Design by Danforth Prince

Distributed Worldwide through Ingram,
Amazon.com, and online vendors everywhere.

Blood Moon Productions
Proudly Defines This Book as
Volume Six of its
Magnolia House Series

CONTENTS

PREVIOUS WORKS BY DARWIN PORTER
PRODUCED IN COLLABORATION WITH BLOOD MOON

BIOGRAPHIES FROM BLOOD MOON'S
MAGNOLIA HOUSE SERIES

Marilyn: Don't Even Dream About Tomorrow
(a 2021 revised version of the best-selling
Marilyn at Rainbow's End: Sex, Lies, Murder, &
the Great Cover-Up (2012)

The Seductive Sapphic Exploits of Mercedes de Acosta
Hollywood's Greatest Lover

Judy Garland & Liza Minnelli, Too Many Damn Rainbows

Historic Magnolia House: Celebrity & The Ironies of Fame

Glamour, Glitz, & Gossip at Historic Magnolia House

***

BIOGRAPHIES FROM BLOOD MOON
NOT ASSOCIATED WITH ITS MAGNOLIA HOUSE SERIES

Burt Reynolds, Put the Pedal to the Metal

Kirk Douglas, More Is Never Enough

Playboy's Hugh Hefner, Empire of Skin

Carrie Fisher & Debbie Reynolds,
Princess Leia & Unsinkable Tammy in Hell

Rock Hudson Erotic Fire

Lana Turner, Hearts & Diamonds Take All

Donald Trump, The Man Who Would Be King

James Dean, Tomorrow Never Comes

Bill and Hillary, *So This Is That Thing Called Love*

Peter O'Toole, *Hellraiser, Sexual Outlaw, Irish Rebel*

Love Triangle, *Ronald Reagan, Jane Wyman, & Nancy Davis*

Jacqueline Kennedy Onassis, *A Life Beyond Her Wildest Dreams*

Pink Triangle, *The Feuds and Private Lives of Tennessee Williams, Gore Vidal, Truman Capote, and Famous Members of their Entourages.*

Those Glamorous Gabors, *Bombshells from Budapest*

Inside Linda Lovelace's Deep Throat,
Degradation, Porno Chic, and the Rise of Feminism

Elizabeth Taylor, *There is Nothing Like a Dame*

J. Edgar Hoover and Clyde Tolson
Investigating the Sexual Secrets of America's Most Famous Men and Women

Frank Sinatra, *The Boudoir Singer. All the Gossip Unfit to Print*

The Kennedys, *All the Gossip Unfit to Print*

The Secret Life of Humphrey Bogart *(2003), and*
Humphrey Bogart, The Making of a Legend *(2010)*

Howard Hughes, *Hell's Angel*

Steve McQueen, *King of Cool, Tales of a Lurid Life*

Paul Newman, *The Man Behind the Baby Blues*

Merv Griffin, *A Life in the Closet*

Brando Unzipped

Katharine the Great, Hepburn, *Secrets of a Lifetime Revealed*

Jacko, His Rise and Fall, *The Social and Sexual History of Michael Jackson*

Damn You, Scarlett O'Hara,
The Private Lives of Vivien Leigh and Laurence Olivier

FILM CRITICISM
Blood Moon's 2005 Guide to the Glitter Awards
Blood Moon's 2006 Guide to Film
Blood Moon's 2007 Guide to Film, and
50 Years of Queer Cinema, 500 of the Best GLBTQ Films Ever Made

NON-FICTION
Hollywood Babylon, It's Back! and Hollywood Babylon Strikes Again!

NOVELS

Blood Moon,
Hollywood's Silent Closet,
Rhinestone Country,
Razzle Dazzle
Midnight in Savannah

OTHER PUBLICATIONS BY DARWIN PORTER
NOT DIRECTLY ASSOCIATED WITH BLOOD MOON

NOVELS

The Delinquent Heart
The Taste of Steak Tartare
Butterflies in Heat
Marika (a roman à clef based on the life of Marlene Dietrich)
Venus (a roman à clef based on the life of Anaïs Nin)
Sister Rose

TRAVEL GUIDES
Many Editions and Many Variations of The Frommer Guides,
The American Express Guides, and/or TWA Guides, et alia to:

Andalusia, Andorra, Anguilla, Aruba, Atlanta, Austria, the Azores, The
Bahamas, Barbados, the Bavarian Alps, Berlin, Bermuda, Bonaire and
Curaçao, Boston, the British Virgin Islands, Budapest, Bulgaria, California,
the Canary Islands, the Caribbean and its "Ports of Call," the Cayman Islands, Ceuta, the Channel Islands (UK), Charleston (SC), Corsica, Costa
del Sol (Spain), Denmark, Dominica, the Dominican Republic, Edinburgh,

England, Estonia, Europe, "Europe by Rail," the Faroe Islands, Finland, Florence, France, Frankfurt, the French Riviera, Geneva, Georgia (USA), Germany, Gibraltar, Glasgow, Granada (Spain), Great Britain, Greenland, Grenada (West Indies), Haiti, Hungary, Iceland, Ireland, Isle of Man, Italy, Jamaica, Key West & the Florida Keys, Las Vegas, Liechtenstein, Lisbon, London, Los Angeles, Madrid, Maine, Malta, Martinique & Guadeloupe, Massachusetts, Melilla, Morocco, Munich, New England, New Orleans, North Carolina, Norway, Paris, Poland, Portugal, Provence, Puerto Rico, Romania, Rome, Salzburg, San Diego, San Francisco, San Marino, Sardinia, Savannah, Scandinavia, Scotland, Seville, the Shetland Islands, Sicily, St. Martin & Sint Maarten, St. Vincent & the Grenadines, South Carolina, Spain, St. Kitts & Nevis, Sweden, Switzerland, the Turks & Caicos, the U.S.A., the U.S. Virgin Islands, Venice, Vienna and the Danube, Wales, and Zurich.

BIOGRAPHIES

From Diaghilev to Balanchine, The Saga of Ballerina Tamara Geva

Greta Keller, Germany's Other Lili Marlene

Sophie Tucker, The Last of the Red Hot Mamas

Anne Bancroft, Where Have You Gone, Mrs. Robinson? (co-authored with Stanley Mills Haggart)

Veronica Lake, The Peek-a-Boo Girl

Running Wild in Babylon, Confessions of a Hollywood Press Agent

HISTORIES

Thurlow Weed, Whig Kingpin

Chester A. Arthur, Gilded Age Coxcomb in the White House

Discover Old America, What's Left of It

CUISINE

Food For Love, Hussar Recipes from the Austro-Hungarian Empire, with collaboration from the cabaret chanteuse, Greta Keller

This Book Is Dedicated to:

BARBARA PEPPER
For her commentaries on, and loyalty to, Lucille Ball

and to

STANLEY MILLS HAGGART
For his memories of RKO in the 1930s

and to

THE FRIENDS AND FRENEMIES OF
LUCILLE BALL & DESI ARNAZ

OTHER INTRIGUING TITLES FROM BLOOD MOON PRODUCTIONS

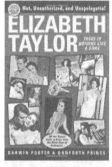

YOUNG AND STAR STRUCK:

HOW I MET LUCILLE BALL & DESI ARNAZ

By Darwin Porter

My research into the lives of Lucille Ball and Desi Arnaz began in the late 1950s, one "otherwise uneventful" weekday during one of their entertainment gigs in Miami Beach.

Their TV series, *I Love Lucy,* had morphed them into two of the most massively famous show biz personalities on the planet. In episode after episode, they had immortalized the names and personalities of Lucy and Ricky Ricardo.

At the time, I was the president of the student body, and also the editor-in-chief of *The Miami Hurricane,* the newspaper at the University of Miami at Coral Gables.

Although fully aware that their schedule might be overbooked, I called their publicist and invited them to a day of recognition and celebration at the University. Frankly, I never expected to hear from him again, but two hours later, he called with news that they had accepted my invitation.

Working hysterically, I set up an itinerary for *Lucy & Desi's Day at the University of Miami,* an event calibrated to welcome them, celebrate them, and entertain them.

As had been agreed with their publicist, I met them in their hotel suite at 8AM. From there, a limousine, scheduled for 9AM, would haul us over to the University's auditorium.

I arrived on time, just as a room service waiter was delivering morning coffee. The stars weren't ready to receive me, but Desi summoned me inside, anyway. Sitting on the sofa in his jockey shorts, he looked haggard from the night before.

He chatted with me about the day's events. Minutes later, Lucille came in. She wore a pink slip with no makeup, looking ten years older, maybe more, than she did on television. Her hair was a tangled mess.

She smiled at me but glared at Desi. I realized that I had entered their suite at an inappropriate moment, and suspected that I had interrupted a serious argument. Then she said to me, testily, "I hope you've made all the arrangements, because I'm in no mood to put up with any shit,"

"Everything's been set up for your visit, and your fans are very excited," I said. "You two are such great performers."

"Yeah, just great!" she snarled sarcastically. Then she whirled around, as she started to cough and headed back into her bedroom to put on her makeup and an orange wig.

From different rooms, their argument resumed. She shouted denunciations at him, at one point calling him a "Spic." She accused him of having sex with two prostitutes the night before.

He didn't deny that, but claimed, "It doesn't mean a thing, my fooling around with some hookers. Peccadilloes don't count. In no way does it threaten my love for you."

Then, in a private aside to me, he said, "All Cuban men play around, including my father, who had a different household and even kids with his mistress, a mile or so down the road from our home in Santiago."

That brought another tirade of denunciations from the bedroom.

En route to Coral Gables in the limousine, the heat in the back seat breached the temperatures of the Sahara Desert. Perhaps irritated by the heat, Desi fought back.

"When I met you, you were an RKO whore, your number passed around from man to man."

"You're one to talk," she shot back. "Fucking Betty Grable, Ginger Rogers, and every *puta* in every bordello in L.A."

I sat between them in the back seat as they seemed to become more agitated. Every time Lucille coughed, she grabbed hold of me and shared it with me. I feared that she should have been in a sick bed that day. Later, I joked to my friends, "I have a new way of describing a star: She's the one who shares her cough with you, right in your face."

After Desi and Lucille arrived on campus, they seemed to bury their fight and emerged from the limo to greet some 300 fans. Acting like well-behaved love birds, they seemed to have instantly transformed themselves into Lucy and Ricky Ricardo.

Wherever they went on campus that fan-worshipping day, they were greeted with love and enthusiasm, looking like the most devoted wife and husband in human history. But in moments when we were alone, they reverted to the battling Arnazes.

That afternoon's luncheon in the University's cafeteria went off splendidly. They each gave speeches that were followed by a special band concert and a one-act comedy, hastily produced by the drama department.

By five o'clock, with the understanding that they'd scheduled a joint appearance for that night on Miami Beach, it was time to leave.

En route back to their hotel, Desi, too, had begun to cough. Lucille was matching him cough for cough, and she generously continued to share her germs in my face.

In the lobby of their hotel, each of them kissed me goodbye, Lucille with dry lips and Desi with sloppy wet ones.

The next morning, I woke up coughing and ill with what I defined as "The Lucy Virus."

And thus, I began what might be called my decades-long research into the turbulent lives of Lucille Ball and Desi Arnaz.

Months later, news of their divorce hit the newspapers, magazines, radio, and television. Millions of their fans were shocked. I was not.

In future years, I encountered them in locales ranging from backstage at the Roxy in Manhattan to the Cocoanut Grove in Los Angeles.

Once, with novelist James Kirkwood (author of the musical *A Chorus Line*), I visited Lucille's home in Beverly Hills. She had set up a meeting with Kirkwood in reference to a film adaptation of his latest novel, *There Must Be a Pony*.

She wanted to play its female lead, that of a once-celebrated Hollywood star attempting a comeback after a stay in a mental hospital. Lucille's association with the film fell through; the role she wanted was assigned to Elizabeth Taylor; and the film adaptation of Kirkwood's novel was eventually released in 1986.

In time, as all of us slid into other crises and other dreams, Desi and Lucille faded from my life, only to be revived within the pages of this biography (Volume One) and its upcoming sequel, Volume Two.

I refer to both of them as "Memory Books," filled with my own observations and the candid opinions of dozens of other people who worked and played with them; made love to them; feuded with them…whatever.

To most of them, Lucille and Desi were flawed but fascinating— truly great American stars.

YESTERDAY, WHEN HE WAS YOUNG

DARWIN PORTER

A social historian fascinated by biographies and the ironies of the American Experience.

CHAPTER ONE

THE JAMESTOWN HUSSY

Millions of fans devoted to the *I Love Lucy* television series believed that its star, Lucille Ball, had been born Lucille McGillicuddy. But that was just the fictional maiden name of the character she played. Likewise, Ricky Ricardo, a Cuban bandleader, was the fictional name of her actual husband, Desi Arnaz, a real bandleader.

She had been born Lucille Desirée Ball on August 6, 1911, in Jamestown, in western New York State, some seventy miles south of the better-known city of Buffalo.

Once known as "the furniture capital of the world," Jamestown lies between Lake Erie to the northwest and the Allegheny National Forest to the south. Fishermen, boaters, and naturalists are attracted to nearby Lake Chautauqua, a small body of water named after the now extinct Erie language once spoken by the Iroquois tribe.

Lake Chautauqua, decades later, was mentioned in an episode of *I Love Lucy*. In the Ricardo attic, she finds a stuffed and mounted fish in a trunk, recalling that Ricky caught it on Jamestown's nearby lake.

***

By the time of Lucille's death at the age of seventy-seven in 1989, the world had changed remarkably from what it was when she entered it in 1911.

Back then, on January 14, 1911, Roald Amundsen's South Pole expedition made landfall. In Washington, work began on the Lincoln Memorial. The Mexican Revolution began, as Pancho

On the left, **Lucille**, at age three, is pictured at the time of her father's untimely death.

On the right, little **Lucille**, with a big ribbon in her hair, sometimes felt her Teddy Bear was her only true friend.

Villa's troops battled the armies of the dictator, Porfirio Díaz. The very first Indianapolis 500 car race was held. In Belfast, the hull of the ill-fated *Titanic* was launched.

In London, George V was crowned king. On August 21, Da Vinci's *Mona Lisa* was stolen from the Louvre. On September 29, Italy declared war on the Ottoman Empire. In Detroit, the first Chevrolet was manufactured to challenge Henry Ford's monopoly.

Many sources still identify Lucille's birthplace as Butte, Montana. Actually, she did live there as a little girl with her parents, and when she broke into show business, she called herself "Montana Ball," thinking that was a more glamourous background that a dull industrial town in western New York.

As time moved on, Lucille Ball became the most famous redhead on the planet. But that was not her natural color. As a very young child, her hair was blondish, later turning chestnut. She would become known for her facial features of blue eyes and a mouth with what was referred to as "Cupid lips."

Lucille's mother, Desirée Evelyn Hunt (1892-1977), had both French and English ancestors, and, in Lucille's words, "a touch of Irish from her father's side that showed up in her porcelain complexion and auburn hair."

As a teenager, DeDe (her nickname) dreamed of becoming a concert pianist. But she abandoned that goal when, at the age of seventeen, she met and later married Henry Dunnell Ball, a telephone lineman who was twenty-four.

Henry had descended from landed gentry in Hertfordshire, England. Many members of the Ball family arrived in America during the late 17th Century. There was even some Ball blood in Mary Ball, the mother of George Washington.

Nicknamed "Had," young Henry was slim and tall, with piercing blue eyes. His

Henry ("Had") Ball, circa 1910. As a little girl, Lucille adored her father, a telephone line man. He caught the grippe in a Detroit sleet storm and died.

DeDe Hunt, Lucille's mother, circa 1907. She was five months pregnant when her husband died. She later gave birth to Lucille's younger brother, Fred.

face was once described as "almost like a Plains Indian's, with a stoic expression that seemed ready to accept life's difficulties."

After Henry married Desirée, he took her west to Butte, Montana, which had been established in the closing months of the Civil War as a mining camp. It was known as one of the largest copper boomtowns in the American West.

As a telephone lineman, Henry was soon transferred to Anaconda, also in Montana, lying at the foot of the Anaconda Range. The Continental Divide lay about eight miles south of the bustling little community. Most of its men worked in a "smelter," processing copper extracted from the mines at Butte. Henry supervised a crew of men bringing phone service to the fast-growing town.

He and DeDe dreaded when winter came as temperatures sometimes dropped to 40° below zero, and the little community was struck by blizzards. Working conditions were rough, and when DeDe told her husband goodbye every morning, she feared he might be electrocuted as some linemen had been before.

Many other local men were employed by the Anaconda Copper Company, with its smoke-belching chimneys. In contrast, summers were scalding hot.

Tiring of Montana's brutal weather, the couple, with Baby Lucille in tow, moved to Wyandotte, Michigan, where Henry was employed again as a telephone lineman, this time for the Michigan Bell Company. That small city lies eleven miles south of Detroit. From the 1920s to the Eisenhower era, Wyandotte was the largest manufacturing site for toy guns and pistols in America, a dubious claim at best.

In this small, industrial town, with its steel factory and blast furnace, Henry rented a small apartment, for a monthly fee of $10, for his wife and daughter. The Detroit River ran through the town. For open-air summer pleasures, the residents headed for Lake Erie.

Tragedy came early in Lucille's life before she was four years old. The Balls were celebrating Christmas of 1914 when DeDe announced that she was pregnant again. When Lucille and her parents opened their presents around a Christmas tree, it was their last happy occasion together.

By February of the following year, Henry took to bed, complaining of an oncoming cold, perhaps the flu. But when a severe storm swept across Wyandotte and the phone lines blew down, he rose from his sick bed to help his men repair them.

Under hazardous conditions, he worked all day in the brutal cold, returning home that night with a temperature of 104°F.

In the next two days, he developed typhoid fever, which in those days was not curable. He soon drifted into death, a devastating blow to DeDe and a shock to his infant daughter. Because she was so young, Lucille retained only vague memories of her father, mainly about how he used to toss her into the air, rescuing her right before she hit the floor.

Henry died on February 28, 1915, and his pinewood coffin was shipped back to Jamestown in a railway boxcar for burial.

Accompanying the coffin was DeDe with Lucille, who soon appeared there on the doorstep of DeDe's parents, Fred and Flora Belle Hunt.

Known as a "jack of all trades," Grandpa Fred was the town character, who sometimes invited his neighbors to dig up carrots, beets, and potatoes from the garden behind his house. He was remembered with a pipe in his mouth, smoking Prince Albert tobacco. In cooler weather, he wore a weather-beaten cardigan with buttons missing.

He drifted from job to job, including one as a mail carrier. Once hired in a factory, he became a labor agitator, urging his fellow employees to go on strike for higher pay and better working conditions. An ardent socialist, he later joined the Communist Party. In the 1930s, he got Lucille to sign up as a member of the Communist Party too.

Lucille's maternal grandmother was Flora Belle Hunt. As an adolescent, she had worked as a maid in a hotel. She was also a midwife, like her mother had been. When she wasn't "birthing babies," she worked as a practical nurse. Orphaned at the age of thirteen, she'd had a rough life, working to support her siblings, who included five sets of twins.

She struggled to put food on her family's table, telling Lucille, "Night after night I had to put more water into the soup. I went to the local butcher and begged him for bones to feed my dog. In reality, I needed the bones to flavor the soup."

As Lucille remembered her grandmother, "She was a dreamer and a planner. No task was too much for her, no hours too long, no time better spent than doing things for her family."

When DeDe arrived with Lucille at the home of the Hunts, she was pregnant. By July 17, 1915, she gave birth to a baby boy named Fred Henry Ball, nicknamed Freddy. Lucille came to love her brother, but in the early stages of her life, she was very jealous of him for taking all the attention away from her.

As a toddler, she was a very mischievous girl. "If trouble lurked somewhere, my daughter would find it," DeDe said. Although Lucille was allowed to play in the backyard by herself, DeDe hooked her up to a dog leash tied to the line so she wouldn't run off. Once, she climbed a nearby tree and got tangled in its branches until a mailman rescued her. She then ran off and was rounded up hours later by the police and hauled back to the Hunt house in a van.

Grandpa Hunt became a surrogate father to Lucille. Every evening when he came home from work, she rushed out to greet this fat, balding, kindly figure. He always wore clothing too small for his

This is Lucille' maternal grandfather, **Fred Hunt** (1865-1944) with his wife, **Flora Belle**.

Lucille called him, "cunning, cute, and cocky." Flora Belle was known as the best midwife in Jamestown.

4

corpulent body, and he had a gold watch chain stretched across his ample waistline.

***

DeDe went three years before she found another husband. She showed up one afternoon in Jamestown with her new man, Edward Peterson, a big, strapping, thirty-five-year Swede. At first, Lucille called him Daddy, but he quickly corrected her: "My name is Ed—call me that."

His parents had emigrated to America from their native Sweden. Lucille remembered him as "big, blonde, and ugly-handsome. He was devoted to the bottle, and I don't recall a night when he wasn't drunk."

In pursuit of higher-paying jobs in Detroit, DeDe and Ed left their children, Freddie staying with the Hunt family, and Lucille was delivered to the home of Ed's parents, the stern-faced, puritanical Petersons.

As she recalled, her time in the Peterson home, "was the most miserable time of my life. They were unforgiving, and any little thing I did was viewed as a transgression. They saved on their food bill because night after night I was sent to my room without supper as my punishment."

"They were deeply religious and viewed the simplest pleasure as the work of the devil. They were always talking about fire and brimstone. I was so unhappy."

"Often sent to bed hungry, I would sit by my window looking out at kids playing in a neighbor's yard and wanting to join them. I cried a lot."

Every day, she was assigned a daunting roster of chores, including dishwashing, kitchen and bathroom scrubbing, and clothes washing. I even learned how to pluck a chicken."

As Lucille remembered it, "Grandmother Peterson was

In 1894, local newspapers heralded the opening of Celoron's waterfront amusement park like this: *"Grand Opening to Take Place of a Playground for Jamestown and All Creation*. It will have all the wonders of electricity and this giant toboggan slide, magic, mirth and soft drinks on tap, and shows every thirty minutes."

Modeled after equivalent parks in Atlantic City and Coney Island, its promoters promised "the liveliest place in Western New York, the greatest amusement part between New York and Chicago, but entirely free from objectionable features, with harmless amusement for all."

Celoron Park, as depicted in this postcard from the Belle Epoque, had declined by the time Lucille strolled here with her then-boyfriend Johnny DaVita during the Depression.

A fire destroyed part of it in 1930, its baseball stadium closed in 1939, its ferris wheel was dismantled in 1952, and by the late 1960s, it was only a shell of its former hopes and dreams. Yet thanks in part to self-promotion, it's indelibly linked to the memory of young Lucille Ball during her formative years.

my first real critic." She mocked Lucille's big feet, small hands, ungainly posture, squeaky voice, and crooked teeth. There was only one mirror in the house, and it was in the bathroom, used only for Grandpa Peterson's shaving. Once, her grandmother caught Lucille studying her face in the mirror and punished her "for being so silly, so vain."

Their hopes dashed in Detroit, DeDe and Ed returned to Jamestown and moved in with her parents, Flora Belle and Fred Hunt, who had bought a new home in the Jamestown suburb of Celoron. It was a modest house, costing only $2,000.

They found Grandpa Hunt making his living as a chiropractor, even though he had had no formal training. Some of his critics called him "a quack doctor."

At the age of eight, Lucille was greatly relieved to be freed from the stern control of the Petersons.

On the western border of Jamestown, fronting the southeastern edge of Lake Chautauqua and named in honor of the 18th-Century French explorer, Pierre-Joseph Céloron de Blainville, the village of Celoron had been incorporated only in 1898, when it became the home of the Acme Giants baseball team. [*Founded by businessman Henry Curtis, it played within the then-thriving Iron and Oil Leagues. The team's initial incarnation was as the Acme Colored Giants, a team consisting solely of black players.*]

After many decades, locals erected a Lucille Ball statue in Celoron's town square.

DeDe's marriage to Ed was not working out. He was drinking more heavily and coming home later and later. She heard that he was having affairs with two sisters who worked in his factory. DeDe filed for divorce, and Ed moved out of their lives.

Lucille's link to **Jamestown** is indelibly "branded" into the town's identity and aggressively promoted by New York State's Tourist Board.

The photos above, showing a "historic landmark' signpost and a large outdoor mural downtown, are only a few of the many references to Lucille prominently positioned throughout the city center.

***

Then the first in a string of tragedies struck: Grandmother Flora Belle came down with cancer. Since there was no cure, it was inevitable that she would die. Lucille tended to her every day as "she just wasted away."

Lucille would forever remember "the cries of agony" from her grandmother during the final stages of her death. Death came as a relief on July 11, 1922. She was fifty-five years old.

With no husband and two children to support, DeDe went to work as a sales clerk in Jamestown's most stylish dress shop.

As a schoolgirl, Lucille showed little interest in her studies. "I flunked algebra five times," she said. Instead of classroom assignments, she began to daydream about being an actress and entertainer. Grandpa Hunt suggested she perform in an Apache dance at a Jamestown Masonic social. Her young dance partner, who was much taller than she was, and heavily muscled, taught her the routine. One the night of the performance, he slung her too far, and she fell into the orchestra pit, dislocating her shoulder. She was in pain for months to come.

Nonetheless, she got her first-ever review in the *Jamestown Post-Journal,* the critic claiming that she was "chock full of talent."

In the summer of 1925, as Lucille turned fourteen, she fell hopelessly in love with the town hood, Johnny DaVita, who was twenty-three years old. DeDe objected strongly to her dating him because he had a bad reputation. He was a gambler and made his living running booze from Canada across the state line into the United States, which was going through a dry spell known as Prohibition.

He was an inch or two shorter than her, but other than that, he was good-looking and very masculine. Local girls labeled him a "walking streak of sex." An Italian, he had dark curly hair, one lock of which dangled over his forehead. He also wore a white T-shirt two sizes too small, which showed off his gym-trained body. His blue jeans were so tight it left little to the imagination.

He looked at Lucille with his penetrating black eyes flecked with gold, and decided, "She's the gal for me." He could have had practically any girl in town, but there was something about Lucille that obviously turned him on.

An avid movie fan, Lucille did not see anyone on the screen who resembled DaVita until she saw John Garfield in the 1940s. "Johnny could be his younger brother." Years later, when she saw John Travolta performing in *Grease,* she said, "He reminds me of Johnny."

John Garfield from the era (the 1940s) when he most reminded Lucille of her former beau, **Johnny DaVita.** Her boyfriend was known as "the town hood."

Although many biographies of Lucille spell Johnny's surname as "De Vita," she always claimed it was "DaVita."

Unknown to Lucille when she started dating him, DaVita was a highly desirable hustler, receiving cash from two of the town's aging widows and three closeted homosexuals in their fifties.

One night, after they had gone out on a few dates, he drove Lucille in his roadster to an out-of-the-way motel a few miles outside Jamestown. There, he took her virginity. As she described to a girlfriend, "He was sweet and gentle, although at the end he used too much force." He would repeat that act on and off with her for years to come.

Actually, she admired him, claiming, "He became a man while he was still a boy."

She was referring to the loss of his father, who had been shot by an unknown assassin. He died instantly and DaVita, with younger brothers and sisters to support, became the breadwinner of his family.

Lucille raised only one objection: "He was too short," which became obvious whenever they danced together at the Celoron Pier Ballroom, often to the music of a midsummer visiting band whose music imitated the style of Harry James.

Johnny also taught her to drive, usually along country roads, even though she didn't have a license. Although he urged her to slow down, she usually stepped on the gas, preferring higher speeds.

Some evenings in summer, DaVita took her on a five-cent streetcar ride to Celoron Park, one of the first amusement parks in America,. Here, they would stroll around eating pink cotton candy on a stick, taking in the sights. They rode the Phoenix Wheel some hundred feet above the earth, and listened to imported bands, none more famous than John Philip Sousa, known at the time as America's most illustrious bandleader. She and DaVita rode a Shetland pony to the entrance of the zoo, where she saw animals she'd only read about in books.

Other attractions included a boardwalk, a roller coaster, shooting galleries, fortune tellers, freak shows featuring a grossly overweight fat lady, and vaudeville performances.

It was here that Lucille became a dedicated movie fan for life, laughing through any Charlie Chaplin or Buster Keaton movie. She also thrilled to every serial of *The Perils of Pauline,* starring Pearl White.

As she told DaVita, she found inspiration in all of these shows, and began plotting how she might become a performer herself. She loved the attention and also liked making people laugh.

Vaudeville, a theatrical genre that had been born in France in the 1890s, fascinated her. Acts were varied: a dancer, a singer, a comedian, an acrobat, a magician, a strong man, a female impersonator, a juggler, and most definitely a clown. Sometimes, one-act plays were presented, often melodramas with a villain attired in a black cape. Minstrel shows were all the rage, with white actors appearing in black face. Vaudeville was eventually killed off by the coming of "the flickers."

With a group of students, Lucille took charge of staging a three-act production of *Charley's Aunt.* First performed in London in 1892, it held the record for years of the longest-running play in the world. Its plot centers around a young man who dresses in drag as a means of being near the woman he loves. Two friends, Jack and Charley, persuade another undergraduate to impersonate the latter's aunt. Complications arise when the real aunt arrives. There's also a comedic attempt by a fortune hunter to woo the bogus aunt, not knowing that he's a man.

"I played the male lead," Lucille said. "Not only that, but I sold tickets, printed the posters, and moved my family's living room furniture to serve as stage props."

"Performing in *Charley's Aunt,* I knew for the first time that wonderful feeling that comes from getting real laughs on a stage," Lucille said. "The play was a big success. Tickets sold for a quarter, and we grossed twenty-five dollars."

She often parted from DaVita whenever she migrated to and from New York City, hoping to find a break on Broadway, even as a chorus girl. Often he drove down to see her, always finding her short of money which he supplied to her. Because of his bad reputation as a local hoodlum, news of her affair with the town stud soon spread across the village. Some of her gossipy critics referred to her as "The Jamestown Hussy."

"My love for Johnny was real, and it haunted me for many years—at least until I came to Hollywood."

***

Tragedy struck the Hunt family in the summer of 1927. Lucille's brother, Freddy, had a birthday coming up, his twelfth, and Grandpa Hunt purchased a gift for him, a .22 rifle loaded with real bullets.

Even before his birthday cake emerged, he was invited into the backyard where tin cans had been arranged in the distance for target practice. A neighborhood girl, Joanna Ottinger, also twelve, attended the party. She wanted to go first in firing at the tin cans.

As she pulled the trigger, the boy next door, Warner Erickson, ran in front of the target and was shot in the back, the bullet lodging in his left lung. He fell to the ground, as everyone in the yard rushed to his side, including his mother from next door. She began to scream hysterically. An ambulance was summoned.

Ten days later, the Hunts received the bad news: Warner had been paralyzed for life and would never walk again. The Erickson family sued, and Grandpa Hunt lost his only asset—his home. He then had to move his family into a crowded apartment within a building at 20 East Fifth Street in Jamestown.

As a teenaged ingenue, **Lucille** dreamed of becoming an actress.

In Manhattan, as a chorus girl, she was fired time and time again and told to go back home, perhaps to work as a soda jerk.

***

9

When Lucille turned seventeen, DeDe gave her daughter permission to study acting in New York City at the John Murray Anderson-Robert Milton School of Drama and Dance. Johnny DaVita drove her to the train station in Buffalo. After a tearful goodbye, she boarded the train that would take her to Grand Central in Manhattan.

Her tuition had cost $350 for five months and had eaten up most of DeDe's savings. For living expenses, Lucille carried fifty dollars sewed into her underwear.

DaVita had promised to drive down to see her within a month, and she hoped he'd bring her some cash from his gin-running from Canada.

DeDe had arranged for her to live with two senior citizens who had a small apartment on Manhattan's Upper West

Lucille enrolled in a class of "Interpretive Dance" taught by a then-struggling choreographer, Martha Graham. She later became "The Mother of Modern Dance."

"Please drop out of my class," Graham told her. "You are hopeless as a dancer."

side. DeDe had once worked for them when they lived in Jamestown. Lucille would have to sleep on the sofa.

The school's star pupil, Bette Davis, was getting all the praise. "I was in awe of how she tackled a role, although personally I found her snobbish and intimidating. After studying at our school, she moved to Hollywood, or so I heard. Who knows what happened to that then-blonde bitch?"

[Lucille was joking, of course. The whole world knew what happened to Bette Davis, who became one of the biggest movie stars in film history.]

One section of the school was devoted to modern dance under the guidance of the avant-garde Martha Graham, who would go on to be called "The Mother of Modern Dance." Lucille attended some of her classes for a few days before Graham asked Lucille to remain behind after the other students left. "Please drop out of my class," Graham asked her. "You are hopeless as a dancer. You're like a quarterback taking up ballet. Perhaps you could find work as a soda jerk."

"So many girls wanted to come to Broadway to be a dancer, and I could immediately tell if one of them had any talent," Graham said. Later, she recalled, "I was deadly accurate in my cruel assessment of Lucille Ball. That girl never could dance."

As Lucille remembered it years later, she was embarrassed and—perhaps in a style she'd later recycle as a slapstick routine in one of her TV episodes—quipped, "I tried that once but got fired because I kept forgetting to put a banana in a banana split."

Before her enrollment, she knew very little about the John Murray Anderson-Robert Milton School of Drama and Dance, having selected it because it had the cheapest tuition. Its brochure claimed that Milton had been born in Russia and had worked in British films before coming to New York, where he wrote and directed plays for the stage. He had also helmed a number of films, including Ferenc Molnár's *The Devil* in 1908 and Richard Bennett's *He Who Gets Slapped* in 1922.

Born in Newfoundland, Milton had studied in Edinburgh and worked in the theatre industry in London. He seemed to know how to do anything: direct, produce, act, write screenplays, dance, and design lighting.

Lucille was publicly coached by Milton on her first day at the school, where he mocked her midwestern accent in front of the class, asking her to pronounce certain words such as "horse" as her classmates giggled. Those put-downs made her more insecure than ever, as she was painfully shy.

When Milton asked her to memorize some pages from a script and perform in front of her classmates, she was terrified, almost tongue-tied. She flubbed her recitation, forgetting her lines. That afternoon, Milton wrote to DeDe back in Jamestown: "Your daughter is wasting our time and your money. She has no talent as an actress...She's far too reticent and timid. In front of an audience, she seems to panic... Your tuition money is not refundable."

Stunned by the rejection, Lucille, during her train ride back to Buffalo, cried for most of the trip across New York State.

Her spirit was enlivened somewhat by Johnny DaVita, who was waiting for her at the railway station in his speedy roadster. Together, they checked into a motel, where they spent the next two nights together, making love time and again. "You got rejected by some queen in New York, but I find you highly desirable."

Then, instead of taking her back to live with her family, he moved her into his apartment in Jamestown. During her time there, she got to know the other young hoodlums in his gang, all of whom seemed engaged in some illegal enterprise. The better-looking ones were male hustlers, catering to older men and women.

Life with DaVita was rough, as he was known for his violent temper, often bursting into rages. She tried hard to please him. When she didn't, she sometimes ended up with a black eye. After a fight, he always brought her a present and then took her to bed to make up. She always forgave him.

Little is known about the details, but Lucille later admitted to friends in Hollywood that DaVita once drove her across the Canadian border for an abortion, thereby avoiding her evolution into a pregnant and unmarried teenaged mother.

At times, he begged her to settle down with him in Jamestown and abandon her dream of being a performer in New York City. Yet she held onto that goal, warning him that when she felt the time was right, she'd once again attack the theatrical citadels of Manhattan.

Despite DaVita's objections, she continued plotting to return to "The City." Her refusal to acquiesce led to one of their most violent fights.

Living with DaVita catalyzed some personality changes in her. She developed a foul mouth to match his own and those of his hoodlum friends. She also took up smoking and drinking and was often the only female present at some of the parties for his gang. She had lost most of her shyness, having learned to defend herself against DaVita's assaults, and was no longer tongue-tied.

After a final night with DaVita, he reluctantly drove her back to the train station in Buffalo, where she boarded a rail car headed once again for Grand Central Station in Manhattan. This time, she found a dreary, closet-sized room in a boarding house on the Upper East Side priced at six dollars a week. She had to share a lone bathroom on the corridor with all the other lodgers. Most of them were actors, or at least wannabe actors. She was surprised that the males weren't shy, often walking nude down the hallway except for a towel around their necks.

She was still going by the name of "Montana Ball," during auditions, hoping to get cast in the chorus line of a Schubert or Ziegfeld production.

One morning, she had planned to ride the subway to the theater district, but found only four pennies in her purse, one cent short of the five-cent fare. For the first time, she became a panhandler, begging for just one penny. She approached an older man with a mustache, who offered to give her ten dollars if she'd go back with him to his hotel room. She rejected his offer, but eventually got a penny from a kindly older lady.

In the Times Square district, she pounded the pavements, but was rejected at most of her auditions, She was skinny and underweight, having to compete with voluptuous, big-breasted showgirls who arrived almost daily from the hinterlands, hoping to get cast, perhaps even in the Ziegfeld Follies.

Finally, a breakthrough came when she was cast as a chorus girl in an upcoming musical called *Step Lively*. Apparently, she did not step lively enough, as the director fired her after two weeks of unpaid rehearsals. "You can't do toe work," he told her. "We're hiring girls who trained for the ballet."

Without money for food, she learned how to survive. A cup of coffee and two doughnuts in those days cost a dime. Some men at the counter would drink a cup of coffee, eat only one doughnut, and leave the other, along with a nickel tip. When a waitress wasn't look-

Times Square in the 1920s, when Lucille, as an untested actress and would-be chorine, literally had to beg a dime.

ing, Lucille would move quickly on the vacated stool, eat the doughnut, and order a cup of coffee with the nickel tip.

She dated on occasion, and her suitors took her to dinner. She carried a large handbag with a plastic liner. Throughout the evening, she would slip bread rolls and pastries into her purse along with stalks of celery, olives, or whatever. She also ordered a large steak, eating only half of it and slipping the rest into her bag for tomorrow's food.

Just as she was about to give up, she got a lucky break when she was cast in Fred Stone's *Stepping Stones,* a musical comedy revue that featured "Roughette Hood," a street-smart adaptation of "Red Riding Hood."

Stone had first gained recognition when he'd appeared on Broadway in the 1902 stage version of *The Wizard of Oz.* He later became a minor star in Hollywood. In an unusual twist of fate, Lucille in 1934 would play a script girl in *The Farmer in the Dell,* in which Stone was the star.

This time around, Lucille survived three weeks of rehearsals until the choreographer fired her. "You can't dance, Montana. I suggest you head back west, and become a cowgirl rounding up the herd."

Crying all the way, she walked back to her rooming house near Columbus Circle.

"Lesser and less foolish mortals might have given up at this point— but not me," she recalled. "I got another job as a soda jerk, and yes, I had learned to put a banana in a banana split."

"When I saved up the train fare, I went back to Jamestown to see my family and to stay with Johnny," she said. "For the next few months, I came and went back and forth. Another cheap rooming house with cockroaches, out-of-work actors, and drunks."

"A lot of the actors and actresses were selling their young bodies to support themselves, and I may have been tempted but held out."

She decided that the name "Montana" no longer fitted her, and she chose the more elegant logo of "Diane Belmont," a name inspired by Belmont Park, the race track in Long Island.

After moving unsuccessfully from audition to audition, she finally landed a job in the chorus line of Earl Carroll's latest musical revue, *Vanities,* an extravaganza competing with Flo Ziegfeld's *Follies Girls.*

Author Kathryn Brady wrote, "Carroll was a bald man in his forties, with a domed forehead and a nickname of 'Bathtub Man,' as a result of having caused a scandal at a party that featured a naked chorus girl

Fred Stone and
Dorothy Stone
Forrest.

Fred and Dorothy Stone in one of their vaudeville *schticks.* Much of "later Lucy's" comedic style was influenced by these Ragtime Broadway pros.

splashing in a bathtub of champagne." After two weeks of rehearsal, Carroll dismissed Lucille, or "Diane Belmont," as she was then being called.

After two more unsuccessful auditions, she was cast by Stanley Sharpe in the then-current production of *The Ziegfeld Follies*. The rather obese Sharpe was known as "Flo Ziegfeld's right-hand man."

"I weeded out the gals before Flo gave them the once-over, deciding if they merited going to bed with him. He was casting the third road show company of the musical *Rio Rita*."

After two weeks, he also fired her, telling her, "You've got no tits, and you can't dance. Are you sure you want to be a chorus girl? You're not sexy at all. With your figure, you might attract stage-door Johnnies...if they're into boys."

Out of a job, she wandered the streets, desolate and desperate. She wondered if she should return to Jamestown and make a career as a gun moll. "I could join Johnny on his liquor runs down from Canada, with the police chasing after us."

"At the age of seventeen, I came to New York to break into show biz," **Lucille** recalled. "We dream of going on the stage because we want to be loved. Guess what? We pick a profession where we can be rejected by the largest number of people."

In her rooming house, she lived across from an aspirant actress, Jeannie Halburne, who recommended that she might try for a job as a model. "You may not be as voluptuous as a Ziegfeld Girl, but fashion editors like slim figures to advertise their clothes."

Lucille thought that might not be a bad idea. "In the meantime, while you're waiting to be discovered, you can go out with me on some dates. I know several guys who might want to date you. Not all men I've found like big-busted sexpots. Some men prefer a date who looks more like a schoolgirl, perhaps fresh out of a convent. I could fix you up. At least you'd never have to go hungry again, surviving on a stale bread roll and a celery stalk."

The next time Lucille heard that line was in 1940 when she attended a showing of *Gone With the Wind* in Los Angeles. Delivered with passion by Vivien Leigh as Scarlett O'Hara was the immortal and wrenching line, "I'll never go hungry again."

THE PRINCE OF SANTIAGO FLEES TO MIAMI

On every continent of the world, and in any language—Greek, Finnish, Hungarian, Portuguese, even Bantu—Desi Arnaz became known as Ricky Ricardo on the *I Love Lucy* show, where he played a Cuban bandleader, as he was in real life.

His real name was too long for the marquee, and he shortened it. He was born on March 2, 1917, in his country's second-largest city, Santiago de Cuba, and named Desiderio Alberto Arnaz y de Acha III. His father (1894-1973) was Desiderio Alberto Arnaz y de Alberni, and his mother (1896-1988), Dolores de Acha, came from a rich family. Her father was one of the men who presided over the Bacardi Rum ("The King of Rums") Empire.

Nicknamed "Lolita," Dolores was hailed as "one of the most beautiful women in Latin America."

At the age of twenty-nine, Desi's father was the youngest mayor in the history of Santiago, and his uncle, Manuel Arnaz, was its chief of police. "We had things pretty well sewed up in my hometown," Desi recalled.

Born into wealth and power, Desi was called "The Prince of Santiago," his father its "King," and his mother, its "Queen."

The family owned three ranches, a palatial home in Santiago, and a vacation villa on a private island in Santiago Bay.

As a schoolboy, Desi was fed the rich history of his then-prosperous native town. Santiago lies in the south-eastern area of Cuba, 540 miles from Havana. Hernán Cortés set out from here to discover the wonders of Mexico. French forces plundered the city in 1552, the British Navy ravaged it again in 1603. French and English refugees fled here in the

Santiago, a city known for colonial architecture, revolutionary history, and Afro-Caribbean music, the kind that Desi, then almost destitute and "exiled" to the U.S., brought to the nightclubs of Miami, New York, and Los Angeles.

late 18th and early 19th centuries when Santiago was still a slave colony.

During the Spanish American War (1898), Colonel Theodore Roosevelt's Rough Riders stormed San Juan Hill. After a fierce battle, Spain surrendered, its remaining fleet returning, defeated, to Europe. Cuba declared its independence, although American troops remained in place there for several years.

[Another momentous event, with more far-reaching consequences, occurred in Santiago on January 1, 1959, long after the Arnaz family had fled: Fidel Castro stood on the balcony of Santiago's City Hall and proclaimed the victory of the Cuban Revolution.]

Early in its history, Queen Isabella of Spain granted Desi's ancestors vast tracts of land in California, including Beverly Hills, the Wilshire Boulevard district of Los Angeles, and Ventura County. "They should have held onto it, and I could have been the richest man on Planet Earth," Desi claimed, years later.

Desi's grandfather, Don Desiderio, had been the medical doctor for the Rough Riders. He was a well-respected figure in Santiago, having guided the city through epidemics of cholera, yellow fever, and smallpox. His funeral was the largest in the city's history.

Right before he passed on, Desi visited him for a final goodbye. He said, "I want you to make the Arnaz name known throughout the Americas."

"I'll give it a hell of a try," Desi promised.

As a teenager, Desi spent a lot of time fishing and going horseback riding. On his tenth birthday, he'd been given a horse, a Tennessee walking pinto. Even before he was old enough to qualify for a driver's license, his father taught him to drive their family car, an Essex, one of the last cars manufactured by that company's founders before they sold it in 1922.

"The world was my oyster," Desi recalled. "If I wanted something, I had only to ask for it. Ambition, incentive, opportunity. Self-reliance. Appreciation of what I had meant little to me. I had a fast-swelling case of what, in a language I couldn't speak at all then, is called a fat head."

As a schoolboy, Desi was taught by the stern Jesuits, who knew how to discipline the rambunctious youth. He looked forward to the family's retreat every summer to their vacation villa, a home set on the oddly named "Cayo Smith" in the Bay of San-

Fidel Castro *(depicted as the center figure, above)* was so deeply associated with the city of Santiago, Desi's hometown, that its Santa Ifigenia Cemetery became his final resting place after his death in 2016.

Santiago was at the center of many key moments in Fidel Castro's revolutionary and personal life. When Batista, the U.S.-backed dictator, fled on New Year's Day 1959, the triumphant guerilla fighter, depicted above, came down the nearby Sierra Maestra Mountains, site of his guerilla strongholds, and delivered his first victory speech from a balcony above what was then Santiago's city hall.

tiago, one of the most beautiful in the world. Elegant villas were built there for the privileged class. They contrasted sharply with the rows of shanties along the shore, where fishermen fed their families from the "fruits of the sea."

Desi took long walks exploring the island, its beaches, and its groves of mangoes, bananas, guavas, and coconuts. The island also produced pineapples. With all its tropical flowers and bird life, it was a fantasy for the young boy.

His father had a speed boat, which he maintained for his transits back and forth to Santiago, and Desi had his own motorboat for fishing. Every autumn, he had to return to school, where he struggled to keep up his grades. His father planned to send him to study at the University of Notre Dame in Indiana after his graduation from high school, hoping he'd follow in his footsteps as an attorney and politician.

"The world was my oyster," said a mature **Desi** about his formative years as a child of privilege during the final years of Cuba's Colonial excesses.

***

At the age of twelve, Desi decided that it was time for his first sexual experience. The African American cook, who worked for the family preparing lavish meals, had a daughter who was Desi's age. "She was very cute, and I lured her into the women's dressing room at the boathouse, where I bolted the door."

"I stripped down and let her play with my thing, and I helped her out of her dress. But there was a problem. No one explained to me how to take a girl's virginity. Everything we tried didn't work."

After about ten minutes of failure, there as a loud knock on the door. It was the girl's mother, the cook, calling out for her daughter and demanding that the door be opened.

"The small proof of my ardor disappeared," Desi recalled. "I put on my trunks and escaped through a window by jumping thirty feet into the water. I swam fifty yards from the scene of my crime without surfacing. I had stamina in those days. I surfaced at the pier, where my Uncle Salvadore was waiting for me. I forgot that I had promised to go fishing with him that day. I figured that if there was any problem, I could plead innocence, claiming that it couldn't have been me in the boathouse because I'd gone fishing."

Salvadore and Desi headed out in his fishing boat to the wreck of the *Merrimac,* the only U.S. vessel sunk during the naval battles of the Spanish-American War. The area was a good fishing ground for red snapper, yellowtail, and bass.

During their fishing, Salvadore told him that his mother had seen him go into the boathouse with the little girl, and had sent the girl's mother, the cook, to investigate. "You'll have to go home tonight and face the music. I know she will tell your father."

"Nothing was said during the family's dinner that night. But after dinner, his father took him into his study and lectured him severely, warning him never to do that again with the little girl, or with any other little girl.

He assured his son that on his fifteenth birthday, he would arrange for Salvadore to escort him to the Casa Marina, the best bordello in Santiago. It was staffed by a madam who employed nine girls, none of whom came from any local family. Two of the young women were from the Dominican Republic, and one was a white girl from Florida. The others were delivered from Havana. The madam didn't think she would be shut down, since Salvadore was a regular patron, and his brothers included not only the city's mayor but its chief of police, too.

Desi's father kept his word, and on his fifteenth birthday, he lost his virginity to an experienced prostitute. She called him "a sweet lover, ever so gentle." She also complained about the rough week she'd had, citing how her bordello had been overrun with Cuban sailors from Havana. "I had to service twenty *hombres*," she complained.

Desi became a frequent visitor at the whorehouse, arriving every weekend until he'd sampled all the girls, and then started the process again. As he grew more experienced, and since he had plenty of money, he began ordering two of them at the same time. He always requested "First Chance" at any new *puta* in the bordello. That included a girl imported from Jamaica who proved very popular.

Desi later claimed that taking a teenaged boy to a bordello was better than "the kid doing it on his own in the back seat of his car, where he might impregnate her. If I ever have a son, I'll be dragging him off to the whorehouse on his fifteenth birthday."

As a teenager, Desi became aware of the tenets of Latino macho culture that were practiced by men of means. What he learned during those years would not go over very well with his future wife, Lucille Ball.

Many of the more prosperous men in

Adolescent, entitled, privileged, and horny: **Desi Arnaz.**

18

Santiago maintained two separate households—his main residence where he lived with his wife and children; another a *casa chica,* the abode of his mistress and his illegitimate children.

Desi's grandfather, Don Desiderio, lived with his wife, Rosita, and his seven "official" children at his main residence in Santiago. He also maintained another household on the outskirts of town for his mistress and their nine illegitimate children. Desi suspected that Rosita knew of this second home, but it was never mentioned.

Years later, Desi tried to find out if his father also maintained a separate household, but it was too late by then. "I was left wondering if I had any half-brothers and sisters."

***

In May of 1925, swept into office by a widespread popular vote, and with the full support of the Arnaz family (Desi's father had contributed money to his cause), General Gerardo Machado became president of Cuba. Prior to his election, Machado had promised to serve only one term. He was viewed as a "puppet" of the U.S. government. In the 1920s, Cuba, especially Havana, became a popular tourist destination for travelers from the U.S. mainland, luring thousands upon thousands of *"norteamericano"* visitors, many of whom arrived by air or by ship from nearby Key West or from Miami. Prohibition was being strictly enforced on the U.S. mainland.

In marked contrast to the puritanical rigidity of the U.S. mainland, in Cuba, gambling casinos flourished, as did night clubs and taverns serving liquor. There were many bordellos, including some that catered exclusively to homosexuals.

As the Cuban regime—with Machado at the center— became corrupt, its top officials began sending lots of government money to private banks in South Florida.

When sugar prices dropped and a recession set in, Machado's popularity waned. But he was determined to stay in power at any cost. He reversed his promise about being a one-term president, and ran for re-election in 1928, winning his second term with rigged ballots. His regime became bloody, and he came to be known as "The Presi-

Nightlife and prostitution flourished during Batista's spectacularly corrupt regime in the 1950s. Regardless of its moral implications, thousands of *norteamericano* tourists were thrilled to partake of its exotic charms, less than a ninety-minute boat ride from Key West.

Closeted sex addicts sometimes referred to Havana as "The Camelot of the Libido."

dent of a Thousand Murders." He ordered the Cuban Army to kill many of his most outspoken critics. This corrupt regime continued to inflict damage on Cuba.

But two parties rose up to challenge him, one called the ABC Party, the other the Communist Party.

Like America itself, Cuba was plunged into a depression in the wake of the Wall Street stock market crash of 1929. Political unrest and poverty swept across the island. In the midst of this, Machado lived lavishly. At the presidential palace, he dined on gold plates and drove a $50,000 armored car with bodyguards armed with grenades and machine guns.

To compound the sufferings of the "average Cuban," an earthquake struck Santiago on June 1, 1932, killing dozens of people. Desi escaped death by fleeing to his parents' bedroom for protection. They were safe there, but a brick wall crashed into his own bedroom, and—had he remained there— he surely would have been killed.

Desi's father continued to support Machado, a policy he maintained during his successful bid for a seat in the House of Representative from his district in 1932. He then purchased a house in the most exclusive district of Havana.

The new Arnaz home stood in the elegant Vadado section of Havana. One of the most popular gathering places in the city was the waterfront seawall known as the Malécon. The best hotels in the capital were also lo-

January, 1959: **Victorious rebels i**n the Havana Hilton after the flight of Cuba's U.S.-supported dictator, Fulgencio Batista. Politicians and investors throughout North America were horrified.

cated here, including the Riviera, the Hilton, and the Nacional de Cuba, as well as the Embassy of the United States. On the east, the district was bordered by the Alemendares River.

But as the months went by, the Machado government was nearing collapse. The newly elected President of the United States, Franklin D. Roosevelt, sent his savvy Latin American policy advisor, Sumner Welles, to work out some sort of compromise.

At first, Machado supported him, but in time refused to give in to the U.S. government's demands for reform. Machado soon expelled Welles from Cuba, attacking "the colonial adventures of the United States."

Even as a teenager, Desi realized that his family's luxurious way of life might be coming to an end.

Machado, envisioning the end, transferred as much Cuban gold as he could to his private banks in Miami, He fled the country on August 12, 1933, never to return. Before he left, he phoned Desiderio II, urging him to flee with his family to Florida, but Desi's father did not think such a drastic move was necessary, as he believed that he still retained his popularity in Santiago because of all the good he'd done to improve the city.

He was wrong. From their new home in Havana, Desi and his family learned that members of the ABC Party, in league with the communists, had marched on their home in Santiago. After sacking and looting it, they virtually wrecked the building and smashed the family's Essex automobile into pieces. They also invaded the family's ranch, slaughtering every animal there, from chickens to horses.

Then a former Army sergeant, Fulgencio Batista (1901-1973), staged a military coup. As one of his first orders of business, he commanded the arrest and imprisonment of any high government officials who had not already fled.

With a hundred dollars in his pocket, Desi joined refugees in a boat headed for Key West, the nearest part of the U.S. to Cuba. His mother remained behind in Cuba, retreating to her father's home in Santiago to await news regarding the fate of her husband, who had also chosen to remain behind.

Safe but emotionally tormented, Desi found a refuge in the home of some distant relatives in Miami where he, too, awaited news about the fate of his parents.

Desiderio, senior, languished in prison for six months until he was freed with orders to leave the country at once. He had been warned that the communists had targeted him for assassination, so he was told to disguise himself.

Awaiting him at the pier in Key West was his son, Desi. When his father emerged from the boat, Desi ran to him. Each held the other in his arms.

"My dear son," he said to him. "We're starting life anew with nothing. God bless and keep us."

His father spoke English, and he demanded that from now on, Desi do the same. "I obeyed my father's orders and ever since, my tongue has been fighting a losing battle with that language. I only speak Spanish when I'm raging mad."

PILLARS OF SPANISH COLONIAL SOCIETY: Long ago and far away: a double portrait of Desi's paternal grandparents, **Rosita** (left) and **Don Desiderio** (right), Santiago's doctor, when life expectancies were low, mortality rates were high, and surgeries were living hell. The hard-to-see portrait in the middle is of Desi's father, the youngest mayor in the history of that city.

Young Desi Arnaz: An extroverted young prince on the dawn of unimaginable changes.

22

CHAPTER THREE

AS A HOT MODEL, LUCILLE SEDUCES HER WAY ACROSS MANHATTAN

In Manhattan, Lucille devoured the want ads in the New York newspapers, checking out the sections labeled MODELS WANTED. At the time, having failed to find work as a Broadway chorus girl, she was sharing a hotel room with another model. Her friend set up a meeting for Lucille with an agency that eventually hired her.

"A job that paid five dollars a day came through for me," she recalled. "I modeled coats which concealed my skin and bones." She worked for an elderly Jewish couple who ran a clothing store on Seventh Avenue.

Her next modeling assignment involved posing for a company that sold dresses and gowns. She also posed for advertisements touting such products as Yardley English Lavender Soap, "Iron Clad Stockings," and Torrain Coffee.

"I made friends with some of the models, who were a lot friendlier than those Ziegfeld Girls," Lucille said. "Some of them passed me on to their surplus supply of beaux."

Soon, she was a fixture at the posh nightspots of Manhattan, showing up on the arm of boxer Hymie Freedman or else that of designer Hugo Bruno.

Lucille later, and only to her most intimate friends, credited Lela Rogers, the mother of Ginger Rogers, with urging her— if she wanted to make it to Hollywood for a starring role in films— to make herself available for "casting couch duties."

"You're a good-looking young woman," Rogers told her. "If you want to be a star within two years, get auditioned on the casting couch. That's the

Young Lucille—before she got glam.

A dress designer told her, "You've got a good body and a little bit of personality. You can model beautiful clothes, but in private, you dress like a lesbian."

advice I gave my own daughter."

"I've been dreaming of stardom for years," Lucille said.

"Then take the direct route," Rogers answered.

"I'll think about it."

[Lela was later hired by RKO to train new talent. She often staged plays in The Little Theater *on the RKO lot, and producers or directors would drop in to observe new talent under contract.*

IS IT TRUE? That an actress's best friend is REALLY her stage mother?

In the case of **Lela** (left) and **Ginger** (right) **Rogers**, it might, indeed, have been true.

At one point, executives considered dropping Lucille by refusing to renew her option. Lela later took credit for saving Lucille's career at the studio: "You fire Lucille and I'll quit," Lela threatened them. "Lucille Ball is one of the most promising young women you have under contract. If you're stupid enough to fire her, the minute you let her go, I'll snap her up and take her to another studio, which will see to it that she gets the roles she deserves."]

As Lucille told some model friends, "I hate having to sing for my supper. Sometimes I go for weeks without turning a trick. But you miss eating. When you're hungry, you'll pull off some stunts you'd rather not do. But what the hell. At least I learned that not all men prefer big-busted, voluptuous women. Some prefer young girls. In a few cases, I told a beau that I was still

Rogers with Astaire, doing what they became famous for doing: Dancing.

a senior in high school approaching graduation."

"Many of these men also liked to go out with young actors out of work," Lucille said. "For some reason, they preferred dancers."

She also posed for artists and photographers, including one bare-breasted assignment for which she was paid fifty dollars. That was the same fee Marilyn Monroe earned years later for posing for her nude calendar.

A pivotal moment in Lucille's life came when she launched an affair with Roger K. Furse, who had been born in England in 1905. A commercial and portrait artist, he was tall, dark, and distinguished, sporting a Van Dyck beard. He coached Lucille on her make-up, camera angles, and wardrobe choices.

"With Roger, I got rid of that 'Girl from Buffalo' look," she said. "The sex wasn't bad either."

It was Furse who arranged for her to have her biggest modeling assignment to date, as a clothes model for Hattie Carnegie, for which her salary rose to thirty-five dollars a week.

[By 1934, Furse went on to become a stage designer for Broadway plays. In the early 1940s, he moved to Hollywood. Later, he joined the Navy. In 1943, he was granted temporary leave to design costumes and armor for the Laurence Olivier film, Henry V. *After the war, Furse was united once again with Olivier and worked with the Old Vic Company in London. Both Furse and Olivier were bisexual, and there were rumors of an affair.]*

An artist at work, one of enormous help to young, career-building ingenue, Lucille Ball. **Roger Furse**

Hattie Carnegie, from the 1920s into the 50s, was the leading fashion entrepreneur in the United States. Born in Vienna in 1886 into a poor Jewish family, her birth name was Henrietta Kanengeiser. She "stole" her adopted surname from Andrew Carnegie, at the time, the richest man in the United States.

In time, she emigrated to New York, where at the age of thirteen, she was hired as a messenger girl at Macy's. By 1919, she had evolved into a designer of women's hats, many of them worn by gossip maven Hedda Hopper.

In time, Hattie began migrating at frequent intervals to Paris for expositions of the latest fashions, and would rip off and replicate their designs at her workshops in New York.

Hattie Carnegie was the diva of high fashion in New York, and she hired Lucille to model her elegant lines of clothing.

"There was a side benefit," Lucille confessed: "I got to meet the most eligible bachelors in Manhattan."

Carnegie became so successful that she later purchased a building just off Park Avenue at East 49th Street. Before the stock market crash of 1929, her fashion house was grossing $3.5 million dollars a year.

"The Carnegie Look" in the fashion world stood for good taste and superb workmanship. Hattie became celebrated for dressing women "from hat to hem."

Many designers who worked for her went on to find glory in the world of fashion themselves, notably Norman Norell and Jean Louis.

"Hattie was difficult to work for, and at least once a week she fired me," Lucille said. "She even kicked me in the shins to remind me to bend my knees properly. She also pinched my ribs to make me raise my chest higher."

"I went through at least three dozen wardrobe changes a day, even modeling for socialites from the families of Vanderbilt, Rockefeller, and Whitney. One day, the Woolworth heiress, Barbara Hutton, arrived to spend lavishly, even making off with the three most expensive furs in the

Carnegie collection."

Lucille also modeled fashion shows at such hotels as the St. Regis, the Pierre, and the Plaza.

She soon began to meet celebrities, modeling clothes for such screen personalities as Gloria Swanson and Joan Crawford. One day, the actress, Gertrude Lawrence, came into the shop and Lucille modeled clothes for her all day. The star ended up spending $22,000 on wardrobe, a huge sum back then.

Hattie didn't like Lucille's "mousy brown" hair, suggesting that she dye it blonde. She also ordered her to make herself look as much like the film star, Constance Bennett, as possible. *[Constance was the sister of another fabled star, Joan Bennett. Recipient of $30,000 a week, Constance was the highest-paid female film star in the world, and one of the most popular.]*

Lucille could hardly imagine that within months, she, too, would live in Hollywood, appearing as a showgirl in a movie that starred Constance herself.

"My transformation into a dime store Constance Bennett was approved by Hattie," Lucille said. "I tried to look like her, walk like her, and dress like her."

Constance—who famously insisted on never wanting to be photographed twice in the same outfit—made at least three trips a year from California to New York for new wardrobes.

"Before Constance, I modeled such items as a thousand-dollar hand-sewn sequined dress and a $40,000 sable as casually as a rabbit."

The first time Constance showed up at Hattie Carnegie's showroom, she was escorted by James

The Hattie Carnegie "Look" and her flair for *haute mode* is reflected in this ad she commissioned in 1934. Young Lucille had the perfect figure for the *luxe, soigné* allure that many said was inspired by Carnegie's training in Austria and France during the peak years of the Jazz Age.

Two views of Constance Bennett (left), as a 20th-Century Fox "clothes horse," and (right) in a press and PR photo with "The King of Hollywood," **Clark Gable.**

Fortunately for Lucille's employment potential, her body measurements matched those of Bennett almost exactly, making her the perfect sales mannequin for upscale merchandise aimed at the star's voracious spending patterns.

Henry Le Bailly de La Falaise, Marquis de La Coudraye, to whom she was married from 1931 to 1940. Whereas his friends called him "Henry" or "Hank," the rest of the New World tended to be awed by his spectacularly prestigious title.

[A year after her divorce, Constance went on to marry the handsome movie star, Gilbert Roland. Born in Mexico, he was billed as one of the screen's leading "Latin Lovers."]

While Constance was in one of Hattie's dressing rooms, the Marquis asked for and got Lucille's phone number. Then, although he'd been scheduled to escort his wife to a premiere the following night, he bowed out, claiming that he didn't feel well. After Constance had left for the evening, the Marquis invited Lucille to his hotel suite, where he seduced her, giving her a thousand-dollar bill, the most she'd ever been paid for sex. Lucille later recalled that this sleazy European aristocrat and trophy boy told her, "Don't be astonished—Constance has a lot more where that came from."

After Henri had informed Lucille of his full formal title, she said, "I can't remember that."

"Don't worry about that, he said. "You can call me 'Hank.'"

The Marquis had been awarded France's *Croix de Guerre* for heroism during World War I. Actress Lillian Gish referred to him as "a genuine war hero. In a bathing suit you can see that he's been cut and shot and covered with scars."

Lucille was extremely flattered that "Hank" found her an exciting date, since he was and had been married to two of the most alluring actresses on the planet. "I couldn't believe it," she confessed to Hattie. "Here I was with this high society French aristocrat. God, he was charming. Only problem was, I was his Back Street romance, and could not be seen with him in public."

James Quirk, editor of *Photoplay*, wrote, "The Marquis is of medium height, athletic build, and blonde—

Constance Bennett was a girl with Lucille Ball's measurements and a gift for marriages to handsome, dashing, stylish, and interesting men—five of them, in fact.

Left photo: Bennett with husband #4, Latin heartthrob, **Gilbert Roland** (married 1941-1946); and with husband #3, (right photo) **Henry de La Falaise, Marquis de La Coudraye**, (married 1931-1940), with whom Lucille sustained a brief affair.

Was he attracted to Lucille because she had almost the exact physical dimenstions as Constance?

27

not at all the tall, dark, haughty figure of traditional nobility. I'm inclined to think that the Irish blood in him is predominant, for he wins you at once with the frank, easy smile and easy manner. That laugh of his is natural and infectious, and more than once, I have seen him laugh Gloria out of her troubles when she was sorely beset with a multitude of worries and harried by a score of people intent on talking business with her."

Others thought that Henri was a mere gigolo, although he could talk Napoleonic history with Charlie Chaplin, or discuss The Great War (World War I) with director Cecile De Mille.

Although Lucille modeled clothes for Gloria Swanson from time to time, she never let her know that she was acquainted with her former husband. "Swanson was at the twilight of her once-glorious film career, and sometimes she'd stay on in Hattie's salon talking about the 1920s in Hollywood and all the grand parties she used to attend."

Swanson described one of her favorite costume parties, a spectacular event hosted by William Randolph Hearst and Marion Davies in their one-hundred room Ocean House in Santa Monica.

Mary Pickford dressed as Lillian Gish in *La Bohème;* Douglas Fairbanks as Don Q from *Son of Zorro;* Chaplin as Napoléon; Madame Elinor Glyn was Catharine of Russia; and Marshall Neiland and Allan Dwan as the bearded Smith Brothers of cough-drop fame.

"The Marquis and I came as ourselves." Swanson said.

Gloria May Swanson, a vintage Silent-era actress known for her extravagance, famously visited Cartier, the Parisian jeweler, in 1932, and bought two of its inventory of six Art Deco style rock crystal bracelets.

According to publicity associated with 2009's hundred-year anniversary of Cartier in the U.S., the platinum bracelets each have 25.35 carats of round and baguette cut diamonds that are set on half discs of rock crystals. Each bracelet is unique, with a different size and number of opaque rock crystals.

Gloria, one of the highest paid actresses in the late 1920's to the early 1930's, wore the bracelets on stage and off as her "signature" look. Charlie Chaplin and Cecil B. De Mille were her directors and close friends. She danced the tango with Rudolph Valentino and was the mistress of Joseph Kennedy, Sr.

In 1950, in *Sunset Blvd.* as an aging recluse desperate to be cast in another movie, she rides to Paramount wrapped in furs in her chauffeured convertible Rolls Royce, wearing both bracelets over long black gloves smoking a cigarette. At that point in her career, jewelry from Cartier had became part of her legend.

This was the client whom Lucille Ball had to placate during her shopping sprees at Hattie Carnegie's dress emporium where Lucille was modeling clothes, trying to break into show biz, and doing her best not to get into trouble.

One night while modeling at Hattie's salon, Lucille collapsed on the runway. There have been many conflicting stories about this event from her past, and over the years, Lucille has contradicted previous descriptions. Allegedly, she'd succumbed to a crippling form of rheumatoid arthritis. The doctor who examined her warned that "you might not walk for many years."

During his treatment of her, he gave her daily injections of horse urine, an unusual treatment, even at the time. "Nothing worked," she said. "My body was riddled with pain."

She went back to tell Hattie goodbye at her fashion house. "She gave me a chic hat, coat, and dress, and kissed me farewell."

"When you recover, you're welcome to come back here," Hattie promised. "I've made you into one of our best models."

According to Lucille's account, she was in a wheelchair when a medical attendant helped her onto a train at Grand Central headed for Buffalo. "I never knew at the time if I'd ever return to Manhattan, much less resume my career as a model.:"

When the train rolled into Buffalo, Johnny DaVita was waiting for her at the station. She was shocked by his appearance. Even though he had not yet turned thirty, he looked much older. The rough life he'd led seemed reflected in his face, which had become embittered.

She claimed that she was driven from Buffalo back to Jamestown where she remained virtually crippled for 2½ years. If indeed she had had rheumatoid arthritis, it was not likely to go away, as it did in her case. Perhaps she had rheumatic fever instead, the symptoms of which were relieved by a new sulfa drug.

Her assertions were contradicted by other stories that claimed that she wasn't paralyzed at all during this time and that she was living, in good health, in an apartment subsidized by DaVita. It was also rumored among Jamestown residents that she underwent another abortion at this time. One story that won't go away is that Lucille was riding in a car one night when her hoodlum boyfriend pulled out a gun and shot an innocent young boy—"just for the fun of it." Whatever the truth, it may never be known as all eyewitnesses are now dead.

Even Desi told friends what he thought: "Lucy was always covering up something in her life—and maybe she got sick too. Who knows? She never gave me a straight answer as many times as I asked her."

During her time in Jamestown, her affair with DaVita began to wind down. As surprising as it seemed, she had grown "too old" for him, as he preferred thirteen or fourteen year-olds who were much younger than her. Although she still cared for him, he rarely visited, and all the news about him seemed bad.

In the autumn of 1930, she learned that he had almost been killed when the car he was driving sustained a head-on collision with a delivery truck as he was being chased by a police car. His vehicle at the time was filled with illegal "hootch" imported from Canada.

After his recovery in a hospital, he was hauled off to jail for a year, yet was released after only three months.

Shortly before Christmas, of 1931, DaVita was a victim of a stop-and-frisk procedure. A police officer discovered that he was carrying an illegal pistol and that he did not have a permit for it. On February 17, 1932, he did more jail time but, as before, he was released early after serving only three weeks.

Then he got a job as a security guard. He'd stand outside on the sidewalk in front of a gambling den with the task of alerting the men inside of any possible police raid.

In the back of the "casino" was a blackboard on which, in chalk, would be written the racing results, as phoned in from the local racetrack

One night his father ran up a gambling debt of $5,000 but had only three-hundred dollars on him at the time. He was given forty-eight hours to come up with the money, but he could not raise that much. His son didn't have that kind of money, either.

When DaVita, Senior couldn't meet the deadline, he was gunned down as he emerged from his home one night. Apparently, at the approach of the hit man, he, too, pulled out his pistol. But before he could discharge it, eight bullets riddled through his body. His killer was never found, and DaVita, according to Lucille, suffered greatly from the loss of his father.

Around that time, a surprise offer came in.

A local resident, William Bemus, had been a professional actor on Broadway, and the Jamestown Players asked him to direct and produce a fast-paced stage melodrama, *Within the Law*.

He cast Lucille into its leading female role of Aggie Lynch, a fast-talking, hard-boiled dame. At one point, the script called for her to disguise herself as an elegant and demure debutante, a challenging transition for any actress.

For the first time, she was asked to dye her hair black, but Bemus wanted a streak of gold. When that black hair was dyed a second time, the streak didn't come out gold, but red. According to Lucille, "with that streak of red in my hair, one might say it was the meager beginning of my lifelong career as a redhead."

Within the Law opened in Jamestown at the Nordic Temple on June 24, 1930. The local paper praised Lucille's performance, even citing her as "a budding Jeanne Eagels." Lucille didn't know who that was.

[Eagels was a famous stage actress whose most memorable performance was as

As a brunette, **Lucille** looked more like actress Joan Bennett than her blonde-haired sister, Constance Bennett.

the prostitute Sadie Thompson in W. Somerset Maugham's Rain.]

Lucille's production was later moved to the Chautauqua Institute, some twenty miles outside of Jamestown. This was a cottage community that flourished in summer. Nearly all of its thousand residents showed up at the Norton Auditorium to see *Within the Law.*

The *Chautauqua Daily* wrote: "Lucille Ball lived the part of the underworld girl with such realism as if it were her regular existence. In a role that required action, and a good deal of it, she exhibited remarkable maturity and poise."

After her triumph, she felt renewed and once again was ready to storm the citadels of Manhattan. She wrote to Hattie Carnegie to tell her that she had recovered and wanted to resume her career as a model. She was rehired.

Before leaving Jamestown, she spent the day with DaVita. Together, for the sake of "old times," they visited the ruins of what had been the Celoron Amusement Park. *[It had burnt to the ground.]* It had been the scene of their summer romance, and its vaudeville programs had sparked her interest in show business.

"I felt my girlhood was buried in those ashes," she recalled. "Johnny and I stood there, looking at our early life somewhere in the ashes, but not finding it."

"He kissed me goodbye and put me on the train to Manhattan. I always kept a soft spot in my heart for Johnny, because he was my first lover," Lucille claimed. "He believed in 'Live fast, die young.' In time, he'd remind me of the actor, James Dean, who had the same motto."

"I never thought much about Johnny after I left Jamestown. So many other men entered my life and stole my heart while I was working my way up the ladder in Hollywood. I was always falling in love with the next Tim, Dick, or Harry. Perhaps I should add a Johnny or two or three to that list."

***

Back in Manhattan, Lucille resumed her job as a model at Hattie's, appearing again on the fashion runway in front of Constance Bennett. As far as it is known, Constance never learned about Lucille's affair with her husband, and the Marquis was hardly the only beau Lucille dated in her pre-Hollywood days as a model.

At night, she frequented the speakeasies with the man of her choice, often a lowlife, but on a following evening, she might be seen with a well-dressed, rich suitor at a golf club, a far

"When I wanted to, I could look like a thirteen-year-old girl," **Lucille** said. "Some of my rich suitors were actually pedophiles in their hearts."

more refined escort. In other words, she was known, in the vernacular of that era, as "a gal about town." According to some of the other models, "Her phone number got passed around a lot."

Lucille became an expert on Manhattan after Dark. She danced at the Cotton Club in Harlem to the music of Louis Armstrong. Still fully dressed in her evening clothes, she often watched the sun rise over Central Park, sometimes—after a long night—ordering breakfast in Greenwich Village as the drag queens retired after their late-night theatrics.

She was a familiar sight at supper clubs and at lavish parties in brownstones. In a borrowed gown, she often showed up with a tuxedo-clad escort at a Broadway opening.

Montana, Diane Belmont, and its latest incarnation, Lucille Ball, became known as a "Manhattan Baby," who sometimes greeted the milkman early in the morning as she was returning to her apartment.

One affair led to another, and sometimes, they were conducted at the same time. One of her biggest involvements was with a New York born and bred entertainment mogul-in-the-making, Albert E. Broccoli, nicknamed "Cubby."

He became one of her least attractive beaux, but he had a charismatic personality. He was born into an Italian family and, as he grew older, experimented with a number of careers, including the ghoulish one of being a casket maker.

In time, he signed on as a "gofer" for the aviator/producer Howard Hugues. He worked on the set of the notorious film about Billy the Kid, entitled *The Outlaw* (1943), that morphed the big-busted Jane Russell into a major-league Hollywood sex goddess before being dethroned by Marilyn Monroe.

Broccoli, along with the Canadian producer Harry Saltzman, produced the first James Bond film, *Dr. No*, in 1962, that transformed the Scottish actor, Sean Connery, into an international star.

Broccoli followed that with such other big hits as *Goldfinger* (1964); *From Russia with Love* (1964);) *Thunderball* (1965); and *You Only Live*

For many years, **The Cotton Club** represented "Harlem chic." Some of the most celebrated stars and the richest men and their dates showed up here late at night. They were treated to some of the best musicians in America—perhaps Louis Armstrong, Billie Holiday, or Ella Fitzgerald.

"I dated **Cubby Broccoli** for a while," Lucille said, "although on our first date I told him my favorite green vegetable was Swiss chard, not broccoli."

"At the time, I never dreamed he'd launch all those James Bond movies with Sean Connery. My only fault with him was that he did not make me a Bond Girl."

"What does Ursula Andress have that I don't have?"

Twice (1967).

[In 1941, Cubby would marry actress Gloria Blondell, the younger sister of Joan Blondell.]

Cubby introduced Lucille to his cousin, the mobster hustler, Pasquale (Pat) DiCicco. By then, Cubby's interest had drifted on to other showgirls, and her introduction to his cousin was perhaps his attempt to dump Lucille. The sleazy DiCicco was only too willing to assume stud duties.

Lucille would know DiCicco on and off for many years during the 1930s. Sometimes, the two of them would slip away for weekends in Palm Springs, hosted by the bisexual aviator and film producer Howard Hughes.

"Pat was filled with humor and sophistication," Lucille claimed, "and he made a thrilling escort." She once confided to Joan Blondell, "Pat taught me tricks in bed I think he learned in a brothel in Shanghai."

Over the years, many reporters asked Lucille about her involvements with Cubby and DiCicco, but she had nothing to say, other than "I may have met them once or twice at a party. I know nothing about them."

Both men were involved in one of the most shadowy scandals in Hollywood, the murder of comedian Ted Healy, the creator of The Three Stooges, outside the Hollywood nightclub, Trocadero, in 1937. A source alleged that actor Wallace Beery, Cubby, and DiCicco beat Healy so badly in an alley that he died. The case was investigated, but no charges were ever filed.

Two views of mob-connected gigolo **Pat DiCicco,** more famous for marrying **Gloria Vanderbilt** (lower photo) and for suspicions of murdering Thelma Todd than for seducing Lucille.

Sexy, charismatic, and studly, DiCicco would go on to marry two famous American women, film star Thelma Todd and heiress Gloria Vanderbilt.

A native of Massachusetts, Todd was nicknamed "The Ice Blonde" and "Hot Toddy," for her profit-generating screen roles. She starred in 120 films between 1926 and 1935, the year of her death. She was known for appearing with comedians such as The Marx Brothers, Buster Keaton, Jimmy Durante, Laurel and Hardy, and Wheeler and Woolsey.

Todd had also appeared as a prominent supporting character in the original version of *The Maltese Falcon* (1931), starring Ricardo Cortez. *[In a 1941 remake, Humphrey Bogart assumed the Sam Spade role in a newer version, Todd's role being played by Mary Astor.]*

Lucille, accompanied by her *beau de jour,* later became a regular patron of Todd's Sidewalk Café at Pacific Palisades. They knew each other well, and often gossiped about DiCicco.

At that time, Todd had moved on from DiCicco and was involved with Roland West, her business partner and lover. On the night before her death, DiCicco showed up at the club, and the two had a violent public argument.

Thelma Todd with the man she loved (was he her murderer?) **Pat DiCicco.**

In time, Lucille went from being a lover of DiCicco to one of Todd's best friends. She never shared her views about Todd's notorious death.

The next night, Todd was found dead in her car, a victim—it was said—of carbon monoxide poisoning. An investigation concluded that she had locked herself inside the car with its engine running, parked at the time within a garage with the doors and windows sealed, thereby committing suicide, but the legend lingers that she was murdered. [*Although a grand jury ruled that Todd had committed suicide, it was unable to explain her broken nose, the bruises around her throat and two cracked ribs.*]

Six years later, an even more famous woman, heiress Gloria Vanderbilt, the mother of CNN news anchor Anderson Cooper, succumbed to the charms of DiCicco, too. Marrying him in 1941, she denounced him as a gold-digging hustler and divorced him four years later.

Vanderbilt, an artist, author, actress, and socialite, was once one of the most famous women in America, known for dating Frank Sinatra and for marrying Leopold Stokowski and Sidney Lumet. She later became celebrated as a fashion designer. Half of America seemed to be wearing her designer blue jeans.

"Although Lucille was dating and falling in love every week, she was not the kind of girl who threw herself at men," claimed Kay Vaughan, one of her best friends. "If a man propositioned her, he had a good chance of getting somewhere. Lucille told me she had wanted to marry DiCicco, but he never proposed."

She was probably lucky he didn't. He had bigger game in mind than Lucille, who was "a nobody" at the time she was going with him, just one of hundreds of starlets banging on the doors of Hollywood and moving between casting couches.

***

DiCicco wasn't the only one to get involved with a Vanderbilt. Lucille herself started to "heavy date" Arthur O'Neill, a photographer and member of the Vanderbilt dynasty. Living on a trust fund, he was an imposing figure, immaculately groomed with sandy-colored hair and a pencil mustache.

She found him debonair and ultra-sophisticated. For a long time, he indulged in photographic portraiture at his studio on the Left Bank in Paris. It was he who produced many of the fashion photos that appeared in the French edition of *Vogue*.

As the final curtain came down on their affair, a new man entered her life, actor Hugh Sinclair, a Londoner, the son of a clergyman. As an actor, he was known for playing variations of himself—that is, a character who was handsome and suave and also witty enough to excel in light comedy.

The British actor, **Hugh Sinclair,** "heavily dated" Lucille for a while.

"She would make an appearance looking like a glamourous figure from a fashion mag. Within five minutes, she had you laughing at her jokes, many of which made me blush like a virgin."

Sinclair said, "Lucille had become one of the most popular models in Manhattan. She had a great sense of humor and was living well at a time when millions of Americans were hardly surviving during the Depression. Somebody was supporting her because she resided in an elegant apartment. Not only that, but she became known as a soft touch, often giving a friend about to be evicted from his or her apartment a hundred dollars during the depths of the Depression."

Sinclair later revealed that Lucille had some links with gangsters in Manhattan even before she moved to Hollywood.

"I don't know what was going on, and it was never revealed, but she was in trouble and seemed afraid. Once night, we were dancing in this club in Harlem when she grabbed my arm, and said, 'Let's get the hell out of here.' She was right. The hoodlum, we learned later, came into the club, gunned a man down, and then escaped and was never caught."

If Lucille is to be believed, there was an attempt on her life, too, during her residency at Manhattan's Kimberly Hotel. She was taking a bath. While she was soaking in the tub, she was fired upon and the bathtub was riddled with bullets, Miraculously, she escaped injury, but the room downstairs was flooded.

Lucille's patron at the time was Sailing P. Baruch, Jr., a nephew of the famous financier, Bernard Baruch, the stock investor, statesman, and political adviser to such presidents as Woodrow Wilson and Franklin D. Roosevelt.

It seemed that in Lucille's case, Sailing wanted a mistress, not a wife. At any rate, Lucille was not the type of girl a rich man wanted to take home to mother. Sailing later became the president of the multi-million-dollar Bernard Baruch Company.

***

A big break came for Lucille when she posed for a freelance painter named "Ratterman." He outfitted her in a lavishly flowing blue chiffon dress borrowed from Hattie Carnegie's fashion house. With it, she wore a matching picture hat. To the painting he crafted of her, Ratterman added, by her side, two gray Russian wolfhounds.

He then sold his oil painting to an advertising agency that was hyping Chesterfield cigarettes, at the time one of the biggest tobacco products in America. "Suddenly, without my knowing it, my image was posted all over the country, most significantly in Times Square on a giant billboard," she said.

Processed with a blend of Turkish and Virginia tobaccos, Chesterfield cigarettes had been an American staple since 1926. It became a pioneer at aiming its product at women, beginning with an ad

Russell Markert rehearsing his Rockettes.

Hw found Lucille enticing enough to bed, but unqualified to be a Rockette. "I guess I just didn't measure up," she lamented.

whose artwork suggested to a woman's husband (or male friend), "Blow some my way." The Roaring Twenties had broken down some of the era's judgments against women smokers.

Lucille became a trailblazer who was later followed by Chesterfield sponsors who included Bob Hope, Bing Crosby, Perry Como, Arthur Godfrey, and Humphrey Bogart. In his 1944 movie, *To Have and Have Not,* in which he co-starred with his future wife, Lauren Bacall, Bogie smoked Chesterfields.

Lucille remained a dedicated smoker of Chesterfields. However, during her starring stint in *I Love Lucy,* her sponsor was Philip Morris. She got around having to change to another brand by emptying a pack of Philip Morris cigarettes and refilling it with Chesterfields.

Two people entered her life at around the same time, each taking credit later for having "discovered" the future bigtime star, Lucille Ball.

One was Russell Markert, the founder and director of the fabled Rockettes at Radio City Music Hall. She began an affair with him, even though she did not qualify as a Rockette. [*A candidate had to have a shapely figure and a rigorously enforced height of between 5'5" and 5'8. She also had to be adept at ballet, tap, and soft shoe, and to be able to kick at least six inches above the level of her head.*]

So even though Lucille didn't qualify as a Rockette, during their lovemaking, Markert promised to arrange an introduction to James Mulvey, the New York-based agent for Samuel Goldwyn, who, at the time, was lining up a coven of beauties and redefining them as Goldwyn Girls.

During one of her lunch breaks, Lucille wandered to Times Square to gaze up at her chiffon-draped image on the Chesterfield billboard. As she was taking in her larger-than-life blow-up, someone called out to her, "Hey! You're the Chesterfield Girl!"

The woman who recognized her turned out to be Sylvia Hahlo, a talent scout. She, too, promised to arrange an audition with Mulvey, but this time with the intention of including her in the process of booking a dozen show-girls for Goldwyn's new Eddie Cantor movie, *Roman Scandals* (1933). What this meant for Lucille was that Mulvey received recommendations from both Markert and Hahlo. He, too, found Lucille striking as the Chesterfield Girl.

Within an hour of meeting her, he signed her to a $125-per-week contract for a six-week engagement. Terms of her contract included her train fare to Hollywood. DeDe came down from Jamestown to Grand Central to see her daughter off to Hollywood.

With dreams of stardom flashing through her mind, Lucille rode the Super Chief, which originated in Chicago, across the plains and mountains of North America. Known as "the train of stars," because of the dozens of celebrity entertainers who traveled along its route, it was the flagship of the Atchison, Topeka, and Santa Fe Railway that Judy Garland would sing about in the years to come.

On the train, Lucille spotted Douglas Fairbanks, Sr., the swashbuckler of the silent screen. He and his wife, Mary Pickford, were widely known as the two most famous people on the planet.

Little could she have imagined at the time, but she would become very well acquainted with his son, Douglas Fairbanks, Jr., in her near future.

Not only that, but in time, she would get to know Pickford's next husband, the musician, Charles ("Buddy") Rogers, who came to be labeled "America's Boy Friend."

Waiting for Fairbanks in Los Angeles was Mary Pickford, who in all her silent movies had been hailed as "America's Sweetheart." At the end of the line, Lucille watched as Fairbanks dashed off the train and into her waiting arms. She had driven her baby blue convertible to the station to haul him away.

Lucille had daydreamed during most of her cross-country transit, imagining a world of riches, glamour, sex, and worldwide adoration when she, too, would become a movie star. She also planned to marry a Viking God, standing tall, blonde, and muscled in green tights.

Emerging from the Super Chief,

Douglas Fairbanks, Sr., married **Mary Pickford** in 1920. As an ingenue breaking into show-biz as a model and wannabe actress, Lucille recognized him on the Super Chief more than a dozen years later.

Lucille entered into the fast-changing Hollywood of 1933. It was churning out Talkies and recruiting a new armada of stars with voices and faces. Silent screen stars who had faces but unacceptable voices were watching their careers vaporize overnight.

Even though the years she spent as a fashion model weren't remembered as the happiest period of **Lucille's** life, the skills she developed in showing the most photogenic aspects of her physicality served her well during later phases of her acting career.

The three lower photos show Lucille "getting glam" and showcasing the often elaborate clothing she was assigned during the course of her film career,.

CHAPTER FOUR

DESI SHAKES HIS MARACAS AND HIS SALAMI AT MANHATTAN

By the time Desi and his father arrived in Miami, they had almost no money. A tip led them to a seedy, hurricane-battered boarding house on the southwestern fringe of the city, where a group of Cuban immigrants had settled. "Lousy food, lousy cots shared with bed-bugs, and a smelly communal bathroom," Desi said. "But it costs only five dollars a week."

"Once we enjoyed one of the finest homes in Santiago, and now we were reduced to this creaky old dump hastily constructed back in the 1920s as food for termites."

When Desi and Desiderio settled here, Miami had only a few hundred Cuban refugees. That was long before hordes of them arrived to completely alter the demographics of the city, almost mandating that Spanish become the language of the land.

Gone With the Wind

For upper-class Cuban so-cialites in 1938, as represented by this elaborately dressed landowner with her dog and by the Arnaz family, everyday life was *"La Dolce Vita."*

Here are **formerly prosperous Cubans** newly ar-rived at Florida's Opa-Locka Airport, the first wave of thousands, exiled or self-exiled from the ravages of outrage and horror to come.

Because of the Arnaz family's gilt-edged associations to the former regime, they were among the first to exit .

Desiderio missed his wife, and Desi longed to see his mother again. But they could hardly send for her to come over from Cuba until they could afford a decent house for them to live in, and that would cost $5,000 at least. She was still living with her aging father in Santiago.

Desi was having a hard time communicating with his father, who demanded that he speak only English. One night, he sent him out to have dinner on his own in Miami, not joining him. Desi wandered about until he saw a little greasy spoon, Edna's Kitchen, hyping a meal for just fifty cents.

His former Jesuit teachers had provided him with a limited English vocabulary, but had neglected to teach him how to read anything written in English. Not wanting to show his ignorance when the cute waitress approached him, he pointed to four items on the menu. She seemed mildly surprised but wrote down his order.

By 1960, **emergency emigrations** from Cuba to Florida had become more frantic, less well-funded, and to those displaced persons who experienced it, more terrifying.

He was served four kinds of soup that night—chicken noodle, green pea, tomato, and black bean. Later, he found a small tavern that had a sign—*Se Habla Español (Spanish is spoken here)*—and he and his father dined there on occasion when the boarding house food became intolerable. They liked the Cuban dive because the cook, like Desiderio himself, was a native of Santiago.

For the summer of 1934, an arrangement was made for Desi to enroll at St. Leo's Catholic School, forty miles fromTampa. He'd have preferred to remain in Miami to help his father earn some money, but Desiderio was insistent.

"My lack of English led to my getting the beating of my life," he recalled. He was approached by the coach, an athlete who had, a few years before, won Florida's middleweight amateur boxing championship. He invited Desi into the ring in a match before his schoolmates the following night. Not really understanding, Desi said, "Yeah, sure."

The next night as he came into the arena for a boxing lesson, he saw that the seats were filled with spectators from St. Leo's. The coach helped him on with his boxing gloves. It seemed that he had agreed to face off against an amateur boxing champ who weighed 250 pounds and stood 6'3".

Desi wanted to flee from the arena but knew he'd be branded as a coward if he did. When the bell rang, he faced off with the boxer nicknamed "Killer."

At first, he tried to dance around him "until I got a blow to my gut that caused me to fall on my ass. When I was able to get up again, I was in pain but couldn't escape those lethal punches. Three times, I landed on my ass, and was completely knocked out in the third round. I also got a concussion. For the next two weeks, I couldn't hold down solid food. More than ever, I knew Dad was right. I'd better learn English."

"After my defeat, I decided I didn't want that to happen to me again. Over the course of my youth, I'd have some violent encounters. This time, I was ready to take on guys even bigger than me. I must admit I did not follow the Marquis of Queensberry rules. Before a thug knocked me on my ass again, I grabbed his *cojones* and squeezed as tight as I could. I had the fucker screaming in pain as I pounded his nose until blood spurted."

As summer came to an end, Desi returned to live with his father on Miami Beach, staying at another little hotel that catered mostly to refugees from Cuba. While he was away, Desiderio had formed the Pan American Importing and Exporting Company, with two partners—one the former governor of Santa Clara in Cuba. The other had been the governor of Camagüey.

With hopes of attending Notre Dame gone forever, Desi enrolled in St. Patrick's Catholic High School at 3700 Garden Avenue on Miami Beach, the parish school for St Patrick's Catholic Church.

It soon became apparent that Desi was the poorest kid in the class. His classmates seemed to come from well-off families, many of whom could afford to live on Miami Beach during the winter months and head back to New York in the late spring before the stifling summer heat blanketed Florida.

Although today, its Florida campus houses a liberal arts university, **Saint Leo College Preparatory School** operated from 1929 to 1964.

Strings were pulled and arrangements were made for Desi to attend within a few months of his exit from Cuba. As a "stranger in a strange land" and as a "newly imnpoveriished newcomer" speaking very little English, he had to fight, hard and frequently for acceptance.

Desi volunteered to help out with the new company, which sold ceramic tiles from Mexico. Regrettably, after pooling their assets, the three partners had only five-hundred dollars. They couldn't import more tiles until they sold all of their stock to the building trade.

A seedy old warehouse was rented on Third Street in Southwest Miami. At the rear was a rat-infested space with a sink and a toilet. Both Desi and Desiderio came up with the same idea at once: They'd flee from their present room in that hotel since it was filled with drunks and drug dealers.

Father and son set out to make the rear of the warehouse fit for habitation. They brought in two cheap army cots and a two-burner stove. "We didn't have a shower, but we could take a whore's bath in the sink. I learned that expression. It's what a *puta* calls washing her wares in a sink after sex with a 'john.'"

For food, they shopped for bargains, finding the best deal in a market where cans of pork and beans sold for fifteen cents each. "Every night, we ate those pork and beans. It kept us alive, but when things got better, I swore off pork and beans for life."

With no real money coming into the imported tile business, their partners drifted off to seek other jobs. Desiderio was left with only a pile of broken tiles.

> Then and now: Complications for Desi and for those who followed.

He and Desi went into the banana business, buying a small shipment from Puerto Rico, which they planned to sell on the street for five cents a banana. The first shipment sold out, but trouble began when Desi drove down to the Port of Miami in a cheap, battered old pickup truck they'd bought for eighty dollars. All the bananas in this shipment had turned black during their transit from Puerto Rico.

Despite these setbacks, Desiderio bought a second-hand radio for his son. At night, Desi would listen to American music, which bored him. "Who did this Rudy Vallee think he was? He couldn't sing worth a damn."

In their warehouse remained a pile of broken ceramic tiles. They sparked another of Desiderio's creative ideas about how to make money. He designed a tile mosaic with the intention of embedding the broken tiles in rectangular blocks of wet cement. They were then sold to building contractors who were told that they were all the rage in Latin America.

Sales took off, and soon, father and son had to import more tiles. Desi deliberately broke them into "artistic-looking" shards by placing them in the back of his pickup truck and driving them along bumpy roads through and around the Everglades.

Just as some of their problems were being solved, an agent from the U.S. Department of Immigration arrived at their warehouse. Although Desi and Desiderio had lived in Florida for almost two years, they had never filed for residency. They were, in fact classified as illegal immigrants. They were immediately warned that if they didn't have their paperwork in order within ninety days, they'd each be deported.

They faced an immediate hassle. Applications for residency had to be filed from outside the United States. Desiderio feared that if he returned to Cuba, he might be re-imprisoned, so he flew to San Juan instead and filed papers from there. Desi felt that it was safe for him to fly to Havana to file his own paperwork, which he did, filling out the documents there. He then rented a car and drove to Santiago for a reunion with his mother. He promised that Desiderio would send for her as soon as they could save enough money to buy a small house.

***

Back in Florida, Desi managed to combine work with attendance at high school. He concentrated on learning to speak and write English, and he also joined both the swim team and the baseball team. This athletic endeavor built up his body, and he attracted girls, especially cheerleaders.

"I went girl crazy—girls, girls, and more girls. I screwed and screwed and then screwed some more. On some nights, I had at least three orgasms, when some of my buddies had a hard time managing just one."

Meanwhile, as Cuba collapsed, **Florida** and its image as a sybaritic paradise for beach bunnies and their voyeurs flourished. Here's a promotional photo for **Cypress Gardens** in the early 50s, Desi's beach-bunny heyday

"To serenade my gal of the moment, I did what young *Cubano* men often do: I bought a guitar. For only five dollars, I picked up this instrument that had palm trees and bikini-clad girls painted on it. At beach parties, I played it and sang Cuban love songs to whatever hot *puta* I was dating at the time. Sometimes, under the 'Moon over Miami,' we'd strip down and race to the ocean. Later, on the beach, we'd make love like it was going out of style."

***

At school, Desi acquired a new best friend, Alphonse Albert Francis Capone, Jr., whom he called Sonny. He was the son of America's most famous gangster, who was serving time in Alcatraz. The Feds had already nailed him for tax evasion.

"My buddy Sonny had been born right before Christmas in 1918. In addition to having Capone as a Dad, his mother was Mae Coughlin, who had married the gangster the year Sonny was born. Although he screwed around with hundreds of *putas,* Capone married only once."

When Capone, Sr. was sent to Alcatraz, doctors examined him. A psychiatrist reported that he had the mentality of a twelve-year-old. Blood tests showed that he had suf-

Gangster kingpin **Al Capone, Sr.** with his son, nicknamed **Sonny** (later, Desi's best friend), and some very tense security guards.

This photo was snapped on September 9, 1931, at Chicago's Comiskey Park. The event was a charity event configured as a match between the Chicago White Sox and the Chicago Cubs. The Cubs won 3-0

fered for years from both syphilis and gonorrhea, as well as withdrawal symptoms from years of cocaine addiction.

Sonny had been born with congenital syphilis and a serious mastoid infection. As an infant, he had to undergo brain surgery. It left him deaf in one ear.

Desi was seen riding up and down Lincoln Road in Sonny's gold Cadillac convertible. On most occasions, as many as four bathing beauties would also be in the car with the two teenaged boys.

Even though Desi was still living in virtual poverty within the moldy warehouse, he was surrounded by luxury whenever he was with Sonny. Both Desi and his father sometimes dined within the lavish Capone mansion of Miami Beach's most exclusive island. "Except for fear of going to jail, I sometimes daydreamed about becoming a bigtime gangster myself."

Most of the kids in high school shunned Sonny because of the notoriety of his father. Desi also faced racial prejudice and was constantly mocked as a "Spic."

Sometimes a gang of boys would entrap Desi and beat him up, even though he fought back like a hungry tiger. But those occasions were rare. His nights were filled with love-making, often on the beach with Sonny beside him on a blanket, having sex with their pickups.

[After he was graduated from high school at the age of nineteen, Desi and Sonny went their separate ways. Desi thought he would never see Sonny again But Sonny, years later, re-entered his life, much to Desi's regret.

In Hollywood, as head of Desilu Productions, Desi launched a hit TV series called The Untouchables.

Broadcast on the ABC Television Network (1959-1963) and starring Robert Stack as Detective Eliot Ness, it became a landmark in TV crime series. Stack played a Prohibition agent fighting crime in gangster-soaked Chicago in the early 1930s.

In high school, Sonny often told Desi stories about his father during his gangster heyday. One of his tales had Capone ordering the severe beating of three of his men for plotting against him. After suffering bone-breaking violence with a baseball bat, the men were shot by Capone's bodyguards. Some of the stories Sonny had told Desi reappeared again in scripts for The Untouchables.

Here is a recent view of the pool house on the grounds of the Palm Island (Miami Beach) mansion that was purchased for $40,000 in 1928 by America's then-most-famous mobster, **Al Capone,** and which his widow, Mae, sold in 1952, five years after the mobster's death, in prison, in 1947.

When it was built, it boasted the largest swimming pool in Miami (30' x 60'), one that was used frequently by Desi Arnaz during his high-school visits to Capone's complicated, partially deaf son, Al Capone ("Sonny") Jr.

Although popular with the public, the series set off a furious reaction from thousands of Italian Americans, who objected to the negative stereotypes of their race, always depicting them as gangsters or mobsters who murdered at will.

Sonny sued for a million dollars, naming Desilu, the TV network, and the sponsor, Westinghouse Electric Corporation. The lawsuit was later thrown out of court, but Desi's life was threatened by anonymous callers.

One night, Frank Sinatra, an Italian American, encountered Desi at the Cocoanut Grove night club in Los Angeles. Sinatra punched Desi in the face, bloodying his nose.

Faced with the loss of sponsors and the threat of public boycotts, Desi directed his lawyers to draw up a manifesto, which he hoped would meet favor with the Italian American Defamation League. Three of the most pertinent points in their manifesto included the following:

> 1) There will be no more fictional hoodlums with Italian names in future productions.

> 2) There will be more stress on the law-enforcement role of "Rico Rossi," Ness's right-hand man on the show.

> 3) There will be an emphasis on the "formidable influence" of Italian American officials in reducing crime and an emphasis on the "great contributions:" made to American culture by Americans of Italian descent.]

In addition to attending English language classes; breaking ceramic tiles; chasing girls with Sonny; and singing to the sounds of his guitar; Desi made another friend in Teddy Whitehouse. He began to date his sister, Lucy.

"Later on," he said, jokingly, "another Lucy would enter my life. My Miami Beach teenage Lucy was a hot blonde. The other Lucy was a dynamic redhead, fiery as a furnace. I don't recall her last name—just joking, folks."

Mr. Whitehouse, Lucy's father, was an American married to a Cuban wife. His hobbies included breeding canaries, and he had a large garage filled with these yellow birds. He came up with a money-making scheme for which he would hire Desi at a salary of fifteen dollars a week.

Whitehouse purchased a hundred birdcages. Into each of them, he put a reasonable sampling of live, exotic-looking canaries, and placed them in stores throughout Coral Gables, Miami, and Miami Beach.

Desi's job involved moving from store to store, cleaning out the cages and supplying the birds with food and water. He defined his employment as "my bird shit job." He became jittery when he entered two outlets near his high school, fearing that one of his classmates might spot him and that he'd then be mocked throughout his school.

"When all those canaries were sold, my shitty job ended," Desi said. "I shed no tears for losing the work. I also decided to dump Lucy and move on to a richer opportunity."

Months before his graduation, Desi fell in love and quit chasing "after a gang of *putas* every night."

The object of his affection was a Latina beauty, Gabriella Barreras, the granddaughter of the former president of the Cuban Senate during the brutal reign of Gerardo Machado. Unlike Desiderio, Antonio Barreras had fled Havana with three million dollars in government gold.

Gabriella was a beautiful, olive-skinned, brown-eyed girl who could have qualified as a Miss Havana contestant.

Desi didn't need any more menial jobs, as he became the kept boy of teenaged Gabriella, who was given $150 a week as an allowance, and more, if she needed it.

Desi was soon seen driving her Cadillac. She bought him suits of clothing and five pairs of alligator shoes.

"Dad and I rarely had to cook on that two-burner stove any more," Desi said. "At least three nights a week, they dined lavishly at the Barreras mansion on Miami Beach, elegant dinners served by three formally dressed black men.

"Miami Beach was filled with kept boys being supported by older women, but I think I was the only stud supported by a teenaged girl."

It might have been Gabriella who supplied Desi with the five-thousand dollars he needed to buy a house for himself and his parents. At long last, Desiderio could send for his wife, who soon after arrived from Santiago, happy that her family was gathered together under one roof again.

It was through Mr. Barreras that Desi was offered his first gig in show business. It happened during the final months of his senior year in high school. It was with the resident band in the night club at the Roney Plaza, an upscale hotel preferred by movie stars and politicians.

"I had gotten pretty good at singing and accompanying myself on my guitar," Desi said. "I tossed away that cheap five-dollar guitar with the palm trees and bikini beauties painted on it. It was replaced by one of the best guitars on Miami Beach, compliments of my darling Gabriella, who couldn't seem to get enough of what I called 'my Cuban salami.' Her father heard me serenade his daughter one night, and set me up for a possible hook-up with the cats who had a band at the Roney Plaza."

"I was eager to take the gig—a new English word for me—and I did so over Dad's objections," Desi said. "He equated musicians on the same level as thieves, thugs, and child molesters. He still clung to the dream that I might one day go to college and on to law school."

Desi went to work at this deluxe hotel, which had opened in 1926 at 3200 Garden Avenue on Miami Beach.

"I never set out to go into show business," he recalled. "Who could have imagined how far I would climb in the entertainment business? As time went by, the history of Hollywood could not have been written without a section about me—and, oh yes, that redhead whose damn name I could never remember."

***

It seemed that Antonio Barreras, that exiled former Cuban politician, liked to play the numbers game. The guy who sold the numbers to Barreras had a small rumba band that played second billing at the Roney Plaza, the top night spot on Miami Beach.

Barreras hooked Desi up with the gambler/musician, and he passed the audition. He became a member of the hotel's resident group, the Siboney Septet, even though they included only six (not seven) members.

The Cuban rumba band included a bongo player, a singer/guitarist (Desi), a pianist, a bassist, a maracas shaker, and the band leader, who played the marimbula, a wooden box with four metal strips over a hole in the center.

It became the second-tier nightlife attraction at the Roney Plaza. The featured orchestra was conducted by Charles (Buddy) Rogers, a good-looking, wavy-haired movie star and musician, who had been nicknamed "America's Boyfriend."

As an orchestra leader, he reached the peak of his fame in the late 1920s and early 1930s. In 1927, he had co-starred with Mary Pickford in *My Best Girl,* and he had begun an affair with her even though she was married at the time to Douglas Fairbanks, Sr.

[Pickford would divorce Fairbanks in 1936, marrying Rogers the following year.

In 1927, Rogers also co-starred with Clara Bow, the "It Girl," in Wings, the first movie to win an Oscar as the Best Picture of the Year.

Rogers was bisexual, and Desi, years later, claimed that the band leader had made a pass at him, which he did not intercept.]

In his new job, Desi was paid thirty-nine dollars a week. The Siboney Septet played the rumba *[also spelled rhumba].* At the time, it was not well-known in North America. When the Rogers band played a foxtrot, or any of the swing tunes popular at the time, the dance floor was full. But when Desi and his associates played a rumba, the floor would suddenly empty. The Cubans quickly realized that they had to do something fast or they'd lose their gig.

It was Desi, not the band leader, who persuaded Rogers to end his set with his own rendition of that rumba, "The Peanut Vendor *(El manisero)."*

Since it was Rogers' band playing it, most of the dancers stayed on the floor. The women took to it faster than the men. Desi claimed that "the gals liked it because it showed off their whirling skirts and ankles to good effect."

Desi (second from left) as leader of the **Siboney Septet,** only six of whom are represented in this photo.

47

The males eventually got into step, and the rumba gained popularity in America.

The 1935 film, *Rumba,* brought the dance to its largest audience. Ballroom rumba was derived from a Cuban rhythm and dance called the *bolero-son.*

Ironically the movie would star George Raft, Lucille Ball's future lover, and Carole Lombard, one of her best friends.

***

In one of those coincidences that sometimes occur in show business history, the celebrated bandleader Xavier Cugat dropped into the Roney Plaza one night to hear Desi's newly formed Cuban band. *[Cugat was always on a search for new and exciting Latino talent, sometimes hiring it for his own orchestra. At the time, Cugat ("The King of Rumba") was also the undisputed King of Latino music in North America.]*

Born in Spain, Cugat spent his formative years in Havana. At the age of nine, he'd been hired as a violinist in a silent movie theater. As he grew up, he became the "first chair" violinist for the Teatro Nacional Symphonic Orchestra. By 1915, he had settled in New York, appearing in recitals with Enrico Caruso, and specializing in violin solos.

In the 1920s, Cugat starred at the Co-

Carole Lombard and George Raft getting tropical and Latin together in *Rumba* (1935), the film that helped launch the dance craze that Desi played long, hard, and until its dying gasp.

coanut Grove in Los Angeles, where Charlie Chaplin advised him to add the tango to his repertoire. In 1928, he was cast in a movie entitled *Xavier Cugat and his Gigolos,* which introduced him to his widest audience yet. In his spare time, he was a cartoonist, his caricatures enjoying national syndication.

In 1931, he moved to Manhattan, opening at the Waldorf-Astoria, where he became that hotel's resident bandleader. For the next thirty years, he would fly between New York and Los Angeles. His trademark gesture was to hold a chihuahua in one arm while waving a baton with the other. Over the years, he made a number of screen appearances, beginning with *Gay Madrid* in 1930.

Knowing that Cugat was in the audience, Desi delivered his best performances as a singer and guitar player that night. When his act was over,

Cugat remained seated at table and did not get up to greet the members of the Siboney Septet.

Desi walked past Cugat's table several times. Nothing. He even stopped and lit a cigarette near him. Again, nothing.

Finally, as Desi later admitted, "I thought to myself, 'What an asshole I am. Why should he want me in his orchestra?'"

But as Desi headed for the door, Cugat called out to him: "Hey, Chico! You're good, kid. How about showing up tomorrow afternoon at the Brook Club for an audition?"

"Mr. Cugat, I'll be there with bells on."

"Just haul your ass over. No bells."

The Brook Club was the most exclusive in Miami Beach, patronized by the elite of South Florida and visiting dignitaries, both theatrical and political.

Skipping his history class, Desi, with his guitar, arrived at the club. He walked in and went over to the balding, mustachioed maestro. Without saying hello, Cugat asked him, "Do you know '*Para Vigo Me Voy?*'"

Desi said that he did. The song's English-language title was "In Spain, They Say *Si, Si.*"

"I have never performed the song," Desi said.

"Here's your chance, kid."

"I was nervous as hell, but I didn't plan to blow my big chance," Desi said. "My Cuban blood was flowing like Niagara Falls. As I sang, my hips were revolving. I think Elvis Presley in the years to come stole my gyrating hips act. My heels clicked, and I shook ass. I've got a pretty damn hot ass. I sang the shit out of that 'Si, Si' number."

He wasn't particularly handsome, and he's less well-known today than his competitors, big band leaders Harry James and Tommy Dorsey.

But in his heyday (1935-1950) **Xavier Cugat** managed to charm women as diverse as **Carmen Miranda** (above) and the sultry singer/actress **Abbe Lane** (right), who became famously linked as his fourth wife.

Each of the photos show the obsessively hardworking entertainer with his trademark dog breed, a chihuahua.

When he was finished, Cugat came over to him and hired him on the spot. But there was a problem. The band leader was startled to learn that such a grown-up young man like Desi was still in high school and would not graduate until June. "I was held back because of the Cuban revolution," Desi said. "Not because I'm retarded."

After Desi's graduation in June, he feared that Cugat had forgotten all about him. He wrote to him at the Waldorf-Astoria Hotel in New York, and by return mail, the band leader's secretary sent Desi a one-way Greyhound bus ticket to Manhattan.

He had, weeks before, broken up with Gabriella. Actually, she was the one who tossed him aside, having fallen for the tall, blonde captain of the University of Miami's football team.

"I was a spendthrift and had gone through all my money except for fifty dollars," Desi said. "My Dad was broke and barely getting by. He didn't want me to go to New York. I set out and by the time I reached New York, I had only ten dollars left."

Arriving at the Port Authority Bus Terminal, he wandered around until he found this seedy hotel where rooms rented for only a dollar a night.

"My fellow residents looked like *putas* and drunks," he said. "My room was the size of a closet, and there was a communal bathroom. When I showered, I attracted unwanted stares. Late at night, there were knocks on my door, but I buried my head in the pillow. I never answered the door. I knew what strangers wanted from me, and I wasn't going to put out."

The following afternoon, he headed for that forty-seven story Waldorf-Astoria at 301 Park Avenue between 49th and 50th Streets. Completed as recently as 1931, it had become an Art Deco landmark, an icon of glamour and luxury. For years, it would remain the preferred temporary residence of visiting movie stars and politicos from other countries. In time, suites were named for former guests who included Cole Porter and the Duke and Duchess of Windsor. General Douglas MacArthur took up residency; Winston Churchill stayed here, and ex-president Herbert Hoover lived here for thirty years after his retirement from the presidency.

At the Waldorf-Astoria's welcome desk, Desi was directed to the Starlight Roof, where Cugat was rehearsing a new number with his band.

His stunningly beautiful wife, Carmen Castillo, whom he'd married in 1929, spotted Desi and his guitar and beckoned him over to her table. From afar, and in error, Desi mistook her for the glamourous, porcelain-skinned Mexican movie star, Dolores del Rio.

Desi's mistake wasn't at all surprising: During her Hollywood days, Carmen had been the stand-in for Del Rio on the sets of some of her movies.

Instead of taking in Cugat's musicians, Desi's eyes were transfixed on Carmen, "the most beautiful woman I had ever seen."

During a break, Cugat joined them at table. Then, he revealed to Desi that he would pay him twenty-five dollars a week as part of a two-week tryout during which he'd observe but not actually play alongside Cugat's musicians. He reserved an option that Desi could be fired after the two-week "tryout" if he didn't fit in.

Cugat also invited Desi to dine with Carmen and himself in their suite after reminding him that he had paid for Desi's bus transit to Manhattan.

***

Desi's first real chance to perform with Cugat came at Billy Rose's Aquacade, a music, dance, and swimming show produced by, as its name implied, Billy Rose. Featured at the time were swimming greats such as Eleanor Holm and Johnny Weissmuller. *[Weissmuller was later replaced by Buster Crabbe. Rose married Holm after divorcing his first wife, Fanny Brice.]*

An entertainer herself, **Carmen Castillo** was married to bandleader Xavier Cugat. But as it happened, her lustful eye could occasionally be aimed at a handsome young musician from Cuba.

Performances were at a 10,000-seat amphitheater whose stage extended out onto the waters of Lake Erie in Cleveland. The event would feature Cugat and his orchestra, alongside vaudeville acts, some Olympic swimmers, and a cast of 500. Struggling to adapt to the circumstances, Desi was hardly noticed.

He had a lot to learn from Cugat, "who taught me how to put on a show. He would come out in a tux wearing a sombrero with little bells around the brim."

During Desi's rendition of "In Spain, They Say *Si, Si,*" which he delivered on an elevated stage built out over an artificial lake, he nearly fell off the platform. He would have if he hadn't been grabbed by the scruff of the neck by one of the other musicians.

Desi was very impressed with Crabbe, who had won a 1932 Olympic Gold Medal after a 400-meter freestyle swimming event. Between 1933 and the 1950s, he would turn his fame as an athlete into movie stardom. He became famous for portraying comic strip heroes such as Tarzan, Flash Gordon, and Buck Rogers.

One night, he confided to Desi how he earned money on the road to stardom. "I rented myself out to queers but allowed them to enjoy me only from the waist down. While I let them do me, I closed my eyes and conjured up beautiful girls."

"If you want to get ahead in show business, consider going that route yourself—it's a quick way to stardom. My rival, Johnny Weissmuller, would perform jerk-offs at homo parties. The guys formed a circle around him to watch a show that ended in a blast-off. He'd never let guys touch him, but he became famous for his two-foot shots into the air."

According to Desi, "I didn't go that route in Cleveland. I was too busy having a good time. Never in my life have I been surrounded by so many heavenly aquamaidens. I had a different one every night. Oh, man, what a summer! I should have paid Cugat for letting me be in the show."

After Cleveland, Cugat and his orchestra traveled to the Arrowhead Inn at Saratoga in New York State. During Prohibition, it had been an en-

Two views of **Billy Rose's Aquacade**, part of the Great Lakes World Exposition (1936-37) beside the shores of Lake Erie in Cleveland. *Left:* its futuristic exterior; *right:* its stage, where dozens of good-looking swimmers, male and female, put on a show combining *oooh-la-la* athletic skills, waterworks, and show-biz razzmatazz.

Desi, as a then-unknown minor member of Xavier Cugat's Orchestra, provided some of the music.

tertainment venue for summer visitors who had included the Vanderbilts, the Whitneys, the Du Ponts, and a scattering of Rockefellers.

Celebrities, including Bing Crosby, flocked to the resort. A horse-racing aficionado, he was drawn to Saratoga for the thoroughbred racing. On hand were nightclub entertainers who included Sophie Tucker ("The Last of the Red Hot Mommas"), Jimmy Durante, and a rare appearance from Claudette Colbert.

One night, after Desi sang *Quiereme mucho (Yours),* he was invited over to Crosby's table. As it turned out, he was a devotee of Latin music. He agreed to get up on the stage and perform three numbers alongside Desi.

When Cugat appeared to thank Crosby for becoming part of the show, Crosby asked him, "What is a penny-pinching jerk like you paying this talented boy?"

"Twenty-five big ones a week," Cugat said.

"Dammit, that's a starvation wage," Crosby said. "Give him a raise."

"I will, I will, Bingo, as soon as we get back to Manhattan."

Before leaving Saratoga, Crosby shook Desi's hand. "We'll meet again, kiddo," he promised.

Crosby remembered his promise to Desi, and years later, invited him to appear with him on his *Kraft Music Hall Radio Show,* marking the

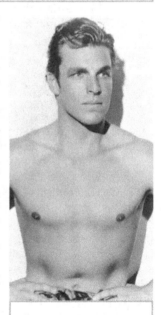

The screen's future Tarzan, **Buster Crabbe**, bragged to Desi, "I'm the sexiest and best-looking guy in America, an Olympic swimming champ. I get at least eight offers a day from both men and women. Sure beats hell out of working for $8 a week at Silverwood's clothing store in Los Angeles."

first time Desi ever starred in a nationally broadcast radio show.

Even after Cugat's five-dollar (per week) raise, Desi was finding it harder and harder to sustain life in Manhattan.

"I was paid so little that I didn't have enough to eat," Desi said.

"To reach the stage, I had to walk through the Waldorf-Astoria's kitchen. As I went along, I harvested food. Those multi-colored rumba shirts had wide, full sleeves with big ruffles. In those sleeves, I harvested food, all sorts of goodies to eat back in my dreary hotel room."

Desi learned that for the extra five dollars generated by Crosby, he had to perform certain duties. They included walking Cugat's dogs, fetching them from the music director's suite at the Waldorf three times a day. They included two Mexican chihuahuas and a "bloodthirsty" German shepherd. "I learned not to piss off this ferocious dog, or he'd have me for dinner. I later got my revenge on Cugat, the fucking cheapskate."

By now, Desi was becoming a star in his own right, enough to make his boss jealous. He went over big with the ladies, and became known for his sex appeal, something which Cugat seemed to lack. *[This was in stark contrast to Cugat's bandleading competitor, Artie Shaw, famous for romancing and marrying both Lana Turner and Ava Gardner.]*

"A lot of the gals came to see Cugat and his orchestra just to watch me shake my ass," Desi said, years later. "I wore black pants too sizes too small. As I gyrated on stage, I jutted my hips forward, my Cuban salami clearly outlined. I think the gals at the ringside tables could tell I still had my foreskin. Years later, that Welsh singer, Tom Jones, stole my 'tight pants' act."

One day, when Desi arrived at Cugat's suite for one of his three-times-per-day dog-walks, he found Carmen, Cugat's wife, there alone. She was lying on the sofa in the living room, wearing a black, see-through *négligée*. She didn't bother to cover herself when Desi entered the room. "I've come for the dogs," he said, slightly nervous.

"How can you mention the word dog when you're looking at a luscious beauty like me?" she asked.

Desi didn't know what to say. "I....ah, I mean.....I mean.... My English is not very good."

The Arrowhead Inn, reputed to have been linked to the mob operations of Meyer Lansky, was one of a half-dozen nightclubs operating on the east side of Saratoga Springs, New York, from the 1920s until the early 1950s. Collectively known as "The Lake Houses," they offered fine dining and top quality entertainment, along with illegal liquor during prohibition and illegal gambling.

Xavier Cugat, who employed Desi Arnaz as a member of his orchestra during the early part of the Cuban's career, entertained there frequently.

Displayed above is a promotional poster for some of Cugat's featured entertainers there.

"I think a man should take advantage of a pleasant encounter when he comes upon it."

"Yes, ma'am," he answered, moving closer toward her.

"Come here, you big sexy Cubano stud."

That was all the invitation he needed.

***

After six months, Desi admitted he'd learned a lot from Cugat but wasn't getting richer. It was time to move on to another gig.

The Cugat musicians were released every night after their gigs at 2:30AM. After that, Cugat usually headed to the Waldorf's midnight café, which stayed open until dawn, for breakfast. Desi asked if he could join him.

Over eggs and bacon, Desi told him that he was leaving the band and heading back to Miami where he planned to form his own band. At the time, the Latin music craze was sweeping the country, and Desi wanted in on it.

"But instead of being one of the boys in the band, I want to be the band leader and its singing star, too." he told Cugat.

"You'll have some lean and hungry days on your own," Cugat warned. "Launching a new band isn't easy, and you're talking to a man who would know. So OK, you god damn Cubano *hombre,* strike out on your own. If I know anything about show biz, you'll probably come back here starving, begging for your job back. But I'm in a position to make a deal with you. I'll let you bill yourself as Desi Arnaz and his Xavier Cugat Orchestra, direct from the Waldorf-Astoria in New York."

"And that is more than I could hope for," Desi answered, reaching for Cugat's hand."

"But there's a catch to my offer," Cugat said. "I'll want a commission, *Chico.* You know…for the use of my name."

"You've got a deal," Desi said.

"How much are we talking about?" Cugat asked.

"Twenty-five fucking big ones, to be paid to you every week," Desi answered. "Miami, here I come, right back where I started from."

Young, new to the sleaze aspects of show biz, and impressionable: **Desi Arnaz**.

54

CHAPTER FIVE

LUCILLE LAUNCHES HER ACTING CAREER AS A NAKED ROMAN SLAVE

"A girl's gotta do what a girl's gotta do." —Lucille Ball

Lucille arrived in Hollywood in 1933 as one of the Goldwyn Girls, a stock company of female dancers employed by producer Samuel Goldwyn.

Being a Goldwyn Girl did not guarantee success as a future film star, as most of the hopefuls eventually drifted into obscurity and returned to their hometowns. Lucille would be among the select few who emerged as a star. *[Others included Betty Grable, Virginia Bruce, Ann Sothern, Paulette Goddard, and Jane Wyman, who would later marry Ronald Reagan.]*

Born in Poland, Goldwyn (original name Goldfish) was one of the greatest producers of Hollywood's Golden Age. Even though he lent his name to Metro-Goldwyn-Mayer, the greatest studio, he never had any link to its management. Instead, in April of 1924, he established his own company, Samuel Goldwyn Productions, and became one of the richest producers in Hollywood history.

Lucille launched her Hollywood career as one of **The Goldwyn Girls**, each personally selected by Samuel Goldwyn, who maneuvered many of them onto his casting couch—"but not little me," she said.

"Eddie Cantor commended me for putting comedy first, despite the risk to my glamour, a rule that I follwed throughout my long career."

Lucille was eager to work for him. She fully expected to be summoned to his office for a starlet's obligatory "audition" on a casting couch.

En route by train to the West, a fellow Goldwyn Girl asked Lucille if it were hard to give up all her boyfriends in Manhattan.

"No way!" she answered. "Hollywood has the most beautiful men in the world, and I can have my pick."

When Lucille and the other Goldwyn Girls arrived at the train station at Pasadena, three dozen reporters and photographers were waiting "to ambush us."

Driven by limousine to the Roosevelt Hotel, Lucille faced the Hollywood press for the first time. "I made a big mistake, giving my right age of twenty-one. Had I said 'seventeen,' I could lie about it later when I'm older."

She spent one night at the Roosevelt before moving to a one-room apartment with a Murphy bed on Formosa Street. She could walk three blocks to United Artists, where the Eddie Cantor film, *Roman Scandals,* was being shot.

The Hollywood she encountered in 1933 had gone through its revolution from silent pictures to the talkies. An emerging star, Katharine Hepburn, won the Best Actress Oscar that year for *Morning Glory,* and the gay English actor, Charles Laughton, walked off with the gold for *The Private Lives of Henry VIII.*

The Goldwyn Girls were superficial, glittery, and anonymously glamourous, each dreaming of stardom. This is the world into which a young newcomer to show-biz (in this case, Lucille) was thrust.

A slightly plump, forty-year-old sexpot from vaudeville, Mae West, had arrived in town and had shot to stardom after only a fifteen-minute appearance in *Night After Night* (1932). Her co-star had been the Valentino lookalike, George Raft, soon to become Lucille's lover.

At the time, the industry's reigning sex goddess was Jean Harlow, famous as a fast-talking platinum blonde. It seemed that every actress in Hollywood was dyeing her hair blonde, and Lucille followed the trend long before she became America's favorite redhead.

"The Divine Garbo" vied with Norma Shearer as Queen of MGM. At that studio, Joan Crawford and Clark Gable were "electrifying" both on and off the screen.

The sultry blonde *femme fatale,* Marlene Dietrich, had created a sensation in Hollywood after her emigration from Germany. She had defied Hitler, who wanted her to stay in Berlin making political propaganda films.

Clara Bow, the "It Girl" of silent films, seduced an emerging new star, Gary Cooper, who became known as "The Montana Mule." Bow proclaimed, "Gary is hung like a horse...and can go all night." After that, he was pursued by members of Hollywood's homosexual set and by hordes

In this view of the chorines in **Roman Scandals,** critics have noted that, as in many line-ups by Busby Berkeley, moviegoers see not only the costumes and body parts, but fleeting views of everyone's face, too.

of devouring females, too. They ranged from the "Mexican Spitfire," Lupe Velez, to that "Wham from Alabam," Tallulah Bankhead.

Reporting for work on her first day, Lucille was nervous about being given a skimpy bathing suit before she joined an "inspection line" with other beauties for a viewing by the star of the picture, Eddie Cantor. She had seen him doing vaudeville on Broadway.

A New Yorker and the star of *Roman Scandals,* Cantor was known as "The Apostle of Pep," and as a singer, dancer, actor, and comedian who often appeared in black face. His hit songs included "Makin' Whoopee" and "If You Knew Suzie."

Cantor's eye-rolling song-and-dance routines had earned him the nickname of "Banjo Eyes." On Broadway he'd made his stage debut in *The Ziegfeld Follies of 1917* and stayed with the *Follies* troupe for a decade.

When Lucille joined the line-up of Goldwyn Girls, she realized she was the only one who was not voluptuous. Weighing 111 pounds, she was quite skinny. As she surveyed the busts of her competitors, she was overcome with the fear that she would be la-

Eddie Cantor was autocratic, self-important, and according to Lucille, "Way too peppy."

57

ROMAN SCANDALS: Lucille is on the right in what appears like a macabre assembly line of enslaved women, a sadist's *smörgåsbord* of sexual fantasies and perversions.

ENSLAVED LUCILLE, chained to her Hollywood ambitions and naked except for her "Lady Godiva" wig.

beled "Miss No Tits."

Before inspection by Cantor, Lucille did a very strange thing: She tore up little pieces of red crepe paper, tongued them, and applied the dye from them to her face and arms, as if she had a severe case of giant measles. She could have been dismissed on the spot for that stunt, but Cantor found it funny.

"That Ball gal is one hell of a riot, and she'll be my pick to pull all the stunts in the film, including wearing a mud pack," he said. "The other gals will probably maintain an aura of beauty. Ball will be the daredevil of the film."

***

In her day, Lucille Ball would seduce many sexy, handsome, desirable men. But one afternoon, years later, in a candid conversation with Marilyn Monroe, the blonde goddess told Lucille—and she agreed—that on the way to stardom there are a "lot of piggies you have to sleep with as well."

On the set of *Roman Scandals*, Cantor didn't even make a pass at Lucille. When she met Samuel Goldwyn,

Stacked up against the big-breasted glamour girls of her day, **Lucille** came in a distant No. 22 in the lineup. Nonetheless, Busby Berkeley saw talent behind her steely determination.

A fellow actress, Kay Harvey, gave her a harsh critique: "In those days, Lucille, even if she was a Goldwyn Girl, was actually a plain Jane with nondescript brown hair. She had no legs, no breasts, only a high energy drive. Then she became a Harlow blonde."

he chased her around his desk, trying to seduce her. She didn't let him, although later she wondered why. "I slept with every other producer. Why not dear old Sammy?"

Instead of Goldwyn, Lucille told friends, "I much prefer going to bed with Fred Kohlmar." She was referring to Goldwyn's personal assistant, who was also a casting director. "I don't really like his body, but I sure like his job," she said.

Although her part was uncredited, Lucille set out to introduce herself to the stars of the picture. Cantor's leading lady was Gloria Stuart as Princess Sylvia; corpulent Edward Arnold was Emperor Valerius; David Manners was Josephus; singer Ruth Etting was Olga; Veree Teasdale was the Empress Agrippa; and Alan Mowbray was Majordomo.

Frank Tuttle was the director of *Roman Scandals*. A director and writer, he had helmed his first film, *The Cradle Buster* in 1922.

Like Lucille herself, Tuttle would join the American Communist Party later that decade, mainly as a reaction to Hitler's rise to power. That idealistic decision brought a halt to his career later on. In 1951, in an attempt to restore his career, he named, in a testimony in front of the House Un-American Activities Committee, thirty-six colleagues and associates who had also joined the Communist Party. They included Lucille. But in a radical departure from the norm, her career would survive her long-ago involvement.

Frank Tuttle, the much-maligned director of *Roman Scandals*, would later be hauled in front of HUAC *(House Un-American Activities Committee)* for his purported ties to the Communists.

Unlike Lucille (who also registered as a communist), his career ended, even though, in attempts to placate the committee, he betrayed many of his collaborators trying to save his career.

Lucille's colleague in *Roman Scandals*, Gloria Stuart, a native of Santa Monica, was—like Lucille—new to films and filmmaking. Previously, she had appeared in a horror film, *The Invisible Man*, released the same year (1933) as *Roman Scandals*. Three years later, she gained far greater exposure co-starring with Shirley Temple in *Poor Little Rich Girl* (1936) and *Rebecca of Sunnybrook Farm* (1938).

[Stuart came out of retirement in 1997 to appear as Rose Dawson Calvert in James Cameron's disaster drama, Titanic *(1997), the highest-grossing film to that point in movie history. Playing a 101-year-old who threw a priceless 18th century heirloom into the sea "where it belonged," she was nominated for an Oscar as Best Supporting Actress.]*

Nebraska-born Ruth Etting was a singing star of the 1920s and '30s. Her signature tunes being "Shine On, Harvest Moon" and "Ten Cents a Dance." She became nationally known when she appeared in *Ziegfeld's Follies of 1927*. In 1955, Doris Day would impersonate Ruth Etting opposite James Cagney in *Love Me or Leave Me*.

Also in *Roman Scandals* appeared a still "undiscovered" New Yorker, Edward Arnold, who would soon shoot to stardom as *Diamond Jim* in 1935, reprising the role of Diamond Jim Brady in the 1940 film *Lillian Russell*. He eventually abandoned his attempt as a leading man, going for character roles instead. "The fatter I got, the better character parts I was given."

David Manners was a handsome, blonde-haired leading man from Nova Scotia. He'd shot to fame in Tod Browning's 1931 horror classic, *Dracula,* with Bela Lugosi in the title role. The (gay) film director, James Whale, maneuvered him onto a casting couch, and he soon became a popular leading man opposite such actresses as Barbara Stanwyck, Myrna Loy, Loretta Young, and Katharine Hepburn.

Lucille bonded with him during the filming of *Roman Scandals*. "He wasn't in any scene with me, but he did invite me to supper. He was mobbed by fans. All the time, he kept telling me I had personality. He said that if I persevered, I'd get somewhere in Hollywood. Not once did he ever hint he'd like to take me home to his boudoir. He was charming, but he preferred our handsome male waiter."

A Londoner, Alan Mowbray made his Broadway debut in the 1926 *The Sport of Kings*. His film debut came in the 1931 *God's Gift to Women,* playing a butler as he would so often be cast in so many other movies. That was the same year (1931) he portrayed George Washington in the film *Alexander Hamilton.*

"With all that talent in one film, who would ever notice me?" Lucille lamented.

According to the script, Cantor, cast as "Eddie," is a low-paid delivery boy in West Rome, Oklahoma. When he uncovers corruption in City Hall, he's run out of town. He wonders if such injustices occurred in ancient Rome, too. At that point, he drifts back in the pages of history,

Two views of heartthrob **David Manners,** lower photo, as a pinup and male model for sportswear and swimwear. In 1935, his fan club had 200,000 members, and four secretaries who labored to answer his fan mail.

When his star dimmed, he famously retreated to the desert as a spiritualist.

Ruth Etting, cast as Olga in *Roman Scandals*, evokes "the beauty of cigarette salesgirls" in *Ziegfeld Follies of 1931*.

arriving in (ancient) Rome right at the point where he's about to be sold on the slave market to the highest bidder. Josephus (Manners), who sets him free.

Cantor (playing Eddie) is then hired as the official food taster for the tyrannical emperor, Valerius (Edward Arnold). This is a dangerous job because dozens of people want to poison the ruler. As Princess Sylvia, Gloria Stuart is the prisoner of the emperor.

Four screenwriters labored over the script, based on a story by George S. Kaufman and Robert E. Sherwood. Lucille prevailed on one of the scriptwriters, Nat Perrin, to give her at least one line of dialogue. The first words she ever uttered on the screen were these: "He said the city put us here, and we should live here."

"All of the chorus girls were trying to look like Harlow," Lucille said. "Cantor found my eyebrows bushy, and I shaved them off. They never grew back. From that day forth, I never went anywhere without my eyebrow pencil."

Lucille, originally hired as a bit player for six weeks, worked for six months, as the musical became the most expensive ever made to that point in Hollywood history.

The dance director of *Roman Scandals* was Busby Berkeley, nicknamed "Buzz." For Americans mired in the misery of the Great Depression, he offered a two-hour escape from their woes with several iconic musicals during the 1930s, including *42nd Street*. He

Film director/choreographer **Busby Berkeley,** was famous for artfully underdressed chorus girls and "gleeful cinematic excess"

As described by film critic Tom Huddleston, in reference to this still photo from *Gold Diggers of 1933*, "**Busby Berkeley** could pack more inspired ideas and indelible images into a seven-minute dance routine than most directors managed in a full-length feature.

The quintessential Berkeley frame depicts a circle of dancing girls – scantily dressed, perfectly synchronised, beaming from ear to ear – making kaleidoscopic patterns for a downward-facing, God's-eye camera. It's such an idiosyncratic and unusual image that it's almost unsettling: the only other place you'll find such precise choreography en masse is in footage of the Nuremberg rallies, and it's no surprise that *[Nazi Germany's Propagand Minister]* Joseph Goebbels was a huge Berkeley fan."

became celebrated for sequences that featured kaleidoscopic dances with multiple beauties scantily clad in exotic costumes.

In *Roman Scandals,* he developed the technique of a "parade of faces," which individualized each chorus girl with a loving close-up. This was Lucille's first on-screen close-up. "I gave it my best Jean Harlow come-hither look," she said.

Originally, Buzz dressed the slave girls, including Lucille, in body stockings, their figures covered by long, absurdly oversized wigs. (Lucille's was blonde). He then ordered that all the girls strip naked, concealing their body parts behind the strands of their wigs. He arranged for the scene to be filmed on a closed set at night to escape the ogling of Peeping Toms.

Lucille joined the chorus of the song "Keep Young and Beautiful." Later, as part of the continuity of *Roman Scandals,* she appeared in a contemporary scene set in Oklahoma as one of the townspeople in a song called "Build a Little Home."

"Nothing was beneath me during the filming," she said. "Even covering my face with that damn mudpack. I'd scream, I'd yell, I was getting my education in filmmaking, and putting my foot in the door."

Berkeley later claimed, "I saved her career. I think that at one point, Goldwyn wanted to boot her out of the studio, but I took up for her. She was a bundle of energy, taking all assignments offered and running with them. I told her I thought she was going to go far in Hollywood. She owed me one, if you get my drift, and she didn't turn me down."

As its director, Berkeley presented happy faces during filming and on the screen, but in real life, his own face was often sad. Thanks to his passion for liquor and women, he was mired in scandal. In 1935, while driving drunk, he was responsible for a terrible accident where two people were killed and five others severely injured. Eventually, after several court appearances, he was cleared of manslaughter charges.

Roman Scandals was a big hit at the box office. *Variety* defined it as "The hokiest kind of hoke," and *The New York Evening Post* claimed, "The picture is full of *harum-scarum*, also exhibiting the Goldwyn Girls in all their gorgeousness. It is cleaning up at the box office."

***

Lucille's early reputation as a "gun moll" for the mob began during her brief involvement (and brief appearance) in a film called *The Bowery,* shot during the

Lucille had only a bit part in *The Bowery,* and had to leave most of the girl/guy emoting to **George Raft and Fay Wray**, that film's romantic leads, depicted above.

summer of 1933. It was a Pre-Code comedy and action movie set on the Lower East Side of Manhattan during the "Gay Nineties" of the late 19th Century.

Directed by Raoul Walsh, it starred Wallace Beery, George Raft, and the child star, Jackie Cooper. Fay Wray, fresh from her worldwide success in *King Kong* (1933), had the female lead of Lucy Calhoun. Lucille had only a brief, uncredited role in a beach scene.

Samuel Goldwyn lent some of his Goldwyn Girls to the then-newly emerging studio, Twentieth Century Fox, run by Joseph Schenck and Darryl F. Zanuck. *The Bowery* was the first film issued by that new studio.

As was his custom then and in the future, Zanuck seduced some of the Goldwyn Girls, but skipped Lucille because he was a self-style "big breast" man.

Originally, Lucille was told that the movie would star Clark Gable, the King of Hollywood, but at the last minute, he dropped out and was replaced by Raft.

The plot pits saloon keeper Chuck Connors (Wallace Beery) against his rival, Steve Brodie (Raft), whose character in the film, as part of a wager and a stunt, jumps off the Brooklyn Bridge. Beery and the young Cooper had scored a big hit together in *The Champ* (1931), the highest-grossing film of that year. According to the plot, Wray falls in love with Brodie.

Colorful Bowery characters populate the film, speaking local street jargon, much of the language considered, by today's standards, politically incorrect. In one scene, a sign in the window reads, "Nigger Joe's." Throughout the course of the film, Chinese people are routinely called "Chinks."

At one point, an actress playing temperance activist Carrie Nation appears with a roiling mob of angry women to destroy Connors' saloon with axes and hatchets.

The New York Times reviewed the movie as "punctuated with ribald mirth, brawls, fights, noises, and vulgarity."

Director Walsh, a New Yorker, had achieved fame when he starred as John Wilkes Booth in *The Birth of a Nation* (1915). Before meeting Lucille, he

Raoul Walsh in 1928, before he injured his eye and before he had to wear an eyepatch.

Here, he's depicted as a horny U.S. Marine courting Sadie Thompson, a South Seas hooker portrayed by **Gloria Swanson**, in one of the most famous silent films of its era. It was also directed by Walsh.

Mack Grey was the "sidekick and henchman" of George Raft. Grey became one of Lucille's first lovers in Hollywood, and was partially responsible for her early reputation as a "gun moll."

Carole Lombard, Lucille's friend, nicknamed Grey "killer." She and Raft were lovers at the time.

On Broadway, Grey was known as "The Tango King," and he later became Dean Martin's "Dirty Deeds Man."

had starred in and directed Gloria Swanson in W. Somerset Maugham's *Sadie Thompson* (1928), the story of a straight-talking prostitute.

Walsh's acting career ended when he was driving through the desert one afternoon and a jackrabbit broke through his windshield, whose shattered glass blinded him in his right eye. After that, he concentrated on directing, always wearing a black patch over his damaged eye. He had generated critical, but not box office, success in helming *The Big Trail* (1930), an epic wagon train saga that had starred an unknown actor named John Wayne.

Lucille had begun to date Mack Grey, the bodyguard for Raft, who was still connected to the mob in New York. She and Grey were seen driving around Hollywood in Raft's bulletproof limousine. She told actress Carole Lombard, who was dating Raft at the time, "Mark doesn't have a pretty face, but once he strips down, he can have any woman he wants in Hollywood."

The bisexual Raft often summoned Grey into his bed, so he knew why Lucille was so appreciative of his bodyguard's seductive power.

On several occasions, Grey had been accused of being Raft's "hit man," but he had never been charged. Lombard nicknamed him, "The Killer."

Grey might do dirty deeds for Raft and the mob, but Lucille found him a considerate gentleman. On the night of August 27, 1936, they showed up as a "loving couple" at the Cocoanut Grove, the most popular nightclub of its day. Lucille was spotted chatting with actresses Gail Patrick, Margaret Sullavan, and Ann Sothern (a future rival in TV comedy). Later Lucille became so amorous at table with Grey that the manager approached and sarcastically suggested, "Why don't you two rent a room?"

Lucille and Grey often double-dated on nights out with Raft and Lombard, who were starring together in the film, *Bolero,* which was released in

Known as :The Hoosier Tornado" from Fort Wayne, Indiana, **Carole Lombard** reigned as the mistress of screwball comedies in the 1930s. In the years before she married Clark Gable, she and Lucille often double-dated and were called "Hell Raisers."

1934.

At the time, Lombard was in the process of divorcing actor William Powell. *[Their marriage lasted from 1931-1933.]* One day, Lucille visited the set of *Bolero,* where she was introduced to an old-time vaudevillian named William Frawley. Only forty-six at the time, he would later become Fred Mertz, married to Ethel, on the *I Love Lucy* TV series.

Lombard told Lucille that before she signed for *Bolero,* she'd been offered the female lead in *It Happened One Night* (1934). After she rejected it, the role went to Claudette Colbert, who won the Best Actress Oscar for her performance in it. *[Her co-star, Clark Gable, took home the Best Actor Oscar for his performance in that film, too.]*

Lombard had co-starred with her then-husband, William Powell in *Man of the Year* (1931). Ironically, a year later, she'd also co-star with her future husband, Clark Gable, in *No Man of Her Own* (1932), but their love affair and subsequent marriage (1939-1942) would come later. Howard Hughes, the aviator and film mogul, "had been the first man to deflower me," Lombard confided to Lucille.

George Raft claimed, "Carole has one of the most sensational figures I've ever seen in my life," However, she was relatively flat-chested, and had to be equipped with falsies in most films. She would yell at her wardrobe women, 'Bring me my god damn tits!'"

Her tongue was often referred to as "blue." When she was quite young, so many men made advances at her, she asked her brothers to teach her every vulgar word they knew, hoping that would turn off her would-be suitors.

When Harry Cohn of Columbia Pictures put the make on her, she shot back, "I've agreed to be in your shitty little picture but fucking me isn't part of the deal!"

She got the role anyway since he admired her spunk.

Raft learned that both Lucille and Lombard weren't natural blondes. One night, he caught Lombard whipping up a peroxide solution to dab over her pubic hair. She told him, "I'm just making my cuffs and my collar match."

Raft would be but one in a series of affairs Lombard had before her marriage to Gable. Lucille stayed in touch with her until her untimely death in 1942 in an airplane crash. In the meantime, John Barrymore came and went from her boudoir, as did singer/actor Russ Columbo, director Ernst Lubitsch, David Niven, John Gilbert, Charles (Buddy) Rogers, Cesar Romero (who was mostly gay and frequently lusting after Desi Arnaz), and even producer David O. Selznick and director Preston Sturges.

Lucille and Lombard were known for getting together "to dish" their various suitors and for bonding as friends. The more experienced Hollywood player advised Lucille on how to dress better and urged her to seek "roles with more meat on them. Those fucking bastards should give you a break."

Grey apparently relayed many stories to his boss, Raft, about how great Lucille was in bed. Consequently, Raft decided to try her out for himself. At first Lucille resisted, but he couldn't understand why. "C'mon," he told her, "I'm irresistible. Even Mae West says so."

Finally, Lucille confessed why she kept turning him down: "Tallulah Bankhead says she got gonorrhea from you. She told me her weight went down to just seventy pounds by the time she checked out of the hospital. Then Tallulah laughed hysterically and said that contracting a bad case of V.D. hadn't really taught her a lesson and that she went right back to her 'bad girl' ways."

"But that was so long ago, and I'm completely cured now," Raft assured her. He finally won her over, and she went to bed with him. Later she told Grey, "Now I know why Valentino nicknamed your boss 'Black Snake.'"

Rudolph Valentino and Raft had been lovers and roommates when they worked together as "taxi-dancing gigolos" during their early days in New York.

Grey told Lucille, "Screwing is Raft's game. He can get it up first thing in the morning and put in a whole day of it, going on into the night, on and off. He averages at least two women a day, most often three."

In Hollywood, he quickly developed a reputation as a "Ladies' Man," seducing Mae West, his co-star in *Night After Night* (1932). After her first romantic encounter with Raft, she said, "That guy can come up and see me sometime...anytime."

Usually, he seduced hookers and chorus girls, but occasionally, he dated from the A-list—Norma Shearer, Billie Dove, Ann Sheridan, and Marlene Dietrich.

One of his girlfriends, however, cast a dissenting voice. Betty Grable told Lucille, "George is probably a latent homosexual broken in by Valentino when they were roomies in New York. He never touched me except to beat me up."

Lucille would know Raft for many years. He had been born in Manhattan's Hell's Kitchen in 1905. In the 1920s, during Prohibition, he had been a "runner" for mobster Owney Madden, and known to such gangster kingpins as Al Capone and Bugsy Siegel.

His screen career began in 1929 with the movie, *Queen of the Night Clubs.*

It was his 1932 performance in *Scarface,* in which he played a coin-flipping gangster, that made him a bigtime star. Signed by Jack Warner and noted mostly for his gangster films, he competed with Edward G. Robinson, James Cagney, and later, Humphrey Bogart for roles in mob epics.

He told Lucille, "Instead of a gangster, I could have been the first X-rated dancer. I was very erotic. I used to caress myself, even fondle my cock, often enough to produce an erection in my tight pants. I was never a great dancer, no Fred Astaire, but I was a stylist, unique. I also did the fastest Charleston of any male dancer. Joan Crawford and I should have gone on tour together."

In London, while watching him perform, the Duke of Windsor (the former King Edward VIII) was said to have developed a crush on Raft.

Raft always carried around a roll of hundred-dollar bills. One night when Lucille complained to him that she was flat broke and behind in her rent, he lent her two hundred dollars. Years later when she was rich and heard that he was heavily in debt, she repaid the loan, and even offered to pay interest, but he wouldn't hear of it and returned the money to her.

She remained friends with him. "He never listened to my career advice," she once said. "As a man, he thought he knew more than I did." She read three scripts that Raft rejected and urged him to star in each of them. After thinking it over, Raft decided not to appear in *High Sierra, The Maltese Falcon,* and *Casablanca,* the roles going, of course, to Humphrey Bogart. When Raft encountered Lucille at a nightclub in Hollywood in 1946, he said, "If only I had listened to mama."

Both Raft and Lucille went on to other loves, but she still remembered her good times with him. When he died of leukemia at the age of 85 on November 25, 1980, Lucille paid a secret visit to the mortuary where his body lay in state. To her surprise she discovered that Raft and his long-ago lover, Mae West—the two stars of the 1932 *Night After Night*—"were having a posthumous reunion," in her words. West had died only two days before, and her body was resting in peace beside that of Raft's.

In *Blood Money,* **Frances Dee** and **George Bancroft** were lovers, enough so that it became the first film banned by the Legion of Decency of the Catholic Church.

At night however, Dee sought shelter in the arms of Joel McCrea, whom she eventually married "for love everlasting."

Tallulah Bankhead had been set to play Dee's role, but backed out.

"In my next picture, *Blood Money* (1933), I was merely part of the scenery," Lucille said. "This was another film for Fox, and Darryl Zanuck had yet to summon me to his casting couch. *[He never would.]*"

Zanuck had success with producing gangster films, including (in collaboration with Hal Wallis) *Little Caesar* (1931) starring Edward G. Robinson.

Blood Money was written and directed by Rowland Brown, who, like George Raft, had underworld ties. As a bootlegging teenager during Prohibition, he'd developed a reputation as a tough guy, having once knocked out boxing champ Jack Dempsey in a sparring match.

Blood Money became Brown's favorite Pre-Code film. Years later, director Martin Scorsese recalled, "Rowland Brown is a largely forgotten figure today, but he made sardonic crime movies in the 1930s, each dealing with city politics, corruption, and the coziness between cops and criminals."

Long after working briefly with Lucille, Brown would helm *Angels with Dirty Faces* (1938), starring James Cagney, Pat O'Brien, and Humphrey Bogart. He was nominated for an Oscar for Best Original Screenplay.

Lucille Ball as a bit player, impersonating a gun moll, in *Blood Money*.

In her role, she is paid to keep Chick Chandler, cast as Drury Darling, company at the race track...and elsewhere.

The star of *Blood Money* was George Bancroft, a former Merchant Marine, who later worked on Broadway, where he became known for his blackface routines and impersonations of celebrities. In 1929, he'd been nominated for a Best Actor Oscar for his film *Thunderbolt*. In *Blood Money*, he played a bail bondsman who falls for Elaine Talbert (Frances Dee).

The Dee role had originally been cast with Loretta Young, and later, with Tallulah Bankhead, but Brown dropped both of them before the debut of filming and hired Dee.

Lucille met Dee only briefly, having seen her in the 1931 film adaptation of Theodore Dreiser's novel, published in 1925, *American Tragedy*.

[Twenty years later, in 1951, Dreiser's novel would be adapted once again and retitled A Place in the Sun. *Elizabeth Taylor would reprise the role that Dee had pioneered.]*

During the filming of *Blood Money*, Lucille talked with Dee's beau, actor Joel McCrea. Dee married him in 1933, a union that lasted until his death in 1990.

The character that Dee played, a role that Lucille coveted, was described as "a kleptomaniac, a nymphomaniac, and everything in between."

Blood Money also marked the film debut of the Australian actress, Judith Anderson. She would later immortalize herself as the psychotic lesbian housekeeper, Mrs. Danvers, in Alfred Hitchcock's 1940 thriller, *Rebecca*. Almost two decades later, she played "Big Mama" in the 1958 film adaptation of Tennessee Williams' stage play, *Cat on a Hot Tin Roof,* with Elizabeth Taylor, Burl Ives, and Paul Newman.

Blossom Seeley, known as the "Queen of Syncopation," had a brief role in *Blood Money* as a singer. Every time Lucille walked by the entrance to her dressing room, Blossom would be playing two of her singles again and again and again: "Way Down Yonder in New Orleans," and "Yes, Sir, That's My Baby."

In *Blood Money,* Lucille was cast as a gun moll paid to keep Chuck Chandler "company." The role of the gangster went to an actor with the unusual name of Drury Darling.

Critic Mordaunt Hall reviewed *Blood Moon* as "flat stuff, a whimsical tale of thievery, thuggery, and attempted slaughter that Zanuck mistook for entertainment."

Another critic labeled it "Deliciously perverse, a tale of double-crosses and dark desires."

This "shockingly subversive" film had the dubious distinction of being the first movie ever banned by the Catholic Church's Legion of Decency.

Lucille Meets the Brain Squad, an Intellectual Jackpot:

S.N. Behrman was a playwright, a biographer, and a longtime writer for *The New Yorker.* For that magazine, he became known for his profiles of notable figures such as composer George Gershwin, entertainer Eddie Cantor, and the Hungarian playwright, Ferenc Molnár.

In later years, Lucille compared her link with him to Marilyn Monroe's unhappy affair (and later marriage) to Arthur Miller.

***

In the 1930s, no matter how torrid the affair, Lucille did not confine her attentions to just one boyfriend.

Later in life, she recalled her affair with the famous author, S.N. Behrman. "Marilyn Monroe had her Arthur Miller; I had my Behrman."

She claimed she met Behrman by accident . . . literally. It was a rainy afternoon—Lucille didn't remember where—and he was coming out of a building. He slipped on the pavement and fell, his glasses bouncing into the street where they were run over by a taxicab. Since he was near-sighted, he appealed to her to help him. She didn't know who he was at the time of their first meeting.

Taking him to a coffee shop, she learned over coffee and a grilled cheese sandwich that he had just written the film script of *Queen Christina* (1933) for Greta Garbo. Duly impressed, she wanted to know more about him.

He was very willing to tell her that he was one of Broadway's leading authors of "high comedy," having written for such stars as Katharine Cornell, Ina Claire, and Jane Cowl, even for the acting team of Alfred Lunt and Lynn Fontanne. Lucille later admitted that she hoped he might write a high comedy for her because she'd grown tired of her silly walk-ons.

She drove Behrman back to his home and, when he invited her to stay over, she did.

Lucille later told actress Ann Sothern, "It is not Sam's looks that attract me to him, but his mind. He's a hell of a lot smarter than I will ever be, but he never talks down to me. There is much I admire about him. He's very owlish-looking and quite erudite."

"He's not homo himself, but he's a very tolerant fellow," she said. "He has a lot of homo friends and shares in their trials and tribulations. Over the years I knew him, I met some of his best friends, W. Somerset Maugham, Laurence Olivier, Noël Coward, and Jean Giraudoux."

One reporter described Behrman as "slim, dark-eyed, and curly-haired, with the brooding melancholy of a young Jewish intellectual." Critic Brooks Atkinson labeled him as one of the Theater Guild's most adored authors, ranking up there with Elmer Rice, Gavin Maxwell, Robert E. Sherwood, and Sidney Howard.

In addition to Garbo's *Queen Christina* (1933), Behrman worked on the script for other pictures with her, including *Conquest* (1937), in which she played the mistress of Napoléon opposite Charles Boyer. Behrman also wrote the screenplay for Garbo's last film, *Two-Faced Woman* (1941), in which she starred with Melvyn Douglas and Constance Bennett.

Ralph Forbes with **Clara Bow** in *Her Wedding Night* (1930)

During their marriage, **Ralph Forbes** and **Ruth Chatterton** co-starred in *The Lady of Scandal* (1930), just as the Talkies were taking over Hollywood. .

***

In 1933, love entered Lucille's hectic life, at least love expressed by one of her suitors. She wasn't sure of her own emotions. She had never really been in love except once back in Jamestown with Johnny DaVita.

In Los Angeles at the Cocoanut Grove Night Club, Carole Lombard stopped at Lucille's table and introduced her to her escort of the evening, Ralph Forbes, the English matinée idol. Later, while Lombard was dancing with her future husband, Clark Gable, Forbes— a blonde-haired, blue-eyed Englishman—came over and asked Lucille to dance.

Holding her close to him on the floor, he whispered in her ear, "There's nothing between Carole and me. I'm just her escort for the evening. I want you. I've got a good memory. Whisper your phone number in my ear."

Strongly attracted to him—she was lured by his wit, charm, and looks—she did what he'd requested.

He phoned her late the following morning, and they began to date.

She soon discovered who this dashing stranger was who had entered her life so abruptly: An actor, he was born in London in 1904 to a stage and film actress, Mary Forbes. Lucille noticed a scar on his cheek, the result of a football injury he'd sustained in college in Staffordshire.

He'd launched his film career in silent pictures in 1921 and had then worked steadily throughout the rest of that decade.

He arrived for the first time in the United States in 1924, and, at the age of twenty, appeared on the Broadway stage with Ruth Chatterton, who was thirty-two at the time. The couple fell in love and were married that same year on December 19, when she was accused of "robbing the cradle."

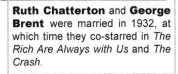

Ruth Chatterton and **George Brent** were married in 1932, at which time they co-starred in *The Rich Are Always with Us* and *The Crash*.

As a couple, they gravitated to Hollywood, where Chatterton became a leading movie star in the early '30s, second in box office appeal only to Norma Shearer, the Queen of MGM.

Chatterton's first critical film success involved her starring in the 1929 *Madame X*, for which she received an Academy Award nomination as Best Actress. Her second Best Actress Oscar nomination came the following year when she starred in *Sarah and Son* (1930), the story of an impoverished housewife who becomes an opera singer. Her son was played by the child actor, Philippe de Lacy.

Meanwhile, Forbes reinforced his image as an actor of considerable talent in plays by Noël Coward and Henrik Ibsen.

When Lucille met him, he was co-starring with Katharine Hepburn in *Christopher Strong* (1933), in which she played a female airplane pilot.

Tiring of Forbes, Chatterton divorced him in 1932. That same year, she married actor George Brent, who would later get

Lucille's brief but torrid romance with British actor **Ralph Forbes** had long ended by the time they co-starred as supporting players in *Annabel Takes a Tour (1938)*.

She introduced him as "my old flame."

involved in a torrid affair with Bette Davis.

One night on a date at the Cocoanut Grove, Brent and Chatterton encountered Forbes with Lucille. Deeply threatened, Chatterton immediately became catty. "Ralph, who is this whore you've taken up with?"

"How dare you call me a whore?" Lucille shouted at her. "You fucking lezzie."

She had heard many rumors about how Chatterton—one of the first women pilots—was an intimate of a far more famous aviation pioneer, Amelia Earhart. Gossip had swept through Hollywood that they were involved in an affair.

[Earhart, as the world found out, disappeared on July 2, 1937, during a circumnavigational flight around the world with navigator Fred Noonan. Their bodies were never found.]

Shortly after that confrontation at the Grove, Forbes proposed marriage to Lucille. "I had to turn him down, as I was not ready for marriage," she said. "I was playing the field and had no intention of getting locked into wedded bliss. Besides, he was a dignified Englishman, and I was not the rarefied British type—you know, the type who drinks from a teacup with a dainty crooked finger extended in the air? There was another reason for not marrying him. I decided I didn't really love him."

Broadway Thru a Keyhole: It was Pre-Code, frothy, and racy. Lucille had a very minor (i.e., ornamental) role in it.

Forbes recovered quickly from the rejection. To Lucille's dismay, within days, he'd run off to Yuma, Arizona, to marry the British actress, Heather Angel. "Ralph sure got over his heartbreak quickly," Lucille claimed.

***

Her next brief appearance in *Broadway Thru a Keyhole* (1933), a saucy Pre-Code film from 20th Century Fox, was as an uncredited "chorine" and beach bunny" in a scene filmed on the sands of Santa Monica. She delivered a line that was said to be her first on-screen joke. When her companion is slighted by the film's leading lady (Constance Cummings), Lucille quips, "Well, you certainly were the life of the party, Louie, while it lasted."

After the release of *Broadway Thru a Keyhole*, Lucille waited for three years before seeing herself in it. "My role was so small I didn't think it was worth my time. Months and months later, when I saw it advertised on the second bill of another movie, I said, 'What the hell,' and dropped in to see

72

it. I was not impressed."

Its script had been written by the sometimes acerbic newspaper columnist Walter Winchell. For inspiration, he drew directly from the life of Ruby Keeler, who, in 1933, had scored big with her noteworthy and ground-breaking musical hit from Warners, *42nd Street*. In it, she played a sweet young thing who takes over the lead role from the injured star.

Keeler's husband, Al Jolson, was so angered by Winchell's having ripped off an episode from his wife's life that he challenged him to a boxing match.

There was personal tragedy, even death, associated with some of the stars of *Broadway Thru A Keyhole*.

Lowell Sherman was brought in as director. Born in San Francisco, and noted also for his skills as an actor, he had emerged from a theatrical family. His grandmother, an actress, had co-starred with the noted actor Edwin Booth, the brother of John Wilkes Booth, the assassin of Abraham Lincoln.

Sherman also directed Mae West in her first starring role, *She Done Him Wrong* (1933), and he'd followed that the same year by helming Katharine Hepburn in her Oscar-winning role in *Morning Glory*. Lucille always credited Sherman for giving her encouragement about how she might one day become a star. Sherman would die at the peak of his career in 1934, only a year after the release of *Broadway Thru a Keyhole*. He's most frequently remembered today as both an actor and director for his 1932 performance with Constance Bennett in *What Price Hollywood?*

In a nutshell, *Broadway Thru a Keyhole* depicts racketeer Frank Rocci (Paul Kelly) falling in love with showgirl Joan Whelen

In Manhattan during Prohibition, **Texas Guinan** was hailed as "The Queen of the Night Clubs." Regrettably, she died only days after the release of the movie she'd co-starred in, *Broadway Thru a Keyhole*.

Her early promoters, the Frohman Amusement Corporation, described her as "the most compelling, original, and captivating character of the screen."

"Texas Guinan: She came out of the vast unknown regions of th West with the spirit of the desert and plains. [She has] the power and brawn of those compelled to defend their own by force of might and will, and yet she possesses all the graces and charms of a woman. Her films attain a new high-water mark in Photo Dramatic Creation."

Guinan appears above in a pistol-packing still shot from her 1920 silent film, *Wildcat*. Ironically, forty years later, Lucille would make her Broadway debut in a musical with the same name.

(Constance Cummings), a dancer from a famous Broadway night club inspired by the flamboyant "girl about town," Texas ("Tex") Guinan. Rocci uses his influence to make her a star, hoping that she'll fall in love with him. When he proposes marriage, she accepts more out of gratitude than love.

When she migrates to Miami Beach, she falls in love with a handsome crooner, Clark Brian (Russ Columbo). The question is, can she let the psychotically jealous Rocci know she's in love with another man, and a handsome and charismatic one at that?

A former chorus girl on Broadway, Cummings had been discovered by Samuel Goldwyn, who lured her to Hollywood, where she would make twenty movies. She never really made the top tier in Hollywood but fared better in England. She eventually moved to London, where she acted on both the stage and in films. Her most famous role was in the supernatural comedy, *Blithe Spirit* (1945), starring Rex Harrison.

In the early 1930s, **Russ Columbo** was dubbed "The Vocal Valentino" as he rivaled Bing Crosby in "The Battle of the Baritones." On the dawn of what might have been a brilliant acting and singing career, he met "a wayward bullet." His death is still a mystery.

Its male star, Brooklyn-born Paul Kelly, broke into show business as a child actor in 1911. *Broadway Thru a Keyhole* was his first Talkie.

[Kelly had made headlines in 1927 because of a fight he had with actor Ray Raymond over Kelly's affair with Raymond's wife, actress Dorothy Mackaye. Kelly bashed in Raymond's head and killed him. For the actor's death, Kelly was sentenced to ten years in San Quentin, but served only twenty-five months.

After his release, he married Mackaye. In their review of Broadway Thru a Keyhole, *even The New York Times had applauded the acting talents of "Jailbird Kelly."]*

During the filming of *Broadway Thru a Keyhole,* Lucille maintained her friendship with Carole Lombard, who was also slated for an early death. Around this time, Lombard dumped George Raft and began "heavy dating" Russ Columbo, the bandleader, actor, and songwriter known for such compositions as "Too Beautiful for Words." Columbo worked in movies with such stars as Lupe Velez and Gary Cooper and became known in other broadcast media as "Radio's Valentino."

[Columbo, too, was slated for an early death, fatally shot at the home of his friend, photographer Lansing Brown. The shooting still remains a mystery, but apparently, he was "playing around" with Brown's antique gun collection. The weapon accidentally discharged, a bullet lodging in his brain just below his left eye. He was rushed to the hospital for surgery, but it was too late.

Although it was thwarted by his early death, Variety had predicted that Russ Columbo would "go places."

Lucille offered Lombard whatever comfort she could and attended Columbo's funeral along with such Hollywood luminaries as Bing Crosby.]

She would recall another ill-fated star who appeared in *Broadway Thru a Keyhole*, Texas Guinan, "the most fascinating character I had ever met."

A daughter of Waco, Texas, born to Irish immigrants, she had become the most famous nightclub hostess on Broadway, welcoming customers to her illegal speakeasy, greeting them with what became her legendary refrain, "HELLO, SUCKERS!"

At the time, Guinan reigned over a sea of highly visible flappers who included Joan Crawford dancing the Charleston. The club was frequented by Al Jolson, boxer Jack Dempsey, Rudolph Valentino, George Raft, Mae West, Ruby Keeler, the Prince of Wales, and President Harding.

[Guinan died on November 15, 1933, shortly after meeting Lucille, at the age of forty-nine. It was exactly one month before Prohibition was repealed.

In 1945, Betty Hutton would bring a highly sanitized adaptation of Guinan's life story to the screen in Incendiary Blonde.*]*

Minor roles in *Broadway Thru a Keyhole* featured the Russia-born Gregory Ratoff, a character actor in the 1930s. He had played Mae West's lawyer in *I'm No Angel* (1933), but his greatest performance lay in his future when he was cast as producer Max Fabian in *All About Eve* (1950), starring Bette Davis.

Singer Blossom Seely also had a role. Lucille had just worked with her on the set of *Blood Money*.

***

If Sam Goldwyn can, with great conviction,
Instruct Anna Sten in diction,
Then Anna shows,
Anything goes.

Anna Sten played *Nana*, based on Émile Zola's novel of the same name.

It was the then-risqué story of an impoverished French girl who rises to became a high-class prostitute.

—Lyrics (*"Anything Goes"*) by Cole Porter

Nana (1934), a Pre-Code drama produced by Samuel Goldwyn, was a celluloid bastardization of Émile Zola's controversial French novel, published in 1880, with the same name. Goldwyn conceived it as a vehicle for the Ukraine-born Hollywood ingénue, Anna Sten, whom he had discovered during a talent hunt in Europe. He decided to hire her and put her under contract at his studio, where he would bill her as "The New Garbo."

Lucille recalled *Nana* as "My first big break in Hollywood."

She had two scenes with Sten in which the actress talks of her great love for a soldier. Offscreen, the star and the would-be star became friends, "and I had to ease her into her adjustment in Hollywood," Lucille said. "I never saw her after the movie wrapped. Not only that, but I never saw myself on the screen except as a fleeting glance as an extra. My scenes with Sten ended up on the cutting-room floor. I burst into tears, vowing that 'my day will come'—but when?"

Goldwyn had made the decision to engage the beauty, who spoke no

Two views of **Dorothy Arzner,** upper photo: Directing, and (lower photo) with **Joan Crawford.**

English, after seeing a screening of *Der Mörder Dimitri Karamassof (The Murderer, Dimitri Karamazov),* a German-language film (released in 1931) loosely based on motifs from Fyodor Dostoyevsky's literary classic, *The Brothers Karamazov.*

Goldwyn had decided that once he got Sten to Hollywood and under contract, he'd keep her out of sight for a year, supervising her instruction in English, acting, singing, and dancing. Meanwhile, he continued to promote her in the press, suggesting that she would soon enter the pantheon of those screen goddesses who included not only Garbo, but Mae West, Jean Harlow, Norma Shearer, and Marlene Dietrich.

"Talk about high expectations," Lucille said. "I wondered at the time

In her "golden age" role with **James Cagney** in *The Public Enemy*, **Mae Clarke** was immortalized for having a grapefruit smashed into her face by a psychotic gangster played by James Cagney.

Decades later, she re-invented herself as a key player in the daytime soap opera, *General Hospital,*. She appears in this photo with (right) **John Beradino** in 1963.

if all that superhype might doom Sten if she ever got around to actually making a movie."

At first, Goldwyn decided to choreograph Sten's debut with an American adaptation of *The Brothers Karamazov,* but eventually abandoned that idea. He thought she would be better showcased playing the French courtesan, Nana, based on the female protagonist (described as a "precociously immoral prostitute who destroys every man who pursues her") in Émile Zola's best-selling French novel.

In *Nana*, the heroine is pursued by rich and powerful men, but her heart belongs to a handsome young soldier, played by **Phillips Holmes.**

To showcase his exotic new star, Goldwyn rounded up some top designers and technicians—wardrobe by Adrian, cinematography by the innovative Greg Toland, and music by Rodgers and Hart.

At first, Goldwyn hired George Fitzmaurice as director, but fired him after three weeks and discarded all his footage. Then, in a surprise move, he hired the lesbian director, the very mannish Dorothy Arzner, ordering her to start shooting from scratch.

"I heard that Joan Crawford put out for her, but that wasn't my scene," Lucille said.

At the time, Arzner was the only female director working in Hollywood, and she'd become a key figure in launching the careers of Katharine Hepburn and Rosalind Russell. She had also helmed Clara Bow, the "It Girl" of silent films, in her first Talkie, *Wild Party* (1929).

Arzner would later play a

Actor **Richard Bennett** in 1918 with his three daughters, future stars **Constance** (left), **Joan** (center), and **Barbara** (right)

major role in launching Lucille into stardom during her direction of *Dance, Girl, Dance* (1940).

Phillips Holmes, cast as the handsome leading man, a soldier, Lt. George Muffat, was Sten's co-star. His most successful film to date was *An American Tragedy* (1931), based on the novel by Theodore Dreiser.

It was during the shooting of *Nana* that he became involved with actress Mae Clarke, who had a supporting role of "Satin."

Clarke had immortalized herself on the screen when her boyfriend, James Cagney, had crushed a half grapefruit into her face in *The Public Enemy* (1931).

After filming *Nana*, Holmes was driving Clarke to a secret rendezvous when he crashed into a parked car. She suffered facial cuts and a broken jaw, and she sued him, claiming that he was drunk at the time of the accident. She dropped the suit, however, when he agreed to pay her medical bills.

Holmes' life would end tragically. At the start of World War II, he joined the Royal Canadian Air Force, but was killed in a mid-air collision over northwestern Ontario.

In *Nana*, Richard Bennett played a show-biz impresario, Gaston Greiner. As early as 1905, he'd been a leading man on the stage. But in time, he became better known as the father of three budding actresses, Constance, Joan, and Barbara Of course, Constance and Joan Bennett became superstars.

A Londoner, Lionel Atwill was cast as André Muffat, the brother of the character played by Holmes. The year he met Lucille, he also starred in three horror movies: *The Vampire Bat, Murders in the Zoo,* and *Mystery of the Wax Museum.* After working on *Nana* he was cast by Josef von Sternberg as the leading man opposite Marlene Dietrich in *The Devil Is a Woman* (1935).

In 1930, Atwill married Louise Cromwell Brooks, who had once been married to one of history's most famous generals, Douglas

Lionel Atwill with **Marlene Dietrich** in *The Devil Is a Woman.* "My movie offended not only the censors, but the rest of the world, too," Dietrich lamented. "A boresome botch."

Constance Bennett with **Franchot Tone** in *Moulin Rouge* (1934).

Privately, he said, "So many women to serve at the time...and an occasional male."

MacArthur. That marriage lasted from 1922 until their divorce in 1929.

In 1942, Lucille read about Atwill's indictment for perjury after lying to a grand jury about a sex orgy he'd staged at his home.

For the most part, reviews for *Nana* were respectable but not exciting. Even so, the public stayed away in droves. Goldwyn did not give up so easily on Sten and cast her into two more movies: *We Live Again* (1934) with Fredric March, and *The Wedding Night* (1935) opposite Gary Cooper.

Both pictures bombed at the box office.

Critics called the latter picture "Goldwyn's Last Sten." He fired her, releasing her from her contract and sending her back to Europe. She continued to act occasionally until her final film appearance in 1962.

***

In *Moulin Rouge,* a Pre-Code 1934 musical released by United Artists, Lucille had a small part as a showgirl. On its set, she had a reunion with its star, Constance Bennett.

As a model for Hattie Carnegie back in New York, Lucille had been designated to model clothes for her whenever she arrived for one of her

Devoted Lucille Ball fans have tried to identify her among the chorines of this scene from the naughtily voyeuristic dance scene "Boulevard of Broken Dreams" from *Moulin Rouge (1934).*

Some of the best guesses place her as the left-hand figure in the front row, a portrait that we've expanded and inset on the lower right.

spending sprees. Lucille had dyed her hair blonde and used makeup to try to transform herself into a Constance Bennett lookalike.

Sidney Lanfield, the director, cast Lucille with blonde curls and gave her some closeups. Dance routines were staged by Russell Markert, who had been her lover during a brief fling with her in Manhattan.

[In 1949, Lanfield would co-star Lucille with Bob Hope in Sorrowful Jones.*]*

Originally, *Moulin Rouge* was set to star Robert Montgomery, but when he was reassigned to another film, the lead role went to Franchot Tone, who was dating Joan Crawford at the time and would marry her in 1935.

As Lanfield asserted, "Franchot always had his eye out for the next hot broad, and his roving eye focused on Lucille. From what I gathered, he took her one night to a remote motel in the San Fernando Valley, where Crawford might not find out. Because of the rumored size of his dick, Franchot was known in both homo and straight circles as 'Jawbreaker.'"

In 1947, when Lucille was a well-established star, she would be billed above Tone in *Her Husband's Affairs,* a Columbia release.

In *Moulin Rouge,* Bennett played a former vaudevillian, Helen Hall. She marries Douglas Hall (i.e., Franchot Tone), a famous composer. She has a strong desire to return to the stage, but he refuses to allow her to do it. Tone and his producer, Victor Le Maire (Tullio Carminati), have just imported Madam Raquel, a star at the Moulin Rouge in Paris, to Manhattan as one of their performers.

As a means of thwarting her husband's refusal, Helen (Bennett) persuades the French star to let her impersonate her as a means of fooling her husband. Up until then, Bennett has worn a black wig, but she "goes blonde" in an attempt to impersonate Raquel.

As the plot lumbers on, romantic matters get complicated when Douglas (Tone) falls for "Raquel," never realizing

In *Hold That Girl!,* **Claire Trevor** was cast as an "enterprising newspaper gal." Her leading man, James Dunn, played an affable, easy-going Irish detective.

Hoping for a comeback after a long alcoholic binge, **James Dunn** returned to the screen as a drunken father in *A Tree Grows in Brooklyn (1945)* with **Peggy Ann Garner.**

Dunn won a Best Supporting Actor Oscar for his performance.

that the woman who's impersonating her is actually his wife.

Helen Westley, an actress from the Theatre Guild, made her film debut cast as Mrs. Morris, an *aide-de-camp* to Bennett.

The plot of *Moulin Rouge* was ripped off from a flicker released seven years earlier, *Her Sister from Paris* (1925). It had co-starred Ronald Colman and Constance Talmadge. That plot was recycled again in the 1940 film, *You Can't Fool Your Wife*, except that this time, Lucille had top billing. [*The same plot was also replicated in Greta Garbo's adieu to the screen in* Two-Faced Woman *(1941) in which Bennett had third billing. Her star power had, by then, greatly diminished.*]

Before the end of 1934, Lucille made an astounding ten more films, none of which made her a star. In fact, she went from one picture to another at such rapid speed that she hardly knew the plots of the movies in which she had bit parts.

***

In advance of her next picture, Fox's *Hold That Girl!,* a 1934 comedy, Lucille wanted to know "What role will I play?"

She was disappointed to learn how meager her part was, so fleeting that her character was identified only as "Girl."

"Another nameless walk-on," she complained. "When, oh when, am I going to get a star role?"

with ~
SPENCER TRACY
PAT PATERSON
JOHN BOLES

HERBERT MUNDIN
SID SILVERS
HARRY GREEN
THELMA TODD
PRODUCED BY B G DESYLVA
DIRECTED BY DAVID BUTLER

Even though **Lucille** had only a small role in *Bottoms Up*, someone in its press department decided to release this photo as if to prove that, indeed, the film included LOTS of attractive extras.

The leads in *Hold That Girl!* were played by James Dunn and Claire Trevor, who had, the year before, co-starred together in a modest hit, *Jimmy and Sally* (1933).

The son of New York stockbroker, Dunn had made his screen debut in *Bad Girl* (1931). Now at the height of his popularity, he was referred to in the press as "America's Boyfriend." He and Sally Eilers were teamed together in five successful films. He also appeared with Shirley Temple in three of her films.

[*In a short time, having descended into alcoholism, Dunn would fade into ob-*

scurity for five years. He was eventually called back to appear as the drunken father in A Tree Grows in Brooklyn *(1945), for which he won an Oscar as Best Supporting Actor.]*

The charming (and durable) female lead in *Hold That Girl!*, Claire Trevor, would appear in sixty-eight movies from 1933 to 1982, winning an Oscar for her role as a washed-up night club singer and gangster moll in the *Key Largo* (1948), starring Humphrey Bogart, Lauren Bacall, and Edward G. Robinson.

The director of *Hold That Girl!* Was Hamilton McFadden, known mainly for his Charlie Chan detective movies. Lucille would always remember his depressing and incorrect advice: "You'll never make it in the movies. Get yourself a waitress job in the commissary."

In February of 1934, **Spencer Tracy** was getting kidnapping threats. He was so upset that the director had to write him out of several scenes until he "could get hold of himself." without delaying production.

In *Hold That Girl!*, Dunn played an easy-going detective, Trevor an enterprising "newspaper gal," both of them investigating a gang of jewel thieves.

After that "nothing role" (Lucille's words), she was put in another picture where she would be instructed to "look beautiful."

L'Amour à l'Anglaise: This press photo from 1939 shows British beauty **Pat Paterson** with her husband, the Franco-American star **Charles Boyer**, a year after his successful "career-maker," *Algiers* (1938), with Hedy Lamarr.

Seventeen years later, in 1956, Boyer would appear as a guest star in an episode of *I Love Lucy*.

***

Lucille's next picture, *Bottoms Up* (1934), with its sexually suggestive title, gave her a chance to look lovely and elegantly gowned along with other gorgeous chorus girls. She was especially glamourous, clad in early 20th-Century garb, during one of its production numbers, "Waitin' at the Gate for Kathy."

In a nutshell, the male star of the picture, Spencer Tracy, in the only

82

musical comedy he ever appeared in. He portrays a fast-talking, flimflam artist. Smoothie King, whose scam involves passing off a B-list extra, Wanda Gale (Pat Paterson) and forgery expert, Limey Brook (Herbert Mundin) as British nobility. His intention involves getting them (and himself) lucrative gigs in Hollywood. Romantic imbroglios abound.

Tracy was just months away from "deflowering" a virginal and teenaged Judy Garland. Lucille was told that he often made passes at both young actresses and, on occasion, young (male) actors like Lew Ayres.

But when she met him, sex seemed the last thing on Tracy's mind. The police had just left his dressing room. He was receiving threats that he'd be kidnapped, or else that his children would be abducted if he didn't come up with eight-thousand dollars and drop it off at a point to be later designated. He was also threatened, if he didn't pay the ransom, with the kidnapping of an actress he was dating. That meant Loretta Young, with whom he was engaged in an adulterous affair at the time.

Tracy was not pleased with his "second fiddle" role in this Pre-Code musical comedy, as he felt it was tailored more to exploit the talent of his British co-star, Pat Paterson, a beauty from Yorkshire, England.

Lucille noted that every day at lunch, the French matinee idol, Charles Boyer, would show up to take Paterson to lunch.

She would marry Boyer later that year, their union becoming one of the most successful in Hollywood, lasting until her death in 1978. It was marred by the death of their only child, Michael, who died from a self-inflicted shotgun wound at the age of twenty-one.

During the shoot, Lucille met and befriended a future star, Lynn Bari, a cool brunette climbing the Hollywood ladder

In *Bottoms Up*, in something approaching a scene you might expect in a "drawing-room comedy," **Pat Paterson** (left) embraces **Thelma Todd.**

What did **Thelma Todd** have in common with mega-millionairess Gloria Vanderbilt? They both married mobster/hustler Pat DiCicco!

John Boles with **Rosalind Russell** in *Craig's Wife* (1936).

It was not Russell, but Lucille whom this married man secretly dated during the filming of *Bottoms Up*.

83

rung by rung. In 1943, she would marry and (in 1950) divorce Sid Luft before he became Judy Garland's third husband.

Its director, David Butler, had co-authored the script of *Bottoms Up*. A former actor, he'd made a string of musicals and comedies, including three for Shirley Temple. [*As the producer and director of That's Right—You're Wrong! (1939), he would cast Lucille into one of its parts.*]

The producer of *Bottoms Up*, Buddy DeSylva, a New Yorker, had been a songwriter on Tin Pan Alley in Manhattan. [*Roughly designated as West 28th Street between 5th and 6th Avenues in Manhattan, between 1885 and around 1920, it was widely recognized as the densest concentration of popular music publishers in the world.*] He had worked frequently with George Gershwin and written songs for Al Jolson. He is remembered today chiefly for writing "California, Here I Come."

Before the filming of *Bottoms Up*, **Lucille** (center) began a life-long friendship with **Barbara Pepper** (left).

In this publicity still, the unknown starlet on the right poses with them.

On several occasions, Lucille lunched with actress Thelma Todd, cast in the minor role of Judith Marlowe, who is upstaged by Wanda Gale. Todd and Lucille had plenty of talk about, mainly Pat DiCicco, with whom Lucille had had an affair back in New York. Todd was in the process of divorcing him. DiCicco would go on to marry heiress Gloria Vanderbilt, and he would also become the lover and sex partner of Howard Hughes, the (demented) aviator and movie mogul.

In the film colony, Todd was known as "Hot Toddy" and "The Ice Cream Blonde." From 1926 to 1935, she would make 120 feature films with such comedians as the Marx Brothers, Jimmy Durante, Laurel and Hardy, and Buster Keaton.

In 1935, at the age of twenty-nine, Todd was found dead in her car, which was parked in a sealed garage. Although police reports defined her as a victim of carbon monoxide poisoning. Lucille, along with a host of other people in the film industry, always believed that she'd been murdered.

In the third lead of *Bottons Up*, John Boles, is remembered for his performance as Victor Moritz in *Frankenstein* (1931). He'd also worked in silent pictures, starring opposite Gloria Swanson in *The Love of Sunya* (1927). He later appeared opposite Irene Dunne in the 1934 adaptation of Edith Wharton's novel, *The Age of Innocence*.

Boles was married to Marcelite Dobbs, and would remain so until her death, but he secretly dated Lucille on the side, taking her to out-of-the-way places where they would not be recognized.

He later said, "Lucy was going out with a different beau almost every evening and was seen at all the night clubs. Her phone number was passed around a lot. She was about twenty-three when I met her and hot to trot, a regular little spitfire with changing hair color. Word got out in Hollywood, and guys were lined up at her door. At the end of an evening, she rarely disappointed."

***

In her next film, *Murder at the Vanities,* a saucy, sexually provocative Pre-Code 1934 release from Paramount, Lucille almost got lost in another bit part. She was swimming in a sea of scantily clad chorines collectively billed as "The Most Beautiful Girls in the World," a bit of an overstatement. A theatrical version, based on a crime comedy/drama by Earl Carroll, had already run for six months on Broadway.

Although Cary Grant had been announced as the male lead, at the last minute, he dropped out. His role went instead to the Danish actor and singer, Carl Brisson, who had already made two

Kitty Carlisle, long before she became a staple of the game-show circuit.

Photo above shows a chorine scene from *Murder at the Vanities* with its star, **Kitty Carlisle**, on its right. The photo on the right is a blow-up of **Lucille,** who's positioned within the oval on the bigger photo's left.

silent films for Alfred Hitchcock. Before that, he was middleweight boxing champ of Europe.

In *Vanities,* the dashing Dane introduced the hit song, "Cocktails for Two."

On the set, Lucille had lunch with another of the extras, Ann Sheridan, the future "Oomph Girl" with the come-hither look and a deep, suggestive voice. At the time, the two aspiring actresses could only dream of the super-stardom that awaited each of them around the corner.

Another star on the rise was Gail Patrick, often cast as "the bad girl" in films between 1932 and 1948, notably *My Man Godfrey* (1936), and *My Favorite Wife* (1940).

Director Mitchell Leisen was also a costume designer. He insisted that Brisson strip naked every morning so that he could fit him with his clothing, beginning with his underwear.

"Mitch often had me try on eight different pairs of underwear before making up his mind," Brisson later said. "What's odd about that? In no scene did I appear in my underwear. Whatever turns you on, I say."

Although married, Leisen was known to have had a long-lasting affair with Billy Daniel, the dancer and choreographer. The director's career highlight was *Hold Back the Dawn,* nominated as the Best Picture of 1941. It starred Charles Boyer, Olivia de Havilland, and Paulette Goddard.

The plot of *Vanities* unfolds on opening night as Eric Lander (Brisson) and Ann Ware (Kitty Carlisle in her film debut) announce that they are engaged. That causes great pain to Rita Ross (Gertrude Michael), who had hoped to snare the hunk for herself.

As an example of the many ironies associated with Pre-Code Hollywood, *Murder at the Vanities* included a surreal, bacchanalian dance with *chiaroscuro* shadows and animated Latino dancers wearing Carnival Costumes.

Its highlight was a song sung by **Gertrude Michael** (photo above) whose lyrics, to everyone's surprise, got past the censors. Here are the then "very avant-garde" lyrics, as penned by Sam Coslow.

SWEET MARIJUANA

Soothe me with your caress
Sweet marijuana, marijuana

Help me in my distress
Sweet marijuana, please do

You alone can bring my lover back
to me
Even though I know it's all a fantasy

And then you put me to sleep
Sweet marijuana, marijuana

During the stage play, Ann escapes two near-fatal accidents. That brings in police lieutenant Murdock (Victor McLaglen). This English film actor, who held a dual citizenship, was known for his character roles, having won an Oscar for Best Actor in 1935 for *The Informer.* He also made seven films with John Ford and John Wayne.

During the run of *Murder at the Vanities,* Rita and a private detective are murdered, much to the horror of Jack Ellery (Jack Oakie).

When he was five, Oakie's family moved to Muskogee, Oklahoma, and he adopted "Oakie" as a stage name. In 1923, he made his Broadway debut as a chorus boy in *Little Nelly Kelly* by George M. Cohan. Oakie made Silents in Hollywood beginning in 1927, later appearing in his first talkie, *The Mummy,* in 1929.

In the 1930s, he became known a "The World's Oldest Freshman," since he appeared in numerous films with a collegiate theme.

His great moment came when he did a burlesque of a boisterous dictator, Bensino Napaloni (read that as "Mussolini"), tyrant of Bacteria, in Charlie Chaplin's *The Great Dictator* (1940). For his parody, Oakie won an Oscar nomination as Best Supporting Actor, losing to Walter Brennan in *The Westerner.*

In a particularly provocative kind of "inside secret," Rita (Gertrude Michael) sings an ode to "Sweet Marijuana," although some members of the audience might not have known what the weed was. *[A censor later zeroed in on it, ordering that the song be deleted.]*

This detail from a press photo that featured "The Duchess of Florence," **Constance Bennett** in the foreground shows **Lucille**, as a mousy brunette, cast as a lady-in-waiting "standing around' with her life and career on hold for *The Affairs of Cellini.*

One of the highlights of *Vanities* was an appearance by Duke Ellington, the composer, pianist, and leader of a jazz orchestra. Famous for his appearances at the Cotton Club in Harlem, he became a pivotal figure in the evolution of American Jazz.

Vanities fared poorly at the box office, in spite of its barely dressed

87

showgirls, lewd dialogue, and, yes, murders. One critic claimed, "The movie has something for anyone looking to see just how outrageous films could be in 1934 before the censors moved in for the kill. *Vanities* is so strikingly offbeat and off-color that one can quickly forget how dreadful it really is."

***

Lucille's next picture, *The Affairs of Cellini,* was a Fox bedroom farce that in some way evoked the swashbuckling adventures of silent screen star, Douglas Fairbanks, Sr. The *Los Angeles Times* referred to it as an "Ernst Lubitsch type of comedy transferred to another era."

Lucille's first question was, "Just who in hell is Cellini?"

[She must have slept through Art History 101 not to know who Benvenuto Cellini was. Born in the Republic of Florence in 1500, he was an Italian goldsmith, sculptor, draftsman, soldier, musician, and artist. As one of the great masters of Mannerism, he's celebrated for such sculptures as the world-famous Perseus with the Head of Medusa.

He also wrote a famous autobiography in which he spoke of his loves, hatreds, passions, and delights.

Over the centuries, his name has been evoked countless times, even in Herman Melville's Moby Dick. *He even figures in Ian Fleming's James Bond thriller,* Goldfinger. *Fleming wrote, "Goldfinger was an artist—a scientist as great in his field as Cellini and Einstein were in theirs."]*

Gregory La Cava, who in three years would direct Lucille in *Stage Door* (1937), cast her as handmaiden to Constance Bennett, who played the Duchess of Florence. Veteran actor Frank Morgan was the Duke of Florence, and Fredric March was cast in the title role of Cellini.

Morgan was offered the role only after Charles Laughton turned it down. Brooklyn-born Louis Calhern, cast as Ottaviano, had just starred in *Duck Soup* (1933) with the Marx Brothers.

Modeling hats or modeling topless, to break into show business, "A girl's gotta do what a girl's gotta do."

Photographers criticized **Lucille's** "boyish figure," but she desperately needed the money. At the time that this was taken, she was billing herself as "Diana Belmont' and surviving on tomato soup made from catsup.

Fay Wray, a successful frenemy of the sometimes envious Lucille. Wray appears here in her scantily clad "acting out' of her most famous celluloid love/hate relationship: She was the girl who captured the heart of King Kong.

Morgan virtually stole the picture from Bennett and March and was nominated for a Best Actor Oscar that year, losing to Clark Gable for *It Happened One Night.* Of course, Morgan's most celebrated part would come in 1939 when he appeared in the title role of *The Wizard of Oz* with Judy Garland going over the rainbow as Dorothy Gale.

Fox producer Darryl F. Zanuck approved the cast, suggesting Fay Wray for the role of Angela, one of Cellini's models. Wray had just immortalized herself in *King Kong* (1933) as "the beauty who tamed the beast."

[Wray told Lucille that she was paid $10,000 to star in King Kong, *a film that saved Lucille's future studio, RKO, from bankruptcy. Wray also let Lucille in on a secret: "RKO at first didn't want me for* Kong *and sent the script to Jean Harlow, who rejected it."]*

Lucille said, "In *Cellini,* all I had to do was look gorgeous in elegant finery, and I attracted the eye of an old horndog like March, who was known for seducing women on pictures in which he starred. He made a pass, but I didn't intercept," she said, "although he may have bedded Wray."

"I went from modeling clothes in New York for Constance Bennett to being her handmaiden in that Cellini Flick," Lucille said. "When will I be the star of a picture, with Bennett as my servant as her career wanes? Frankly, I think her brunette sister, Joan Bennett, is the more talented actress. Don't quote me!"

Irene Mayer Selznick, daughter of Louis B. Mayer and the wife (1930-1949) of David O. Selznick, claimed, "Constance Bennett was crazy about two things—first, money, her real passion, and then sex, her hobby."

In response to Selznick, and probably with the intention of launching some barbs at Lucille, too, Bennett said, "Hollywood's gossipmongers have gleefully reported me as being in the arms of first one, then another. Anyone who habitually reads the fan magazines and newspaper chatter columnists might well conclude that I am a female Casanova, and that I announce my loves from the roof-

Ronald Colman and **Lorette Young** in *Bulldog Drummond Strikes Back.*

"I always had a schoolgirl crush on this suave English actor," Lucille said. "I never got really intimate with him, but he had the best speaking voice in Hollywood."

By the mid-1930s, despite her frustration about the lack of speaking roles for her in Hollywood, **Lucille** had amassed an astonishing portfolio of press and publicity shots.

"Before my next picture, I made a quick visit to Jamestown," she said. "My former boyfriend, Johnny DaVita, made love to me morning, noon, and night."

tops. That description more accurately describes the servant girl in my latest picture, one Miss Lucille Ball. She's already building a reputation for attracting the husbands of other women. What a trollop!"

***

"Dammit!" Lucille said when told she'd been cast in the Fox film, *Bulldog Drummond Strikes Back* (1934), a mystery tale featuring the master detective.

"It seems I'll be used as decoration at a wedding reception, gabbing with the other bridesmaids. Big fucking deal! I'm not getting any younger, you know."

The film was a sequel of sorts to *Bulldog Drummond* (1929), which had starred the English actor, Ronald Colman, earning him an Oscar nomination. Before reporting to work once again as Drummond, Colman learned that he had been voted the handsomest actor in Hollywood, beating out Clark Gable and Fredric March.

Although he'd been born in Sweden, **Warner Oland** became the screen's famous Asian sleuth, Charlie Chan.

While making the film, he learned he'd been cast in two more films, each of which would become a screen classic: *A Tale of Two Cities* (1935) and *Lost Horizon* (1937).

In *Bulldog Drummond Strikes Back*, he took time out to play a villain, Prince Achmed.

According to Hollywood gossip at the time, Colman was said to be shy around women. If true, that didn't stop him from seducing several stars with whom he co-starred or would appear in his future. They included Bessie Love (with whom he co-starred in the 1925 silent, *The Dark Angel*), and in his future, Marlene Dietrich, Merle Oberon, and Shelley Winters.

"On the set, I gave Colman my best 'Ann Sheridan come-hither' flirtation, but he looked at me as if I had indigestion," Lucille said.

Produced by Darryl F. Zanuck, *Bulldog Drummond Strikes Back* had Roy Del Ruth helming a very talented cast, with a coterie of actors who were household names to the movie-going public. During their heydays, millions were flocking to movie theaters to escape their Depression-era blues.

As "Algy" in *Bulldog*, **Charles Butterworth** was described as "long faced, befuddled, tight-lipped, and deadpan."

Filmmaker Del Ruth had begun his Hollywood career as a scriptwriter for Mack Sennett in 1915. His first triumph came with the release of *The Desert Song* (1929), the first color film ever issued by Warner Brothers. That same year, Del Ruth also directed another hit, *Gold Diggers of Broadway*, Warner's second "Two-Strip Technicolor," all-talking feature film.

He'd gotten the Bulldog Drummond gig mainly because of his success helming Dashiell Hammett's *The Maltese Falcon* (1931), starring Ricardo Cortez. Del Ruth had also helmed James Cagney, Edward G. Robinson, and Bette Davis.

The female star of Bulldog Drummond was Loretta Young, cast as Lola Field, the daughter of the man whose murder was being investigated. The detective had found his corpse in the mansion of Prince Achmed. Achmed was played by the Swedish actor, Warner Oland. Despite the fact that he wasn't Asian, Oland became known for his portrayal of Chinese characters, most notably as police detective Charlie Chan.

Character actor Charles Butterworth played Algy, Drummond's partner. A familiar presence on the screen, he was noted for his distinctive voice. His career was cut short by an early death in an automobile accident in the spring of 1946.

From her second-tier role in *Drummond*, Loretta Young, a former child actress, would go on to become one of the biggest stars in Hollywood, winning a Best Actress Oscar for her role in *The Farmer's Daughter* (1947).

After that, she starred opposite Clark Gable in *Call of the Wild* (1935), during whose filming he impregnated her. A devout Catholic who opposed abortion, she mysteriously and discretely disappeared from the Hollywood scene. In the months that followed, she gave birth and nurtured her infant, Judy Lewis. In the years after that, she rigorously and frequently asserted that Judy was her adopted child.

The distinguished Londoner, C. Aubrey Smith, had the part of Captain Reginald Nielsen, an actor whose niche involved the portrayal of "officer and gentleman" types. He set the tone for that in the first Talkie version of *The Prisoner of Zenda* (1937).

At the end of filming, Ronald Colman bid *adieu* to the Bulldog Drummond character, which was later taken up by actors who included Ray Milland, Walter Pidgeon, Ralph Richardson, and John Howard.

***

Lucille, still a Goldwyn Girl, learned that she was to appear in another bit part in the latest Eddie Cantor movie, *Kid Millions,* also set for a 1934 release by United Artists.

Roy Del Ruth, who had just helmed her in

Even as a chorus girl, **Lucille** (left-hand figure in the grouping above) began to receive more fanfare, as in this crowd scene with **Eddie Cantor**, the "perhaps overexposed" star of *Kid Millions.*

Perhaps it was over-hyped. In advance of its release, a frenzied press campaign pre-defined it as "Uproarious, fun-filled, and eye-dazzling, a million dollars worhty of beauty, laughter, and song for an evening of unlimited gaiety."

By the end of filming, Lucille considered it frenetic, forced, and exhausting.

Bulldog Drummond Strikes Back, cast her again in this comedy. It starred Ann Sothern, Ethel Merman, and George Murphy.

As one of the Goldwyn Girls, Lucille would join a lineup that featured Lynne Carter, Barbara Pepper, and Paulette Goddard.

As a Samuel Goldwyn Production, *Kid Millions* would be the fifth Goldwyn comedy for Cantor. Ads for this new feature promised "dames and giggles," as well as "music, mirth, and madness," particularly a finale featuring an "Ice Cream Fantasy" that was screened in the newfangled "Three-Strip Technicolor," one of the earliest uses of this then state-of-the-art technology.

Perhaps in an attempt to celebrate their "esprit de corps," the dance director of *Kid Millions* (**Seymour Felix**, center) posed as a Pasha against a backdrop of the girls he'd choreograped.

One of them, **Lucille Ball**, a blonde, is highlighted with an oval.

Although his style of comedy would go out of style, Cantor at the time was the highest-paid actor in Hollywood. Remembering Lucille, he called her aside and delivered some career advice. "I think, gal, you've got a knack for comedy, but you're going nowhere as a Goldwyn Girl. You've got a sense of timing that's priceless for comedy. You should break free of Goldwyn's harem."

Actually, Lucille didn't have any trouble breaking free of Goldwyn. When her work on the picture ended, he called her to his office and fired her. "You've showed no promise at all. Maybe you can get a job as a sales clerk. Show business is not for you. Ann Sothern, who is in *Kid Millions,* is a gal who's going places. You were lackluster in all the chorister chores I gave you."

"Thanks for the career advice," Mr. Goldwyn," she said. "I'll take my leave and thanks again for the memory."

The plot of *Kid Millions*, written in part by Nunnally Johnson, had Cantor playing Eddie Wilson, Jr., journeying to Egypt to claim a $77 million inheritance. According to the script, the fortune derived from his late father, who as an archeologist, had plundered tombs from the heyday of ancient Egypt.

"Like me, **Paulette Goddard** had a bit part in *Kid Millions,*" Lucille said. "But soon, she was to marry Charlie Chaplin (perhaps). When I visited her in 1945 on the set of *Kitty* with Ray Milland, she had seduced everyone from Clark Gable to Gary Cooper."

There was trouble ahead on the set: Ethel Merman was cast as a flimflam artist who tries to con orphan Eddie out of his inheritance. The movie was filled with gags and funny scenes, including one where Merman, wearing a hat and veil, sits on Cantor's lap, insisting that she is his dear old Mom.

Two views of "The Belter," **Ethel Merman**, as a flimflam huckster in *Kid Millions*.

The photo on the right is with **Eddie Cantor**, and yes, they're escaping into the Sahara on a camel.

She heard Cantor virtually beg Goldwyn to get the scriptwriters to create a romantic scene for him. "Forget it, Eddie," Goldwyn said. "You have absolutely no sex appeal...I mean, none whatsoever."

"Then how do you explain my having five daughters?"

A compromise was reached. Cantor was to have a scene with Princess Fanya, the Sultan's daffy daughter, who falls for him as he saves her from a small dog. He recommended Lucille for the role, but Del Ruth and Goldwyn preferred an actress named Eve Sully.

Sothern was cast as Joan Larabee, niece to Colonel Harrison Larabee (Berton Churchill), a Southern gentleman from Virginia who had funded Professor Wilson's expeditions in Egypt for the discovery of buried treasures.

Sothern's character is in love with Jerry Lane (George Murphy), who had been an assistant to the deceased professor. Murphy later became a leading song-and-dance star in many big budget Hollywood musicals. A longtime friend of Ronald Reagan, in time, he entered politics, becoming the U.S. Senator (1965-1971) representing California.

Louella Parsons announced

LOOK! WHO'S ON YOUR RADIO!

ANN SOTHERN in "MAISIE"

Presented by
EVERSHARP
TONIGHT
AT 7:30
on
KGLO
And Every Thursday Night!

Ann Sothern in *Kid Millions*.

"She was cast as the ingenue, Joan Larrabee, in a role that should have gone to me," Lucille said. "Alas, when will Hollywood realize I'm a star?"

WOMEN WE LOVE: Ann Sothern later emerged as a star herself in a series of ten *Maisie* movies released between 1939 and 1947.

In them, she was an All-American asset to anyone in trouble, a wise-cracking, fast-talking showgirl with the body of a goddess and a heart of gold. A critic from *Time* magazine described Sothern as "one of the smartest comediennes in the business," words that many believed could equally have been applied to Lucille.

Murphy's arrival in Hollywood with this: "Having just heard this new boy from New York sing, I think Bing Crosby had better look at his laurels."

Seven years after *Kid Millions* was wrapped, Lucille and Murphy would co-star in the RKO film, *A Girl, a Guy, and a Gob.*

In time, Lucille might have forgotten working on *Kid Millions* were it not for friendships formed near the end of her gig as a Goldwyn Girl.

Her relationship with Paulette Goddard, however, was relatively superficial. Two years after working with Lucille, Goddard was said to have married Charlie Chaplin—although perhaps it was a common law union without an actual wedding ceremony and marriage license.

The **"Ice Cream Fantasy Finale"** from *Kid Millions*. Was it perhaps too campy and/or politically incorrect, even for its era?

It included suggestive bovine references, milking pails, appearances by happily assimilated Egyptian slaves, and two or three dozen milk-complexioned Los Angeleans pretending to be Dutch.

Lucille made it into this novelty sequence, but wondered, "What was I? Vanilla, chocolate, or strawberry?"

Goddard gave Lucille some career advice, which she never followed: "Never sleep with a man until he gives you a pure white stone diamond of at least ten karats."

Goddard went on to marry actor Burgess Meredith and, finally, the novelist Erich Maria Remarque. Along the way, she had a string of other lovers ranging from Gary Cooper to Bruce Cabot, from Clark Gable to director John Huston, from novelist Aldous Huxley to Sir Alexander Korda, even David Niven, Spencer Tracy, John Wayne, and the Greek shipping magnate, Aristotle Onassis.

As fellow Goldwyn Girls, Barbara Pepper and Lucille became lifelong friends, as Lucille watched her devolve from a blonde bombshell of the 1930s into an overweight alcoholic by the late 1940s. At that time, Lucille considered her for the role of Ethel Mertz in *I Love Lucy,* but found that she was too deep into alcoholism.

Ann Sothern, the female lead in *Kid Millions,* and Lucille also bonded, even though as rival comedians, they could have viewed each other as competitors.

Arriving at Union Station in Los Angeles, Sothern had escaped from the cold winds of North Dakota. Although she began her career in the late 1920s, a decade went by before Sothern starred as Maisie in 1939. The role had been written for Jean Harlow, but she had died in 1937. *Maisie* became such a hit that it spawned a series of sequels, making Sothern a star.

In *Congo Maisie,* the script was inspired by the 1932 movie *Red Dust.* It had starred Harlow with Clark Gable.

Years later, Lucille told the press, "Ann is the best comedian in the business, bar none."

After leaving Goldwyn, Lucille moved over to Columbia, even though it meant a cut in her weekly salary, which fell from $75 a week to $50.

Money was tight, but she rented a home at 1345 North Ogden Drive, a street lined with trees.

She missed her family. She sent train fare to her mother, DeDe, so that she along with her Lucille's brother, Fred Ball, and her grandfather, Fred Hunt, could come to Hollywood to live with her in her modest home. She would support them for the rest of their lives.

***

For her next picture, a thriller *The Fugitive Lady* (1934), Lucille walked through the gates of Columbia for the first time. On her first day there, she was told that she would appear only briefly, at the beginning of the movie, playing a beautician in a cosmetic salon.

Although disappointed, she was relieved that at least she was working, having feared that she might be pounding the pavement for months, looking for another gig after being dumped by Samuel Goldwyn.

She was quite photogenic and was often called upon to pose as a model for publicity photographs. She was also "attacked" by The Three Stooges in a twenty-minute slapstick short, *Three Little Pigskins* (1934). As one critic later phrased it, "This was Lucille's first appearance in a knockabout comedy."

She watched scenes from *The Fugitive Lady* being shot at the time under the direction of Albert S. Rogell, an "Oakie" born in Oklahoma City. In Hollywood, at the age of fifteen, he was helming shorts and B pictures. By 1923, his brother, Sol Rogell, was the producer of *The Fugitive Lady,* and would become one of Lucille's bosses when she moved over to RKO.

Lucille's latest picture starred Neil Hamilton, Donald Cook, and Florence Rice: Collectively, they were hardly an A-list cast. As Ann Duncan, Rice played a beautician who falls in love with Jack Howard (Cook), not knowing that he's a

Yet again, Lucille had a minor role in a minor film, *The Fugitive Lady.* Its stars included (left to right) **Donald Cook, Florence Rice,** and **Neil Hamilton.**

Cook was cast as Jack Howard, a suave thief who marries Rice, who runs a beauty shop. During their honeymoon, he steals a cache of jewelry and flees into the night, leaving her to take the rap.

There's a happy ending: Hamilton plays Donald Brooks, a wealthy man with whom she falls in love.

jewel thief. The police move in on him after his latest heist, and he flees, leaving his young bride to take the rap. Hauled off to prison, her train crashes. She flees from the wreckage and later pretends to be the *fiancée* of a rich young man who died in the crash. She is taken in by Donald Brooks (Hamilton), who falls in love with her. Then the real fiancée shows up, as does her jewel thief of a husband.

With melodramatic style, everything eventually works out in the end for the Rice character.

A rather dashing leading man, Hamilton started his career modeling white shirts before joining several stock companies. His big break came when D.W. Griffith cast him in *The White Rose* (1923). He soon became one of the leading men at Paramount, often appearing in vehicles starring Bebe Daniels. In *Beau Geste* (1926), he played the brother of Ronald Colman.

That same year (1926), he starred in the first screen adaptation of F. Scott Fitzgerald's classic 1925 novel, *The Great Gatsby*, a silent film now lost to history. A few years later, Hamilton was billed above newcomer Clark Gable in *Laughing Sinners* (1931), starring Joan Crawford. He is remembered more today for playing the craggy-faced Police Commissioner James Gordon in the *Batman* TV series from 1966 to '68.

Florence Rice launched her career on Broadway before going to Hollywood, where she starred in some fifty films between 1934 and 1943. She was often paired with Robert Young. Before fading into oblivion, she worked with William Powell, Myrna Loy, Jeanette MacDonald, and even the Marx Brothers. She would appear with Lucille again in the upcoming *Carnival* (1935).

In the third lead, Donald Cook flourished in Pre-Code films and on Broadway, and was seen in gangster pictures such as *The Public Enemy* (1931) and *Baby Face* (1933). He was also noted for playing detective Ellery Queen on the screen.

On the set of *The Fugitive Lady,* Lucille met character actor William Demarest, who would appear in some 140 movies beginning in 1927. That meeting might have been insignificant except he was once considered for the Fred Mertz role in *I Love Lucy.* Instead of that gig, he was cast as Uncle Charley in the TV series *My Three Sons,* starring Fred MacMurray. Ironically, William Frawley, who won the role of Fred Mertz, was replaced in the MacMurray series by Demarest, who was hired when Frawley became uninsurable because of his failing health.

***

On her next picture, *Men of the Night,* a 1934 release by Columbia, Lucille joined the list of two dozen actors (and the characters they would play) in this drama written and directed by Lambert Hillyer. Her role of "Peggy" was so insignificant (a walk-on part at the end) that it didn't even appear on the list.

She went to Hillyer, requesting that she be given a line or two of dialogue, but he rejected the idea.

She wasn't very impressed with him, as he was mostly known for directing westerns with cowboy stars like Tom Mix, the stoic William S. Hart, and Buck Jones. He would later helm the first screen depiction of *Batman* (1943), a fifteen-episode serial conceived as a diversion for wartime audiences.

The three leads in *Men of the Night* included Bruce Cabot as Detective Sergeant Kelly, Judith Allen as Mary Higgins, and Ward Bond as detective John Connors.

The picture marked Lucille's first encounter with Cabot, who would appear again in her life after she became a big star, Cabot playing third lead during her stint with Bob Hope in *Sorrowful Jones* (1949) and again in *Fancy Pants* (1950).

A handsome leading man, Cabot had immortalized himself in screen history, starring with Fay Wray in *King Kong* (1933). Before that, he had been an oil field worker, a prize fighter, a used car salesman, a surveyor, an insurance salesman, and a butcher in a slaughterhouse decapitating pigs.

[A close friend of "bad boy:" Errol Flynn, he later became the subject of lurid gossip. At Flynn's orgies, he was a noted exhibitionist. Later, their relationship soured when Flynn refused to pay him money owed. Cabot retaliated by threatening to expose the gay life of the swashbuckler. He also had incriminating pictures of Flynn sodomizing a fourteen-year-old boy.]

At one point during the filming of *Men of the Night,* Lucille was summoned to Cabot's dressing room. She found him sitting naked at his makeup table. She had hoped that he would intercede in her campaign to get her part expanded. As she later revealed, "He shook his dick at me and asked me if I wanted to try it on for size. I fled instead."

Judith Allen, *Men of the Night's* leading lady, had arrived in Hollywood and made three films in 1933. *Men of the Night* would be one of five movies she'd star in in 1934. She'd never graduate beyond B pictures, such as *The Port of Missing Girls* in 1938 with Milburn Stone. Before the coming of World War II to America, she had faded into oblivion.

Ward Bond became one of the most famous character actors in Hollywood, starring in some 200 films and in the hit NBC-TV series *Wagon Train* from 1957 to 1960. He is best remembered for his performance as Bert, the cop, in Frank Capra's *It's a Wonderful Life* (1946) starring James Stewart in

Bruce Cabot with **Fay Wray** in *King Kong* (1933). During the filming of *Men of the Night*, Lucille visited him in his dressing room. He wanted her to appraise his physical assets.

Beautiful **Judith Allen** said, "I worked steadily in films in the 1930s, but suddenly, it was 1940, and the world was at war. It was time I faded away."

Old Cowboys Never Die: **Ward Bond** (right) with **Robert Horton** (left) in an episode of *Wagon Train* (1957)

his most memorable role, Bond is also known for his long association with John Wayne and director John Ford.

Not giving up hope for a big break to come her way, Lucille received notification that Columbia had earmarked her for two more films before her lackluster 1934 ended.

"I'm a bigtime movie star, but only to my family," she said. "They rave about me starring in pictures all the time."

***

Lucille had moved to Columbia hoping for better parts. Again, she faced disappointment when she reported to the set of *Jealousy*, a 1934 drama directed by Roy William Neill and starring Nancy Carroll, George Murphy, and Donald Cook. She had worked with Cook and Murphy before but was meeting Carroll for the first time.

In a nutshell, its plot (conceived by four writers) told of an insanely jealous boxer (Larry O'Rourke) played by Murphy. The boxer murders his manager when he finds him alone with his fiancée, played by Carroll. She is the one charged with the crime by police.

Larry eventually confesses to the murder and is sentenced to die in the electric chair. But he wakes up and realizes that everything that happened was only a dream.

Lucille's part was so small that her character wasn't even assigned a name. *[She appeared on the cast list as "Extra."]* She met with the Irish-born director, Neill, asking if he could enlarge her part.

[In time, Neill would helm 107 films, 40 of them silent, beginning in 1917. He was a busy man. In the year he met Lucille, he also directed six other films. He seemed impatient with her and denied her request.

As a director, his chief claim to fame was his direction of the last eleven of the fourteen Sherlock Holmes films that starred Basil Rathbone between 1943 and 1946, the year of Neill's death.]

An Irish lassie with a baby face, New Yorker Carroll had burst onto the scene, beginning her career in Broadway musicals. In 1928, alone, she'd made eight films, her performance in *Easy Come, Easy Go* with Richard

Lucille moved from RKO to Columbia, hoping for better parts.

In this minor *whodunit*, she didn't find one.

Nancy Carroll (upper photo), during her flapper years, and (lower photo) **the Kennedys**, (left to right), Joe Jr., Joe Sr., and JFK.

The title of her movie, *Jealousy*, could also be applied to Carroll's private life. At the time, she was competing with Gloria Swanson for the bedtime antics of Joseph Kennedy, Sr., bootlegger and movie maker.

Dix (Lucille's future co-star) shooting her to stardom.

[Around that time, she began an affair with Joseph Kennedy, the bootlegging, stock manipulating father of a future U.S. President. The horndog patriarch was also engaged in a torrid romance with Gloria Swanson.]

Carroll had been nominated for a Best Actress Oscar for her 1930 film, *The Devil's Holiday*. She also co-starred with Cary Grant and Randolph Scott in *Hot Saturday* (1932), which marked the beginning of a long-term affair between those two (male) actors.

Around the time that Lucille met her, Carroll was beginning her decline as a film star. But in the early 1930s, she received the most fan mail of any star in Hollywood.

As 1934 was coming to an end, Columbia notified Lucille that she would join the cast of an upcoming film, *Broadway Bill.*

"What role do I play?" she asked its casting director.

"An unnamed telephone operator."

"Oh, goodie, goodie," Lucille said. "I can't wait."

***

Director Frank Capra had scored one of his biggest hits when he'd helmed Clark Gable and Claudette Colbert in *It Happened One Night* (1934). It brought Oscars to both stars, and the film won an Oscar for Best Picture of the Year.

Written by columnist Mark Hellinger, *Broadway Bill,* Capra's latest movie, was the story of a man's love for his thoroughbred racehorse and of the woman who helps him achieve his dream.

It was announced that Gable would be the star, but at the last minute, he dropped out and was replaced with Warner Baxter. That actor assured Capra that he was a devotee of horses, but as filming began, Capra discovered the awful truth: Baxter was terrified of horses.

As a leading man, Baxter had starred in some fifty films in the 1920s, most notably *The Great Gatsby* in 1926. Cast as "the Cisco Kid" in *In Old Arizona* (1928), Baxter won the Academy Award for Best Actor at the second Academy Awards ceremony. When Lucille met him, he was the highest-paid actor in Hollywood, a position he would not hold for long.

Myrna Loy met Lucille and, as they talked, she told her that, "I made the mistake of my life when I turned Frank Capra down. He wanted me for the Claudette Colbert role in *It Happened One Night.*"

Loy launched herself playing vamps of Asian descent. She hit her stride as Nora Charles opposite William Powell in *The Thin Man* (also 1934). That would lead to five sequels.

She had been discovered by Natacha Rambova, the ultra-flamboyant second wife of Rudolph Valentino, and the two women had engaged in a lesbian affair.

Born in Sicily ("and I was never a gangster"), Capra had a "rags to riches" story that he claimed personified the American Dream.

For *Broadway Bill,* he selected a stellar cast: Walter Connolly, as J.L Higgins, had also starred in *It Happened One Night.* Helen Vinson, as Margaret, starred in forty films between 1932 and 1943. A Texas beauty, the daughter of an oil man, she had brown eyes and naturally curly hair. Unlike her leading man, Baxter, she had "a passion:" for horses and loved working on the picture. Before her career came to an abrupt halt at the end of World War II, she would appear with many big stars, including William Powell, Kay Francis, Carole Lombard, Cary Grant, and Gary Cooper.

Cast as "Edna," Margaret Hamilton, before the decade's end, would immortalize herself as the Wicked Witch of the West, terrifying Dorothy (Judy Garland) in *The Wizard of Oz* (1939).

Frankie Darro as "Ted Williams" had launched his career as a child actor in silent pictures.

As he grew older, producers considered him too short for leading man status, as he stood only five feet, three inches. His wiry, athletic frame often led him to being cast as a horseracing jockey.

After serving in the U.S. Navy's Hospital Corps, where he contracted malaria, he returned to Hollywood and ended up on "Poverty Row," working for Monogram in *Bowery Boys* comedies.

***

As 1934 came to an end, Lucille had a final dinner with Barbara Pepper. "I've made a serious decision. While I'm still under contract to Columbia, I plan to cooperate and lie like a good girl on a casting couch for the big enchilada, Harry Cohn. I've resisted so far, but other gals like Joan Crawford did all right. At a party one night, I heard her tell some people that the casting couch was better than the cold hard floor."

Two views of **Lucille** in the 1930s. She was growing increasingly discouraged about the actor's rat race, despite her obvious (sometimes blonde, sometimes brunette) beauty.

100

A "CONSTANT CHORINE" AND A "PULCHRITUDINOUS PROP," LUCILLE PROVIDES CONTEXT TO OTHER PEOPLE'S HEADLINES

"At this rate, I'll never become a movie star."

—Lucille Ball

Lucille's new boss at Columbia Pictures was the notorious Harry Cohn, famous for his casting couch, the most battered and overused in Hollywood. He was called "The Jewish Howard Hughes." She'd been told that Cohn was ruthless, self-centered, and mean-spirited, and that every female under contract to him had to submit to him sexually.

She'd heard all the rumors about starlets summoned to his office. He maintained a secret passageway that let directly from Columbia's main dressing room directly into his office and that it was used for unregistered access to his office by starlets under contract to him. By accessing that passage, they didn't have to transit through his waiting room, thereby attracting unwanted attention.

Cohn was also infamous for his vulgarities and foul language, uttering such statements as "Lemme tell ya what show biz is about—it's about cunt and horses."

Born into a working-class Jewish family in New York City, Cohn was first a streetcar conductor and then a song plugger [*i.e., a salesman of sheet music in an era before it could be recorded*] before migrating to Hollywood, where he got a job at Universal Pictures. In 1918, with another partner and his brother, Joe, he founded the Cohn-Brandt-Cohn (CBC) Film Sales Corporation (also known, especially to its critics, as "Corned Beef and Cabbage.)

Eventually, with Cohn as president and production manager, it was renamed Columbia Pictures. Because of his harsh way of doing business, he became known (and frequently reviled) as "King Cohn."

Thanks in large part to the artistic sensitivities of director Frank Capra and others, Cohn would later employ such stars as Cary Grant, Mae West, Katharine Hepburn, Humphrey Bogart, Mickey Rooney, and Dorothy Lamour. Rita Hayworth became his biggest star.

Over the years, Columbia turned out many prestigious films, including *Mr. Smith Goes to Washington* (1939), starring James Stewart; and *Gilda* (1946), Hayworth's most memorable role.

Gossip maven Hedda Hopper claimed that Cohn "was the man you stood in line to hate." Actor Henry Mollison said, "He reels off smut like a berserk, unexpurgated Chaucer."

Cohn once told comedian Red Skelton, "I'm entitled to the broads because I have them under contract."

Years later, director Elia Kazan weighed in with his opinion: "Cohn liked to be the biggest bug in the manure pile." Producer Budd Schulberg pronounced him "the meanest man I ever knew—an unreconstructed dinosaur."

Biographer Bernard F. Dick wrote: "Ben Hecht called Cohn 'White Fang.' Director Charles Vidor took him to court for verbal abuse. The image of Harry Cohn as a vulgarian is such a part of Hollywood lore that it's hard to believe there were other Harry Cohns: The only studio president who was also head of production, the ex-song plugger who scrutinized scripts and grilled writers at story conferences, a man who could look on actresses as either 'Broads' or 'Goddesses.'"

Lucille was a broad, Hayworth a goddess.

Lucille had been told how crude Cohn was. But even for a Broadway veteran of the casting couch, she was stunned by his approach. After she'd entered the office and had been ordered to take a seat, Cohn got up from behind his desk and approached her. He unbuttoned his pants and pulled out a circumcised penis. "Suck it, bitch!" he commanded. Wanting to succeed in Hollywood, Lucille dutifully did her duty, as Marilyn Monroe would do in an equivalent setting in years to come.

Lucille claimed that Columbia chieftain, **Harry Cohn** (above, with his chic and *soignée* wife, actress **Joan Perry**), "was crude, uneducated, as foul as a big fart, and on his best day, merely abrasive."

Perry was signed to a Columbia contract in 1935 the same year as Rita Hayworth,. According to Perry, Cohn told her that (whereas) "Hayworth will be a star, you'll be my wife." Married in 1941, the marriage lasted until Cohn's death in 1958.

That didn't stop Cohn from sexually abusing a LOT of ingenues and established stars. "I kiss the feet of talent," Cohn told Lucille. "But in your case, I'll merely fuck your much used pussy. And don't forget one thing: I don't have an ulcer. I give them."

Lucille shot back, "So you're the head of the studio? I guess that's better than being a pimp!"

***

Shot at the Mack Sennett Studios in Hollywood during the autumn of

1934, *Carnival,* a Columbia release, was the first picture to give Lucille on-screen billing, though in the actual footage, she appears very briefly as an unnamed nurse.

A gifted studio writer, Robert Riskin, often worked with director Frank Capra. He eventually won an Oscar for his script of the Gable/Colbert romance, *It Happened One Night* (also 1934). In 1942, he married "scream queen" Fay Wray.

A son of Tennessee, director Walter Lang would go on to a grand career, producing musicals for Fox, none more notable than *The King and I* (1956), starring Yul Brynner and Deborah Kerr.

In *Carnival,* the male lead, Lee Tracy was trying to rebuild his career after having been fired by MGM in 1933 in Mexico after filming *Viva Villa!* starring Wallace Beery.

[Desi Arnaz, in his autobiography, A Book (1976), wrote about the incident that got Tracy fired: He claimed that in Mexico City, Tracy stood on a balcony and urinated on a military parade passing below. Others denied that the incident ever took place.]

Tracy often portrayed hard-boiled newspaper reporters. In *Blessed Event* (1932) his character evoked Walter Winchell, a then widely popular gossip columnist.

Sally Eilers poses in *Carnival* in the seductive role of "Daisy." She had a brief reign in the early 1930s as a movie queen, shooting to stardom in the title role of *Bad Girl* in 1931

In *Carnival,* as "Chick" Thompson, Tracy loses his wife during childbirth. He wants to keep his newborn son—"Dickie" Walters starring as "Poochy"—but his father-in-law objects because Tracy, who's a carnival performer, is considered "unworthy."

He flees with his infant son, dodging the authorities until there is a happy ending.

Sally Eilers, cast as Daisy, becomes his romantic interest. Jimmy Du-

Lee Tracy (1898-1968), according to film critic J. Hoberman, was "the brashest, cleverest motor-mouth newshound to ever slang a source or elbow his way through the urban jungle."

"Skinny and feral... with slicked back hair, a self-satisfied smirk and a foghorn bray...he was the original Hildy Johnson in the 1928 Broadway production of *The Front Page*...He often appeared as a shill or an ambulance-chasing shyster."

rante is "Fingers," a reformed pickpocket.

Eilers, like Carole Lombard, got her start appearing in "flaming youth" shorts for Mack Sennett. In the early 1930s, she starred in crime melodramas with George Raft and Spencer Tracy. Her first husband was the famous Western star, Hoot Gibson.

Florence Rice, cast as Miss Holbrook, had recently worked with Lucille in *The Fugitive Lady* (1934).

Thanks partly to his gravelly voice and humor, Durante became a household name and remained one for almost fifty years, famous for his *schnozzola* (big nose) and his theme song, "Inka Dinka Doo."

The New York Times reviewed *Carnival* as "an enjoyable sentimental comedy."

Jimmy Durante, when he was young, opening his night-time act by calling attention to his proboscis (his long nose), which he dubbed his "*schnozzola.*"

***

Lucille's next picture for Fox was *Behind the Evidence* (1935), a crime drama directed by Lambert Hillyer, who had previously helmed her in *Men of the Night* (1934). She was given a screen credit, but not a name, appearing as "Secretary."

The film starred Norman Foster, Sheila Mannors, and Donald Cook, with whom Lucille had worked on the set of *Jealousy* (1934).

Foster was cast as a globe-trotting millionaire Tony Sheridan, who has lost his money. He takes a job as a society reporter for *The Daily Herald*. As the plot unfolds, he finds himself shielding an old flame of his, Ruth Allen (Mannors), from her shady fiancé, Donald Cook. He was cast as Ward Allen, a gang leader.

Ultimately, Tony is kidnapped by Cook's gang, but it all works out in the end in his favor, The gang leader is dispatched with a shotgun.

Foster was also a director and screenwriter, helming several Charlie Chan and Mr. Moto movies as well as projects for Orson Welles and Walt Disney. In 1926, he married screen legend Claudette Colbert, divorcing her in 1935 to wed Sally Blane, the older sister of Loretta Young.

During his marriage to Colbert, they lived at different addresses, which allowed her to

Behind the Evidence, once reviewed as "a harmless little specimen of the wood-pulp school of film melodrama," lay lost in Columbia's archives for many years until, one day, it was "re-discovered."

carry on with her lesbian liaisons. Colbert had an affair with Gary Cooper when they co-starred in *His Woman* (1931) and was known for a number of affairs with women, including Marlene Dietrich.

Sheila Mannors, a daughter of San Francisco, billed herself under five different names, including Sheila Bromley, and was best known (if at all) for her B movies, often westerns. The cowboys came and went from her life: John Wayne, Hoot Gibson, Johnny Mack Brown, and Bill Cody.

Lucille remembered her and years later, cast her as Helen Erickson Kaiser, a childhood friend of Lucy Ricardo in *I Love Lucy.*

The *New York World-Telegram* called *Behind the Evidence* "a thin and wispy piece of murder entertainment with nickel-weekly clichés about hold-ups and reporters who solve crimes that baffle the police."

"If I don't get a breakthrough role soon, I'll end up in oblivion," Lucille lamented.

***

Hope bloomed anew when Lucille was notified by Columbia that she was going to appear in their 1935 film, *The Jail Breaker,* co-starring two A-list actors, Edward G. Robinson and Jean Arthur.

[During the shoot, the title was changed to Passport to Fame. *Then, before its release, its title was changed once again to* The Whole Town's Talking. *The picture had nothing to do with a 1926 film with the same name.]*

Lucille confided to her friend, starlet Barbara Pepper, "Those sessions in Harry Cohn's office seemed to have paid off. I'm getting cast in a Grade-A picture at last."

She received more good news: Cohn had hired John Ford as the director, with a script by Robert Riskin, who had penned the screenplay for her earlier picture, *Carnival.*

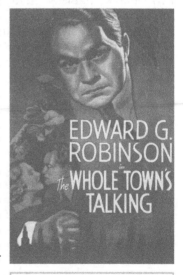

Born in 1894 at Cape Elizabeth in Maine, Ford was the son of an Irish bootlegger. In 1913, he migrated to Hollywood, where he began an illustrious career in the film industry. Greater works lay in his future, when he'd win five Oscars for churning out classics that included *The Grapes of Wrath* (1940) with Henry Fonda.

Closely associated with John Wayne, Ford starred him in *Stagecoach* (1939), the film that made "The Duke" a star.

Ford had a reputation as a hard-driving, hard-drinking, profane, crusty, and brilliant director. He was also highly intelligent, erudite, sensitive, and sentimental.

Years later, when asked, **Edward G. Robinson** did not remember Lucille appearing in this John Ford-directed melodrama with comic overtones. "Today, when I see her on TV, she makes me laugh, and I don't laugh easily," he said.

105

He wore dark glasses and a black patch over his left eye, and was always seen with a pipe in his mouth.

Lucille was among the first to hear gossip about Ford's sexual preference. Rumors spread that the director had put Wayne on the casting couch years ago. In Maureen O'Hara's 2004 memoir, *'Tis Herself*, she claimed that she walked in on Ford when he was deep kissing a famous male actor. She didn't name him, but that actor was the bisexual Tyrone Power.

Lucille was extremely disappointed when she learned that she was only an extra, one of those people off the street hired for ten dollars a day. When her family went to see the picture, they couldn't spot her in a crowd scene.

Robinson had shot to stardom in *Little Caesar* (1930), but he was tiring of gangster roles. Having no immediate work for him, Warners lent him to Columbia to portray two separate characters in the same movie.

In *The Whole Town's Talking,* he'd play a gangster, but for only half of the picture. In one of his roles, he's a sociopathic killer, but in the other part he plays, he's a mild-mannered drone in an advertising agency. The gentle, decent character he portrays is a lookalike who closely resembles the gangster. The similarities lead to a series of plot twists that threaten his (character's) life.

His romantic interest centers on Jean Arthur, cast as Miss Clark, a role that demonstrated her flair for comedy. Capra would soon showcase her talent, casting her in such classics as *Mr. Deeds Goes to Town* (1936); *You Can't Take It with You* (1938); and *Mr. Smith Goes to Washington* (1939).

Arthur specialized in playing hardworking girls with hearts of gold. Cohn ordered that she be photographed only from her left side. "Her right side is half-horse," he tactlessly said.

Her first marriage (1928) to photographer Julian Anker lasted only one day. She was married to Frank Rose, Jr., from 1932

Like Lucille, it took **Jean Arthur** a long time to hit her stride in the movies.

In one of her early films, she had to battle Clara Bow, cast as her sister, for the love of the same man. In another movie (a Philo Vance mystery) the plot called for her to kill a millionaire.

When John Ford cast her in *The Whole World's Talking*, the world finally took notice.

John Wayne (left) with director **John Ford.** The world may never know the full implications of the published information and sometimes compelling rumors about the early relationship of Duke and the closeted director.

Did Ford really maneuver and/or coerce the then-young John Wayne onto the casting couch?

to 1949, but was said to have had numerous affairs with women during its tenure. .

Lucille's three-month contract with Columbia was quickly coming to an end, and as such, she'd appear in only one more picture for them. Oddly enough, in it, her character would be given the name of Lucille.

***

She'd previously worked as an extra on the set of *Jealousy*, which had co-starred an unlikely duo, Nancy Carroll and George Murphy. Now Lucille was assigned yet another walk-on part in their latest picture, *I'll Always Love You*, set for a 1935 release by Columbia. Murphy and Carroll would unite one more time for the 1935 *After the Dance*.

Murphy later claimed that Carroll was not an easy actress with whom to work. "She enjoyed making me uncomfortable. She never quite made it in the movies, perhaps because she relied on stage tricks instead of her own God-given talents. As for Lucille, I thought she would just disappear into that sea of broken dreams."

"Harry Cohn told his associates that I was the only son of a bitch in Hollywood that liked him," Murphy continued. "During the shoot, he called Lucille to his office at around one o'clock one afternoon to render her services on his casting couch."

The director of *I'll Love You Always* was Leo Bulgakov, who had emigrated to the United States in the 1920s, after having appeared on the stage in the Soviet Union. In the 1940s, he turned to acting, appearing in

George Murphy and **Nancy Carroll** in "*I'll Love You Always*"

"On a personal level," Murphy said, "the title of our movie could not have been more misleading. I detested working with Carroll."

such pictures as Ernest Hemingway's *For Whom the Bell Tolls* (1943), starring Gary Cooper and Ingrid Bergman.

The trite little tale (*I'll Love You Always*) should have been better than it was. Its screenplay was authored by Sidney Buchman, who wrote the script for the 1938 hit, *Holiday*, starring Katharine Hepburn and Cary Grant. The other writer, Vera Caspary, would go on to pen the classic thriller *Laura* (1944), starring Gene Tierney.

The plot has Nora Clegg (Carroll) giving up her stage career to marry Carl Brent (Murphy), a struggling engineer. His job requires him to work in Russia for several months, but the deal falls through. In the meantime, he steals money from his prospective employer and is convicted and sent to prison.

Somehow, believing he's in Russia, his wife doesn't find out. Contributing to the deception is one of his Russian friends, who mails his letters, written in prison and funneled through Moscow, back to her in the United States. In the meantime, to pay the bills, she takes a job in a "taxi dance" hall.

It all works out in the end, at least according to the standards of the mid-1930s. Murphy is released from prison, and she becomes pregnant.

At the end of the shoot, Lucille got her pink slip from Columbia. Cohn told director Bulgakov, "Cocksuckers like Lucille Ball are a dime a dozen in Hollywood."

She had a date on the night of her dismissal with Richard Green, the brother of songwriter Johnny Green.,

When she told him she'd been booted, he informed her of a "cattle call" that very evening at RKO. "I heard that you were a model in Manhattan. Have you ever modeled clothes for Bergdorf Goodman?"

She said that she hadn't.

"Well, claim that you have," he said. "Bernard Newman, who used to hire models there, is picking girls from the lineup. He'll be impressed if you were a Bergdorf gal."

At the audition, as instructed, she told Newman she'd been one of the top models at Bergdorf.

"You're hired!" he said. "I used to pick the models for Bergdorf, but I've never seen you before, and I've got a great memory. But you lied so convincingly, I think you can make it as an actress."

That encounter led to a three-month contract at RKO, which, with renewals, continued for the next seven years.

"*I'll Always Love You* was a trite, Depression-era story that marked my ungraceful exit from Columbia," **Lucille** said.

"After some of the casting directors who mattered went to see it, they told me to marry some fellow with dough and settle down as a housewife, abandoning any hope of a movie career."

A critic for *Liberty* magazine wrote: "*Roberta* stands in a good way of being the best musical comedy to come out of Hollywood. It is so thoroughly lively, so exciting to the eye and ear, and so imbued with an unstrained-for-gaiety that it glides smoothly and pleasantly through the vaguely motivated tale."

***

At RKO, Lucille made her film debut in a hit musical, *Roberta* (1935). Her involvement wasn't particularly memorable: She played a fashion model in an uncredited role.

Roberta starred Irene Dunne, Randolph Scott, Fred Astaire, Ginger Rogers, and Helen Westley. Music was by Jerome Kern and conducted by Max Steiner. Hermes Pan and Astaire were the dance directors.

Left to right, **Ginger Rogers** and playwright **Garson Kanin** on the set of *Roberta*, chat with **Pandro S. Berman**, its producer.

As Ginger later claimed, "Pandro was very turned off by Lucille. But she soon changed his mind, and office scuttlebutt revealed that they were having an affair."

The musical was based on a hit Broadway show, opened in 1933, that had starred Bob Hope, George Murphy, and Lyda ("the Polish-Hungarian bombshell") Roberti.

Pandro S. Berman was its producer. The first time he spotted Lucille, he couldn't understand why his fashion coordinator, Bernard Newman, had hired her in the first place. He told his director, William A. Seiter, "Bernie has put this kid under a short-term contract. She's great at parties, or so I hear, a real funny kid, but I can't see any future for her in the movies."

[Berman would not only radically change his mind about Lucille. He'd soon be having an affair with her.]

Because of the negative opinion of his boss, Seiter was skeptical of Lucille when he met her.

A New Yorker, he had broken into films in 1915 in Mack Sennett's Keystone Studios, doubling as a cowboy. In the mid-1920s, he earned a reputation directing popular Reginald Denny vehicles, many of them starring his wife, Laura La Plante.

Over the course of his career, he would helm such A-list stars as Rita Hayworth, Barbara Stanwyck, John Wayne, Henry Fonda, and the Marx Brothers.

During her first week together at RKO, Lucille renewed her friendship with Lela Rogers, the powerful mother of Ginger. *[In Manhattan, she had advised Lucille to make use of the casting couch if she wanted to advance herself in show business. Lela repeated that advice at RKO.]*

"Berman told me he has a bad opinion of you," Lela said. "Why don't you flirt with him, make yourself available, and perhaps you can make him change his mind. You could become the biggest star at RKO—other than

MEET THE ROGERS

A MOTHER-DAUGHTER SHOW-BIZ TEAM

LEFT PHOTO: **Ginger**, left, and **Lela**, right) celebrating at home (yes, one of them had a soda fountain) . Resting on the countertop is the Oscar Ginger won for her role in *Kitty Foyle* (1941).

RIGHT PHOTO: Ferociously loyal but argumentative as only mothers and daughters can be, the Rogers matriarch and her daughter are shown here rehearsing for one of their occasional stage performances.

According to Ginger, in reference to Lela, " I traveled with my mother, and there was never enough money. I always had to roll down my silk stockings and carry a doll when we bought train tickets so I coudl go half fare. If we had $3, we always figured how to tip for the trunks and still eat."

Decades after it was filmed, a LOT of glamour continues to pulse through celluloid replays of *Roberta*.

Astaire and Rogers executed dance maneuvers that are now part of the "religious canon" of Golden Age Hollywood.

On the left in the photo above is **Lela Rogers,** mother of Ginger, who was hired to train, groom, and rehearse emerging starlets at RKO.

One of her pupils was **Lucille Ball,** who was attired in pants, which was rare in Hollywood at that time.

Ginger, of course."

"I'll think about it," Lucille promised.

"Lela was the first person to see me as a queen with glamour," Lucille said. "She pulled my frizzy hair back off my brow and had of couple of my side teeth straightened. Then she sent me to a voice coach who got me to lower my squeaky voice by four tones."

"As I finally became a star, I heeded the advice not only of Ginger, but of Carole Lombard," Lucille said. "Never cast anyone younger and prettier than yourself—hence, my future selection of Vivian Vance."

From 1938 to 1945, Lela would be in charge of RKO's new talent, working as an assistant to Charles Kerner, the studio's vice president overseeing production.

Berman himself had been impressed with the way Lela handled her daughter. "When Ginger faces the camera, Lela barges around the set like a rhinoceros protecting her young."

Lucille found Lela "petite, dynamic, and shrewd, and also quite sexy and beautiful like her daughter."

Lela also revealed that her daughter, Ginger, did not like working with Astaire. As a perfectionist, he sometimes had her dancing in rehearsal eighteen hours a day until her feet were bleeding. *Roberta* was the third of the musicals in which they danced together.

Years later, in a *tsunami* of nostalgia, **Lucille** (left) and **Ginger Rogers** co-starred together in an episode of *The Lucy Show.*

In *Roberta*, **Lucille** had never looked more glamourous onscreen.

In an elaborate fashion show sequence, she gracefully preened and strutted to the tune of the Oscar-nominated "Lovely to Look At."

Referring to themselves as "Two Old Broads," they danced the Charleston and evoked their days at RKO in the 1930s.

Their fans went wild.

"As a leading man, Fred left much to be desired," Lucille said. "I saw no romantic appeal in him at all. He was skinny and balding, but that runt could really dance."

Astaire recalled meeting Lucille on the set of *Roberta:* "I liked her very much. She was a lady determined to make good. I could see that she had talent. She was just doing small bits in my pictures, but you knew somehow or other that there was a lot of something going on there."

Lucille and Ginger became lifelong friends, even though Lucille once ruefully asserted, "I should have been a star years before I became one. All the roles that would have shot me to stardom back then went either to Ginger or else to Ann Sothern."

In 1971, almost forty years after their inaugural meeting, Ginger appeared on an episode of *I Love Lucy* and danced the Charleston.

Lucille loved gossip, and Ginger kept her abreast of her five marriages—one of them (1934-1940) to Lew Ayres—and her many affairs. What she kept from Lucille was that during her estrangement from Ayres, Desi Arnaz had impregnated her with a child she had arranged to abort.

Lucille found that Ginger's most charming and desirable husband was the French actor Jacques Bergerac, the sexiest of her mates. Ginger confided that when she and Bergerac visited Noël Coward at his residence on the French Riviera, the playwright escorted the actor upstairs to his bedroom for a two-hour audition without his jockey shorts.

Lucille also heard about Ginger's other affairs with such men as director Mervyn LeRoy, attorney Greg Bautzer, French actor Jean Gabin (when he wasn't involved with Marlene Dietrich), George Gershwin, Cary Grant (trying a woman for a change), singer Rudy Vallee, Burgess Meredith (Paulette Goddard's ex), another director, George Stevens, and actors George Montgomery (married to Dinah Shore), David Niven, James Stewart, and producer/aviator Howard Hughes.

Years after the demise of his marriage (1953-57) to Ginger Rogers, the handsome Frenchman, **Jacques Bergerac**, appeared as "Freddy the Fence" in an episode of *Batman.*

Irene Dunne was promoted, in advance of the release of *Roberta*, as its headlining female lead. In the years that followed, however, Ginger Rogers emerged as its real female star, largely because of her dances with Fred Astaire.

RKO's publicists made it a point to promote the value of the gems in Dunne's tiara to movie audiences: $6,000 (*aka* $115,000 in today's dollars)

The plot of *Roberta* unfolds as John Kent (Scott), a former Harvard football player, arrives in Paris with his close buddy, Huck Haines (Astaire). Astaire heads a dance band, the Wabash Indianians, but their hoped-for gig falls through.

To help out, Kent goes to his Aunt Minnie (Helen Westley) who owns a chic house of fashion. He soon falls in love with his aunt's chief assistant, Stephanie (Irene Dunne).

Huck, too, encounters his hometown sweetheart, Lizzie Gats (cast with Ginger), who is posing as the Polish Countess Scharwenka. She gets his band a gig playing at a Parisian night spot where she is a featured dancer. He promises to keep her real identity (a hometown American girl) a secret.

Then Aunt Minnie dies. Kent—although he knows nothing about *haute couture*—inherits her house of fashion. Although the plot gets complicated, everything works out happily in the end, including his romance.

Uncredited, Lucille appears in her most glamourous role to date. She descends an elegant staircase, her hair dyed a Jean Harlow shade of platinum and attired in a flamingo pink ostrich cape over a form-fitting gown embellished with plumage.

As was her custom, Lucille set about to get to know the stars, including Westley, who that same year had been cast in a big hit, *Anne of the Green Gables*. Born in 1875, she would also star in four Shirley Temple movies and the 1936 version of *Show Boat*.

The Belle of Louisville, Kentucky, Irene Dunne (cast as Aunt Minnie's assistant and the firm's chief designer), was one of the leading stars of Hollywood's Golden Age. She had set out to become an opera singer, but the Met in New York rejected her twice. After migrating to Hollywood, she became a movie star, making her debut in 1930 in the musical, *Leathernecking*.

Over the course of a long career, she'd be nominated for a Best Actress Oscar five times, including for such classics as *Love Affair* (1939) and *I Remember Mama* (1948). In her heyday, she was one of the highest paid stars in Hollywood.

After she surrendered her title, "First Lady of Hollywood," President Eisenhower named her as a U.S. delegate to the United Nations.

A son of Virginia, the lantern-jawed Randolph Scott began his film career in 1928 and became known as a stoic man of the West as he hemmed and hawed his

According to Pandro S. Berman, the handsome, macho star, **Randolph Scott** (left) had an affair with Fred Astaire, "That was during the day. At night, he came home to his in-house lover, **Cary Grant.**" (right photo)

way through many an "oater." Sixty of his 100 movies were Westerns, and his leading ladies ranged from Mae West to Marlene Dietrich, even Shirley Temple.

Actress Anne Baxter said, "Scott is tall, blonde, and handsome. Who cares if Cary Grant is his better half?"

Scott himself (ungrammatically and awkwardly) said, "If a man is for men, and it's in most walks of life, I can buy that."

In spite of his preferences, Scott married two socially prominent heiresses, Marion DuPont and Patricia Stillman, Other than Cary Grant, his numerous affairs included involvements with Gary Cooper, Howard Hughes, Dorothy Lamour, and Margaret Sullavan, who called him "an ignoramus."

He not only married well, but ended up with $100 million in real estate, securities, and oil wells.

Even though Fred Astaire was hardly a sex symbol, he became one of the most influential dancers in the history of cinema. His career as a performer spanned a period of seventy-five years, during which he starred in thirty-one musicals.

As a dancer, he was known for his uncanny sense of rhythm and his innovations, having an impact on such other dancers as Rudolf Nureyev, Michael Jackson, George Balanchine, Bob Fosse, and Jerome Robbins. His sister, Adele, also rose to fame as a choreographer and dancer, having first appeared with her brother on Broadway in 1917.

Berman paid $65,000 for the screen rights to *Roberta* and ordered scriptwriters to combine the roles of Murphy and Hope into a single character. Dunne sang the musical's breakaway pop hit, "Smoke Gets in Your Eyes." Also retained from the stage play were other favorites such as "Yesterdays" and "Let's Begin." Two songs were added, including "Lovely to Look At" and "Three Sisters." Both of them became hit songs of 1935, and "Lovely to Look At" was nominated for a Best Song Oscar. Another hit song was called "I Won't Dance."

A critic asserted that the on-screen pairing of Astaire with Rogers converted a continental operetta into an All-American musical, also noting that "Fred and Ginger" in "I'll Be Hard to Handle" turned the pair into screen deities. This was also the first number in which both stars danced in pants.

Bob Thaves later made a famous remark. "Sure, Astaire is great, but don't forget Ginger Rogers, who did everything he did backwards...and in high heels."

The film rights to *Roberta* were later acquired by MGM and released once again in 1951 under the title of *Lovely to Look At,* starring songbird Kathryn Grayson and Howard Keel, a studly baritone.

A Bostonian, Benny Rubin, is hardly a household name today, but he can still be seen on reruns of *I Love Lucy.*

Long before they actually worked together, he and Lucille had a brief fling. Born in 1899, Rubin made his first film appearance in *Daisies Won't Yell* (1928) and worked in movies until as late as 1979. He died of a heart attack, in Los Angeles on July 15, 1986, and Lucille sent flowers.

Rubin had been a show business veteran for some seven decades—a comedian, character actor, and dialectician. Lucille once jokingly said, "The only difference between Desi and Benny when they took off their shorts was a tiny piece of skin."

Lucille and Rubin added a footnote in Hollywood history one night in San Francisco when they attended a performance at the Club Bal Tabarin. Lucille was dating Rubin at the time, perhaps hoping he could use his influence at RKO to get her better parts. He was a leading talent scout for the studio at the time, hardly realizing that his date would one day own the studio.

At the Bal Tabarin, Lucille was impressed with "a tap-dancing babe and wise-cracking chorus girl" by the name of Ann Miller. She was so impressed with Miller's machine gun taps that she urged Rubin to get her a screen test at RKO.

"Pussy whipped," as Rubin described himself, he ultimately agreed, and as in the aftermath, "Sugar Baby" got her first contract with a big Hollywood studio.

[In 1940 Miller appeared in Too Many Girls with Lucille and Desi Arnaz.]

Benny Rubin was a comedian, character actor, dialectician, and a veteran of almost 70 years in show business. He also had a brief fling with Lucille.

She later told Ann Miller. "I thought the bastard would get me better parts, but he didn't. Oh, well."

***

Lucille's next big part was in a college musical, a genre that was wildly popular in the late 1930s. This one, the badly titled *Old Man Rhythm*, was released by RKO in 1935. It starred bandleader Charles ("Buddy") Rogers, hailed as "America's Boyfriend" in the late 1920s and early '30s when he reached the height of his popularity.

"When I met him," Lucille quipped, "'ZING! Went the Strings of My Heart.' He was handsome and charming. Only problem was that he was dating Mary Pickford. Once known as 'America's Sweetheart' in silent pictures, she was rich as Midas."

Lucille had first "fallen" for Buddy when she'd gone to see *Wings* (1927), an aviation flick in

Lucille Ball always claimed that she had personally discovered the dancing sensation, **Ann Miller,** at a night club in San Francisco.

Miller, the greatest tap dancer in the history of cinema, also had an affair with Desi Arnaz, which—for a while, at least—remained a secret from Lucille.

115

which he had appeared opposite Clara Bow. The movie was the first ever to win an Academy Award as Best Picture of the Year.

After *Wings,* Buddy made *My Best Girl* (also 1927) with Pickford. The two fell in love and began an affair.

[Before her astonishing success as silent screen star, Pickford had been married (1911-1920) to actor Owen Moore. At the time she met Buddy, she was still married (1920-1936) to the swashbuckling star of silent pictures, Douglas Fairbanks, Sr. In 1937, she married Buddy, a union that lasted until her death in 1979. During the course of her marriage to Fairbanks, Pickford sustained affairs with other leading men, including Johnny Mack Brown, her co-star in Coquette (1929), and Leslie Howard, her co-star in Secrets (1933).]

As Lucille found out years later, Buddy was bisexual, operating his own version of the casting couch for aspirant musicians wanting to join his band.

Lucille's fling with Buddy was brief. When *Old Man Rhythm* was finished, so was Buddy. "The competition for him was more than I could handle. I knew he'd ultimately go for the money—namely, Miss Pickford—and so he did."

Urged on by Lela Rogers, Lucille had tried to convince director Edward Ludwig to let her play one of the girls competing for Buddy's attention.

"I wanted Grace Bradley's role of Marion Beecher, the campus vamp. But Ludwig wouldn't have that and cast that Brooklyn bitch, who was a pianist more than an actress. She was pulling in $150 a week to my $75, which had been raised by $25 from my origi-

Old Man Rhythm was a "campus comedy," elaborating on then-prevalent beliefs that college students were entitled to endless fun, and that the college experience would be remembered years later as the romantic and glamorous high point of every graduate's life.

Mary Pickford and **Buddy Rogers** in the scene above, evoke the then-current perception of college life. They were married in 1937, two years after the release of *Old Man Rhythm.*

Marketed for years as "America's Sweetheart," Pickford told the press, "I only want to be one man's sweetheart, and I'm not going to let him (i.e., Rogers) go."

That's not exactly the way things worked out. She sustained some adult affairs during the course of her married life, notably with actor Johnny Mack Brown and later, with the English heartthrob, Leslie Howard. Buddy, her bandleader husband, was bisexual and conducted a number of flings with some of his musicians.

nal salary."

Lucille also tried out for Barbara Kent's role of Edith Warren, but Ludwig rejected her for that role, too.. "Kent was a petite, Canadian brunette who stood four feet, eight inches," Lucille said. "A real midget. She'd played a *femme fatale* in the Greta Garbo movie, *Flesh and the Devil* (1926). I thought she was a bit long in the tooth for a campus cutie."

She then continued, even more sarcastically, "When Kent was a little girl and wanted to come into the house, her daddy always warned her, 'Wipe the dinosaur shit off your feet.'"

[Actually, Kent had been born in 1907. Lucille in 1911.]

"What did Ludwig know about life on an American college campus?" Lucille wondered. "He was born in Ukraine. As the years went by, I heard that two of the hottest studs in Hollywood, John Payne and Rory Calhoun, ended up on his casting couch. What chance did I have?"

"Hermes Pan took time off from Astaire to teach a lot of extras—part of the student body—some dance steps. I was one of the students, seen on-screen roasting marshmallows and swaying to the band music, a role that called for the talent of Sarah Bernhardt," Lucille quipped, sarcastically.

Once again, as she had in other pictures, she set out to meet fellow members of the RKO family. The cast included Erik Rhodes, who had been born in El Reno, Indian Territory, part of Oklahoma. She would later work with him in the upcoming *Top Hat* (1935) and *Chatterbox* (1936).

Rhodes had appeared on Broadway in *Gay Divorce* (1932) with Fred Astaire, where he played a spirited feather-brained, thick-accented Italian eccentric. RKO later cast him in its film adaptation, the title by then modified to the more appealing *The Gay Divorcée* (1934), co-starring the dance team promoted as "Fred and Ginger."

The English actor, Eric Blore, had appeared on Broadway in Cole Porter's *Gay Divorce* with Astaire and Clare Luce. Blore had made a career out of playing a butler. He was widely quoted when he said, "If I were not a gentleman's gentleman, I could be cast as a cad's cad." He'd work with Lucille again in *Top Hat*.

Lucille had a surprise encounter with Erich von Stroheim, Jr., who'd been assigned a small part. "Talk about living in the shadow of a famous father," she said, referring to the legendary actor/director Erich von Stroheim, Sr., billed at the time as "The Man You Loved to Hate." Both a director

Erich von Stroheim, father (right) **and son** (left).

On the set one day, Lucille had a chance encounter with the younger of these two men. "I didn't dare ask him what growing up with his father, the tyrannical director, was like. I imagine it was like having Hitler as a dad."

and star of silent pictures, his last silent, *Queen Kelly* (1929) starring Gloria Swanson, had not been completed.

Von Stroheim, Sr. had co-starred with Greta Garbo in 1932 in *As You Desire Me*. In 1950, he would immortalize himself "in that dumb butler role" with Gloria Swanson in *Sunset Blvd*.

On the set, Lucille "hung out" with songwriter Johnny Mercer, who had been cast as one of the singing students. In the early 1940s and early 1960s, respectively, as a lyricist, Mercer would pen some of her favorite songs, such as "Moon River" and "That Old Black Magic."

She emerged, after *Old Man Rhythm's* release, with a long-lasting relationship with Betty Grable, not knowing of her affair with Desi Arnaz.

At age twelve, Grable had begun her film career in Hollywood, and by the 1930s, she had already appeared in a string of B musicals, mostly cast as a college student.

She seemed headed for oblivion, a feeling all too familiar to Lucille as well. But Grable replaced Alice Faye in *Down Argentina Way* in 1940, and shot to stardom, appearing in movies with John Payne, Don Ameche, Victor Mature, and Tyrone Power. By 1943, she became the highest paid star in America.

One of her photos, shot from the rear, elevated her into one of the most visible pin-up girls of World War II, surpassing even Rita Hayworth. That photo was carried to every battlefield where Americans fought, from Berlin to Tokyo. Her legs were voted the most beautiful in the world. As Grable later quipped to Lucille, "I became a star for two reasons, and I'm standing on them."

She and Lucille liked to indulge in "girl talk" about men (but never about Desi Arnaz). Grable got down and dirty whenever she discussed her sex life. She told Lucille that her first husband (1937-1939), Jackie Coogan, "taught me more tricks than a whore learns in a whorehouse."

She had an affection for homosexual chorus boys and dancers, but preferred "rough trade," some of them truck drivers whom she'd fellate at truck stops east of Los Angeles.

She'd be famously married to Harry James (1943-1965), but managed affairs with Tyrone Power, Artie Shaw (she aborted his baby), Rory Calhoun, cross-dressing Dan Dailey (he wore her gowns), Dick Haymes (her co-star in *The Shocking Miss Pilgrim* (1947), Victor Mature ("the biggest endowment") Mickey Rooney ("The Little Runt"), Robert Stack, and George Raft.

It was surprising that Lucille and Grable became chums," as they called

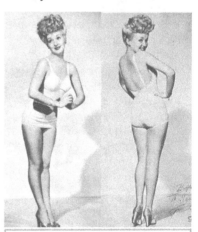

Two views of **Betty Grable**, the most popular pinup girl of World War II.

"It was impossible to sit next to her and not want to get to know her better," said Desi Arnaz.

it. Actually, Grable was her chief rival at RKO, and whereas she could dance, Lucille could not. It was because of Grable that Lucille eventually quit being a blonde and dyed her hair red to look different.

"It was also because of Grable that Lucille quit yawning her way through a picture and did some real acting," said Kay Harvey, an actress and model.

In February of 1958, Grable with her husband, bandleader Harry James, appeared on the fourth *Lucille Ball-Desi Arnaz Show.* The segment was named "Lucy Wins a Racehorse."

***

Lela Rogers directed RKO's Little Theatre where she cast aspirant starlets in plays to keep them in practice before they had to face the camera. Directors and producers attended these plays, some perhaps hoping to cast young women in a film, others with different intentions, perhaps an audition on a casting couch.

Sometimes, Lela's daughter, Ginger, would appear with Lucille in a play. Soon, the two began to go out on double dates, hitting the leading night clubs of Hollywood. In those days, whereas Lucille preferred masculine, studly stagehands, Ginger tended to date "names," especially leading man Lee Bowman, Henry Fonda, James Stewart, and the formidable Orson Welles.

In a memoir, obviously designed to protect Lela's reputation, Lucille denied that Lela ever "pimped out" any of the girls under her supervision. Such a denial was to be expected.

One week, Lela cast Anita Colby in *A Case of Rain,* and Lucille played a minor role. Before its opening on Saturday night, Colby came down with a severe fever and could not go on. Since Lucille had attended every rehearsal, Lela asked her to take the lead, even though she had only hours to prepare for the performance.

That Saturday night, Pandro S. Berman, head of Production at RKO, slipped into the theater and sat by himself in the back row. Nicknamed "Pan," he was six years older than Lucille, and was fairly good looking, and a rather forceful "macho man."

Berman had been born into a Jewish family in Pittsburgh, As "Pan" grew older, his father moved his family to Hollywood.

Following in his father's footsteps, Pan joined the film industry, becoming a movie editor at RKO before working himself up to one of its assistant producers. He was so effective in that spot that management advanced him to head of Production.

For this publicity shot, **Lucille** was instructed to act like a *femme fatale*, "a seductress moving from one male animal to her next catch."

119

Many of the Astaire/Rogers musicals were made during his steward-ship, as were some of Katharine Hepburn's best pictures. In the greatest year of movie releases, 1939, Berman entered the sweepstakes with *Gunga Din,* starring Cary Grant, and *The Hunchback of Notre Dame* with Charles Laughton.

Berman became known as RKO's "Boy Wonder," the same name ap-plied to Irving Thalberg at MGM before his untimely death.

After sitting through Lela's play, *A Case of Rain,* Berman rose to his feet and began his exit from the theater. At that moment, Lela approached him and said, "Lucille Ball, under contract to you, played the lead and was called in at the last minute. I think she did a damn good job. Maybe you can give her more to do in her next film."

"I'll see what I can do," he said. "She looks like a hot little spitfire. Tell her to come over to my office around nine tomorrow night. I'll be working late."

Dressed and made up most seductively, Lucille arrived at the ap-pointed time. What happened next has not been revealed. However, on those lists of Hollywood seductions, Berman's name appears on Lucille's roster, following Desi Arnaz, writer S.N. Behrman, and Milton Berle.

The day after Lucille's appointment, Berman called director Mark San-drich *[He'd been designated as helmer of the next Astaire/Rogers musical,* Top Hat*]*, and ordered him to give Lucille some lines.

For most of the coming months, she was known to make several evening visits to the small hideaway apartment that Berman maintained a few blocks from RKO.

Author Kathleen Brady wrote: "Unlike Sam Goldwyn, Berman was definitely Lucille's type—dark, broad, and fleshy. He was energetic, force-ful, and loved gambling."

Lucille's cousin, Cleo Smith, later said, "Pan really went for Lucille and helped her career, although he was slow in doing so. She was more of a pal to him than a vamp. She liked men, and there was no war of the sexes with her. He didn't offer her any star roles at first. He told Lela Rogers that if he did give her the lead and she flopped, it would mean the end of her Hollywood career. But if she improved, he'd give her better roles."

"The casting couch only gets a gal in the door," he said. "What she does in front of the camera is what really counts."

Although married to Viola Newman, Berman continued to meet Lu-cille at his hideaway near RKO. Soon everyone on the lot knew they were an item, and the staff treated her with great respect, not wanting to anger "the boy wonder."

Even though he was sleeping with her, he kept her in limited roles, and didn't seem overly jealous. In fact, he wanted her to be seen dating other men, hoping that this would keep his wife from finding out about his affair. "To Pan," as Ginger recalled, "Lucille was just a hot piece of ass. He was smitten with her in the beginning but it was all about sex—not love. The trouble was, Lucille wanted to get married, and she began to 'try out' other candidates. She knew there was no future with Pan."

Berman was later accused of using Lucille as a virtual hooker, ordering her to date RKO's financial backers coming in from for "inspections" and fact-finding trips from the East Coast. But Ginger always claimed that going out with these rich men was Lucille's idea, and Berman agreed to set it up, since he wanted word to get around that she was dating plenty of men.

Although details are scarce, it appears that Lucille slept with a number of these men from New York but turned quite a few down, too. Bernie Kahn, a stockholder, claimed he seduced Lucille on the same night he took her to the Cocoanut Grove. "I didn't force her, but she went along with it. In my hotel suite, she pulled off all her clothes and went about having sex with me as if duty bound. It wasn't much fun for me, and I had a hard time maintaining an erection because of her indifference."

Berman stayed on at RKO until the end of the decade, departing in 1940 for "greener pastures" at MGM. As one of its major producers, he turned out some of the biggest hits from that studio, beginning with *The Ziegfeld Girl* in 1941. He became a figure in the career of Elizabeth Taylor, casting her in *National Velvet* (1944) when she was still a child, and later in *Father of the Bride* (1950). She didn't want to play a prostitute in *BUtterfield 8* (1960) but Berman insisted, and it brought her a Best Actress Oscar.

***

Top Hat (1935), a screwball musical comedy from RKO, has been called "the quintessential Fred Astaire/Ginger Rogers musical, a premier Americana example of show-biz nostalgia." For Rogers and Astaire, it was their fourth movie appearance together.

Top Hat, a Fred Astaire and Ginger Rogers musical, is hailed even today as one of the top musicals of Golden Age Hollywood.

"The dialogue has more genuinely funny gags than all the rest of screen musicals put together," a critic proclaimed.

Lucille was given a small role, the part marking her second appearance on the screen with the dancing duo.

Combining glorious music by Irving Berlin with memorable dance routines, *Top Hat* became the studio's highest grossing film of the 1930s, taking in $3.5 million at the box office.

In an opening scene, Lucille, as a flower peddler, was assigned a few "smarty-pants" lines delivered in a Cockney accent.

But repeatedly, she flubbed her lines and could never get the accent right. Losing his patience, director Mark Sandrich summoned Lela Rogers.

"I was extremely nervous," Lucille said. "I had virtually begged for some lines of dialogue. Now that I had them, I was screwing up the scene, requiring eight takes—and still not delivering. Lela convinced Sandrich that the dialogue didn't suit Lucille as the flower clerk and more appropriately belonged to the salesman to whom she was talking. After the scene was rewritten, it worked. All Lucille had to do was react. Her dialogue was reduced to "What can he say?" and "Really?"

Lucille would always be grateful to Sandrich for not booting her. Years later, she hired Jay Sandrich, his son, fresh out of the U.S. Army, as assistant director on the *I Love Lucy* TV series. He would later helm *The Mary Tyler Moore Show* and *The Crosby Show*.

A New Yorker, Sandrich was not only a director, but a writer and producer. In 1927, he'd launched his career by helming comedy shorts. He'd first worked with "Fred and Ginger" in their debut, on the set of *Flying Down to Rio* in 1933. He'd also directed *The Gay Divorcée* and would later helm others of their musicals, too.

Helen Broderick was the mother of actor Broderick Crawford. "Wait until you meet my son," she told Lucille. You'll fall head over heels in love with the guy."

He would die young at forty-four, but not before churning out several other classic films, including *Holiday Inn* in 1942 starring Astaire and Bing Crosby, who introduced Irving Berlin's "White Christmas."

The most memorable Berlin song in *Top Hat* was "Cheek to Cheek," which became a classic. Another song, "Top Hat, White Tie and Tails," became Astaire's most celebrated solo. Also memorable was the song "Isn't This a Lovely Day (To be Caught in the Rain)?"

Eric Blore (left) and **Edward Everett Horton** emoting as eccentric fussbudgets in *Top Hat.*

After she'd gotten through her scene, Lucille hung out on the set for the next two weeks, hoping she'd learn something. Astaire remembered her from *Roberta* and approached her.

Finding her discouraged over the failure to get her career launched, he advised her not to give up and told her, "When I did my first test for Paramount, the director evaluated me like this: 'He can't act, he can't sing. Balding. Can dance a little.' Most people don't know this, but it took me a long time to make it in the movies. In 1914, when I was about thirteen, I made my film debut in a two-reeler, *Fanchon, the Cricket,* starring Mary Pickford."

The following day, as she was watching Astaire dancing with Rogers, Katharine Hepburn walked up and stood before her, taking a break from a nearby set. At the end of their number, Hepburn turned to Lucille and said, "Fred gives her class, and Ginger gives him sex appeal."

Director **Mark Sandrich** was remembered by Lucille for his kindness to her when she screwed up her lines.

At the time, Lucille could not have imagined that she would soon be working in a Hepburn picture.

The *Top Hat* script by Dwight Taylor and Allan Scott was hardly special. An American dancer, Jerry Travers (Astaire), arrives in London, where he's set to star in a play on the West End, a musical put on by Horace Hardwick (Edward Everett Horton), who is married to Madge (Helen Broderick.) Travers soon falls for Dale Tremont (Rogers). A case of mistaken identity ensues, and she thinks he's already married.

On the set of *Top Hat,* Lucille renewed her relationship with Eric Blore, the valet to the bumbling producer, Horace Hardwick (Horton). Erik Rhodes, as Alberto Beddini, was cast as a designer and rival for the affection of Dale Tremont (Rogers).

The "oh so gay" Horton, a son of Brooklyn was the beak-nosed plain-looking actor who had a patented *schtick,* always exclaiming, "Oh, dear!" in many scenes in his nervous, jittery voice.

Blore and Rhodes had recently worked with Lucille on her last picture, *Old Man Rhythm.*

Born in 1891, Helen Broderick had begun her career as a chorus girl in the 1907 version of the *Ziegfeld Follies.* By the 1920s, she had become a featured player on Broadway, appearing in the early 1930s in such stage musicals as *The Band Wagon* and *As Thousands Cheer.*

Helen was the mother of Broderick Crawford, and she decided to do a little matchmaking and arrange a date with her actor son and Lucille. "I predict it will be love at first sight."

Opening at Manhattan's Radio City Music Hall in late August of 1935, *Top Hat* attracted such a large audience that more than two dozen policemen had to be summoned to control the crowd.

Rotten Tomatoes reviewed the film as "a glamourous and enthralling depression-era diversion, a nearly flawless film, with acrobatics by Astaire and Rogers that make the hardest physical stunts seem light as air."

Top Hat was nominated for a Best Picture Oscar, losing to MGM's *Mutiny on the Bounty,* starring Charles Laughton and Clark Gable.

The movie also received Oscar nods for Best Song ("Cheek to Cheek"), Best Dance Direction ("The Piccolino"), and Best Art Direction.

***

RKO decided to make the first American talking version of *The Three Musketeers* (1935), based on the 1844 novel by Alexandre Dumas. Over the 20th Century, any number of actors would take on the role of D'Artagnan, beginning with Douglas Fairbanks, Sr. Other stars would follow: Don Ameche, Louis Hayward, Gene Kelly, Cornel Wilde, Michael York, and Chris O'Donnell.

For the 1935 version, Pandro S. Berman had originally cast the Czech-born actor, Francis Lederer, but at the last minute, he became unavailable.

RKO then gave the role to Walter Abel, who was known mainly as a character actor. He'd made his Broadway debut in *Forbidden* in 1919 and over the years built up an impressive list of theater credits, performing in plays by Eugene O'Neill and Anton Chekhov.

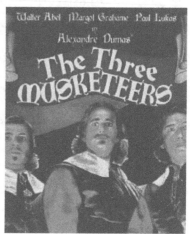

The most distinguished member of the cast was Paul Lukas, interpreting the role of Athos. Born into a Jewish family in Budapest, he'd made his stage debut in 1916 in Hungary, which led to his playing star roles, often cast as a smooth womanizer, both in his native land and in Germany and Austria, where he'd worked with Max Reinhardt.

By 1927, Lukas had emigrated to Hollywood. He became a naturalized American citizen a decade later.

In the year he met Lucille, he was portraying the series detective, Philo Vance, in *The Casino Murder Case* (1935). He would go on to win a Best Actor Oscar for his performance in the film *Watch on the Rhine* (1943).

Lucille had an awkward encounter with two of the other stars: Ralph Forbes, cast as the Duke of Buckingham, and

Left: **Walter Abel** and right **Margot Grahame** in the lackluster 1935 version of *The Three Musketeers.*

124

Heather Angel, who played Constance, the queen's lady-in-waiting.

[Months before, Lucille had had a serious affair with Forbes, but they had broken up and some bitterness lingered between them. By the time of their reunion on the set of The Three Musketeers, *the British actor was sharing his charms with Angel, and the couple had gotten married.]*

The blonde English actress, Margot Grahame, played Milady de Winter, a part that would be more famously portrayed by Lana Turner a decade later. A New Englander, Brian Keith, was cast as Count de Rochefort.

The Three Musketeers was shot in the scalding furnace of the San Fernando Valley in midsummer. Attired in heavy 17th Century regalia as an uncredited lady of the court, Lucille fainted twice in the heat. "All my seven petticoats were soaking wet. I hoped that this would be my last costume drama."

Pretentious and overly accessorized, here's a scene from the 17th Century costume drama, *The Three Musketeers*, where the actors suffered through a California summer clad in their aristocratic finery.

Lucille, once again playing a lady-in-waiting, appears within the oval as an ornamental and cooperative "accessory."

Since then, film critics have interpreted the 1935 RKO adaptation of Dumas' novel "the most uninspired."

***

Lucille's next film—again only a bit part—was the 1935 RKO release of *I Dream Too Much*. Pandro S. Berman had already noted the success of opera diva, Grace Moore, in a singing role in *One Night of Love* (1934), and he was hoping to duplicate it with a showcase featuring Lily Pons, the diminutive French coloratura soprano.

Born in France in 1898, she'd grown up near Cannes on the French Riviera. As a teenager, she'd sung for French troops during World War I. By 1928, she'd made her operatic debut. Her greater fame came at the Metropolitan Opera in New York City between 1931 and 1960, where she would appear almost 300 times (a record) as its principal soprano.

[As her career advanced, Pons became skilled at promoting herself as a marketable cultural icon. Her opinions on cuisine and fashion were frequently reported in women's magazines, and she was featured in advertisements for Lockheed, Knox gelatin, and various food and beauty products throughout America.]

Hoping to replicate with Pons the success he was having with the Astaire-Rogers musicals, Berman hired some of the best talent in the business, notably Henry Fonda as her leading man. He also signed Max Steiner as the project's music director; Hermes Pan as its choreographer; and Jerome Kern, backed up by lyricist Dorothy Fields, to write four new songs. Berman even employed Pons' famous husband, André Kostelanetz, to conduct the movie's operatic sequences.

Supporting roles went to Eric Blore, who had previously worked on a film with Lucille, as Roger Briggs. Osgood Perkins was cast as Paul Darcy. He'd been a leading man on Broadway, but Hollywood saw him more as a character actor. He later became far more famous as the father of actor Anthony Perkins, who immortalized himself in Alfred Hitchcock's *Psycho* (1960).

Other roles were essayed by Mischa Auer as Darcy's pianist, and by child actor Scotty Beckett as "Boy on the Merry-Go-Round."

With her hair dyed blonde, Lucille was given a thankless (very small) role of an American tourist in Paris. Fonda is her tour guide. It's obvious that she'd rather sample the night life with him than see any of the historic monuments.

As a gum-chewing American tourist, Lucille had only one line: "Culture makes my feet hurt."

The movie would receive an Oscar nod for sound recording. In spite of that, critic Grahame Green reviewed its musical score as "ponderous."

Hired as the director who would pull together this percolating stewpot of talent

Henry Fonda and **Lily Pons** in *I Dream Too Much.*

The New York Times wrote: "*I Dream Too Much* suffers from inaction and a limited sense of humor. But it is amiably played, and provides a reasonably painless setting for the gifted soprano."

was John Cromwell. His career had started in the early days of sound and lasted until the 1950s when he was "blacklisted" as a Communist during the McCarthy witch hunt.

Although Lucille had been mesmerized by Cromwell's direction of Bette Davis in the screen adaptation of W. Somerset Maugham's *Of Human Bondage* (1934), she considered their picture together as a comedown for him.

The plot had Annette Monard (Pons), an aspiring singer, falling in love with and marrying Jonathon Street (Fonda), a struggling young composer. He urges her into a singing career, and she becomes a star, leaving him after his career totters and fails. Although the plot in some ways evokes that of *A Star is Born,* everything works out happily in the end.

Lucille found Fonda unassuming, very kind, and quite handsome. When she met him, he had recently ended his marriage (1931-1933) to his first wife, actress Margaret Sullavan, and he had not yet married his second wife, Frances Seymour Brokaw (the mother of both Jane and Peter Fonda.)

Henry spent most of his time with his longtime "best pal," James Stewart, and had once lived with him in New York when both of them were struggling and virtually unknown.

In her pre-Desi days. Lucille often double-dated with her then "best pal," Ginger Rogers. One night, their respective beaux were "roomies," James Stewart and Henry Fonda. They lived together in Brentwood just as they had roomed together during their poorer days in New York. Ginger got James, leaving Lucille stuck with Henry.

Henry cooked dinner while Ginger, in the living room, taught James and Lucille how to dance the carioca. As Lucille remembered it. "I ended up doing the dishes." After dinner, the quartet headed for Cocoanut Grove at the Ambassador Hotel to dance to Freddy Martin's band, later going for hamburgers at Barney's Beanery on Santa Monica Boulevard. Here they ate under a misspelled sign that read NO FAGOTS ALLOWED.

Their double date lasted until dawn when Fonda looked at Lucille's nighttime makeup in the morning sunlight and said "Yuk!" He later claimed. "Shit, if I hadn't said that they might have named the studio Henrylu instead of Desilu."

Although the romance between Fonda and Lucille would have to wait for another day, Ginger got lucky. Leaving Lucille to get home on her own, she headed back to Brentwood with James and Henry. There, she disappeared into James' bedroom. The next morning. Ginger had already left for the studio before James emerged to join Henry for breakfast. There. James gleefully informed Henry. "I lost my cherry last night."

Henry looked skeptically at his friend. "You can't lose what you don't have. Remember all the others? Marlene Dietrich? The abortion? And for all I know, you lost your cherry to me. Remember?" Their interchange was later repeated by them to their mutual friend, director Josh Logan.

***

Although it was still a minor part, Lucille was assigned to her most substantial role to date when director George Nicholls, Jr., cast her in RKO's comedy, *Chatterbox* (1936).

Anne Shirley, the female lead, played an aspirant actress, Jenny Yates. *[Shirley had launched her career as Dawn O'Day, but in 1934, when she starred as the title character in* Anne of Green Gables, *she started billing herself as Anne Shirley. Right after working with Lucille, she was cast in* Stella Dallas (1937) *opposite Barbara Stanwyck. That brought Shirley a Best Supporting Oscar nod.*

About a year after working with Lucille, Shirley married screen heartthrob John Payne, whom Lucille considered "the sexiest, handsomest, and hottest stud ever to set foot in Hollywood."]

According to the script, Phillips Holmes, portraying a struggling actor, arrives in Shirley's rural community with a stock company. As a troupe, they're rehearsing an old melodrama with dreams of its possible transfer to Broadway.

A tangled web of complication follows, including Jenny's transit to New York. There, she replaces the temperamental, already established star Lillian Temple, portrayed by Lucille. The role gave her a few lines of dialogue and some wardrobe changes.

Lucille knew Holmes, having worked with him before on the ill-fated *Nana,* the picture in which Samuel Goldwyn had attempted to forge a star out of Anna Sten.

The director, George Nicholls, Jr., had followed in his father's footsteps. In a talk with Lucille, he told her that his dad, born while the U.S.'s Civil War was still raging, had appeared in 221 films between 1908 and 1927, the year of his death. Not only that...He had directed 103 movies between 1911 and 1916.

On the set, Lucille had a reunion with Erik Rhodes, cast as a stage manager. They had last worked together on *Top Hat.*

She also lunched with Margaret Hamilton, who had been cast as "Tippe" Tipton.

In *Chatterbox,* **Lucille** was cast as a mercenary leading lady. In this scene, the actor (**Erik Rhodes**) who'd been cast as her director pleads with her to save the show on opening night.

Anne Shirley with her husband, **John Payne.**

Shirley may not have known it at the time, but her spouse was also sharing his formidable sexual allure with Jane Wyman both in "reel" and "real" life, as well as with Alice Faye, Betty Grable, Sonja Henie, Linda Darnell, Gene Tierney, and Susan Hayward.

This notorious "crotch shot" of **John Payne** from *Kid Nightingale* (1939) became an underground collectors' item for American homosexuals.

As actor Roddy McDowall recalled, "It did for John what the Betty Grable pin-ups did for her in World War II."

Over ham sandwiches, Lucille poured out her woes about her stalled career, and confessed that she was considering "marrying a husband who is also a breadwinner. I could be standing at the door every night as he comes home from work. Of course, I'd have martinis waiting for him."

There would be many ironies associated with Lucille's ongoing struggle for better roles at RKO. In her words, "I ended up buying the fucking studio."

Two views of **Margaret Hamilton**. Upper photo, as she appeared in *Chatterbox*, and (lower photo) as the Wicked Witch of the West with **Judy Garland** in *The Wizard of Oz* (1939).

***

In her next film, a detective drama entitled *Mess 'Em Up* (1936) from RKO, Lucille was demoted to being an extra once again. "My mother and the rest of my family went to see the movie when it opened in Los Angeles and couldn't even find me in a crowd scene."

A noted director, Charles Vidor, was tapped to cast it. Born to a Jewish family in his native Budapest, he rose to fame in Hollywood during the silent era. One of his most memorable films lay in his future. In it, he'd helm Rita Hayworth in her most famous film, *Gilda* (1946). Vidor's battles with Columbia's Harry Cohn became part of Hollywood legend and lore.

In a career that spanned four decades, Preston Foster played the lead character, Tip O'Neill, a private detective hired by a megamillionaire to solve baffling events associated with a kidnapping, police abuse, assault, and ransom payments.

Lucille usually liked dating "rough, tough guys," and Guinn Williams, nicknamed "Big

During the filming of *Chatterbox*, Lucille strolled over to the set of another film being shot at RKO, *Muss 'Em Up.*

Director Charles Vidor spotted her and asked her if she'd appear in a scene as a departing train passenger.

That afternoon, she met movie tough guy Guinn (Big Boy) Williams, who played "Red" Cable in Vidor's movie. "I made a really stupid mistake and went out on a date with him," she later lamented.

Boy," seemed to fill the bill. She later regretted it. Over time, Big Boy would team onscreen with his close friends John Wayne and Alan Hale, Sr. He'd also appear frequently as a celluloid "sidekick" to Errol Flynn.

Lucille accepted Big Boy's invitation to a night club with "hot jazz" in San Fernando Valley.

En route, he stopped at a remote location and, as she reported to Vidor, "He raped me. I fought back, but he is, after all, named Big Boy and he overpowered me."

HALL OF SHAME: Lucille repeatedly claimed that **Guinn (Big Boy) Williams** once raped her on a date. He later boasted of that "conquest" to his boozing pal, Errol Flynn.

Williams had recently starred with Flynn and Olivia de Havilland in *Dodge City* (1939). The portrait of him from that film appears on the right.

As she later reflected, "Back in those days, struggling young actresses rarely reported cases of rape, and sexual harassment was virtually unheard of. All men, except the gay ones, sexually harassed young women as proof of their manhood."

***

Shooting began on *Follow the Fleet*—another musical that teamed Fred Astaire with Ginger Rogers—in October of 1935. Once again, Pandro S. Berman hired Mark Sandrich (director of *Top Hat*) to helm the new production.

This would mark the third time Lucille had appeared in an Astaire/Rogers musical, the previous two having been *Roberta* and *Top Hat,* which, around this time, opened at Radio City Music Hall in Manhattan, playing to packed audiences.

Lucille shared Ginger's dressing room and listened to the star's complaints about her director. "He regards me like a mere clothes hanger who can dance a few steps with Fred. He thinks Fred is a talented genius but dismisses me as a bubblehead."

Follow the Fleet, inspired by a 1922 play, *Shore Leave,* had been crafted by three screenwriters. *[One of them, Dwight Taylor, was the son of the legendary stage actress, Laurette Taylor, who generated critical acclaim in 1945 as the demented mother in Tennessee Williams stage production of* The Glass Menagerie.*]*

Follow the Fleet's music was by Irving Berlin and Max Steiner. Hermes Pan, as the production's dance director, worked out Astaire's routines.

The third lead went to Randolph Scott, who had previously co-starred with Astaire and Rogers in *Roberta.* Throughout the course of its filming,

Cary Grant, on occasion, showed up to take Scott to lunch.

Cast as Kitty Collins, Lucille was allowed to make a few quips. Just before a dance number, she appears with an unwanted admirer, a sailor, and says, "Tell me, little boy, did you get a whale or a baseball bat with that sailor suit?"

She had a reunion with Betty Grable, whose superstardom lay just around the corner. They spent time with singer Harriet Hilliard, cast in the fourth led as Connie Martin. *[In her future, Harriet would marry Ozzie Nelson and become the mother of David and Ricky. Collectively, from 1952-1966, they'd star together in the hit TV series* The Adventures of Ozzie and Harriet.*]*

In *Follow the Fleet*, Astaire was cast as Seaman "Bake" Baker, whose best buddy is "Bilge" Smith (played by Scott). They show up together at a San Francisco dance hall where Baker has a reunion with his former dance partner Sherry Martin (Rogers), now working as a dance hall hostess at a joint named "Ballroom Paradise."

The convoluted plot includes mistaken identities and multiple misunderstandings. Everything is resolved in the end.

Two of the songs in the musical ended up on *The Hit Parade*: "Let's Face the Music and Dance" and "Let Yourself Go."

Making his film debut was the singer Tony Martin, who immediately caught Lucille's roving eye. They went out on three dates, each time with a promise of hitting the nightclubs, but ending up each time in a motel room.

Apparently, she raved about Martin's boudoir skills so much that Grable, too, wanted in on some

Three ambitious bit-part players in a press and PR photo for *Follow the Fleet*:

Left to right, they're **Lucille Ball, Harriett Hilliard** (aka Harriet Nelson of the TV series, *The Adventures of Ozzie and Harriet*), and **Betty Grable**.

All of them would blossom into major movie or TV careers.

Bosom buddies **Randolph Scott** ("Bilge') and **Fred Astaire** ("Bake"), each expressing their opinion of life in the Navy.

of it. She jokingly said, "Lucille must have broken him in for me."

At the time that Martin was slipping around seducing both Lucille and Grable, he was married to actress Alice Faye, the reigning singing sensation of 20th Century Fox until Grable replaced her during the war years.

[Ironically, when Follow the Fleet *was remade in 1955 with its title changed to* Hit the Deck, *Martin played the male lead opposite Jane Powell.]*

Follow the Fleet was a success, generating mostly good reviews, although *Variety* found its running time "way overboard." As high praise, indeed, critic Graham Greene claimed that Astaire and Mickey Mouse were alike in the sense that they were always "breaking the laws of nature."

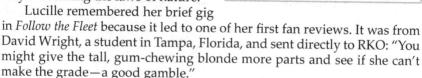

Bandleader **Tony Martin,** Lucille's "extra-curricular" during the filming of *Follow the Fleet.*

In her words, "I always had a weakness for musicians."

Lucille remembered her brief gig in *Follow the Fleet* because it led to one of her first fan reviews. It was from David Wright, a student in Tampa, Florida, and sent directly to RKO: "You might give the tall, gum-chewing blonde more parts and see if she can't make the grade—a good gamble."

***

Lucille would also remember her brief appearance in RKO's *The Farmer in the Dell* (1936), as "my last time as a Jean Harlow blonde. Miss Harlow was soon to die, and with her passing, all the showgirls in Hollywood switched from platinum blonde to something else. I was getting damn tired of all that bleaching. I had to come up with another look."

She was cast as a script girl, Gloria Wilson, in this homespun comedy. Director Ben Holmes placed Fred Stone, Jean Parker, and Esther Dale in the lead roles. Stone and Dale were an unsophisticated "Ma & Pop" who feel that their daughter, Adie, is pretty enough to break into movies.

The convoluted plot was nailed by the *New York World-Telegram,*

Portraying a script girl, Gloria Wilson, Lucille's brief scene in **The Farmer in the Dell** was filmed outdoors.

It was almost purely ornamental, but "Lucille Freaks" memorialize it as her last appearance as a Jean Harlow-inspired blonde.

which wrote: "The film is a satire that cruelly razzes the insanities of Hollywood as well as some of those who want to crash its loony portals."

Born in 1873, Stone was often compared to the America's then folk hero, Will Rogers. He'd begun his career in show-biz in circuses and minstrel shows, eventually working his way onto the stages of vaudeville. When Lucille met him, he'd just played Katharine Hepburn's father in *Alice Adams* (1935).

Jean Parker, too, had worked with Hepburn when George Cukor cast both of them in *Little Women* (1933).

For Lucille, a memorable moment on the set involved her reunion with Tony Martin, who had also been cast into a bit part. She suggested that the two of them slip away for a discreet reunion.

She told him, "If I could package what you've got, I'd make a fortune."

[During World War II, Martin was assigned to Glenn Miller's band. Its conductor considered Martin the best singer in the Armed Services.

In 1948, Martin entered into one of the most successful marriages in Hollywood, wedding actress, dancer, and singer Cyd Charisse, a sixty-year union that lasted until her death in 2008.]

***

Around this time, Lucille had to move out of the house she shared with her grandfather, Fred Hunt, DeDe (her mother), and her brother, also named Fred. She needed privacy, and she felt cheap slipping in and out of motels with the men she'd dated.

Grandfather Hunt was seventy-one years old and in poor health, having recently suffered a stroke. A dedicated socialist, he was a faithful reader of communist *The Daily Worker* and "deplored" the Depression era reforms of President Roosevelt, denouncing them as "completely inadequate."

No member of the family shared his dedication to communism, but to pacify him, each of them agreed to register as a member of the Communist Party. Lucille, for one, had little interest in politics, but to please her granddad, she registered as a member of the party on March 19, 1936, an act that would later return to haunt her and almost derail her career.

In the meantime, she was still working with Lela Rogers at RKO's Little Theater. Lela, the mother of Ginger Rogers, cast Lucille as one of the leads in a play, *Hey, Diddle Diddle*.

Lucille's Grandfather, **Fred Hunt,** was a dedicated member of the Communist Party. As such, he was frequently denounced as a "Commie Pinko."

As someone who deeply mistrusted the potential corruption and greed of capitalism, he persuaded Lucille, back when she was still a late teenager, to join the Communist Party.

Its author was Bartlett Cormack, who would later move on to work for both Howard Hughes and Cecil B. De Mille. He had achieved success on Broadway in 1927 with his play, *The Racket,* an exposé of political corruption in the 1920s. It had starred Edward G. Robinson. Gangster Al Capone had managed to get it banned in Chicago.

Since Lucille had a month off between pictures at RKO, she accepted Lela's offer to go East with the cast of the road show version of *Hey, Diddle Diddle.* It opened in Princeton, with the hope of moving on after that to Broadway.

She'd been cast as Julie Tucker, one of three roommates laboring in the entertainment industry, each coping with neurotic directors, confused executives, and grasping stars.

The star of the play was Conway Tearle, a former child prodigy. When he was ten, he could recite twelve Shakespearean plays from memory. His big break came at the age of twenty-one when in the Midlands of England, without any rehearsals, he was called upon to play Hamlet after

Lucille appeared briefly with **Fred Astaire** in *Follow the Fleet.* She worked on it over the Christmas holidays of 1935. In one scene, she played a saucy dancer who's maneuvered into "glamourizing" Ginger' Rogers' mousy onscreen sister, as portrayed by Harriett Hilliard.

Hilliard later evolved into Harriet Nelson, one of the focal points of the long-running (1952-1966) TV series, *Ozzie and Harriett.*

the lead actor took ill before the first act. *[Decades later, in Hollywood, Tearle appeared in* Romeo and Juliet *(1936), with an aging and stagey John Barrymore cast as Mercutio. At one point, Tearle briefly became the highest-paid actor in Hollywood.]*

On Broadway, he had achieved renown in 1932 in a production of a hit play, *Dinner at Eight,* but when Hollywood adapted it into a movie with an all-star cast, Tearle's part went to Barrymore, instead.

The Little Theater's production of *Hey, Diddle Diddle* premiered at Princeton with successful reviews, but by then, Tearle's health had begun to fail, and he had to drop out of the cast. Instead of replacing him with another actor, the producers shut the play down entirely.

One local newspaper wrote that "Lucille Ball has become another Katharine Hepburn."

During its run, she befriended a young actor, Keenan Wynn, who would later become a star in Hollywood films and an intimate friend of Van Johnson, Lucille's future co-star.

Since Lucille had another three weeks of furlough from RKO, and as she'd saved up quite a bit of money, she remained in New York for some binge shopping. She strolled along Fifth Avenue, site of her previous modeling gigs. This time, however, she was the customer.

She also returned to Jamestown for a brief visit to her hometown for a reunion with her aging grandmother. The town was still mired in a repressed economy, a legacy from the (recent) Great Depression, with dozens of stores shut down.

She spent an afternoon there with her long-ago lover, Johnny DaVita, finding that he had fallen on hard times. He pleaded with her for the money to pay the premiums on his ailing mother's life insurance policies, and she came through for him. She later said, "Johnny still carried a torch for me, but my feeling for him was but a small candle, the kind you put on a birthday cake."

Her new wardrobe didn't go unnoticed after her return to Hollywood, where she posed for countless publicity pictures, each in a different dress or gown. Soon, the Hollywood press corps named her as "Best Dressed Girl in Town," beating out other stars who included the very well-dressed Kay Francis. After that, RKO had her pose for more publicity pictures and touted her as "a clotheshorse."

Even though **Lucille's** speaking roles during the mid-1930s were very limited, studio photographers seemed to delight in snapping hundreds of publicity photos of her, perhaps since she made what was called a "photogenically perfect" model.

Here's one of them from around the period of her greatest frustration from lack of good parts.

***

In Hollywood, Lucille's string of minor parts continued as RKO cast her in *Bunker Bean* (1936)

"I played another gum chewer," Lucille said, "this time as Rosie Kelly, an office secretary with a biting wit." No longer a platinum Jean Harlow blonde, she darkened her tresses to a shade she called "chestnut." Her hairdresser further experimented with her coiffure, giving her bangs.

As she soon learned, *Bunker Bean* had been inspired by a writer named Harry Leon Wilson, and adaptations of it had been filmed twice before. For its silent film version of 1918, it had starred Jack Pickford, the brother of Mary Pickford. Its second filming was for Warner Brothers in 1925, when it

Bunker Bean

OWEN DAVIS Jr.
LOUISE LATIMER
ROBERT McWADE · JESSIE RALPH

135

had starred Matt Moore. *[Between 1912 and 1958, Moore would appear in 221 movies. His brother, Owen, had been the first husband (1911-1920) of Mary Pickford.]*

On this, the plot's third incarnation, the lead role of Bunker Bean was cast with Owen Davis, Jr., the son of the dramatist who had won the Pulitzer Prize in 1923 for *Icebound. [In Hollywood, Davis, Jr. often starred with Walter Huston. His life would be cut short when he drowned in Long Island Sound at the age of forty-one.]*

Bunker Bean is a meek office clerk with grandiose dreams. A fake fortune teller convinces him that in former incarnations, he was both Napoléon and an ancient Egyptian pharaoh. This gives him a sense of power and the courage to pursue his boss's daughter, Mary Kent, cast with a minor actress named Louise Latimer, who never rose to the level of star. Her career highlight was when she co-starred with John Wayne in *California Straight Ahead* (1937).

In *Bunker Bean*, **Lucille** was cast as Rosie Kelly, a gum-chewing secretary with a biting wit. Here, she's surprised by the aggression of **Owen Davis, Jr.**, a formerly timid office worker whom a fortune teller has convinced was once Napoléon.

Later, Bunker realizes that his newfound success derives from his own courage, confidence, and spunk, and not from any particularly aristocratic bloodlines.

On the set, Lucille met veteran actor Berton Churchill, cast as Professor Balthazer. A Canadian, he usually played stern or pompous characters—bankers, governors, or land barons. In 1932 alone, he appeared in thirty-four films, surely an annual record for any actor.

Over the years, he'd be directed by John Ford, Frank Capra, and Otto Preminger, Jr. in movies that included Bette Davis, John Wayne, Tyrone Power, Edward G. Robinson, Will Rogers, and Jeanette MacDonald.

The frequently treacherous future gossip columnist, Hedda Hopper, was cast in it as society lady, Mrs. Dorothy Kent.

Playing a telephone operator, Joan Davis, like Lucille, had a very small role. Also like Lucille, she'd become a household name on TV when she appeared in the hit TV series, *I Married Joan* (1952-1955). Even though it evolved into a hit, it failed to achieve the ratings of *I Love Lucy*. Davis' career was cut short when she died at the age of fifty-three in 1961.

***

Winterset (1936), a crime drama, would mark the last time Lucille appeared in a film without dialogue or credit. In it, clad in a sweater and skirt, and wearing a hat, she watches townspeople as they dance to the music of a barrel organ.

George Stevens was its original director, but he bowed out to helm Katharine Hepburn in the period costume comedy, *Quality Street* (1937). He was replaced by Alfred Santell, who was known mostly for his two-reeler comedy shorts for producer Hal Roach.

Three stars were announced: Lionel Barrymore, Sylvia Sidney, and Anne Shirley, but each of them was replaced before shooting began. In its revised version, the leads were assigned to Burgess Meredith (in his film debut); Margo, the Mexican actress; and Eduardo Ciannelli. Mischa Auer, who had worked with Lucille before, appears briefly in it as "A Radical."

John Carradine stars in it as Bartolomé Romagna, who is sentenced to death for a murder he did not commit. Meredith plays his son, Mio Romagna, who has worked for years to clear his father's name, believing he was innocent.

In spite of his less-than-matinee idol looks, Meredith would go on to a distinguished film career. Soon, he'd star in John Steinbeck's *Of Mice and Men* (1939); and as the war correspondent Ernie Pyle in *The Story of G.I. Joe* (1945). His range of roles would be varied, indeed, as he appeared in works by Shakespeare, Eugene O'Neill, and Beckett. He'd even portray Elvis Presley's father; an arch villain, The Penguin, in the TV series, *Batman;* and Sylvester Stallone's boxing trainer in the *Rocky* series.

A horndog, he propositioned Lucille during filming. She rejected him, saying, "I'm not in the mood."

"I understand," he said. "I know I'm not a dashing swain, but a kind of mongrel chasing the foxes."

His chase paid off. In 1944, he married sultry Paulette Goddard after Charlie Chaplin gave her her walking papers. Unlike Lucille, other stars were more accommodating. Meredith would sustain future romantic associations with Ingrid

Publicity portrait of **Margo** with **Burgess Meredith.**

Years later, Meredith arrived at the Shannon Airport in Ireland to perform the stage version of *Winterset by* Maxwell Anderson. His visit had been preceded with passionate editorials in the local press about his associations with John Steinbeck, widely perceived as a communist/socialist because of novels that had included *The Grapes of Wrath.*

At the airport, a hostile mob awaited him, pounding on the windows of his limousine.

In a story that was widely bruited around Hollywood, Burgess' wife at the time, Paulette Goddard, called out to the driver, "Roll down the window and I'll hit them with my diamond necklace."

Bergman, Olivia de Havilland, Marlene Dietrich, Norma Shearer, Ginger Rogers, and a *ménage à trois* with a wealthy and mysterious lady from Berlin and her lesbian lover.

During Meredith's seduction of Tallulah Bankhead, she is alleged to have yelled at him, "For God's sake, don't come in me. I'm engaged to Jock Whitney!"

The plot of *Winterset* was based on the 1935 play by Maxwell Anderson, a playwright, author, poet, journalist, and lyricist. He based his work on the notorious case of Sacco and Vanzetti. In 1920, these two Italian anarchists (recent émigrés to America) were convicted of murdering a guard and a paymaster during an armed robbery. Seven years later, both of them were marched to the electric chair.

Their suspected innocence became the core of one of the largest *causes célèbres* in modern history. It sparked protests throughout the U.S. and in such faraway places as Buenos Aires and Auckland. Supporters included Albert Einstein, George Bernard Shaw, H.G. Welles, and Mussolini.

The governor of Massachusetts, Alvan T. Fuller, faced last-minute appeals, but denied them. A package bomb addressed to him was intercepted by the Boston Post Office.

Two views (one idealized, one real-life) of **Lily Pons.**

When it became clear that *The Girl From Paris*, RKO's second attempt to morph her into a film star, had failed at the box office, she began making plans to desert Hollywood, a place she disliked, and move back to the art form she knew best: Grand Opera.

***

Even though her first film had failed at the box office, Pandro S. Berman decided to give the French singer, Lily Pons, a second chance at American stardom.

He cast her as a singer, Nikki Martin, in RKO's latest musical comedy, *That Girl from Paris* (1936).

[In Pons' first American film, I Dream Too Much *(1935), co-starring Henry Fonda, Lucille had had only a small part. In this newer film, Lucille had a much larger role playing "Clair" Williams, a rival for the love of Windy McLean, as portrayed by Gene Raymond.]*

Jack Oakie, the film's male lead, was cast as "Whammo" Lonsdale. Ironically, he had starred in the first version of this comedy, too. Shot in 1929, it had starred Betty Compson. In another irony, Desi Arnaz would star in the plot's final remake, *Four Jacks and a Jill* (1942).

Lucille had first worked with Oakie when she had a walk-on in *Murder at the Vanities* (1934).

138

She also found herself working once again with character actor Mischa Auer, who was cast as "Butch," even though he was anything but. She also met and talked to Herman Bing, the German-born son of opera star Max Bing. In the 1930s, Herman became known for his wide-eyed factious expressions and thick German accent. But with the coming of World War II, German accents were no longer funny, and Bing could not find work in American films. He committed suicide (with a gunshot to his head) in 1947.

The plot of *That Girl from Paris* is convoluted and rather silly. Pons, in her portrayal of Nikki Martin, flees from the altar in France. The runaway bride-to-be stows away on a ship heading for America. She meets Windy McLean (Gene Raymond). After a series of mishaps, including arrests, she ends up in his arms. The viewer has already figured that out before the end flashes across the screen.

This was one of the publicity shots for which **Lucille** posed for *That Girl from Paris*. Nearly all critics agreed that she was far lovelier than the star of the picture, the opera diva, Lily Pons.

Pons would be offered a final role before deserting the film colony to return to the opera stage. With the coming of World War II, movies with opera stars and opera themes had become passé, a pretentious relic of the 1930s.

In Lucille's best review to date, the *New York Daily* singled her out for special praise, defining her as an "able actress and dancer" and praising her for her "soap shoes" in one comic scene on a slippery floor. "She is worth the whole price of admission." The critic predicted a rosy future for her as a *comedienne*.

Lucille interpreted Raymond as a somewhat bizarre footnote in Hollywood history. Handsome and blonde, he had worked with such luminaries as Jean Harlow, Clark Gable, Carole Lombard, Joan Crawford, Fred Astaire, and Loretta Young. In the year he was appearing with Lucille, he was dating Jeanette MacDonald and would marry her in 1937.

With his starkly blonde hair and "pretty boy" look, New York actor **Gene Raymond** shows why he was "the darling" of gay men in Hollywood.

He continued his affairs with men throughout the course of his marriage to Jeanette MacDonald.

During their honeymoon, MacDonald caught her new husband in bed with Buddy Rogers, the new husband of Mary Pickford.

Throughout MacDonald's marriage to him, he continued his affairs with men. They led to entrapments and three arrests by vice squads. Their marriage endured, fitfully, until MacDonald's death in 1965.

***

Lucille had hoped for a bigger role in her next picture, RKO's *Don't Tell the Wife* (1937), but settled for eighth billing. Cast as Annie Howell, she played a chicly dressed secretary and the sole female in a gang of con artists.

The zany plot by Nat Perrin focuses on a scheme to con New Yorkers into investing in a gold mine thought to be worthless.

Lucille wore a suit she'd bought on Fifth Avenue during her previous visit to Manhattan and would wear that same suit again in her upcoming film, *Stage Door*.

Its director, Christy Cabanne, assembled an impressive cast that included some of the best character actors of the 1930s. *[Cabanne had begun his career in 1911 with an appearance in silent films before becoming a director. He had helmed Shirley Temple in her first credited feature-length movie,* The Red-Haired Alibi *(1932). Temple's appearance in this "forgettable" film lasted no more than five "perky" minutes.]*

Cast in its starring role was Guy Kibbee, who played "Dinky" Winthrop. A Texan from El Paso, he had starred in a number of high-profile movies such as *Rain* (1932) with Joan Crawford and *Captain Blood* (1935) with Errol Flynn.

In the lead female role, Una Merkel played Nancy Dorsey, appearing opposite Lynne Overman in the role of her shyster husband.

Merkel had a reputation as the second female lead to such bigger stars as Jean Harlow, Carole Lombard, Loretta Young, Ginger Rogers, and tap-dancing Eleanor Powell. Merkel was also known for her "kewpie doll looks, her strong Kentucky accent, and her wry deliveries."

After working on her latest picture, she

According to its plot, much of the time, Lucille, cast as a "fashionable secretary," Ann Howell, is heard but not seen as a voice over the intercom.

When she does appear, she's the sole female in a gang of con artists.

Una Merkel was the female lead in *Don't Tell the Wife*. When she was close to completing it, she was told that her MGM contract had only months to go and that she'd soon be out of a job.

But thanks to frequent rebounds, her squinty eyes and perky smile would be seen on the screen for many years to come.

Merkel ended her screen career in 1966 opposite Elvis Presley in *Spinout*.

would go on to screen immortality in 1939 when she appeared with James Stewart and Marlene Dietrich in the western comedy, *Destry Rides Again* (1939). In the role of Lily Belle, she gets embroiled in a "cat fight" with Frenchie (Dietrich) that became one of the most iconic scenes in motion picture history.

Merkel bid *adieu* to films after her appearance in *Spinout* (1966), opposite Elvis Presley.

Other supporting players in *Don't Tell the Wife* included Guinn ("Big Boy") Williams, cast as "Cupid" Dougal.

"Some damn Cupid!" Lucille complained to director Cabanne. "The bastard took me out on a date and raped me. I'll stay clear of him."

In contrast, Lucille bonded with character actor Thurston Hall, who, beginning in 1915, would appear in 250 films, dying in 1958. Early in his screen life, he was a leading man to Theda Bara, the original vamp of the silent screen.

Lucille already knew William Demarest, cast as Horace Tucker. She found working with Hattie McDaniel a delight. She'd been cast as the maid to Nancy (Merkel).

This picture of **Hattie McDaniel** was taken when she was involved in a lesbian affair with Tallulah Bankhead (of all people).

Hattie told Lucille that she had once had "a white man lover," and that when she came home early from the studio one afternoon, she had caught him in bed with another woman.

"I not only tossed both of them out on their asses, but tried to burn down the house."

[McDaniel was only months away from playing her iconic role of Mammy in Gone With the Wind (1939). First Lady Eleanor Roosevelt had urged producer David O. Selznick to cast her own maid, Elizabeth McDuffie, into the role, but he rejected the suggestion.

As Mammy, McDaniel would become the first African American to win an Oscar, in this case, for Best Supporting Actress of the Year.]

Years later, civil rights activists would attack her for promoting racial stereotypes. McDaniel always responded "Why should I complain about playing a maid and making $700 bucks a week? If I didn't do that, I'd be a maid getting $7 a week."

***

The beginning of 1937 marked a turning point in the life of Lucille Ball. Not only would she be given her first major role, but a serious romance (pre-Desi Arnaz) with a screen actor would soon be looming in front of her.

Hey Diddle Diddle

A cigarette-smoking **Lucille Ball** (far right) wore slacks in the stage play *Hey, Diddle Diddle,* which opened in Princeton, New Jersey, on January 22, 1937. It was a satire on the movie industry and wannabe starlets who try to storm the gates of the big studios.

Lucille was cast as Julie Tucker, one of a trio of "roomies" who deal with a "crazed director" and other industry bigwigs.

Lucille got the best reviews in the play. *Variety* claimed that "She outlines a consistent character and continues to give it a logical substance. Ball, making her first stage appearance, fattens her part and almost walks away with the play."

The critic for the *Washington Post* noted, "If there is any young person who is going to add to her professional standing in *Hey, Diddle Diddle,* it is Lucille Ball, just about the slickest trick you ever saw in slacks."

Its producer and director, Anne Nichols, was also the author of *Abie's Irish Rose,* which ran for an astounding five years on Broadway.

Conway Tearle (far left) had the lead role as a beleaguered film director. Standing beside him are **Alice White** and **Don Beddoe**. Seated and looking bewildered in a tux is **Alfred White**. Beddoe not only played the assistant director, but was Lucille's boyfriend at the time.

Tearle, veteran of a distinguished theatrical background since childhood, was in ill health and could not perform at a satisfactory capacity. Playwright Bartlett Cormack wanted to replace him, but Nichols thought that the play should be rewritten to exclude his character completely.

After many arguments, the play was shut down, never making it to Broadway. Lucille called it "a stillborn."

On February 15, she migrated back to Hollywood, ready to to return to making films.

KING OF THE CONGA: DESI ARNAZ

In New York, having decided to head south to Miami to seek work, Desi Arnaz bid Xavier Cugat goodbye. For a stipend of twenty-five dollars a week, the bandleader had granted Desi permission to use his name in his upcoming billings in and around Miami: "Desi Arnaz and his Xavier Cugat Orchestra direct form the Waldorf-Astoria in Manhattan."

But there was a problem: Desi didn't have a band.

During his gigs with Cugat in New York, Desi had formed a close bond with Louis Nicoletti, whose official job was as Cugat's secretary. As Nick told Desi, "My job means I walk his dogs, gather up his urine-stained underwear for laundering, answer his mail, and secure hot young *putas* for him. I'll go with you to Miami. We'll make it on our own."

With absolutely no prospects, the two men piled into Nick's battered old Plymouth. Between them, they had forty dollars, which they figured would barely pay their gas bill. In the back seat, they had stored enough food for the trip, the groceries smuggled out of the Waldorf-Astoria's kitchen.

Nick had volunteered as manager of the as-yet-unformed band that they hoped to pull together. Having spent their last dollar on gas, Nick and Desi finally arrived in Miami. There, they headed directly for the battered, four-room bungalow where Desi's parents, Desiderio and Lolita, lived.

As Lolita later revealed, "My boy and his friend Nick cleaned out my refrigerator when I served them supper. They ate like they hadn't had any food in a month. Such appetites!"

The next day, Nick and Desi set out to form a band and to investigate any possible gigs that might open for them. Miami Beach was gearing up for its winter season, waiting for "snow

Searching for a Style:

Young Desi, shortly after his arrival in Miami/ called it "*cidade maravilhosa*, a marvelous city where there is magic in the night."

He borrowed that description from the then-popular Brazilian singer, Aurora Miranda, whose lyrics were actually describing Rio de Janeiro.

birds" to fly down from the North. Dozens of resort hotels along Miami Beach had remained virtually empty throughout the stifling heat between May and October.

The following week, they secured a booking even before they'd organized a band. A Cuban friend of Desi's father had heard that Bob Kelly was opening a 250-seat nightclub adjacent to the Park Central Restaurant, which in winter drew some of the top entertainers from the North, everyone from George Jessel to Sophie Tucker, "The Last of the Red Hot Mommas."

With one hundred dollars borrowed from Desiderio, Nick and Desi arrived at the club. It had been in business for only two weeks. Their intention involved charming Kelly, hoping to convince him they were seasoned (and bigtime) musicians from the Cugat band.

Desi ordered champagne *[Cordon Rouge, extra dry]*—the kind that he'd seen actor George Raft demand at the Waldorf.

Soon, Kelly came over to greet these "big spenders." They told him they were on vacation and that they intended to return to New York for some upcoming gigs at the Starlight Room at the Waldorf. During their talk, Kelly revealed that he intended permeating his club with a Latin motif. "With your *Cubano* background, you'd be perfect for it,"

After about an hour of negotiations, Nick convinced Kelly that he could persuade Cugat to extend their holiday on Miami Beach through till the end of January. That meant, he said, "that Desi and I and our band can be the

Millions of Hispanics from Desi's heyday knew the lyrics from a Cuban folksong, "Il Manisero (The Peanut Vendor)", but very few Anglos knew about it until "The Rhumba Lady" (**Marion Sunshine**, depicted in the upper photo as she appeared in 1914) translated and published it after working as a showgirl for Florenz Ziegfeld.

Born in Louisville, Kentucky in 1894, her Spanish-to English translations of Cuban Rhumba staples did a lot of the "heavy lifting" needed to acquaint *norteamericanos* with the dance that Desi Arnaz helped turn into a national craze.

In 1930, Havana's Casino Orchestra, in their rendition of her translated lyrics for *The Peanut Vendor*, morphed it into the first million-selling single in the history of Latin music.

144

opening act in your new club." In addition to enthusiastically agreeing, Kelly promised to take out a full page ad in *The Miami Herald*.

Then, after some debates over money, it was agreed that Desi and his (still non-existant) five-piece band would work for $650 a week. *[In that era, individual musicians could be hired for $70 a week, meaning that based on the terms of this deal, some money would be left over for Desi and Nick.]*

By the time the two "refugees from Cugat" left the club, they had to immediately begin assembling a band. That would be tough going, because the post-Christmas season had already begun in South Florida, and nearly all musicians, at least those with any talent, already had bookings.

At the Arnaz family's bungalow, Lolita was already sewing flamboyantly ruffled "rumba shirts" for the band. As its leader, Desi had brought his white tuxedo jacket and a red bow tie down from Manhattan.

The next morning, Desi saw the ad for Kelly's about-to-open nightclub in *The Miami Herald*. He compared it to ads touting its competitors. They included the bands of Buddy Rogers and Guy Lombardo, both of whom were already household names.

In desperation, Desi phoned Cugat in New York, finally getting him to agree to send five musicians from Manhattan to Florida since his band at that time was "overstocked."

In a station wagon borrowed from Desiderio, Desi drove to the train station in Miami to retrieve them. Each had brought his own instruments.

But after Desi greeted the men and talked with them *en route* back to Miami Beach, he was terribly disappointed. "It was obvious that Cugat had dumped these losers on me. I would have been better off hiring the Salvation Army band."

The newcomers included a hopeless Spanish drummer who could only play an old-fashioned *paso doble.* "He'd have been better suited playing at a *corrida* (bullfight) in Madrid than at a swanky nightclub on Miami Beach. Others in the motley crew included two Jews from Brooklyn, one a pianist, the other with a saxophone. The other two musicians were both Italians from the Bronx. One played the bass, the other, a violin. The only *Latino* number they knew was that tired old *cliché*, "The Peanut Vendor."

"In Cuba,
Each merry maid wakes up with this serenade:
Peanuts (they're nice and hot)
Peanuts (she sells a lot)
Peanuts!
If you haven't got bananas, don't be blue.
Peanuts in a little bag are calling you"

Before they opened a short time thereafter, Desi had desperately tried to teach them a half-dozen *Latino* numbers. "I feared that the only things Latin about these guys was their rumba shirts, compliments of Lolita."

By midnight, Kelly, who had planted himself in the audience, hurried backstage. "You're fired! That's the worst god damn band I've ever heard. You've ruined me!"

145

Based on a ruling from the musicians' union, Desi's band could not be legally fired until a "cooling off" period of two weeks. "I fear, Bob *ol' boy*, that you're stuck with us," Desi told him. "We'll get better...and that's a promise."

In the meantime, Desi had hired a trumpeter and an accordion player, each of whom had previously been associated with the band at the University of Miami.

New Year's Eve was fast approaching, and Desi, in desperation, knew that he had to come up with something major. At the time, the conga was virtually unknown in the U.S., As a boy, growing up in Santiago, he remembered the Carnival season when the entire town turned out to dance the conga, led by the town's mayor...in this case, Desi's father, Desiderio.

To help release his band members from their "North European and Anglo inhibitions," he got them drunk on Bacardi. Then, quickly and with humor, he ordered his violinist to put aside his instrument and switch to banging metal spoons against an iron frying pan.

That historic and somewhat desperate night, the conga was introduced to Miami Beach. Desi led the line-up. At first, patrons were reluctant to join the line, but after three young couples dared to try, the rest of the club joined in, forming a long, sinuously rhythmic queue. "I wiggled my hips and ass to the beat, and the patrons joined me," Desi said. "It wasn't long before I had the whole god damn club dancing the conga. Bob Kelly was delighted. We even made the papers. From then on, Kelly's club was packed to the rafters every night."

[Sometimes called a tumbadora, *a conga is a single-headed drum believed to have been developed in the Western Hemisphere by Cubans descended from the people of Africa during the late 19th Century.*

Slaves who'd unwillingly been hauled over from Africa to the West Indies brought with them the street dance known as the conga.

This novelty Cuban carnival dance became popular in the United States in the late 1930s

Social historians and hip bandleaders like Desi knew that social gatherings of "the uptight bourgeoisie" desperately needed someone to tell them how to "innocently unwind."

These photos from the 1930s show how, thanks to the Conga, it was suddenly okay for repressed Anglo-Saxons to have a good time.

largely because of Desi Arnaz. Dancers arrange themselves into a long, sinuously moving line which (according to tradition) bends into a circle. Dancers move rhythmically through three shuffle steps, each on a downbeat, followed by a kick that begins slightly ahead of the fourth beat.

Most Americans became familiar with the conga when they saw it depicted by Desi in the film, Too Many Girls *(1940), in which he was cast as a conga-playing student from Argentina. Xavier Cugat also did much to popularize the dance.*

Soon, conga sequences were being added to other movies, notably It Started with Eve *(1941), the Deanna Durbin movie co-starring Charles Laughton.*

Around that time, Kelly conjured up a new name for his club: "Desi's Place."

"I was modest," Desi said. "I got him to call the club 'La Conga.'"]

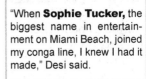

"When **Sophie Tucker,** the biggest name in entertainment on Miami Beach, joined my conga line, I knew I had it made," Desi said.

In the late 1930s, celebrities were found on virtually every block along Miami Beach, and every major hotel had its own night club, and all of them seemed to have hired famous names as performers. During their nights off, many of them began showing up at La Conga.

One night, Desi danced with Sophie Tucker, a voluptuously curvy "Jewish Momma" much admired as the Queen of Miami Beach. She liked Desi and occasionally volunteered at La Conga to sing her theme song "Some of These Days."

One night, Harry Richman, who had once been the piano accompanist to Mae West, arrived with two beautiful showgirls, one on each arm. Born in Cincinnati to Russian Jewish parents, he was a popular actor, singer (a nasal baritone), dancer, comedian, pianist, songwriter, nightclub performer, and, on occasion, bandleader. He liked Desi so much, he promised to bring Bob Hope, his best friend, into the club two weeks later, during his upcoming visit to Miami.

On Broadway, Richman became famous after his appearance in *George White's Scandals* in the 1920s, and in *The Ziegfeld Follies* in the '30s. He made his movie debut as vaudeville-style singer in *Puttin' on the Ritz* (1930). At La Conga, he agreed to sing its theme song for Desi's audience. "I was getting topnotch entertainers who were singin' for nothin'," Desi said. "Only as a favor to me. I felt like hot shit."

An even bigger entertainer than Richman showed up at La Conga the following night, "Banjo Eyes" himself, Eddie Cantor, the famous performer, comedian, dancer, singer, and songwriter. Desi had loved his eye-rolling song-and-dance routines and such hits as "Makin' Whoopee" and "If You Knew Suzie."

Cantor gave Desi some advice: "You'll have to come up with a better first name than Desi. Sounds too much like a fag. My first name was Isadore, and the kids called me Izzy. I had to change that to Eddie. You take my advice. Change it to Diego. You do this sexually suggestive dance. That requires a macho name like Diego instead of that faggy Desi."

"I will, Mr. Cantor, I will," Desi promised.

The quintessential torch singer, Helen Morgan (1900-1941), was nearing the final years of her life when, while clutching the swaying hips of "sexy Desi," she joined the conga line two nights later.

In the 1920s, Morgan became a legend on the Chicago club scene, a favorite of gangsters like Al Capone. A peak in her career came when she starred as Julie LaVerne in the original Broadway production (1927) of Hammerstein and Kern's musical, *Show Boat*.

Desi wasn't surprised when she showed up drunk at La Conga. *[Her struggle with alcohol had long been tabloid fodder.]* After dancing the conga with him, "she gave me a sloppy wet kiss and an invitation to come to her suite when I got off from work. I knew she was a big star, and young hopefuls on the rise like me should always go to bed when a famous star like Helen Morgan invites you, but I was not attracted to her. At one point, she stumbled and almost fell. At that time in my life, Helen just wasn't my idea of a sexy dame."

[Years later, in 1957, Desi went to see Ann Blyth star in The Helen Morgan Story, *based on the Playhouse 90 drama that Polly Bergen had put on television. "Neither Blyth, nor Polly for that matter, had anything to do with the Helen Morgan I encountered that night on Miami Beach," he said.*

Although Desi didn't know Morgan, other than through their casual meeting in his conga line, he was saddened to learn about her early death at the age of forty-one. She was trying to make a comeback in October of 1941 in George White's Scandals of 1942, but she collapsed onstage during a performance and died of cirrhosis of the liver shortly thereafter.

"All those years of heavy drinking caught up with her," Desi mourned.]

Joe E. Lewis learned a bitter lesson, which he relayed one night to the up-and-coming Desi Arnaz: "Never refuse a request from the Mob."

To retaliate after Lewis refused their invitation to perform at one of their clubs because he had a better-paying gig somewhere else, "Machine Gun" McGurn cut out a piece of his tongue.

Helen Morgan onstage in 1929.

According to Desi, "She was the leading torch singer in America in the 1920s and '30s, and she wanted what I had dangling, but a drunken broad always turned me off."

By the time Desi Arnaz made dancing the Conga his main source of income, it had already been configured as an expression of vivacity and joy.

With the White House as its backdrop, the photo above was snapped in Washington D.C.'s Lafayette Park a few minutes before then-President Harry S Truman announced the surrender of Japan at the end of World War II.

Almost as a patriotic act, sailors and marines learned the Conga's footwork—on the double. A critic at the time, in memory of the victims of the atomic bombs unleashed a few days before on Hiroshima and Nagasaki, announced: "**THE CONGA HAS GONE NUCLEAR**."

LET'S LEARN THE CONGA!

Even **Rita** ("The Love Goddess of the '40s) **Hayworth** did it, leading a conga line for dozens of bored and horny U.S. sailors as part of a morale-building assignment.

149

Of the many celebrities who visited La Conga, Desi formed his closest bond with "The King of Clubs," Joe E. Lewis. He visited La Conga whenever he could. *[At the time, he was working as a stand-up comic at a club down the street.]* Lewis was a comedian, actor, and singer who in time became a close friend of Frank Sinatra.

In 1957, Ol' Blue Eyes portrayed Lewis in a movie loosely based on his (Lewis's) life. *The Joker Is Wild* depicts an entertainer who falls foul of the mob. In Chicago of 1927, Lewis had rejected a request from "Machine Gun" McGurn, a henchman of Al Capone. Lewis refused to star at the mob-owned Green Mill Cocktail Lounge, having previously accepted a better-paying gig at a club run by a member of a rival gang.

"Machine Gun," along with two other thugs, one of whom was San Giancana, broke into Lewis' hotel room and mutilated him, cutting his throat and removing part of his tongue. He survived the bloody attack, but for several years could not speak.

One night, Lewis warned Desi, "As you become a big star, you'll attract the attention of the mob. They no doubt will demand that you cut them in on your earnings. Be warned!"

***

As an entertainer, and "as I continued to shake my ass," Desi attracted admirers, both male and female. "Every night I got offers to go to bed with this one or another. Some of them I accepted, others I politely turned down, trying not to offend whoever it was that desired me. Actually, it was flattering."

One night an internationally acclaimed movie star showed up to dance in the conga line with him. She was Sonja Henie, a three-time (1928, 1932, and 1936) Olympic ice-skating champion, winner of more Olympic and World titles than any other ladies' figure skater in history. In Hollywood, thanks to a then-popular craze for song-and-dance "Queen of the Ice" routines on skates. she was one of its highest-paid stars.

When Desi met her, he had not seen any of Henie's movie hits. They included *Thin Ice* (1937), *Happy Landing* (1938), and *My Lucky Star* (also 1938).

Henie, sometimes referred to as "a Degas ballerina on skates," was already a controversial figure. In the

Because Desi's family name ended with an "A," he leads the long list of famous men the ice-skating star, **Sonja Henie**, seduced.

"She was to ice skating what Esther Williams was to swimming," Desi said. "She was an insatiable nympho, just couldn't get enough. She had to have it at least three times a day."

years and months prior to World War II, she had frequently performed and competed in Germany, and was a widely celebrated personal favorite of Adolf Hitler. *[She had famously greeted the Führer with a Nazi salute at the 1936 Winter Olympics in Garmisch-Partenkirchen. Later, she accepted his invitation for lunch at his nearby retreat at Berchtesgaden, a move that led to strong denunciations from the international press, including from media outlets in her native Norway, a nation soon to be overrun by the Nazi war machine.]*

Henie was immediately attracted to Desi as he taught her the hip-swaying nuances of the Conga. She invited him back to her hotel suite that night, and he accepted. He continued accepting her invitations (again and again and again) during Henie's future Miami presentations of her *Hollywood Ice Revue.*

Desi had read about Henie in the gossip columns. In time, her lovers would include the (usually) gay actor, Van Johnson, and an up-and-coming congressman from Massachusetts, John F. Kennedy. She and Tyrone Power became lovers. *[They assigned, it was rumored, specific nicknames to their respective genitalia: His was "Jimmy" and hers was nicknamed "Betsy."]*

Screenwriter Milton Sperling, who wrote the script for Henie's movie hit, *Thin Ice,* claimed, "She was one sexy, voracious broad who liked to fuck anything in pants."

During their fling, Henie tried to teach Desi to skate, "but I kept falling on my ass," he lamented.

As he told Joe E. Lewis, "When Sonja captures you with those ice-skating leg muscles, you're in for the duration...and beyond. She loves encores."

Fox chairman Darryl F. Zanuck, said, "Slap some keys on her and you'll have a grand piano." He was referring to the strength of the leg muscles that had already entrapped Desi.

After Henie left Miami Beach and Desi, she became the first entertainer to perform the conga on skates.

***

As was inevitable, Desi's reign as the Conga King of Miami Beach ended with that year's winter, when the "snow birds" collectively flew north and the hotels and their night clubs along the beachfront shuttered and grew dark.

Staffs and entertainers abandoned Miami Beach *en masse,* most of them headed for interim jobs at various summer resorts in the north.

Desi not only lost his gig but his business partner, Louis Nicoletti, who ran off with an heiress to a Detroit automobile dynasty. "I'm fixed for life," he told Desi over a farewell drink. "All I have to do is plow her once a day. Instead of wondering where your next buck is coming from, I suggest you find some rich bitch and become her kept boy, too."

Each member of Desi's ragtag group of musicians had also headed north, scoping out their next gigs. One of them told Xavier Cugat about Desi's plight, and the bandleader sent him a contract agreeing to pay $200 a week for five years as his band's featured soloist.

At first, Desi was tempted, since the contract offered a kind of security blanket, but before signing it, he decided to show it to a lawyer friend of Desiderio. After reading it, the attorney advised him not to sign it. "The only thing this contract doesn't grant Cugat is the right to plug you in the ass. I haven't read the fine print yet. Maybe he's included a clause about that in it, too. If you sign this damn contract, you're fucked. Even if you get a movie offer at $5,000 a week, Cugat is obligated to give you only $200."

Cugat was surprised when Desi turned him down, claiming, "My offer is very, very generous, more than twice what I'm paying my other musicians."

Nonetheless, Desi opted to remain unemployed, even though he had only forty dollars left. Fortunately, he ran into Caesar De Franco, who had been his bassist during their midwinter gig at La Conga. For five dollars a week, Desi could rent the spare room in a Brooklyn apartment he shared with De Franco's Italian wife.

According to Desi, as it turned out, "That was the best deal I ever made. Mrs. De Franco treated me like her son. The five dollars included three meals a day, and she also did my laundry."

On their building's ground floor was a barbershop where "a gorgeous blonde worked as a manicurist," Desi said. "She was a lookalike for Ginger Rogers, and I'm partial to blondes. So what if she dyed it? She even bleached her pussy hair so she could be blonde all over. Her name was Betty Mayne, and I began to heavy date her. We hit the clubs. Since I had no money coming in, she picked up all the tabs."

At the time, Desi's workday regime involved a round-trip pedestrian transit across the Brooklyn Bridge into Manhattan to save the nickel subway fare. Every day, he searched for a gig, ending up playing in a German band at a restaurant in Yorkville on Manhattan's Upper East Side.

[Although Britain and France had declared war on Germany after its invasion of Poland, the United States had not yet entered the carnage. In the dance hall was a large picture of the Führer. It disappeared after Nazi Germany declared war on the United States after the invasion of Pearl Harbor on December 7, 1941. Before that happened, and in full view of the portrait of Hitler, Desi introduced the conga to the restaurant's German-speaking clientele. Ironically, they took to it brilliantly. "If I'd been appearing in Berlin, I'm sure I would have had Hitler and Goebbels joining my conga line, too," Desi boasted.]

With the coming of warm weather, Desi was offered a booking at a seasonal nightclub in Upper New York State called Fan & Bills, opening onto Lake George.

As it happened, the owner of the club, Bill Pryor, had vacationed in Miami Beach the previous January and had visited La Conga. "He tracked me down through the musicians' union," Desi said.

Before heading up to Lake George, "the Queen of American Lakes," Desi had to round up another band and arrange for their transit deep into the Adirondack Mountains.

In reference to his sexual adventures, Desi later reminisced, "I didn't count them, but I think I went through eighteen virgins that summer, including twin sisters who had driven down from Montréal. I never thought I looked like Clark Gable or was any body beautiful, but the broads were attracted to me, including some married ones. Some days, in addition to dancing the conga, I overbooked myself. It was love in the late morning, love in the

Fan & Bill's Steakhouse

Here is a replicated postcard showing the then-innovative Art Deco design of the Lake George branch of **Fan & Bill's Famous Steak House of Miami Beach**..

In a resort heavily patronized by the mob, it became an important stage for the development of Desi's flair and syncopation as a nightlife entertainer.

afternoon, and love after midnight. Thank god for youth."

For his upcoming winter season, Desi and his band of mismatched musicians returned to Miami Beach for another successful engagement. "Once again, we brought conga fever to the beach, and it spread like an epidemic."

In Miami Beach, vacationing there at the time with a trio of "gun molls," Mafia kingpin Mario Torsatti had visited The Conga Club frequently before meeting with Desi late one Sunday morning in his suite at the Roney Plaza. During their meeting, a pair of gun molls were sunbathing, nude, on his terrace.

Joe E. Lewis had already warned Desi that if he made enough money, he'd begin attracting the scrutiny of the mob. Now, that was happening right before his eyes.

Torsatti mentioned that the $150 million New York World Fair of 1939 would be opening soon. He had invested in a building on Broadway at 51st Street in Midtown Manhattan and was having it decorated to evoke a tropical garden, complete with fake palms and exotic plants imported from Jamaica. "I want a Manhattan version of La Conga. I think the dance will attract a lot of international visitors who'll be in town for the World's Fair."

A deal was struck and within six weeks, the New York La Conga Club opened "on the wrong side of Fifth Avenue." The club did very little business from the World's Fair crowd, since the fairgrounds featured their own night clubs and after dark amusements.

Instead, a fashionable set of Manhattan-based trendsetters, sometimes known as the "*demimonde*," regularly patronized such nightspots as the Stork Club and El Morocco. Word soon spread, and the denizens of the Social Register began showing up at La Conga for what they referred to as "slumming."

At the time, Brenda Frazier was the most gossiped-about, widely publicized debutante in America, featured on the society pages of newspapers almost daily. One night with her *beau du jour,* she ventured into La Conga, and within an hour, she was dancing behind Desi in the conga line.

She spread the word among her friends, and Desi's "New York La

Conga" began to attract other debs and their gigolos, each suitor hoping to "marry into money."

When he first met her, Desi didn't know who Brenda Frazier was, but he soon found out. As she and her friends began to patronize La Conga, news of the club spread though newspaper columns, and the joint was packed nightly.

Desi soon learned more about Brenda: As was said at the time, she was "famous for being famous." Newspaper columnist Walter Winchell defined her as "the world's first *celebutante*."

Other members of the press dubbed her "Poor Little Rich Girl," and she joined the gilded social elite that included the tobacco heiress Doris Duke and the Woolworth heiress, Barbara Hutton.

Born in Québec in 1921, Brenda Diana Duff was the daughter of two alcoholic, dysfunctional parents. Almost immediately after her birth, her father, Frank, who'd been born into a wealthy Bostonian family, disappeared for several months.

Her ambitious, "easy-to-dislike" mother, also named Brenda, was the daughter of the general manager of the Bank of Montréal. He'd been knighted by Edward VII, eldest son of Queen Victoria, in 1910.

Daughter Brenda was widely photographed as the debutante of the year in countless magazines, even appearing on the cover of *Life*. She pioneered the "white face" look, her powdered skin contrasting with her dark, silky, perfectly coiffed hair, and with her luscious red lips that competed with those of any Techni-

The interior of the New York City nightclub everybody was talking about: **La Conga.**

"Our club was an unbelievable success," Desi said. "The Charleston was the rage in the Roaring Twenties, but we made the conga a national dance craze."

November 14, 1938 edition of *Life* magazine, with **Brenda Frazier** on its cover.

"This famous heiress and I had the hots for each other the first night we met at La Conga." Desi claimed. "She was incredibly beautiful. She looked at me with those X-ray eyes of hers. I mean, I had a feeling she could see through my pants and underwear to what lurked beyond."

color screen queen in Hollwood.

Before meeting Desi, Brenda had been pursued by a very young John F. Kennedy and more ardently by the aviator billionaire, Howard Hughes. She also had another ardent admirer in Joan Crawford, who began to send her flowers and expensive perfumes. Soon, Brenda and Crawford were photographed arriving together at the Stork Club and El Morocco.

In print, Walter Winchell wondered, "What's wrong with the red-blooded men of America that these two legendary beauties have to arrive stag?"

Brenda ultimately rejected Crawford's lesbian advances. From that point on, the (offended) screen diva publicly referred to Frazier as "a debutramp."

Around the time Brenda was dating Desi, the volume of her fan mail exceeded that of both Ginger Rogers and Alice Faye. As proof of her fame, she told Desi that she once received a fan addressed simply to "SHE, NEW YORK." The legendary stage actress, Tallulah Bankhead, quipped, "That snot-nosed Frazier kid is more famous than yours truly, and God knows, I'm the world's most famous pussy since Cleopatra."

Brenda could make headlines just by showing up. "It was because of her that La Conga was put on the map," Desi claimed. As he later confessed, "I fell in love with Brenda when she first came into the club wearing a white silk gown with cascading ostrich feathers—what a sight!"

After Brenda made La Conga famous, you never knew who might show up from high society, even Mrs. Cornelius Vanderbilt in her trademark fox fur or perhaps Condé Nast, the publisher of *Vogue*.

Brenda's lovers came and went, even Douglas Fairbanks, Jr., who succeeded in seducing her. *[Some gossips noted that in that endeavor, whereas he succeeded, Fairbanks' bisexual ex-wife, Joan Crawford, had notably failed.]*

The first time Desi visited Brenda's swanky Fifth Avenue apartment he was surprised to see a portrait of Adolf Hitler. "Don't get the idea that I'm a Nazi," she told him. "I'm not. That was a portrait that *Der Führer* personally presented to my grandmother. It made little difference to her if a man were a beast or a national hero, as long as he was head of state."

Brenda Frazier (left) and Desi's sidekick **Peter Arno** (right) were ideal examples of the decadent, frivolous, and gossiply leftovers of café society.

If it appears that Brenda has a stiff neck, it probably derives from the heavy tiaras and headdresses she was maneuvered into wearing as part of her *haute* society status as a *fashionista*.

One night at Manhattan's La Conga, Brenda showed up with Peter Arno, a commercial artist who was much older than herself. Arno, the most famous cartoonist in America, was known at the time for satirizing New York's elite while nonetheless remaining one of high society's most dashing figures. He was notorious for his scandals, brawls, and affairs with newsworthy young women, including Brenda.

Desi began to buy weekly copies of *The New Yorker* magazine just to look at Arno's cartoons. Soon, Brenda, Desi, and Arno, were seen out on the town together as a trio. Sometimes, Arno and Desi, without Brenda, would pile into Arno's Duesenberg and head together for Atlantic City.

Asked if she were jealous, Frazier snapped, "Let the boys have their fun."

Dorothy Kilgallen, in her column, made a veiled reference to the configuration of Desi, Brenda, and Arno as "a threesome."

One night at La Conga, Arno showed up not with Brenda, but with Carmen Miranda, and introduced her to Desi. According to reports, Desi and Miranda (aka "the Brazilian Bombshell") adored each other from the first time they met. That night, together, they worked as a team in leading the conga line.

As closing time neared, "The Lady with the *Tutti Frutti* Hat" invited Desi back to her suite at the Waldorf-Astoria. He gladly accepted.

As he later relayed to Arno, "I didn't mean to take her from you, but I knew you were booked up at Polly Adler's whorehouse, so with Carmen, I promoted friendly relations between Brazil and Cuba."

Years later, in Hollywood, Carmen became a neighbor of Lucille and Desi, presumably his tryst with the flamboyant entertainer having faded with the memories of yesteryear.

Desi later claimed that the last time he dropped in to visit Carmen, "she looked depressed, that perpetual smile gone from her face. She said to him, "I've told so many lies about myself, worn so many masks, I no longer know who I am."

In time, Desi lost touch with Brenda Frazier. Writer Raquel Lanier in the *New York Post* wrote, "She spent much of her last two decades addicted to drugs and alco-

Carmen Miranda: The "Brazilian Bombshell" had actually been born in Portugal. With her self-satirizing humor delivered in fractured English, she became an outrageously flamboyant fixture in escapist musicals during World War II.

"*American men are so tall, so sexy. Dey are de type for me. As soon as I seen Hollywood, I love it. Soon, I had both Johns—Payne and Wayne. Payne had three inches more than the guy they call Duke.*"

"*I didn't give up on Latin men, however. I managed to seduce the homo actor Cesar Romero. Desi told me that screwing me was better sex than getting a blow-job from Romero.*"

"*I did have one thing that got me into trouble,*" she confessed. "*I could never bring myself to wear underpants.*"

hol, languishing away in her home in Beacon Hill and Cape Cod. Her arm bore slashes from her thirty suicide attempts. Emaciated but still convinced she was fat, she refused to eat and would even take her feeding tubes out if she couldn't wrap her index finger and thumb around her upper arm. She once quipped that she 'invented' anorexia."

Frazier finally died in 1982 at the age of sixty.

[One of the last times Arno invited Desi out was in 1942, during the course of his marriage to Lucille Ball. Arno escorted both of them to the Cocoanut Grove in Los Angeles. His date was Oona O'Neill, the seventeen-year-old daughter of playwright Eugene O'Neill and the future wife of Charlie Chaplin.]

***

Polly Adler visited La Conga one night with, according to Desi, "six of the most beautiful gals I'd ever seen in my life." At the time, he didn't know who Adler was, but he was soon to find out. The club owner quickly informed him, "Polly is America's most famous madam. Behind the scenes, her influence is second only to our First Lady, Eleanor Roosevelt."

Desi learned that Adler appeared as a means of "showcasing" her beautiful *putas* to politicians, bankers, press barons, Wall Street titans, and out-of-town oil men from Texas, all of whom had started to frequent The New York branch of La Conga.

During one of Adler's subsequent visits, Desi greeted her after dancing the conga. By now, he knew she was nicknamed "The Jewish Jezebel."

Adler's notorious house of prostitution on Lexington Avenue had flourished throughout the 1920s and into the war years, despite frequent raids from the police. She learned how to cope with raids by paying off corrupt politicians and police officials.

Born in 1900 in Belarus, then part of the Russian Empire, she was one of nine children in a Jewish family. She emigrated to New York at the age of twelve with the understanding that she'd eventually be joined by her family, but their emigrations were stymied by the outbreak of World War I. She lived with a family in Massachusetts as their servant, moving within two years to join distant cousins in Brooklyn.

There, she dropped out of school for a job as a seamstress at a clothing factory. After saving up enough money, she moved in with a showgirl on Riverside Drive in Manhattan. To pay their rent, they allowed their apartment to be used for off-the-record sexual trysts by a local gangster with a preference for showgirls. Partly because Adler liked to hang out with theatrical crowds, the mobster asked her to procure young women for him.

That launched her career as a madam, and led, in 1920, to the opening of her first bordello under the protection of two newly minted friends, gangsters Dutch Schultz and Lucky Luciano.

In time, her brothel catered to many prominent men, including Desi's friend, the *New Yorker* cartoonist, Peter Arno. Heading for her bordello after dark were, depending on the era, Harold Ross, George S. Kaufman, Robert Benchley, Franklin Roosevelt, Jr., and in the late 1930s, actor John Garfield. Jimmy Walker, mayor of New York, was a frequent visitor, too. And al-

157

though it was hushed up, Joseph Force Crater, a New York State Supreme Court Justice, suffered a heart attack in her brothel in August of 1930.

In 1944, after her retirement from "active duty," Adler wrote a biography. Entitled *A House Is Not a Home* it was published with lots of attention in 1953. *[Actually, it had been ghost written by Virginia Faulkner.]* Two years later, it was made into a sanitized movie starring Robert Taylor and Shelley Winters.

One of her frequent visitors, Milton Berle, one of Lucille Ball's future lovers, liked to brag to his male friends, "All of Polly's gals assure me that I'm the best-hung man in New York."

In addition to Lucille, Berle's list of conquests included screen vamp Theda Bara, actress Wendy Barrie, Lila Gray Chaplin (ex-wife of Charlie), Linda Darnell, Betty Hutton, Veronica Lake, and, ultimately, a young Marilyn Monroe, plus countless others. Sometimes, Desi and Berle visited Adler at the same time. "The world knew Polly as a madam," Berle said, "but her friends like Desi and me knew her as an intelligent woman, fun to be with, and a good cook."

"One night at La Conga, I fell in love at first sight," Desi claimed. "She was one of Polly's *putas,* the most ravishing redhead who ever lived. She went under the name of Anita Daven. After La Conga closed that night, Polly and I went back to her lavish apartment, where I got to know Anita very well indeed."

Born in Tampa, Daven had attended the University of Florida but dropped out after her freshman year. She'd come to Manhattan, hoping to become a Ziegfeld Girl, but didn't

Polly Adler is depicted here in Atlantic City in 1920. Slightly overweight, she was being lifted by one of her boyfriends. In Manhattan that year, she opened what became the most famous bordello in America.

"Desi was my best customer, one night seducing six of my girls in one evening alone," she claimed. "That guy was amazing. He told me that he also went for nurses, starlets, secretaries, local pickups on the street. He insisted they be well built and blonde. Amazingly, he ended up marrying this dish who was a redhead with no tits."

qualify. Evicted from her room on the Upper West Side for failure to pay the rent, she met one of Polly's girls, who lured her into prostitution. In time, she became the most requested girl in Adler's stable of beauties.

Recalling it years later, Desi compared Daven's looks to two specific movie stars: Rhonda Fleming and Arlene Dahl, both of them widely promoted as "Queens of Technicolor."

"When I first went to bed with Anita, I thought I was an experienced *hombre,* but she taught me tricks I'd never learned before. No wonder she was so popular. I was madly, passionately in love with her, at least during the first five visits. We carried on and on, but I was not faithful. After all, she was a *puta,* and at La Conga, blondes kept throwing themselves at me. Temptation is not something to resist. 'Go for it.' At least that's always been my motto."

As the world would eventually learn, Desi Arnaz had nothing against redheads, "but to tell the truth, I'm partial to blondes," he said. "Millions of Latin males share that passion. Besides, what red-blooded male would ever turn down Betty Grable or Ginger Rogers?"

***

Inaugurated close to the beginning of World War II, the spectacular 1939 World's Fair was the last big celebration that the world would know for many years. Sprawling across Flushing Meadows in Queens, it was the second most expensive fair ever staged, drawing forty million visitors to "The World of Tomorrow."

As part of the World's Fair opening, NBC commissioned Desi, along with starlet Diosa Costello, to dance the conga as it was recorded for a new medium known as "television." Thanks to NBC's film project, millions of visitors passing through the fairgrounds would see a display of this new invention. At the time, there were only about one-hundred television sets in all of New York City.

On November 12, 1939, Desi, who one day would be nicknamed "Mr. Television" himself, made his debut in the medium he would eventually dominate.

In their video, Desi and Costello introduced the conga. At the time, she was appearing regularly with him at his nightclub. Born in Guayama, Puerto Rico, she was known as "The Latina Bombshell."

As an entertainer, Costello had gotten her start at seedy clubs in Spanish Harlem. She eventually came to the attention of Desi, who hired her to perform with him at La Conga. She was single at the time, and members of the band claimed that "on and off" she was having a fling with the boss.

She would soon make her debut on Broadway in *Too Many Girls* with Desi. In time, she'd become known as the "first Latina on the Broadway Stage," years before Chita Rivera or Rita Moreno. On several occasions, she rejected offers from Hollywood, claiming, "I'm reluctant to move to Los Angeles. New York is my home."

She eventually became a club owner herself in Manhattan, where her sultry beauty and low-cut gowns helped to attract a devoted list of admirers. Years later, when asked about Desi Arnaz, she said, "I don't think he fell in love with me, but with my breasts. He once told me they were the most beautiful the world has ever known."

Amazingly, although Costello spent most of her life in smoke-filled clubs, she lived to be a century old, dying in Hollywood, Florida in

2013.

After dancing with Costello on television for the World's Fair, Desi was not impressed. "I see no future in it," he told the press. "For one thing, a television set costs about $675. You can buy a simple Ford motor car for that kind of money. Take my word for it: Television will never replace radio as some are predicting."

On some weeks, Desi pulled in a thousand dollars a week. He moved from his lowly room in Brooklyn with the De Francos and into a luxurious penthouse apartment he sublet from the boxer, Barney Ross. Living on one of the building's lower floors was the famous composer, Lorenz Hart. He would soon play a major role in Desi's future.

Another big star, Ethel Merman, occupied an apartment in the same building. Desi would often stand in front of the picture windows overlooking Central Park, realizing how far he had climbed in the world from his original job cleaning out bird shit from canary cages in Miami.

At the age of forty-five, Desiderio had met a younger woman and had moved her into his Miami home, asking his wife, Lolita (Desi's mother), to leave. Furious at his father, Desi sent Lolita bus fare and moved her possessions into his penthouse.

She could sometimes be spotted sitting at a lonely table at La Conga, watching her beloved son perform.

She never remarried and wore her wedding ring until the day she died in 1988.

***

One night, it was not a beautiful blonde, but three men who requested that the owner of La Conga, Mario Torsatti, send Desi over to their table so they could talk to him.

"What the hell?" Desi asked. "I'm attracting

Rising from the flatlands of Flushing Meadows, Queens, are the skeletal frames of the then very avant-garde Trilon and Perisphere, key components of "The World of Tomorrow" at the **New York City World's Fair of 1939.**

Desi, as a Conga expert, demonstrated his skills as a Conga Kingpin for the then-experimental medium of television.

Diosa Costello once claimed that "My dancing partner, Desi Arnaz, was the greatest breast devotee of all time."

"One night, he spent two and a half hours at my breasts before moving downstairs on me for further business. When he was a baby, suckling at his Mama's breasts, he may have developed this life long tit passion back then."

homos—and three of them at that?"

"No, you silly fool," Torsatti said. "They're Rodgers and Hart."

"Never heard of them," Desi said.

"They're only the top musical writing team on Broadway. God, how stupid you can be."

"I've never seen a Broadway show in my life," Desi said.

"Then shake your *Cubano* ass over to their table," Torsatti ordered. "They're staring at us now."

Not knowing what he was in for, Desi headed their way, (neurotically) planning to make it clear that he was a red-blooded heterosexual.

At the table, among others, he met Lorenz Hart and his composer-partner Richard Rodgers. He was also introduced to the third man, George Marion, Jr., who, as it turned out, had written the stage version of a new musical, *Too Many Girls.*

As the evening wore on, Desi learned that Hart had discovered him when he was leading the conga line on Miami Beach. He had attended the club, intensely focusing on Desi's act, without ever introducing himself.

It seemed that all three of them had agreed that Desi would be ideal in the play's role of an eighteen-year-old college football player from Argentina named Manuelito.

"I hear that you're girl crazy," Marion said. "One line I wrote seems tailor-made for you: 'Football is not the important thing for me in trying to decide on a college. The place has to have a lot of girls, too.'"

As it turned out, Hart lived in the same apartment building as Desi. It was agreed that he'd call on him tomorrow in the late morning for discussions about the play, followed by lunch.

In the meantime, Desi set about learning just who Hart, Rodgers, and Marion were. One of the dancers at La Conga, Maria García, had once worked in a Rodgers and Hart musical, and she remained behind after the trio left to talk to Desi about these three strangers who had suddenly entered his life.

Born in Harlem in New York City in 1895, Hart had Jewish immigrant parents with German backgrounds. As he grew up, he attended Columbia University's School of Journalism, but in 1919, he met Rodgers. At the time, he was working for the legendary Shubert Brothers, translating German-language plays into English.

Rodgers and Hart bonded and soon joined forces to write songs for amateur productions.

By 1920, six of their songs were featured in the musical comedy, *Poor Little Rich Girl,* with music by Sigmund Romberg. After writing the score for the 1925 Theatre Guild's production of *The Garrick Gaieties,* the song-writing team was off and running, writing the music and lyrics for twenty-six Broadway musicals during a two-decade partnership that ended shortly before Hart's early death.

As time went by, one hit followed another, their famous music featuring "Blue Moon," "The Lady Is a Tramp," "Bewitched, Bothered, and Bewildered," "My Funny Valentine," "This Can't Be Love," "With a Song in My Heart," and many more.

The essence of Hart's works was captured by Stephen Holden in *The New York Times* in an article read by Desi: "Many of Hart's ballad lyrics conveyed a heart-stopping sadness that reflected his conviction that he was physically too unattractive to be lovable. In his lyrics, as in his life, he stands as a compelling lonely figure. Although he wrote dozens of songs that are playful, funny, and filled with clever wordplay, it is the rueful vulnerability beneath their surface that lends them a singular poignancy."

Over the years, many singers have made hit records with Hart's lyrics, notably Ella Fitzgerald, Billie Holiday, Doris Day, and Frank Sinatra. Hart became known as "The expressive Bard of the urban generation that matured between the wars."

Lorenz Hart, lyricist (left) with **Richard Rodgers** (right). Critics have said that you can hear the tragic words of an unrequited lover in many of Hart's lyrics.

Although Desi formed an amicable relationship with Hart, his dialogues with Rodgers always remained more superficial, even though he respected him greatly as an artist. Rodgers was younger than Hart, having been born in New York City in 1902. Like Hart, he had come from a German Jewish family. A child prodigy, he could give a piano concert at the age of six.

In time, he would write forty-three Broadway musicals and more than nine hundred songs, making him one of the genuinely towering figures among American composers of his era. In the 1920s and '30s, he and Hart would create such Broadway shows as *Pal Joey, A Connecticut Yankee, On Your Toes,* and *Babes in Arms.* After Hart's early death, Rodgers teamed with Oscar Hammerstein II. They went on to create such 1940s and 50s musicals as *Oklahoma!, Carousel, South Pacific, The King and I,* and *The Sound of Music.* In time, Rodgers would win an Emmy, a Grammy, an Oscar, a Tony, and a Pulitzer Prize.

A Bostonian, George Marion, Jr. was born in the final summer of the 19th Century. As a screenwriter, between 1920 and 1940, he'd churn out some creative aspect of a staggering 118 (some sources say "106") movies, either their scripts or their subtitles if the movies were silent. His father, George F. Marion, Sr. (1860-1945), was an actor (stage and screen) and also a director. He appeared in the classic *Anna Christie* (1930), cast in the role of Greta Garbo's father.

The famous director, George Abbott, forbade any

Director **George Abbott** (circa 1930) helped launch Desi's career. "In my first audition, I was pretty lousy. He gave my first review, which he shared with Dick Rodgers:"

"Well, at least the kid is loud enough," Abbott said.

According to Desi, "I thought I was gonna be shown the door, but no way! They cast me in a leading role!"

actor to rehearse a script before his or her audition for a part, but behind his back, Hart spent the following day coaching Desi on the nuances of *Too Many Girls*. He learned, and later said, "Abbott would raise holy hell if he thought an actor had rehearsed the scene before showing up for his audition."

Before and after their lunch, Desi and Hart went through every scene he'd have to play in the upcoming Broadway musical.

When Desi finally appeared before Abbott late the following morning, the director quickly figured out that he'd been pre-rehearsed and yelled at Hart for maneuvering behind his back. As for Desi's emotive style, Abbott told him, "Manuelito is a hot-blooded, girl-crazy Latino, but from what I just saw, you seem to be aping John Barrymore."

Despite that "early negative review," Desi got the part. It paid $300 a week in an era when there were very few *latino* actors on Broadway to give him competition.

"George gave me the role, but never got my name right, always calling me 'Dizzy.' He loved to dance, and he showed up that night at La Conga, leading the line himself. He took to that conga, yelling and hollering at me to work it into our Broadway show."

For Desi to appear on Broadway, he had to work out exit terms with Mario Torsatti and his gangster partners, but an agreement was reached.

"George developed the hots for my former girlfriend, Diosa Costello," Desi said, "and he made a deal to cast her in *Too Many Girls* too."

After the first week of rehearsals, Desi finally learned what a powerhouse in the theater Abbott really was.

Born in 1887 in Forestville New York, he had a career that would span nine decades before his death at the ago of 107 in Miami Beach. He became one of the great legends of the theater as a producer, director, and playwright, and he also branched out into films. His stage career began in 1913, as he made his debut in *The Misleading Lady*. The first play he wrote was *The Fall Guy* in 1925.

Desi and his partner, **Diosa Costello**, almost worked themselves to death.

Their nights would begin with a high-energy performance of *Too Many Girls* on a Broadway stage. When it ended, they'd rush over to La Conga Club as the headlining stars of two back-to-back shows, one starting at midnight, the other at 2:30AM.

Desi recalled, "Sometimes the club stayed open till 5AM. After that, I'd go home and collapse until two or three the following afternoon."

Abbott became Broadway's most famous and sought-after "show doctor," called in to iron out any difficulties uncovered during a play's tryouts and previews. He was said to have saved many a show with last-minute re-castings, the insertion of new material, and the deletion of certain scenes. Virtually every year, he was connected to some fast-emerging Broadway show.

His "fast-paced, tightly integrated style" was said to have influenced many directors, notably Hal Prince, Bob Fosse, and Jerome Robbins. He was not only a key player in the launch of Desi, but a figure in the careers of Betty Comden, Adolph Green, Leonard Bernstein, Gene Tierney, Jules Styne, Elaine Stritch, Stephen Sondheim, Fred Ebb, John Kander, Carol Burnett, and Liza Minnelli.

He published his autobiography, *Mister Abbott*, in 1963, but at that point in his career, according to Desi, "his life had only begun.".

Abbott later (cruelly) gossiped to his associates, "Hart is besotten with this sexy *Cubano* and during rehearsals goes around with his tongue hanging out."

One of the lesser-known aspects of Desi's career, though printed in several sources, is his "arrangement" with Hart. Both the composer and the actor-singer lived in the same apartment building, and Desi was seen coming and going from Hart's apartment late at night.

The Conga King soon found himself living rent free. When Hart submitted his

Two views of **Diosa Costello** with **Desi Arnaz** in the Broadway version of *Too Many Girls*.

"I had never seen a Broadway show, and here I was starring in one," Desi said. "Everybody was right on target, even me. I got all my laughs. At curtain time, all of us got a standing ovation."

monthly check to the landlord for his own rent, he tacked on the cost of Desi's penthouse apartment too.

Unlike some Latin men, Desi did not have any particular prejudice toward homosexuals, although swearing, "I am one-hundred percent straight."

As he confessed one night to Abbott, "I have this deal with him (Hart) to give him a little fun on occasion. He can get at me below the belt. I just lie back and think it's Ginger Rogers, my dream gal. I haven't met her yet."

In spite of the sexual overtones, Hart and Desi became friends of sorts. Desi felt a sympathy for him because of his heavy drinking. Sometimes, he'd be absent for days at a time, disappearances he'd define as "hustler and alcoholic binges."

"One night, he told me that he considered himself an undesirable freak," Desi said. "He claimed he'd never been able to find anyone who really loved him."

Hart was known to have maneuvered many an aspirant actor onto a casting couch, preferring "sexy, beautiful men," types with bodies that stood in distinct contrast to Hart's, which he claimed he loathed. He stood only four feet ten inches tall, was not particularly handsome, and always reeked of cigar smoke.

"We're in the middle of a Depression," he told Desi, "but I'm pulling in at least $60,000 a year. It's amazing how many good-looking studs will get an erection at the sight of a hundred-dollar bill when some guys are selling it for only five or ten dollars a throw."

Because of Hart's frequent and unannounced disappearances, Desi often witnessed arguments between Rodgers and him. By 1943, they had ended their partnership. Before the year itself ended, Hart was dead. On a snowy midwinter night in Manhattan—still devastated by the death, a few months before, of his mother and sodden drunk—he collapsed in a back alley. He wasn't discovered until the next morning, but by then it was too late. He had caught pneumonia and died shortly thereafter.

Desi was saddened to learn of his death, news of which went out across the wire services and onto virtually every news broadcast in the middle of World War II.

According to Desi, "One of Hart's best-known songs was 'My Heart Stood Still.' Well, one night it did. The theater will miss him and so will I. More than anyone, he was the sparkplug who launched my career, and I will always be grateful to him for that."

***

On the first day of rehearsal for *Too Many Girls,* director George Abbott informed Desi, "You were the only Spic who showed up to audition for the role of Manuelito. I'm going to work your ass off."

"I never planned to be an actor on Broadway," Desi said. "But Lorenz Hart entered my life and changed everything. In contrast, Richard Rodgers was sort of indifferent to my *Cubano* charm."

Rehearsals for *Too Many Girls* were at the Imperial Theater, an enter-tainment showcase at 249 West 45th Street. A Shubert Theater, it was de-signed for big musical production numbers. Over the years, it would host such mega hits as *Annie Get Your Gun* (1946); *Call Me Madam* (1950); *Oliver* (1963); *Fiddler on the Roof* (1964); and *Cabaret* (1967).

Gracing its stage over the years were John Geilgud, Montgomery Clift, Ray Bolger, Shelley Winters, Hugh Jackman, Zero Mostel, and, after the passage of many years, Lucie Arnaz, daughter of Desi and Lucille.

In September of 1939, during rehearsals for *Too Many Girls,* World War II began after Britain and France declared war on Nazi Germany after its invasion of Poland.

Onstage, Desi joined that Latin bombshell from La Conga, Diosa Costello. Other players included Richard Kollmar, Van Johnson, Marcy Westcott, Hal Le Roy, Leila Ernst making her Broadway debut for forty dollars a week, and—most noteworthy of all— Eddie Bracken. His future would be sealed a few years later when, in 1944, he starred in two classics, *Hail the Conquering Hero* and *The Miracle of Morgan's Creek.*

He'd later return to Broadway as an acknowledged star and become increasingly famous on radio and in television. *[Bracken had the distinction of appearing in films with two future presidents: Ronald Reagan in* The Girl from Jones Beach *(1949) and with Donald Trump (a later intensely politicized eight-second cameo) in* Home Alone 2: Lost in New York *(1992)]*

Desi was assigned a dressing room with Richard Kollmar, who at the time was dating columnist Dorothy Kilgallen ("The Voice of Broadway"). Also in the cast was the red-haired, freckle-faced Van Johnson, who in a few years would become a matinee idol in Hollywood billed as "America's Sweetheart."

As Desi later relayed, much to the amusement of Abbott, "Are you playing a joke on me? The first time I dropped my shorts to take a shower, both of those boys had their tongues hanging out when they saw my Cuban salami. I haven't decided yet if I'm gonna let them have some fun, 'cause I need to save it up for Polly Adler's gals."

On opening night, Adler herself showed up, having booked seats for herself and seven of her beautiful *putas*. At the end of the show, she went backstage to congratulate Desi, inviting him to a late night supper of champagne and caviar at her bordello "to celebrate your success. My girls are on the house tonight."

Sipping champagne, Desi reviewed his performance in the show: "I strummed a guitar and played a bongo drum, and the audience, as you know, seemed to go wild. If I have to say so myself, I was a sensation."

The leading critics of New York (including Kilgallen, Kollmar's *fiancée*) appeared that night in the audience.

It was while Desi was being entertained in bedroom No. 3 of Polly's bordello that the madam herself knocked loudly on his door. "*Cubano!*," she shouted through the locked door. "The morning newspapers have arrived. The critics loved you!"

When Desi showed up at the Imperial Theater the following night, Abbott appraised him: "Spic, you look like hell, like you've been beaten up in an alley and robbed."

"In the last twelve hours, I *schtupped* eight of Polly Adler's gals."

"Don't do that again," Abbott warned, callously. "You need all your energy for the show. Next time, just settle for a blow job from Kollmar or Johnson."

Desi was beginning to bond with Kollmar, because the actor was using his liaison with Kilgallen to introduce Desi to the other entertainment columnists of Manhattan. Kolmar arranged

A closeted bisexual, **Richard Kollmar** appears with his wife, **Dorothy Kilgallen**, a Broadway columnist for the *New York Journal-American.*

Their morning radio show, *Breakfast with Dorothy and Dick*, was a precursor to the morning talk shows that permeate network TV these days.

meetings at La Conga with some of these other gossip mongers.

Kollmar was also seen coming and going from Desi's penthouse apartment late at night. Desi confessed to Abbott, "Dick gives the greatest massage in all of New York.:"

"Massage?" Abbott queried. "So that's what it's called these days?"

One of the first journalists Desi met was George-Jean Nathan, the drama critic and co-founder of both *The American Mercury* and *The American Spectator.*

Like Desi, Nathan had a reputation as a ladies' man, seducing starlet after starlet. The fictional character of Addison DeWitt, the arch and waspish theater critic in Bette Davis' classic *All About Eve* (1950), was based on Nathan. In that movie, it was George Sanders who played the Nathan role, appearing at a party with a budding young starlet, the then-relatively unknown Marilyn Monroe.

At the time, many Broadway insiders believed that Kilgallen was aware that her beau, Kollmar, was bisexual. Nevertheless, she would marry him in 1940. By 1945, the couple would host a 45-minute breakfast radio show, listened to by twenty million Americans.

During a rehearsal of *Too Many Girls,* Desi returned to his dressing room to pick up something. He walked in on Kollmar and Johnson having sex on the sofa. "Come and join us," Kollmar called out to Desi, who declined the invitation.

Kollmar advised Desi to "go out of your way" to charm Brooks Atkinson, theater critic for *The New York Times.* "He has the power to make or break any actor," Kollmar claimed.

"I tried to win him over with my charm," Desi claimed, "but it didn't work. Atkinson seemed cold and distant. He told me he preferred drama to musicals, and that Eugene O'Neill, whoever in hell that was, is his favorite playwright."

Desi was at his best during drinks with Ed Sullivan at La Conga. The then-author of a column named "The Toast of the Town," Sullivan would go on to host a television show seen by millions. Ultimately it became the vehicle for the introduction to American audiences of Elvis Presley and The Beatles, along with a lot of cornball vaudeville acts.

George-Jean Nathan, an early reviewer of Desi's work, became the most important theater critic of his day. He had a snobbish disdain for actresses, but was won over by the D.W. Griffith star, **Lillian Gish**.

Obsessed by her beauty and style, he launched an affair with her that lasted a decade. He had a huge influence on her movie career, but never walked down the aisle to marry her.

"During our meeting, I put my best foot forward, although, frankly, Ed has the personality of a flea," Desi said.

Leonard Lyons was an early devotee of Desi, promoting him in his nationally syndicated column for King Features.

A New Yorker, Walter Winchell

was the most popular syndicated newspaper columnist in America, read by an astounding fifty million people daily and distributed through two thousand major newspapers.

Winchell made several visits to La Conga, deserting his usual post at the Stork Club. He had also delivered a favorable review of *Too Many Girls*. *[After watching Desi lead a conga line, Winchell jokingly suggested that it should be renamed "A Desi Chain," because of all the women drawn to him.]*

Winchell could also make or break a celebrity, damaging the reputation of famed aviator Charles Lindbergh, accusing him of Nazi sympathies, and attacking the African American cabaret entertainer, Josephine Baker.

One morning, when Desi stepped out of the shower, he noticed that his right foot had turned blue. After dressing, fearing blood poisoning, he went to a nearby hospital so that it could be examined.

Walter Winchell was one of the most important newspaper columnists and radio stars of his day, delivering his celebrity scandals with a New York accent at rat-tat-tat-tat speeds.

He was the first columnist to expose Lucille for having registered as a communist in the 1930s. Even so, perhaps because of his utterly humorless "directly from the crime scene" style, Desi made him the narrator of his hit TV series, *The Untouchables*.

He was confined to a hospital bed for a few days, and as such, he was forced to call Abbott so that his understudy, Van Johnson, could replace him, temporarily.

Within the hour, Johnson arrived at Desi's bedside, urging Desi to "talk and jabber. I want to hear your accent." Finally, after Desi chatted on and off for a while, Johnson said, "I can't do it. There's no way I can be convincing speaking your Latino lingo."

Finally, an agreement was reached whereby the doctor would deaden the pain in Desi's foot, allowing him to go on stage. An ambulance drove him from the hospital to the Imperial Theater, then waited for him near its stage door for the curtain to fall and to haul him back to the hospital.

After four nights in the hospital, his doctor delivered bad news: "We can clear up the infection in your foot, but we can't cure your other affliction. You have a bad case of syphilis."

"Wasn't that the disease that killed Al Capone?" Desi asked.

Then, he panicked. Penicillin had not yet been invented, and he feared he might have infected a large number of women, including all the girls in Polly Adler's whorehouse. "Polly always bragged that her *putas* were clean," he said. "Could I have made them dirty with this disease?"

He later asserted, "I considered jumping from the fourth floor of my hospital room to my death. I cried that night, and then cried some more. But when my doctor came for his next mid-morning visit, his news had changed. It seems that the blood sample that led to his earlier conclusion had been misidentified. The doctor's diagnosis of syphilis had derived from the blood of a young man who occupied the bed next to mine. Although my foot was still infected, I did not have syphilis, and as soon as it healed, I could return to seducing every beautiful showgal in New York."

***

Ever since Desi had watched Ginger Rogers dance with Fred Astaire in *Top Hat* (1935), he'd been in love with her screen image. "Blondes are my thing," he always said, "with an occasional redhead thrown in for spice."

When he read in Dorothy Kilgallen's column that Rogers had embarked on a short visit to New York, he collaborated with Kollmar, devising a plan to steer her toward both La Conga and *Too Many Girls* during her time in Manhattan. It had already been announced that she'd be staying in a suite at the Waldorf Astoria. Kollmar agreed to have tickets to *Too Many Girls* sent to her at the Waldorf, along with a "celebrity VIP" invitation to La Conga for after the show.

Somewhat to everyone's surprise, Rogers accepted both invitations. After appraising Desi during his performance of *Too Many Girls,* she came backstage to congratulate him. Her escort that night was a chorus boy who, it seemed, had already arranged a date for himself with Van Johnson. That left Desi free to escort her directly to La Congo for his midnight show.

[At the time, she was married to her second husband, Lew Ayres. According to reports in the press, although they had not yet filed for divorce, the couple had separated. At the time, she was also engaged in an on-again, off-again affair with the (demented) aviator billionaire Howard Hughes. Although they had discussed marriage, nothing was definite, even though he had given her a five-karat diamond engagement ring.]

Rogers told Desi that she was enjoying "my pre-divorce freedom. I feel like a single

During the Broadway run of *Too Many Girls*, **Van Johnson** developed a powerful crush on Desi, who once admitted, "Van always managed to show up in my dressing room when I was stripping down for a shower."

As a red-haired, freckle-faced heartthrob, Johnson rose to fame during the war years as "The Boy Next Door." He and June Allyson became "America's Sweethearts."

According to the Broadway producer, George Abbott, "I never understood it, but at one time in the late 1930s, that annoying Spic, Desi Arnaz, was dating two of the most desirable blondes in show business."

He was referring to that dancing sensation, **Ginger Rogers** (depicted above), famous as Fred Astaire's dance partner, and later, Betty Grable, the pinup queen.

girl again."

She also confessed to Desi that back in Hollywood, she was dating James Stewart, and that although she'd done everything she could to persuade him to join her during this trip to New York, he was shooting a picture back in California. "Jimmy is a real charmer and a joy to be with," she said. "And he loves to go dancing."

"You don't have to worry," Desi assured her. "I'm the only dancing partner you'll need...I'm no Fred Astaire, of course."

"Jimmy and I have double-dated with his best pal, Henry Fonda," she said. "A starlet, Lucille Ball, had been Fonda's date, but that romance is going nowhere."

Her mention of her close friend, Lucille, then inspired her into asking if Desi had seen her non-dancing film, *Stage Door* (1937).

He confessed that he had wanted to, but with his overburdened schedule, he had not been able to get away.

"Lucille Ball is in it with me," she said. "It's her first big part. Katharine Hepburn is the star, but she detests me. In addition to Hepburn and Lucille, it's got quite a lineup of women: Andrea Leeds, Gail Patrick, Eve Arden, and Constance Collier. When he wasn't hitting the bottle, Gregory La Cava directed it."

At midnight, at La Conga Club, Rogers quickly learned how to dance in a line with Desi. Then she remained on site for his 2AM late late show. They were seen leaving the club together at 4:30AM. From there, they headed to her suite at the Waldorf-Astoria.

As Desi later confessed to George Abbott, "Ginger found my *Cubano* accent amusing, but she was mostly attracted not just to my voice, but to another part of my body, too. We didn't get to sleep until around 10AM."

He also claimed that she told him, "Whereas Lew Ayres during their marriage always remained a gentleman, even in passion," I preferred a robust kind of sex. When I first kissed Lew, I felt the earth moving under my feet. It turned out that at that moment, Los Angeles was in the throes of an earthquake."

She also confessed that one of the reasons that Howard Hughes took

HOWARD HUGHES
Hell's Angel

America's Notorious Bisexual Billionaire

By Darwin Porter

In 2005 and again in 2010, Darwin Porter, through Blood Moon Productions, published a biography of **Howard Hughes** that some critics defined as the most complete overview of his "slightly psychotic prominence" in the film industry ever published.

With 812 pages and scads of positive literary reviews, it was marketed like this:

"From his reckless pursuit of love as a rich teenager to his final days as a demented fossil, Howard Hughes changed the worlds of aviation and entertainment forever. This biography reveals inside details about his destructive and usually scandalous associations with other Hollywood players. Set amid descriptions of the unimaginable changes that affected America between 1905 and 1976, this critically acclaimed biography gives an insider's perspective about what money can buy—and what it can't."

up with her was that he preferred "wet decks."

"What in hell is a wet deck?" he asked.

"It's a reference to sexually experienced, recently divorced women, no virgins, please."

"If I'm not mistaken, I think you Americans call that 'sloppy seconds.'"

"How hideous," she said. "That sounds awful."

Ultimately, Desi agreed with the assessment of George Gershwin about Rogers. "She has a little love for a lot of people, but not a lot of love for anybody."

Desi and Rogers would encounter each other for years to come, as she remained a friend of Lucille. RKO once proposed casting Desi and her in a musical together, but the deal fell through.

He was amused when MGM remade *Grand Hotel*, its original version, released in 1932, starring John Barrymore, Greta Garbo, and Joan Crawford. This newer version was renamed *Weekend at the Waldorf* (1945).

As Desi told Van Johnson, who also starred in the remake, "If it was the story of Ginger and me, it would have to be renamed 'Two Weeks at the Waldorf.'"

"Like most of my affairs, my fling with Ginger went the way of the summer winds," Desi said. "But, lucky for me, there was enough passion left between us for a quickie, 'last-gasp' fling when I reached Hollywood."

***

Desi's career was on the rise, and Columbia Records took notice. That company's origins went back to 1889, making it the oldest surviving brand in the record business and the second major company in America to produce records.

When Desi was asked to record for them, he joined a deeply respected line-up of singers and musicians. Over the decades, it had included Al Jolson, Count Basie, Louis Armstrong, cowboy star Gene Autry, Tony Bennett, Duke Ellington, Billie Holiday, Miles Davis, Leonard Bernstein, Johnny Cash, and, eventually, Janis Joplin and Barbra Streisand.

"In addition to being a stage star and a nightclub entertainer, maybe I'll become a jukebox favorite," Desi said. For Columbia, he agreed to record two singles, each of the four sides devoted to Latin favorites. The records sold rather well, especially to America's ever-growing Latin population. He speculated that he might have a future as a Columbia recording artist.

In New York, although overworked and stressed out, he still had time to take up with another blonde goddess.

Desi had first met the blonde-haired starlet, Betty Grable, at Dinty Moore's, a bistro hangout for Broadway entertainers. At the time, that curvaceous twenty-three-year-old whose legs were later voted as "the most beautiful in the world," was the third lead in a Broadway musical: Cole Porter's *Du Barry Was a Lady,* starring Ethel Merman and Bert Lahr. *Life* magazine, at the time the largest circulated periodical in America, had run a cover story about her, accurately predicting that if she went to Holly-

171

wood, she'd become one of the biggest stars in America.

Desi always dropped into Dinty Moore's for lunch, and he often went table-hopping charming Broadway personalities with his own graciousness and eagerness to live life to the fullest.

Suddenly, he plopped down at a table with three actors he knew and found himself sitting next to Grable, the vivacious blonde herself.

He introduced himself to her, and she said, "I know who you are. I hear that, like me, you're destined for stardom."

"I certainly hope so," he said. "I got my start in Miami, cleaning bird shit from canary cages. I figured I could only go up from there."

She laughed and patted his cheek, just like she'd done the previous evening with baseball great Joe DiMaggio at El Morocco. Grable would one day co-star in a movie with his future wife, Marilyn Monroe.

"Seated next to Grable, I never wanted to leave," he recalled. "She was the sweetest-smelling woman I'd ever met. She smelled sweeter than a rose garden."

But for the moment, at least, they had to part. Before her exit, he invited her to La Conga that night, scheduling her arrival for after the curtain went down on their respective starring roles in *Too Many Girls* and *Du Barry Was a Lady*.

As Desi later told Van Johnson, "I fell hook, line, and sinker for this peroxide blonde beauty. One look into her sky blue eyes and I melted."

That night at La Conga, Grable joined the lineup of dancers as a fast learner, dancing the conga better than any other patron in the club. "I was in heaven dancing with her," Desi said. "She was gorgeous, even better-looking and far sexier than Ginger Rogers. She had such a seductive smile, she could even give a homo a hard-on."

Seated together at the same table after the dance, Desi and Grable ordered drinks. "We'd hardly downed our first drink when I felt her delicate hand under the table, fondling my most prized possession. I guess she liked what she felt, since she invited me to visit her suite at the Essex House after La Conga shut down in the early morning. There, we were still making love after the sun had risen. I knew she had a peachy color to her face, but I learned that her skin was peachy all over. She had all the right curves, delicate breasts, and legs to die for. Her nipples would harden when gently bitten. I'm sure I made her forget all about her first husband, Jackie Coogan."

After their first night together, they began to date. He didn't enjoy some of her more athletic pursuits, which included visits to an all-night bowling alley and time together on wheels at a roller-skating rink. Once again, he found himself with a blonde skater, evoking his brief fling with Sonja Henie.

[Later, when Darryl F. Zanuck learned of Grable's expertise as a skater, he told his staff, "We'll hold her in the wings in case the temperamental Henie fucks up. Grable can replace her in our skating movies."]

When Desi wasn't sleeping over at Essex House, Grable was dating millionaire playboy Lex Thompson. He owned a widely publicized custom-made motor home, the largest in America, with space enough to house

172

WOMEN WE LOVE: BETTY GRABLE

[She's depicted in the left and right photos, above. The center photo—a poster for Down Argentine Way *(1940)—promotes the film that first endeared her to the American public. In 2014,* Down Argentine Way *was deemed "culturally, historically, or aesthetically signifi- cant" by the Library of Congress and selected for preservation in the National Film Reg- istry.]*

"I'm always surprised at how easy it was for newcomers to confuse Ginger Rogers with **Betty Grable**," Desi said. "I guess *cutesy-putesy* was in vogue when they each became stars."

The Harvard Lampoon designated Grable as "The worst actress to give the most consis- tently bad performances."   But in spite of that, Grable became the biggest star of World War II.

Around the time Desi began dating her, bandleader Artie Shaw impregnated her. *[She had an abortion when she heard Shaw was about to marry Lana Turner, and that he was fre- quently seducing the teenaged Judy Garland.]*

Again, because his name begins with an "A," Desi is usually the first on the list of who was "hanky-pankying it" with Grable. That list also included Rory Calhoun, Oleg Cassini, Dan Dailey, Dick Haymes, Tyrone Power, George Raft, Mickey Rooney, and Robert Stack.

a chef and a chauffeur, even a butler.

"He wasn't the jealous type," Desi said. "He didn't mind sharing Grable with me—in fact, some nights, we rode out of town in this incred- ible motor home. Each of us got our turn with her."

As it turned out, Grable was also sharing her favors with the famous bandleader, Artie Shaw. In fact, he made her pregnant, leading to her hav- ing an abortion. Desi's affair with Grable would continue in Hollywood.

[Shaw would also sustain a fling with a then-underaged Judy Garland.

Both Grable and Garland would eventually get shoved aside when yet another newly emerged sexpot, Lana Turner, emerged into the national spotlight. Shaw eventually eloped with Lana. The disastrous marriage that ensued was one of the shortest in Hollywood.]

Movie stardom would come to Grable before it was bestowed on Desi. Fox had been set to produce a musical called *Down Argentine Way* for a 1940 release. Alice Faye, Fox's reigning number one box office musical star, had dropped out because of illness. Irving Cummings, its director, and Zanuck himself, had seen Grable in *Du Barry Was a Lady,* and offered her the role instead. She eagerly accepted.

Although Grable had already appeared in minor roles in more than thirty films throughout the 1930s, *Down Argentine Way* shot her to stardom.

Grable's leading man in that film was Don Ameche. It also introduced the flamboyant "Brazilian Bombshell," Carmen Miranda, to the North American public.

Desi's affair with Grable would resume when he, too, migrated to Hollywood.

Ironically, Desi perhaps could have become a star much sooner had he accepted the role that went to Don Ameche in *Down Argentine Way.* Irving Pincus, the chief talent scout for Fox, was on his annual "hunting expedition" in New York, looking for the stars of tomorrow.

He had gone to see Desi in *Too Many Girls* and made up his mind, on the spot, that Desi was the actor who'd portray Ricardo Quintano. (Ricardo, as in "Ricky," was the name of the character that Desi would one day make famous). Ricardo was an Argentine who journeys to New York to sell his father's prize horses. Pincus wanted "a real Latin" to appear opposite Grable.

Ironically, Desi rejected the Pincus's offer of $1,500 a week. It carried a guarantee of forty weeks of work.

"It was a great offer," Desi said, "but I was terrified of facing the camera. I was just learning how to perform on the Broadway stage, and I was afraid that I'd fall on my ass as a movie star. The critics might mock me. The idea of going to Hollywood intrigued me, but, as I told George Abbott, 'I wasn't ready yet.'"

"We'd hate to lose you from our cast, but you're turning down a break that most actors only dream of," Abbott told him.

A close-up of **"Freckles" (Renée) De Marco:**

In spite of her talent and her frequent bookings as a nightclub entertainer, she never evolved into a Hollywood star.

Style, Razzmatazz, and Grace: Exhibition dancers **Renée De Marco** and her husband, **Tony.**

Tony enforced a very strict mandate: "I never dance with another man's wife." Therefore, his dancing partner had to be either his wife or an unmarried performer.

Desi never really regretted his decision, because while still on Broadway, "I fell in love for the first time in my wasted life as a roving Romeo."

***

One night at La Conga, playboy Peter Arno and debutante Brenda Frazier showed up with the vivacious dancer, Renée De Marco, one of the most agile and graceful entertainers of her era. She was fifty percent of a husband-and-wife team, "The Dancing Marcos," whom some critics asserted were more skilled and more entertaining than Fred Astaire and Ginger Rogers.

"Talk about love at first sight," Desi said. In his memoir, he identified her only as "Freckles," her nickname. He claimed, "She was the most charming woman I ever met. Her love, her tenderness, her disposition were unbelievable. There isn't any doubt. She was my first real love. Suddenly, the memory of the lyrics of a Lorenz Hart song rang true:"

> *"I took one look at you.*
> *That's all I meant to do.*
> *And then my heart stood still."*

Although still performing together as professional ballroom dancers, Renée and her husband and dance partner, Tony De Marco, were heading for the divorce courts. They were hardly speaking to each other, communicating only when it was essential for their performance. She had met him when she was sixteen and he was twenty-nine. While dancing, she was said to be "making love," and he was praised for bringing back the dancing image of yesteryear's most sensuous seducer, the late Rudolph Valentino. The De Marcos had appeared together on Broadway in 1930 in *Girl Crazy* with Ginger Rogers.

The attraction between Freckles and Desi was mutual. After La Conga closed for the night, he headed with her back to her suite at the Hotel Pierre. During the days and weeks to come, he was seen so frequently with her that the manager, when he encountered Desi in the lobby, asked, "Don't you think I should start charging you rent?"

In an interview that appeared in *Variety*, Desi had read of Renée's measurements: Five feet, three inches tall; weight: 102 pounds; measurements of 32-23-24."

As Freckles became more intimately involved with Desi, she told him, "Tony makes more love to me on the ballroom floor than he does in the boudoir."

Desi was soon deeply involved in the most serious affair of his life. "I was still a hot-blooded Cuban, and when the occasion arose, I screwed around a bit on the side. But she never confronted me with any jealous accusation. She just seemed to accept with a certain grace that a man will stray from the love nest."

Years later, he lamented, "If only my future wife, Lucy, had been that forgiving and understanding."

175

Although it was Renée's facial beauty and luscious body that lured Desi, New York fashion critics cited her as the most chicly dressed woman in the city. She designed her own expensive gowns, sometimes accessorizing them with layers of chiffon or sprays of semi-precious stones.

Tony De Marco spent very little time mourning the loss of his wife, quickly signing to dance onscreen with Joan Crawford, with whom he had a fling, when he wasn't "heavy dating" Dorothy Lamour.

When Renée dropped out as his partner, he took up with a ballerina, Sally Craven. As one of her claims to fame, she had doubled for Vivien Leigh in long shots during the filming of Scarlett O'Hara in *Gone With the Wind* (1939).

Renée would head to Hollywood while Desi was still performing in the tail end Broadway performances of *Too Many Girls*. He had already signed as the male lead of its movie adaptation, so he hoped to be reunited with "My Freckles in California."

Entertainment journalist Stella Star wrote that in Hollywood, Renée was hired to tutor Judy Garland when Garland's "handlers" learned that she was the young star's favorite dancer. A dance director at MGM had discovered how to get her to dance with more vigor and passion: "Just pretend you're Renée De Marco."

Before leaving Broadway, Desi told Van Johnson, "The title of our musical, *Too Many Girls,* is the story of my life. Women just throw themselves at me. As I've always said, 'Temptation is something a man should give in to.'"

Renée had a realistic outlook about the disadvantages of a marriage to Desi: "If one day a woman is foolish enough to marry him, she'll have to get used to sharing him. Hell, I bet that even on his honeymoon, he'll at least manage to seduce two peroxide blondes on the side."

She could have moonlighted as a fortune teller.

After the close of his play, Desi had two weeks to report to the studio to begin filming the screen adaptation of *Too Many Girls* in Hollywood. Consequently, he decided to drive across America to see more of the land he'd adopted.

He made it as far as Detroit in a rented car. There, he bought a Buick Roadmaster with a black top, black upholsteries, and an exterior color painted in what he described as "pussycat gray."

In his new, state-of-the-art convertible, he headed West, asserting, "California, here comes Desi Arnaz."

En route, wondering if females in the American West were different from those in New York or Florida, he resolved to sample as many as he could for one-night stands.

"In L.A., I'm sure I'll find out," he predicted.

CHAPTER EIGHT

LUCILLE BALL BECOMES QUEEN OF THE "Bs"

"Love! I was always falling in love." —Lucille Ball.

At RKO's Little Theater, the stage curtain had gone down on a play, *Breakfast for Venora,* starring Lucille Ball. After her performance, she went to her dressing room and was soon followed by the play's director, Lela Rogers, mother of Ginger. She carried a bouquet of roses, Lucille's favorite flower.

"I've come to say goodbye," Lela said. "After two years of working with you, I've taught you all I know. The studio is sending over new girls, each dreaming of stardom, for me to work with."

Knowing that the time had come to end their working relationship, tears welled in Lucille's eyes. "I'll always be grateful to you."

"As my farewell, I've persuaded the director, Gregory La Cava, to cast you in an upcoming movie, *Stage Door.* You'll have only eighth billing, but it's a star-making role. You'll get a lot of attention if you pull this off. Stardom will be around the corner. The stars of the film will be my darling daughter, Ginger, and that conceited New England snob, Katharine Hepburn."

In all her years in Hollywood, Lucille had never been cast with such an array of talent: Hepburn and Ginger Rogers, Adolphe Menjou, Gail Patrick, Constance Collier, Andrea Leeds, Eve Arden, Ann Miller, Franklin Pangborn, and Jack Carson.

The plot for *Stage Door* (1937) centered on a Manhattan boarding house. Its tenants for the most part were wannabe actresses, each hoping for that big break. Its script was widely different from that of the stage play that had inspired it. After reading it, Hepburn, who had already seen *Stage Door*

Variety wrote, "There's fire in the players, in the lines that sparkle through the piece like the gems they are, fire in the directing, and it follows, the blaze communicates itself to the audience."

on Broadway, asserted, "Our drama should be titled not *Stage Door* but *Screen Door.*"

Shooting began on June 7, 1937, the same day that Hollywood went into shock from the sudden death of the then-27-year-old platinum blonde, Jean Harlow.

The following day, Lucille met with Ginger, who seemed delighted to be in the cast. Unknown to Lucille, she had just returned from a trip to Manhattan, where she'd begun an affair with a rising young Cuban musician and stage star named Desi Arnaz.

"As you know, Hepburn and I are rivals for the title of Queen of RKO," Ginger said. "I think the time has come for me to wear the crown. Whereas all my recent films have been box office hits, most of Hepburn's recent movies have bombed."

Based on the stage play by Edna Ferber and George S. Kaufman, *Stage Door* had been adapted for the screen by scenarists Morrie Ryskind and Anthony Veiller. RKO had paid $125,000 for the film rights.

W.C. Fields had called La Cava

CHEEK-TO-CHEEK **Ginger Rogers** and **Kate Hepburn** hardly managed to conceal their loathing for each other when they made *Stage Door* in 1937. Kate had utter contempt for "Miss Ginger Snap," and often told friends, "If you have anything good to say about Ginger Rogers, don't say it in my presence."

Kate found herself competing with Rogers for some of the same men—Howard Hughes, George Stevens, Jimmy Stewart.

Kate also went after Ginger's husband Lew Ayres, but Howard Hughes got to him first.

"the best comedy mind in the business—except for yours truly, of course. Both of us are known to take a tipple or two from time to time."

Born in 1892, La Cava had made numerous silent films and had scored two successes with Talkies: *She Married Her Boss* (1935), co-starring Claudette Colbert and Melvyn Douglas; and *My Man Godfrey* (1936), with William Powell and Carole Lombard.

Gregory La Cava is sometimes described as the oddest of the oddball Hollywood directors of the 1930s. He never watched anybody else's films—only his own—and was almost unbelievably unfamiliar with the names of even major Hollywood stars.

"He doesn't know Ginger Rogers from Lucille Ball," Producer Pandro S. Berman said. "I don't dare ask him if he knows who Clark Gable and Greta Garbo are. He doesn't read *Variety*. No newspapers, no fan magazines. He only reads the cartoons. He really wants to create cartoon characters for the screen."

It was only after signing a contract that Hepburn learned that Berman had cast Ginger Rogers as her co-star. Not only that, but Ginger, she learned, would get star billing over her.

Furious, she stormed Berman's office to protest this "outrage." He told her the truth: "You were lucky that RKO renewed your contract after that dismal flop, *Quality Street* (1937). You were awful in it. I can't invest any more of the studio's money in your name alone. I need more box office assurance, and Ginger can bring it. Yes, I'm hedging my bet. We have absolutely no assurance that your name can carry any picture, even a good one if you ever got around to making one. But people will buy tickets if Ginger's name is on the marquee. She'll become the new queen of RKO.

Your reign is over. But in the event that you and Ginger aren't enough for the marquee, I've also lined up some brilliant gals for extra support: Gail Patrick, Eve Arden, Andrea Leeds, Constance Collier. A great team. Even that little whore, Lucille Ball. Mostly we've been calling on her up till now to fuck any out-of-town dignitaries that we have to entertain. But I think that Ball has more talent than shaking her moneymaker at a lot of fat, married bankrollers from back East."

The next week Hepburn learned more bad news: She'd no longer be billed second to Rogers. Berman had reduced her to third billing. Playing the role of *Stage Door's* producer, Anthony Powell, Adolphe Menjou would share second billing with Rogers.

To compound her pain, Hepburn realized that Menjou "at his oiliest," (her words), would be playing a character based on the dreaded Broadway producer, Jed Harris. Hepburn not only detested Harris, but also loathed Menjou ever since they'd co-starred in *Morning Glory* back in 1933. She'd often referred to him as a "right-wing fascist."

When Hepburn once again stormed Berman's office to protest the Menjou billing, he was uncharacteristically rude to her. "Listen, you'd be lucky to get sixth billing in a successful film after your track record." She was devastated.

When Lucille met La Cava again, she had to remind him that she'd been in a picture he'd previously directed, *The Affairs of Cellini* (1934).

"Forgive me," he said. "I don't remember you."

To Lucille, La Cava was a compelling personality with battleship gray hair, and dark, almost black eyes. Despite his heavy drinking, she found him a skilled director of almost boundless energy. He gave her permission to rewrite some

GARBO?
NO, it's **HEPBURN** Shielding her face from photographers (they weren't called *paparazzi* back then), Kate was consistently voted the most uncooperative actress in Hollywood by the members of the women's press corps.

Columnist Hedda Hopper once said, "The damn dyke always claimed that she wanted nothing more than to be famous. Once famous, she went psychotic when someone tried to take her photograph. You figure! Dames. I'm glad I'm not one!"

179

of her lines if she felt she could improve on them.

One of her friends, the photographer Robert De Grasse, told her, "La Cava's face shows all the emotions he's ever felt, both good and bad." Lucille would get to know De Grasse better in the 1950s when he became a cameraman on the set of the TV series, *I Love Lucy.*

In *Stage Door,* Lucille played Judy Canfield, an aspirant actress. The role evoked her own early days as she struggled to find a footing on Broadway.

The plot centers around the Footlights Club, which houses a coterie of poor but beautiful young women intent on a career in show business. Each girl is waiting for her big break.

As Terry Randall, Hepburn, a rich, smug, and self-confidant debutante, moves into the boarding house merely to "soak up atmosphere."

La Cava carefully showcased Hepburn's entrance on the screen, just as meticulously as George Cukor had introduced her to the world in *A Bill of Divorcement* (1932). In *Stage Door,* she makes a dramatic entrance dressed in black with a hat, standing out immediately in the midst of the rapid-fire barrage of dialogue that characterized the other struggling actresses living at the Footlights Club.

One of those wannabes is Judy Canfield (Lucille). In a saucy role, delivering wisecracks, she showed perfect timing. She would win critical praise for her performance, although later admitting to Ginger, "I was not happy with my performance." La Cava had insisted that the girls wear their

Katharine
The Great

a lifetime
of secrets...
revealed   *by*   Darwin
Porter

In 2004, **Blood Moon Productions** published the till-then most revelatory biography of Katharine Hepburn ever printed. Its allegations of Ms. Hepburn's bisexuality were loudly bruited throughout Hollywood and the publishing industry, and discussed frequently, with something approaching passion, on talk-show TV.

Controversial and shocking at the time, and several book awards later, the allegations about Ms. Hepburn's gender preferences are now routinely accepted throughout America, and the book remains widely viewed as one of the best biographies of Miss Hepburn's hardscrabble rise to prominence, ever published.

own street clothes to look more natural. Lucille later sent wardrobe a bill, which they refused to pay.

Of all the tenants in her rooming house, she had the least pretense, telling her housemates, "I prefer *Amos 'n' Andy* to Shakespeare."

Hepburn took notice of her: "I don't think Ball in any way thought she was beautiful. For most of the 1930s, no one seemed to notice her screen work. In private, she always had some male waiting to take her home...or whatever...Even so, I think the girl had 'it,' although I wasn't sure what 'it' was. I'll say this for her: Ball has a lot of spunk."

Unlike the other would-be stars at the boarding house, Lucille's character of Judy eventually leaves Manhattan and heads for the wilds of Oregon, after the other actresses give her a sendoff party.

"My character is the only clear-eyed realist in the batch," her character says. "Instead of exaggerating my talent, I realize my limitations. No Sarah Bernhardt me. My role in life will be somewhere in Oregon, living as a dutiful housewife raising a batch of snotty-nosed brats."

A belle from Alabama, Gail Patrick was cast as Linda Shaw, a wannabe actress involved in an affair with the influential producer, Anthony Powell (Menjou). From 1932 to 1948, Patrick had made some sixty movies, often cast as the cool and aloof "other woman." In *My Man Godfrey* (1936), she played Carole Lombard's spoiled sister. After she quit working as an actress, she became executive producer of the hit TV series, *Perry Mason* (1957-1966).

Starlet wannabees in *Stage Door*. **Lucille**, left, as the smart-aleckey truth-teller, with **Ginger Rogers** and a hard-to-recognize-without-her-tap-shoes-and leotard **Ann Miller**.

Samuel Goldwyn lent Andrea Leeds to RKO to play the doomed actress, Kaye Hamilton. *The New York Times* called her "the real discovery of *Stage Door*," although Lucille had hoped she would be singled out for that citation. Despite of her success, within three years, Leeds would tell Hollywood farewell.

Eve Arden, cast as "Eve" (no last name), was assigned her first major screen role in *Stage Door*. The high point of her film career would come in 1945 when she won an Oscar nod for Best Supporting Actress in *Mildred Pierce*, with Joan Crawford walking off with the Academy Award for Best Actress.

Arden later became a household name when she starred as the sardonic, fast-talking high school teacher in *Our*

Two views of **Eve Arden**. Upper photo: As a dancehall harlot in *Last of the Duanes (1941)* and (lower photo), with Gregory La Cava on set of *Stage Door* holding the temperamental but "plot-central" cat.

Miss Brooks (1952-1956) a hit TV series for which she won an Emmy. *[Ironically, it was Desilu Productions, owned by Desi and Lucille at the time, that ended up producing* Our Miss Brooks.*]* "Thank God our director hasn't walked in and caught me taking a crap," Eve Arden said with her usual arch, wry humor: "The way he is, La Cava would have me dumping the big one in front of his damn cameras."

Ann Miller was the then-newbie actress who portrayed "Annie" in *Stage Door*. Ironically, it had been Lucille who had first "discovered" her. On a date with talent scout Benny Rubin in San Francisco, Lucille had gone to the Black Cat Club, where she spotted tap-dancing Miller.

Later that evening, Lucille and Rubin met with her and told her she should be in pictures. That led to Miller getting cast in *Stage Door*. It was followed by her attention-grabbing role in Frank Capra's *You Can't Take It With You* (1938), starring Jean Arthur and James Stewart. The film won the Best Picture Oscar that year.

Even Hepburn bestowed her greatest kindness on the teenaged Miller, who came to her one day, sobbing. "They claim in wardrobe I'm flat-chested," Miller said. "I'm only fourteen. Mine haven't grown yet."

Although she felt sorry for the youngster, she was horrified to learn her true age. Miller had falsified the birth certificate she'd given Berman after claiming she was eighteen years old. "For God's sake," Hepburn warned her. "If RKO finds out your age, or worse, some authorities, they might shut down production. We might get arrested for employing child labor."

"But I need the money," Miller pleaded. "Please help me."

"Help yourself by not blurting out your true age anymore."

Miller kept her mouth shut about her real age after that.

La Cava took notice of Miller's casual gum-smacking and later improvised a similar scene for her in *Stage Door*.

Miller once told Lucille that while making *Stage Door*, "Katharine Hepburn came on to me real strong. She was impressed with my long legs, I think." Miller also claimed that during the making of Frank Capra's *You Can't Take It With You* (1938), "Jean Arthur tried to seduce me."

Miller once cited the reason she never became a top star was

In her Oscar-winning performance in *Mildred Pierce* (1945), **Joan Crawford** opens a small restaurant with **Jack Carson**, a blunt and vulgar type who tells unfunny jokes and who's always making passes at her.

To the right, **Butterfly McQueen**, as a waitress, repeats her squeaky-voiced, addlebrained maid act of Prissy in *Gone With the Wind* (1939).

that "I never slept with any of the producers." *[Perhaps by then, she'd forgotten about Louis B. Mayer, or else, as the head of MGM, maybe she didn't classify him as a producer.]*

Lucille agreed that it was a mistake not to sleep with producers. "When I start getting a little flabby, I'm going to become a producer myself—and that way I can command any man I want to come join me in bed."

In the minor role of Mr. Millbanks, Manitoba-born Jack Carson started out in vaudeville before ending up in minor roles in Hollywood films. In time, he became a star, appearing in such classics as *Mildred Pierce* (1945) and in Tennessee Williams' *Cat on a Hot Tin Roof* (1958) with Paul Newman and Elizabeth Taylor.

Self-satirizing and fussbudgety, and to modern viewers, closeted but proud, **Franklin Pangborn**.

"Jack really came on strong to me," Lucille said. "He was a big guy standing six feet two and weighing 220 pounds. The jerk wouldn't take 'no' for an answer. I finally had to slap his face really hard."

[In Carson's future, unlike Lucille, Doris Day would be far more cooperative.]

Lucille also met and befriended Franklin Pangborn, whom she found "terribly amusing, with a dry, wry wit." In an era when homosexuality could not be depicted (or discussed) openly on the screen, he nonetheless maneuvered himself into a gay stereotype before the word 'gay' came into common usage. Pangborn was most often cast as a prissy, officious, fastidious, nervous and somewhat fluttery fussbudget used for comic relief.

As Hepburn's roommate, Ginger Rogers played a flippant, cynical dancer named Jean Maitland. In the view of snobbish Terry (Hepburn), Jean (Rogers) was just a chorine of inferior breeding as opposed to her own cultured background.

Facing massive competition from her fellow co-stars, lovely **Andrea Leeds** was cited as "the real discovery" of *Stage Door* by *The New York Times*.

Playing the malnourished, defeated actress, Kay Hamilton, Andrea Leeds, almost stole the picture from Rogers and Hepburn. Leeds attributed her success to "The director treated me like his daughter, bringing out the best in me."

But within three years, she deserted Hollywood.

As the plot progresses Terry (Hepburn), wins a major Broadway role because her wealthy father is the secret "angel" of the play, having provided the money to produce it.

Having competed for the same role and now bitter and disappointed, Kay (Andrea Leeds), commits suicide on opening night.

Although she's a bad actress, Hepburn (as Terry) is so upset by the suicide that, on opening night, she gives a magnificent performance.

Years later, Lucille said, "The way Hepburn talked was terrifying to me. They called it 'Bryn Mawr diction.' I didn't even know how to pronounce Bryn Mawr, much less know where in the fuck the place was. Hepburn never looked into my eyes or spoke to me directly. Sometimes, though, she'd talk in my presence if other people were around. I guess I wasn't worthy of such a *grande dame*. Somehow she managed to ignore me throughout the whole God damn filming."

Constance Collier, an aging and imperial *duenna,* was cast as the superannuated drama coach in *Stage Door*. The moment Hepburn met this heavyset *grande dame*—whose hair had often been described as "gypsyish" in print—Collier became her lifelong friend. Collier had just finished shooting *Wee Willie Winkie,* directed by John Ford and starring little Miss Shirley Temple.

Collier had a wicked sense of humor and "more talent than any actress deserves," Hepburn later said. "From the beginning, we 'bonded at the hip.'"

Noël Coward had branded Collier as "the great dyke of the Western world." *[The very stylish playwright had been in the vanguard of using that word, which would not gain universal popularity until 1942.]*

Although she'd never been a great beauty, Collier personified theatrical glamour. A witty and brilliant conversationalist, Collier mesmerized Hepburn. Coward had yet another appraisal of Collier: "She comes toward you like

IN COMMEMORATION

Four views of a very *grande dame,*
Constance Collier,
a genuine, much-revered relic
of the Edwardian stage.

Upper photo is with **Hepburn** in *Stage Door.*

Middle and lower-right photos are from 1907, when she played a Native American princess in *The Last of His Race.*

Lower left view of her is as Cleopatra, also from 1907.

184

a runaway antique armoire, her mouth oddly evoking a galosh. But once that mouth opens, pure poetry flows out."

Born in 1878 at Windsor, outside London, Collier had made her film debut back in 1916 when D.W. Griffith had cast her in *Intolerance*. Before meeting Lucille, she'd been in some twenty films, mainly typecast as an outspoken *grande dame*.

The theatrical diva had also appeared with the Barrymores in the theatrical version (1917) of *Peter Ibbetson* and as Gertrude to John Barrymore's 1925 London stage version of *Hamlet*. She'd also starred as Charlotte Vance (the Marie Dressler screen role) in the 1932 stage version of *Dinner at Eight*.

Hepburn with **Menjou** in *Stage Door*, delivering the illusion of amiable chitchat from actors who despised each other.

Collier was a charter member of the famous and so-called lesbian "sewing circle," some of whose members included Katharine Cornell, Alla Nazimova, Laurette Taylor, Diana Wynward, and Mercedes de Acosta.

"Almost immediately, Constance became my mother, my mentor, and my drama coach—and mainly a shoulder I could lean on with my many woes," Hepburn said.

She also became her pupil, joining an *alumnae* that over the decades would range from Mae West to Marilyn Monroe.

Even during its previews, Hepburn knew she had broken her box-office jinx and had a good movie on her hands. Film critics have claimed that *Stage Door* presented Hollywood's best spin on backstage drama until the release of *All About Eve* in 1950 with Bette Davis. Movie audiences had never seen anything quite like *Stage Door*. Its armada of female players, including Lucille, each spoke richly and idiomatically, their voices interrupting each other as if to drown each other out.

When the film previewed in Pasadena, Menjou and Ginger Rogers shared star billing. But before it went into general release, after many of the audience review cards defined *Stage Door* as the best Hepburn film ever made, Pandro Berman finally gave in to Hepburn's urgings and restored her to star billing.

After its opening at Radio City Music Hall in October of 1937, *Stage Door* took in nearly two million dollars. RKO officials, however, interpreted the film not as a triumph for Hepburn, but as a group effort, with the added dynamite of a new big name like Ginger Rogers helping to carry the picture.

Both Hepburn and Rogers lost out when the Academy Awards were announced. Andrea Leeds was nominated as best supporting actress, losing to Alice Brady for *In Old Chicago*. La Cava was nominated for best director but lost. *Stage Door* was nominated for best picture of the year but it too lost.

***

At RKO, Lucille met a young contract player who was appearing in *New Faces of 1937*. It was Milton Berle. When he first encountered Lucille, "She was in a pair of white slacks, and I'd never seen a woman in white slacks before. Only Robert Taylor wore them. I asked her out. We danced at the Trocadero. Back at her place, when I took off my underwear, she ran screaming into the bathroom, locking herself inside. It took me two hours to persuade her to come out. I promised I'd be gentle with her."

Milton Berle was called "the first great drag queen of television."

On the left he impersonates Cleopatra. As one critic noted, "Uncle Miltie made a far better Serpent of the Nile on TV than Tallulah Bankhead did on the stage."

His relationship with Lucille lasted for decades. The photo on the right shows them camping it up long after their memories from the 30s lay in their distant pasts.

She later joked to Bob Hope that "seeing wasn't believing."

Lucille later confessed that a romance with the man who became known as "Uncle Miltie" was impossible because of his domineering mother who was always around. A frustrated wannabe actress herself, Sarah Gloantz Berlinger was the quintessential stage mother, and Lucille detested her.

She confided to Ginger Rogers that Berle once told her that a hostile actor had challenged him once, saying he didn't believe stories that he was that exceptionally endowed. "Go ahead, Milton," an unnamed friend said to Berle. "Just take out enough to win!"

Lucille's rival at RKO, Betty Grable, once said, "They say the two best hung men in Hollywood are Forrest Tucker and Milton Berle. What a shame. It's never the handsome ones. The bigger they are, the homelier."

Berle apparently was the first person to talk to Lucille about the potential of television, a medium that both of them would dominate for years. The world knows that Berle launched *The Milton Berle Show* in 1948 when many Americans didn't have sets. What is less known is that he was the first entertainer ever to appear on TV in an experimental broadcast—in 1929.

In 1947, there were only 17 TV stations in the U.S., broadcasting to 136,000 sets. Partly because of the example established by Berle's success, by the end of 1948 there were 50 stations broadcasting to 750,000 sets.

Berle agreed to appear on the monthly Lucille Ball-Desi Arnaz show in 1959, the first show of the 1959-60 season. It required a "tradeoff" that all parties endorsed: NBC agreed to Berle's appearance on CBS with the understanding that Lucille and Desi would then appear on Berle's show.

The episode (*Milton Berle Hides Out at the Ricardos*) aired on September 25, 1959. In it, Berle appeared disguised in drag as Ethel Mertz's dear friend, Mildred. He later told Lucille, "For me, drag is another way to get laughs. My drag is too gay to be gay!"

In July of 2000, two years before his death, Berle sued OUT magazine and Century 21 Real Estate for running the 1959 picture of him in Carmen Miranda drag in one of their ads. The caption read:

OUR TEAM OF FRIENDLY PROFESSIONALS
KNOW HOW TO CATER TO ROYALTY.
AFTER ALL, EVERY QUEEN DESERVES A CASTLE.

In his lawsuit, Berle cited a violation of privacy and defamation, claiming that every "reasonable person looking at the ad would think I was a homosexual." According to the prostitutes of Polly Adler's famous whorehouse in New York City, Berle was "very straight and very big," although the madam heard that he'd once had a brief roll in the hay with Bob Hope in their younger, more sexually experimental days.

Lucille once said that her biggest laugh once came when Berle introduced her at the Friars Club. He announced to the rowdy audience that he would wear kid gloves and have a silken tongue when he honored Lucille. "So here she is—Lucille Testicle!"

***

Lucille always claimed that she never liked pretty boys and proof of that came when she started having affairs with both Broderick Crawford and Paul Douglas. "Even though she was trying to get Broderick to marry her," Ann Miller once said, "she was often arranging two dates in one night with both of them—but never at the same time, of course."

Douglas had come to Hollywood to break into films in the late 1930s, but it would be 1949 before he got his big break in Joseph L. Mankiewicz's *A Letter to Three Wives*, playing Linda Darnell's husband. Lucille called him a "likable lug," and in time would pronounce him a cross between William Bendix and Wallace Beery. She also said he "was great sex—missionary position, nothing too experimental."

Lucille found it a "hoot" that Douglas had rejected the role of Harry Brock in *Born Yesterday* (1950), which brought screen immortality to her other lover, Broderick Crawford. In memory of times gone by, Lucille sometimes employed him. One of the gigs he accepted included his appearance in a 1959 episode of *The Lucy-Desi Comedy Hour*.

Broderick Crawford is mainly remembered today for his machine-gun delivery of dialogue in *Born Yesterday* in 1950, in which he co-starred with

Judy Holliday, who beat out Bette Davis (*All About Eve*) and Gloria Swanson (*Sunset Blvd.*) to win the Oscar.

In 1949 Crawford won the Oscar for his leading role in *All the King's Men*, his character based on the spectacularly corrupt Louisiana governor Huey Long. In a disappointing 2006 remake, Sean Penn's portrayal of the Huey Long role which Crawford had originally made famous was generally viewed as unsuccessful.

Paul Douglas, who looked a lot like, and emoted a lot like....(see below)

According to Crawford, "It was my mother, the actress, Helen Broderick, who arranged for me to go out with Lucille. "I fell for the hot tamale that very night at the Cocoanut Grove."

Soon, Crawford and Lucille became a fixture at Hollywood clubs.

"I wanted her the first night I went out with her, but she held me off for a while," Crawford claimed. "I finally got her up to my apartment one night, where she turned out to be a wildcat."

As she recalled, "Broderick was very much like the character he played on screen, burly and brutish, but sexy in some remote kind of way."

"You might call me a pugilist," Crawford said. "I could play villains and tough guys. When I made *Seven Sinners* (1940), with Marlene Dietrich and John Wayne, I think the director had me beat up fifty guys. I became a tough guy when I dropped out of Harvard after three weeks and became a stevedore on the New York docks."

Broderick Crawford, shown here aimiably interacting with **Lucille Ball.**

According to Crawford, "Paul Douglas and I showed the world you didn't have to be a pretty boy to become a movie star."

Lucille's affair with Crawford heated up enough to talk about a possible marriage. He even went so far as to give her an engagement ring.

"At the last minute," Lucille said, "I chickened out and didn't go rolling down the aisle with him. It wouldn't have worked out because he was drunk most of the time. But we had some really fine rolls in the hay. That was one man who really knew what to do with a woman when he was sober, which wasn't all that often."

During their dating, Crawford was known to the Los Angeles police department as "Old 502," the California radio code for drunken driving. He was notorious for driving under the influence of alcohol. A policeman tried to arrest Crawford and take him to the station one night, but Lucille talked the cop out of it, promising she'd drive him home.

Hollywood insiders said that Crawford was just a "beard," covering up her secret affair with Pandro S. Berman. In a private talk with author Darwin Porter in Barcelona in the 1960s, Crawford denied this. "Lucille and I almost went to the altar. But she broke it off when her affair with Gene Markey heated up. I'd given her an engagement ring, but the bitch refused to return it. For that, I gave her a black eye."

"With Broderick and Paul Douglas," Lucille told Markey, another one of her lovers, "it's like getting the same fuck twice. They have almost identical equipment and plow the same way. It's amazing. Only difference is, Paul likes to keep his tongue in your mouth all during the screw. You end up swallowing a quart of spit—or drowning. Take your choice!"

After dumping Douglas and Crawford, Lucille took up with Markey, and would entertain the idea of marrying him. This Hollywood writer and *raconteur* had been a Rear Admiral and was known in Hollywood for his talent in attracting beautiful women.

Having just emerged from a five-year marriage (1932-1937) to Joan Bennett, Markey was looking around for another trophy wife. He liked to marry movie stars but told his cronies that Lucille "wasn't big enough a name for me." He married two other trophy wives, Hedy Lamarr (1939-1941) and Myrna Loy (1946-50), although each of these two women had had extensive lesbian involvements.

Lucille found it a "riot" that she was dating Joan Bennett's husband throughout the final year of her failed marriage. "I used to model clothes for Joan and her bitch sister,

The very sophisticated (some said "demented") **Hedy Lamarr** with her new husband, **Gene Markey** in March of 1939.

The big question in Hollywood was: "What did the pudgy and relatively plain Gene Markey have that so deeply fascinated some of the greatest beauties of Hollywood?"

Collectively, they were known as "The Beauty and the Beast." Admittedly, Markey was not overly handsome but as an author, producer, screenwriter, and highly decorated Naval officer, he had brilliant conversational skills and a lot of charm.

The *Washington Times* reported that Markey, soon after he arrived in Hollywood in 1929, "became the most sought-after unattached man in the cinema firmament, so sprinkled with far handsomer, richer male stars."

Before Hedy Lamarr, he'd been married to the sultry brunette, Joan Bennett.

He later married (1946-1950) another screen queen, Myrna Loy.

Lucille Ball briefly fell under his spell. She later agreed with Loy's assessment. "He could make a scrubwoman think she was a queen, and he could make a queen think she was the Queen of Queens."

189

Constance," Lucille told Markey.

Markey is best known today for producing that circa 1937 late-show favorite, *Wee Willie Winkie,* starring Shirley Temple. He finally got it right when he married Lucille Parker Wright in 1952, staying wed until his death in 1980. She owned Calumet Farm, the most famous horse-racing stable in Kentucky. By marrying her, he became part of America's premier racing dynasty. Perhaps to show off, he invited Lucille and Desi to Kentucky.

Markey once told Desi, "I love racing horses more than I do fucking movie stars." His sexual orientation is listed as straight, although on one drunken night he admitted to his best friend, John Wayne, that "Douglas Fairbanks—Junior, that is—and I did a little sexual experimenting."

Years later, when Lucille encountered Joan Bennett at a Hollywood party, the fading star told her: "By the time you took up with my husband, we were sleeping in separate bedrooms. I don't know what I saw in the son of a bitch. Maybe he had some hidden talent he showed you—and not me. Besides, I've found Walter Wanger."

Old jealousies aside, both Joan and Lucille laughed about their auditions for the role of Scarlett O'Hara in *Gone With the Wind,* which they both lost to Vivien Leigh. "In the case of Vivien, it was type-casting," Bennett told Lucille. "A bitch cast as a bitch."

A few months later Lucille was saddened when a gunshot in 1951 brought a screeching halt to Joan's movie stardom. While she and her agent, Jennings Lang, sat in a parked car outside Marlon Brando's apartment, Joan's jealous husband, Walter Wanger, showed up with a pistol. He accused Lang of being a home wrecker and shot him in the testicles. De-balled, Jennings survived, but Wanger served 100 days in a minimum-security prison. Regrettably the studios, blaming Joan, blacklisted her. She told the press, "It was almost like I pulled the trigger myself."

***

In 1937, Lucille launched her longest-running pre-Arnaz affair with the Boston-born director Alexander Hall, a noted helmer of light comedies who is best known today for that charming fantasy, *Here Comes Mr. Jordan* (1941). He had divorced Lola Lane the year before he began dating Lucille.

Born in 1894, Hall was older than Lucille. She was impressed that he'd made his stage debut at the age of four. She was a much experienced 26 when she took up with this 43-year-old director.

Hall was not known as a nice man, and he and Lucille had knock-down, drag-out fights. "She was just rehearsing for her marriage to Desi," Ann Miller said. Rumor had it that on a weekend visit to Hall's ranch, Lucille fired a gun at him, wounding him. He was rushed to the nearest hospital, where he claimed some hunter had accidentally shot him in the arm.

Hall liked to show off Lucille in front of his friends, and it is said that she learned many tricks from his show business cronies, which she would later use in her *I Love Lucy* series. On weekends with him at his 75-acre

190

turkey ranch in in the Simi Valley, she often tended barbecue at the parties he hosted for George Burns, Gracie Allen, Charles Ruggles, Fred Allen, Buster Keaton, Arthur Treacher, and Eddie Sedgwick who had directed *The Keystone Kops*. Even though she learned old vaudeville tricks from this clan, Lucille told them that the way to stardom for her would be through dramatic roles, claiming she didn't have the right timing to become a *comedienne*.

Although officially engaged to Hall, Lucille continued to date and have her flings, but, as she told Ginger, she was still "looking for the love of my life. When I see him, I'll know him at once."

***

While flitting from picture to picture, especially during the late 1930s, Lucille spent her nights making love. "It wasn't exactly a *beau du jour,* she said. "Some dudes stuck around a little longer for fun and games. *'Love 'em and leave 'em,'* I always said back then."

One afternoon, a Latin lover entered Lucille's overscheduled life. As it turned out, Desi Arnaz would not be her first conquest in this genre.

His name was Gilbert Roland, and it was love at first sight. Born in Mexico, he grew up wanting to become a bullfighter. But when all the girls told him he was handsome enough to become a film star, he moved to Los Angeles to break into the movies, beginning with a bit part in *The Lady Who Lied* in 1925. In it, he was billed by his real name of Luis de Alonso.

The leading female stars of that day, including Norma Talmadge, heard of his charm

Lucille's most unlikely candidate for romance was director **Alexander Hall.**

Lucille's love affair began late in 1937 when she was 26 years old. Hall, a riper 43, had been twice divorced. He was enjoying success for having directed Shirley Temple in *Little Miss Marker* (1934). Author Kathleen Brady said that the director's "slicked back hair and his pouchy eyes gave him the face of a disengaged owl."

Garson Kanin suggested that Lucille was dating Hall just to advance her career. "The man was a beast. He okayed one script that had a black man spitting in another's face. When I protested, Hall said, 'What in the hell do you mean? It's nigger to nigger, isn't it?'"

and "bedside manner," and were in hot pursuit of him. Soon he was seducing "legends," including Clara Bow, who whipped him in *Call Her Savage* (1932), and Mae West for whom he performed gigolo duties both on and off the screen during the filming of *She Done Him Wrong* (1933).

Constance Bennett had appeared with Roland in *Our Betters* in 1933. Their love affair was on again, off again as the years went by. It wasn't until Lucille met Desi that Constance finally "won." She married Roland in 1940, a union that lasted for five troubled years.

Roland always maintained a soft spot for Lucille and would sometimes stop over for the night when Desi was on the road with his band and shacking up with show-girls.

***

During the filming of Lucille's next picture, *Having Wonderful Time,* released in 1938 by RKO, she encountered familiar faces. Alfred Santell, its director, had recently helmed her in *Winterset.* In her picture, *Stage Door,* she had worked with Eve Arden, Ann Miller, and Jack Carson. *[Carson continued to pursue her, and she still rejected him. "I just don't find you sexy at all," she told him.]*

As the autumn

Two views of **Gilbert Roland,** one of them with **Constance Bennett.** In reference to their five-year marriage (1941-46), Hollywood cynics said he he had become the screen queen's most recent accessory and ornament.

Roland was always aware of his good looks. In his maturity he said, "I was devastatingly handsome, but as a young man just escaping boyhood, I was more beautiful than any girl." George Cukor directed both Gilbert and Constance Bennett in *Our Betters* (1933).

When Cukor encountered Lucille, she said, "*Amigo* told me that I was much better in bed than that bitch, Constance, and I believe him."

Lucille had previously dubbed Gilbert "*Amigo,*" a nickname that stuck.

winds of 1937 were blowing, cast and crew were driven to Big Bear Lake in the San Bernardino Mountains of California. "At seven thousand feet, I felt on top of the world," Lucille said. "At least before I went back to Hollywood, where everybody kisses your cheek and tells you how much they adore you while stabbing you in the ribs."

Actually, those western mountains were a substitute for the Catskills of New York, where the original Broadway play by Arthur Kober had been set.

Kober had agreed to write its screenplay but ran into trouble with the censors. The play on which his screenplay had been based was populated with mostly Jewish characters, the main demographic then visiting the Catskills, but censors objected to the "*risqué* Jewish dialogue and idiomatic slang" in the play.

RKO ordered Santell and Kober to render the characters into Gentiles. The two leads had already been assigned to Ginger Rogers and Douglas Fairbanks Jr. Kober had to change their names: The character played by Ginger was changed from Teddy Stern to Teddy Shaw; Fairbanks' from Chick Kessler to Chick Kirkland. *[In its original Broadway incarnation, John Garfield had portrayed that character as Jewish.]*

Robert De Grasse, the future cameraman of the TV series, *I Love Lucy,* also photographed *Having Wonderful Time.*

At the summer camp where the dynamics unfold, Lucille was cast as Miriam, the cabin mate of Ginger. She has her flirtatious eye trained on Buzzy Armbruster, who seems to have his fickle eye trained on every pretty girl at the camp in that role. Lew Bowman played a successful New York businessman who rents his own private cabin.

Lucille also met and worked with her future co-star, Red Skelton, who was making his movie debut. "The big bosses at RKO did not appreciate Skelton's broad, slapstick style, and they sliced his part down to the barest minimum," Fairbanks said.

She was very attracted to Fairbanks, Jr. who had had a recent hit in *The Prisoner of Zenda* (1937). Previously married to Joan Crawford, he was the son of Douglas Fairbanks, Sr., the long-reigning swashbuckler of the Silent Screen, previously married to Mary Pickford. Lucille had first seen the young actor and had developed a crush on him when she went to see him in *A Woman of Affairs* (1928), a silent movie co-starring Greta Garbo and John Gilbert.

Over lunch with Ginger and Lucille, Fairbanks told them, "Hollywood has become a grind for me. I had some years where I turned out five, even six pictures. Some of them looked okay on paper, but when they came out, they were so bad they were listed as second stringer features, an 'also ran.' Only occasionally would I get a part I liked, such as when I appeared with Katharine Hepburn in *Morning Glory* (1933)."

"I go up a few rungs on the ladder, then fall back three. There's nothing stable about a career in Tinseltown."

At first, Lucille was jealous about how **"Ginger Rogers stole Doug from me"** during the filming of *Having a Wonderful Time* (1938). She was referring to **Douglas Fairbanks, Jr.**

Lucille was attracted to the handsome young actor, but became angry at him during the farewell party for the cast and crew.

"He came right up to me and put his hand in my bra. He felt my tits before suggesting I should have used ice on my nipples before attending the party."

"He claimed that his former wife, Joan Crawford, did that before making an entrance."

"You can say that again, kiddo," Lucille archly replied.

"When I told my Dad I was going to become a movie star like him, he shot back, 'There's only one Douglas Fairbanks!'"

Lucille found Fairbanks charming, sophisticated, and attractive. The press referred to him as a *bon vivant* and raconteur, dubbing him the American Prince of Wales. Over a period of years, he would become known for his powers of seduction, bedding such formidable women as Tallulah Bankhead, Marlene Dietrich, and Rita Hayworth.

"Jack Warner claims I have 'too many faggot friends,'" Fairbanks lamented. "But I've learned to go out clubbing with a coterie of elegant homos while avoiding their boudoirs. Laurence Olivier, Clifton Webb, and Noël Coward come to mind."

[A few years before, Coward had written his famous song, "Mad About the Boy," as an ode to Fairbanks, Jr.]

In his memoir, *Salad Days*, Fairbanks wrote: "Both Ginger and I were adept at imitating Brooklyn-born accents as well as local Jewish slang uttered by residents of New York's boroughs. But when the picture was previewed in the Middle West, few could understand the language. RKO recalled the picture and had us dub it with our own voices. Abroad, European audiences were mystified by this *N'Yawk* pilgrimage (*haji*) to the Catskills."

He also added that Lucille was a hit in her small supporting role in *Having Wonderful Time* and that "Ginger and I got along happily and well."

"There was more to it than that," Lucille quipped. "When not needed on the set, Ginger and Doug would spend long hours in her dressing room...perhaps he was just helping her put on her lipstick. I adored Ginger but was jealous of her for stealing this handsome hunk from me."

Who was **Lee Bowman**? A forgotten name today, he never rose above the status of second-tier leading man. He is seen above starring opposite **Susan Hayward** in *Smash-Up: The Story of a Woman* (1947), her breakthrough role after a decade in Hollywood.

At a party, she compared notes with Lucille about Bowman: "I found going to bed with him as uninspired as having sex with my husband, Jess Barker. Frankly, I'd like to fry both of them in deep fat."

In his memoir, Fairbanks wrote, "There was never anything romantic between Ginger and me."

When Lucille heard that, she said, "If you believe that, I have this bridge to Brooklyn, and I'll sell it to you for only a hundred dollars."

After losing Fairbanks to Ginger, Lucille turned her romantic radar onto another handsome actor, Lee Bowman, who had made his film debut that year in *I Met Him in Paris* (1937) for Paramount. "I got to him before Rita Hayworth devoured him in *Cover Girl* (1944). Poor Lee always dreamed of bigtime stardom, but usually ended up as the third lead who loses the girl at the end."

"I had three dates with Lee," Lucille confessed to Ginger. "How was it? Let's settle for satisfactory."

[After his screen career faded, Bowman often turned to radio and also appeared on Broadway. He was the original actor who played Lucille's mate in a pilot for My Favorite Husband *on CBS Radio in 1948. However, he was not available for*

the full series when CBS eventually greenlighted the project. The role went to Richard Denning.]

When *Having Wonderful Time* opened at Manhattan's Radio City, *The New York Daily News* found that Lucille "turns in another grand performance," a reference to her previous role in *Stage Door. The New York Times* claimed, "Ball is faultless as Miriam, one of the harpies."

On a negative note, *Variety* found that "much of the charm, romantic tenderness, and social problems featured in Kober's stage play are missing in the screen version."

***

In the late 1930s, Lucille sustained a brief fling with the Irish actor, Brian Donlevy, the son of a whiskey distiller. The affair was short and relatively insignificant, but Mart Martin's book, *Did She or Didn't She?*, lists Donlevy as one of her many lovers.

Lucille dated him at the height of his career, during the course of his marriage to his second wife, actress Marjorie Lane. "But we were in the closet," she confessed to her confidante, actress Barbara Pepper.

With some notable exceptions, Donlevy is most frequently cited for his portrayal of dangerous tough guys, often in trouble with the

"Everyone knows the *cliché*, 'ships that pass in the night,'" Lucille said. "That was the case with **Brian Donlevy** and me."

"He was a movie star. I guess that's what you might call him. He came and went briefly from my life. When three weeks had passed, and I had not heard from him, I phoned his home. Someone on the other end told me, 'Mr. Donlevy will no longer be receiving your calls, Miss Ball.'"

law, from the 1930s to the 1960s. Among his best-known film roles were that of Sergeant Markoff in *Beau Geste* (1939) opposite Gary Cooper. For his performance, he received an Oscar nod as Best Supporting Actor. He lost to Thomas Mitchell for his portrayal of Scarlett O'Hara's father in *Gone With the Wind*. That same year (1939), Donlevy played the villain in that classic western, *Destry Rides Again*, opposite Marlene Dietrich and James Stewart.

At the age of fifteen, Donlevy had run away from his Wisconsin home and lied about his age so he could join General Pershing's army in the fight against Mexico's revolutionary, Pancho Villa. During World War I, Donlevy was a pilot in France for the Lafayette Escadrille.

After military service, he worked on Broadway before going to Hollywood. In one of his first screen appearances, he had an uncredited part in *Monsieur Beaucaire* (1924) opposite Rudolph Valentino.

From that point on, he was cast in film after film. Another career highlight occurred when Cecil B. De Mille cast him in *Union Pacific* (1939) opposite Barbara Stanwyck and Joel McCrea. The following year, he was assigned the title role of *The Great McGinty* at Paramount, marking the directorial debut of Preston Sturges.

"Of all the actors I ever met, and I've met thousands, Brian (Donlevy) was the only one I ever heard claim 'I stink in all my pictures,'" Lucille said. "Of course, that wasn't true, but I appreciated his modesty. Nearly all actors I've known tell me how great they are."

"Brian was my secret date and a lot of fun as we went to out-of-the-way places where we wouldn't be recognized," Lucille confessed to Pepper, not the most discreet of witnesses.

"He knew how to bed a lady. He had his physical flaws, however. He was short so he wore platform shoes. He ate and drank too much, which gave him a bit of a gut, which he concealed on camera by wearing a girdle. That wavy brown hair of his was actually a *toupée,* but his flashing smile was winning, as were those piercing blue eyes. The teeth were false like those of Clark Gable, but all the junk below the belt was real."

At the time Lucille was dating Donlevy, she was also carrying on a secret affair with another man, a married Cuban with a wife and three kids. She identified him only as "Mario," and gave few other biographical details about his origins, other than a detail about his having been born in Havana.

As she told Pepper, "He worked as a grip at RKO, and after my first night with him, I decided that he was the sexiest man I ever knew. Some men are good for only two or three times a week, some are daily shack-ups. But on one occasion, Mario, within a period of twenty-four hours, went five times. I mean he'd get this sudden urge and had to have it. I was a goner."

"If you ever decide to trade him in, send him over to me," Pepper said.

Her affair with Mario lasted only three months. "After he drifted off, I was left with the impression that Cuban men make the greatest lovers of all. If I ever meet up with

The Joy of Living

In the upper photo, a dumbfounded **Lucille Ball** (left) learns that the breadwinner of her family, her sister, stage star **Irene Dunne**, is turning over her starring role on Broadway to her. Cast as their brother, actor **Frank Milan**, just looks on.

In the lower photo, **Irene Dunne** and **Douglas Fairbanks, Jr.** were cast in the lead roles. *The New York Daily Mirror* found Dunne, "all charm, wistfulness, and womanliness." Fairbanks was reviewed as "an engaging hero."

It did not do well at the box office. Dunne later recalled it as "one of my lesser endeavors."

another Cubano male, he's a goner."

***

Lucille hoped to move up to at least a co-starring role in her next picture, but that didn't happen. In fact, RKO for a 1938 release gave her seventh billing in a comedy called *Joy of Loving*. Her role was not sympathetic. She was cast as Salina Garret Pine, playing the grasping and dependent sister of Maggie Garett (Irene Dunne), a musical comedy star on Broadway. Lucille had worked with Dunne before in *Roberta* (1935), co-starring Astaire and Rogers.

Dunne had won applause for her dramatic role in *Cimarron* (1931). But after she made *Theodora Goes Wild* in 1936, RKO also knew that, in addition to singing, she could also do comedy. A hit song, "You Couldn't Be Cuter," by Jerome Kern emerged from the musical.

On her first day of work, Lucille talked with her director, Tay Garnett. He would never win an Oscar, nor even a nomination, although he'd helm many a film.

He had joined the industry in 1920, becoming a screenwriter for Mack Sennett. Over the years, he'd worked at many studios with many producers, including Cecil B. De Mille. In his future, for Universal, he would direct *Seven Sinners* (1940) with Marlene Dietrich, Randolph Scott, and John Wayne. His best-known film became *The Postman Always Rings Twice* (1946), starring Lana Turner with John Garfield.

He told Lucille that the name of the film he was directing had been changed to *Joy of Living*, as those censors at the Hays Office interpreted the original title, *Joy of Loving*, as suggestive and objectionable.

"Those damn censors," Lucille said. "I gather that a person is to experience the *Joy of Living* without the *Joy of Loving*. When is Hollywood going to get rid of those bastards censoring the slightest thing?"

Two elements pleased Lucille: Her salary had been raised to $125 a week. And once again, she'd co-star with Douglas Fairbanks, Jr. "I struck out with Doug the second time around," she lamented. "Guess I wasn't his type, but neither was Irene Dunne."

Dunne would come to regard *Joy of Living* "As one of my lesser endeavors." However, she went from there into her next picture, *Love Affair* (1939) with Charles Boyer, which became one of her most memorable movies.

During the second week of shooting, Lucille learned that she had been the second choice to play the annoying sister. Ann Sothern had turned it down, wanting more romantic parts. "Ann became my chief rival as a 'drop-gag gal,' on the screen," Lucille said. "First a role would be offered to her. If she rejected it, I got a phone call. One day at lunch, I encountered her in the commissary, and she assured me 'Your day will come.' I hope that day comes before I'm suitable only for Granny roles."

Her director (Tay Garnett) later told the press, "Ball attacks her role like a hungry stray dog who hasn't eaten in three days. Her goal is to outact Doug and Irene, and she is one scene stealer. Actually, she felt trapped in

197

our picture, because RKO had refused to lend her out to two other films she preferred."

[Those "two other films," both released in 1938, included an offer from Universal to co-star with Andrea Leeds and Adolphe Menjou in Letter of Introduction, and Paramount had wanted her to appear in Artists and Models Abroad with Jack Benny.]

During the shoot, Garnett noted considerable tension between Dunne and Lucille. "We didn't click together," Lucille said. "My role was that of a temperamental, money-grabbing starlet envious of my older sister's stardom. I enjoyed spending her money. Actually, I was envious of Dunne and her big success while I had struggled on for most of the decade."

Cast in the movie as a temperamental Broadway star, Dunne earns $10,000 a week, which her greedy family quickly spends. Cast as her father, Dennis Garret, character actor Guy Kibbee had worked with Lucille before on Don't Tell the Wife (1937).

Alice Brady played the mother, Minerva. Brady was the daughter of the famous theatrical producer William A. Brady, and was at the peak of her career, having recently starred as the flighty mother of Carole Lombard in My Man Godfrey (1936). She'd also make In Old Chicago (1938) portraying Mrs. O'Leary, the owner of the cow which started the Great Chicago Fire. It brought her an Oscar nod as Best Supporting Actress. Her career was cut short in 1939 when she died of cancer.

Lucille also found herself working again "with those two old queens" (her words), Eric Blore and Franklin Pangborn.

Joy of Living lost $325,000. Time Out reviewed it as "Faintly tiresome

Upper photo: cover of **Radio News**, April, 1938.

According to **Lucille**, ""[Radio] gave me a name in the trade as a good feminine foil. I could flip a comedy line, which a lot of actresses couldn't do. In radio I couldn't depend upon props or costumes or makeup; I had to rely on timing and tone of voice for comic effects, and this was invaluable training."

and full of flat stretches, but the excellent supporting cast helps."

***

While making films at RKO in the late 1930s, Lucille also made her debut on radio. She began broadcasting with comedian Phil Baker, who had launched his career in vaudeville, later branching out to become an accomplished composer, songwriter, and accordion player.

On radio, he starred in his own series, *The Armour Jester*, for NBC Radio. He would later host a radio quiz show, *Who's Who*, which bombed.

Jack Haley heard her broadcasts with Baker and hired Lucille for his own broadcast series, *The Wonder Show* (1938-39), named for its sponsor, Wonder Bread. Lucille became a regular on the show, which was broadcast on CBS Radio every Friday night at 7:30PM and sometimes hosted by Gale Gordon.

[Unknown even to most of Lucille's devoted fans, she first worked with Gale Gordon on Haley's The Wonder Show *back in 1938. He would star with her a decade later in her CBS Radio show,* My Favorite Husband *with Richard Denning. He and Lucille also starred years later in her TV series,* Here's Lucy.*]*

"Gale Gordon and I became friends for life," she said. "He taught me a lot. Throughout the 1930s, he was the highest-paid radio star in Hollywood."

"That was no big deal," he recalled. "I made fifteen dollars for every show, and Lucille was paid two bucks per performance. We were grossly underpaid. Sometimes, I'd do two radio shows a day. The studios back then were huddled together on Sunset Boulevard, and I could run quickly back and forth from one broadcast to another."

The star of the show, Jack Haley, had been both a vaudeville comic and a song-and-dance man. In the late 1930s, he was a star at 20th Century Fox, earning $3,000 a week and appearing in such movies as *Alexander's Ragtime Band* starring Alice Faye and Tyrone Power.

Buddy Ebsen had originally been cast as *The Tin Man* for the 1939 release of *The Wizard of Oz* starring Judy Garland as Dorothy. As it happened, to his everlasting regret, Ebsen was later hospitalized with a severe allergic reaction to the aluminum-based makeup the studio had applied during his performances in that film.

At the last minute, MGM had hired Haley to replace him, thereby immortalizing himself as the iconic Tin Man seen by millions, many of them young, around the world for decades to come.

"I loved working with both Judy and Lucille," Haley recalled. "I could hardly imagine that those talented gals would become two of the most legendary entertainers of all time."

***

Producer David O. Selznick paid Margaret Mitchell $50,000 for the film rights to her all-time best-selling novel, *Gone With the Wind.* The saga was narrated from the Southern point of view, beginning in the antebellum era and moving through the ravages of the Civil War that left the South in ruins. The story also depicted Reconstruction.

All of Hollywood was buzzing with speculation about who would play the novel's male and female leads, the dashing Rhett Butler and the seductive, conniving Southern belle, Scarlett O'Hara.

Women's clubs throughout the South overwhelmed Selznick's office with demands that he cast Alabama-born Tallulah Bankhead as Scarlett.

Selznick wavered in his choice, pondering whether he should cast a major-league Hollywood star, or perhaps one of the budding starlets from MGM, Paramount, or RKO. He even considered the possibility of assigning the role to an unknown. When news of that got out, young Southern women—many attired in 1860s costumes, often wearing gowns from their grandmother's attics—bombarded him with pictures of themselves.

Various male-female teams were recommended, particularly Bette Davis and Errol Flynn, but then Davis balked at the idea of playing opposite Flynn, whom she loathed.

Among the early considerations were Katharine Hepburn and Myrna Loy. Joan Crawford wanted to play Scarlett opposite her off-screen lover, Clark Gable, who didn't want the role. Gary Cooper was the second leading choice for Rhett, but he notified Selznick that he wasn't interested, either. Ronald Colman, however, told the producer he thought he'd be ideal as Rhett.

Which actor was Margaret Mitchell's choice? To everyone's disbelief, she recommended Groucho Marx, asserting that he might excel at drama, a radical change from his usual slapstick. She also confessed that he evoked her image of the physicality of the character she'd crafted.

Selznick and his associates interpreted her recommendation as "demented."

Norma Shearer over at MGM was suggested, and items about her suitability for the role of Scarlett made the gossip columns. The news provoked an avalanche of mail, denouncing the idea of a fine (Canadian-American) lady like Shearer having anything to do with "a Southern bitch like Scarlett."

Even though she was too old for the role, Miriam Hopkins, a native of Georgia, was recommended. So were many other actresses. The list is long, but a few of them included Margaret Sullavan, Ann Sheridan, Claudette Colbert, Barbara Stanwyck, Carole Lombard, Jean Arthur, and Joan Bennett.

Rising starlets like Susan Hayward and Lana Turner were also in the running. Even the English actress, Vivien Leigh, was recommended, although Selznick didn't know if her British accent could be overcome.

If Groucho Marx had been an improbable choice for Rhett Butler, Marlene Dietrich was one of the most unlikely selections for Scarlett. Joan Fontaine met with Selznick, pitching herself as a Scarlett, but, as it turned out, he wanted her to play Melanie. That role of Melanie ultimately went to her alienated sister, Olivia de Haviland.

For a while, Selznick thought the best choice among established actresses would be Paulette Goddard, but he feared a scandal. Was she really married to Charlie Chaplin?

Pandro S. Berman at RKO was asked to name eight of his starlets as a possible Scarlett. He put his former mistress, Lucille Ball, at the top of the list. She had never read *Gone With the Wind*, but she felt familiar with the role of Scarlett because of all the publicity the character had received in the press.

The starlets, including Lucille, were given several pages of dialogue for Scarlett to read at various periods in her life, including the iconic scene at the end where Rhett walks out on Scarlett and utters the famous line: "Frankly, my dear, I don't give a damn."

Lucille thought she would be completely wrong for the role of Scarlett, but, on orders from Berman, she set out to learn the dialogue for her audition with Selznick. Berman even hired one of his studio's vocal coaches to help her with the Georgia dialect.

En route to her car on the day of her audition, Lucille met a sudden cloudburst that drenched her. With the understanding that the timing of her audition had already been estab-

When Lucille Ball went to see **Clark Gable** and **Vivien Leigh** emote as Rhett Butler and Scarlett O'Hara in *Gone With the Wind* (1939), she knew how wrong she would have been as that film's female lead.

"Pandro Berman must have been out of his mind when he thought I could play Scarlett," Lucille said. "I knew from the beginning that I was wrong for the part. But I went through the audition anyway, looking like a drowned rat."

lished, she arrived at Selznick's studio dripping wet. Inside his office, she met his associate, Marcella Rabin, who, coincidentally, was a close friend of Judy Garland and was recommending Garland for the role of Scarlett's younger sister, a role that was eventually assigned to Evelyn Keyes.

Shivering and soaked, Lucille stood in front of Rabin, who secured a wrap for her and escorted her into Selznick's office and sat her down in front of a fireplace where logs were burning. "You can dry out here. Mr. Selznick is out to lunch but should be back soon."

So absorbed was Lucille in rehearsing her dialogue that she didn't see or hear the producer enter through a side door. He arrived just as she was delivering part of the line: "*Ah do declah, Ashley Wilkes, ah don't foh the lahf of me undastand what you see in that skinny lil' Melanie.*"

Suddenly, she became aware of Selznick's presence. "That's fine, go on," he said.

She repeated the rest of the dialogue, and then rose to her feet. Only then did she realize that she'd delivered the entire routine on her knees.

Selznick thanked her and told her he'd get back to her. He did hear Scarlett's final lines, "I'll think about it tomorrow at Tara. I'll think of some way to get him back. After all, tomorrow is another day."

In one of the many ironies of Hollywood, Lucille and her husband, Desi Arnaz, would one day buy Selznick's old studio. Not only that, but Lucille would take over the producer's former office, morphing it (and branding it) as her own.

More beautiful clothes and another stupid role: **Lucille Ball** with **Joe Penner** in *Go Chase Yourself* (1938).

She played the wife of a dim-witted bank teller. The *New York Evening Journal* reviewed her performance as "thoroughly diverting."

***

At last, Lucille got her long-sustained wish of co-starring in a picture as the female lead. *Go Chase Yourself* was a second-rate farce set for a 1938 release by RKO with plenty of gags and an exciting chase scene.

The New York Times accurately summed it up as "a lively bit of nonsense much in the style of old silent movies that starred Harold Lloyd, Buster Keaton, and Harry Langdon."

That evocative style used in the silent era was the result of the director, Edward F. Cline. He began his career in 1914, working for Mack Sennett at the Keystone Studios, where he was credited with creating, in 1915, the fabled Sennett Bathing Beauties.

He supported Charlie Chaplin in his early short films, and also played a major role later in the career of W.C. Fields. He helmed both Fields and Mae West in *My Little Chickadee* (1940) and also directed Fields' last two movies, *The Bank Dick* (1940) and *Never Give a Sucker an Even Break* (1941).

The star of *Go Chase Yourself* was Joe Penner, who had been a featured player in vaudeville until it went out of style in 1932. Although a forgotten figure today, he was a household word during the Depression, the equivalent of a latter-day Pee-Wee Herman. Born in Serbia, he also became a 1930s radio and film comedian, uttering his famed catchphrase, "Wanna buy a duck?" His familiar laugh was called "a low *hyuck-hyuck.*" By 1934, he'd become radio's top comedian. From 1934 to 1936, he was the namesake and star of *The Joe Penner Show* for CBS. It was at CBS's studio that he met Lucille and was impressed with her comic timing. He asked RKO to make her his leading lady in *Go Chase Yourself.*

In it, he was cast as a dim-witted bank clerk who is kidnapped by rob-

202

bers. Lucille plays Carol, his domineering wife. They inherit a trailer, although they have no car to pull it.

The modest trailer in the movie is a far cry from the luxurious trailer used in the 1954 film, *The Long, Long Trailer,* starring Lucille and Desi.

The screenplay of *Go Chase Yourself* was by Bert Granet, who in later years was hired by Desi as a producer at his studio, Desilu.

June Travis was cast as Judy Daniels, a runaway heiress evocative of the character portrayed by Claudette Colbert in her Oscar-winning performance in *It Happened One Night* (1934). When Travis met Lucille, she had just wrapped a film called *Love Is on the Air* (1937) that introduced Ronald Reagan.

Dick Lane played "Nails," a gangster. He often starred as fast-talking "swindlers and slickers" in some 150 movies up until 1951. He was best known as Inspector Farraday in those Boston Blackie mystery comedies.

By 1947, Lane became one of the first newscasters on the then-novel medium of television, the first reporter to broadcast news of an atomic explosion on TV.

At the completion of *Go Chase Yourself,* Penner requested Lucille as his leading lady once again in *Glamour Boy* (1941), but the cast envisioned by him, and eventually his deal itself, collapsed.

***

RKO had high hopes for Lucille's next picture, *The Affairs of Annabel,* her first really big co-starring part in a title role. The producers hoped it would be successful enough to generate a series of sequels, following a trend set by other studios. Filmmaking began at RKO on May 23, 1938.

[Peppy movies with sequels (a work that continues the story or develops the theme of an earlier film) were all the rage at the time. Ann Sothern, Lucille's friend and rival, was shooting Maisie, *a spunky romantic comedy that led to eight sequels that each focused on the same theme and which each starred Soth-*

Even in this streamlined version of the posters advertising *The Affairs of Annabel,* consumers recognized **Lucille**, who at last was getting name recognition and better roles.

As an actress preparing for her upcoming role as a maid, **Lucille's** press agent, Jack Oakie, has arranged a job for her as a "domestic assistant" with the Fletcher family.

There, as a celebrity known to thousands of movie goers as "Annabel Allison," she must conceal a recent issue of *Photoplay* where her photograph graces the front cover.

ern. At MGM, Mickey Rooney *was starring in the* Andy Hardy *series, and over at Warners, the Dead End Kids were turning out strings of inter-related films, each a continuation of the one that had preceded it.*

Many of them were detective or mystery dramas—Bulldog Drummond *at Paramount;* Charlie Chan *at 20th Century Fox; and* The Thin Man *starring William Powell and Myrna Loy at MGM. RKO even had its own detective series,* The Saint.]

The New York Times nailed the plot of Annabel as an "amusing trifle about an actress and a zany press agent with a Svengali complex. But his schemes backfire."

Jack Oakie as a press agent was united with Lucille, playing an irrepressible, accident-prone actress. Each of them had had supporting roles opposite opera diva Lily Pons in *That Girl from Paris* (1936).

Once again, Bert Granet, long before he became a producer at Desilu, was the screenwriter.

Ruth Donnelly, who had the third lead, had enjoyed a career on Broadway before becoming a film star, often in supporting roles in such movies as *Footlight Parade* (1933).

Lucille had long been influenced by the actress-sisters, Constance and Joan Bennett. *[Even as a model, Lucille had dyed her hair blonde in imitation of Constance.]* But in Annabel, she was influenced by her sister, Joan, a brunette. Lucille darkened her hair and had it set like Joan's.

To complicate matters, Lucille was dating Gene Markey at the time. *[Markey had been married to Joan in 1932, but they subsequently divorced. Markey would later dump Lucille for Hedy Lamarr, then hailed as "the world's most beautiful woman."*

The New York Times wrote that "Miss Ball is rapidly becoming one of the brightest *comediennes,* and in *The Affairs of Annabel,* she plays her role broadly and without a disruptive trace of whimsy."

After it was wrapped, RKO notified Lucille that an *Annabel* sequel was being prepared, and that she would be its star.

Room Service (1938): Every slapstick piece of *schtick* needs a pretty girl as a foil: In this case, and thanks to her comedic gifts, it was **Lucille.**

In 1944, Frank Sinatra and Gloria DeHaven presented the musical version of *Room Service.* Their picture, *Step Lively,* was far better (and less annoying) than the original Marx Brothers' rendition.

***

Director William A. Seiter, from his office at RKO, phoned Lucille to inform her that he had cast her and her friend, Ann Miller, as the female leads in the latest Marx Brothers film, *Room Service,* set for release in 1938. Seiter had directed *Roberta* (1935) in which Lucille had a brief walk-on in a film that had starred Irene Dunne, Fred Astaire, and Ginger Rogers.

An hour later, Lucille phoned Miller, telling her, "We might as well face it: Those Marx pranksters will not only steal every scene, they'll eat up the sets."

In the minor role of Hilda, Ann Miller was the other female in the story. On the set, she expressed her gratitude to Lucille for having discovered her in San Francisco. She was also thrilled at the role she had recently played in *You Can't Take It With You* (1938), a movie Lucille was anxious to see. Like Lucille, Miller had to put up with the off-screen pranks of the Marx Brothers, particularly Harpo, who was always chasing after her.

During *Room Service's* first week of shooting, Seiter told Lucille, "All you have to do, for the most part, is to look beautiful and run in and out of scenes, letting those zany brothers do their *schticks.* You'll also have to cope with their pranks, which sometimes are funnier off screen than on camera."

She learned more about that the following week when a group of priests and nuns, then on a tour through RKO, were invited to the set to watch the filming of a scene. Groucho loudly objected to the presence of "this heavenly brood" but was overruled.

The scene being filmed that day had Lucille enter a room, see the brothers, and then rush off as they chase after her. As an act of revenge for going over his head and allowing "these damn Catholics" to oversee their working routine, he and Harpo stripped completely naked and chased after Lucille. Horrified, the priests and nuns quickly exited from the set.

That "unofficial" clip wherein the Marx Brothers appeared nude was smuggled out of the studio and frequently, in months to come, screened at Hollywood parties. Lucille saw it for the first time at the raunch-soaked home of Errol Flynn. "Harpo," she later recalled, "was the best hung."

The Marx Brothers, born to Jewish emigrants from Germany and France, worked in motion pictures from 1905 to 1949, scoring their biggest hits with *Duck Soup* (1933) and *A Night at the Opera* (1935). Irving Thalberg at MGM had both nurtured and promoted them, but after he died, negotiations did not go well with his successors, and the brothers migrated to RKO.

Anticipating that they would continue with their hits, RKO paid $100,000 for the screen rights to a then-recent hit Broadway play, *Room Service* (debuted in 1937) by John Murray and Allen Boretz.

In it, Groucho was cast as Gordon Miller, a flat-broke theatrical producer who feels he has a hit play for Broadway if only he could find an "angel" (i.e., "investor"). He and his cast are facing eviction from their hotel, confronting past due rent of $1,200, which they cannot pay.

On his staff is Harry Binelli (Chico Marx) and Faker Englund (Harpo). Groucho did not like the script. "My brothers and I usually write our own material and situations. In *Room Service,* other writers created characters that don't adhere to our style of comedy. We can't do gags and play characters that aren't ours."

His assessment seemed right. The film version of *Room Service* failed at the box office.

The New York Post reviewed some of its *schtick:* "Groucho's mustache and rolling eyes *[are]* footnotes in phoniness." *The New Yorker* claimed, "There were no moments that blew the roof off."

[Of course, they wouldn't have said that if the nude scene with Lucille had been included. Variety *noted that there were "some strong laugh interludes."]*

"I was virtually ignored by the critics," Lucille said, "but I did get one review: The bastard who wrote it called me 'leaden.'"

Groucho was never an admirer of Lucille. "She can't be funny on her own. She has to have someone write the gags for her."

During the shoot, it became obvious that neither star liked the other.

She got on far better with Harpo, and would, years later, cast him in a television episode of *I Love Lucy.*

Film historian Kathleen Brady later wrote: "As an actress, Lucille Ball did not have the gift of pretended fragility that Carole Lombard did, the willing suspension of strength of Ginger Rogers, or even the ultimate tamability of Katharine Hepburn."

As his brothers' agent, Zeppo Marx had negotiated a sweetheart deal with RKO. It stipulated that his brothers would receive $250,000 for their work on *Room Service.* He also pitched himself as a future agent of Lucille. He told her to let him know if she heard of any upcoming roles she'd like to play.

In the second of her Annabel movies, **Lucille,** cast as a film star, Annabel Allison, asks her press agent (Jack Oakie) to ride in their train's baggage car as a "bodyguard" for her precious puppy.

A self-styled "dedicated Chesterfield smoke stack," **Lucille Ball**, in a touch of irony, was sponsored during her most successful TV endeavors by Chesterfield's ferociously competitive rival, Philip Morris cigarettes.

She quickly rattled off the titles of three pictures in which she'd like to star, then later noted that he'd alerted three other actresses who "stole the roles from me. Zeppo betrayed me. I never spoke to the shit ever again."

***

In August of 1938, Lucille solidified her position as Queen of the Bs at RKO by making a sequel to *The Affairs of Annabel.* A few months later, on a blistering midsummer day, she began work on *Annabel Takes a Tour.*

Two days later, a luncheon was hosted at RKO where she mingled with other female contract players, each a formidable rival. Spearheaded by Joan Fontaine, the guest list also included Wendy Barrie, the Mexican spitfire Lupe Velez, Sally Eilers, Anne Shirley, and Frances Mercer, who played Lucille's rival in this latest Annabel movie

In it, Lucille was joined by co-stars from the film's previous sequel. Jack Oakie was cast as her "dangerously resourceful" publicist, and character actress Ruth Donnelly played Josephine.

Annabel Takes a Tour was directed by Lew Landers, a New Yorker who had starred in the D.W. Griffith silent drama, *The Escape* (1914). Before helming the first Annabel sequel, Landers had directed a thriller, *The Raven* (1935) starring rivals Boris Karloff and Bela Lugosi.

Although **Lucille** started her career as a "Constance Bennett blonde," by the time she made *Annabel Takes a Tour* (1938), she had switched and became a "Joan Bennett brunette."

Eventually hailed as "The Queen of the Bs" at RKO, this photo made her a star.

The plot called for Lucille to portray a movie actress midway through a promotional tour. To generate publicity, she leaks a story about how she's having a romantic fling with a famous romance novelist, a viscount, Ronald River-Clyde (Ralph Forbes).

[On the set, she shared a reunion with him, remembering how he had set her heart fluttering back in 1934. Her passion by now had long-ago faded. Since her romance, he had married and divorced actress Heather Angel.]

For her performance as the newest incarnation of Annabel, Lucille's hair had changed from platinum blonde to the darkest it had ever been, and her wardrobe had evolved into the most glamourous she'd ever worn on screen.

"Oakie tried to steal the picture right out from under me," she later claimed. "But we remained friends. In fact, he helped Desi Arnaz and me, as newlyweds, find our dream house near his in San Fernando Valley."

Upon release of their picture, which did not do as well at the box office as the first *Annabel, Variety* wrote: "Miss Ball handles her assignment as a film actress in a capable fashion."

Her reaction to that? "Faint praise indeed."

The New York Times reviewed her as "one of the more attractive colloquial comediennes." The *Daily News,* also in New York, called her as "easy to look at and a capable actress."

For a number of reasons, the *Annabel* series was scrapped after its second installment. RKO rejected the salary demands of Oakie, who wanted $50,000 for his involvement in another sequel. *[Oakie, citing the proposed sequel's low budget, eventually left RKO and moved to MGM.]*

During its final week of shooting, executive producer Lee Marcus came to the set to inform Lucille that she'd get star billing as the most important player in *Next Time I Marry*, a film set for release in 1938.

***

At long last, as the decade neared its end, Lucille, for the first time, after years of struggle, would lead the cast of *Next Time I Marry*, her seventh movie of that year. She'd be the focal point of its plot, playing against two handsome leading men, James Ellison and Lee Bowman, with direction from Garson Kanin.

She learned that she'd been the second choice for the role of Nancy Crocker Fleming. Miriam Hopkins had turned it down.

Next Time I Marry is a screwball romantic comedy. As a madcap heiress, she said, "The plot was in the genre of *It Happened One Night*, which had brought a Best Actress Oscar to Claudette Colbert."

Lucille's character stands to inherit $20 million if she marries "a plain American." With that premise, she marries virtually the first Yankee she runs across. He's James Ellison cast as Anthony J. Anthony. Regrettably, the character she plays is in madly love with someone else, a gold-digging artistocrat, Viscount Georgi De Volknac (Bowman). As for the Yankee played by Ellison, she plans to divorce him as soon as her inheritance is secured.

When the money comes through, the bickering All-American newlyweds take a trailer cross-country to the divorce courts of Reno. Along the way, after a series of (adorable and comic) mishaps, they begin to fall in love.

Portraying Lucille's American (new) husband, Ellison never became a matinee idol like Robert Taylor or Tyrone Power. But in 1938, a movie magazine had voted him one of the handsomest actors in Hollywood.

A native son of Iowa, he appeared in seventy films between 1932 and 1962. Although Lucille was attracted to him, he had wed Gertrude Durkin the year before. As it happened, he was still in love with his new wife, and wasn't playing the field like so many other leading men of that era.

Much of his career to that point

According to the plot of *Next Time I Marry*, when Anthony J. Anthony (**James Ellison**) marries heiress Nancy Crocker-Fleming (**Lucille**), he is mocked in the press as "Cinderella Man."

She hated this scene. "It was shot outdoors in 110°F heat. and I was wearing a fur coat.

had been spent "riding high in the saddle" as the sidekick of Hopalong Cassidy (William Boyd). Ellison's biggest role to date had been as Buffalo Bill in Cecil B. De Mille's *The Plainsman* (1936), co-starring Gary Cooper and Jean Arthur. Even though the film was a hit, De Mille detested Ellison's performance and threatened to use his power to destroy his screen career.

At the time that the actor worked with Lucille, he had completed *Vivacious Lady* (1938) with her friend, Ginger Rogers and James Stewart. A few months later, he'd be cast again as a co-star with Lucille.

Bowman had worked before with Lucille on *Having Wonderful Time* (1938), the comedy that had starred Rogers and Douglas Fairbanks, Jr.

Once again, Lucille and Bowman had "a couple of dressing room flings," according to Ellison.

Director Kanin had once led his own band, The Red Hot Peppers, and had pursued an acting career, although he became better known as a director and playwright.

Kanin directed his first film when he was only twenty-six, in the same year he met Lucille, *A Man to Remember*. It was later hailed as one of the best movies of 1938.

In 1942, he married actress Ruth Gordon, who became his collaborator on screenplays such as *Adam's Rib* (1949) starring Spencer Tracy, Katharine Hepburn, and Judy Holliday.

In future years, Lucille would meet with him, urging him to help get her cast as the daffy blonde in *Born Yesterday,* a film adaptation of his 1946 play with the same name. *[Kanin preferred Holliday for the role. As mentioned before, for her performance, Holliday went on to win the Best Actress Oscar of 1950, beating out stiff competition from Gloria Swanson in* Sunset Blvd. *and Bette Davis in* All About Eve.*]*

Next Time I Marry was released on December 9, 1938 as RKO's final offering for that (movie-packed) year. Each of the leading newspapers of New York reviewed it. *The New York Times* said, "The former lanky and glass-eyed *comedienne,* Lucille Ball, has prettied herself up, put her eyebrows on in the wrong place, and everything."

The *Daily News* found that "Miss Ball has individuality and wears smart clothes exceptionally well. She's a very interesting addition to Hollywood's roster of madcap heiresses."

The *Post* found her "as screwy and spoiled as any of Hollywood's poor little rich girls."

When Lucille read these critiques, she said, "With reviews like this, I'm going nowhere."

***

Even though 1938 was coming to an end, Lucille would be assigned two more films during what was later historically defined as the busiest year of her life.

Beauty for the Asking, set for a 1939 release, teamed her with two handsome leading men, Patric Knowles and Donald Woods, with her taking star billing. All of them were under the direction of Glenn Tryon.

So many screenwriters were involved in the final production that Lucille said, "We never knew who wrote what."

She was cast as a beautician, Jean Russell, her character obviously inspired by those hawkers of beauty products, Elizabeth Arden and Helena Rubinstein.

The pre-publicity at RKO touted the film as "an *exposé* of the beauty racket," which it really wasn't. It was more like any other love triangle whose genre was familiar to movie audiences of the 1930s.

Originally, this story of manufactured glamour was called *The Glorious Graft*, its title later altered to *The Beauty Racket*.

As a casting oddity, a minor actress from Texas, Leona Maricle, played a character named Eve Harrington. That name became associated with one of the most famous roles in movie history when Anne Baxter played Eve Harrington in *All About Eve* (1950). In it, she competed with her co-star, Bette Davis, for the Best Actress Oscar that year.

Beauty for the Asking's director, Glenn Tryon, a son of Idaho, began his career as an actor in silent films, starring in *Her Dangerous Path* in 1923. When his career waned, he turned to screenwriting and directing.

The producer, B.F. Fineman, told him that Lucille might develop into "another Gail Patrick," no great compliment.

Lucille was delighted with her role in that it evoked her goal as a teenager back in Jamestown, when she wanted to grow up to become a beautician. In her childhood home, she had organized her own little beauty salon, inviting her girlfriends at school to come over for "makeovers."

As the movie opens, Jean Russell (Lucille) has

Lucille never got to pursue her original career goal as a beautician, but she got to play one in *Beauty for the Asking*.

A beautician at last (at least on the screen), she turns an anti-wrinkle cream into a cosmetics empire.

As "cosmetics queen," Jean Russell (**Lucille**), fans wondered if she'd been inspired by Elizabeth Arden or Helena Rubinstein.

The photo above was widely displayed in the lobbies of movie theaters nationwide. Although Lucille is in the arms of fortune-hunting **Patric Knowles** (left), she casts a wistful eye at the man who really loves her, **Donald Woods** (right).

been romanced by Denny Williams (Patric Knowles) for three years. To her chagrin, as a gold-digger, he dumps Jean to marry a multi-million-dollar heiress, Flora Barton-Williams, played by Frieda Inescort.

Jean then becomes involved with Jeff Martin (Donald Woods) an advertising executive who helps turn her invented cold cream into a million-dollar business.

Coincidentally, the investor in her "fiscally appealing" new company is none other than the heiress, Flora, who is unaware that her husband had ever been romantically involved with Jean. Denny (Knowles) comes back into Jean's (Lucille's) life, professing love for her and telling her he never really loved his (wealthy) new wife.

By now, the audience has figured out the future of this cosmetics-soaked love triangle. Will Jean take Denny, the cad, back into her life? Or will she build her dreams with Jeff, the advertising genius who has fallen in love with her?

During the course of its filming, Lucille worked smoothly with her two leading men without getting romantically involved. Knowles had been born in Yorkshire, England, and exported to Hollywood to play Kay Francis' married lover in *Give Me Your Heart* (1936). That same year, he was cast as Errol Flynn's younger brother in *The Charge of the Light Brigade*. He worked with the swashbuckler again in *The Adventures of Robin Hood* (1938). Critics often referred to his roles in the films as "second fiddle."

Donald Woods, who had migrated to Hollywood from Manitoba, Canada in 1928, was the centerpiece of a career that spanned six decades. Most of his career was spent in B pictures, but he did get feature roles in two classics, *A Tale of Two Cities* (1935) and *Anthony Adverse* (1936). Like Lucille herself, he would become known for his vast career on TV, joining the new medium early in 1951.

Critic Leonard Matlin found that *Beauty for the Asking* "suggested an unusual feminist viewpoint for its time, and that "Ball delivers a strong performance." The *New York Evening Journal* called Lucille "one of Hollywood's most promising players."

Variety noted that she showed promise but might not get anywhere unless her scripts improved.

The *New York Daily News* wrote, "Miss Ball rises high enough above the material to remind us that she is the stuff stars are made of."

Variety also announced that Lucille was set to star in another comedy with Joe Penner. Entitled *Glamour Boy,* it was eventually released, with an entirely different cast, in 1941.

In lieu of that, Penner went on to make a movie, *The Day the Bookies Wept,* with Lucille's rival, Betty Grable. Grable was still "dating Desi Arnaz on and off."

Before the end of 1938, Lucille would shoot one more film, a total of eight that busy year.

***

For a 1939 release by RKO, Lucille was cast as the female lead in a taut

211

crime drama, *Twelve Crowded Hours,* an interlude in her career that allowed her a respite from romantic comedies.

The lead in the picture was Richard Dix, a former big name in Hollywood. He had launched his career in silent pictures, having been a football hero in college. In 1923, he became well-known when he starred in Cecil B. De Mille's grandiose silent film, *The Ten Commandments.*

When talkies came in, he made an easy transition, winning a Best Actor Oscar in 1931 for his performance in *Cimarron* opposite Irene Dunne.

In a change of pace from all those recent and rather silly romantic comedies, **Lucille** found herself cast as Paula Sanders in this very *noir,* very dark crime drama.

There's a problem: Her boyfriend, Nick Green **(Richard Dix)**, sends her brother to prison for a crime he didn't commit.

Dix and Lucille would co-star in one of her upcoming movies. He was steely-eyed, square-jawed, and solidly built, but many critics noted that he was "beyond his expiration date," and was even referred to as a "has-been."

The third lead in *Twelve Crowded Hours* was Allan Lane, who had played the boyfriend of Lucille's roommate in *Having a Wonderful Time.* Although she didn't get too involved with him then, during the making of their latest film, she dated him three times.

"It was nothing serious," she told Barbara Pepper. "He told me he might get married one day but he isn't really the marrying kind." *[Previously, he had predicted, in front of Lucille, "Probably the day I get married, I'll fall for the maid of honor and commit adultery before my honeymoon is over."]*

She found Lane "good looking, very masculine, and with a great body." He'd been a sports hero at the University of Notre Dame and had done nude modeling for art classes.

"Whenever he wasn't needed on camera, Allan often worked out," said Lucille. "He was determined to keep that body of his in good shape for his next adventure."

In *Twelve Crowded Hours,* Dix played Nick Green, an investigative reporter who mistakenly sends Dave Sanders (Lane) to prison for a crime he didn't commit. There was a problem: Dave was the brother of his girlfriend Paula Sanders (Lucille). Nick learns his mistake and reconciles with Paula when he gets Dave out on parole and finds a job for him. But once again, he is convicted of yet another crime.

Nick suspected that the man behind the crime is George Costian (Cyrus Kendall), the head of a numbers racket. Hot on his trail, Nick is later abducted with Lucille, their lives menaced. But everything works out in the end.

As critics noted, Lucille didn't have a lot of dialogue, but she used her hands and eyes most efficiently, more than she had in her previous movies.

The New York Times asserted that Lucille played her role "with just the appropriate air of somnambulism." The *New York World Telegram* found that she was "exactly what a heroine in distress should look like."

Twelve Crowded Hours emerged as a diverting crime drama that moved fast across the screen, lasting only sixty-four minutes of suspense.

***

Film historians consider 1939 the greatest year for movie production in the history of Golden Age Hollywood. Although *Gone With the Wind* emerged as the Oscar winner for that year's Best Picture, the competition was stiff. Other noteworthy claimants included *Dark Victory* with Bette Davis; *Goodbye, Mr. Chips* (its hero, Robert Donat, won the Best Actor Oscar that year, having beaten the early favorite, Clark Gable as Rhett Butler); *Love Affair* with Irene Dunne and Charles Boyer; *Mr. Smith Goes to Washington* (a career-defining movie for its male lead, James Stewart); *Ninotchka* ("Garbo Laughs"); *Of Mice and Men* (based on the John Steinbeck classic novel); *Stagecoach* with John Wayne; *The Wizard of Oz* with Judy Garland; and *Wuthering Heights* with Laurence Olivier and Merle Oberon.

As these classics were released, Lucille turned out some undistinguished movies, beginning with *Panama Lady*, an RKO release. A quirky irony associated with this movie was her name: In it, she played "Lucy," a character she would make legendary in her *I Love Lucy* TV series of the 1950s.

In *Panama Lady*, RKO teamed her once again with Allan Lane, with whom she'd made two previous films and who she got to know much better during the shoot of their latest movie. Together, they drove to Palm Springs for two weekends in a row, occupying a villa borrowed from a friend of his.

She wanted to know more about Lane's career in movies: It had begun at the dawn of the Talkies when he'd been cast with June Collyer in *Not Quite Decent* (believed, today, to be lost). He made some films for Fox before going over to Warners. With a career seemingly going nowhere, he abandoned his dream of becoming a leading man and dropped out for two years.

But he came back in supporting roles, playing opposite Shirley Temple in *Stowaway* (1936).

After working with Lucille, he would go into the 1940s playing in a series of Royal Canadian Mounted Police Dramas. After WWII, he starred as Red Ryder seven times, replacing Wild Bill Elliot.

The last time Lucille encountered him was in 1961 when he was the voice of the talking horse on the popular TV series, *Mister Ed*.

She knew the director of *Panama Lady*, Jack Hively, because he'd edited her film, *Next Time I Marry*. After helming Lucille, he turned out many more films, including *Father Takes a Wife* (1941) starring Gloria Swanson,

213

Adolphe Menjou, and (surprise) Desi Arnaz. Hively also made the *film noir, Street of Chance* (1941) with Claire Trevor and Burgess Meredith. Like Lucille herself, he eventually drifted into television.

The script of *Panama Lady* was the work of Michael Kanin, the brother of Garson Kanin, who had directed Lucille in *Next Time I Marry. Panama Lady* was a remake of the 1932 RKO-Pathé movie, *Panama Flo,* co-starring Helen Twelvetrees and Charles Bickford.

According to the plot, Lucille, cast as "Lucy," is a nightclub hostess. She is stranded in Panama by her ex-lover, Roy Harmon (Donald Briggs). He is an arms smuggler who pulls a shakedown on an oil rigger (Dennis McTeague) as portrayed by Lane.

Left penniless, Lucy is caught stealing money from McTeague. He gives her a choice: Go to jail or come with him to his oil-rigging camp and work as his housekeeper.

She departs with him to the remote camp, where she encounters a jealous native girl, Cheema, who was cast with Steffi Duna, a Hungarian actress and dancer.

Lucille also met the sultry Evelyn Brent, who played Leonore in the film. Brent was a big star of yesterday who was now reduced to minor roles. Lucille feared that she herself would following her footsteps.

[A native of Tampa, Florida, born in 1895, Brent had been a fabled beauty in silent pictures. Her film career had begun in 1915 when she made The Shooting of Dan Mc-Grew.

In 1922, after success on the London stage, she returned to America to star in some two dozen films. A career highlight came in 1928 when director Josef von Sternberg cast her in The Last Commandment. *That war drama brought a Best Actor Oscar to its star, Emil Jannings.*

Brent's first Talkie was Paramount's Interference (1928), *a picture in which she co-starred with William Powell. She held on in B pictures as her star fell dras-*

GLAMOR OF THE TROPICS!

...THAT FADED INTO SINISTER GLITTER!

PANAMA LADY

with
LUCILLE BALL
ALLAN LANE
DONALD BRIGGS
EVELYN BRENT
R-K-O RADIO PICTURE

Having received top billing in *Panama Lady,* **Lucille** ended 1939 with this melodrama. It marked the eighth film she'd made that year.

Her leading man, **Allan Lane,** was cast as an oil prospector in some remote outpost in South America. As his housekeeper, Lucille fends off his advances, but love wins out in the end.

The actor became better known as "Ricky" Lane, starring in a number of Westerns for Republic.

The "voice overs" he crafted for the talking horse, *Mister Ed (1961-66),* became familiar to millions of TV viewers.

tically in the 1940s. She abandoned her career in 1950, retiring after making 120 films.]

In *Panama Lady*, the oil rigger, Lane, soon falls for his new housekeeper, Lucille, but complications follow when her ex-lover Roy returns to reclaim her. She gets implicated in his fatal shooting.

After it was screened by censors at the Breen Office, *Panama Lady* had to delete several scenes. One censor demanded that references to Lucy being a former prostitute be cut.

It wasn't well received by critics. The *New York World Telegraph* wrote, "Save for the presence of the lovely Lucille Ball, there is little to recommend in this tropical melodrama."

Variety noted that Lucille's "dramatic emoting is a far cry from her more sprightly, recent comedy roles."

The *New York Daily News* best summed up the dilemmas of Lucille's career. "*Panama Lady*, although a bit of a tawdry drama, is another minor triumph for Lucille Ball. But it's high time RKO recognized her potentialities and put her in something more deserving of her ability than the last things she has appeared in. I don't contend that she is Eleonora Duse, but she is one of the most up-and-coming young players around. Even when the story runs amok, in melodrama, she makes you believe in the unfortunate Lucy."

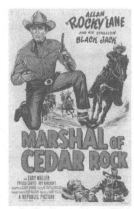

In 1953, a few years after the completion of his films with **Lucille, Allan** (by then also known as **"Rocky"**) **Lane** went on to star in this vaguely remembered B Western.

***

As the 1930s neared their end, Lucille finally adapted to Hollywood. That means she bought her first fur, a "bushy" silver fox with square shoulders four feet wide.

She also hired a personal maid, Harriet McCain, who accompanied her everywhere except out on dates. Before joining Lucille's household, she'd worked for Jack Benny for fourteen years.

Almost every weekday, in Lucille's red Buick convertible, Harriet drove her during the early morning hours to RKO. There, in the kitchen of Lucille's dressing room, Harriet cooked her a "lumberjack breakfast," consisting of eggs sunny side up with a thick juicy steak.

The smell of the food often lured the "Mexican spitfire," Lupe Velez, over to join them. Since she

Meanwhile, **Lucille**—always practical when it came to making a dollar, and perhaps pessimistic about the future of her career—signed as an advertising spokesperson for "Shinola Shoe Cream."

was strenuously trying to diet, she always complained to Lucille for tempting her with such a heavy breakfast.

Occasionally, Carole Lombard would drop by for a visit, too, always amusing Lucille with her ribald jokes. According to Lucille, "Lombard was incredible, so foul mouthed that it shocked the fowl in the air. She uttered such shocking statements as 'If Clark (Gable) had one inch less, he'd be the Queen, not the King, of Hollywood.'"

RKO had already scheduled its tense drama about a doomed airplane and its passengers, *Five Came Back,* for a 1939 release.

Originally, *Variety* had announced that it would star Cary Grant as its pilot and Ann Sothern as a not-very-well-disguised prostitute. Neither of those stars was available, so the pilot role went to Chester Morris, with Lucille once again getting cast in one of Sothern's "sloppy seconds."

In *Five Came Back* (1939), **Lucille** played Peggy Nolan, a beautiful young woman with an immoral past. Her plane crashes in a jungle where headhunters roam.

She is seen holding child actor **Casey Johnson**, and she is flanked by the co-pilots, **Chester Morris** (left) and **Kent Taylor.**

Director John Farrow rounded up a talented roster of players. They included some of the finest character actors in Hollywood.

Its script was the combined work of three writers, two of whom became famous.

One of them, the New York born author and screenwriter, Nathanael West, had become known for two darkly satirical novels, each suggesting that "The American Dream had been betrayed." He'd published *Miss Lonelyhearts* in 1933. When Lucille met him, he'd recently finished his masterpiece, *The Day of the Locust,* published in 1939. Regrettably, West didn't have long to live, dying right before Christmas in 1940. He was only thirty-seven when he suffered a fatal car crash in El Centro, California.

The script's other famous writer, Dalton Trumbo, from Colorado, would become even more famous because of his show trials before Congress, and for his industry-wide blacklisting during the McCarthy witch hunt for alleged sympathies for communists.

Trumbo was usually forced to write under a pseudonym during his creation of such classics as *Roman Holiday* (1953) starring Audrey Hepburn and Gregory Peck. In contrast, for the script he crafted for *Spartacus* (1960), the star of the picture, Kirk Douglas, insisted that the film be credited under Trumbo's real name.

The plot of *Five Came Back* unfolds as *The Silver Queen,* an airplane bound for Panama, takes off from an airport in South America. Aboard are nine passengers, two pilots, and a steward who's doomed for an early death.

As it traverses the Andes, a fierce nighttime storm attacks the plane, and it crashes in a remote jungle location inhabited by headhunters whose arrows shoot poisonous darts.

After many struggles to survive, the pilots manage to salvage the plane so that it can fly again.

As the plot unfolds, the logistics of the salvaged wreck demand that only four passengers and a boy can safely escape. The question is, who will fly to safety and who will be left behind to die?

It was a motley crew who took off in *Five Came Back*. Lucille was cast as Peggy Noland, a hooker with a shady past, who is snubbed by some of the other passengers. Piloting the aircraft is "Bill" (Chester Morris), with Joe Brooks (Kent Taylor) as his co-pilot. The sole steward, Larry (Dick Hogan), will be the first to die as, midflight, he falls through an open door to his death in the Amazon jungle.

On board is wealthy Judson Ellis (Patric Knowles), who is eloping with Alice Melhorne (Wendy Barrie) because their respective families object to their marriage.

C. Aubrey Smith was cast as Henry Spengler, a professor of botany, flying with his wife Martha (Elisabeth Risdon). Tommy Mulvaney (Casey Johnson) is the young son of a gangster who is being escorted by a warm-hearted bodyguard named Pete (Allen Jenkins). Vasques (Joseph Calleia) is an anarchist being extradicted. He's facing a death sentence for killing a high-ranking politician. His guard, "Crimp" (John Carradine), is dreaming about collecting a big reward.

Since this was a B picture and because shooting on location was too expensive, some trees were imported to evoke a jungle. During filming, Lucille leaned against one of them, and almost immediately, a pair of deadly black widow spiders fell on her head. After brushing them off, she ran screaming toward her dressing room. The crew and other members of the cast laughed.

"That was just part of the fun of working with our director, John Farrow," Lucille said. "He was a real brute, very demanding, every fourth word a curse. He also had a violent temper. Nothing seemed to please him. As we tried to get this picture in the can, we had several fights."

A native of Australia, Farrow was married at the time to the Irish actress, Maureen O'Sullivan ("Me Tarzan, You Jane"). One of their daughters, Mia Farrow, born in 1945, became even more famous than her parent as the movie star (her most famous film was *Rosemary's Baby*) who married Frank Sinatra.

On the set, Lucille had a reunion with Patric Knowles, who had been her leading man in *Beauty for the Asking*. Now, he was reduced to playing a supporting role.

Her new leading man, Chester Morris, had made a big name for himself in the 1930s in cops-and-robber flicks. His tough, street-bred mug, with its furrowed brow, flat nose, and round chin, became familiar to movie-goers.

"I've never had a worse co-star," she lamented. "He would not take 'no' for an answer. He was horribly aggressive, sneaking up on me and slipping his hand up my dress. Even slapping his face didn't help. The next day he'd try again."

He kept telling her, "You know you want it, baby, so give in. All you have to do is lie back and enjoy it. I've thrilled stars in Hollywood far bigger than you."

Then hustle your ass back to them," she snapped.

Born in New York, Morris quit school when he was fifteen to star on Broadway, in a role opposite Lionel Barrymore in *Copperhead* (1915). He always claimed that the closeted homosexual made several passes at him. By 1917, Morris made his first silent film, *An Amateur Orphan.*

After more Broadway plays, Hollywood beckoned, eventually casting him in his first Talkie, *Alibi* (1929), for which he was nominated for a Best Actor Academy Award.

In the early 1930s, he starred with many A-list stars, appearing with Norma Shearer in *The Divorcée* (1930); with Wallace Beery and Robert Montgomery in the prison drama *The Big House* (also 1930); and with Jean Harlow in the 1932 comedy/drama, *Red Headed Woman.*

By the 1940s, Morris was reduced to B pictures, notably playing Boston Blackie, a criminal-turned-detective in fourteen features for Columbia.

Like so many other stars, Morris came to a bad end. He was found dead in a motel room in 1970 after succumbing to a barbiturate overdose.

On the set of *Five Came Back,* although he had struck out with Lucille, he hit a home run with Wendy Barrie, cast in the third lead.

Born to English parents in British Hong Kong, she had red-gold hair and piercing blue eyes. She'd become known to movie-goers when she played Jane Seymour in *The Private Life of Henry VIII* (1933) starring Charles Laughton.

In the 1930s, Barrie became a serial seducer of Hollywood's leading men. They included Spencer Tracy, Richard Green, George Sanders (Lucille's future lover), and James Stewart. Eventually, she became the girlfriend of gangster Bugsy Seigel.

Although its director, John Farrow, didn't impress Lucille, its roster of character actors did.

C. Aubrey Smith, born in England in 1863, usually played "officer-and-gentleman" type roles. He was also one of the world's leading cricket players, teaming in matches with David Niven, Laurence Olivier, Leslie Howard, and Boris Karloff.

Few actors in the history of entertainment had as many film and TV credits as John Carradine, a New Yorker. Having begun his career as a member of Cecil B. De Mille's film company, he appeared in 351 productions, many of them high-profile adaptations of Shakespearean plays, horror movies, and Westerns.

Maltese-born Joseph Calleia was an actor and singer on stage, in films, and on radio and TV. In Hollywood, he usually played a villain, popping up on occasion in a classic such as *Algiers* (1938) with Charles Boyer or in *Gilda* (1946) with Rita Hayworth. One of the highlights of his career was his role in Orson Welles' *Touch of Evil* (1958).

Allen Jenkins, a Staten Islander, made his first appearance on stage in a chorus line with James Cagney, who sometimes worked as a drag queen. He arrived in Hollywood in 1931 at the dawn of the Talkies and became a familiar face on the screen playing comic henchmen, stooges, policemen, taxi drivers, and tough guys. *The New York Times* labeled him Hollywood's "greatest scene stealer," and he was also a member of Tinseltown's "Irish Mafia" that included not only Cagney but Spencer Tracy and Pat O'Brien.

The New York Times described *Five Came Back* as "a rousing salute to melodrama, suspenseful as a slow-burning fuse, exciting as a pinwheel, and as spectacularly explosive as an aerial bomb."

Variety found the movie "admirably restrained yet tremendously persuasive."

The New York Daily News claimed, "Lucille Ball gives a fine performance as a mysterious young woman whose interesting past is vaguely suggested." *[The character she played, of course, had a background as a prostitute with "a heart of gold."]*

Time magazine found the suspense worthy of Alfred Hitchcock.

The aircraft used in the picture was recycled as a prop in 1942 when John Wayne made *Flying Tigers. Five Came Back* was later retitled, partially re-scripted, and re-released as *Back from Eternity* (1956), co-starring Robert Ryan and Anita Ekberg, who was cast into the role previously played by Lucille.

***

Lucille's next film, RKO's *That's Right—You're Wrong* (1939), was a musical vehicle for Kay Kyser, one of the most popular bandleaders and radio entertainers of the 1930s and '40s. His show, *Kay Kyser's Kollege of Musical Knowledge* (1938-1949), was one of the first to combine a quiz show with music. *[Its format would be imitated several times in the future by other hosts.]*

Kyser played "The Ol' Professor," who often repeated the show's catchphrase, "*That's Right—You're Wrong,*" which, of course, became the title of the film.

Lucille was displeased that her star status had been diminished to the fourth lead. The top three roles went to Kyser himself, Adolphe Menjou (her former

Almost everyone agreed that **Kay Kyser** (left) would have a hard time "carrying " the romantic lead, of the weakly plotted *That's Right—You're Wrong* (1939).

In an attempt to compensate, RKO commissioned this press and PR shot of him with **Lucille**, hoping that her glamour would lend the OOOMPH he desperately needed.

"most despised" co-star), and veteran character actress, May Robson.

The movie also showcased the band's lead female singer, Ginny Simms, who went on to a successful career acting and singing after leaving Keyser's band.

Menjou played producer Stacey Delmore, who worked alongside his screenwriters, portrayed by Hobart Cavanaugh and prissy Edward Everett Horton, with whom Lucille had worked before.

The male lead (played by Kyser) called for a handsome and dashing matinee idol, which the bespectacled, rather bland-looking Kyser was not.

Meanwhile, Delmore (Menjou) is unable to devise a script that effectively showcases Kyser's appeal, and Kyser plots to get rid of him.

First, he instructs him to dump Simms, as he plans to replace her with the glamourous Sandra Sand (Lucille). Delmore, however, is fully aware that the (somewhat nerdy) bandleader can't live up to his billing as "Casanova Kyser."

He orders a screen test between Kyser and Sandra. For Lucille, the episode becomes her comic highlight in "the movie within the movie."

Expect zany twists and turns before Kyser and his musicians happily return to "their own backyard," (i.e., their hit radio show).

Interrupting all these shenanigans is the guest appearance of two of the leading Hollywood gossip columnists of their era, Hedda Hopper and Sheilah Graham.

Its director, David Butler, a son of San Fran-

Cast as Kyser's Grandma, veteran actress **May Robson**, born in Melbourne before the American Civil War, befriended Lucille.

She told Lucille many intriguing stories of her past when, at the age of sixteen, she had married and moved to America.

Her husband died young, and she spent most of her life in films, cast as prickly old ladies with wagging fingers and tongues.

One of her most famous film clips was recorded when she played Katharine Hepburn's aunt in *Bringing Up Baby* (1939). When she confronted Cary Grant clad in women's lingerie, he tells her that he's suddenly turned gay.

cisco, was also a producer and screenwriter. He'd launched his career working in silent pictures for D.W. Griffith. In the 1930s, he would helm Shirley Temple in four of her films when she was one of the leading box office draws in the world.

Butler also guided Walter Brennan to a Best Supporting Actor Oscar for his performance in *Kentucky* (1938). In time, Butler would direct Doris Day in some of her best-known films, including *Calamity Jane* (1953).

The fifth lead of Chuck Deems, the band's manager, was assigned to Dennis O'Keefe. A one-time vaudeville star, he would, over a period of years, make one-hundred films.

Originally billed as Bud Flanagan, he snagged an impressive small role in *Saratoga* (1937), Jean Harlow's last picture, made with Clark Gable around the time of her death. O'Keefe would go on to play tough guys in the 1940s *film noir,* but he was versatile, also appearing in comedies.

May Robson, born in Australia way back in 1858, was most convincing as Kyser's "Grandma" in *That's Right—You're Wrong.* She'd become a stage actress in 1883, and eventually gravitated to Hollywood, where she emerged as one of the industry's most enduring stars.

Robson had been awarded a Best Supporting Actress Oscar nod for her performance in *Lady for a Day* (1933), losing to Katharine Hepburn. *[Ironically, she would later star with both Hepburn and Cary Grant in* Bringing Up Baby *(1938). Robson had starred in that film right before working with Lucille.]*

That's Right—You're Wrong evolved into a big hit at the box office. That would prompt RKO to cast Kyser in a musical every year until 1943.

***

Five Came Back started out as a "sleeper thriller" that eventually woke up at the box office. After its premiere at the Rialto in Manhattan, it drew so many crowds that the manager started showing it twenty-four hours a day. Even in the wee hours, the seats filled up with a late night crowd, many arriving at the theater drunk after a night of partying.

At long last, Lucille felt she'd reached stardom, and was almost certain that RKO would upgrade her roles, giving her first choice before Ann Sothern. She was provided with transportation expenses and train tickets, with a hotel suite waiting for her. She headed for Manhattan to promote the film.

An executive told her that RKO had bought the screen rights to the Broadway musical, *Too Many Girls,* and suggested that she attend the show because she was being considered for the female lead in its screen adaptation.

For her first publicity stunt, she was sent to Rockefeller Plaza, where she rehearsed a pratfall on the smooth ice of the skating rink. She was provided with a ski outfit—something similar to what Sonja Henie wore in those ice-skating movies. In Lucille's case, it was midnight black trimmed with white fur.

Russell Markert, the choreographer who had launched the Rockettes, was a former beau of hers. He agreed to be her escort during her time in Manhattan, perhaps resuming their long-dead affair. He knew how to rehearse her pratfalls in ways that wouldn't injure her.

But when she didn't follow his instructions, she fell hard on her ass. As she put it, "I heard a loud crack in my sacroiliac *[i.e., pelvic joints]."*

Her pratfall was captured by photographers for the next day's press. There was even a photo of her being carried out of Rockefeller Plaza on a stretcher. She was confined to a hospital bed for the next ten days.

For the evening of the first day of her release from the hospital, Markert had secured front-row Broadway seats to *Too Many Girls* and invited her to see it with him. Anxiously, she agreed, mostly to ascertain if she could play its female lead in a screen adaptation. She'd also heard rave reviews for its 22-year-old Cubano lead, Desi Arnaz, who was supposed to be a sensation. She had long had this "thing" for Latino men.

As she later confessed, she could not take her eyes off Desi after he walked onto the stage. She later wrote about his "broad shoulders and chest" and "his narrow hips in tight football pants," and "how he swayed to the catchy rhythms of the bongo drums."

She told Markert, "The kid has star quality and an electrifying charm."

When he first spoke, she burst into laughter, finding his accent "both hilarious and adorable," suspecting that as a performer, it would serve him well, especially if he ever opted for comedy.

After the curtain went down, in lieu of visiting him backstage, she asked Markert to take her to the Club La Conga. Markert had already told her that La Conga was the hottest and sexiest dance craze in the country.

She was disappointed when she arrived at the club, where a staff member told her that it was Desi's night off. She'd be returning to Hollywood early that morning to report to the set of her next picture.

There, she was told that RKO could not release a film adaptation of *Too Many Girls* until the Broadway musical it would be based on had "run its course."

She realized that her involvement and (perhaps) seduction of this sexy Cuban would, therefore, have to wait.

Both Get The Bandits But Only One Gets The Blonde!

Leathernecks on the loose in the haunted hills of Central America!... Two lusty sons of the fighting legion ...comrades in action but rivals in love ... riding the clouds to glory in a land of hot adventure!

RICHARD DIX
CHESTER MORRIS
LUCILLE BALL
IN
The MARINES FLY HIGH

with
STEFFI DUNA
JOHN ELDREDGE

Power-drive drama... Loop-the-loop romance... Sky-high thrills, down where the senoritas are sweeter, the outlaws are bolder, and a fighting man has room to roam!

RKO RADIO Picture

Produced by ROBERT SISK. Directed by GEORGE NICHOLLS, Jr., and BEN STOLOFF. Screen Play

***

It was October of 1939. The decade was coming to an end. It had been monumental for Lucille Ball, who had, during its course, been cast in an amazing forty-six motion pictures in roles small and large.

Producer Robert Sisk ordered that she be cast in one final adventure yarn. It was his last hurrah at RKO, as he would soon exit from the studio. George Schaefer moved in to take his place.

"Sisk wanted to get the last drop of blood out of me, even though I needed a rest," she said. She resented that she was given third billing, having hoped that from now on, she'd be cast either as number one, or as the leading lady

"The problems we had in the plot of *The Marines Fly High* seemed so trivial when it opened, usually on a double bill," Lucille recalled.

"France and England had declared war on Nazi Germany after Hitler ordered the invasion of Poland. Many movie-goers went to our relatively harmless picture thinking it was about World War II."

in the number two slot.

She was surprised that her co-stars once again would be actors who had recently made films with her: Richard Dix and Chester Morris. "With Morris, I'll have to wear iron underpants to shield my vital zones from his roving hands."

Lucy's next film, *The Marines Fly High,* slated for a 1940 release from RKO, had initially been directed by George Nicholls, but when he died in a car crash, he was replaced with Ben Stoloff, who had helmed her in *The Affairs of Annabel.*

Everyone involved knew that the script was weak, but the cast hoped that all the acting in the movie would conceal that embarrassing truth.

According to the plot, Lucille (playing Joan Grant) is the owner of a cocoa plantation in Central America. The foreman of her ranch is John Henderson, played by actor John Eldridge. She is menaced by a cutthroat gang let by the mysterious "*El Vengador.*"

As it happened, a military outpost of the U.S. Marine is nearby: Joan appeals to it for rescue. Arriving on the scene are Lt. Danny Darrick (Dix) and Lt. Jimmy Malone (Morris). A love triangle develops as both of them fall for Joan.

As it turns out, El Vengador is really the (disguised) foreman (John Henderson) of her ranch. He later kidnaps Joan and sets a trap for the Marines.

To beef up the plot, Danny's ex-flame, Teresa (Steffi Duna), shows up to complicate the life of Danny, who's torn between two rival women. Lucille had just worked with the Hungarian actress and dancer in *Panama Lady.*

During filming, she lunched with Lucille, inviting actor Dennis O'-Keefe who had also been Lucille's recent co-star. Both of them would get married in 1940. Duna would soon abandon Los Angeles for London for the filming, with Vivien Leigh, of *Waterloo Bridge* (1940), a taut tearjerker in which the former Scarlett O'Hara plays a remorse-soaked prostitute.

After the release of *The Marines Fly High, Variety* noted its thin plot but stated that "Lucille Ball again demonstrates she's an up-and-coming actress."

The *New York Daily Mirror* did not find the movie worthwhile "unless you admire pretty faces like that of Lucille Ball."

With her family, Lucille celebrated the end of 1939, Hollywood's greatest year for the production of memorable film classics. "The trouble was," Lucille lamented, "I wasn't in any of the hits. Perhaps I should do like so many other actresses of the 1930s did: Marry a rich man and settle into a luxurious home in Beverly Hills with six servants and a choice of Rolls-Royces to drive me to lunch with ladies who like to gossip about who's sleeping with whom in Tinseltown."

***

Lucille was delighted that her next picture was a comedy and even more impressed with the fact that she'd get top billing in *You Can't Fool Your Wife* (1940).

Her co-star would be the handsome leading man, James Ellison, who'd been her co-star in *Next Time I Marry*. When she'd worked with him previously, she'd been attracted to his looks and manly charm. He'd recently married Gertrude Durkin and at the time, still seemed madly in love with her. Lucille didn't want to interfere.

However, on this second go-around, his newlywed passion for marital harmony had faded, and he seemed more receptive to Lucille's advances. That was true, at least on the three occasions when the cast noted his prolonged visits to her dressing room.

The plot of *You Can't Fool Your Wife* was very complicated. In a vastly different form, it had been depicted before. Actually, it was a loose interpretation of Ferenc Molnár's *The Guardsman*. In 1931, it was a Pre-Code film that had starred the Broadway legends Alfred Lunt and Lynn Fontanne, both of whom had appeared in its 1924 stage version.

It would be the only time Lunt and Fontanne ever teamed in a film together, and both of them would receive Academy Award nominations for their performances. But although each actor was lavishly praised, the picture flopped. In the aftermath, they left Hollywood and returned, as a team, to future triumphs on Broadway.

The ill-fated Ray McCarey was its director. He'd had a long background in comedy, beginning his career at Hal Roach Studios. He worked on *Our Gang* and Laurel & Hardy comedies, and also with Fatty Arbuckle. Between 1930 and 1948, he would helm sixty-two movies.

His brother, Leo McCarey, in 1934, had directed Lucille in a short, *Three Little Pigskins,* starring The Three Stooges.

Those comedians had never impressed her: She agreed with author Charles Higham's assessment: "The idea of comedy for The Three Stooges was tweaking noses with large crunching sounds, upsetting paint pots over

In reviewing **You Can't Fool Your Wife**, *the New York Daily News* wrote: "Lucille Ball and James Ellison, in their second and final re-teaming, are good at comedy, and it's bad that the picture lets them, as well as us, down with a climax that I thought had been put away in moth balls. "

In this tale of suspicious wives and husbands, and, wandering off with a gleam in their eyes, **Lucille** is torn between **Robert Coote** (left) and **James Ellison**.

other people's heads, crushing toes with boots, slamming doors on fingers, and poking fingers into eyes."

At one point during the shoot, Ray McCarey fell ill and had to be replaced with John Farrow, whom Lucille openly detested. The animosity had begun when he directed her in *Five Came Back,* and it resumed on the set of her latest film. Fortunately, McCarey recovered and returned to work.

[McCarey's ill health began in 1940 and would last for most of the rest of that decade. In 1948, his body was found dead kneeling beside his bedside, with two empty prescription bottles at his feet. His brother Leo told the San Bernardino police that Ray had been suffering from ill health for several months. His death was legally defined as a suicide.]

In *You Can't Food Your Wife,* Lucille and Ellison headed a cast of relatively unknown actors: Richard Coote, Virginia Vale, Emma Dunn, and Elaine Shepard.

The script opens when two college sweethearts, Andrew and Clara Hinklin (Ellison and Lucille), have been married for five years. Their life has become unexciting, even boring, and it is not helped by the fact that they live in a small apartment with her annoying mother, a character portrayed by Emma Dunn.

Their dull life is about to change when Andrew is ordered by his boss to entertain a visiting "party animal," "Batty" Battincourt (Coote). His father is a major stockholder in the company. Night after night, he entertains Batty on the party circuit. Clara soon suspects her husband of being unfaithful on the till-dawn-breaks party circuit. She kicks him out, and he moves in with Batty.

At one point, Batty (Coote) meets Clara (Lucille) finding her an unglamorous housewife. He decides that she urgently needs a makeover and transforms her into an Argentine glamour girl with a Spanish accent and sexy clothes.

After her transformation into Mercedes Vasquez— "a hot spitfire from Buenos Aires"— she attends a party where she tries to maneuver Andrew back into her orbit. What follows is a series of deceptions, ticklish farces, mistaken identities, and comic routines. Eventually, Clara (Lucille) and Andrew (Ellison) fall back into each others' arms.

At its cliché-soaked ending, **Lucille Ball** and **James Ellison** are on a second honeymoon at Niagara Falls.

"Our picture seemed so trivial, so lost in yesterday," Lucille said. "All of us, one way or another, would soon be sucked into the most horrendous war of all time. Millions would die."

Although this was Lucille's last movie with Ellison, she'd work with Coote again in 1947 when he was assigned a role in her movie, *Lured*.

The New York Sun reviewed *You Can't Fool Your Wife* with: "The plot is fairly complicated for such a small picture. Lucille Ball has to don a Spanish mantilla and play a dual role. She manages it quite well. Miss Ball and Mr. Ellison keep natural, even in the face of the usual, high-pitched farce situations."

Some critics dismissed the comedy as just another depiction of an average married couple with a mother-in-law trouble.

***

Thrilled with her recent success, Lucille realized that she was no longer getting Ann Sothern's rejected scripts. "The situation has changed," she told friends. "I've come up in the world. Now I'm getting Ginger Roger's rejects."

After a few days back home, an urgent phone call came for her.

The voice on the other end of the line said, "Lucille, this is Orson Welles. It's urgent that I meet with you tonight."

When she wasn't actually working on a movie, **Lucille** posed for dozens of publicity pictures. Many of them sold her as a bland but stylish paragon of sophistication and glamour (left).

But she also liked stills that depicted her as an actress well-suited for comic and dramatic roles (center and right).

CHAPTER NINE

LUCILLE BALL MARRIES DESI ARNAZ

To prepare for her meeting with Orson Welles, nicknamed "The Boy Genius," Lucille decided to dress demurely, avoiding flash and cleavage but to attire herself in well-tailored taste and refinement. In the event that he'd had her in mind for a movie role, which she suspected he did, she wanted to look like a lady, not like the hooker or showgirl she'd played in so many B movies. Thus, she wore a minimum of accessories and was adorned only with subtle touches of makeup.

When he arrived at her residence, she invited him in for a drink. She found him reasonably handsome and most eloquent. Long before he became grossly debauched and overweight, author Peter Noble described him as "a magnificent figure of a man, over six feet tall, handsome, with flashing eyes, and a gloriously resonant speaking voice. His eyes were green, his hair brown, and his voice a bass-baritone."

Of course, she was familiar with his name—much of America was—but she knew little of his career. Before meeting him, she read a magazine profile of him, discovering, to her surprise, that he was four years younger than herself.

A native of Wisconsin, he was still married, but in the process of divorce from his first wife, Virginia Nicholson, the Chicago-born actress and socialite. He would remain what he termed "a free man" until 1943, when he married the love goddess of the 1940s, Rita Hayworth, one of the most popular pinup girls of World War II, rivaling Betty Grable.

Two views of **Orson Welles,** from around the time of his *War of the Worlds.*

Producer Erich Pommer convinced Welles that he could turn Lucille into one of the biggest stars in pictures and that she'd be "a combination of Mae West and Jean Harlow."

Lucille learned that in 1937, in collaboration with actor-producer John Houseman, he'd founded the Mercury Theatre, an independent repertory company known for its world-renowned production of prestigious, avant-garde, and sometimes experimental plays. One of them was *Caesar* (1937). Inspired by a work by Shakespeare, it was presented with an entirely African American cast.

In 1938, he'd achieved nationwide notoriety with his radio series *Mercury Theatre on the Air*. Broadcast across America, he narrated an adaptation of H.G. Welles's novel, *The War of the Worlds*. Thousands upon thousands of listeners tuned in. Except for its introduction, it was presented as real and immediate, an accurate news report about the landing of a Martian spaceship on farmland in New Jersey, with hideous and malevolent creatures emerging from its armed and fortified capsule.

In countless homes across America, families went into panic, and many fled, creating miles-long traffic jams. Car accidents, broken legs, nervous breakdowns, and even miscarriages followed in the wake of the broadcast. Numerous lawsuits were launched against CBS. One husband discovered his wife on the verge of poisoning herself as a means of avoiding a possible rape from monster aliens. New Yorkers, as in other cities, ran through city streets in panic, terrified of an imminent Martian takeover.

To many, it was the end of civilization as they had known it. The word being bandied around on everybody's lips was "Doomsday."

Over dinner with him, Lucille found Welles eloquent, although he kept consuming one glass of Scotch on the rocks after another. That was followed by a gargantuan dinner in which he alone consumed two bottles of wine. Lucille merely sipped from her glass.

He told her that he had seen *Five Come Back* (1939) and that he was most impressed with her acting, so much so that he wanted her to play the lead in his upcoming pilot for an avant-garde movie, *The Smiler With a Knife*. Based on a plot about a Fascist takeover of the United States, Welles had written the original script, but it had been doctored a lot by screenwriter Herman Mankiewicz.

Based on how he described her character in lofty terms, she assumed that if she could pull off the role, she might be nominated for an Oscar. However, she warned him that he'd have to get permission from RKO, since she was under exclusive contract—that is, if he couldn't get RKO to produce it.

What he didn't tell her was that he had already offered the role to both Carole Lombard (who had flatly rejected it) and to Rosalind Russell (who had a scheduling conflict).

Lucille's meeting with Welles went well. They were so compatible that he asked her out on a date the following evening. This time, he drove her to a remote restaurant in San Fernando Valley, where, once again, he consumed a large amount of booze and another (for him, at least) two-fisted dinner, this one with two large Texas-bred steaks, cooked rare.

After dinner, he invited Lucille to a nearby motel, and she accepted. However, once they checked in, he fell into bed and almost immediately went to sleep. She lay beside him for about an hour, listening to his drunken snoring until she, too, drifted off.

In the morning, after each of them had showered, he had recovered his sexual prowess and made love. As she later confessed to Barbara Pepper, "Orson made up for the previous night. He's quite a man."

Welles had been engulfed in some form of sexual relationship since the age of nine, when he went to live with two female cousins in the wake of his mother's death. In Woodstock, Virginia, they seduced their new housemate. He later recalled, "The girls had their way with me to whatever extent that may be."

As time went by, his trail of seduction was littered with an array of bodies, including a teenaged Judy Garland. Other conquests would include the French actress, Corinne Calvet; actor Jack Carter; Marlene Dietrich; African American singers Lena Horne and Eartha Kitt; heiress Gloria Vanderbilt; actor-producer John Houseman; Maria Montez ("The Cobra Woman"); and Marilyn Monroe. His seductions also included a bevy of prostitutes in the bordellos of Singapore and Shanghai.

He told Lucille, "I always seduce actors I cast. I make them fall in love with me—even Joseph Cotten who, ironically, is homophobic. You might call me a male Lillie Langry to the homo set in Hollywood."

[Presented at the English court to Queen Victoria, and noted for her charm, beauty, and social connections, Lillie Langtry (1853-1929) was an Edwardian-age actress, theatrical producer, adventuress, and mistress to the then-Prince of Wales.]

Later, to the press, Welles recalled his wartime experience in Hollywood. "During the War, I had everybody. All the able men were on the battlefields of Europe or at sea in the Pacific. There was almost no competition."

Regrettably, as it turned out, RKO refused to release Lucille to make that thriller with Welles. He soon abandoned the project and began work to create *Citizen Kane* (1941), which some critics hailed as the best film ever made, at least on the level of Humphrey Bogart's *Casablanca* (1942).

***

In 1940, Pandro S. Berman, Lucille's former lover and one of her biggest boosters at RKO, departed from that studio for greener pastures at MGM. He was replaced by a new executive, George Schaefer, an intelligent and cultivated man who said something that was widely bruited around within RKO, "I have no interest in Lucille Ball at all. She's just another girl under contract to us."

When Lucille heard that, she feared either that her days at the studio might be numbered, or—even worse—that she'd stagnate at RKO in one unworthy picture after another.

During Schaefer's second week on the job, although she'd requested a private meeting with him, his secretary told her that it wasn't possible. Schaefer was well-known in the film industry, having become general manager of Paramount in 1933 and later, Vice President of United Artists.

Alas, instead of pictures featuring Lucille Ball, his interests lay elsewhere, particularly with the release of *Gunga Din* (1938) and *The Hunchback*

229

of Notre Dame (also 1938). He was president of RKO when Orson Welles made *Citizen Kane* (1941), but was fired the year after, based on the artistic feuds and commercial failure of Welles' second picture, *The Magnificent Ambersons* (1942).

Fortunately for Lucille, producer Erich Pommer took over the reins at RKO and cast her in an upcoming drama, *Dance, Girl, Dance* (1940). He predicted that she had great potential as a star, and that perhaps she'd evolve into what Jean Harlow was to MGM and what Mae West was to Paramount.

As a producer, Pommer had been a leader in the German Expressionist movement of silent films of Germany's Weimar Republic. He'd been involved in the production of film classics that included *The Cabinet of Dr. Caligari* (1920) and *The Blue Angel* (1930), the film that introduced Marlene Dietrich to international audiences.

During an interlude in 1926, he went to Hollywood, directing such stars as Pola Negri, Lon Chaney, Sr., and Norma Shearer.

After that, Pommer returned to his native land to supervise production at UFA *[Universum-Film Aktiengesellschaft]*, where he became a pioneer in German Talkies. After the Nazi takeover of Germany in 1933, Josef Goebbels, the Nazi Minister of Propaganda, fired him, prompting Pommer's return to Hollywood, where he spotted the potential of Lucille.

Around 1941, he became seriously ill, and his contract at RKO was not renewed.

After World War II, Pommer returned to Germany to help revive that war-torn country's film industry. Lucille remained forever grateful to him for the boost he gave to her career.

Dancing the Hootchie-Kootchie—Lucille's most iconic moment in **Dance, Girl, Dance (1940).**

Cast as "Bubbles," Lucille was told by producer Erich Pommer to watch *The Blue Angel*, the famous movie that Josef Von Sternberg had made to launch Marlene Dietrich into international fame.

Lucille (left) was cast opposite **Maureen O'Hara**, who plays a classically trained ballerina in a burlesque house. "Wrong script, wrong actress," O'Hara later recalled.

In America, the Irish lass had shot to fame in 1939 as Esmeralda in *The Hunchback of Notre Dame* (1939) starring Charles Laughton.

Roy Del Ruth had been designated as the director of *Dance, Girl, Dance* (1940), but creative differences between Pommer and him led to his firing. He was replaced by Dorothy Arzner, one of the few women directors in Hollywood. She was already known to Lucille, who had appeared briefly in her 1934 film, *Nana*.

Arzner had previously directed such stars as the bisexual actresses Katharine Hepburn and Rosalind Russell and was rumored to have had lesbian affairs with both of them. Arzner was also said to have had affairs with Billie Burke and Nazimova, once the queen of Metro.

Dorothy Arnzer directs the floozie version of **Lucille** in *Dance, Girl, Dance*.

At the time of its filming, she was that rarity in Hollywood: A female director. She started out as a secretary for Famous Players-Lasky, but soon rose to helm *The Wild Party* (1929). **Clara Bow's** (see poster below) first talkie.

Biographer Charles Higham wrote: "As before, Lucille felt uncomfortable and uneasy with Arzner. She was embarrassed by the widespread gossip about the director's lesbianism and felt ill at ease when confronted by a severe, well-tailored crop-haired, mannish woman who barked directions with the toughness of John Ford or Henry Hathaway. No doubt, Lucille was also tense because Arzner was known to have sexually approached more than one leading lady in her pictures."

The original story of *Dance, Girl, Dance,* had been written by Vicki Baum, an Austrian writer famous for her novel, *Menschen im Hotel (People at a Hotel),* published in 1929. In 1932, MGM adapted

the story into a film, *Grand Hotel,* starring Greta Garbo, John Barrymore, and Joan Crawford.

In a nutshell, the drama follows two dancers, Judy O'Brien (Maureen O'Hara) and "Bubbles" (aka Tiger Lily), a role that cast Lucille as a burlesque queen. They vie for the attention of a rich young suitor, Jimmy Harris (Louis Hayward), who is still in love with his estranged wife, Elinor (Virginia Field). Steve Adams, a ballet impresario who rescues Judy, was played by veteran actor Ralph Bellamy.

Dublin-born Maureen O'Hara became Ireland's first superstar in Hollywood. The famous redhead, sometimes promoted as "The Queen of Technicolor," would often play heroines in adventure or Western films. She'd launched her career with Alfred Hitchcock's *Jamaica Inn* (1939) and *The Hunchback of Notre Dame* (also 1939), each starring Charles Laughton. In time, however, she'd become more closely associated with the movies she made with John Wayne, none more notable than *The Quiet Man* (1952). The Duke told the press, "She's big, lusty, absolutely marvelous—my kind of woman."

For the male lead, RKO borrowed dashing Louis Hayward, who was born in Johannesburg, South Africa, and was at the time married to actress Ida Lupino, sometimes called "the poor man's Bette Davis."

Early in Hayward's career, he had been the *protégée* of Noël Coward. He had launched himself after many sessions on Coward's casting couch.

After appearing in several British films, Hayward made his Broadway debut in 1935 in Coward's *Point Valaine* with Alfred Lunt and Lynn Fontanne.

Although it was poorly received, it led to Hayward getting a four-picture deal with MGM, where he co-starred with actors who included Paul Muni, Miriam Hopkins, and Douglas Fairbanks, Jr.

Right before working with Lucille, he had starred in one of his most famous films, cast in a dual role in *The Man in the Iron Mask* (1939). After *Dance, Girl, Dance*, he headed for another swashbuckling role with Joan Bennett in *The Son of Monte Cristo,* a sequel to *The Count of Monte Cristo* (1934).

A native of Chicago, Ralph Bellamy had a career that spanned six decades, playing both leads or supporting roles, often portraying *beaux* who didn't get the girl at the end of the picture. The year he worked with Lucille, he also made *His Girl Friday* (1940) with Cary Grant and Rosalind Russell. His first film was *The Secret Six* (1931), co-starring Wallace Beery, Jean Harlow, and Clark Gable. By the end of 1933, he'd made nearly two dozen movies, notably *Rebecca of Sunnybrook Farm,* starring Shirley Temple. After making *Dance, Girl, Dance,* he was set to star in the horror classic, *The Wolf Man* (1941) with Lon Chaney, Jr.

Born in Tula in 1876, then part of the Russian Empire, about 120 miles south of Moscow, character actress Maria Ouspenskaya emigrated to America, where she began performing on Broadway in 1922.

In films, with her marked Russian accent, she played European characters of various nationalities, starring in such pictures as *The Rains Came* (1939) with Tyrone Power. After working as Lucille's manager in *Dance, Girl, Dance,* she was set to co-star with Vivien

Louiis Hayward was an odd choice as the male lead of *Dance, Girl, Dance*. With his aloof smirk and rather handsome face, he was better known as a swashbuckling hero in such movies as *The Man in the Iron Mask* (1939).

In *Dance, Girl, Dance*, he takes up a collection for out-of-work showgirls.

Ralph Bellamy, cast as Steve Adams, a ballet producer, takes both a professional and romantic interest in Judy (Maureen O'Hara).

As it turns out, he rescues her from the burlesque parlor and makes her dream come true by hiring her as a "legitimate" ballet dancer with a "respected" ballet troupe.

Leigh in *Waterloo Bridge* (1940). That would be followed by *Kings Row* (1942) in which Ronald Reagan, in his best film performance, woke up after the surgical amputation of his legs by a sadistic doctor to say, "Where's the rest of me?"

Virginia Field, a Londoner, was born into a family related to the Confederate General, Robert E. Lee. As a stage actress in Vienna, she'd worked with Max Reinhardt. At the age of sixteen, she appeared in her first film role, a British comedy entitled *The Lady Is Willing* (1934). Her involvement led to a contract in Hollywood.

In 1936, David O. Selznick cast her in *Little Lord Fauntleroy*. A critic once reviewed her breasts as having "such robust and luscious proportions" that censors demanded that one of her scenes be removed from the film's final clip.

Ironically, in 1942, she'd marry actor Paul Douglas, one of Lucille's former lovers.

Walter Abel, cast as a judge in *Dance, Girl, Dance,* had played the lead role of d'Artagnan in the 1935 version of *The Three Musketeers.* Lucille was also in *Dance, Girl, Dance,* noted that he'd been demoted from star roles to minor parts.

In *Dance, Girl, Dance,* Lucille had to perform a striptease in a controversial scene that somehow managed to slip past the censors. O'Hara, during an "onscreen audition" for a job as a dance hall hostess, had also been asked to perform a striptease, but was later rejected by the club owner, who found her too demure and ladylike, preferring the vulgar, scantily clad Lucille instead.

"I'm prudish," O'Hara told Lucille. "I would never pose in a bathing suit. After all, I'm not Lana Turner. I'm a cold piece of marble, and you would never find me warming

The formidable **Maria Ouspenskaya,** cast as the showgirls' hard-selling manager, "Madame Basilova," was the second choice for the role.

As an actress, she got her practical training by touring through the Russian provinces during the reign of the last Tsar "of all the Russias."

The original director of *Dance, Girl, Dance,* Roy del Ruth, cast a male, Maurice Moscovitch, in the part.

Moscovitch fell ill and died soon after.

During his direction of *The Sound of Music* (1965), **Robert Wise** became famous for replicating the flair and beauty of Austria and its political dilemma prior to World War II.

Here he is with the marionettes the Von Trapp children used to present their puppet show in the Von Trapp's Tyrolean *schloss,* when Julie Andrews played a country girl on loan from the nearby convent.

a casting couch. I'm glad you're playing the whore in this picture—and not me."

O'Hara always claimed that she never had an extramarital affair. Actor Anthony Quinn disagreed.

The film editor of *Dance, Girl, Dance* was Robert Wise, who had worked on previous movies with Lucille, including *Winterset, Stage Door*, and *Having Wonderful Time*. After he finished work on her latest picture, he edited Orson Welles' *Citizen Kane* (1941).

Wise would later win Oscars for Best Director for *West Side Story* (1961) and Best Picture for the film he'd produced, *The Sound of Music* (1965).

Variety noted that *Dance, Girl, Dance,* became one of Arzner's most celebrated films. "It was an unlikely female burlesque, a movie that conceals a withering attack on the male gaze under its showgirl wardrobe of sequins and feathers."

Another critic wrote, "The film is yet another example of the ways in which Arzner subverted and complicated traditional depictions of women and female relationships, as well as social mobility. The movie foregrounds dance as women's avenue to self-expression and economic independence. In a scene about midway through the film, O'Hara's character of Judy stops her stage performance to directly address members of the male audience. Judy confronts the men with a striking admonishment of their objectifications of women."

The New York Times, in a review by Bosley Crowther, panned the movie: "With the exception of Maureen O'Hara, who is sincere but badly miscast, the roles are competently filled and the film is pretentiously staged. *Dance, Girl, Dance,* is just a cliché-ridden, garbled repetition of the arches and pains in a dancer's rise to fame and fortune. It's a long, involved tale told by a man who stutters, Nevertheless, it is Miss Ball who brings an occasional zest into the movie, especially that appearance in a burlesque temple where she stripteases the Hays Office. But it isn't art."

Variety wrote that "Miss Ball is on for extensive periods and is credible on the hoof, in looks, and in singing, her vivacious personality virtually relegating the weak story."

The New York Herald-Tribune found the story "rather confused but Ball is swell as the burlesque queen."

As the years went by, *Dance, Girl, Dance* has undergone a popular revival and critical assessment, and is often cited in film studies as an example of empowered women. It is now listed among the "Top 100 Essential Films" of

The first time **Lucille** (right) saw **Desi Arnaz** on stage in *Too Many Girls*, she realized, "He has an electrifying charm." But she didn't know him (as Bathsheba knew David) until she starred with him in the movie version.

On the right is **Ann Miller**. Unknown to Lucille at the time, she had already discovered what was below Desi's leather belt.

234

the National Society of Film Critics, where it's represented as a "bona-fide feminist masterpiece."

The New Yorker wrote: "The movie lives up to its title—its subject is really dancing. Arzner films it with fascination and enthusiasm, and the choreography is marked by the point of view of the spectators and the dancer's awareness that they're being watched. Arzner, one of the few women directors in Hollywood, shows women dancers enduring men's slobbering stares. The very *raison d'être* of these women's performances is to titillate men. That's where the story's two vectors intersect—Art vs. Commerce and Love vs. Lust. This idealistic paen to the higher realms of creative and romantic fulfillment is harshly realistic about the degradations that women endure in base entertainments."

***

When Desi Arnaz arrived in Hollywood late in 1939 to make *Too Many Girls*, he complained that his main problem was expressed by the title of the movie.

"Females hankering for my body overtaxed me," he said. "How would I find the time to make that damn movie?"

In those days, Hollywood was still a small town, and word soon spread that a "hot new Cuban stud" had joined the film-making colony. "I was getting a lot of calls in my room at the Roosevelt Hotel. Unlike Cuba, where the male calls the female for a date, in Hollywood it's the women who call the men for a date. Of course, I soon learned that sometimes certain men also try to book you for a date...or whatever."

"Some of the gals I had seduced in Manhattan, and I had agreed to see them again. I'm talking Betty Grable and Ginger Rogers. It was no secret: I favored blondes. There was a new gal on the scene, and there was nothing blonde about her. She was hailed as a great beauty in spite of her overbite. I'm talking about Gene Tierney. Dark haired, radiantly beautiful, desirable. So, she was not a great actress, I heard, but looks alone can carry you far in Tinseltown."

He had met her in Manhattan after George Abbott brought her into La Conga. During a break in the show, Desi joined his director and Tierney for a drink. When Abbott went to the men's room, Tierney gave him her phone number. Abbott had cast her in a Broadway play, *Mrs. O'Brien Entertains*, which had led to her joining the cast of *The Male Animal*. Hollywood took notice and sent for her.

"I heard that the casting couch is a way of life, but I don't expect that will be a problem for me," she told Desi. "Mr. Abbott has already taken my virginity. I have a whale of a crush on him. But it's going nowhere and I'm looking around. Of course, I'm only eighteen, and he's fifty-three." She looked up. "Here he comes now. Note that he walks like a panther."

With a promise to meet again if Desi ever made it to Hollywood, Tierney headed west to make her first motion picture, *The Return of Frank James* (1940), in which she played a newspaperwoman in love with an outlaw played by Henry Fonda, all in Technicolor.

In a memoir, Tierney admitted she transferred her crush on Abbott to Fonda, whom she found "gentle and thoughtful."

Her fling with Fonda was brief, and she was, therefore, available to go out with Desi when he called her from his lonely room at the Roosevelt Hotel. It would be the first of a hundred visits to the Cocoanut Grove. Apparently, based on reports, it took three dates before she was seen by a bellhop entering his hotel room.

Abbott, Fonda, and Desi were just the beginning of a long line of Tierney seductions. In time she'd have affairs with three famous men: John F. Kennedy (who refused to marry her), Prince Aly Khan (competing with Rita Hayworth), and aviator/producer Howard Hughes (competing with dozens of other beautiful women and matinee idol men).

In the 1940s, **Gene Tierney** was the reigning beauty at Fox. She emerged from a role as a player in the shady, trashy *Tobacco Road* (1941) , and was eventually cast as the female lead in the classic *Laura* (1944).

It was about a mysterious woman whose portrait obsesses and entrances detective Dana Andrews.

Desi later boasted, "I broke her in for John F. Kennedy, a lieutenant in the U.S. Navy."

"I dated a lot in my early days in Hollywood," Tierney admitted. "Even some time spent with that horndog Charlie Chaplin. Men are wonderful, and I adore them. They always give women the benefit of the doubt."

"One night after dinner, Desi confessed to me that he had fallen for this actress, Lucille Ball, and it was time for him to move on," Tierney said. "I wanted to move on, too. My God, I was even dating Eddie Albert at the time. I was also dating Tyrone Power, but soon learned that my other beau, Howard Hughes, was dating him, too. That's Hollywood for you. Soon another more serious man entered my life, the fashion designer Oleg Cassini, who at the time was earning $200 a week at Paramount."

"A first marriage was in the cards for me, but so were many other lovers—perhaps too many: Darryl F. Zanuck, Victor Mature, Rudy Vallee, and even Kirk Douglas. They came and went. It was hard to keep up. Much later, add Spencer Tracy."

Desi saw Tierney only rarely in the years ahead, usually at Hollywood parties. He noted with sadness the news of her mental collapse. She struggled with doctors, and made a long, slow recovery from "the black tunnel of mental illness," during which she spent seven years in and out of sanitoriums.

***

As Betty Grable's biographer, Tom McGee, wrote, "Desi Arnaz was believed to be besotten with her." He had seduced her in New York, and she was the first beauty he phoned to renew their affair after he migrated to

236

Los Angeles.

Grable had not fully recovered from her affair with bandleader Artie Shaw, but she was dating, nonetheless. She had a motto: "The best way to get over a broken love affair is to begin a new one."

McGee later claimed that the arrival of Lucille Ball in town soon put an end to Desi's budding romance with Grable. But there was another reason, and it's not for the faint of heart to learn.

At the time that Desi was dating Grable, she was also having a torrid affair with matinee idol Tyrone Power, the devilishly handsome star who set millions of female (and gay male) hearts fluttering every time they went to one of his movies.

As author Mart Martin revealed, "Unknown to Grable, until it was 'discovered' and removed by her gynecologist, she had a condom lodged within her vagina. Over time, it created such a bad odor that Power ended his affair with her."

Desi experienced the same disillusionment with the star, although neither beau revealed anything to her about their disenchantment.

To the surprise of both Desi and Power, Grable, once the condom was surgically extracted, shot to almost unheard-of stardom around the globe, especially among soldiers fighting World War II. She beat out Rita Hayworth to become the number one wartime pin-up girl.

In her famous cheesecake picture, which went around the world, she posed with her back to the camera, showing an over-the-shoulder smile. That was necessary because she was visibly pregnant at the time. Soonafter, she married trumpeter Harry James in 1943, a union that lasted for twenty-two years, though it was rife with alcoholism and infidelity.

The year she posed for that picture—one of the one-hundred most influential photographs of all time—she was the reigning box office champion of the world.

Martin also wrote, "She had a lifetime affection for chorus boys and dancers, many of whom were homosexual. When she couldn't find other sex partners to service her, she'd press her demands on 'the boys.' She really preferred rough men, calling herself 'a truck driver's delight.'"

Two American actors (**Tyrone Power** and **Betty Grable**) were beautiful and wholesome in or out of uniform.

In *A Yank in the R.A.F.*, they defended freedom and—according to some—a highly sexed version of the American way, both at home and abroad.

Later, much to Lucille's annoyance, Desi kept that pin-up poster of Grable in his dressing room. She removed it three times, but he always found a replacement for it.

Despite their youthful indiscretions and jealousies, both Lucille and Desi maintained a lifelong friendship with Grable and James: In fact, they were honored guests at the tenth anniversary celebration of Lucille's marriage to Desi.

Both Grable and Lucille shared their lament of being married to bandleaders, who were always on the road touring. "Our guys are out in a new town every night doing God knows what to whatever bitch," Grable said. "Even though he plays around, Harry is still extremely jealous of me, accusing me of having all sorts of affairs."

"Ditto for Desi," Lucille chimed in. "But he always comes home to his redhead."

***

As they'd mutually agreed, Desi contacted Ginger Rogers in Hollywood, calling her for a date at the number she'd provided. He felt she had become such a big star that she might not even remember him. But she did, and plans were arranged for dinner at the Brown Derby, followed by dancing at the Cocoanut Grove.

By now, Desi had seen *Stage Door*. He lavishly praised Ginger's performance in it, telling her, "You beat out Katharine Hepburn. That Lucille dame was hot stuff, too, but no one looked at any other gal after you came onto the screen."

"Flattery will get you anywhere," she warned him. "Lucille likes me as much as Hepburn detests me. I told her about you, telling her you're one good-looking and hot Cuban stud. You see, she digs Latin men. You might want to date her when I'm out with Jimmy Stewart, who's not free every night to see me. He likes to have sex without commitment. Strangely, he refers to the sex act as 'polluting myself.'"

Ginger's rising power as a star became obvious whenever they'd enter a club such as Cocoanut Grove. Wherever she went with Desi, she was given star treatment. "When you're a gal who's big at the box office, like Ginger was, she's treated like a goddess in Hollywood," Desi said. "If there's one thing this town respects, it's anyone, male or female, who could have them lined up at the box office."

Despite her success, she found things to complain about: "I want to prove myself as a dramatic actress, but I'll be forever linked to Fred Astaire. The public thinks he's my Svengali and that I'm his dancing Trilby, obeying every command of my master. That's hardly the case. Let's face it: Astaire is a great dancer, perhaps the best, but he has less sex appeal than Gabby Hayes...you know, the sidekick of that cowboy who has my

Although she went on to more famous dramatic roles, **Ginger Rogers** never escaped being half of the greatest dance team in movie history. "**Fred and Ginger**" became cinematic legend, each of them viewed as a screen immortal.

last name…Roy Rogers with the beady eyes?"

"When Astaire and I made *Follow the Fleet* with Randolph Scott, it wasn't me he was interested in. He chased after Randolph Scott and made several visits to his dressing room. I hope Cary Grant didn't find out. You may not know this—even though half of Hollywood already does: Grant has staked Randy out for himself."

[Ironically, Ginger would have a brief fling with the bisexual Grant when they co-starred in Monkey Business *(1952) with Marilyn Monroe.]*

On every date with Desi, Ginger talked about Astaire: "Some of our fans think we're married," she said. "I must confess, one night after rehearsal, we got together. To put it bluntly, it was a case of my asking, 'Are you in yet?' How unlike the case with you, sweetheart. You always carry that pistol around in your pants. My nickname for it is 'Ever Ready.'"

"Thanks for the compliment, doll," he said.

Rogers began seeing Stewart less and less because of his filming of *Destry Rides Again* (1939) with Marlene Dietrich. Their off-screen affair led to her having an abortion.

Although Rogers continued to date Desi on and off for a few more weeks, her romantic attentions soon began to focus on David Niven, with whom she was making *Bachelor Mother* (1939). Desi had seen this dapper, urbane, Scottish actor with the pencil-thin mustache in several movies.

By the time Stewart entered the Air Corps in World War II, he and Ginger were each involved elsewhere. The homespun actor kept a diary of all the beautiful glamour girls he'd seduced, and whereas Ginger's name was near the top, other conquests included Jean Harlow, Rosalind Russell, Lana Turner, Norma Shearer, June Allyson, Olivia de Havilland, and Grace Kelly. He'd lost his virginity to Margaret Sullavan, who later married his best friend, Henry Fonda. Eventually, he settled down into a long and happy marriage to Gloria McLean.

One night, Ginger defined her relationship with Desi: "What I like about you is that we can have sex without commitment. It seems that every showgirl in Hollywood thinks of marriage after she's dated a guy a few times. My friend, Lucille Ball, and I share something in common: We believe in 'love 'em and leave 'em.'"

"My philosophy exactly," he assured her.

Desi and Lucille were alert to one of Ginger's recent victories: She had received a Best Actress Oscar for her dramatic role in *Kitty Foyle* (1940), for which she beat out both Katharine Hepburn and Bette Davis.

Ironically, on that same night, her former lover, James Stewart, won the Best Actor Oscar for *The Philadelphia Story*, "stealing" the picture from Hepburn and Cary Grant. As sometimes happens in Hollywood, he competed against his best friend, Henry Fonda, who had been nominated for his performance in the movie classic, *The Grapes of Wrath* (1940).

***

The first time Desi spotted Lucille Ball, he didn't know who she was. He mistook her for "some broken-down hooker." She had taken a lunch break from a fight scene with Maureen O'Hara during the filming of *Dance, Girl, Dance* (1940).

"I thought she was just some whore who'd been beaten up by her pimp," Desi recalled. "Her tousled hair was real frowsy, and she had on this burlesque outfit that only a floozie would wear. In Havana, she'd have to work the back streets, hoping to pick up a drunken sailor in dim light at three o'clock in the morning."

When he met her, he was having lunch with his friend, George Abbott, who had cast him in *Too Many Girls* on Broadway and wanted him to repeat his performance in RKO's upcoming film adaptation, slated for release in 1940.

Lucille sported a fake black eye after her onscreen fight with Maureen O'Hara in *Dance, Girl, Dance*. When Desi met her off set, she wasn't wearing the ermine coat, and her hair was a lot messier.

"She looked," he said, "like a beat-up, two-dollar whore."

She stopped by their table and greeted the director. "This is Lucille Ball," Abbott said to Desi. "Lucy, meet Desi Arnaz."

"Hi ya, Dizzy," she said.

"It's 'Desi,'" he said.

"Okay, Daisy, but that sounds like a girl's name."

"Daisy is a flower," he said, harshly. "I'm Desi. D-E-S-I"

"Whatever," she answered. "Nice to see you, George. Looking forward to working with you and Daisy Mae here."

"You mean you've cast that thing as our star?" Desi asked when she'd gone. "Why not Marcy Westcott? She was terrific on Broadway."

"RKO wanted one of its up-and-coming stars," Abbott answered. "Don't judge her too harshly. She's been in a fight scene in *Dance, Girl, Dance,* where she plays a burlesque prostitute."

At around six o'clock that evening, Desi was in the studio rehearsing "She Could Shake the Maracas" (later dropped from the film) when this beautiful girl with reddish-gold hair walked in. She wore a sunflower-yellow sweater and tight-fitting beige slacks.

It took him a moment to realize that this was the same girl he'd met in the commissary earlier that day. As he later told Abbott, "What a change in looks. The way she looked now was designed to give me a hard-on."

"Glad to see you again, Daisy, I'm excited to be working with you in my next picture. I saw you on Broadway. I thought you were terrific."

"Thanks," he said, flirtatiously. "Now that I've met the real you, I'm gonna demand that Abbott write in some hot love scenes with us."

"That's very flattering." She looked him up and down. "Are you Mexican?"

"No, from Cuba originally," he said. "I grew up in Miami." Then he decided to make his pitch to her. "Do you know how to rumba? I think Abbott is gonna require it of us in the picture."

"I don't, but I bet you do."

"Some of the cast is meeting tonight at this swinging little Mexican joint, El Zarape. It's a restaurant, but they have a small band and dance floor. Will you join us? I'll teach you how to rumba. Do you like Mexican food?"

"It's okay," she said. "But it makes me fart. I'd love to learn to rumba."

At the restaurant, Desi, Lucille, and five members of the cast danced, drank, and ate until four that morning. Cast members included Hal LeRoy, Libby Bennett, Ivy Scott, Bryon Shores, and an emerging star, Van Johnson. From her seat in the audience, Lucille had seen all of them in the Broadway production.

She later relayed the details of that night to Ann Miller, who had played the third lead in *Too Many Girls* but who hadn't attended the party. "Before dawn, I flipped for this Cubano stud. I might as well confess, we retired to the corner of the dive and talked. After five minutes, I was in love. BANG! Just like that. I adored the way he rolled his r's. I was ready to invite him for a sleepover at my apartment, but I had to meet my family for some urgent business that morning. I had him drop me off at my family home, not at my secret hideaway."

Desi, too, recalled the night to Abbott: "On her doorstep, I fed her some tongue and got her hot, but I couldn't go inside. Her mother was already in the kitchen, she told me, cooking breakfast."

Later that afternoon, Eddie Bracken, repeating his starring role in *Too Many Girls,* had invited members of the cast to his rented villa opening onto the beach at Malibu.

By ten o'clock, a somewhat exhausted Desi drove to Union Station in Los Angeles to pick up Renée DeMarco, the ballroom dancer and his New York lover.

Normally, he might have invited her back for a long-delayed makeup session, but both of them needed some emergency sleep. He told her he'd pick her up later at her hotel and take her to Eddie Bracken's party.

Hours later, he returned to her hotel, picked her up, and drove her to Malibu, where the Bracken party was in full swing. In the bathroom, he changed into his bathing trunks, but she would remain in the house as he headed for the beach. Her nickname was "Freckles." Because she freckled so easily, she avoided the sun.

He introduced her to Van Johnson, who was reprising his uncredited Broadway role in the film adaptation of *Too Many Girls.* He, too, freckled easily, so he, too, stayed behind, in the house, to talk to her.

As Desi was leaving, "a good-looking young kid with blonde hair arrived with drinks for the two freckled ones," Desi said.

After he wandered down to the beach, to his surprise, he discovered Lucille, wearing a one-piece bathing suit in shocking pink, lying on a blanket by herself. He appraised her figure with a hungry, well-trained eye.

"You've got a body designed for bathing trunks," she provocatively said. "Personally, I think men's suits are designed to hide too much, especially those baggy pants." She patted the sands beside her, inviting him to join her.

He eagerly accepted her invitation. Then they talked for two, maybe three hours, as they had the night before at the Mexican dive. Finally, although he didn't want to leave her side, he headed back to the living room to check on Freckles, promising Lucille he'd return soon.

In the living room, he found Van Johnson sitting alone and nursing a beer. "What happened to Freckles?" he asked.

"That damn bitch ran off with that hunk, the pool boy, and I wanted the kid for myself," Johnson replied. "I'm lonely. Maybe you'd like to come back to my hotel room tonight?"

"Forget it," Desi answered. "I'm taking Lucille Ball back to her private apartment."

This time, after driving her back, she invited him inside. No more family. Not only did he get supper, a catered affair from a Chinese delivery service, but he was invited to spend the night, an intimacy he knew was inevitable.

The only source for what happened next came from their director, George Abbott. He spread the word among the male cast members of *Too Many Girls* that Desi had "plugged" Lucille, their star, three times in one night. "I already knew she went for Latin guys."

Obviously, she liked what he had to offer, because he moved into her apartment the very next night. For appearances' sake, he rented an apartment of his own, where he installed his devoted, divorced *Cubana* mother. His father was still living with his new love in Miami.

After his second night with Lucille, Desi phoned Freckles at her hotel. He apologized for deserting her at Bracken's party, later adding, "It was wrong of me, but I heard you didn't have to go home alone."

In the upper photo, **Lucille** and **Desi** were snapped on a press junket promotiong their co-starring roles in *Too Many Girls*. They looked like a happy couple.

The lower photo shows how their attraction continued from reel into real life, at the buffet table of a cast party. There, the studio cameras continued to click to record the offscreen dramas associated with the upcoming film release

"No need for an apology," she said. "I'm not a fool. We'll have our memory of New York, but we're in Hollywood now. I'll soon be a free woman, and I've started to shop around. My God, I think Hollywood has the handsomest guys ever put on earth. Each of them wants to be Clark Gable, if they're macho, or Tyrone Power or Robert Taylor if they're pretty. Better watch out! One of them might snare you!"

"That isn't likely, I can assure you," he

said. "I'm a hopelessly dedicated ladies' man."

"That's obvious," she said. "We fell for each other, we made passionate love, and now it's time to move on. Good luck, Desi, with your career and your personal life."

"The same to you, Freckles," he said as she put down the receiver.

In the late afternoon, Lucille asked him to drive her to Alexander Hall's turkey ranch in San Fernando Valley. She wanted to break off their affair and pack up some suitcases with her belongings.

The older Hollywood veteran was most understanding, shaking Desi's hand and wishing him luck with Lucille. "She's a hell of a gal. You could do worse, you sneaky Cuban bastard. No hard feelings. Come out back with me."

He took Desi for a walk around the grounds and showed him where he raised turkeys. Then he caught one of his biggest birds, took it, fighting and squawking, to a chopping block where he cut off its head. When the bleeding stopped, he bagged the bird and gave it to Desi as an engagement present.

Lucille spent an hour privately with Hall, presumably telling him farewell and ending their affair. When she returned to Desi, who was waiting in the car, he told her about the dead turkey in the trunk and put her suitcases on the back seat.

"I'm not taking that damn turkey into my apartment," she said. "We'll stop off at the Salvation Army and give it to their cook."

They rode in silence for the next half hour until she asked him, "Just how old are you, kid?"

"I'm twenty-three," he answered. "Is that too old for you?"

"Hell, no! I'm pushing thirty. Everybody's gonna accuse me of cradle snatching."

***

When Lucille began steadily dating Desi, she was well known in Hollywood, "pigeonholed"—in distinct contrast to fast-emerging A-list players like Lana Turner and Betty Grable— as an actress best suited for B pictures.

Although completely unknown except by those who had seen *Too Many Girls* on Broadway, Desi soon became recognized as "the new boy in Tinseltown."

In his black Buick convertible, he had been seen speeding down Hollywood Boulevard, often getting a ticket, which he always tossed away. Beside him might be

In *Too Many Girls*, **Ann Miller** poses in what she called "my crotch shot."

Behind her is Desi Arnaz. She was having a good time on screen and off with this handsome new man in town,

Miller was one of the many stars Desi seduced before a certain redhead—cast in the same movie— came into his life.

243

Ann Miller, Betty Grable, Lana Turner, Gene Tierney, and, finally, Lucille herself. Miller never told Lucille, one of her best friends, that Desi "deflowered me before he got around to plucking her—that's 'plucking,' darling."

During the filming of *Too Many Girls,* many members of the cast warned Lucille against getting serious with this *Cubano* exotic: "Just use him like a piece of meat before you move on to the next juicy steak," Van Johnson advised. A survivor of the Broadway show, he was repeating his stage role in the film. "He's too young and wild for you, a real skirt chaser. If you fall for him, I can almost guarantee he'll break your heart like he did that of Renée DeMarco."

"Oh, Van, you're just jealous," Lucille told him. "You want him for yourself. He told me you've made several passes at him."

Desi liked chili and Barney's Beanery was said to make some of the best in Hollywood. The first time they stopped there, they ate under a hand-lettered sign that read NO FAGOTS *(sic)*. During that first visit, the waitress came over to Lucille while Desi was in the men's room. He had just ordered a beer. "Is your boyfriend an Indian?" she asked. "Barney has a policy of not serving alcohol to Indians."

"Yes, he's a Cherokee, and I'm his squaw. Now bring him that god damn beer and shut your fucking face."

She already knew much of Southern California, having lived there for most of the decade, and she was eager to show it to him. On weekends, they went exploring. She soon learned what a dangerous driver he was.

"The only speed he knew on an open road was a hundred miles an hour. Once, he hit something jutting out on the highway, which took off his left fender, but he didn't stop to retrieve it."

Sometimes, she screamed, and at times, that became a ritual: *i.e.,* he'd drive fast, and she'd scream.

In addition to panic, she had another reason for screaming: "Katharine Hepburn, when we made *Stage Door,* warned me that my voice was too high-pitched. She suggested I go to the beach and scream every day for an hour to lower the register of my voice and make it more suitable for possible dramatic roles. So, as Desi drove like a bat out of hell, I screamed. Miss Hepburn was right: I did eventually lower my voice, making better roles suitable

Upper photo: In *Too Many Girls*, Lucille appears with (center) **Eddie Bracken**, who looks at her adoringly. **Richard Carlson** (right) plays a shy football hero who slowly falls in love with her.

Lower photo: Carlson is flanked by Lucille (left), cast as an heiress, with a "Mexicana-accessorized" **Ann Miller**.

for me."

Once, she invited him to drive her to Big Bear Mountain, where previously, she had been on location, filming *Having Wonderful Time.* They even drove south to Tijuana, where Desi became intrigued with the art of bullfighting.

Whenever they could, they escaped to a "nude weekend" in Palm Springs, where they began to dream about their future, perhaps buying a small villa there for retreats. It was agreed that if they ever got married, and both of them were certain that they would, they'd have three children—two boys to carry on the Arnaz name, and a girl who'd grow up to be a beautiful movie star like Carole Lombard.

To this point, RKO had not succeeded at transforming Lucille into a publicity machine, although every now and then they got a cheesecake shot of her into the papers. At this point, however, their publicity department began to have one of its photographers follow them, as a couple, around on dates with the intention of getting their pictures into newspapers. They promoted Desi as a new Latin lover, perhaps even another Valentino.

One night, he told Lucille that RKO opposed his getting married until at least five years had passed. "RKO feels that gals will attend my pictures more, and make me their pinup dream boy, but only if I'm single. That way, they can fantasize about me being their lover."

During the filming of *Too Many Girls,* Lucille and Desi often double-dated with their co-star, Ann Miller and their director, George Abbott. She was too young, and he was in his fifties, but it didn't seem to matter to Miller, who even dated Louis B. Mayer. "Ann believed in reincarnation," Lucille said. "She often told us of when she reigned over Egypt as Cleopatra. One night, she ordered 'seductions' (if you could call it that) from eighty of her sex slaves before the break of dawn."

Both Abbott and Desi taught Miller and Lucille how to rumba, and they were often seen at that Mexican dive, Zarape, which, at Desi's request, had imported a band from Havana.

In his opening scene for *Too Many Girls,* as his character met his romantic counterpart (Lucille) for the first time, Desi was required to facially register the visuals of her gorgeous body and then swoon in ecstasy. "I got paid for doing what came naturally."

According to Miller, "Whenever the two of them weren't on camera, but scheduled to go on together soon, you could see them sitting off somewhere in a corner, practically making out. They couldn't seem to get enough of each other. In the bluntest of terms, they had the hots for each other, seemingly not able to wait until they returned to her dressing room, which they did frequently. Was I jealous? Okay, I admit, a little bit."

Eventually, Lucille and Desi met their co-stars, Richard Carlson and Frances Langford.

Carlson, the son of a Danish lawyer, was cast in the lead as Clint Kelly. Richard Kollmar, who had portrayed that character on Broadway, remained back in New York to marry columnist Dorothy Kilgallen. Carlson, meanwhile, was on the dawn of a big career in feature films and later on television as both an actor and director.

He'd become known on Broadway when he co-starred with Ethel Barrymore in *Ghost of Yankee Doodle* (1937-1938). In Hollywood, MGM cast him opposite Lana Turner in *These Glamour Girls* and *Every Inch a Lady*, each released in 1939.

After working with Lucille and Desi, Carlson would go on to perform with such luminaries as Bob Hope, Cary Grant, Abbott & Costello, Hedy Lamarr, Judy Garland, and Elvis Presley. *[In Presley's case it was in his 1969 film,* Change of Habit.*]*

Carlson never obtained the major stardom he so desperately desired. One of the drawbacks was that he bore a striking resemblance—both physically and in voice register—to another actor, Hugh Marlowe. Autograph seekers often approached him saying, "Mr. Marlowe, may I have your autograph?"

Marlowe had starred as the playwright and husband of Celeste Holm in *All About Eve* (1950). One critic who must have had a few drinks before seeing the film, cited Bette Davis, Anne Baxter, and Holm as the stars of the film, praising "Richard Carlson for his brilliant performance as the double-crossing playwright." *[The critic had foolishly mistaken Carlson for Marlowe.]* Marlowe was furious, Carlson merely amused, as he had originally auditioned for the role himself.

Florida-born Frances Langford was also a singer, achieving her greatest success during the Golden Age of Radio. In World War II, she became a "G.I. Sweetheart," entertaining servicemen during tours with Bob Hope, with whom she sustained an on-again, off-again affair. Her signature songs included "You Are My Lucky Star" and "I'm in the Mood for Love." *[After its release, in a delayed reaction to their titles, dozens of soldiers called out to her, "You've come to the right place, Baby."]*

When she met Langford, Lucille asked her, "How does it feel to be married to Jon Hall, a living doll that half the world desires?"

In one of the most iconic scenes from *All About Eve* (1950), two mink-clad divas, **Celeste Holm** (left) and **Bette Davis** are caught in a snow storm. The driver is **Hugh Marlowe,** cast as a Broadway playwright.

In her greatest role, Davis played the irrepressible volcano Margo Channing. In this scene, she is being betrayed by her so-called "best friend."

Richard Carlson, years after his almost-forgotten involvement in *Too Many Girls*, protects **Julie Adams** in *Creature from the Black Lagoon*.

In the years following their respective demises, even the most skilled of Classic Movie geeks got Marlowe and Carlson confused. Could it have had something to do with the bland regularity of "buttoned-down" men during that conformist era of Sputnik-era history?

Langford's answer was provocative: "I have to line up—and there's always a long line waiting—just to get him to fuck me."

On the set of *Too Many Girls*, word spread among the crew that Desi was slipping around and seducing Langford, who vehemently denied it.

[From 1955 to 1986, Langford was famously married to Ralph Evinrude, the president of the Outboard Marine Corporation. At her Florida home she often threw lavish, star-studded parties attended by the co-author of this book, Darwin Porter, then employed as a reporter and entertainment columnist for The Miami Herald.

During World War II, when *Too Many Girls* was made, singer **Frances Langford** was hailed as "The G.I. Nightingale," a sweetheart of the Armed Forces, whom she entertained during tours with Bob Hope.

At the time she worked with Desi and Lucille, she was married to heartthrob Jon Hall. But did she cheat on him with Desi?

In later life, Langford became a sort of (eccentric) philanthropic legend in Florida, donating acres for the opening of Langford Park and helping fund research programs of the Florida Oceanographic Society.]

Garson Kanin, who had directed Lucille two years earlier in *Next Time I Marry*, was an assistant to George Abbott during the filming of *Too Many Girls*. He became the first professional in Hollywood to realize that Desi might have more potential than beating bongo drums and singing "Babalu."

"Unlike most actors, Arnaz set out to learn everything he could about how films were made," Kanin said. "Of course, he was a pain in the ass on the set, always interfering, wanting to set up every scene himself and even direct it. He was also giving Abbott and me suggestions about what to do in every scene."

A writer and director, **Garson Kanin** was a colleague of Thornton Wilder and in 1942 married actress Ruth Gordon. She became his frequent collaborator.

His greatest play, *Born Yesterday,* ran for 1,642 performances after its Broadway opening in 1946.

Kanin also revealed that Lucille had been cast in the film "under a cloud of rejection." Lee Marcus, the man in charge of RKO's "B" movies, didn't find her right for the role, citing, among her other inadequacies, that she was too old to play a coed. He suggested that RKO should look for a younger star who hadn't previously played a lot of hookers on-screen. "It was with reluctance that he signed Lucille for the role, although he thought Arnaz was perfectly cast."

***

After a day's work on the set, Desi and Lucille frequented the hot spots of Hollywood and Los Angeles. On Saturday nights, they often hit as many as three separate showrooms before retiring for Desi's pre-dawn maneuvers in the bedroom of her apartment.

The popular gossip columnist, Sheilah Graham, lived in the same apartment building as Lucille. At the time, she was engaged in an affair with F. Scott Fitzgerald, the fabled author of such novels as *The Great Gatsby*.

"Out on our balcony, Scott and I could hear Lucille's frequent arguments with Desi," Graham asserted. "Most of their arguments centered on his roving eye. Even though he seemed madly in love with her, he just couldn't seem to keep it zipped up."

"He would accuse her of having an affair with her handsome co-star, Richard Carlson, and she would claim that he was banging Frances Langford. They would really go at it, setting an early pattern for their combative upcoming marriage."

Apparently, their makeup sessions following a bitter fight were very vocal. "Scott and I could hear the sounds of their lovemaking through the open doors of their balcony, drifting down to our landing. Lucille seemed like a director in bed, giving him guidance on what spots to hit."

Early in their lives together, Lucille ascertained that Desi was an exhibitionist. At Ciro's, for example, he would get up and sing "Babalu" as Earl Coleman's band backed him up. One night, he also performed "Spic and Spanish," "You're Nearer," "Conga," and "'Cause We Got Cake," all of them songs from their upcoming film.

RE-INVENTING THE SARONG

Frances Langford was married to **Jon Hall**, known as "The Body Beautiful" after he appeared on the screen with **Dorothy Lamour** (depicted above) in *The Hurricane* (1937)

In it, Hall asked its director, John Ford, to let him appear in a revealing, bikini-like sarong" but was refused.

The New York Times asserted that the movie "is a hurricane to blast you from the orchestra pit to the first mezzanine. It is a hurricane to film your eyes with spin-drift, to beat at your ears with its thunder, to clutch at your heart and send your diaphragm vaulting over your floating rib into the region just south of your tonsils."

Hall later made films with Maria Montez, the queen of cinematic camp, in such kitsch features as *Arabian Nights* and *Cobra Woman*.

The romantic duo also became a regular at Cocoanut Grove in the Ambassador Hotel on Wilshire Boulevard in Los Angeles. They watched as emerging screen goddesses such as the very blonde Lana Turner made their spectacular entrances. It was a setting of artificial palm trees purchased from the long-ago set of Rudolph Valentino's most celebrated film,

The Sheik (1921). If a patron looked up, he or she saw toy monkeys in the trees, along with *pâpier-maché* coconuts.

The Grove became their favorite hangout, a stamping ground where they introduced themselves to the legendary stars of the era, especially those who had survived the 1930s. It was here that Mack Sennett discovered Bing Crosby, and it was here that years before, during the flapper craze, that Joan Crawford won (almost) every Charleston contest she entered.

Desi and Lucille often lunched at the Vendome at 6666 Sunset Blvd. One day, they spotted an unexpected pair of famous blondes dining together and gossiping: Mae West and Marlene Dietrich.

At the age of 44, the author of *The Great Gatsby*, **F. Scott Fitzgerald** (left) died in California just before Christmas 1940 after a high-excess, alcohol-soaked literary life.

One of the great literary figures of his generation, he defined himself as "straight 1850 potato-famine Irish," and became known for ambivalent feelings about American life which seemed to him both dazzlingly promising and spectacularly vulgar.

His last great love was the American newspaper columnist, **Sheilah Graham**, right, who had a lot to say in later years about the "knock-em-down" fights between Lucille Ball and her live-in boyfriend, Desi Arnaz.

The Trocadero, which Desi called "The Troc," also became another much-frequented hangout for Desi and Lucille. It was the brainchild of Billy Wilkerson, publisher of the *Hollywood Reporter.* This was a venue for the film colony's moguls: Samuel Goldwyn, Joe Schenck, and Louis B. Mayer. It is believed that it was here that Mayer saw Lucille dancing with Desi. Their union that night, it's believed, inspired him to lure her away from RKO and to sign her at MGM.

One night, Fred Astaire, who rarely went out, showed up with his wife, Phyllis, and invited Lucille to dance. Reportedly (and perhaps he said it only flirtatiously), as he whirled her around the floor, he told her, "You, not Ginger Rogers, should have been my dance partner."

"My god," Lucille said. "Two filet mignons at the Troc would set you back by about fifteen bucks, which was the weekly take-home pay of many workers of that day."

When she wasn't with him, Desi developed a fondness for prostitutes. After all, it was a whore in Cuba who had first introduced him to sex. He was sometimes seen coming and going from Club Mount-Aire on Harold Way. Seven buildings away, Brenda Allen ran a bordello where she costumed and made up her ladies as movie stars.

"If an *hombre* couldn't get Lana Turner or Betty Grable 'on the hoof,' he could get a lookalike from Miss Allen," Desi said. "Just to see what it was like, I sampled 'Shirley Temple' one night. The kid went for my lollipop, a term she used based on Shirley's song, 'On the Good Ship Lollipop.'"

Lucille and Desi often ended their own nightclubbing by popping into Schwab's Pharmacy, a retail outlet with a luncheonette and diner usually patronized with out-of-work actors and young starlets hoping to become the next Lana Turner. Located on the (Sunset) Strip, Desi always ordered his breakfast favorite: Scrambled eggs with fried onions.

Sometimes, they'd stop at Nate 'n Ale's classic deli, ordering well-stuffed pastrami sandwiches on rye to go. One night, they found Groucho Marx there. *[Lucille had appeared with him in* Room Service *(1938).]*

That was also the setting where they met Frank Sinatra, an emerging singer from Hoboken. Waiting for him in the car outside were both a redhead and a blonde.

He told Desi, "I'm trying to break into the movies. Otherwise, I might have become a mobster in Jersey."

Sinatra and Desi had a lot in common, each of them preferring prostitutes, waitresses, showgirls, secretaries, and script girls.

Very Formal, Very Connected, and Very Posh:

THE COCOANUT GROVE

Once-resident F. Scott Fitzgerald referred to The Ambassador Hotel as "the greatest, gaudiest spree in American history."

Built in 1921 and demolished in the 1980s, it could accommodate 4,000 diners and revelers at a time. Adela Rogers St. Johns recalled Joan Crawford as she danced the night away one enchanted evening, standing out "as though the light was too bright for anyone but her."

In its night club, Lucille and Desi made it a point to see and be seen as a career-building networking tool during its grandest era.

Desi and Lucille also started to get invited to A-list parties. They never knew who they might meet at these parties: Humphrey Bogart, Charlie Chaplin, Howard Hawks, Howard Hughes on rare occasions...perhaps the Nobel Prize-winning novelist (in 1949), William Faulkner.

"Desi was so jealous," Lucille said. "He always demanded to know if I had slept with any of these bigshots. I always denied it, especially when I introduced him to Orson Welles."

***

Romanoff's became another hangout for Desi and Lucille. Bogart, who was sitting alone in his private booth one night, invited Desi and Lucille to join him on three separate occasions. They'd each, years later, remember some of his pronouncements:

ON LOCATION AT ROMANOFF'S WITH HUMPHREY BOGART

"I don't go for these top-heavy dames; They're not sexy to me. I'm not a bosom-man...more of a leg man."

"I'd had enough women by the time I was twenty-seven to know what I'm looking for in a wife, if I marry again."

"Women are weird just because of that little triangle they possess. They think because of that they can get away with anything."

"To have an outside love affair breaks a bond between a husband and a wife, even if she doesn't know about it. The relationship invariably will be less open, so something very important will be missing from the bond."

Bogart may have said that, but even throughout the course of his upcoming marriage to Lauren Bacall, he continued for years to have an affair with his mistress, Verita Thompson, who was also his hairdresser.

***

Desi discovered another place which would become a hangout for them: The Café Swiss. It stood on North Rodeo Drive, and Desi would sometimes sing there as Joe Marino played the piano. Any night he showed up, the owner requested that he sing "Babalu." Later, Desi would introduce the "Boogie Woogie Conga" there.

Sometimes, Clark Gable was a patron. After his big success as Rhett Butler in *Gone With the Wind,* he could have any actress in Hollywood, and he more or less did, providing she was a star at MGM. Even so, his heart still belonged to Carole Lombard, Lucille's friend. Yet Gable often showed up at the Café Swiss by himself, always ordering the same item: a corned beef sandwich with lots of mustard.

When Desi wasn't escorting Lucille around, he was often seen betting on the horses at Santa Anita. As his reputation as a card player grew, he began to receive invitations to private poker games.

Lana Turner, in her most famous movie role, heated up the screen with **John Garfield** in *The Postman Always Rings Twice* (1946). They not only ignited the screen in this bristling *film noir,* but sizzled off screen too.

After Lucille complained to George Raft about Desi's on-again, off-again dalliance with Lana, the *Cubano* newcomer to Hollywood was warned to "lay off" Lana after a terrifying night in the desert at the hands of "goons" sent by Bugsy Siegel.

By the way, the authors of this book have sustained a decades-long infatuation with "The Sweater Girl," aka Lana Turner.

In 2017, they published history's definitive biography of her life, her legal troubles, and her often thwarted passions.

Some were hosted at the homes of producers Joe Schenck or Samuel Goldwyn. Sometimes, he arrived with his new friend, whom he called "Bogie." On occasion, Jack Warner or David O. Selznick showed up for all-night games.

For a big event in Lucille's life that year—her 29th birthday on August 6, 1940—Desi threw five separate surprise parties for her. They included a family gathering with its own separate birthday cake; a 5PM celebration with the cast and crew of *Too Many Girls* collectively honoring her; and a lavish gathering at Slapsie Maxie's nightclub, where everyone sang "Happy Birthday" to her. The sun was rising by the time that evening's final party concluded.

When chilly winds from the north signaled the debut of autumn, Desi took Lucille to Tam O'Shanter, a restaurant that emulated an inn in Normandy, with small, cozy rooms by art director Harry Oliver. Desi booked a private table in front of a roaring fireplace. There, he proposed marriage and she accepted as he put an engagement ring on her finger. He also vowed, "with all my heart to remain faithful to you." Perhaps he had his fingers crossed.

When Lucille was needed at the studio, and Desi had the day off, he sometimes went out with Lana Turner, that seductive blonde whose fame as a movie star was growing daily. They were spotted together at the Santa Anita racetrack and over "zombie cocktails" at Don the Beachcomber's.

Lucille heard about this, and a big fight ensued. He promised never to see Turner again, but a week later, someone spotted them together entering a joint along the Strip.

Lucille decided to take drastic measures and phoned her former beau, George Raft, the ex-gangster who had become a big star, rivaling Bogart for roles at Warners.

"That's My Boy!" by VAN JOHNSON'S DAD

To Desi's rage, after the release of *Too Many Girls*, it was Anglo-blonde and closeted gay **Van Johnson** who emerged in the fan magazines, as the romantic heartthrob of the film, not Desi.

Raft came to her aid. He was a close friend of bigtime gangster Bugsy Siegel, who, over the course of his career, would seduce Jean Harlow and Mae West, and in later years, Marilyn Monroe, too. Raft had a reputation as "God's gift to women."

He always carried a locket containing five pubic hairs from Harlow. He had bought them for $500 each. They'd been plucked by an orderly while she was laid out, unconscious, on a hospital bed.

Raft came up with a plan to scare Desi from dating Turner: One night, the *Cubano* parked his car and was headed to his own apartment to be with his mother. Two of Siegel's henchmen approached him. With a gun pointed at this head, he was forced into the back seat of their car and driven out into the remote California countryside. There, he was stripped of his clothes and left nude, with no money to get back into town.

No one knows for sure what happened that night, but Turner later heard that no motorist wanted to stop in the desert, in the middle of the night, to pick up a naked man—that is, until two gay men stopped for him and invited him into their car. They had a home two miles away, and Desi was asked in for drinks and to spend the night.

He never discussed what happened later that night, but he showed up at his own apartment late the following morning, having been clothed and driven there by one of his benefactors, who—as it happened—worked in the makeup department at Warners.

Even though Lucille, with Raft's help, seems to have ended Desi's affair with Lana Turner, she knew there would be others, certainly whenever he went on the road with his band, traveling from town to town and meeting lots of young women. If she agreed to marry him, she'd have to accept his philandering.

After discussing it with Ann Miller, Lucille decided she might fit into a pattern of many Hollywood marriages. Even though she eventually married him, she didn't want to sit at home knitting and pining for him.

Miller told her, "There are more handsome young men in Hollywood than anywhere else in the world, and some are actually straight. Maybe you'll go out on a few dates when Desi is away doing what he does. Live it up, girl. Don't sit at home waiting for any man. After all, you and I aren't getting any younger."

***

As a movie, *Too Many Girls* fell far short of the critical acclaim set by the Broadway play. Lucille blamed any failure on George Abbott, its director. "He though he was shooting a picture with his Kodak camera in his hotel room. He gave our movie a static quality. Also, the censors screwed us, cutting our best scenes."

Even so, it was predicted by some Hollywood insiders that the movie would make stars out of both Desi and Van Johnson.

"No one can really nail down what makes a star," Desi said. "It is someone, male or female, who jumps out at you on the screen and wins your heart. When *Too Many Girls* was previewed, many females in the audience filled out those reaction cards. They wanted to know, not who the sexy *Cubano* was, but that handsome, red-blonde fellow with all the freckles. Yes, I was jealous of Van for stealing the thunder. Those gals should have asked about me."

Variety found the film "lively, fast-moving, gay and nonsensical, and studded with good tunes. Ball is a beauty for the lead."

The New York Daily News noted that "Desi beats the bongo with Latin American fervor. The producers couldn't have selected a better Connie than Lucille Ball, who plays the willful heiress of the story with zest."

Bosley Crowther of *The New York Times* found the film "pleasant and light-hearted, and with enough snap and bounce to attract a young audience." It claimed that Lucille Ball, Frances Langford, and Ann Miller were "dangerous co-eds." The critic went on to blame George Abbott for "letting the movie sag in the middle, at which point the thin spots badly show. Many of the dance numbers look sad and gloomy. It is a simple, conventional rah-rah picture. Desi Arnaz is a noisy, black-haired Latin. His face, unfortunately, lacks expression, and his performance is devoid of grace."

In contrast, the critic at *Time* magazine labeled him a "terpsichorean Rudolph Valentino."

On the last day of the shoot, Lucille hosted a cast and crew party on the set of *Too Many Girls.* At the end of the gathering, the troupe vowed to stay in touch, even if they never made another movie together.

Driving back to their apartment, she told Desi, "Promises like these are made at the end of any shoot in Hollywood—that is, if the stars got along and didn't fight. No one lives up to that promise of 'we'll meet again.' All of us have to move on."

"That goes for me, too," he said. "I'm heading with Van Johnson to Chicago for the stage version of *Too Many Girls.*"

***

It had been agreed that after the film version of *Too Many Girls* was wrapped, Desi would fly to Chicago to appear in a live reprise of the show as it had originally been performed on Broadway.

As he later told Van Johnson, "I spent my final night with Lucille making love to her until dawn. I got on the plane worn out, the last drop drained from my trusty friend below the belt."

Richard Kollmar had played the lead on Broadway, but he had rejected any link to the Chicago booking so that he could remain in New York with his bride, Dorothy Kilgallen. Van Johnson, who had had a bit part in the Broad-
way production, now assumed the male
lead.

Lucille, because of film commitments
to RKO, would be able to join him for
only one weekend during his entire sojourn in Chicago. Her visit to Desi in
Chicago set the stage for their later married life. "We fought furiously and then
made love furiously. Most of our fights
were jealous rages, each accusing the
other of various affairs."

At the Colony Club in Chicago, Desi
and Lucille were dining together when a
waiter arrived with a note from the formidable British actor, Charles Laughton,
who had just scored a worldwide hit as
The Hunchback of Notre Dame (1939). Also
in Chicago at the time, he had virtually
demanded in his note that Lucille come
over to his table, and she obeyed. Excus-
ing herself from Desi, she was soon in the
presence of this fleshy English actor, face-

People you wouldn't expect to run into in Chicago:

Dotty, über-eccentric, British, and memorable: **Charles Laughton** and **Elsa Lanchester** in the 1930s.

255

to-face with his jowly cheeks and beady eyes. He introduced her to his wife, actress Elsa Lanchester, who usually played batty eccentrics with quavering voices.

At RKO, Erich Pommer had come up with the idea of starring the three of them (Laughton, Lanchester, and Lucille) in an upcoming film. In reference to that, the portly Englishman apologized to Lucille: "We are sorry to tell you that Elsa and I have backed out of the deal. Horrible script. Perhaps we'll work together in the future on some other film."

After she thanked them for their considerations, she returned to Desi. She found him fuming for being left alone for forty-five minutes. "The only attention I got was when I went to take a leak and two fellows got up and followed me to the urinal."

That led to a fight, and she walked out of the restaurant without him. But after paying the bill, he chased after her and made up with her on the sidewalk after twenty minutes.

When the curtain went down on Desi's final live performance in Chicago, he went on the road to promote the film version of *Too Many Girls*, touring from town to town. As a gimmick, they decided to stage a rumba contest for the best dancer in various towns, including Lexington, Kentucky. There, he could find no woman who could dance the rumba, although he did discover one blonde beauty who told him she knew how to square dance.

At the end of his promotional tour, he headed back to Manhattan, where he had a booking at a posh nightclub, the Versailles. It would be a solo act without a band. It was here that he would have a much longer reunion with Lucille, one that would lead to marriage. But first, she had to finish her latest picture for RKO, a comedy.

Desi got good reviews for his act at the Versailles. *Variety* hailed him as "the hottest vaude and nitery bet since Carmen Miranda hit these shows."

***

Lucille's latest film, RKO's *A Girl, a Guy, and a Gob (1941),* started life without her.

Originally entitled *Three Girls and a Gob,* it was to star Maureen O'Hara, Lucille's former co-star in *Dance, Girl, Dance* (1939), and Jack Carson. But the script underwent a number of revisions, and at least six writers could claim co-authorship. George Murphy, the star of the new script, now entitled *A Girl, a Guy, and a Gob,* remembered working half the night with its di-

WHAT'S A GOB?

This was the first film that Harold Lloyd produced but in which he did not star.

He had achieved screen immortality in silent pictures, his most iconic image being his daredevil stunt in which he dangles from a giant clock near the summit of a New York City skyscraper.

rector, Richard Wallace, creating new dialogue to give to the actors in the morning.

Producer Harold Lloyd had seen two pictures with Lucille and decided that she had not been properly showcased, based on her talent as a *comedienne*.

Born in the bowels of Nebraska in 1893, he had become a master of comedy on the silent screen—a challenge even to Buster Keaton and Charlie Chaplin. In all, Lloyd would star in some 200 comedies, both Silents and Talkies, always as a bespectacled, straw-hatted success-seeking go-getter who matched the *Zeitgeist* of the Roaring Twenties. As a sideline, he liked to photograph nude female models, his subjects ranging from the pin-up queen Bettie Page to, years later, Marilyn Monroe.

Lloyd continued as a player in Hollywood for years to come, helping to launch the careers of both Debbie Reynolds and Robert Wagner. When asked which actor would be best suited to play him in the eventuality that a biopic was ever made of his life, he answered that he'd probably pick Jack Lemmon.

Lucille and **George Murphy** in *A Girl, a Guy, and a Gob*.

Murphy played the titular "Gob," and bore the wacky nickname of "Coffee Cup." He's a flighty sailor and amateur wrestler.

Lucille is his favorite gal, and he calls her "Spindle."

Even before he designated its director, Lloyd personally selected the cast. As its star, he opted for the song-and-dance man, George Murphy, as a flighty sailor and part-time wrestler, Claudius J. Cup (aka "Coffee Cup"). He develops a yen for Dot Duncan (Lucille). In the third lead was actor Edmond O'Brien, cast as Steven Herrick, a sedate, mild-mannered shipping magnate, who in time also falls for Dot.

In a nutshell, the theme for *A Girl, a Guy, and a Gob* was based on a love triangle.

Its director, Richard Wallace, had worked for the Hal Roach studios in the1920s, often with comedian Stan Laurel. Later, when the talkies came in, he helmed three Shirley Temple pictures and directed Katharine Hepburn in *The Little Minister* (1934).

He was hardly Lucille's favorite director. Halfway through the shoot, she gave him her candid opinion: "This movie stinks. A real bomb. I hope my career doesn't explode with it."

However, when the picture was released, it was a big hit, and Lucille falsely asserted how much she enjoyed working with its cast and crew.

According to the constantly revised script, she was a poor working girl from a screwball

Edmond O'Brien was cast in the third lead, playing Steven Herrick, an affluent businessman who falls in love with Dot Duncan (Lucille).

257

family whose quirks had been inspired by the zany relatives of Jean Arthur in the hit movie, *You Can't Take It With You.* (1938).

Murphy and Lucille had known each other for years, beginning when she had bit roles in three of his movies in the 1930s. Now, she had graduated to leading lady status. By the 1950s, as owner of RKO, she was in a position to hire him as a public relations executive. At the urging of his best friend, Ronald Reagan, Murphy would run for the office of U.S. Senator from California, serving from 1965 to 1971.

Edmond O'Brien, Brooklyn born and of Irish descent, got his big break in 1939 when Pandro S. Berman, Lucille's former lover, cast him as the romantic lead in *The Hunchback of Notre Dame.* He later hung around Hollywood long enough to drink a lot, gain a lot of weight, and go to seed. But when he worked with Lucille, he was handsome and slim. A national organization of spinsters voted him as having "more magnetism" than any other male actor in Hollywood. They unanimously agreed that O'Brien stirred their "imaginative impulses." The runner-up was Ezio Pinza, the Italian singer.

O'Brien's biggest critical success came when he won a Best Supporting Actor Oscar for his role in *The Barefoot Contessa* (1954), starring Ava Gardner and Humphrey Bogart.

Lucille became close friends with O'Brien. After she married Desi, they often entertained him.

[In 1985, she was saddened to read a comment by his daughter, Maria, published in Variety. *She had recently visited her father when he was in a straitjacket at Veterans' Hospital. "He was screaming. He was violent. I saw him walking around like all the other lost souls trapped there."*

At the age of 69, O'Brien died of complications from Alzheimer's disease.]

In one of her first films, Marguerite Chapman, a former switchboard operator and Powers model, had the third female lead as snobbish Cecilia Grange. She attracted the attention of Howard Hughes, who gave her a screen test, and she went on to make a number of pictures with leading stars like Edward G. Robinson and George Sanders.

She never rose to A-list star status, and by the 1950s, she was playing minor roles, one of them opposite Marilyn Monroe in *The Seven-Year Itch* (1955).

Lucille worked once again with the prissy Franklin Pangborn, cast as the owner of a pet store. She was more impressed with veteran character actor Henry Travers, cast as Able Martin. He had a long career, often playing slightly bumbling but lovable old men. He's seen every Christmas on TV playing the guardian angel, Clarence Odbody, to James Stewart in the classic, *It's a Wonderful Life* (1946).

Although Lucille told the press that she'd had a wonderful time making her latest film, that was not the case. She confessed to being miserable since Desi left Hollywood to work at various nightclub venues across the country.

The lovers ran up big phone bills and wrote love letters to each other. In one of them, he expressed how "lonely and alone" he felt without her. In Knoxville, he lamented that he could not find even one young woman who knew how to rumba.

A reunion was planned when RKO booked her as part of a publicity visit to New York for the promotion of her previous film, *Dance, Girl, Dance.*

After that, and months later, *A Girl, A Guy, and a Gob* opened to respectable reviews.

It premiered in Manhattan. A critic for *The New York Times* asserted, "The lady's family is a little touched. They play cops and robbers in the parlor and dance an impromptu conga. Lucille Ball may not be made of rubber, but she has as much bounce. Harold Lloyd's rib-ticklish little comedy makes perfect nonsense."

The *New York Morning Telegraph* claimed that Ball, Murphy, and O'Brien "get under your skin and make you like everybody." *The New York Times* wrote, "Miss Ball has been good for quite some time and now she's better. Bigger pictures than this are calling her."

The *Hollywood Reporter* found that she handled her role with "charming ease and skill."

***

With *A Girl, a Guy, and a Gob* wrapped, Lucille, as negotiated with RKO, headed East with Maureen O'Hara to attend premiers of their joint venture, *Dance, Girl, Dance.* Although they were friends, Lucille was nonetheless jealous of the flame-haired Irish beauty for attracting more attention than she did at stopovers along the way.

After his successful gig at The Versailles, Desi had signed a month-long deal to present four daily shows at the Roxy Theatre, near Times Square in Manhattan. The largest theater in the world at the time, it seated 5,836 people. Publicized as the "Cathedral of the Motion Picture," when it opened in 1927, it hosted the premier of *The Love of Sunya,* produced by and starring Gloria Swanson, and marketed as "A Drama of Invincible Destiny." The theater, noted for its lavish stage shows, was demolished in 1960.

Between live shows, The Roxy screened films on a huge screen. Desi remembered it as *Alexander's Ragtime Band,* starring Alice Faye and Tyrone Power, but that movie had been released two years earlier. Actually, the film shown was *Tin Pan Alley,* starring Faye, Betty Grable, and John Payne, (Lucille's alltime "swoon").

Lucille looked forward to her long-delayed reunion with Desi. "I had heard rumors that all the debutantes on the East Coast were after him, but in our calls at night he steadfastly maintained that he was being true to me. Of course, I didn't believe one word coming from his lying tongue, but I was too madly in love with him to give him his walking papers."

A musician friend of Desi said, "My pal didn't know the difference between sex and love. To put it bluntly, he saw love as something that could come and go within an hour. He might be in love with Lucille Ball, but he could fall in and out of love with the pickup of the hour. Having sex was just a casual thing with him, like the brushing of your teeth or taking a crap in the john. The moment the gal left his hotel room, he forgot all about her and began plotting his next conquest."

Once, in Manhattan, Desi took the elevator up to Lucille's suite (paid for by RKO) at the Pierre. He hardly had time to greet her before he hauled her off to the bedroom.

She was eager to see his show at The Roxy, and he asked her about how her publicity tour was going. "The press treats Maureen like the lady she is and seems to regard me like the burlesque hooker I play in the film."

In the afterglow of the sex act, there was talk of marriage, and she started to raise some potential problems: "I'm several years older than you. When I'm old and gray, you'll still be jack-rabbiting it around town."

She also raised a possible conflict based on their different religions, his being Catholicism and hers being Protestantism. "In what religion will we raise our children?" she asked him. He had no answer for that.

"We come from such different backgrounds," she said, stating the obvious "I'm a very independent woman, but I've been told that women in your native country are trained to provide a man with sex whenever he wants it, to raise his children, and to have a hot meal on the table at his command. That's not who I am."

An even bigger problem reared because of their conflicting schedules. RKO had signed him to a three-picture deal, making $10,000 for each film. He would also be allowed six months a year for whatever gigs he could arrange, independently of RKO.

"I'm no orchestra wife, trailing after her hubbie. I've got a film career of my own, which will keep me in Hollywood all year, except for short vacations. That means that with your road tours, I'll have a husband for only half a year."

"I'll call you every night and write you every morning," he promised, "and I'll be true blue, as you Yankees say, although I don't know where the 'blue' comes from. In fact, before you flew here, did you get my telegram?"

"Indeed I did, a lovely sentiment," she said.

In it, he'd wired, "I loved you yesterday, and I love you today, and I will love you *mañana.*"

Erich Pommer at RKO warned her, "Don't marry Arnaz. I think he has talent and that's why I signed him. But as a husband, forget it! I'm told he's left a string of broken hearts stretching from Times Square to Sunset Boulevard."

After their reunion, and after she'd sat in for four of his shows at The Roxy, she met members of the press for interviews, denying that she was planning to marry

Joseph Cotten,. during a publicity tour in Milwaukee, encountered Lucille in the lobby of the hotel where they were staying.

According to a bellhop, he spotted Cotten leaving her hotel room in the pre-dawn hours.

Cotten had made his film debut in Orson Welles' *Citizen Kane* (1941), hailed as the greatest movie ever made..

Desi. She also gave an interview to a reporter for a feature article, "Why I Will Always Be a Bachelor Girl."

After a final night with Desi, she continued on her publicity tour for *Dance, Girl, Dance*. One stopover scheduled for two days in Milwaukee stretched into a week because of the number of events added during the course of her stay there. She and Desi would have several phone fights. At first, he accused her of having an affair with the handsome mayor of Milwaukee after seeing them together in a newspaper photo.

Two days later, he accused her of having an affair with Joseph Cotten, one of the stars of Orson Welles' *Citizen Kane* (1941).

"Don't be an ass!" she shouted back at him over the phone. "I don't even know Cotten!"

He, too, was in Milwaukee promoting one of his movies. By coincidence, right after she'd put down the phone and descended into the lobby, she spotted Cotten coming through the door from the street to confront a barrage of reporters. He recognized her and called out to her. When he came over to introduce himself, she was caught by photographers who snapped away. She could no longer pretend she didn't know him, especially when he invited her to dinner, during which she found him a charming companion.

Although later she denied having had a fling with him, a bellhop reported that he spotted Cotten sneaking out of her hotel suite at 3AM. It turned out that they shared something in common: Each of them had been seduced by Orson Welles. On the morning of the following day, Cotten drove Lucille to the airport for her departure to New York.

She wore a simple black dress, a rip-off of a Chanel. Her maid, Harriet, would follow with her two trunks on a train headed to Grand Central in Manhattan.

After checking into her suite at the Pierre, Desi was her first visitor, spending the night with her. He called it "a preview honeymoon seduction," and told her why he'd said that. He'd arranged for them to be married in Greenwich, Connecticut, and they had to be up at 6AM. He warned that he'd have to be back in Manhattan at 11AM for his first performance of the day at The Roxy.

Since Harriett had not yet arrived with most of her clothing, she told him she'd have to get married "in my black widow's weeds." To her relief, at least, she had boarded the plane from Milwaukee wearing her silver fox

As a newlywed, **Lucille** claimed that "November 30, 1940 was the most momentous day of my life."

Referring to her marriage to **Desi Arnaz.** "Friends gave our marriage six months. As for me, I gave it a week."

coat, a large fur pompon, and a hat.

A limousine was outside the hotel to carry them to Greenwich. Waiting for them was his business manager, Deke Magaziner. Lorenz Hart was supposed to have accompanied them in his capacity as Best Man, but he was too hung over from an alcoholic binge the night before.

In spite of her many reservations about marriage, she was still eager to wed Desi. "He was a jealous, hot-tempered Latino. Beneath all that dazzling charm was a homeless boy who had no one to care for him. I wanted him to be my lover and the father of my children.:"

Although he had forgotten a few arrangements, Desi had planned the details of the wedding while he was in the Midwest. He had arranged for them to short circuit the five-day waiting period required before a wedding could be formalized in Connecticut. However, they were each required to submit samples for a blood test before the ceremony could take place.

It was to have been conducted in the office of John J. O'Brien, the justice of the peace, but he found that too dreary a setting, and he drove them to a more romantic setting at his country club, set in an area with snow-covered pines and a view of a river. It was the Byram River Beagle Club. The date was November 10, 1940, which she would later cite as "the most important day of my entire life."

[Their wedding inspired an episode of a future TV sitcom. In the 1950s, devotees of I Love Lucy *would see Lucille McGillicuddy marry Ricky Ricardo at this same country club.]*

Desi had forgotten to buy a ring, and he sent his business manager out to buy one, but no jewelry store was open. The only ring he could buy was one that cost three dollars at Woolworth's

Because of all the delays, he had to phone the manager of The Roxy to deliver the bad news: Although a long line of patrons waited on the sidewalk, he would not make it back to Manhattan in time for the first show.

After the ceremony, en route back to Manhattan in a limousine, Desi and Lucille heard over the radio news of their elopement to Greenwich. At The Roxy in time for the second show, photographers and reporters were backstage waiting for them.

He brought Lucille out onto the stage to a thunderous ovation as he kissed her.

Small packets of rice had been distributed to patrons when they'd filed into the theater. As Desi appeared with Lucille, "a snowstorm" of rice was thrown at the stage. She later said, "I have only pity for the cleanup crew."

While she retreated to his dressing room, Desi later faced the press. He even showed them a copy of the most recent telegram he'd sent Lucille in Hollywood before her trip east. It read: "I LOVE YOU MORE THAN ANTONY LOVED CLEOPATRA."

After that day's final show at The Roxy, Lucille and Desi rushed to their limousine and instructed the driver to take them to El Morocco, a leading Manhattan nightclub. It was a white tie and tails only event. The club was decorated with flowers and wedding cakes. As the newly married couple entered, the band struck up "The Wedding March."

Friends from the New York and Hollywood "A" list greeted the newlyweds: Brenda Frazier, once America's most famous debutante, accompanied by Peter Arno, was among the first to kiss Desi. *[There had been rumors of a three-way with Desi.]* Lucille was rather chilly when introduced. Lorenz Hart had been too hung over to serve as Desi's best man, but he had sobered up enough to attend the late-night party. By 2AM he was staggeringly drunk once again. Richard Rodgers and George Abbott showed up with friends. Dorothy Kilgallan was there, covering the event for her column. Her new husband, Richard Kollmar, the former (stage) star of *Too Many Girls,* privately whispered to Desi, "I still have the hots for you, kid."

The next day, after Desi had finished his noon show at The Roxy, he rushed back to his dressing room, stripped off his costume, put on his pants (without his shorts) to hustle his way over to the Pierre.

Lucille was there waiting for him with George Schaeffer, the president of RKO. As he rushed in to shake the hand of his boss, he dropped his cigarette lighter. He had not zipped up his pants and his penis flopped out. Lucille took it all in, and quipped, "Forgive Desi. He believes in advertising."

As the days went by in the weeks after their marriage, his jealousy grew worse than ever. When he heard she'd hired a chauffeur to haul her around Manhattan on a shopping spree, he accused her of not only selecting the best-looking driver but of having an affair with him, too. "I'll not have a wife of mine riding around alone with a chauffeur. I've seen those 1930s movies."

"Don't you accuse me, you son of a bitch," she shouted at him. "I know for a fact that you've fucked every girl in the chorus of *Too Many Girls."*

Then her maid, Harriet, arrived from Milwaukee with Lucille's wardrobe trunks. She really did not approve of Desi, having observed firsthand their courtship and the opening days and nights of their ill-fated marriage. "They fought and made up and then fought again," she recalled. "Most of their friends gave the marriage six weeks, if that."

Before Lucille was scheduled to return to Hollywood to begin another picture, she stayed on in New York, sometimes meeting Desi at The Roxy after his late, late show. "We made love in the early morning hours and often after his second show at The Roxy when I visited him in his dressing room and locked the door."

"I was determined to make my marriage work," she said. "Desi had high hopes for a film career of his own, although I feared his accent would hamper his chances except for select roles. He wanted to become the leading Latin lover of his era."

He rigorously maintained his own private theories about marriage, details of which he confided to both Hart and Abbott. "Your wife is your wife, and marriage should in no way hamper a husband's indulging in a little outside ass. That was the world I grew up in in Cuba, My father had a wife and two miles away lived his mistress. He even had kids with his second woman. Marriage is a sacred thing, and a man's pecadilloes shouldn't interfere with a couple's wedded bliss. I don't understand why more people don't get that, especially silly Americans."

"In my first month of marriage, I still paid periodic visits to Polly

Adler's whorehouse," he claimed. "She let me break in any new gal she was hiring. The world was my oyster, and what I wanted I have only to ask for it." _

***

After Desi completed his gig at The Roxy, it was time for Lucille and him to head back to Hollywood for a new phase in their careers. They set out in the early spring of 1941 after reading a headline in *The New York Times:* LUCILLE BALL AND HER HUSBAND DESI ARNAZ TO CO-STAR.

Everything started out as what she described as a "win-win" for each of them. According to the announcement, he would be playing the romantic lead in her latest picture for RKO, *Look Who's Laughing* (1941).

Some industry insiders were even predicting that Lucille and Desi would become the reigning new comedy team of the 1940s, evocative of Burns and Allen.

They left Grand Central in Manhattan aboard the Twentieth Century Limited, changing trains in Chicago for the Santa Fe Super Chief. The cross-country trip evolved into a delayed honeymoon. They ordered champagne and caviar in the Art Deco Pullman dining car. Every day, he arranged the delivery of fresh flowers to their compartment, usually red and white carnations. They had rented two interconnected compartments, and he proudly boasted to his poker-playing buddies, "We made love at least twice a day, maybe more, depending on how I felt."

Late at night, he strummed Cuban love songs to her until well after midnight, at least until the occupants of neighboring compartments began complaining about the noise. He created a new song, "My New World with You," dedicating it to her with the promise that it would be "their song" sung at their future celebrations and wedding anniversaries.

Ventriloquist **Edgar Bergen and his dummy,** a foot-long wooden character named **Charlie McCarthy,** were the real stars of Lucille's latest movie, *Look Who's Laughing* (941).

"The dummy got all the best lines," she said. "Edgar Bergen was the straight man. In the script, I'm supposed be be in love with Edgar, but his heart belongs to his alter ego."

A flirtatious radio exchange on NBC in 1938 between Charlie and Mae West horrified the censors.

***

They faced disappointment when they arrived at her apartment to begin their married life in California.

Financially, RKO was in the doldrums. Allan Dwan, the producer and director of *Look Who's Laughing,* had ordered major script changes from screenwriter James V. Kern. To "guarantee" better box office sales, he didn't want to take a chance on an untested actor with a Cuban accent like Desi. Instead, the new script called only for performers who were already famous on radio.

The star of the picture would be Edgar Bergen, who was celebrated for his skill as a ventriloquist, always in "collaboration" with his dummy sidekick, a wooden puppet known as Charlie McCarthy, who would be billed as Bergen's sidekick. The dummy's "wisecracks" had elicited laughs from radio fans since their act was introduced in May of 1937.

[In later life, Bergen would become famous as the father of actress Candice Bergen. Incidentally, as noted in Ms. Bergen's memoir, her father excluded her from his will, but awarded $10,000 "for sentimental reasons" to the puppet in 1978 after his death.]

Dwan was not impressed with anything he had heard about either Desi or his act at The Roxy. He dropped him. He didn't really consider Lucille a draw, either, although the studio had raised her salary from $500 to $1,000 a week.

In this creepy photo, future movie star, **Candice Bergen**, daughter of Edgar, at the age of four, was photographed with her father's dummy, **Charlie McCarthy.**

According to Candice, "On the stairs, both of us wore 'feely' pajamas. The dummy was a cocky, charming character who went on to become an icon in the 1940s and '50s. While technically an only child, I was always known—as a kid, at least—as Charlie's sister."

In the late 1930s, many big-name stars in Hollywood had been labeled "box office poison," including such notables as Joan Crawford, Katharine Hepburn, Marlene Dietrich, and Fred Astaire, among others. After the failure of *Dance, Girl, Dance,* word spread through RKO that Lucille, too, had become "box office poison."

Although she had appeared in more than fifty movies, a recent Gallup poll showed that forty percent of the movie-going public had never heard of her. Hovering at around the age of thirty, she was older than sixty-five percent of the movie-going public at the time. In general, they preferred stars closer to their own age. In Hollywood, if a starlet hadn't made it big by the time she reached thirty, she was often put out to pasture. Even established, deeply entrenched female stars, by the time they approached forty, were escorted to the studio gates and dismissed.

At the time, Toronto-born Dwan had a lot of power at RKO. Although hardly known today, he was a legend in the early film industry, opening Flying A Studios in 1911, one of the first organizations to begin churning out Silent Films. He made a series of comedies and westerns, later starring Mary Pickford and Douglas Fairbanks, Sr. He went on to direct Gloria Swanson in eight silent pictures. When talkies came in, he directed child star Shirley Temple in *Heidi* (1937) and *Rebecca of Sunnybrook Farm* (1938). As late as 1949, he was turning out such hits as *Sands of Iwo Jima* starring

John Wayne.

To back up Bergen and his puppet, Dwan cast other big names from radio, notably a real-life husband-and-wife team known across the country as "Fibber McGee & Molly," (aka Jim and Marian Jordan), one of the most popular radio teams in show-biz at the time. *[The couple started out in radio in the 1920s and launched their Fibber McGee and Molly series in 1935, going off the air in 1956. For two years in the late 1930s, Jim had to work without Marian because of her long battle with alcoholism.]*

Another popular radio character with a pivotal role in *Look Who's Laughing* was Harold Peary, who had become famous for his playing "The Great Gildersleeve" (first name, Throckmorton). His sonorous voice and flustered catchphrases became his trademark.

Lucille was very disappointed to find herself cast as Julie Patterson, secretary to Bergen, with fourth billing.

If she were dismayed, she could imagine how Neil Hamilton (as Hilary Horton) felt. In 1934, when Lucille had been relegated to a bit part in *The Fugitive Lady*, he'd been the star of the picture. In advertisements, he'd been publicized as "The Arrow Collar Man," and he could only dream of the early 1930s when his name had been billed before Clark Gable's and Joan Crawford's.

Neil Hamilton, a big star in the 1930s, was awarded a small part (eighth billing) in *Look Who's Laughing*. For years, he'd been "The Arrow Shirt Man." This ad (which featured his likeness) appeared in national magazines.

The big question for movie audiences screening *Look Who's Laughing* was "Will Hamilton, cast as businessman Hilary Horton, build an aircraft factory in sleepy Wistful Vista?"

***

Living in Lucille's new apartment, Desi made it clear to her that a Cuban man expects his wife to "play second fiddle." Deeply in love, her judgment wasn't clear. She became a housewife for the first time.

She had never been much of a cook, but soon learned to make his favorite dishes such as *arroz con pollo* (chicken with rice) and black beans with *pecadillo*. As it turned out, he was a better cook than she was. It was he who prepared the first meal to which they invited guests, in this case, her family and Lolita, his mother.

Desi got to know her communist grandfather, her mother, DeDe, and her brother, Fred. Sometimes, Cleo, her cousin, would visit, too.

Cleo was more like a sister to Lucille than a first cousin. She often came over with her husband, Artie Auerbach, who was known for his radio appearances as Mr. Kitzel on *The Jack Benny Program*. After Cleo divorced him, she remarried and introduced Lucille and Desi to her new husband, Kenny Morgan. He served as an Army captain during World War II, and in the

1950s, Desi put him in charge of public relations at Desilu Productions.

As Desi soon learned, Lucille's grandfather (Grandpa Hunt) was a dedicated communist. The only newspaper he read was *People's World*, which had been founded by communists, socialists, union members, and other activists in Chicago in 1924. Its aim was "to raise the standards of struggle against the few who rob and plunder the masses."

Hunt was a disciple of Eugene V. Debs (1855-1926), the best-known socialist in America.

The fiery oratory of American Socialist **Eugene Debs** is depicted in this photo, snapped during one of his speeches. His socialist views were passionately endorsed by Lucille's grandfather.

[Born in Terre Haute, Indiana, Debs became one of the founding members of the Industrial Workers of the World, a key organizer of railway workers' strikes in the 1880s, and the Socialist Party's five-time presidential candidate in their races for the White House. A brilliant orator who opposed America's entry into World War I, he was arrested and convicted of sedition in 1918. After the courts convicted him of prison time, President Woodrow Wilson denounced him as a traitor and stripped him of his U.S. citizenship. In the 21st Century, Vermont Senator and former presidential candidate, Bernie Sanders, had long been an admirer of Eugene Debs, too.]

"When Debs spoke, he had a tongue of fire," Grandpa Hunt maintained, "and when he wrote, he had a kinship with all living beings." *[One of Debs' more famous quotes? "While there is a lower class, I am in it; while there is a criminal element, I am of it; and while there is a soul in prison, I am not free.]*

Grandpa Hunt urged Desi to join the Communist Party, but he refused. Earlier, her grandpa

In the aftermath of a botched plastic surgery, which caused her pain for the rest of her life, **Carmen Miranda** was rumored to carry around a stash of cocaine in her trademark platform shoes.

In the second of these two photos, she whirls around, *sans culottes*, with **Cesar Romero**, scandalously revealing to the world that she wore no underwear.

had persuaded Lucille to sign up for membership. She did it only as a favor, perhaps just to humor him. Actually, she was a strong supporter of President Roosevelt.

***

Carmen Miranda was one of the first visitors to the apartment of the newlyweds, and Desi himself prepared a Cuban dinner for her. "She came through the door without her signature *tutti-frutti* hat, but she was glamourous nonetheless, wearing a red dress that would have gotten her arrested in my native Santiago. Lucy adored her as much as me, except I gravitated to her music. In fact, I labeled her 'The Queen of Samba.'"

Voted the third most popular personality in America, Miranda had risen to fame during World War II. By 1945, at war's end, she was the highest paid woman in the United States, earning $200,000, the equivalent of $3 million in 2021.

During her heyday, Miranda had numerous affairs and a very brief marriage to David Sebastian. Among her many conquests were both John Payne and John Wayne, as well as Dana Andrews and a brief fling with Desi.

She even had an affair with the gay actor Cesar Romero, who had a lifelong crush on Desi himself. As one writer said, "Carmen believed that panties restricted her dance movements for which she wore 'flying skirts' and focused on fast dancing steps."

As she whirled around, the crew on her pictures often caught a glimpse of what one grip called "the Brazilian tropics south of the equator."

One afternoon during a dance with Romero for their latest movie, *Weekend in Havana* (1941), he lifted her legs up into the air, revealing that she, as usual, wore no panties. One of the mischievous cast members held a camera at a low angle and photographed her private parts.

Hundreds and hundreds of copies of that scandalous picture, through means and methods that weren't quite clear, were mailed out across the country. It was seen by thousands of men, and eventually, found its way into Kenneth Anger's book, *Hollywood Babylon*.

***

Sometimes, Constantin Bakaleinikoff, the musical director at RKO, would arrive to visit Desi and Lucille with five members of his band for a Cuban dinner and a musical evening. He always brought along some choice Russian vodka and caviar. Desi, with as many as three guitar players, sang "Babalu," which he'd perform thousands of times in his future. "Babalu" did for Desi what "Over the Rainbow" did for Judy Garland.

One night, Bakaleinikoff arrived with the latest press release from RKO. It read, "Desi Arnaz, the newcomer, may be just what the doctor ordered for RKO. He may bring back the heyday of the Latin Lover in the 1920s, which has gradually died out since the death of Rudolph Valentino in 1926. Unlike The Sheik, Desi can also sing and dance, more than just the Tango, and if teamed with his new wife, Lucille Ball, they'd make an ideal comedy team."

Their first big night out was when her longtime friend, Carole Lombard, invited them to a champagne dinner at Chasen's. There, they had a drunken reunion with Lombard and her new husband, Clark Gable, who held the title at the time as "The King of Hollywood."

***

Desi drove through the studio gates of RKO to accept the supporting role of Steve Santo in *Four Jacks and a Jill,* set for a 1942 release. Its director, Jack Hively, hoped that his comedy would be a diversion for moviegoers, who were in despair as America had been plunged into World War II after the devastating Japanese attack on Pearl Harbor the previous December.

The actual stars of the picture were Ray Bolger, Anne Shirley, and June Havoc, the sister of America's most famous stripper, Gypsy Rose Lee.

Cast into the minor role of "Happy," Eddie Foy, Jr. was the son of the legendary vaudevillian, Eddie Foy, Sr., who had maneuvered his son into a position as a key performer in the celebrated act called "Seven Little Foys."

During the first week of shooting, Desi had nothing but high hopes for the film but he soon fell into despair. He later claimed that he had hoped that no one would go see the movie. As for its director, he detested him so much he refused to mention his name in his memoir. "Nobody knows what happened to the jerk," he wrote. "I learned one thing from him, and that was how not to make a comedy. After this picture, I think the director went into hiding. What a stinker he made. The more he called me 'boy,' the more I disliked the creep."

Desi, as one of the available "Jacks," phones the "Jill" in *Four Jacks and a Jill.*

Actually, in real life, Desi wasn't as pulled-together as he appears in this press and PR photo.

One hot afternoon, enraged with the film's director, Jack Hively, he actually slugged him on the set. For years after that, Desi's detractors used that incident as affirmation of his legendary temper.

[He was deliberately trying to mislead the readers of his memoir. Hively did not disappear. Ironically, he was hired as the director of Desi's next picture, Father Takes a Wife *(1941), starring Gloria Swanson.*

Hively had helmed Lucille in the first film for which she got star billing, Panama Lady *(1939). He was also a noted film editor, a position he had performed on a number of Lucille's movies, including Garson Kanin's comedy,* Next Time I Marry *(1938).]*

Ray Bolger was still basking in the praise he'd received for his performance as the Scarecrow in *The Wizard of Oz* (1939). After that movie, he left MGM and joined RKO. Among other talents, he was known for his tap dancing, and his latest movie (which he dismissed as a "harmless bit of fluff") showcased that talent.

Anne Shirley, as Nina Novak, is caught between **Ray Bolger** (left) and **Desi Arnaz.**

Bolger, as Niffy Sullivan, saves Novak from being hit by a car.

As Steve Sarto, Desi is a taxi driver and a dead ringer for King Stephen, European royalty.

Bolger sang and danced with Foy and others in the first rendition of "Boogie Woogie Conga." In *Four Jacks and a Jill*, Desi performed with Havoc.

Actually, *Four Jacks and a Jill* was the second remake of a 1929 film, *Street Girl*, that had co-starred Betty Compson and Jack Oakie. *Street Girl* had been remade in 1936 as *That Girl from Paris. [As mentioned in an earlier chapter, that film, which also starred Jack Oakie, was a showcase for the opera diva, Lily Pons. In another touch of irony, Lucille had also appeared in that movie.]*

In *Four Jacks and a Jill,* Anne Shirley played an (exotic) Continental" named Nina Novak, who—as part of the plot—was required to sing and dance. She wasn't good at either, and her singing voice had to be dubbed by Martha Mears.

Lucille later admitted, "I was jealous of Anne Shirley because she was married *[1937-1943]* to that dreamboat, John Payne, a Southern boy from Virginia. At that time, there were only two actors in Hollywood I'd have left Desi for: John Payne or James Craig.

Despite lobbying to be a co-star with Payne in one of his pictures, Lucille never got cast with him. The equally dashing James Craig, however, would be her co-star in her next picture.

As Steve Santo, Desi had a sort of dual role playing a taxicab driver who at one point disguises himself as a prince, making an appearance at a gala in Manhattan's Waldorf Astoria. He accused Hively of allowing a weak, unclear plot to be filmed. "How is the audience to know if the prince at these highclass functions is the real thing or a cabbie impersonating royalty?" he asked the director. "It's not clear to me: Who is acting, and who is real? And if it's not clear to me, how can it be clear to the ticket buyers?"

Hively ignored his protests.

Desi's concerns were echoed by preview audiences who questioned "Who was who and what was what?"

Hired for a brief cameo appearance was the famous vaudevillian, Lou

Holtz, who was in the same league at the time as Milton Berle or George Burns. In the 1920s, he had been the highest-paid actor on Broadway, earning an amazing (for the time) $6,000 a week.

[Holtz invested most of that money in the stock market. When it crashed in 1929, he emerged with only $500.]

As part of his performance in *Four Jacks and a Jill,* Holtz had to deliver a long monologue, which seemed out of character for him. In take after take he stumbled over the lines, finally pleading with Hively to let him change a few of the words. In one of the hottest days of that year, he was sweating profusely, and a makeup man had to be repeatedly summoned to the set to make him ready for and endless series of retakes.

FALLEN FROM GRACE

Lou Holtz, once the highest paid actor on Broadway, had been reduced to almost abject poverty by the time he appeared with Desi Arnaz.

The culprits, he said, were changing tastes in the entertainment industry and the collapse of the Stock Market in 1929.

Here's how he appeared a decade after the crash.

Yet Holtz continued to flub his lines, and the director denounced him in front of cast and crew. The star seemed to have developed some kind of block. He cursed the director one final time, and then walked off the set, exiting from the studio twenty minutes later.

Holtz, as a minor player in the cast, could have his appearance cut from the movie. Desi, however, proved an even greater problem. His conflicts with his director, Hively, almost let to a fist fight.

One hot afternoon, Desi's Latin temper exploded, and he grabbed Hively by his shirt, calling him a "broken down bum," and a "son of a bitch. You've never done a goddamn thing but a five-and-ten-cent budget piece of shit, you stupid asshole. Who in the fuck ever told you you knew how to direct?"

An attack like this by an actor on a director was almost unheard of. Hively controlled his temper that day, and even allowed Desi to join the cast of his next picture for RKO.

One reviewer of *Four Jacks and a Jill* suggested that Desi's big number, a reprise of "Boogie Woogie Conga," wasn't enough to save the picture. Another critic, years later, wrote that he found Desi "handsome, and quite comprehensive in English, so you do wonder what happened to him in his *I Love Lucy* days. Was his Cuban accent a mere put-on?"

Most movie-goers agreed with a critic who claimed, "The plot creaks and the jokes land with a thud."

RKO lost $113,000.

***

During the filming of *Four Jacks and a Jill,* June Havoc attracted an avid admirer who found her "super sexy, gorgeous, and blonde...a triple threat." He was her co-star, Desi Arnaz. In the film, she played Opal, a tough band singer whose big number was "I Haven't a Thing to Wear."

Desi flirted openly with her, telling her that he loved to see her when she didn't have anything to wear.

Three days before Havoc invited him into her dressing room at five in the afternoon, they'd had lunch together twice and some long talks while waiting for their next scenes.

He found her very insecure. "I don't know how I'm going to photograph with my long Norwegian beak."

He assured her, "You can in no way look other than what you are: A beautiful doll, highly desirable."

"The makeup man even criticized my ears as being too small, but they are larger than my older sister's."

She was referring to Gypsy Rose Lee, the most famous stripper in America.

"I don't think your ears, and especially tiny ears of Gypsy, is

Sexy **June Havoc** was a blonde star whose trim figure and "ready-for-my-closeup" good looks got her included in the ranks of actresses competing with Lucille for some of the same roles.

Comparisons to Havoc's sister, Gypsy Rose Lee, then the most famous stripper in the world, were purely coincidental.

In the left photo, she appears in *Brewster's Millions* (1945), playing an actress who'll "put out" for the the right producer.

In later years, despite Havoc's youthful dalliance with Desi Arnaz, she and Lucille became close friends.

In the right photo, she appears as the focal point of "*Willy*,' a short-lived TV series produced by Lucy and Desi at Desilu.

a problem," he said. "I've seen your sister on the stage. When she comes out as a burlesque queen, no man in the audience is looking at her ears."

"My childhood ended with the death of vaudeville," Havoc lamented. "My girlhood went down the drain with the outlawing of the dance marathon. Now I've hit Tinseltown, where the studio system is already frayed to a cobweb."

Soon, Desi was remaining late at the studio, spending an hour or two alone with Havoc in her dressing room. That meant that he arrived late every night for supper with Lucille, making up some excuse.

His wife had met Havoc on her first week of work on *Four Jacks and a Jill*. According to Lucille, "She was unstrung sitting under a hair dryer and bawling her eyes out. I had never seen so much water coming from a human being. I pulled back the dryer so we could talk."

Havoc poured out her anxieties about becoming a movie star: "On

Broadway, it's called stage fright," Lucille responded. "On camera, and in Hollywood, it's called 'the jitters.' But I think you'll come through. I'll tell you what you need, and that is a friend. Why not come back with me tonight and have dinner at my apartment with Desi and me?"

As Havoc relayed to her sister, she had hoped that with her new contract with RKO, she'd be interpreted as a serious actress like Ingrid Bergman.

"When you're Gypsy Rose Lee," her sister had responded, "You don't have to act, and you don't have to sing. All you have to do is to keep up enough strength to carry your money to the bank, and—oh yes—toss a garter to a bald-headed old geezer in the front row."

Desi was fascinated when Havoc revealed details of her life as a child star. At the age of two, she had worked in Harold Lloyd's short films. Later, prodded by her tyrannical mother, Rose, she became a stage performer. By the age of five, she was a vaudeville headliner, and, later, a model and dancer. Her biggest breakthrough had been her triumph on the Broadway stage in 1940 starring in *Pal Joey*.

"Even if I became a big movie star," Havoc told Desi, "I doubt if I'll ever receive the fame and notoriety of my sister, Gypsy."

Havoc and Lucille had dinner ready by the time Desi arrived two hours later. At first, he seemed shocked to see the emerging star with his wife, but, as they talked, he realized that Havoc had been discreet. They'd each concealed their sexual trysts from Lucille. That evening, however, marked the debut of a lifelong friendship for the trio.

About a decade later, when Lucy and Desi were in charge of Desilu in the 1950s, they hired Havoc as the star of *Willy*, a TV series about an unmarried lawyer ("Willy" Dodger) in a small New England town. Broadcast on CBS at 10:30PM, it had to compete every Saturday night with the very popular TV series, *The Hit Parade*. It survived for only one season (1954-1955).

Also in 1954, Lucille and Desi starred together in a comedy, *The Long, Long Trailer*. The vehicle that inspired its title was one of the longest and most luxurious in America.

After it was wrapped, Desi moved the vehicle to a location at their ranch at Chatsworth in San Fernando Valley. There, it served as a guest house for friends who visited them there. Between acting gigs, Havoc would sometimes move into the trailer and set up housekeeping.

***

Lucille may not have known about her husband's affair with June Havoc, but she was aware that in New York, Desi had sustained a torrid affair with Renée DeMarco, a famed ballroom dancer who usually performed alongside her husband, Tony DeMarco. During Desi's earliest days in Hollywood, Renée had followed him there, and they'd become engaged.

According to Renée, "He dumped me for Lucille. She snatched that Cubano stud right from under my nose."

Amazingly, Lucille and Renée became friends, seemingly not jealous of each other. After her divorce from Tony, Renée began an affair and later married Jody Henderson, who became her dancing partner.

She married him in March of 1943 and two months later the couple produced a baby daughter. In an arrangement that surprised many of their friends in Hollywood, the newlyweds came and lived with Lucille and Desi on their ranch in San Fernando Valley.

Lucille doted on their baby girl, often lamenting that she did not have "a pink-cheeked little girl of her own."

Renée's second marriage did not work out, either. She divorced Henderson and later wed Paul V. Coates, a Hollywood publicist.

As time went by, she faded from the lives of Lucille and Desi. The last they heard of her, she went into oblivion, moving to Bend, Oregon, where she died in 2000.

***

Variety announced that Gloria Swanson, one of the most visible screen

In *Father Takes a Wife*, a 1941 release from RKO, **Gloria Swanson** returned to the screen after an absence of seven years. Her co-stars were **Adolphe Menjou** and **Desi Arnaz.**

Critics immediately began sharpening their knives, calling her return to pictures "woefully inadequate for a once great star." Other words they used included "fluffy," "trifling," "forced," "arch," "insubstantial," and "negligible."

The artist and political cartoonist, James Montgomery Flagg, wrote, "I have an idea that **Gloria Swanson** will always be a beautiful woman."

That was certainly true at the beginning of the 1940s. As the reigning "clothes horse vamp" of the Silent Screen, Swanson remained obsessed with the elaborate finery that had helped make her famous in the 1920s.

Feverishly, she continued her trademark "over the top glamour" during her filming of *Father Takes a Wife.*

vamps of silent pictures, would be returning to the screen to star in a Technicolor musical for Paramount, *Louisiana Purchase,* opposite Bob Hope. Like so many other projects in Hollywood, the deal eventually collapsed, but it was made clear that she might be offered another picture deal if she'd submit to a screen test.

Father Takes a Wife (eventually released in 1941) would co-star Swanson with Adolphe Menjou, her longtime friend and co-worker from the 1920s. Each was known as a "clothes horse."

Jack Hively, fresh from (disastrously) directing Desi in *Four Jacks and a Jill,* conducted the screen test, and subsequently approved casting the legendary and highly temperamental Swanson. Shooting began on April 18, 1941. Swanson's contract stipulated that she'd receive $35,000.

Desi Arnaz was an unlikely co-star in an acting trio that included Adolphe Menjou and **Gloria Swanson**, two veteran (some said "temperamental and way past their prime") stars of another era.

As a stowaway on a ship, he is more or less adopted by Swanson and Menjou, her new (onscreen) husband.

Arnaz emerges as a sort of Cupid, managing to save the new marriage of this bickering, difficult-to-handle, late-middle-aged couple.

[Ironically, two years later, Menjou would co-star with Swanson's long time, equally ossified arch rival, Pola Negri in Hi Diddle Diddle (1943), *a spectacular flop.]*

Although Swanson—once the reigning queen of the silent screen— had not made a picture in seven years, her Talkies, at least six of them filmed in the late 1930s, had each been lackluster, including *A Perfect Understanding* (1933) with Laurence Olivier.

In contrast, Menjou had made a graceful and profitable transition from Silents to Talkies. Whereas in 1926, he'd co-starred with Rudolph Valentino in his most famous silent film, *The Sheik* (1921), Menjou later appeared in a Talkie that became world-famous: *Morocco* (1930) with Gary Cooper and Marlene Dietrich.

In the script by Dorothy and Herbert Fields of *Father Takes a Wife,* Menjou was cast as a widowed and middle-aged shipping magnate who falls in love with Leslie Collier (Swanson), a famous stage actress. After a whirlwind courtship, he marries her and turns over his empire to his son, Junior (John Howard).

They sail away on Menjou's yacht, on which they encounter a young stowaway, Carlos Bardez (Desi), who's trying to get to New York so that he can break in as a singer. He comes off as a bit of an egotistical "singing genius," based on the character's view of himself.

He manages to charm both of them, especially Swanson, who decides to become his sponsor. The young artist moves in with the older couple and eventually tests their patience. Menjou becomes jealous, viewing him as a rival

Years later, some movie-goers decided that Desi—for the first time on screen— showed that comic aptitude he'd demonstrate more than a decade later on television during the 1950s in the *I Love Lucy* series.

John Howard and Florence Rice were credited as Menjou's son and daughter-in-law.

The plot, referred to as "lightweight as a champagne bubble," also cast the formidable Helen Broderick as Swanson's man-hungry Aunt Julie. At that time, whereas Eve Arden was becoming known as the "Queen of the Wisecrack," one reviewer suggested that Helen Broderick should be defined as the "Mother of the Wisecrack."

Helen amused Desi throughout the shoot, telling him about how she had tried to get Lucille to marry her son, the tough, rough, and gruff actor, Broderick Crawford.

Also in the cast was Neil Hamilton, a fading star of yesterday, who appears as Vincent Stewart, Swanson's leading man in some of the plays she starred in on Broadway.

Hamilton talked with Desi about his first-ever meeting of Lucille when he'd been the star of *The Fugitive Lady* (1934), and she played a bit part. Ironically, Florence Rice, now reduced to the bit part of the daughter-in-law, had been Hamilton's co-star in that film.

Throughout *Father Takes a Wife*, the glamourous Swanson appeared in fantastic and outrageous fashions. When she made her first dramatic entrance onto the set, the 200-member crew applauded her return to motion pictures.

During the shoot, word was spreading about the on-screen chemistry of Menjou with Swanson. RKO executives were considering branding them as a co-starring team evocative of all those *Thin Man* pictures with William Powell and Myrna Loy.

Suitable showcase vehicles for them were being discussed, too. Columbia Pictures was considering an offer for Swanson, and even Cecil B. De Mille, her director during her silent film heyday, was thinking about recruiting her again. Louis B. Mayer at MGM also expressed an interest in re-hiring her.

After *Father Takes a Wife*, flopped at the box office, all of these deals and "expressions of interest" vaporized. Swanson would have to wait until 1949 until Paramount, at the last minute, hired her as the fading Silent Screen diva, Norma Desmond, in *Sunset Blvd.*, released the following year.

Appearing opposite William Holden, Swanson, during her performance as the demented has-been, was nominated for an Oscar, losing to Judy Holliday for her "dumb blonde" role in *Born Yesterday.*

Neither Swanson nor Desi got along with Hively. Of course, he remembered Desi's physical assault on him during the filming of *Four Jacks and a Jill*, and he cracked down on Desi in this new movie, sometimes demanding take after take.

Desi's greatest disappointment came when Hively had his voice dubbed in that Latin favorite "Perfidia," a title usually translated as

"Treachery" or "Betrayal." The song had been written by Alberto Dominguez, a Mexican composer and arranger.

Charles Koerner, president of RKO, had heard Desi sing it at a benefit in San Francisco and had purchased the rights to it, telling Hively to insert it into *Father Takes a Wife*.

"I always liked the ballad, and the way I sang it was just with my guitar," Desi said.

However, Hively had other ideas. Although Desi sang it with the understanding that it would be inserted into the context of the film, his voice was later dubbed by an Italian tenor and backed up by a complete orchestra. Years later, many of Desi's Spanish-speaking fans wanted to know why he sang it in the style of an operatic aria, and with an Italian accent.

The song became a standard and was later recorded by dozens of other musicians, including Xavier Cugat, Desi's former boss. Other artists recorded it, too, including Andrea Bocelli, Nat King Cole, Benny Goodman, Glenn Miller, Mel Tormé, and Linda Ronstadt.

Desi later said, "Hively was more of an asshole than ever, except this time I didn't beat him up. I controlled my Latin temper."

In her memoirs, and without a lot of clarification, Swanson gave her impression of Desi: "Desi Arnaz is…well…Desi Arnaz."

A year later, Hively weighed in with his own impressions: "Gloria Swanson was more concerned with her makeup and her gowns than she was with the role she was playing. As for Arnaz, what can I say? He was a total jerk, and I detested him as much as he detested me. I never knew why Lucille Ball married him. Maybe he has a big dick. Even recently married, he was still chasing after every pretty gal at RKO, even our script girl. Fortunately for me, he would soon be gone from my life forever."

RKO advertised the movie with slogans that included: THERE'S GLAMOUR ON THE SCREEN AGAIN BECAUSE GLORIA IS BACK! The secondary headline read, "Star news of the year for every movie fan over seven! You'll see what you missed when you see what Gloria Swanson does to you in this hilariously amorous story of two lovebirds who elope without his children's consent!"

One reviewer noted, "Swanson and Arnaz mixed like oil and water, chemistry wise." Most critics dismissed the movie as "trifling." Even Swanson on her first reading of the script had called it "trifling but suitable."

Unfortunately, the film opened close to the date of the Japanese attack on Pearl Harbor. Hively said, "It was a disastrous time to open our film. Americans had more on their mind than Swanson's wardrobe or the silliness of Mr. Super Ego, Desi Arnaz. I had already told RKO that the Cuban bastard was going nowhere in films."

***

"Desi had dreams about becoming a big-time movie star, and he talked about it all the time," Lucille said. "His dreams were big, but I still felt that his thick Cuban accent would obviously hamper his chances. I urged him to take diction lessons, but he refused. I did everything I knew to advance his career, including giving pep talks to people I knew in the industry, but nothing seemed to help. The fact that his last two pictures were duds didn't exactly advance his prospects. Both of us wanted to make another movie together, but that wasn't happening."

Meanwhile, Lucille was having career problems of her own. With the coming of the war, American military men wanted cheese-cake photos to remind them of the girls they'd left behind. Of course, few could anticipate coming home to the two reigning pinup queens of the day, Betty Grable and Rita Hayworth,

"I posed for cheesecake, but some photographers called me the 'no tit wonder,'" Lucille said. "The painful truth was that there was no way in hell that I'd ever become a rival to these well-stacked dames. God didn't make me that way I felt that because I could do comedy better than those girls, I might have a chance."

She would have preferred using her long-time friend, Carole Lombard (married to Clark Gable), as her role model. It was Lombard who presented her with a script entitled *Ball of Fire,* produced by Samuel Goldwyn. She rejected it but felt it might be a breakout vehicle for Lucille.

Studying it, Lucille agreed that the role was ideal for her. Screenwriter Charles Brackett and Billy Wilder, who would later turn out Gloria Swanson's *Sunset Blvd.,* also contributed ideas to the script. *Ball of Fire* was their twist on *Snow White and the Seven Dwarfs.* It was the story of a burlesque dancer, Sugarpuss O'Shea, who moves into a house occupied by eight prissy professors, led by Gary Cooper, who had already been cast.

Lucille contacted Howard Hawks, the director, who told her that it was too late: "I've given the script to Ginger Rogers, your friend, and I'm awaiting her response. When Ginger informed Lucille that, like Lombard, she had rejected the script, Lucille phoned Hawks again. This time, he told her he'd offered the role to Jean Arthur, the very talented lesbian actress who might have been perfect for the role. One of the screen's warmest personalities, she had already proven herself in such features as *You Can't Take It With You* and *Mr. Smith Goes to Washington,* both in 1939. Lucille said, "Time for me to throw in the towel."

BALL *of* FIRE

"I should have been cast in that comedy, **Ball of Fire**, as the burlesque queen, Sugar-puss O'Shea," Lucille said. "The new picture could have been advertised as LUCILLE BALL IN *BALL OF FIRE*."

To her regret, **Barbara Stan-wyck** was cast instead.

Weeks later, Lucille learned that the film's male lead, **Gary Cooper,** had strongly objected to her getting cast into the role she craved.

Directed by Howard Hawks, the Samuel Goldwyn Production was loosely based on the Walt Disney film, *Snow White and the Seven Dwarfs* (1937).

In this case, Snow White was a burlesque queen, and the dwarfs were a group of university professors researching the nuances of modern American slang.

But then she heard that Arthur, too, had rejected it.

Hawks took Lucille's call once again. "Sorry," he said. "I'm sure you would have been fine for the role, but I've given it to Barbara Stanwyck. She's at the peak of her career and will be big box office. Only trouble for me is that she's one of the highest paid actresses in Hollywood. You would have to come cheap for me."

She later learned that it had been Cooper himself who had "pulled the plug" on Lucille, demanding Stanwyck instead. Lucille claimed that "The 'yup' man is a fucking son of a bitch for dumping me—my one big chance."

Lucille's hunch about the value of the role proved correct at Oscar time. Stanwyck was nominated for a Best Actress Academy Award, losing to Joan Fontaine for *Suspicion.*

***

In 1941, as Lucille moved closer to her thirtieth birthday, she was overcome with career anxiety. What did her future hold for her? "In Hollywood, if a starlet hasn't made it by the time she reaches thirty, she's often shipped home," she said. "Back to the wheat fields of Idaho, the fishing shacks of the Bayou Country, or the job of a librarian in a small town in New England. For the lucky ones, they'll reunite with their high school sweetheart, get married, and have five kids."

She feared that her days as the Queen of the Bs at RKO were winding down. The studio was struggling financially, and massive layoffs were predicted.

George Schaefer had been fired as president and been replaced by Charles Koerner. Almost immediately, Koerner set out to make economies, firing Orson Welles. He had recently made *Citizen Kane,* a film loosely based on press baron William Randolph Hearst, Many critics later heralded it as the greatest film ever made, but it had not immediately made money. In his next production, Welles, "the boy genius," continued to go over budget.

"He had a genius for going over budget," Koerner claimed. "The new motto at RKO is 'showmanship over genius.'"

In time, Lucille became one of the most famous entertainers on the planet, but in the early 1940s, she was not that well known except within the Hollywood colony. RKO conducted a survey of its stars, which among other revelations, had revealed that two-thirds of the movie-going public had never heard of her. Those who had were given a card to fill out with comments about Lucille Ball. Many of them described her as "hussy," "real cheap," or "floozie." They seemed to be describing the role she'd played in *Dance, Girl, Dance.*

She also appeared on a list of stars who were "destined to fail." Sharing the roster with her were such future stars as Ann Miller, Victor Mature, and William Holden.

"It's about time I fled the coop before I'm fired," she said. She began shopping around, contacting other studios as her contract had only a few months to go. Would Fox, MGM, Paramount, or Universal want to hire her? Would Columbia be interested in signing her again?

On the homefront, she faced growing pains in her marriage to Desi. There wasn't a week that went by when their arguments didn't end in major, blockbusting fights. Sometimes, he'd storm out of the house and would be gone for as long as three days. On some occasions, he'd stay in the apartment he rented for his mother, Lolita.

DeDe, Lucille's own mother, became used to being awakened at 4AM and hearing Lucille tearfully claim, "The philandering bastard has left me once again. Why oh why didn't I listen to you in the first place and not marry him? Mother knows best."

One of the growing pains within their marriage was about money. She was thrifty, and he was a spendthrift. Once, he took her for a weekend in Las Vegas. "Call it beginner's luck, but I won $18,000," she said. "I stopped while I was ahead. That Monday morning, I called my new business manager and had him invest it for me. What was Desi's fate that weekend in Las Vegas? He lost $5,000 at the gaming tables: half the fee he'd received for co-starring with Swanson in *Father Takes a Wife.*

When eventually Desi did score big in Vegas, he didn't put his winnings in a bank, but immediately went out and bought a boat.

Desi and Lucille agreed on one thing: Their apartment was just too small, especially if they wanted to have kids. She longed to have children, but he was hesitant about such a commitment. One night, when they discussed their need for a bigger place to live, they dined with Jack Oakie, who had become her friend since they made two successful movies together, *The Affairs of Annabel* and *Annabel Takes a Tour.*

"I know the perfect place for you to settle, Oakie said. "Buy a small ranch in the San Fernando Valley. I'll take you guys there tomorrow."

Little knowing it at the time, their lives were about to undergo a change whose implications would be felt for years to come.

CHAPTER TEN

LUCILLE & DESI FIGHT WORLD WAR II ON THE HOMEFRONT

Jack Oakie, one Saturday morning, took Desi and Lucille on a tour of the San Fernando Valley, which she later referred to as a "wild and woolley open space in those days." Many movie stars, soon to become their friends, were moving there, preferring it to Beverly Hills.

Not far away from where Desi and Lucille eventually settled, they visited the ranch of her friend, Carole Lombard, and "The King," Clark Gable, at Encino.

Sometimes, while Desi and Gable played poker, Lucille and Lombard would go for walks in the country, where she became intrigued with abandoning her cramped apartment in the city and seeking an oasis, perhaps a small ranch for Desi and herself.

The outspoken Lombard confessed a secret to Lucille: "I have only two regrets in my marriage to Clark. I want to be a mother but that hasn't happened, Also, forgive me for saying so, but I wish Clark had two more inches than he does. I love Pa dearly, but I can't say he's a helluva good lay."

The Gable/Lombard ranch house was (facetiously) known as "The House of the Two Gables." Lombard showed Lucille her dressing room and bathroom, which she referred to as "The Most Elegant Shithouse in the San Fernando Valley."

Sometimes, she accompanied her husband on fishing and hunting trips, and he even taught her how to

Clark Gable, "The King of Hollywood," and **Carole Lombard**, "The Queen of Screwball Comedy," enjoy a quiet, sunny afternoon in 1938.

They were photographed in front of a picket fence at their ranch house at Encino in the San Fernando Valley.

Their endorsement of the good life there would in the months ahead lure new neighbors, Lucille Ball and Desi Arnaz.

ride a horse. She told Lucille, "The first time I went riding on a horse, it reminded me of a dry fuck."

Once, when she was alone with Lucille, she spoke of her previous husband, William Powell, and of her many lovers such as John Barrymore, musician Russ Columbo (who died tragically), Gary Cooper, aviator Howard Hughes, David Niven, George Raft, Buddy Rogers (married to Mary Pickford), director Ernst Lubitsch, Preston Sturges, and David Selznick.

As the two married couples sat on Gable's terrace, admiring the view, Lucille and Desi shared their dream of also finding a ranch house and living in the valley.

Invariably, they talked of the movies, suggesting possible roles for themselves or speaking of films already made.

Lucille related how she was tested by Selznick for the role of Scarlett O'Hara in *Gone With the Wind* (1939), in which Gable had starred as Rhett Butler.

Lombard asked Desi what he thought of the movie based on the famous novel by Margaret Mitchell.

"I've heard of that film," he said, "but I never saw it. What's it all about?"

***

A short time later, lured to "The Valley" by the example set by Carole Lombard, Clark Gable, and Jack Oakie, Lucille and Desi set out on their own to explore (and perhaps invest in) the orange-tree studded region about twenty miles north of Hollywood. Occasionally, they'd drive past a ranch-style house with a white-painted wooden fence in front. Years later, they'd remark, almost with incredulity, how sparsely settled San Fernando Valley had been in the months before World War II.

The region's former residents, Native Americas, left behind caves featuring "rock art" and other artifacts. On one occasion, they got out and took a long walk, taking in the mountains of the Transverse Range. They finally found a newly built ranch house they wanted. Set on five acres, it was available for only $15,000. The West Hills lay to the south, the Simi Hills to the north.

The location was in the little town of Chatsworth in the northwestern section of the Valley. The area had been colonized by the Spanish beginning in the late 1760s. It became a U.S. possession after the Mexican-American War (1846-1848).

The area was also the home of the Inverson Movie Ranch, a 500-acre site which became the most filmed movie ranch in cinema history. Dozens upon dozens of Westerns were shot there.

They needed a name for their ranch and preferred a combination of their respective names, finally settling on "Desilu." It later became the name of their film production company, too.

Other movie stars who had settled in the area collaborated on hosting a "welcome-to-the-neighborhood party." They brought much-needed supplies, especially gifts for the kitchen. Milton Berle sent a large box of toilet paper.

With the help of some local carpenters, Desi created a chicken coop, and Grandpa Hunt arrived to erect a barn for Holstein calves. The property already had a swimming pool, and Lucille supervised the planting of a vegetable garden. Its chief crop was Swiss chard, her most preferred vegetable, which she served at practically every meal.

Snapped at the Cocoanut Grove, a rising young star, **William Holden**, and his actress wife, **Brenda Marshall**, were neighbors of Lucille and Desi.

During their frequent visits, Lucille tried hard not to reveal that she had a crush on the handsome young actor.

Two of their favorite guests were the actor/actress team of William Holden and Brenda Marshall. *[Marshall preferred that her friends address her with her birth name, Ardis Anderson.]* She had divorced her first husband and married Holden in 1941.

Lucille considered him (rivaled by James Craig) as "the handsomest, sexiest, and most charismatic macho male in the movies."

She had "fallen in love" with him when she saw him opposite Barbara Stanwyck in *Golden Boy* (1939). Lucille would get to know him far more intimately when she co-starred with him in *Miss Grant Takes Richmond* (1949).

In 1952, the Holdens would be designated as Best Man and Matron of Honor at the wedding of their best friends, Ronald Reagan and starlet Nancy Davis. *[Often, during the 1950s, the Holdens, the Reagans, and the Arnaz's would collectively engage in triple dates, dining and dancing at Chasen's and the Cocoanut Grove.]*

Barbara Stanwyck emotes with **William Holden** in *Golden Boy* (1939), the picture that made him a star. It was the story of a music-minded young man who becomes a prizefighter.

Off screen, the couple launched a torrid affair.

Another neighbor, actor Francis (aka Franz) Lederer, sometimes visited for dinner with his new wife, Marion Irvin, a native of Canada, whom he'd wed in 1941. *[He had previously been married to the actress who billed herself as "Margo."]* In reference to Irvin, he told Lucille, "On the second time around, I got it right."

"Marion and I became close," Lucille said, "and she was a great promoter of humanitarian causes. I got involved whenever I could."

[Lederer would live to the age of 100, dying in 2000 as one of the last surviving

veterans of World War I's Austro-Hungarian Army.]

Richard Carlson and Lucille had been friends since they'd co-starred in *Too Many Girls*. As a neighbor, he and his wife Mona, whom he'd married in 1939, were frequent dinner guests, claiming that Desi made the best spaghetti sauce known to humankind. The Carlsons often provided Lucille with company when Desi went on tour.

In time, Lucille and Desi also became close friends with their other neighbors, Gordon and Sheila MacCrae, who had gotten married in 1941. After serving in the U.S. Army Air Force during World War II, MacCrae returned to Hollywood and starred in two of Rodgers & Hammerstein's most memorable musicals, *Oklahoma!* (1955) and *Carousel* (1956).

Lucille's most memorable moment occurred on August 6, 1941 when she approached the dangerous age (for a film actress) of thirty. "When I woke up that day, Desi made no mention of my birthday. Finally, I needed some groceries, and I drove off to a store two miles down the road."

When she returned, she was greeted with at least two dozen guests, some of whom had driven up from Hollywood. Desi had hired a five-piece Cuban band, and everyone joined in to sing "Happy Birthday" to her.

Suburban social life in the then sparsely inhabited San Fernando Valley was like postwar suburban life everywhere else in postwar America, except that many of the Arnaz family's neighbors were also movie stars.

Pictured above are **Mr. and Mrs. Gordon McCrae** (Gordon and Sheila) in 1952.

All of them were in her front yard. When she entered the house, she was enchanted to see that he had covered the water of their swimming pool with white carnations, her favorite flower.

At the time, Desi was having a hard time getting a new gig. Stardom, which had seemed so certain at one point, looked more elusive. He kept calling his agent, who told him that it was almost certain he'd get cast in an upcoming picture, *The Navy Comes Through.*

"Will I get star billing, and what beauty will be my leading lady?" Desi asked.

"Not so fast," the agent answered. "You'll get seventh billing, and you'll play a Cuban."

***

Desi still had a few weeks before shooting began on his next picture, so he drove Lucille to Taos, New Mexico. There, in the sweltering heat of midsummer, in a hotel without air conditioning, shooting began on her latest movie for RKO, *Valley of the Sun*, scheduled for a release in 1942.

The story had originally appeared in 1940 as a serial in *The Saturday*

Evening Post. It was written by Clarence Buddington Kelland, who had had a big success with his *Mr. Deeds Goes to Town,* made into a hit movie in 1936, starring Gary Cooper and Jean Arthur.

In the Arizona Territory of the 1860s, Lucille plays a saloon keeper at the Busy Bee Café in Yuma.

Her leading man, James Craig as the heroic Jonathan Ware (who disrupts her wedding), has another plan for her, wanting her for himself. Although he's on the lam and evading the military police, he's a friend of the Indians and wants Jagger to return the cattle he's stolen from them.

"I knew she had the hots for her co-star, James Craig," Desi said. "He'd been introduced to her when he co-starred as one of the suitors of Ginger Rogers in *Kitty Foyle* (1940). Lucille raved about him, his looks, his male beauty, and his rugged masculinity. I mean, like I had all those things, too, but better. It was a good thing I was going with her to New Mexico, because I could not trust my wife alone for one minute with this heartthrob."

But once Desi arrived on location, he was clearly bored and had nothing to do. Then, he discovered some Indians beating their drums. He asked to join them, and over the course of a week, he taught groups of them to play the conga. "There must have been five-hundred Indians hired for the shoot, but by the time I left New Mexico, I had the whole tribe addicted to the conga."

Lucille was surprised that RKO had cast her in a Western. Then, she learned that she had not been the first choice for the role. The part had originally been offered to Dale Evans, the Queen of the Cowgirls and the wife of Roy Rogers. A deeply religious person, she turned it down, telling RKO that the character she'd been asked to play was "immoral."

The role had also been offered to Dorothy Comingore, who had recently filmed *Citizen Kane* (1941) with Orson Welles. When negotiations with Comingore col-

Gossip columnists speculated that casting **Lucille Ball** as a saloon keeper in a Western would be a disaster.

Director George Marshall responded, "If I could make that Kraut, Marlene Dietrich, convincing in *Destry Rides Again,* I surely can do it again with Miss Ball."

With war paint on his chest and tied in ropes, the fate of **James Craig** is uncertain in this scene from *Valley of the Sun.*

Craig had faced that same uncertainty in his career when it had been announced that, because of his resemblance, he was the actor most likely to replace Clark Gable—then fighting on the battlefields of Europe--for movies he couldn't make.

lapsed, Lucille emerged as the third choice.

When she learned that her director would be George Marshall, she felt more at ease, convinced that he'd know how to guide her. "After all, he managed to make that German Kraut, Marlene Dietrich, convincing in a Western, *Destry Rides Again* (1939), and I knew he could do the same for me."

John Houseman had said, "George was one of the old maestros of Hollywood. He never became one of the giants like John Ford, but he held a solid and honorable reputation in our industry."

Marshall had launched his career in the early days of the Silents, starting out with Westerns, some starring Tom Mix, but he'd also helmed comics Laurel and Hardy. In time, he'd direct other comedians such as Bob Hope, W.C. Fields, Jackie Gleason, Jerry Lewis, and Will Rogers. On occasion, he'd make pictures with A-list actresses such as Barbara Stanwyck or Loretta Young.

Lucille was intrigued that he had recently directed William Holden and his friend, Glenn Ford, in *Texas* (1941). She also spoke to Marshall about her friendship with Holden and his wife, Brenda: "Before he got hitched, did Bill play around?" she asked.

"He told me he did…and how!" Marshall said. "That mostly lesbian Stanwyck fell for him when they co-starred in *Golden Boy* (1939). He confessed that when he first hit Hollywood, he spent his nights servicing older actresses."

"I was a male whore," Holden admitted. "All actors are whores. We sell our bodies to the highest bidder."

"That's good to know," Lucille said. "If I ever divorce my philandering husband, I might take up with Bill—that is, if by that time he's divorced from his wife."

"Bill is the kind of guy who enjoys his vices more than his virtues," Marshall said. "But he's got a drinking problem. I'll say this about the guy: He's the cleanest man you'll ever meet. He takes at least four baths a day, maybe five."

Lucille was thrilled by her co-star in *Valley of the Sun* (1942), James Craig.

Actress **Fern Emmett** helps **Lucille**—a reluctant bride--get dressed for her character's wedding day.

According to Lucille, "For that scene, I wore more clothes than I did in my last trio of movies: A billowing, floor-length gown, a half dozen petticoats, a smothering, bone-ribbed corset, and of course, the mandatory bustle."

In this publicity shot of **James Craig** interacting with **Lucille** between scenes, his ornamental "Indian drag" wasn't particularly convincing.

286

Handsome, dashing, and charming, Craig, a son of Tennessee, was a married man, having wed Mary June Ray in 1939. That same year, he was tested for the role of Rhett Butler in *Gone With the Wind* (1939). Lucille, as she reminded him, had also tested for the role of Scarlett O'Hara. "Who knows?" she asked. "You and I might have become lovers back then." She quickly added, "On the screen, I mean."

It was noted at the time that Craig bore a striking resemblance to Clark Gable, who ended up playing Rhett. A few months later, MGM signed him to a seven-year contract, Louis B. Mayer viewing him as a possible replacement for Gable, who said that he might join the U.S. Army Air Force.

When Desi returned to Hollywood, Craig had been flirting with Lucille since day one. In the film, during their characters' initial encounter, she catches him taking a bath in her barrel of water at the rear of her saloon. When he starts to emerge nude from the rain barrel, she steps back and demurely retreats until he's dressed.

Saucy but Subliminal

When Lucille, in *Valley of the Sun*, first encounters **James Craig**, he's taking a bath in her rain barrel.

At the end of the scene, when he emerged from the barrel, in front of the cast (including Lucy) and crew, he was wearing a jock strap.

"That jock strap was too damn small," Lucy later commented, "to conceal everything he had."

"He was not totally nude in that rain barrel," she later told her friend, Barbara Pepper. "He was wearing a jock strap, a super-sized one that bulged. I was really turned on. I figured Desi was back in Hollywood screwing around with some chorus girls or hitting the whorehouses."

"James invited himself to my hotel room one night, and left the next morning," Lucille confessed. "He was everything I thought he'd be as a man...and more! We repeated that, night after night, and we spent hours together when it rained for days and we couldn't do any filming."

"I felt I was paying my horndog husband back for his many indiscretions," Lucille said to Pepper.

Lucille's original suitor in the film was Dean Jagger, cast as Jim Sawyer, a government agent for the Indian Territories. He's cheating the tribe out of the cattle promised them by the U.S. government. Craig, in his role of Jonathan Ware, is a champion of the Indians, and he falls for Lucille (the saloon keeper) and breaks up her wedding to Jagger. It's obvious that she doesn't love him.

A former elementary school teacher, Jagger decided to go on the stage in vaudeville before becoming a character actor. He'd once played an Indian himself in a movie, *Behold My Wife* (1935). His most memorable role had been as the Mormon leader *Brigham Young* in that Hollywood biopic released in 1940, right before he worked with Lucille. "I would not be convincing in any love scenes with Jagger," Lucille warned Marshall.

The distinguished English actor, Sir Cedric Hardwicke, had the third lead of Lord Warrick, an enigmatic immigrant to America. He would have been more at home in a play by Shaw or Shakespeare.

The pudgy actor, Billy Gilbert, cast as the stuttering, sneezing Judge Homer Burnaby, provided comic relief. Lucille had seen him recently opposite Marlene Dietrich in *Seven Sinners* (1940), in which she co-starred with John Wayne.

Two big stars of yesterday, Antonio Moreno and Tom Tyler, were each reduced to minor roles: Moreno as Chief Cochise and Tyler as Geronimo. The roles were quite a comedown for them, especially when they had to strip down to display bodies that had been young at the turn of the century. *[Moreno had been born in 1887; Tyler in 1903.]*

Moreno, a native of Madrid, had once rivaled Rudolph Valentino as a romantic hero of the silent screen. He had appeared with such leading ladies as Gloria Swanson, Clara Bow, Blanche Sweet, Pola Negri, and Greta Garbo.

With the arrival of the talkies, he could never overcome his heavy Spanish accent. In *Valley of the Sun,* cast as an Indian chief, he had to wear a prosthetic nose.

To Lucille, no one represented the vagaries and pain of a Hollywood career like Tom Tyler. The cowboy star had once been known to every kid in America, especially to those who attended any of the Western-packed Saturday matinees across the land. He had started out as a merchant seaman, lumberjack, coal miner, and prizefighter.

He landed in Hollywood in 1924, working as an extra. Within a year, he was starring in Westerns for $75 a week. One of his leading ladies was Jean Arthur, who went on to major stardom.

In the 1920s, he became a popular cowboy hero and continued to make "sagebrush quickies" with the advent of Talkies. Once he was considered for the role of Tarzan.

Tyler had been an extra on such pictures as *Stagecoach* (1939) with John Wayne and *Gone With the Wind* (also 1939). He also appeared briefly in *Grapes of Wrath* (1940) starring Henry Fonda.

When he met Lucille, he had a momentary career revival, playing a mummy in *The Mummy's Hand* (1940), and having been cast in the serial, *The Adventures of Captain Marvel* (1941).

Trouble lay ahead, and in 1943, he was diagnosed with severe rheumatoid arthritis, yet struggled on as a bit player in films starring Roy Rogers, Errol Flynn, and John Wayne. He found work on Poverty Row, where some Westerns

By the time he was cast as a bit player in *Valley of the Sun*, **Tom Tyler's** career had fallen on bad days.

It had declined considerably from when he'd appeared (photo above) as a matinee idol in the silent film *Red Hot Hoofs* (1926).

He received more fan mail in the month after it was released than any other actor in Hollywood.

were shot on a budget of only $6,000.

As time went by, his condition didn't improve, and he ended up destitute, dying at the age of fifty in the home of his sister in Michigan.

When *Valley of the Sun* played in Manhattan, *The New York Times* reviewed it as "an ambling and cross-purposed film, wobbling between blood-and-thunder and Western farce." Another critic said the film revealed "why Lucille's movie career never caught fire."

One reviewer, however, called the movie "Lucille Ball's frontier treat. It packs plenty of action, rambunctious humor, and a sparkling romantic chemistry between James Craig (why he didn't become a major star remains a mystery) and luscious Lucille Ball, exuding the volcanic combination of dazzling beauty and an innate flair for slapstick.:"

Regrettably, *Valley of the Sun* did not recoup its $650,000 production cost.

***

When she returned to Hollywood, Lucille was summoned immediately to the executive offices of RKO. There, she heard the bad news of how financially strapped RKO had become. She was informed that in a money-saving cutback, her salary of $1,500 a week would be cut by one-third.

She immediately protested, and, through her agent, Arthur Lyons, she threatened a million-dollar lawsuit, citing breach of contract. Finally, the studio relented and kept her on at her regular salary, but more than ever, she became aware that her reign as "Queen of the Bs" at RKO was nearing its end.

World War II was raging, and new movie stars, both male and female, were emerging, including, among a host of others, Alan Ladd and Veronica Lake. Lucille's co-stars in the 1930s were heading for retirement. In contrast, some of her friends like Betty Grable and Ginger Rogers were becoming bigger than ever.

"My star power just did not exist," Lucille lamented.

Early in 1942, when a break came in their schedules, Lucille and Desi accepted a booking at the Roxy Theater in Manhattan, where he'd been so successful. America had entered the war, and movie-goers needed diversions.

On stage, Lucille sometimes abandoned her "glamour queen" image. Clad in baggy pants and a battered derby, she'd appear in comedy routines that evoked the slapstick routines of Charlie Chaplin. Little did she know that at

To his sometimes chagrin, **Desi** became as inextricably linked to "Babalu" (which sounded increasingly tiresome as he and musical tastes changed) as Judy Garland was with "Over the Rainbow."

Here's the cover of an album exclusively devoted to his hit single.

times, those routines were "warm-ups" for her antics on the *I Love Lucy* TV series of the 1950s.

Usually assigned entirely different routines within the same revue, Desi repeated his previous successes: He played the bongo drums and obeyed calls from the audience to play "Babalu."

After the Roxy in Manhattan, the show was successful enough that it moved to Brooklyn, and later to the Loew's State Theater in New Jersey.

Alert to their success, producers at the Palladium in London cabled an offer for Lucille and Desi to appear at that fabled West End venue. Regrettably, Lucille had to turn it down. The day before, a doctor in Manhattan had informed her that she was pregnant. Her dream of giving birth was about to come true, or so she believed at the time.

All of her future bookings had to be canceled. Then, to her ever-lasting sorrow, she lost the baby during her third month of pregnancy.

The train she rode back to California was overloaded with hundreds of sailors, soldiers, marines, and pilots.

At a stopover along the way, a paperboy came aboard touting the latest news. In "Second Coming" headlines, his newspapers blared: CAROLE LOMBARD DIES IN PLANE CRASH.

The fatal accident occurred at 5AM on the morning of January 16, 1942 after she'd boarded a Transcontinental & Western Airlines flight on a DC-3 leaving from Indianapolis after Lombard had completed a war bonds tour. Hours later, it was a flaming mass of wreckage, with debris strewn across the south side of the Potosi Mountains in Nevada.

In Hollywood, Desi made several attempts to reach Clark Gable but failed. He and Lucille did not know how to contact him. Two weeks later, they heard the sound of his motorcycle speeding up Devonshire Drive toward Chatsworth, and eventually, to their door.

When Lucille answered the door, she found "The King" looking bleary-eyed and haggard. He also seemed drunk.

He talked to them until the early hours of the morning, drinking heavily and falling asleep on the sofa in their living room. Lucille put a blanket over him before switching off the lights.

In the days ahead, Gable became a frequent visitor. Sometimes, he brought along a copy of one of Lombard's screwball comedies, which Desi would show in their den.

Gable confessed to them that he would never love again. "Perhaps I'll get married, but I'll never love any other woman now that Carole is gone from my life."

Lucille worried about Gable for many reasons and was horrified by the reckless way he drove his motorcycle. As she told Desi, "He seems to want to kill himself."

After a weekend where they had met with a grief-stricken Gable, Lucille drove to the offices of RKO. She was told that the script by Damon Runyan for a new film was still in pre-production and not yet ready for the cameras to roll.

Then, since she was still under contract to RKO, she was informed that they'd temporarily "lend" her to 20th-Century Fox to make a movie tentatively entitled *Strictly Dynamite,* starring Betty Grable and Victor Mature. Lucille would play Vicky, Grable's sister, who is murdered.

Fearing that she'd not be free of *Strictly Dynamite* in time for the debut of filming for the Runyon project, which she preferred, Lucille rejected the offer from 20th-Century Fox. That kept her schedule open so that she could work on the (delayed) Runyon film instead. In a tense situation bristling with politics and egos, her decision appeared defiant and forced her into suspension, even though she badly needed the money.

[Retitled I Wake Up Screaming *(1941), the 20th-Century project eventually co-starred Carole Landis, Victor Mature, and Betty Grable. Before the end of the decade, Landis would commit suicide, perhaps over her ill-fated romance with Rex Harrison.]*

Later, Lucille was notified that RKO was at last ready to begin shooting the film adaptation—now retitled *The Big Street*—of Runyon's short story for a release in 1942. She was to report to RKO the following Monday to meet the director and the cast.

To her surprise, she was to play opposite Henry Fonda, her former beau.

Lucille was originally offered the Carole Landis role in the *film noir, I Wake Up Screaming.*

Wanting to star in another picture, she turned down the role, in which she would have played the sister of Betty Grable, a former lover of Desi, and the pinup girl of World War II who emerged as a big star. Lucille had long known of Grable's affair with Desi.

I Wake Up Screaming would have become Lucille's first picture with **Victor Mature.**

Later, she would co-star with him in two 1940s movies. From afar, she had admired his muscular frame, slick, wavy hair, and thick lips opening onto a toothy smile.

***

In 1940, Runyon published a short story in *Collier's Weekly* magazine. It had the ridiculous title of "Little Pinks." RKO purchased the screen rights, engaged Leonard Spielgass to craft a film script, and even named Runyon as the producer.

The studio knew that naming its film adaptation "Little Pinks" would not incite fans to line up at the box office, and two or three other titles were considered before *The Big Street* was chosen. *[Manhattan's Broadway used to be nicknamed "The Big Street."]*

At first, Runyon, the newspaperman and short story writer, had recommended Charles Laughton and Carole Lombard as the leads, but that ended, of course, with the tragic death of the actress in an airplane crash in Nevada.

Born in the small town of Manhattan, Kansas, Runyon wrote about America's entertainment industry (especially its theater industry) during Prohibition. New Yorkers depicted in his work spoke in *rat-a-tat-tat* slang and were a rough and tough gang of gamblers, crooks, hustlers, actors, and gangsters, men nicknamed "Harry the Horse" or "Dave the Dude." He peopled his stories with what one critic defined as "loud-mouth, arrogant twits." Runyon's greatest fame came with the Broadway musical *Guys and Dolls* (1950), which Marlon Brando and Frank Sinatra adapted into a film in 1955.

With Lombard out of the picture, RKO wanted the lead role of a tough-talking gun moll to be cast with either Barbara Stanwyck or Jean Arthur. But before those offers went out, columnist Walter Winchell introduced Runyon to Lucille Ball in the RKO commissary one day at lunch.

On the spot, Runyon decided that she'd be just what he'd had in mind for the character of Gloria Lyons, nicknamed "Your Highness" in his short story.

Henry Fonda had signed on as the male lead, a character cursed with the absurd name of "Little Pinks." Desi felt the name was "faggy." Fonda's character was a simple, naïve busboy who falls in love with Gloria, the gun moll of gangster Case Ables,

During a Barbara Walters interview, Jane Fonda claimed that her father, **Henry Fonda**, had once been deeply in love with Lucille Ball.

"They were very close. Their on again, off again affair didn't end until they completed another picture, *Yours, Mine, and Ours* in 1968," Jane said.

When asked about Ms. Fonda's **comments, Lucille** responded, "I'd rather regret the things that I have done than the things I have not."

portrayed by Barton MacLane. Case and Gloria have a fight, and he pushes her down the stairs, which cripples her for life.

She is befriended by Pinks, who has very little money. He maneuvers her wheelchair during their long transit to Florida, getting picked up as hitchhikers by passing motorists.

Gloria hopes to recuperate in the home of his friends, Violette Shumberg (Agnes Moorehead) and her stocky husband, "Nicely Nicely" Johnson, who is overweight and speaks with the voice of a croaking frog. Moorehead, having recently appeared in Orson Welles' *Citizen Kane* (1941), was on the fast track to becoming one of the most formidable character actresses in Hollywood.

Lucille had reservations about portraying a bitch on the screen. She met with one of her admirers, Charles Laughton, who still was mulling the possibility of co-starring with her one day if they found the right vehicle. "Here's what you do," he advised. "Play the bitch like the bitchiest bitch there is, and you can't go wrong. You might even win an Oscar."

As the vixen, Gloria believes that "love means you'll live in a one-room apartment, develop two chins, and hang your clothes on a tenement washline." Unsure if she'll ever walk again, Gloria is a gold-digger who is just using Little Pinks.

She's got her radar trained on a millionaire boyfriend, Decatur Reed (William T. Orr).

Despite his matinee idol good looks and a physique exhibited on a Florida beach in a bathing suit, Orr never became "another Robert Taylor." But in the long run, he did fine professionally, eventually put in charge of television for Warner Brothers.

Rounding out the cast of *The Big Street* was a string of other well-known character actors, including Ray Collins as "The Professor." Like Moorehead, he too had appeared in *Citizen Kane*.

The African American actress Louise Beavers was cast as Ruby in the film. Throughout the 1940s, she consistently vied with Hattie McDaniel for black maid roles.

Ozzie Nelson and his Orchestra provided the music. His great fame would come later when his family appeared in the 1950s in a hit TV series.

Directing this cast of varied personalities was the relatively untested Irving Reis, who was known mostly for his work in radio, for which he wrote plays. *[He later became a scriptwriter for Paramount Pictures.]* He would receive more renown in 1948 when he helmed Arthur Miller's play, *All My Sons*.

Since he was not working at the time, Desi showed up every day at the set of *The Big Street* as a kind of self-anointed guardian of his wife. "I'm protecting my investment," he told the director. "Lucy used to go out on double dates with Fonda, Jimmy Stewart, and Ginger Rogers. I think a lot of stuff went on when she and Fonda co-starred together in *I Dream Too Much*. I'm here to see that Fonda doesn't bang my Lucy just for old time's sake. He can't be trusted around co-stars. I know for a fact that when he made *Jezebel* (1938) with Bette Davis, he plugged her."

For the most part, Lucille got the best reviews of her career, and she felt she did her finest work. *Life* magazine called her performance "superb—that girl can really act." Also, most reviewers agreed that in some scenes she had never looked more glamorous.

The *New York Herald Tribune* asserted: "Lucille Ball gives one of the best portrayals of her career as the ever-grasping, selfish Gloria, who takes delight in kicking the hap-

Lucille was cast as an overpowering, overwhelming, maneuvering bitch, like Bette Davis in *Of Human Bondage*.

Henry Fonda portrayed a country boy lost within the clutches of a woman who mocks him.

less Little Pinks around."

Time magazine wrote: "Pretty Lucille Ball, who was born for the parts Ginger Rogers sweats over, tackles the emotional role as if it were sirloin, and she doesn't care who is looking. Good shot: Miss Ball, crippled and propped up in bed, trying to do the conga from the hips up."

Her performance brought her to the attention of Arthur Freed at MGM. He was in pre-production of a musical, *Du Barry Was a Lady.* He thought she might be ideal for a role in it.

Her film career was about to undergo a dramatic change as her days at RKO dwindled.

***

Whereas Lucille was working steadily in pictures, Desi's career was going nowhere. "I was a has-been before I was ever a 'been,'" he lamented. "Lucy was finding roles in all those B pictures, and I—virtually unemployed—would have been happy to get cast in a C film."

When he escorted her to their first gala movie premiere, the announcer called out the names of the stars as they arrived in their cars to walk the red carpet. He heard the announcer claim, "Lucille Ball's car has just arrived," to the screaming movie fans.

As a bright note, news kept appearing in *Variety* that Desi would soon be starring with Ginger Rogers in a major musical, or else that he'd be the co-star of Maureen O'Hara in an RKO "extravaganza."

"The only thing I had to show for my time in Hollywood was three lousy pictures," he said. Rumors persisted, however, that he might get the lead in a Broadway musical that in time became known as *The Most Happy Fella,* with both music and lyrics by Frank Loesser.

During the darkest days of the war, in 1942, after Loesser had enlisted in the Army Air Force, he wrote "Praise the Lord and Pass the Ammunition." While still in the service, he also wrote "Baby, It's Cold Outside" which became a big hit. When it was featured in *Neptune's Daughter* (1949), a film featuring the "Aquacade Queen," Esther Williams, it won an Oscar as Best Original Song.

[In 1950, Loesser went on to write the Broadway musical Guys and Dolls, *based on short stories by Damon Runyon. Bob Fosse called it "the greatest American musical of all time."]*

Still thinking he might get cast in *The Most Happy Fella,* Desi took diction lessons for three months in advance of his audition, at which time "They said my Cuban accent was more pronounced than ever."

Finally, with no roles or show-biz prospects in sight, he told Lucille goodbye and headed for New York to seek work in a night club. There, he formed another band and got a job at a new club run by Tom Cassera, a night club impresario. Even though he phoned Lucille every night, Desi was seen dating a number of showgirls. Word soon reached Lucille, and their phone duels became almost legendary, with a lot of slamming down of receivers after lengthy accusations. She told Barbara Pepper, "It's going to be a short marriage, like so many others in Tinseltown."

Whenever he wasn't randomly dating, Desi made frequent visits to Polly Adler's elegant whorehouse, always insisting on trying out "the new *putas*."

After the Japanese attack on Pearl Harbor, Cuba declared war on Japan. Still a citizen of that Caribbean nation, Desi was offered a commission as a lieutenant in the Cuban Army. He turned down the post and attempted to join the U.S. Navy instead. After the U.S. recruiter rejected him, he was told that only American citizens could volunteer. The only way he could join was if he were drafted. "The law made no sense to me. I could become an American sailor if drafted, but not as a volunteer. You figure that one out."

At long last, RKO cast him in another movie, a World War II drama, *The Navy Comes Through* (1942), directed by A. Edward Sutherland. War pictures were in demand as the country mobilized to defeat the Axis powers.

It was the story of the ferocious encounters of the freighter *Sybil Gray*, which, during a perilous transit to England, is attacked by a Nazi U-boat. Later, two planes from the Luftwaffe strafe and bomb the U.S. vessel.

Pat O'Brien and George Murphy, who had co-starred with Lucille before, played the leads alongside Jane Wyatt as

George Murphy and **Desi Arnaz** each appeared in this wartime movie: Murphy as the second lead, Desi in a pithy but much smaller role.

Although he appeared in dramatic roles, **George Murphy**'s claim to fame was as a song-and-dance man, as this publicity still reveals.

the film's only female. *[Wyatt's greatest fame as an actress would come in 1954 when she was cast in the hit TV series,* Father Knows Best, *opposite Robert Young.]*

Jackie Cooper, the former child actor, had the fourth lead. He shared memories of working with Lucille when he met her years before when she'd been cast as an extra in *The Bowery* (1933), a picture he made with Wallace Beery and George Raft.

Another member of the film's cast, Max Baer, had been the world's Heavyweight Boxing Champion in 1934. *Ring Magazine* voted him No. 22 on its list of the 100 greatest punchers of all time.

He told Desi that Joseph Goebbels had banned his movies in Germany, ever since he made *The Prizefighter and the Lady* (1933) with Myrna Loy and Walter Huston. "It was not just because I have Jewish blood," he said, "but because I once knocked out a German boxer, Max Schmeling. After all, they are not always the super-race."

[The Baer-Schmeling fight occurred on June 8, 1933, at Yankee Stadium in New York City. Favored to win, Schmeling had been Adolf Hitler's favorite fighter.]

Unlike his previous director, Desi had great respect for Sutherland, who got his start as an actor playing a Keystone Cop in early Silent comedies. He'd also been directed by Charlie Chaplin in *A Woman of Paris* (1923). In time, Sutherland became a director, helming Stan Laurel, about whom Sutherland said, "I'd rather eat a tarantula than work with that jerk again." In 1926, Sutherland married actress Louise Brooks for a brief union. She later immortalized herself in the silent film, *Pandora's Box* (1929).

Although his roles were small, Desi always made a point of befriending the leads in every picture on which he worked. He had seen Pat O'Brien cast as Knute Rockne, the famous University of Notre Dame football coach in *Knute Rockne, All American* (1940). In that movie, he delivered the eventually famous line "Win one for the Gipper," a reference to the recently deceased football player, George Gipp, portrayed in that film by a young Ronald Reagan. In 1980, when Reagan ran against Jimmy Carter, he used that slogan in his successful bid for the U.S. Presidency.

When **George Murphy** was running for the U.S. Senate seat in California, a woman asked him, "Didn't you used to be George Murphy?"

George Murphy (right) was one of **Ronald Reagan's** best friends and advisers.

He urged Reagan to follow in his footsteps and "go into politics."

With George Murphy, Desi listened to his memories of working with Lucille most recently in *A Girl, A Guy, and a Gob.*

Desi and Murphy became friends, enough so that in the 1950s, he hired Murphy as a PR spokesman for Desilu Productions. However, eventually, there was a clash of personalities, as he found Desi too domineering, and he resigned. Murphy told him, "Arnaz, you and just don't mix....No hard feelings."

Although it did not always get good reviews, *The Navy Comes Through* took in $1.7 million at the box office. With the advent of America's entry into the war in 1942, war was on the mind of millions of Americans except among those who wanted to escape from hearing about the horrors of battle.

Variety labeled the drama "an action-filled, exciting naval adventure with strong romantic interest between George Murphy and Jane Wyatt."

The New York Times, in contrast, found the story "hackneyed," yet *Harrison's Report* viewed it as "a pretty good war melodrama, presented in a thrilling fashion in which interest never sags, masculine entertainment offered with a thunderbolt of excitement."

The Navy Comes Through marked the end of Desi's career at RKO. He was called to the office and told that his three-picture contract would not be renewed. "In other words, I'm fired," he said. "You guys don't have to show me to the gate. Some day I'll be such a big star that you jokers will be working for me."

***

Desi's next gig was without pay, as he was asked by the State Department to join a cast of A-list movie stars on a goodwill trip to Latin America, specifically Mexico. It was part of Franklin D. Roosevelt's newly inaugurated Good Neighbor policy. The purpose was to denounce the previous intervention of the United States in Latin America's political affairs and to replace it with trust and friendship.

A group of stars headed for Mexico City, the plane carrying, in addition to Desi, Clark Gable, Bing Crosby, Robert Taylor, Hedy Lamarr, James Cagney, Norma Shearer, Lana Turner, and Mickey Rooney.

"Norma, at the end of her reign as Queen of MGM, and pint-sized Mickey Rooney were, believe it or not, having a torrid affair," Desi said. "When Mickey stood next to the former screen goddess, he was tall enough to look like he was talking to her knockers."

Columnist Earl Wilson claimed, "Bing and Desi were in a heated contest to see who could score the most." In the past, Desi had had a brief fling with Lana, and he resumed that during the tour—that is, when he wasn't seducing the Austrian beauty, Hedy Lamarr, whom he considered 'the most beautiful woman on the planet.'"

Crosby snidely told Wilson, "That Cuban bastard couldn't keep it zipped up. He had to seduce, in addition to Lana and Hedy, every beautiful *señorita* he encountered."

Of course, the savvy columnist was aware that Crosby was slipping around "and getting more than his share, taking the Good Neighbor Policy very seriously."

Later, Desi became skepti-

Desi never imagined that a casting director might hire him as an instrument of international diplomacy,

But he was suddenly well-positioned as a Latin-America actor who might help heal divisions between FDR's U.S. and the rest of Latin America.

cal of that policy, as Mexicans told him, "Now the United States wants to be friendly to us. War has come, and we're being courted by the Nazis. Roosevelt suddenly wants to make love, not war, on us."

***

Lucille almost didn't get cast in the last picture she made for RKO, *Seven Days' Leave* (1942). This film, a hit at the box office during wartime, would end her reign as the studio's Queen of the Bs.

Its male star was rugged, handsome, muscular Victor Mature, who had been all the rage since he'd bared so much flesh in *One Million BC* (1940), a prehistoric epic in which he "hand-to-hand battled" gigantic lizards.

He had married Frances Charles, but the union was annulled two years later.

With his sensuous "body builder" physique, Mature was a rising sensation on the screen. No wonder that by 1949, Cecil B. De Mille would cast him in the title role of *Samson and Delilah*. Before working with Lucille, he had just filmed *My Gal Sal* (1942), with the 1940s love goddess, Titian-haired Rita Hayworth.

[My Gal Sal is known to some trivia experts as the film where Mature and Hayworth shared their first kissing scene. As the cameras rolled, the scene went on and on, long after the director yelled "cut." Irving Cummings claimed, "I practically had to bring in a bulldozer to pull them apart." That night, Mature and Hayworth began a torrid affair, generating much press. There were reports that they would eventually get married.]

As his female counterpoint in *Seven Days' Leave,* Mature had strongly requested Hayworth, but at Columbia, Harry Cohn famously refused to lease her out. In the aftermath of that, Mature told Cummings, "I'm very disappointed that you cast Lucille Ball as my leading lady. What makes you think I could fall in love with that one, even if it were only make-believe?"

Cummings responded, "Listen, hunk, in this business, men are forced to make love to women even if they're homosexual, even if they hate the woman they're kissing. It goes with the turf. Get used to it."

Tim Whelan was both the director and producer of *Seven Days' Leave,* the work of four different screenwriters. It was a musical comedy about a soldier on leave who will inherit $100,000 from his great-grandfather's fortune if he'll marry a descendant of the Havelock-Allen family, with whom his relatives have feuded for decades. He hopes that such a union will bring a reconciliation.

There's a hitch, of course. *[After all, this is a movie script.]* Johnny Grey, Mature's character, is already set to marry a *Latina* played by the Puerto Rican actress Mapy Cortés, an artist best-known for her many roles in Mexican films during "the golden age of Mexican cinema.' *[Ironically the name of the character Cortés portrayed was also named Mapy Cortés.]*

Lucille, as the heiress, Terry, has a boy-crazy sister, Mickey (Marcy McGuire), who develops a powerful crush on Johnny, too. *[As a romantic complication, Lucille as Terry is also set to marry Ralph Edwards (Walter Reed).]*

Harold Peary, with whom Lucille had worked on the film *Look Who's Laughing* (1941), had been cast in his familiar role of Throckmorton P. Gildersleeve, the lawyer for the estate.

Charles Walters was the film's dance director. He'd go on to greater things, helming Judy Garland and Fred Astaire in *Easter Parade* (1945) and Bing Crosby, Grace Kelly, and Frank Sinatra in *High Society* (1956).

Lucille's favorite photographer, Robert De Grasse, handled the film's cinematography. "I don't know how Bob does it," she said. "But he could always make me look beautiful."

Singer Ginny Simms would appear as herself before the Freddy Martin Orchestra. Additional music would be provided by Les Brown and His Band of Renown.

Hedda Hopper was the first to report that Mature and Lucille, as the male and female leads of the film, were feuding so much during shooting that production was often delayed.

"He seemed to be punishing me for being cast instead of Rita," she claimed. "He tried to sabotage my scenes, and practically turned me into a nervous wreck. In a kissing scene, he virtually assaulted me, biting my lip as he kissed me and running his big hand up my dress to grope me. I ran crying to my dressing room, and the scene had to be reshot the next day. He was a real bastard to me. I was miserable. Making things worse was that Desi was in New York at the time, no doubt being entertained by one of Polly Adler's whores."

RKO released publicity pictures of Lucille and Mature together, seemingly taking delight in each other's company. In fact, they were so successful at pulling off the pretense that they were happy co-stars that Desi later accused his wife of having an affair with Mature.

After completing *Seven Days' Leave,* Mature joined the U.S. Coast Guard, a decision that put a strain on his love affair with Hayworth.

During his enlistment, a fellow serviceman photographed Mature nude as he lay on his cot. The photo shows in grainy detail his thick uncut penis hanging over the edge of the mattress. This underground photograph became one of the hottest, most widely circulated snapshots of any celebrity of that era, and is still being published today. It was also said to have generated what became Mature's following among hordes of homosexuals.

In her exit film from RKO, Lucille was cast with "the Hunk," **Victor Mature**. On screen, he had been Betty Grable's leading man, but after dark found him in the arms of Rita Hayworth.

"I detested him during the shoot, as he mauled me, tonged me, and vagina-groped me," Lucille claimed.

Seven Days' Leave marked Mature's final picture until the end of World War II. Before it was over, he went off and joined the Coast Guard.

In reference to Mature, the gay author Gore Vidal later said, "If the Germans had seen him nude, they would have surrendered far earlier."

The evolution of *Seven Days' Leave* provided Lucille with a graceful exit from RKO. It turned out to be one of the studio's highest-grossing movies of 1942, helping it wipe out some of that year's red ink.

***

In 1942, a few months after the wrap of his most recent picture, *The Navy Comes Through,* Desi joined the Hollywood Victory Caravan for a cross-country "barnstorming" tour of America. *[Editor's Note: This is not to be confused with an equivalent fund-raising tour about a year later, which involved Lucille but not Desi.]*

It was a fund-raising effort by the U.S. Army and Navy Relief to provide financial aid to the widows and children of U.S. soldiers and sailors killed on the battlefields of Europe or on the islands of the Pacific.

Seventeen trains, each donated by the Santa Fe Railroad, set out with two dozen movie stars to raise money in at least a dozen cities. In all, $800,000 was raised.

Its producer was Mark Sandrich, who had built up his reputation with Astaire and Rogers musicals, some of which had cast Lucille in bit parts. *[He had previously directed* Holiday Inn *(1942), with music by Irving Berlin. In that film, Bing Crosby had introduced "White Christmas."]*

Alfred Newman was its musical director, bringing along an orchestra of thirty. In time, this composer became a towering figure in movie musicals, winning nine Oscars and being nominated forty-five times. In a career spanning four decades, he composed scores for some 200 films.

Because his name began with an "A," Desi found himself at the head

Two views of 1942's **Hollywood Victory Campaign**, each of them chock-a-block with actors, including Desi Arnaz, who toured the country as part of a morale-building, fund-raising effort that was strenuously supported by then-First Lady Eleanor Roosevelt.

On the lawn in front of the South Portico of the White House, on April 30, 1942, **Mrs. Roosevelt** appears in a white blouse waving out from a temporary entourage of at least 40 big-name movie stars.

of a cast whose members were listed in alphabetical order. "I was the least-known actor in the crowd," he said. Featured in the troupe were Charles Boyer, James Cagney, Claudette Colbert, Crosby, Olivia de Havilland, Cary Grant, Bob Hope, Laurel and Hardy, Groucho Marx, Merle Oberon, and tap-dancing Eleanor Powell. A bevy of starlets, hopefully the stars of tomorrow, went along to provide cheesecake. None of these beauties could compete with Marie MacDonald, who, as a minor movie star, became known as "The Body Beautiful,' a name later shortened just to "The Body."

As First Lady, **Eleanor Roosevelt** had seen only one movie that included Lucille. That film had been *Stage Door*, in which she had only a minor role, the star parts going to Katharine Hepburn and Ginger Rogers.

When Desi met Mrs. Roosevelt, he was surprised that she even knew who he was.

She'd have been surprised that in years to come, her son, Elliott Roosevelt, would "get to know Lucille quite well" during a boating party off the shores of Balboa Beach in California.

On his first day on the road, Desi's roving eye focused on MacDonald, whom he found very receptive to his overtures. On the troupe's first night in a hotel, he didn't even turn down his own bedcovers, but slept in hers. Thus began a passionate romance that would last for the duration of the tour.

Of the starlets, MacDonald was the only one who ever obtained the status of movie star. She became one of the most popular pin-up girls for the American soldiers and posed for the cover of *Yank* magazine. Her movie career never generated big box office, even *Living in a Big Way* (1947), in which she co-starred with Gene Kelly. At the finale of a lackluster career, she ended up co-starring with fading Jayne Mansfield in *Promises, Promises* (1963).

Desi found her "sexy and amusing...a lot of fun," as he confided to Newman. "She'll do all the things Lucy won't. A lot of people later claimed I was bedding gals in every town we visited, but that was a lie. With a luscious blonde waiting in bed for me every night, why should I be wasting it on other *putas.*"

The caravan's first performance was at Loew's Capital Theater in Washington, D.C. That afternoon, Eleanor Roosevelt had hosted a tea for them at the White House. Standing in line, Desi shook the hand of the First Lady. She greeted him by saying, "Hello, Desi? How is Lucille?"

"I was dumbfounded," he recalled. "The most famous woman in the world knew who I was. That was one of the thrills of my life. I felt really important."

From coast to coast, Desi introduced himself and his song, "Babalu," to thousands of Americans in such cities as Boston, Philadelphia, Detroit, Chicago, Dallas, and Houston. The last show was in San Francisco on the night of May 19, when he "serviced" MacDonald for the final time. The next morning, he was on a plane flying back to Los Angeles to face an irate wife.

***

After she finished "that picture" with Victor Mature, Lucille was called into the office of Charles Koerner, head of RKO. He wasn't rude or harsh the way Louis B. Mayer had been when he fired Joan Crawford. But Koerner was very frank, even realistic.

"There is much that I admire about you," he said to Lucille. "But RKO is going through a rough time financially, and we have no future plans for you. If you stick around until your contract expires, you'll get cast in a dud or two and then you'll be dropped—headed for oblivion."

"Maybe you'll end up as a housewife cooking paella for that Cuban boy of yours—what's his name?—and waiting for him to come home from the local bordello. I've got a couple of vague offers for your services from both Paramount and MGM. With the understanding that there's nothing for you at RKO, which studio do you want me to pursue?"

At first, she was stunned and bewildered. Recovering quickly, she said, "MGM. It turns out the best musicals."

"MGM it is," he said. "I'll get in touch with them this afternoon. A word of caution: Be careful that Mayer doesn't stick his hand up your dress."

Years later, Lucille recalled to Vivian Vance, "And that's how my reign at RKO came to an end. The very next morning, I entered the heavily guarded portals of the greatest studio on earth. Metro-Goldwyn-Mayer, which advertised itself as 'having more stars than in heaven.' The question was, would I fit into its galaxy?"

Many of MGM's early crop of superstars weren't around anymore: Jean Harlow had faced a premature death; and Greta Garbo had slipped away to an early retirement. Mickey Rooney was still around, but his days as a box office champ were over. John Gilbert and Norma Shearer had gone the way of the snows of yesterday, and Clark Gable would soon be off to join in the fighting of World War II. Nevertheless, new stars were emerging at MGM, notably Lana Turner, Hedy Lamarr, and June Allyson, plus an older English import, Greer Garson. Musical stars like Kathryn Grayson and Gene Kelly had appeared on the scene, even a swimming sensation, Esther Williams, and Van Johnson, Elizabeth Taylor, even Peter Lawford, were on the horizon.

MGM's magical kingdom was presided over by the tyrannical Louis B. Mayer, the "Merchant of Dreams." Earning half a million dollars a year, he was the highest-paid man in America. From a Jewish ghetto in the Ukraine, he had climbed rung by rung the ladder to success, becoming the very personification of a Hollywood mogul.

In August of 1942, the first full year of America's involvement in World War II, Lucille signed a contract with MGM for $1,500 a week.

Her first assignment was not for a film, but for a complete aesthetic makeover. She was assigned to Sydney Guilaroff, Hollywood's most fa-

302

mous hairdresser. He had handled many of the biggest stars of the Golden Age, everyone from Barbara Stanwyck to Clark Gable.

Born in London to Russian parents, Guilaroff had left the UK with his parents to settle in Canada. Eventually, he made his way to New York City, where he found himself sleeping on benches in Central Park—like Valentino in his early days. He found work as an assistant to a gay beautician, but later came down with tuberculosis.

Hollywood's master of coiffures, the very gay **Sydney Guilaroff,** gave Lucille her trademark hair color, "Tango Red," which, in time, made her the most famous redhead on the planet.

"I never turned gray," she said. "I always used dye. I never knew what my real hair color was like as the years went by."

After a long recovery, he was back again, creating the signature black bob of Louise Brooks and dressing the hair of such actresses as Corrine Griffith and Miriam Hopkins. At the exclusive Manhattan beauty parlor known as Antoine's, he became known as "Mr. Sydney."

It was here that the gave Joan Crawford a new look. She was so captivated by him that she imported him to Hollywood, where—beginning in 1934—he became the leading hair stylist for MGM.

In the 1930s, Lucille had gone from a blonde at Columbia to a redhead at RKO. Now, at MGM, Guilaroff had a new color for her: "Tango Red."

"I called the hideous shade orange, just like one of the ripe oranges that grow all over Southern California," she said. "I went along with Sydney, but I planned to get rid of it sooner than later. I used to wear my hair long and loose, but he went heavy on the lacquer, so much so you couldn't even crack it with a hairbrush."

Lucille, of course, did not get rid of the color and kept it for the rest of her life, becoming the most famous "redhead" on the planet.

Guilaroff continued on and off to dress her hair for years to come, but his roster of clients changed. In time, the list included Nancy Reagan, Marilyn Monroe, and Frank Sinatra.

Throughout Hollywood it was widely assumed that Guilaroff was gay, and he might have been, even though in his memoir, *Crowning Glories,* he claimed affairs with both Greta Garbo and Ava Gardner.

In 1938, he became the first single man in America to adopt a son, naming him "Jon" in honor of Joan Crawford. The State of California sued to prevent the adoption but lost in court, a loss that prompted Guilaroff to adopt two more boys.

As a continuation of the studio's efforts to give Lucille a new look, they called in the famous costume designer, "Irene," for a new wardrobe.

Irene had been an actress in silent pictures, later switching professions and becoming a costume designer. In the 1930s, she'd dressed Ginger Rogers, Claudette Colbert, and Carole Lombard, later transferring her fashion sense to Hedy Lamarr and Ingrid Bergman. As the leading costume designer at MGM, Irene became known for her "*soufflé*" creations.

One afternoon, she confessed to Lucille that Gary Cooper was the only man she'd ever loved.

She told Lucille that her "Tango Red" hair and piercing blue eyes would photograph beautifully in Technicolor. She had her new client rid herself of all those "Hattie Carnegie grays, blacks, and beiges." Instead, Irene outfitted her in such flamboyant colors as sunflower yellow, fire engine red, sunset pink, ocean aqua, and the shade of orange that streaks a sky at dawn.

"Irene even designed my lingerie," Lucille said, "turning me into a boudoir goddess in silks and chiffons. My favorite color was 'pussy pink,' and what's wrong with Maribou?" *[Editor's note: Maribou is usually a shade of violet.]* "I understand that that African stork feeds on carrion. How very appropriate to use it in the adornment of a woman's body in bed with a man."

[In 1962, Lucille was greatly saddened when news came across radio and TV stations that Irene had checked into the Knickerbocker Hotel in Los Angeles and later jumped to her death from the ninth floor.]

***

Du Barry Was a Lady, was Lucille's first film for MGM under her new contract. Originally, with music and lyrics by Cole Porter and starring Bert Lahr, Ethel Merman, and Betty Grable, it had opened on Broadway in 1939.

For its film adaptation, many of its songs and much of its dialogue had to be rewritten, as the play was considered too *risqué* for a "family-friendly" MGM musical. Louis B. Mayer was strict about that.

Scheduled for a wartime release (in 1943), Roy Del Ruth was designated as the director of a cast that included Red Skelton, Lucille, and Gene Kelly. Del Ruth had first helmed Lucille when she played a minor role as a bridesmaid in *Bulldog Drummond Strikes Back* (1934).

Irene Lentz billed herself in film credits simply as **"Irene."**

She detested "that Hattie Carnegie look" Lucille had assumed in her assemblage of a private wardrobe.

"I don't want to turn you into Carmen Miranda, but I want you to burst out in color. You'll be making pictures in Technicolor. We'll use the rainbow as inspiration for the palette of your gowns."

On August 1, 1942, **Lucille** began working under contract for MGM. She was immediately cast in dual roles with **Red Skelton** (left) and **Gene Kelly**.

"I was scared shitless, but I pulled it off. The press dubbed me 'Technicolor Tessie.' This is the picture in which my public got to see my new hair color of 'Tango Red.'"

He met with Lucille during her first day on the set, visiting her in her dressing room. She was honored to have been assigned quarters which had only recently been occupied by Norma Shearer, who had reigned as Queen of MGM in the 1930s during her marriage to "Boy Wonder," Irving Thalberg.

[Del Ruth would helm Lucille again in a brief sequence in the upcoming Ziegfeld Follies *(1946). He had just lost his position as the second-highest-paid director in Hollywood.]*

He told Lucille that the role had originally been offered to her friend, Ann Sothern, who had had to bow out because she was pregnant. He also told her that MGM had paid $80,000 for the film rights.

"At RKO, I was in the position of getting Ann's sloppy seconds," Lucille said. "Now at MGM, the same thing is happening to me."

Cole Porter had been paid handsomely for his music and lyrics, but he had regrets when he saw how *Du Barry Was a Lady* had been "watered down," in his view.

Time Out expressed it well: "This adaptation of the Cole Porter musical ditches most of the original songs and the lovely bawdiness that went with them. Instead, it fashions a vehicle for Skelton and Lucille Ball to perform more suitable numbers for film audiences."

Charles Walters, one of the best dance directors in Hollywood, would guide Lucille through her numbers, despite her belief that "I can't sing and I can't dance."

During Skelton's reunion with Lucille, he noted her new hair color, likening it to a "pink carrot."

[They had previously worked together in Having a Wonderful Time *(1938). Skelton, a son of Indiana, was fast*

Du Barry Was a Lady (1943), in which she played a tongue-in-check interpretation of an imperial French courtesan, was **Lucille's** all-time glamour role.

MGM stylist Sydney Guilaroff styled her hair for the film, dying it Tango Red. That color, of course, later became her trademark. Ann Sothern was set to play the role of May Daly (Madame Du Barry) but discovered that she was pregnant just before filming started. Lucille was cast instead.

She feared she would not be able to follow in the footsteps of Ethel Merman and the acclaim won in the Broadway version by Cole Porter, but she created a sensation in high powdered wigs and hoopskirts.

As the film revealed, the entire scenario was a dream of **Red Skelton** in which he became King Louis XV after he'd been slipped a Mickey Finn.

rising as a star. Once, he'd been part of a minstrel show, and had entertained on a showboat before working the burlesque circuit as a vaudeville comedian. He'd be one of the first stars to recognize the oncoming invasion of television, and he'd play a role in enticing Lucille to launch her own series in the new medium.]

"My life's dream is to make people laugh," he told her. "But privately, I'm a very unhappy man, finding solace by sitting in my garden for hours." *[He was in the midst of divorcing his wife, Edna Marie Stillwell.]*

Each of the three lead actors had dual roles, both played out with kind of "time travel" theme. Each would portray an occupant of the mid-20th-century and also a figure from the 18th Century French court at Versailles during the reign of Louis XV. Skelton was cast as Louis Blore, a mid-20th Century cloakroom attendant. Someone slips him a Mickey Finn, and he drifts into sleep, dreaming that he is Louis XV.

As May Daly, Lucille is a modern-day nightclub entertainer, but in her dream, she imagines herself as Madame Du Barry, the infamous mistress of the French monarch. He lusts for her, but faces competition from Kelly as Alex Howe, a nightclub dancer. In their shared dream, he, too, lusts for Du Barry in his imaginary role of Black Arrow, a kind of Robin Hood. A love triangle ensues.

The court is entertained by Tommy Dorsey and his Orchestra, each member of which is outfitted in 18th Century drag. Lucille's singing voice was dubbed by Martha Mears, but that's her own voice near the end of the film singing "Friendship" with Dorsey's Orchestra.

The movie's fourth lead was cast with Virginia O'Brien, who portrays a cigarette girl in a modern night club. At the end, the Skelton character ends up not with Lucille, whose heart belongs to Kelly, but with O'Brien.

O'Brien would work with Lucille in future roles, but her career didn't really take off and her star dimmed. Her big number in the film was "Salome."

Some strong character actors took over the supporting roles, including Rags Ragland as Charlie. This Kentuckian was a former truck driver and boxer before breaking into burlesque and later becoming the "top banana" at Minsky's, the leading burlesque house in America. Beginning with *Panama Hattie* (1942), he became a major MGM contract player. He'd also worked with Skelton on all three of his "Whistling" movies, beginning with *Whistling in the Dark* in 1941.

Zero Mostel appears as Rami the Swami. The Brooklyn-born comedian and star of stage and screen would later immortalize himself in the musical, *Fiddler on the Roof*.

Donald Meek, performing as both Mr. Jones and the Duc de Choiseul, had worked with Lucille on *Murder of the Vanities* and on *The Whole Town's Talking*. His two best roles were already behind him: *You Can't Take It with You* (1938) and *Stagecoach* (1939).

In time, Meek would become celebrated for his energetic and athletic dance routines, reaching a pinnacle of his career when he starred in *Singin' in the Rain* (1952).

He told Lucille, "I was appalled at the sight of myself blown up twenty times on the screen. I felt I was a tremendous flop."

Cast as Niagara, Louise Beavers often played a maid or a servant. Like her rival, Hattie McDaniel, she was a "mammy stereotype"—that is, a black domestic servant, generally good natured, often overweight, and loud. Her breakthrough role had come in 1934 when she played Delilah in *Imitation of Life* starring Claudette Colbert.

As a Hollywood footnote, three future movie stars appeared in *Du Barry Was a Lady,* either in a cameo or else uncredited. Lana Turner, by now an established star, had walked on as herself. Ava Gardner was uncredited as the perfume girl. *[Turner had already married, and Gardner would eventually marry, bandleader Artie Shaw, adding to the onset drama.]* And Marilyn Maxwell starred as Miss February, a Vargas calendar girl.

Sultry blonde goddess, **Lana Turner,** was "merely ornamental" in *Du Barry Was a Lady.*

She was kept busier at night, telling her ex-husband, bandleader Artie Shaw, "I dated 150 servicemen in 1942, each a pickup at the Hollywood Canteen."

[Maxwell would achieve minor stardom in the 1940s and '50s, notably starring opposite Kirk Douglas in Champion *(1949). Her affair with Frank Sinatra became notorious. She also had a fling with Bob Hope when they traveled together on USO tours, entertaining the troops during World War II. Rock Hudson once "dated" her to conceal his gayness. Desi, with his roving eye for female flesh, lay in her future.]*

At one point, Desi was on the set waiting to have lunch with Lucille. She caught him in the far corner talking to Maxwell and jotting something down on paper. Was it her telephone number? After all, he was partial to blondes.

Later in her dressing room, she accused him of arranging a secret date with her. He denied it, claiming that she was merely interested in getting him to sing "Babalu" at a charity event and maybe get involved with a USO tour to entertain servicemen. Lucille didn't believe one word of his denial, and a big fight ensued.

Upon its release, the movie made a profit of $900,000.

Bosley Crowther of *The New York Times* wrote: "Producers have given the juicy dame role to Lucille Ball who carries it off well. The whole show has a Technicolor sheen, an eye-filling opulence and splendor, which is fabulous in these rationed wartimes."

Her favorite review appeared in the *New York Herald Tribune:* "To her red-headed and bewigged beauty, Miss Ball's vivaciousness and excellent comedy timing proves once again that she is a musical comedy star of the first magnitude."

Some critics hailed Lucille's "Technicolor triumph," in terms that Irene, the designer, had predicted. One of them temporarily renamed her "Technicolor Tessie."

Lucille credited photographer Karl Freund with much of the success in featuring her in her debut in the color process. Later, she hired him as the director in charge of photography for the *I Love Lucy* series.

***

In a career that spanned 60 years, tall, suave, and sophisticated Cesar Romero (1907-1994) blazed across the screen. In the 1930s he played a Latin lover in seemingly countless musicals and romantic comedies. In a series of low-budget Westerns, he became that rogue bandit, "The Cisco Kid." To the generation growing up in the 1960s, he was the green-haired, white-faced cackling villain, The Joker, of the television series *Batman* (1966-68).

Like Desi, Cesar was born of Cuban parents—not in Havana, but in New York, where, as he grew into maturity, he became a ballroom dancer. The year 1927 found him on Broadway in *Lady Do*. Hollywood beckoned, and he arrived there in 1933 to perform in *The Shadow Laughs*. He's still seen on the late show with Shirley Temple in *Wee Willie Winkie* (1937). In the 1930s, Hollywood columnists defined Romero as "The New Valentino."

The *Cisco Kid* series, including *The Gay Caballero* in 1940, was a hit in the United States but practically caused riots south of the border. Romero played The Kid from 1939 until 1941. In his book, *They Went Thataway*, author James Horwitz wrote: "Romero was no cowboy, but one of those Brill-Creamed Latin Lover types and played The Kid as a smarmy dandy and fop, while Chris Pin-Martin's Pancho (The Kid's sidekick) was a gutbucket slob. Latin American sensibilities were offended by this unlikely

As Latin lovers, Ricardo Montalban and Fernando Lamas heated up the screen. But whenever a director wanted a gay Latin lover, he cast **Cesar Romero** (above).

"I was never stereotyped as just a Latin lover in any case because I played so many parts in pictures, Romero said. "I was more of a character actor than a straight leading man."

Then he paused: "No pun intended."

Cesar Romero with **Carmen Miranda,** in *Weekend in Havana* (1941).

Along with Desi, they became sought after by the U.S. State Department , then devising media aspects of their Good Neighbor program, as the kind of charming, polite, fun, and well-mannered folk a U.S. citizen might meet "South of the Border"

duo. An international incident nearly occurred. Diplomatic cables flew back and forth between Latin America and the State Department. The Cisco Kid, as portrayed by Romero, was, so to speak, queering America's south-of-the-border foreign policy. Darryl F. Zanuck at Fox was more or less ordered by Washington to change Cisco's style or stop making the pictures. He decided to drop the series altogether."

In World War II, Romero left to serve in the Coast Guard. One man who served with him later said, "If one of the guys wanted a great blow-job, they went to call on Romero."

Most of his conquests were unknown men. For some odd reason, he seemed especially to like gas station attendants and cute, smart, feisty, articulate young men. One of his conquests, Nick Carbone, formerly a tax auditor living in a suburb of Harrisburg, Pennsylvania and now semi-retired in Palm Springs, remembers him with fondness and a certain alarm: "There we were, sometime in the 70s, making out in a car somewhere in Los Angeles, with the police banging on the window, and Cesar screaming at them and daring them to arrest him. He was a loud and radical kind of bugger... totally Out and completely unafraid of being identified as gay."

Occasionally, Cesar went after a famous star. He was especially taken with the beauty of Tyrone Power, with whom he appeared in the Technicolor historical epic, *The Captain from Castile* (1947). As the director, Henry King, once said, "Ty gave it away to almost any Topman who propositioned him."

Today, if you search the web, you can find all sorts of outrageous statements, including the assertion that Lucille decided to dump Desi when she caught him fucking Romero. *[She may have caught her husband fucking Romero, but that was not the reason for the divorce.]*

Tyrone Power and **Cesar Romero**, on the debut of their extended trip to South America in 1946.

And although Power said "yes" to Romero, he later, somewhat unchivalrously, confided, "That was no major accomplishment. That dear boy, Ty, said yes to anybody who asked."

Cesar Romero, "The Latin from Manhattan," seldom turned down a role, but always refused to shave his mustache.

"I played any part, a musketeer (above), a Hindu, an Indian, an Italian. There were few pictures where I ended up with the gal. Not that I would know what to do with one."

She tolerated Romero and was aware of the actor's crush on her husband as early as 1940. She considered it a harmless diversion on Desi's part, and preferable to "taking on five of Polly Adler's whores—one by one."

In an interview with Boze Hadleigh published in *Hollywood Gays*, Romero admitted that he'd had sex with Desi. Romero claimed that Desi "knew he was pretty irresistible, and he knew about me. I guess he could see it in the eyes. One day Desi said to me, 'All right, we both know what you want. Let's get it over with.' We did."

What Romero didn't confess to the reporter, but what Lucille found out about, was that their affair lasted for eight years. Reportedly, it was a one-sided affair. Desi would allow himself to be fellated, or else he'd sodomize Romero, who would have to resort to masturbation for his own relief.

Romero suggested that over the years, Desi allowed other gays to fellate him as well, including his co-star on Broadway, Richard Kollmar, husband of the famous columnist, Dorothy Kilgallen. Romero also suggested that when Desi was appearing on Broadway in *Too Many Girls*, he reportedly had an affair with one of its co-authors, Lorenz Hart, the homosexual lyricist.

Lucille later claimed that when Vincente Minnelli (father of Liza) had directed them in *The Long, Long Trailer* (1954), he came on sexually to Desi, who rejected him. "Why not?" Minnelli is reported to have (bitchily) said. "Are you saving it for Cesar Romero?"

With hair the color of stainless steel, Romero became a seemingly permanent fixture on the Hollywood scene, living a long and socially active life. In 1968, *TV Guide* dubbed him "one of the most beautiful men in the world."

Cesar Romero was a frequent escort of aging **Jane Wyman,** the first **Mrs. Ronald Reagan.**

He joked with her about his sexual conquests and even encouraged her "in our mutually shared obsession with young men. How could I dare chastise Jane for falling for younger men when I'd done the same thing every night of my life?"

Ironically, Romero eventually evolved into a favorite escort of Lucille herself. Knowing he was gay, she considered him a safe choice, as did Joan Crawford and Carmen Miranda. In later life, he escorted aging actresses such as Ginger Rogers and Jane Wyman to various media and social events.

Wyman told friends that "Cesar is a far better escort than Ronnie was. Cesar pays attention to the lady, but Ronnie ended up in some corner talking politics to some guys all night." [*She was referring, of course, to her former husband, Ronald Reagan.*] Near the end of his long career. Romero had appeared as Wyman's love interest in the soap opera, *Falcon Crest*, playing Peter Stavros from 1985 to 1987.

He was a "beard" for actresses involved in off-the-record romances. After an event in a public place, he would drop off the actress with her male or female lover before departing for a night in the arms of his current male hunk, which—much to Romero's sorrow—no longer included Desi. By 1948, Desi had told Romero: "Let's cut out all this shit but remain friends."

***

310

Desi's next picture, his first for Metro-Goldwyn-Mayer, was *Bataan* (1943), a stark, brutal World War II drama with a tragic (some said "genocidal") ending in which all the American soldiers are killed, mostly by the invading Japanese forces who overran the Philippines, chasing out General Douglas MacArthur and the allied forces. *[In its bloody aftermath, the general vowed, "I shall return," one of the most famous lines of the 20th Century.]*

The plot, written by several screenwriters, depicts a brave band of men who are killed off one at a time but not before indulging in acts of bravery and heroism.

Malaria-plagued American forces captured by the Japanese were starved, brutalized, and enslaved before forced onto the bloody trails of the Bataan Death March, one of the most cruel genocidal acts committed by the Japanese during World War II.

[The historic moment depicted in the film shows a platoon of under-armed men under the leadership of Sgt. Bill Dane, taking a position in the mountains outside Manila for a desperate last stand, praying for a relief force that never came.]

During its retreat, the U.S. Army focuses on a high bridge spanning a ravine on the Bataan Peninsula. After their escape, an *ad hoc* group of thirteen hastily assembled men from different units are assigned to stay back and blow up the bridge so that the oncoming Japanese won't be able to use it.

Then the unit's Captain, Henry Lassiter (portrayed by Lee Bowman), is killed by a sniper, leaving Sergeant Dan (Robert Taylor) in charge.

No longer is Taylor the "pretty boy" of the late 1930s. He's tough, unshaven, uncharming, and bitter, looking haggard and grim as he barks orders to his doomed men.

In unusual casting, George Murphy, a song-and-dance man, takes the secondary role of Lt. Steve Bently of the U.S. Army Air Corps. He and his Filipino mechanic, Corporal Juan Katigbank (played by Rogue Espirito), work frantically to repair a damaged Beechcraft C-43 aircraft. They manage to do that, but the Filipino is killed and Bentley is mortally wounded. In his dying moments, he's airborne with a plane loaded with explosives. On a suicide mission, he crashes into the bridge with the intention of destroying it, forcing the Japanese to slow their advance.

Desi, cast as Private Felix Ramirez, of the 194th Tank Battalion, is the only other soldier not killed by the Japanese (referred to as "Japs" throughout the course of the movie). Before the last image, he dies from malaria.

Lloyd Nolan (left) with **Robert Taylor** (looking mean and more-than-usually-macho) in *Bataan*.

Taylor later said, "This movie ended forever that pretty boy reputation I had in my films of the 1930s."

At first, the director, Tay Garnett, set up the shot with a mosquito net draped over him, but Desi talked him out of it, wanting his face on full display during his death scene. *[Eventually, it emerged as the single best bit of acting of Desi's entire film career. He even won a* Photoplay *award for his brief performance.]*

Despite his status as a novice on the filmmaking scene, Desi made yet another demand. The script called for him to recite the liturgical *Mea Culpa* in either Spanish or English, but he wanted to do it in Latin like he'd learned as a schoolboy in Santiago. Garnett granted this "final" request. "I'm glad I got to kill off Arnaz early. Otherwise, he'd have wanted to direct the entire picture."

Even when he was no longer needed on the set, Desi remained behind to get to know his fellow actors and their director. He felt that as a rising star at MGM, he might be working with them again.

Garnett was no stranger to the direction of films with military themes. Before *Bataan*, he'd helmed *One Way Passage* (1932), *China Seas* (1935), and *Seven Sinners* (1940), the latter starring Marlene Dietrich and John Wayne.

His most celebrated film lay only a few years away — *The Postman Always Rings Twice* (1946), starring Lana Turner and John Garfield. It became a celebrated classic, one of the most famous *films noir* ever made.

Garnett told Desi that he'd wanted to direct *Bataan* so much that he'd agreed to a drastic cut in salary.

It was shot at the studio, a locale that presented a horrendous challenge during its reconfiguration into a jungle. The fogs that settled over the men caused many genuine medical crises. Fumes emanating from a fog machine

"Ricky Ricardo, we hardly knew you!" fans wrote to **Desi Arnaz** after they watched the re-release on TV of *Bataan* (1943), a grimy World War II saga in which brave U.S. soldiers give their lives fighting the invading Japanese.

In his death scene in *Bataan*—a scene he delivered in English and liturgical Latin—Desi showed the world that he could pull off high drama. He would never have such a moment again in films.

were so toxic that the actors couldn't breathe whenever it was turned on. The director had to shoot his scenes in brief segments so that his actors could rush out at frequent intervals for fresh air.

Taylor later told Louella Parsons that *Bataan* was one of the four most favorite films he'd made, the others being *Magnificent Obsession* (1954), *Waterloo Bridge* (1940), and *Johnny Eager* (1941). Soon, he'd join fellow actors like Clark Gable, Henry Fonda, Tyrone Power, and James Stewart to march off to war.

Desi learned some Hollywood gossip on the set of *Bataan:* A bisexual, Taylor was having a clandestine affair with Phillip Terry, cast as Private Matthew Hardy of the Army Medical Corps. At the time, Terry was married to Joan Crawford, and Taylor was wed to Barbara Stanwyck. The irony was that these two actresses were also having an affair with each other.

Terry, a native of San Francisco, was a handsome, strapping, very masculine young man, the son of German Americans. He'd first had an affair with his future wife when he had a bit part in her film, *Mannequin* (1938), opposite Spencer Tracy. Before that, he'd been a roustabout and rig builder on the oil fields of Oklahoma.

Cast as Captain Barney, Lloyd Nolan was the "wise guy" of the platoon. Like Lucille, he'd previously been confined mostly to B pictures, although he did get to appear opposite Mae West, Dorothy McGuire, and Lana Turner.

Robert Taylor with then-wife **Barbara Stanwyck.** Theirs was called "the most famous lavender marriage in Hollywood."

Each of them was free to have gay or lesbian affairs outside the home. Since each of them were major box office attractions, intimacies with others grew complicated.

Phillip Terry with his then-wife, **Joan Crawford.**

During the course of his marriage to Crawford, the handsome, masculine actor was also engaged in a torrid affair with Robert Taylor.

Meanwhile, the lesbian liaison of Terry's wife, Joan, with Barbara Stanwyck dated back to the late 1920s.

Thomas Mitchell played career soldier Captain Jake Feingold. He was often cast as an Irish con man, although he'd be forever known as the father of Scarlett O'Hara in *Gone With the Wind* (1939). He did get to appear, however, in another classic, *High Noon* (1952), where he played the mayor of the small Western town where Gary Cooper was cast as the sheriff, with

Grace Kelly looking on.

Married at the time to Jennifer Jones, Robert Walker made his film debut as a sailor in the U.S. Navy, a garrulous youngster who carries his emotions on his sleeve.

Barry Nelson, as Private Francis Xavier Matoski, had just co-starred with Taylor in *Johnny Eager*. He would become the first actor to play James Bond in *Casino Royale* (1954, part of the *Climax!* series), a live television adaptation of the 1953 novel of the same name by Ian Fleming.

Desi had several talks with Lee Bowman, who had appeared in two films with Lucille: *Having a Wonderful Time,* and *Next Time I Marry.* What he wanted to learn, and didn't, was whether Lucille had an affair with him during the making of either movie.

Bowman became a leading man during the war years because of the shortage of big name, more widely recognized actors. He was eventually cast opposite Rita Hayworth in *Cover Girl* (1944) and with Jean Arthur in *The Impatient Years* (also 1944).

Bowman played an odd footnote in the saga of Lucille and Desi. He had appeared in the original pilot of what became her radio series, *My Favorite Husband,* playing the lead opposite Lucille. But when it came time to shoot the series, he was not available, and the part went to Richard Denning. Of course, as the world knows, Denning lost the role when the series was transferred to television and renamed *I Love Lucy.*

For the most part, *Bataan* got good reviews and generated a profit of $1.4 million.

Regrettably, the movie would have been even more successful, but Southern film exhibitors objected to its depiction of an integrated platoon. Kenneth Spencer, an African American, was cast as Private Wesley Epps of the Army Corps of Engineers. He is depicted with an appealing dignity and a quiet inner strength.

Bosley Crowther of *The New York Times* did not exactly give it a rave: "*Bataan* is a surprisingly credible conception of what that terrible experience must have been for some of the men who endured it. The film is not without its melodramatic flaws and admitted technical mistakes. But in the end, it doesn't insult the honor of those dead soldiers."

Since Desi had been praised for his acting in it, he sent word to Louis B. Mayer that "I'm now ready for those Latin lover roles you suggested. Bring 'em on."

None was offered.

Instead, he got another notice: "Greetings from Uncle Sam."

***

When Lucille went to pick up her first paycheck at MGM, it was the highest weekly salary she'd ever received: $2,000. Desi was envious. Louis B. Mayer had offered him only $500 a week, but he had finally cajoled him into $650, although he had held out for more.

"In Cuba, where I come from, the men are supposed to be the breadwinner bringing home the pay, not some kept boy like me supported by a redhead movie star."

MGM producer, Arthur Freed, specialized in musicals, and three times a year, he flew to New York to attend all the latest Broadway shows. In 1941, he'd gone to see *Best Foot Forward,* and had liked it so much, he made overtures to buy its movie rights for $150,000. At the end of its run on The Great White Way, he planned to turn it into a Technicolor musical starring Lana Turner and Gene Kelly.

[George Abbott, Desi's former director of Too Many Girls, *had presented* Best Foot Forward *on Broadway at the Barrymore Theatre.]*

Born in Charleston, South Carolina, and a former musical song-plugger, Freed would become increasingly known for producing some of the big movie musicals of the 1940s, including *Meet Me in St. Louis* (1945) starring Judy Garland. He would go on to win Best Picture Oscars for *An American in Paris* (1951) and *Gigi* (1958).

Lucille ended up cast in the film adaptation of the Broadway hit, *Best Foot Forward.* She was cast as a movie star playing herself.

She had not been the first choice for the role. It had originally been announced that Lana Turner would star in it.

By the time *Best Foot Forward* ended its Broadway run, its movie adaptation was ready for filming. Gene Kelly was working on another picture, and Lana Turner announced that she was pregnant.

She would in the months ahead, give birth to her daughter, Cheryl Crane, who would be her only child. Both Lana and her daughter would become involved in one of the most notorious murders of the 1950s, the stabbing death of gangster Johnny Stompanato (aka, Lana's lover). The mystery is still shrouded in controversy. Who killed the hoodlum? Was it Lana or was it her lesbian daughter?

Freed hired Brooklyn-born Edward Buzzell as director of its film adaptation. He was noted for directing the Marx Brothers in *At the Circus* in 1939 and *Go West* in 1940. Both Freed and Buzzell agreed to offer the lead role in *Best Foot Forward* to Lucille, who would portray a glamorous movie star who visits a military academy filled with horny young men lusting for her.

Harry James and his Orchestra would provide the music, performing such numbers as "The Flight of the Bumblebee."

Freed wanted to employ some members of the original Broadway cast, notably June Allyson and Nancy Walker. He was predicting stardom for each of them. He also employed Tommy Dix, Kenny Powers, and Jack Jordan. To that roster of talent, he added a rising young star, Gloria DeHaven and child star Virginia Weidler.

The film's promotional publicity and ads would feature Lucille and Harry James, since her leading man, William Gaxton, had no marquée value.

The story, a somewhat silly piece of fluff, centers around Lucille, who accepts an invitation to the senior prom at a military academy. It's been sent by her most devoted fan, a handsome young cadet, Bug Hooper (Dix). It was merely a fan letter, and he didn't expect her to accept. However, in dire need of publicity to beef up her career, and based on the urging of her agent, Jack O'Riley (Gaston), she accepts.

Bud has also invited his girlfriend, Helen Schlesinger (Weidler). The expected complications follow when Lucille shows up as his "movie star" date. In public, she gives him a smooch.

According to Lucille, "When I was told that **William Gaxton** had been cast as my leading man, I told Arthur Freed, 'You must be kidding.'"

"Then I found out he was to be my press agent, not my on-screen lover. What a relief."

Many in the cast could sing and dance their way through their respective numbers. Dix, in fact, had previously made a hit record with the song, "Buckle Down, Winsocki."

Since Lucille was not an accomplished singer or dancer, her voice had to be dubbed by Gloria Grafton.

June Allyson told Lucille, "I have big teeth and I lisp. My eyes disappear when I smile. My voice is funny. I don't sing like Judy Garland. I don't dance like Cyd Charisse. But whereas men might desire Cyd, they'll take me home to meet Mom."

Within two years, Allyson would marry Dick Powell, Lucille's future co-star.

Even though she was a (barely closeted) nymphomaniac, Allyson would go on to be hailed as "America's Sweetheart."

"No studly studio grip was safe from that darling girl," Lucille once quipped. "But she could also screw from the A-list, notably future presidents like John F. Kennedy and Ronald Reagan. Dean Martin, Alan Ladd, and James Stewart, among others, would flit in and out of her life. When she'd call me, her voice at first made me think it was Jimmy Durante on the phone."

It was Allyson who introduced Lucille to the chorus boy Stanley Donen. With the exception of Vincente Minnelli, he would become the best-known director of classical musicals. *On the Town* (1949),

Here's a view of the actor, **Chill Wills**, as he appeared in 1941.

"He was pure Texas, with that twang and folksy talk," Lucille said.

Royal Wedding (1951), and *Singin' in the Rain* (1952) are among the best examples.

Lucille wasn't particularly dazzled by her leading man, William Gaxton, who played her publicity agent, Jack O'Riley. "I found he had no charisma, although he was known as quite a good performer, having worked with such musical greats as Rodgers and Hart and Cole Porter,

316

too." He'd also appeared with big stars like Ethel Merman.

Lucille met Chill Wills before he became type-cast as the voice of Francis the Talking Mule. One afternoon, he said, "If you want to get a 'poke' from an old cowpoke, call on me. I do it the old-fashioned way."

"And what might that way be?" she asked.

"We come into the room where I've rented a saloon gal for fifty cents. I take off my cowboy hat and my stinking boots. We keep our clothes on, but lower our breeches, and I poke her one. I get up, put the coins on the table, say 'Thank you, ma'am,' and then hit the trail."

Gloria DeHaven was a competent performer during the Golden Age of MGM musicals, but she lacked that "something" that would have made her a leading star.

"At MGM, I went from playing Mickey Rooney's sweetheart (no big deal) to Judy Garland's disagreeable sister."

At the age of seventeen, Virginia Weidler would end her career with her performance in *Best Foot Forward*. As a child, she'd acted alongside some of the biggest stars in Hollywood: Clark Gable, Myrna Loy, Bette Davis, and Judy Garland. One of her more recent screen appearances was as Katharine Hepburn's younger sister in *The Philadelphia Story* (1940). She would soon disappear into oblivion.

A beauty born right in Los Angeles Gloria DeHaven was the daughter of the actor-director Carter DeHaven, a famous name during his heyday in vaudeville. Gloria had first appeared on the screen as a child in Charlie Chaplin's *Modern Times* (1936), but her role as a motion picture star had been late in coming. Although it was predicted that she would be a leading "star of tomorrow," that would never happen. She worked in films throughout the 1940s and '50s, and married actor John Payne in 1944.

Lucille wasn't really joking when she chided Gloria, "Please, please lend him to me at least for one night of passion and depravity."

Gloria told her that she planned to remain forever young, glamourous enough to play *femme fatale* roles until she was ninety. "I will stay beautiful forever because of my organic diet and faith in prayer."

She did not find ever-lasting youth, but she did live to be ninety-one, dying in Las Vegas of undisclosed ailments.

Another star on the rise, Nancy Walker, was a very talented performer on stage, screen, and television. After *Best Foot Forward,* she was cast in *Girl Crazy* (1943) with Mickey Rooney and Judy Garland. Her most high-profile role was that of Mildred, Rock Hudson's maid in his TV series, *McMillan & Wife* (1971-77).

Edward Buzzell became Lucille's favorite director. He'd be called back to helm her in *Easy to Wed* (1946). "Eddie was the first director who really understood my unique brand of comedy," she said.

Best Foot Forward was made for $1.6 million and generated $2.7 million at the box office.

Reviews were mostly good, *Variety* asserting that "The glamourous

Miss Ball is an eyeful in Technicolor, accenting the dazzle of her brilliant red hair." *The New York Daily Mirror* proclaimed, "Long a favorite of ours, Lucille Ball handles the comedy and lines in a manner reminiscent of the late Carole Lombard."

Lucille collected her own raves, recycling them later for advertising and product endorsements. They included such phrases as "the fresh spirit of youth," "sparkling dialogue," "bubbling, rollicking and charming," and "sharp and refreshing."

***

Faced with a choice of which branch of service he wished to join, Desi immediately selected the U.S. Army Air Force, with the dream of becoming a bombardier like he'd seen in World War II movies. When Lucille heard that, she exploded in anger. "You mean you don't want to come back alive? I'd better buy some widow's weeds."

Before the Monday morning when he was to report to induction, he received a call from a casual friend, Arnold Brady, who lived a few miles away. He asked Desi to join him as a player in a baseball game scheduled that Sunday afternoon at the Arlington Reception Center, near Riverside (California).

Although Lucille would have preferred that he spend Sunday with her, he was determined to play baseball. "Although hardly a Joe DiMaggio," he'd been a good player in Santiago as a teenager.

Bonding with the other players, Desi was picked for a team and assigned first base. Finally, it came time for him to step up to bat. Years later, he recalled what happened next: "I don't know how it happened, but when the pitcher threw me a fast ball, I swung wildly at it. I heard this bone-crunching sound. I felt my leg had been broken. There went my one good knee. I'd injured my other knee on a soccer field in Santiago. I was driven to the nearby hospital at Riverside, little knowing at the time that it would become my home for the next three months. Lucille visited almost every day."

His doctor urged an operation, but Desi devised his own cure. With his leg in a cast, he began a daily exercise regime to regain its use.

"My leg never really recovered, and I went

Virginia Weidler depicted here with **Toto**, the Cairn Terrier who appeared with Judy Garland in *The Wizard of Oz.* (1939)

Best Foot Forward was the swan song of this teenaged character actress.

In the immediate future, roles she might have been assigned would be given to Margaret O'Brien.

On stage and screen, **Nancy Walker** was a talented performer and appeared in musicals. But directors deemed her "not beautiful enough" for star roles.

Her greatest acclaim came on TV when she played Rock Hudson's maid.

through the rest of my life with two weak knees. Never again would I be able to shake my ass like I did in the Conga line at that nightclub in New York."

After his discharge, he still had to report to active duty at a recruiting station. Lucille always remembered driving him to the railway station, where he joined other recruits being transported to a training camp. After hugging and kissing him goodbye, she returned to her car, where she cried for an hour before driving away.

After a physical examination, Desi was rejected for the Air Force and assigned to the infantry instead. "There went my chance to bomb Berlin. But the infantry? I was assigned to the god damn infantry with two crippled legs. Made no sense to me at all."

At camp, he mingled with a type of American he had never known before: "Real farmboys. Some had never left Indiana or Kansas…one of those 'flyover' states between New York and Los Angeles. They seemed to have movie houses in some of these states, and the guys in the infantry had heard of Lucille Ball. Word soon spread that I was married to this glamourous redhead."

"These country bumpkins were filled with nothing but prejudice like I'd never known before," Desi said. "They hated Spics, Jews, niggers, and queers. They also felt that all Hollywood actors were faggots. I was always getting into a fight when some of them called me a fag or queer or a pansy or cocksucker. That last label really pissed me off. No one likes the gals more than me. Calling me a Hollywood fag was fighting words."

On three different occasions, his fights led to him ending up in the brig. "Once, I was so badly injured when attacked by four guys that I was in a hospital bed for three days. I always seemed to have a black eye. No sooner would I get rid of one than I'd get another hit."

He later claimed that when he went to see the World War II drama, *From Here to Eternity* (1953), he identified with the imprisoned character of Maggio as played by Frank Sinatra.

Before the end of his basic training, all the recruits had to go on a treacherous ten-mile "training run" with a heavy backpack. "With my bad knees, I felt I'd be experiencing the ordeal that those poor soldiers did on that Death March in Bataan, the theme of my latest picture."

Desi later recalled what happened to him at the end of that rugged ten-mile hike through the wilderness that came at the end of his training for the infantry. "I was very determined and I did make it to the end, but my leg had swollen to the size of a fat ham from a 1,000-pound hog. I was rushed to the hospital."

After his stay at the clinic, he thought he might be judged unfit for further service and discharged. He was called to the office of his commander. The Army needed all the men it could enlist, and the commander had a surprise job for Desi. "I understand you're married to Lucille Ball, and that you've done some entertaining yourself, like singing and playing the guitar."

"Guilty," Desi said.

"You seem like a very smart guy, and I want you to teach a bunch of illiterates how to read and write English. They come from the backwoods of America, remote spots in northern Alabama or West Virginia. Some of them never went to school."

Desi was stunned. "Me, an English teacher? Wait until Lucille hears about this."

The next day, he met his students, some with Southern accents so thick it was hard to understand just what they meant. He apologized for his Cuban accent and set about teaching the young men. He began with lesson number one: How to write their names. "The kids didn't know what I meant by a Cuban accent—in fact, they'd never heard of Cuba."

"After we got to know each other, we bonded," Desi said. "Some of the kids began to look upon me as a father figure, although I wasn't that much older than them. They had never been away from home before, and on several occasions, these harmless boys turned to me for comfort. I did what I could until one day I was called back into the commander's office. I thought, 'What now?'"

"I've come up with an idea," the officer said. "The government sends movie stars, such as Bob Hope, even Marlene Dietrich, to entertain our troops overseas. But we ignore our boys in training camps in California. They're often lonely and depressed before being sent out, many to face death on some god damn Jap-held island they've never heard of. I want you to organize some form of entertainment for these guys."

"Now I can do that better than I can teach English," he answered.

The very next day, he set about putting on a show. First, he called Lucille. She would know what to do.

Indeed, she did, almost becoming director of entertainment herself. She began to recruit friends who were free on weekends and eager to entertain servicemen before they headed off to war.

She booked a rotating all-star cast of enormous talent: Ann Sheridan, Gloria DeHaven, June Allyson, Martha Raye, Lena Horne and Mickey Rooney, who agreed to show up with Judy Garland. Tommy Dorsey and His Orchestra promised to appear whenever they could.

The commander was amazed, telling his lieutenant, "Can you believe it? This little Cuban Spic is bringing some of the top talent in Hollywood to this remote little hell hole."

***

During the final two weeks of the shooting of *Best Foot Forward*, three of its stars were assigned specific additional duties by its producer, Joe Pasternak at MGM. Lucille, Gloria DeHaven, and June Allyson were each wanted for cameo appearances in MGM's upcoming musical, *Thousands Cheer* (1943).

Filmed during the height of World War II, it had been conceived as a morale booster for America's soldiers. It would feature a cavalcade of major stars from MGM: Judy Garland, Ann Sothern, Lena Horne, Red Skelton, and Eleanor Powell. It would be hosted by Mickey Rooney, and in it, the then-famous pianist and composer, José Iturbi, would make his film debut.

The actual stars included MGM's songbird, Kathryn Grayson, and actor-dancer Gene Kelly. He plays an aerialist drafted into the Army, and he falls for Grayson, who is the daughter of his commanding officer. Two Hollywood veterans, John Boles and Mary Astor, starred as Grayson's parents.

In Lucille's cameo, she does a comedy stint with Frank Morgan, who portrays an amorous barber impersonating a doctor giving her a physical examination. Music is provided by the orchestras of Bob Crosby and Kay Kyser.

When *Thousands Cheer* held its premiere in Manhattan, it took in $550,000 from a sale of War Bonds. It would ultimately gross $5.8 million in an era when many theaters charged a quarter for a seat.

The movie's theme song, "I Dug a Ditch in Wichita," ends the picture with Grayson leading an international chorus of men pleading for world peace.

The New York Times defined it as "a virtual grab-bag of delights...there is something for all tastes, from José Iturbi to boogie-woogie."

The *New York Herald Tribune* called it a "prodigal and sumptuous picture, saved by Gene Kelly from being merely a parade of personalities."

Meanwhile, Lucille stepped up her patriotic efforts to raise money through the sale of war bonds.

In September of 1943, she became one of a troupe of stars, part of the Hollywood Bond Cavalcade, touring the country, raising morale, and selling war bonds.

THOUSANDS CHEER

During this film's heyday, this poster was prominently displayed in Allentown, Pennsylvania. Thousands more were distributed nationwide as part of the War Effort.

Their jaunt began in Washington, D.C., later moving on to sixteen cities in three weeks, and ending up in Los Angeles. Along the way, they were mobbed by autograph seekers in Boston, Philadelphia, New York, Cleveland, Detroit, Chicago, New Orleans, and Dallas, among others. The Cavalcade raised forty million dollars in War Bond Sales, In St. Louis, Lucille had to call security to have a love-sick sixteen-year-old removed from under her bed. As he was escorted out, he swore lifetime devotion to her.

When available, Desi joined in, once appearing with Charles Boyer, Joan Bennett, and Joan Blondell. Other stars who signed on included James Cagney, Claudette Colbert, Bing Crosby, Olivia de Havilland, and Cary Grant. Betty Hutton delivered some "boogey woogie," and Judy Garland sang "Blow, Gabriel, Blow."

Lucille appeared with Harpo Marx, as he chases her around the stage in a pretend seduction. *[Back in 1938, she had starred with the Marx Brothers in* Room Service.]

When the Cavalcade crew ended their involvement with it in Los Angeles, a mob of six thousand waited for them at the railway station in Glendale. A Navy band showed up to play "California, Here I Come."

[The same song was performed years later, in 1955, on an episode of I Love Lucy *when Ricky Ricardo and Fred and Ethel Mertz piled into a car en route to Hollywood.]*

***

At the Desilu Ranch, early one morning in March of 1944, Lucille was awakened by the ringing of her bedside phone. She feared any call at this hour meant trouble. Sleepily, she picked up the phone to hear Desi's excited voice. "I'm being transferred to Birmingham."

"Oh, I'll miss you, honey," she said. "But next week, I'm on a bond tour with a stopover in Atlanta. I can arrange to visit you in Alabama from there."

"Not Alabama, wherever in hell that is," he said. "Birmingham, California, only five miles down the road from our ranch! I'll get weekends off!"

Thousands Cheer was based on a winning formula of patriotism and romance, and cheerfully bundled with in an appeal for fundraising.

Here's **Gene Kelly** wooing **Kathryn Grayson.**

According to Kelly, "She could sing and I could dance. What a winning combination of talent!"

"That sounds too good to be true!" she said. "The U.S. Army will actually lend-lease me my husband two nights a week."

"At least that, my sexy redhead doll. And you're gonna get it."

After making plans for their reunion the upcoming Friday night, he put down the phone. As she remembered it, "I felt the happiest I'd felt in years."

Regrettably, her weekends with Desi did not exactly work out as she envisioned. "What ever does?" she later asked. "That's life."

At the military base, Desi no longer had to teach English to illiterate boys. He was given an even more challenging role involving the organizing of entertainment for wounded young men being shipped home from Iwo Jima, Bataan, and Corregidor.

Some of them would be arriving on stretchers, and nearly all of them had broken limbs. The worst of the wounded were the "basket cases" without arms or legs; others arrived in every possible configuration of debilitation and pain. Many of the men had been mentally and/or emotionally damaged by the horrors of war.

Seeing all these wounded men and how they had suffered made Desi feel guilty that he had not been physically fit for active duty abroad. The very presence of some of the wounded reminded him of that embarrassing (to him, at least) fact.

The worst cases were segregated into a separate ward whose occupants required psychiatric help. "Otherwise, I tried to be the shrink to my own men, who were often bitter and filled with resentment."

He cited a tall, handsome, blonde-haired former football player who had lost one leg in the war. He told Desi to go away. But Desi was determined, and he kept pursuing the soldier, despite his verbal abuse, until one day he stopped attacking Desi, worked with him, and learned to walk on an artificial leg.

To entertain the wounded, Desi at first beat the drums or else played his guitar and sang to them. "I think the guys got tired of 'Babalu.'"

He knew they wanted more, so he prevailed on Lucille to come through for him, and she did.

She began to show up with a busload of beautiful starlets to meet and talk with the wounded men. Significantly, when they were asked what they wanted to drink, many of them chose cold milk. The starlets who presented them with it soon became known as "The Milk Girls."

"Most of the guys would drink a whole quart of cold milk," Desi said. "One soldier actually consumed four quarts."

After Lucille persuaded the studios to send over their latest films, Desi arranged to turn one building—"Really a sort of barn"—into a theater with a stage for the screening of movies two nights a week. MGM was especially generous, but so were Paramount and Columbia. Even RKO sent over its Ginger Rogers movies. According to Desi, "My first request to RKO involved shipping us a copy of my film, *Bataan*, in which I die of malaria."

With his military haircut, **Desi** is on leave and spending it "with the love of my life," the emerging movie star, **Lucille Ball.**

Since he was stationed at an Army base less than five miles away, he could usually visit her on weekends, pending his ability to wangle a weekend pass.

At first, only backless wooden benches were provided for the men, and many weren't able to sit on them comfortably for very long. Through an elaborate scheme, Desi figured out a way to get around Army regulations: "If I went through all the red tape, including permission from Washington, the war would be over before those seats arrived."

[According to Desi, he learned that a cute brunette secretary was a key figure in working through the Army's red tape, and to that effect he began to date her, taking her out dining and dancing Eventually, he helped persuade Irving Briskin, an executive at Columbia, to provide conventional seating for the makeshift theater, thanks partly to funds provided by B'nai B'rith.]

Often, during those visits, he was midway between liaisons with other women, compliments of Fox's Darryl F. Zanuck, who sometimes arranged a rendezvous for Desi with one or another of his beautiful starlets.

323

In addition to films, Desi began to present live shows, too. Lucille and Desi performed the same vaudeville act they'd showcased at the Roxy Theater in Manhattan. One night, Lucille appeared wearing a mink coat, which she slipped off onstage to reveal the burlesque costume she'd worn in *Dance, Girl, Dance* (1940). The whistling and yells from the soldiers were so prolonged and so intense that Desi refused to let her repeat the act.

Sometimes Desi, through Lucille, could arrange for an appearance by a major star. Betty Grable became the biggest attraction, but Ginger Rogers went over big, too. Red Skelton, Martha Raye, June Allyson, and Nancy Walker followed.

"We were too small to attract Bing Crosby or Bob Hope, who entertained far more troops than ours," Desi said. "Betty Hutton with her wild boogie-woogie numbers was always a reliable star to depend upon."

She called it "doing one for the boys."

Lucille was disappointed as weekends with Desi at home became increasingly rare. She blamed it on Birmingham being too close to Hollywood.

In the wake of Louis B. Mayer's separation from his wife, the mogul, in 1944, purchased the Marion Davies' mansion in Beverly Hills. There, he threw wild parties. Around the same time, many other studio executives were leaving their wives to party and seduce the legions of starlets who had migrated to Los Angeles during the war.

Somehow, Desi used his charm to ingratiate himself into this notoriously impenetrable circle. He became a vocal admirer of Darryl F. Zanuck at Fox, deciding that of all the studio heads in Hollywood, Zanuck was the one whose example he most wanted to follow.

Stars that Zanuck had famously seduced had included Wendy Barrie, Dolores Costello, Linda Darnell, Ann Harding, and Merle Oberon. He seemed to prefer, however, intimacies with lesser-known starlets. Regular events every day beginning around noon at Fox became known as "Zanuck's fuck break." Two starlets would be summoned to his office, which had an adjoining bedroom. As he told Desi, "I like to begin by watching two gals make love. Then I select the one on which I wish to bestow 'God's gift.'"

["God's gift" was his legendary penis, which he liked to pull out and display to an actress while he was interviewing her. He had even exposed himself to child star Shirley Temple. Ava Gardner told Desi, "The only thing bigger than Zanuck's cigar is his cock."]

On any weekend he wished, Zanuck, not Mayer, arranged for Desi to seduce one or several of the Fox starlets under his command. Lucille bitterly resented Desi's hanging out with such bigtime studio brass, but she was convinced that Mayer, after Desi's discharge from the Army, would promote him as a Latin lover, as he had once considered. She also wanted Mayer to cast Desi in musical comedies with her.

[After the war, Mayer did create two Latin lovers for the screen, but not Desi. They were Ricardo Montalban and Fernando Lamas.]

"My marriage to Desi became a long distance phone call," Lucille lamented.

Sometimes, when Desi visited their ranch, Lucille was gone on a bond tour. In most cases and in most of the stopovers during the tour, the Army would assign her a handsome, star-struck soldier as an escort.

In 1952, when *I Love Lucy* was a regular fixture on television, emerging columnist Mike Connolly wrote an article that was never published. In it, he became the first newspaperman to expose the adulterous affairs of "Lucy and Ricky Ricardo."

At the time, his editor and/or bosses suppressed the *exposé*.

In it, Connolly not only wrote about Desi's affairs, but alleged that Lucille sustained a number of affairs during her bond tours with U.S. soldiers.

When Desi managed to return to the ranch during his tour of duty in Birmingham, he often spent hours talking to Lucille and pondering if he did indeed have a future as a movie star. She tried to assure him that he did, stressing that MGM was still receiving two to three hundred fan letters a week for him, even though it had been more than a year since he'd last appeared in a film, and a minor role at that.

She also told him that during his stint at RKO, the incoming volume of his fan mail was exceeded only by that received by Ginger Rogers.

***

Returning from a bond tour, Lucille was notified by MGM that her next picture, *Meet the People,* scheduled for a release in 1944, would co-star Dick Powell.

A day before she was to report to work on the set of that film, a call came in from a tense and upset June Allyson, who said, in her husky voice, "Just a warning, girl: Dick is private property, and your reputation has preceded you. Hands off! GOT THAT?" Then she slammed down the receiver.

Later, Lucille told her friend, Barbara Pepper, "Imagine getting a call from the Nymph of MGM telling ME to back off."

***

Producer E.Y. ("Yip") Harburg and director Charles Reisner gave Lucille star billing in her next film, *Meet the People* (1944). Her co-star, Dick Powell, had been one of the featured crooners of such hit films as *42nd Street* (1933).

On the first day of shooting, Powell showed up with June Allyson. Later, she visited Lucille in her dressing room.

Responding to Allyson's phone call of the previous day, Lucille told her, "If you're here

Looking proper and very prim, here's **June Allyson,** as she appeared in *The Bride Went Wild* in 1948.

She warned Lucille to keep her hands off Dick Powell, Lucille's new co-star, even though he was still married to Joan Blondell,

Allyson had already staked him out as her next husband.

to protect Powell from my clutches, forget it. On a scale of one to ten, I'd rank his sex appeal as one and a half. Besides, he's still married to my friend, Joan Blondell."

"Not for very long," Allyson retorted. "He's in the process of filing for a divorce. As for my being here now, I've persuaded Yip to give me a part in your picture. Don't worry. I promise not to steal the film from you."

Although Harburg, (aka "Yip") was producing this time, he was best-known as a musician and songwriter. He'd won an Oscar for Best Original Song, "Over the Rainbow," sung by Judy Garland in *The Wizard of Oz* (1939). Regrettably, this talented song lyricist and librettist would, in a few years, be blacklisted for socialist politics.

The film's director, Charles Reisner, had also acted. He had appeared with Charlie Chaplin in *A Dog's Life* (1918) and *The Kid* (1921). He'd go on to direct comedies with such stars as Buster Keaton, W.C. Fields, and the Marx Brothers.

The plot of *Meet the People* spins around a glamourous movie star, Julie Hampton (Lucille), who gets involved with a shipyard worker, Swanee Swanson (Dick Powell), at a manufacturing plant

Cast in *Meet the People* as the glamorous Broadway star, Julie Hampton, **Lucille** poses for a publicity shot with her troupe of dancers. The producer described this wartime "morale builder" as a "musical with a viewpoint, that is, revue plus story."

Much of the film takes place in a shipyard. As *The New York Times* wrote, "They may build iron ships in that shipyard, but they certainly have got a wooden plot."

during World War II. For having raised $10,000 for the government through the sale of War Bonds, he's awarded a date with the star.

During his date with her, he pitches a play he's written, *Meet the People.* He wants to see it mounted on Broadway as a tribute to all the men and women who struggled in manufacturing plants to win World War II.

The idea intrigues her, but the producers set out to glamourize it into a frivious musical. Disillusioned, Swanee withdraws. From here, the plot twists need a road map to follow. A stage version of his script eventually opens on Broadway, and from there, the emotional ups and downs of the plot get tricky, indeed. Fear naught: Everything works out in the end.

Virginia O'Brien, who had recently worked with Lucille in *Thousands Cheer,* joined the cast as a character named "Woodpecker Peg." With her trademark deadpan expression, she sings, "Say That We're Sweethearts Again."

Cast as "Annie," Allyson leads other singers in a rendition of "I Like to Recognize the Tune." "Rags" Ragland does his comic bit as "Smitty" Smith.

Gloria Grafton was hired once again to dub Lucille's voice during musical numbers.

As a musical spoof on Hitler, Spike Jones and His City Slickers perform "Der Fuehrer's Face" and "Schicklgruber."

Other music was provided by Vaughn Monroe and His Orchestra. Bert Lahr is a scene-stealer, cast as "The Commander."

Meet the People was one of the lesser efforts of the flag-waving musicals of the wartime years. The *New York Daily News* commented on how gorgeous Lucille looked as a movie star, but not when she takes a job as a welder in a war plant to get to know the working people contributing to the Allied Cause.

The New York Times found the talent of "Rags" Ragland and June Allyson "Lost in the pile." *Variety* viewed the story as "both innocuous and unimportant, dragging in many parts."

Meet the People bombed at the box office, losing $720,000 for MGM.

Dick Powell, cast in *Meet the People* as "Swanee" Swanson, has won a date with actress **Lucille Ball** as part of a fund-raising contest for War Bonds. As the storyline unfolded, it becomes clear that he and the character played by Lucille don't really get along.

At the time, though still married to Joan Blondell, a friend of Lucille's, Powell was "heavy dating" June Allyson.

***

Before shooting her next picture, Lucille had a sad journey to make back to her hometown of Jamestown, New York. She went there to bury Grandpa Hunt, who had died at the age of seventy-eight.

She cried as she stood in front of the elm-shaded family plot, watching the earth cover the casket of the father figure who had represented so much in her life. She'd wanted him buried next to his beloved wife, Flora Belle, who had passed on before him.

She remained in Jamestown for four nights, receiving old friends, all of whom came to greet her and to comment on her remarkable success. Her former reputation as "The Jamestown Hussy" seemed not to be remembered by anybody. While there, she raised money for a War Bond drive before flying back to Los Angeles to begin work on her next picture, *Ziegfeld Follies*, eventually released in 1945.

Fired with a kind of razzmatazz patriotism, Arthur Freed set out to produce MGM's most spectacular extravaganza of the 1940s. To that end, he drew upon the studio's vast stable of contract players. Lucille was told that she'd have a sequence where she'd dance with one of the picture's two male stars, either Gene Kelly or Fred Astaire. That did not happen.

Fanny Brice was the only member of the cast who had been in any of the many versions of the Follies mounted on Broadway.

Judy Garland "harvested the thunder" when she appeared in one of its musical numbers as a glamorous movie star as she delivered a news interview to "dancing reporters." She was said to be spoofing Greer Garson.

Astaire and Kelly (without Lucille) would be praised for "trading taps and double-takes for a photo finish" in their dance routine, *The Babbitt and the Bromide.*

But it was Lucille herself who stole the most spectacular sequence. She had never looked more seductive than when she rode in on Lone Ranger's horse, "Silver." She cracks a rhinestone-studded whip over the heads of eight starlets dressed as black panthers. Astaire had introduced her entrance with "Bring on the Beautiful Girls."

Flaming red hair is topped by the second most elaborate headdress of her career, as she emerges as a vision in a pink gown supported on towering black high heels. *[The size of her headdress was surpassed only by the headgear she'd worn in* Du Barry Was a Lady.*]*

Other stars in the cast included Kathryn Grayson, Lucille Bremer, Lena Horne, James Melton, Victor Moore, Red Skelton, Edward Arnold, Robert Lewis, Keenan Wynn, Cyd Charisse, and Hume Cronyn.

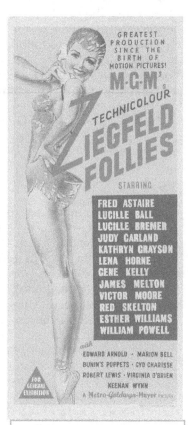

On the set, Lucille met and talked to William Frawley, who would loom so large in her future. In the 1950s, he would be cast as her landlord in *I Love Lucy,* alongside Vivian Vance as his wife. At the time, neither Lucille or Frawley could envision the international fame that awaited them in the television world of the 1950s.

George Sidney had directed Lucille's most elaborate sequence, but he soon left and was replaced by Vincente Minnelli, who arrived on the set with more lipstick than Lucille wore.

During the long time it spent in production, which straddled, with many delays, parts of 1944 and 1945, other directors were also called in: Roy Del Ruth, Lemuel Ayers, Robert Lewis, and Charles Walters, who wrote the screenplay, limited though it was. Instead of being based on a conventionally chronological plot line, it really consisted, for the most part, of a somewhat disjointed series of musical numbers and comedy sketches.

Supposedly a tribute to master showman Flo Ziegfeld (William Powell), **Ziegfeld Follies** (1945) shows him in Heaven looking down at the human frailties (and follies) unfolding below.

When it was first shown in preview, it ran for three hours and got, for the most part, unfavorable audience reactions. Freed called it back for extensive cutting and some reshooting. In the final version (110 minutes long), most of Lucille's comedic sketches were cut, with the exception of the black panther number.

Its actual premiere did not occur until April of 1946 in Manhattan.

Audiences watched William Powell in the opening sequence. Portraying the showman, Flo Ziegfeld, he looks down from heaven to see what the Follies of 1946 looks like. *[Powell had played Flo Ziegfeld in The Great Ziegfeld (1936).]*

The New York Times reviewed the film as "strictly episodic, with its inevitable ups and downs, but it's entertaining." *Cue* wrote, "In show business parlance, Ziggy had his flops as well as boffs. And so this $3 million kaleidoscopic film glorification of Flo Ziegfeld and his lush extravaganzas also has its flops and boffs."

Lucille's own review? "A costly dud."

It took in $5.3 million at the box office, but because of its staggering production costs, it showed a loss of $300,000.

The real-life Flo Ziegfeld may not have liked everything he saw in the new Follies, but he must have been impressed with **Lucille.**

She had never looked more glamourous in her form-fitting pink gown with sequins, "Tango Red" curls, and a towering feathered headdress.

As part of her *schtick*, she rides in on the Lone Ranger's horse, "Silver," with a whip in hand.

***

Ziegfeld Follies was only a minor disappointment to Lucille. More troubling was her failing marriage to Desi. She still maintained that she loved him, but it was a love affair from afar. During the previous five weeks, he hadn't called or come home.

Occasionally, he made the rumor mill, having been seen at various clubs along Sunset Strip with an array of beautiful, often blonde, starlets.

Lucille spent many a lonely weekend until Barbara Pepper, her longtime confidante, began to visit with her new, handsome, and dashing husband, Craig Reynolds. The happy couple made Lucille envious that she didn't have a comparably compatible relationship with Desi.

She had seen only one of the films Reynolds had made, *The Mystery of Mr. Wong* (1939).

[Pepper ended up just as lonely as Lucille after Reynolds went off to war, returning with a Purple Heart. After the war, his film career stalled. In October of 1949, at the age of forty-two, he died in a fatal accident on his motorcycle, leaving Pepper alone with their two sons, John and Dennis. Lucille offered what comfort she could.]

During Reynolds' wartime absences overseas, Pepper and Lucille often went to hear music at one of the clubs. Lucille defined themselves as "the lonely widows."

She confessed to Pepper, "I get offers almost every week from some highly desirable men, often married. I don't think it's fair for Desi to be having all the fun while I stay at the ranch feeding grain to the chickens."

"Are you going to divorce the horndog?" Pepper asked. "You can't call what you have a real marriage."

"I don't want to, but I think I must. It's a sham marriage. His failure as a husband is part of the culture he learned as a boy. His father, so I was told, went whoring whenever he felt like it."

***

One windy afternoon in late September of 1944, Desi received a phone call at his military base in Birmingham.

It was from a law firm in Beverly Hills: "Mr. Arnaz," came the voice on the other end. "I am the attorney that Miss Lucille Ball has retained to begin divorce proceedings against you."

On the set and between scenes of *Zeigfeld Follies* (1945), **Lucille**—still wearing her costume—has a laugh with veteran show biz legend, **Fanny Brice.**

Brice, a somewhat beat-up old pro of yesterday, had actually performed in some of the real-life Flo Ziegfeld's stage revues.

CHAPTER ELEVEN

AVOIDING DIVORCE AMID FAST-CHANGING ENTERTAINMENT TRENDS, THE BALL/ARNAZ LOVEBIRDS CAN'T (OR WON'T) CONTROL THEIR CHEATING HEARTS

Before filing for divorce from Desi, Lucille went through a five-month period where MGM offered no film roles.

"Two or three hot properties came along, but they went to Angela Lansbury." Lucille no doubt was thinking of her role as the Cockney maid of Ingrid Bergman in *Gaslight* (1944) for which Lansbury got an Oscar for Best Supporting Actress of the Year. Among other roles, Lucille also coveted Lansbury's portrayal of Sibyl Vane, a music hall performer in the film adaptation of Oscar Wilde's *The Picture of Dorian Gray* (1945).

"The brass at MGM knew I had something, but they couldn't figure out what," Lucille said. "Mayer seemed to be devoting his casting to a coven of girls he thought might appeal to wartime audiences. There was always an up-and-coming (mostly going) starlet of the month to promote."

According to Lucille, "At the time, were also some hold-over relics from the Hollywood waxworks on MGM's payroll, each a major player from the heyday of silent film. Two of them were Buster Keaton and Edward Sedgwick, each of whom received a monthly stipend."

Lucille had great respect for Keaton's talent in comedy. Once a spectacularly famous star, he had fallen on hard times and was working for a hundred dollars a week as a consultant. She spent several hours with him in his capacity as a coach for MGM. In studio-sanctioned "consultations," he rehearsed her in comedic antics, and screened some of his favorite silent pictures for her.

Many of these classic comedies had been directed by Sedgwick. He also became Lucille's teacher. Born to vaudeville parents, he had first appeared on the stage when he was four years old. He later achieved his greatest success as a director of silent films. She had known him since her days at RKO when she met him on the set of *That Girl from Paris* (1936).

She later recalled, "Buster and Eddie taught me a lot about how to pull off slapstick and how to make use of props. Those lessons came in handy during the long run of *I Love Lucy* on TV."

***

Finally, producer Lawrence Weingarten cast Lucille as the third lead in a film starring Spencer Tracy and Katharine Hepburn. It was based on the Philip Barry

HONING HER CRAFT

Buster Keaton during his silent era heyday in *The General* (1927).

Lucille—always alert to the talents of the vaudevillians who had preceded her—quizzed him (and he counseled her) in his twilight years as an acting coach.

play, *Without Love,* which had had a "less than successful" run on Broadway. Nonetheless, Katharine Hepburn, herself in need of a hot film role, prevailed on Louis B. Mayer to buy the screen rights.

Barry had also written the script for Broadway's 1939 version of *The Philadelphia Story,* in which Hepburn had starred. In the movie version with Cary Grant and James Stewart, she staged a "comeback." *[Its timing coincided with her labeling as "box office poison" in the late 1930s.]*

Screenwriter Donald Ogden Stewart was hired to "work out the kinks in the Barry play before shooting began."

George Cukor was not available to direct Hepburn, so Weingarten assigned Harold S. Bucquet to helm it. *Without Love* (1945) became his last picture, as he was to die in February of 1946. Before that, he was known mainly for helming Dr. Kildare movies. *Without Love* would be released only months before his death.

In it, Hepburn was cast as a lonely widow, Jamie Rowan, living in wartime Washington, D.C., where there was a housing shortage. She opens her home to a military research scientist, Patrick Jamieson (Spencer Tracy), who is developing a prototype for an oxygen-supplying helmet for pilots flying at high altitudes. She goes on to propose marriage to him, suggesting it would be a marital union of mutual benefit but *Without Love.*

Of course, as was inevitable, the couple fall in love. *Without Love* evolves into a friendship "with love."

Lucille reported to work on the set of *Without Love* on October 16, 1944. That was the same day she had to take a break for a court appearance involving her divorce from Desi.

She later told gossip columnist Louella Parsons that she would not mention Desi being "Girl Crazy," a state of mind that most of Hollywood already attributed to him.

"Our failure in marriage is because of our difference in temperaments. I'm just as much to blame as he is. We both can be very difficult, leading to some epic battles. We are often separated at times, even when he has leave from the service."

In the third lead, Lucille played Kitty Trimble, a wise-cracking friend of Jamie. Kitty is involved in a romance with Quentin Ladd, as portrayed by Keenan Wynn. He had been added to MGM's stable of contract actors in 1942. Fully aware that he and Van Johnson had been long-time secret lovers, she had known him for years.

Katharine Hepburn had befriended Lucille when they had co-starred together in *Stage Door* (1937). Over lunch in the commissary, Lucille confided that she was planning to divorce Desi because of his constant philandering.

"I'm not going to cite that in court. Instead, I plan to claim mental cruelty. Do you have a problem with Tracy screwing around?"

Hepburn seemed to take offense at the question: "If you must know, Spence and I are not a sexual couple," she said, coolly. "We are dear, dear platonic friends."

Good, wholesome, family-friendly fun, circa 1945 was the theme in *Without Love*.

Tracy and **Hepburn** maneuver their (muted) intimacies across a bunk-bed divide.

During the filming of *Without Love*, Lucille had one of her recurring fainting spells because of her arrhythmia, a leftover from an adolescent heart ailment.

Always the nurse, Hepburn rushed to her side to help give her air. By the time Lucille regained consciousness, Hepburn had unbuttoned her blouse and was trying to unhook her brassiere.

As Lucille sat up, she said, "Now you know. Mine are no bigger than yours. Even so, when I was starving in New York City, I once posed bare-chested."

Hepburn looked at her and answered, "So did I, and I wasn't even starving."

Lucille told director Bucquet, "Like E.F. Hutton, when Hepburn speaks, you listen—that is, if you're smart. She even lectured me on how to brush my teeth properly. Also how to shell peas. I've never shelled a pea in my life."

Lucille had nothing but praise for the movie's cinematographer, Karl Freund. Years later, he'd help her in her struggle to launch a filmed TV show, unheard of at the time.

As a footnote in Hollywood history, a future star, sultry Gloria Grahame, appeared briefly in *Without Love* as a flower seller with allergies to pollen. When Lucille lunched with her, Grahame shared her dream of future stardom, which she'd first taste in *film noir*.

[Years later, although Grahame appeared on the screen for only nine minutes during the filming of The Bad and the Beautiful *(1952), she was nominated for a Best Supporting Actress Oscar in that picture with Lana Turner and Kirk Douglas.*

In 1948, Grahame would marry director Nicholas Ray. Four years later, he divorced her in 1952 when he came home early from work and caught her in bed with his thirteen-year-old son, Anthony. In 1960, she married the boy.]

Without Love generated $3.8 million at the box office. Its success established Tracy and Hepburn as the leading co-starring team in Hollywood. From there, they'd go on to make other pictures together.

Filmink defined *Without Love* as "absolutely, resolutely, and incredibly unmemorable." *Harrison's Reports* found it "an amusing comedy drama…There's more talk than action, but the sparkling dialogue is a compensating factor."

Wolcott Gibbs of *The New Yorker* stated that although it had been significantly altered from the play that had inspired it, it was "a very witty and engaging picture recommended without hesitation."

The New York Times predicted that Lucille would evolve into a wise-cracking third lead in the tradition of Eve Arden. *The Nation* wrote, "It is good to see Lucille Ball doing so well in a new kind of role for her." In unflattering contrast, *The New York Sun* found that "Miss Hepburn caricatures her part."

***

Lucille met the handsome, sleepy-eyed hunk Robert Mitchum on the back lot of

Lucille appears here as the third lead (after Tracy and Hepburn) in *Without Love*. She received some of the best reviews of her career for her performance as a wisecracking real estate agent dealing with the wartime housing shortage.

Standing behind her, character actor and eccentric, **Keenan Wynn,** pretends to look like a goofball.

Women we love: **Gloria Grahame.**

Although she had only a bit part as a flower girl in *Without Love*, her arched brow and pouting upper lip would soon grace thousands of movie screens of post-war America.

334

Metro in 1944 during his filming of *Thirty Seconds Over Tokyo*. They were introduced by that film's director, Mervyn LeRoy, and they ate together in the commissary. He seemed fascinated by her, and she was turned on by his cool charm. She later told LeRoy, "Bob is the most masculine man I've ever met."

"I've seen you around," Mitchum said when he met her. "I've been dying to find out something that has really bothered me."

"Yes, I know. Desi is fucking every showgal in America."

"No, it's not that. I want to find out if you're a real redhead all over."

LeRoy later described their romance as casual and short-term, involving at the most no more than three separate trysts. During the peak of their involvement, he ran into Lucille in the commissary and asked her, "What do you think of our boy, Bob?"

"He's a real pain in the ass," she said enigmatically.

"It was only years later that I found out what Lucille meant," LeRoy said. "Ava Gardner told me that Bob liked to go in through the rear door. Apparently, Desi is strictly a front door kind of guy, and Lucille had never had it that way before."

[Mitchum faded from Lucille's life until the spring of 1957, when he came to her for advice about launching his album of calypso vocals for Capitol Records. The album was called Robert Mitchum — Calypso Is Like So! *He also wanted to sing on one of her specials.*

She later conveyed that at the time, she told him bluntly, "You're no Harry Belafonte."

When Lucille met Marilyn Monroe, they bonded temporarily one drunken evening by talking about Hollywood studs and by reviewing if they'd ever shared a lover in common. Mitchum was at the top

Even some ardent fans didn't know that **Robert Mitchum** harbored a desire to be a calypso singer.

In 1957, he recorded an album that was ridiculed by some music critics.

River of No Return (1954) started out as a cheap B Western but mushroomed into a big production directed by Otto Preminger and starring **Marilyn Monroe** and **Robert Mitchum**. It was shot at scenic locales which included Jasper, Wyoming and Banff Springs, near Lake Louise in western Canada.

Holding Marilyn in his arms, Mitchum found her over-articulating. Apparently, her "smelly surrogate mother," Natasha Lytess, had recommended this, but it wasn't coming across as "natural."

"She looked like she was doing an imitation of a fish," Mitchum told Preminger before slapping her on the ass and telling her to act like a human being.

He later became more familiar with her famous ass.

335

of their list. Marilyn, who had made River of No Return with him in 1954, claimed that "Bob brags about how he used to share a locker with my first husband, James Doughtery. At the time, both of them were working as sheet-metal workers at Lockheed Aircraft."

"Bob gives interviews about how he used to go dancing with me and my husband in the war years," Marilyn told Lucille. "Actually, I never met him in those days. The closest he came to knowing me was when Jim showed him a nude picture of me he'd taken when I was a teenager standing by the garden gate. And Bob sometimes ate the baloney sandwiches I packed for Jim's lunch."

Marilyn also told Lucille that Jim Dougherty had gotten drunk with Mitchum one night. "If Jim is to be believed, Bob came on to him. Around midnight he told my then-husband that he was a real cute Irishman, and he'd like to plug his ass. Jim told him, 'I don't go that route, not with Norma Jean waiting at the house for me.' Jim said he sorta avoided Bob after that and no longer shared a locker with him."

Close friends of Mitchum's knew that he'd had a number of homosexual encounters during his wild and woolly days as a young man on the road. In Hollywood, he once "rented himself out" to gay actor Clifton Webb.

Marilyn also confessed that on the set of River of No Return (1954), alert to Mitchum's interest in anal sex, she approached him one day with a book on sexuality. She asked Mitchum to explain to her what the author meant by "anal eroticism."

Mitchum might have suspected that James Dougherty, Marilyn's former husband, had told her about his long-ago attempt to seduce him. But regardless, Mitchum behaved like a gentleman and agreed to break her in to the finer points of anal sex. Marilyn went on to appraise Bob as an expert at "back door entry."

She claimed that because she was enduring a particularly debilitating period of menstruation at the time, she had willingly submitted. "I found it a bit of a turn-on and was glad Bob broke me in. It came in handy with later lovers."

Marilyn could have been referring to President John F. Kennedy, who told friends that "I'm never through with a woman until I've had her three ways."

But before wiggling away, Marilyn delivered one final appraisal, noting that "Bob should watch that bad breath. And as you probably already know, he's a lousy kisser."

Lucille would never encounter Marilyn again. She was saddened to learn about her suicide (or murder?) on August 5, 1962.

As for Bob Mitchum, Lucille was surprised, years after their inaugural fling, when he called her and said that he considered her "the most savvy woman in show business" and that he wanted her career advice. She knew he wasn't trying to rekindle their romance from World War II. He expressed his regrets at having turned down the role of "the last cowboy," in The Misfits, which subsequently went to Clark Gable. Released in 1961, The Misfits is best remembered as a somewhat tepid movie best known for having showcased the last film appearances of both Clark and Marilyn.

"I think it would have been a great part for you," Lucille told him. "It would also have been a great learning experience."

"Yes, I think it would have been," Mitchum said. "And we'd have had some laughs too."

"What about?" she asked.

"Huston has this pet monkey," Mitchum said. "He likes to take him out drinking. When everybody's drunk and crazy enough, Huston likes to masturbate the monkey in front of friends. Ol' John and I would have had fun boozing all night and jerking off that damn monkey."]

***

Lucille recalled the first time she tried to divorce Desi, an attempt that occurred in the autumn of 1944 while he was stationed at the military outpost in Birmingham, California. She referred to her divorce as "the shortest interlocutory decree in the history of the California courts."

Lucille's *confidante*, Barbara Pepper, later asserted, "I didn't really believe those two lovebirds wanted a divorce. From what I observed up close and personal, during the many nights I spent at their Desilu Ranch, they had the hots for each other. The sounds coming from their bedroom into my guest room made me hot for Craig."

[She was referring to her husband, Craig Reynolds, who was serving in the military overseas.]

"I think the divorce proceedings were a mere threat from Lucille, a warning bell that Desi should change his ways and stop fucking all the starlets she sent to Birmingham to entertain those wounded soldiers."

"Desi was a real womanizer," said Ken Morgan, a close friend. "Everybody in the Hollywood inner circle knew that. His uncut prick got stuffed into any available hole. He was also reared in the Catholic faith, which interpreted divorce as immoral."

"Desi had strongly objected to his father dumping his mother for a hot little spitfire," Morgan continued, "and he didn't want to follow in his dad's footsteps. But at the time, he seemed fully convinced that he could commit adultery at will, and that Lucille would always take him back."

Before her court appearance in Santa Monica, where she intended to charge Desi with "mental cruelty," she moved out of the ranch at Desilu, assigning its care and maintenance to an older married couple with instructions to take good care of their barnyard animals.

At the time, presumably because of their distance from home, the U.S. Army allowed its enlisted men to postpone any pending divorces until

"Lovers come and go, but friendships last forever," Two views of Lucille's enduring friend, **Barbara Pepper**, from her early days as a (then-svelte) ingenue.

In her own words, she claimed, "I was the dime store version of Jean Harlow."

they returned home from the battlefields. Separated by stress and long distances, many marriages at the time were at the breaking point, and many young women left on the homefront by active duty husbands were taking up with men left behind, many of them classified as 4-F. Desi waived his right of postponement.

It was understood that by insisting on a speedy hearing, Lucille would waive her rights to alimony. Of course, her weekly receipt of a paycheck from MGM assured that she was making far more money than he was, since he drew only a meager soldier's pay.

That meant that she carried all the expenses of running the Desilu ranch. She estimated that for every egg laid by one of their chickens, it cost her $4.50.

The afternoon before she was to appear in court, Desi phoned her at her apartment in Beverly Hills. He did not have her address, but she had given him her phone number, telling him to call only in case of an emergency. Otherwise, he was to communicate only with her Beverly Hills lawyers, who were charging her $2,000 for the divorce action against him.

Desi asked what she was doing that evening. When she answered that she had nothing planned, he invited her for a night of dining and dancing. Bored, she eagerly accepted, and the estranged couple were seen later that evening at the Mocambo on Sunset Strip, dancing the rumba to the music of a band imported from Mexico City.

Their evening together ended back at her apartment, where, as Desi later told Van Johnson, "I spent most of the night plugging her. Never have I performed with such passion."

The next morning, when he woke up in her bed, she was just finishing getting dressed, wearing a new business suit in navy blue, with a large hat acquired only two days before in a Beverly Hills department store. "Where are you going?" he asked her.

"To divorce you," she answered. "I'm due in court in an hour. Reporters and photographers will be there, and I want to look good for the press. An MGM publicist told me that my picture will end up on the front pages. I need to let those damn directors know that Lucille Ball is still alive. I'm getting very little work, with long delays between pictures."

He asked her not to attend her court appearance, and to call it off. Then he made an impulsive move, pulling back the sheet ex-

Actress Wins Divorce

DECREE GRANTED—
Actress Lucille Ball ⟶
shown in court yesterday as she was granted a divorce from Staff Sgt. Desi Arnaz upon describing a turbulent married life with the actor, who is now in the Army.

The fine print of what's readable on the caption of this news story says, "Actress **Lucille Ball** shown in court yesterday as she was granted a divorce from Staff Sgt. Desi Arnaz upon describing a turbulent married life with the actor, who is now in the Army."

338

posing an erection. "Jumbo is waiting for you when you get back,"

"I'll see you later this afternoon," she promised.

Arriving early at the courthouse, she posed for reporters and answered their questions, making a point not to demonize Desi and assuming half the responsibility for the failure of their marriage.

The hearing lasted for only fifteen minutes before the judge granted the divorce. "He gambles all his money away," she claimed. "I have to pay all the bills. He has a violent temper, and we engage in some big battles. He often storms out of the house and is gone for weeks. Worrying about our relationship, I am a nervous wreck, and I'm losing weight."

She made a confession she'd never revealed before. "I also had a miscarriage, which I blamed on my deteriorating physicality."

Later that afternoon, she returned to her apartment, finding Desi wandering around in his jockey shorts. That night, as he made love to her again, he promised, "We'll make a baby. You've always wanted one, and I'm the stud hoss to give you one."

[He was well aware that by sharing cohabitation, he was nullifying the divorce. Under California law, if a couple indulged in sexual intercourse right after a divorce is granted, the court action is nullified.]

Barbara Pepper was Lucille's first visitor at Desilu ranch after Desi's return to his military base. Lucille told her friend, "I'm going to stay married to Desi, and for the next few weeks, maybe even two months, I expect he'll make a pretense of being faithful. Then he'll gradually return to his philandering. I think I've come up with the solution of how to live with that."

"What, pray tell," Pepper urged.

"During his frequent absences, I'll go out on dates, since I get a lot of offers," she confessed. "I don't plan to stay home lonely and crying. I'm at the peak of my seductive powers, but I'm on the road to forty. As you know, that's when a gal is washed up in Tinseltown. The men stop calling, and the roles dry up."

"I'm not going to throw my life away with a man I know will leave one day. At some point, maybe years from now, he'll divorce me, no doubt for a younger piece."

"Well, go, girl, go, and good luck to you," Pepper said.

***

At last, a call came in from MGM for Lucille to report to work. But when she heard what the movie was, she was rather disappointed. This black-and-white comedy, *Abbott & Costello in Hollywood* (1945), was set to go before rolling cameras. At first, she thought she'd been assigned the female lead, as had happened in *Room Service,* starring the Marx Brothers.

She knew that Abbott & Costello would steal the film from her, as they were the most popular comedy team throughout the 1940s and early 1950s. They'd been among the highest-paid entertainers during World War II. Their patter routine, "Who's on First?" was one of the best-known comedy skits of all time.

Director S. Sylvan Simon introduced Lucille to the comedians, but separately. She learned that a rift was unfolding because Costello had fired, without telling him, one of Abbott's domestic servants. In the aftermath, Costello refused to speak to Abbott except when they were on camera.

Simon had built a name for himself working with the Marx Brothers and Red Skelton. Eventually, he'd produce the hit comedy *Born Yesterday* (1950). For that film, Lucille would virtually beg him for the lead role, but he rejected her in favor of Judy Holliday, who won a Best Actress Oscar for her performance.

But within about twenty minutes, Lucille learned that her role was not the female lead, but a brief cameo where she'd play herself. In the same style, cameo roles were also assigned to Rags Ragland, Preston Foster, and actor/director Robert Z. Leonard, who was once married to the silent screen goddess Mae Murray of *The Merry Widow* fame.

He had carried home a Best Picture Oscar for *The Great Ziegfeld* (1936). He'd also helmed Greer Garson and Laurence Olivier in *Pride and Prejudice* (1940).

For her brief time on the screen, Lucille had to perform a skit in which

Lucille cuddles up to **Bud Abbott** as **Lou Costello** looks wistfully on.

The comedy team of Abbott and Costello had been among the top ten box office draws during the war years. But by the time this picture was made, their popularity was sharply declining.

"The same could be said for me," Lucille lamented. "My last five assignments at MGM had been guest cameos."

she is trying to film a scene for the fictional studio called "Mammoth." Her co-stars were actor Preston Foster and director Leonard. Costello appears to disrupt the proceedings.

Lucille and Foster had had a brief fling when she had worked as an extra on his picture, *Muss 'Em Up* (1936). He later asked her, "How about it for old time's sake?"

"Sounds great, but give me a raincheck," she said.

Simon would eventually compensate for having "short-changed Lucille in the Abbott and Costello film by granting her the lead role in *Her Husband's Affairs* (1947) with her co-star Franchot Tone.

She told Simon what he already knew. "My most recent job at Metro was about making guest appearances in films starring other actors. Do you think Mayer is trying to tell me something? Mainly that my days are numbered?"

The *New York Herald Tribune* reviewed Lucille's sketch in *Abbott and Costello in Hollywood* as "bleak and dreary."

***

In Lucille's next picture for MGM, *Easy to Wed* (1946), she was assigned the second female lead. Its stars were Van Johnson and Esther Williams, who would be getting all the attention and publicity because they were big box office. Johnson and June Allyson were being promoted at the time as "America's Sweethearts."

Esther Williams was MGM's "Daughter of Neptune." She had set multiple national and regional swimming records while still in her teens. She'd spent five months swimming alongside Olympic Gold Medal winner and Tarzan star, Johnny Weissmuller, as part of Billy Rose's *Aquacade*. The studio was devising a number of what it called "aqua-musicals" in which she would star.

Ever since his appearance with Desi in *Too Many Girls,* Johnson had been a friend of both Lucille and Desi. She had a reunion with him and also with his lover, Keenan Wynn, who had the fourth lead, as her romantic interest.

She also met again with director Edward Buzzell, who had directed her in *Best Food Forward.*

Research by the Academy Research Institute revealed that Lucille had doubled her name recognition since joining MGM's stable, even though that studio had not given her any really desirable roles. Producer Arthur Freed said, "Lucille just doesn't stir up the fan excitement that so many of our other stars do—take Judy Garland, for instance."

Easy to Wed was a musical re-

"VAN! VAN! VAN!" The publicity posters shouted.

Esther Williams (left) and **Van Johnson** were top box office stars, but **Lucille** stood out in the third lead. She used her full comedic talent in a drunken scene with Johnson where she impersonated a duck she identified as "a red-haired, pintailed widgeon." For that, she received some of the best notices of her career.

make of *Libeled Lady* (1936), which had starred Jean Harlow as Gladys Benton, William Powell, Myrna Loy, and Spencer Tracy. In the remake, Lucille would take over Harlow's role as Gladys.

According to the plot, financier J.B. Allenbury (Cecil Kellaway) plans to file a $2 million libel suit against *The Morning Star* for claiming that his daughter Connie (Esther Williams) was the husband-stealing culprit who broke up a marriage.

The paper calls on Warren Haggerty (Keenan Wynn) to postpone his marriage to Gladys (Lucille) to save the paper from this possibly crippling judgment. A convoluted scheme is devised to turn the libelous scandal into truth.

That devious plot is handed over to reporter Bill Chandler (Van Johnson), who goes to Mexico where he wins the confidence of the wealthy Allenburys, both father and daughter Connie (Williams).

It works out in the end, as Bill falls for Connie, and Mr. Allenbury (in the role interpreted by Kellaway) drops his libel suit against *The Morning Star.*

Born in Cape Town in South Africa, Kellaway later became a familiar face in American movies, and he would be twice nominated for a Best Supporting Actor Oscar: In 1948 for *The Luck of the Irish,* and again in 1967 for *Guess Who's Coming to Dinner?* with Hepburn and Tracy.

Easy to Wed was a hit at the box office, generating revenues of $5.7 million. Bosley Crowther of *The New York Times* wrote, "Perhaps the best things about it are Keenan Wynn and Lucille Ball. Both of these pleasant young people have exceptionally keen comedy senses, and their roles are the most productive in the film. Eddie Buzzell's direction has never been memorable."

Variety reviewed it like this: "Lucille Ball (is) a standout on the comedy end, particularly in her sequence where she indulges in an inebriated flight into fantastic Shakespeare."

The *New York Herald Tribune* praised Lucille as a "superb *farceuse.*"

Keenan Wynn and Lucille had received good critical acclaim when they had appeared in *Without Love*, starring Katharine Hepburn and Spencer Tracy.

In this remake of *Libeled Lady*, Lucille and Wynn assumed the roles previously played by Tracy and Jean Harlow.

By this point in her career, directors and producers understood that many a boring moment in a romantic romp could be perked up by **Lucille** nonchalantly clad in an "over-the-top" bit of fashion whimsy.

Here she is, what a reviewer called "a superb *farceuse*," (a girl who knows how to play slapstick and farce) in *Easy to Wed.*

***

When Lucille and Desi, along with the rest of the world, heard that Hitler had committed suicide and that Nazi Germany had surrendered, it was time for celebration. Desi got a pass from his Army base at Birmingham so that he could perform with Lucille for soldiers at the Hollywood Canteen. It was there that they celebrated V-E (Victory in Europe) Day with Allied soldiers. It was a joyous occasion, as Desi addressed the audience with the assurance that "The Japs are next."

Later, he and Lucille led a conga line that swept out of the Canteen and then moved along a block-long stretch of Cahuenga Boulevard before meandering back into the club.

She was listening to a radio program on August 6, 1945 when the world heard astonishing news: The Atomic Age was launched when an American B-59, *Enola Gay*, dropped an atomic bomb on Hiroshima, killing thousands of Japanese and wreaking hitherto unimagined devastation on the region.

She believed that Desi would soon be discharged and—like almost everyone else—she didn't see how the war in the Pacific could continue for too much longer.

Three days later, news flashed around the world that a second bomb had been dropped on Nagasaki, with destruction described as "Biblical" and hastening, the arrival of V-J Day. The most devastating conflict in human history, with forty-five million dead, had ended.

Louis B. Mayer announced within days that the studio would begin filming *The Beginning or the End*, a documentary eventually released in 1947 about the development of the atomic bomb. Lucille and Desi celebrated V-J day, but he confessed to a lingering guilt based on how, throughout the duration of his military service, he'd never been stationed more than fifty miles from the Desilu Ranch.

This photo shows the U.S. Navy's post-war replica of **'Little Boy,'** the atomic bomb that destroyed Hiroshima.

A newspaper account described how it was made and what it did:

"About 141 pounds of highly enriched uranium-235 was used to create "Little Boy," the first nuclear-fission bomb used in warfare. At 8:15 a.m. on August 6, 1945, the bomb exploded about 1,900 feet over Hiroshima, a city of about 350,000 people situated on a coastal plain in the Chugoku region of western Honshu, Japan. The enormous blast instantly destroyed most of the city and claimed some 70,000 lives,"

For Lucille, Desi, and everyone else on the planet, the world was instantly and permanently changed. Within a few months, both the Cold War and the Age of Television was launched.

Movie studios had prospered during the war, as audiences needed to escape for a couple of hours to watch "the two Bettys—Grable and Hutton," or Rita Hayworth, even Abbott and Costello.

Many studios didn't see much threat in television, although some did. By 1949, there were five million TV sets in America.

Convinced by a number of industry soothsayers, Desi and Lucille would be among the first to understand the unlimited possibilities associated with this fast-emerging new medium—all of this in an era when other big stars wouldn't even agree to appear on it.

After his discharge on November 16, 1945, Desi was anxious to return to work as an entertainer. He had not drawn a salary during his enlistment, but according to the terms of his MGM contract, his pay level had been periodically increased. Instead of his pre-war salary of $650 a week, he'd be drawing $1,000.

He hadn't worked on a film since *Bataan* (1943), and he was eager (some said "desperate") for a role.

During her filming of *Easy to Wed* with Esther Williams, Lucille had learned that Williams' next film, *Fiesta* (1947), would be set in Mexico and that it contained a role that would be ideal for Desi as the male lead.

Williams promised Lucille that she'd lobby to get Desi cast opposite her, and an appointment was arranged with Jack Cummings, the director of that picture. *[Cummings was the nephew of Louis B. Mayer and had a lot of power at the studio.]*

Only five minutes into Desi's interview, Cummings took an axe to Desi's dream: "Actually, I've already cast the male lead, assigning it to Ricardo Montalban. Mayer wants me to build him up as MGM's new Latin lover. Ricardo's got influence, too. He's Loretta Young's brother-in-law. *[In 1944, Mexico-born Montalban had married Georgina (nicknamed "Georgie") Young, the half-sister of Loretta Young. Their marriage lasted 63 years, ending in the deaths of Montalban in 2009 and Georgina in 2007.]*

DOES GOD HAVE A SENSE OF HUMOR? Almost simultaneously with the launch of the Atomic Age came the debut of the Television Age. Lucille and Desi were among the first to see its vast potential.

Heartbroken, Desi returned to the Desilu ranch and into the comfort of Lucille's arms.

She cited fears about her own dismal future at MGM, "Soon, I, too, will be out the door," she accurately predicted. "We'll just have to reinvent ourselves."

"With no movie roles in sight, I'll need to go back to the good old days, organize my own band, and start looking for gigs," Desi said.

Money was a problem, as he needed to help Lucille with personal expenses. He was already $30,000 in debt, mostly to the IRS, as he had not paid his taxes before going into the Army.

While Mayer was in England, Desi decided to set up an appointment with Benny Thau, who was running MGM during the mogul's absence. He wanted out of his contract because he knew he'd make a lot more money with his band taking club engagements.

Before the meeting with Thau, Desi worked to make himself as unattractive as possible, not bothering to shave, staying up drinking all night so he'd look haggard. He even put a pillow under his belt to convey the impression that he was overweight.

"When I walked in the door and Thau looked at me, I knew he was thinking that I wasn't star material. All he said was, 'It looks like Army life was rough on you, kid.'"

"Thau was such a cheap bastard," Desi said. "I had borrowed a puny $1,500 from MGM when I was in the Army. Now, he wanted it back."

Ten days before, Desi had borrowed $8,000 from businessman Tommy Rockwell, the head of GAC. So because he had the cash, he shelled out fifteen one-hundred-dollar bills and, on the spot, bought his way out of his MGM contract.

When he exited through MGM's studio gate, he didn't bother to look back. He had only two weeks to put a new band together and to rehearse its musicians.

His manager had already arranged a booking for him and his band at the chic Los Angeles nightclub, Ciro's.

In her first post-war interview, Lucille spoke to a reporter from the *Los Angeles Times*: "Desi is out of the Army now, no longer a sergeant. I plan to continue making movies, perhaps taking time off to have babies. Desi is predicting that our first kids will be born twins. You know how Latin men like to boast. Right now, I'm making my last movie at MGM, *Two Smart People*, in which I will appear with John Hodiak."

"Desi has also ended his career at MGM. I wouldn't exactly call it a career. He's forming his own band to play at various clubs like Tommy Dorsey or Harry James. Latin music is still the rage."

"As for myself, I'll become a free-lancer selling my ass to whoever wants it. I pray I don't end up on Poverty Row, the studio burial grounds of stars past their prime."

Privately, she shared her fears with her new friend, Esther Williams. "Your star is on the rise, and I know your big box office triumphs lie ahead of you. But I've been a failure, a 'never was.' Big stardom just eluded me, first at Columbia, then at RKO, now at MGM."

"I've also turned thirty-six, which, as you know, is Death Valley for stars who never made it. If David O. Selznick remakes *Gone With the Wind,* perhaps he'll consider me for the Aunt Pittypat role. As for maid parts, Hattie McDaniel and Louise Beavers seem to have those already nailed down."

***

In September of 1945, Lucille reported to work at MGM to star in her next picture, *Two Smart People.* World War II had ended, and her career at Metro was also winding down without her being assigned to any of the roles she coveted.

After *Easy to Wed,* she expected to be cast in another comedy, but that was not the case. Instead, she was assigned the role of a con artist, Ricki Woodner. Her leading man, John Hodiak, would portray Ace Connors, a thief on the run. He had made off with $500,000 in bearer bonds, which he'd hidden in a cookbook.

On his tail was a cop, Bob Simms (Lloyd Nolan). Ace is menaced by "Fly" Felentti, portrayed by Elisha Cook, Jr. in a "type" of role he'd played before: a cowardly and neurotic but dangerous villain.

Its producer, Ralph Wheelwright, was also the author of the short story on which the movie was based. Originally, he entitled the film *Time for Two,* a name that Lucille did not like. Nor did she like its change to *Two Smart People.* "It doesn't even hint at what the drama is about."

Its director, Jules Dassin, was born to Jewish parents from the Ukraine, and had grown up in Harlem and the Bronx. He had joined the Communist Party, as had Lucille, during the depths of the Great Depression. But whereas Dassin would eventually be blacklisted for that, Lucille somehow managed to escape censure.

In the aftermath of his censure, Dassin moved to Europe, marrying Melina Mercouri in 1966. The most famous actress in Greece, Mercouri became

John Hodiak and **Lucille Ball** in a flippant melodrama, *Two Smart People.*

PM magazine reviewed it like this: "It's a neat idea—assembled, of course, from dozens of other previously exploited neat ideas—matching John Hodiak and the always reliable Lucille Ball."

"Any cat-and-mouse film, to hold interest, has to be helped a lot by characterization, smart photography, and direction."

"Two Smart People has both."

celebrated for her performance in, among many others, *Never on Sunday* (1960).

Lucille told Barbara Pepper, "Hodiak is ruggedly handsome, a post-war Clark Gable, but he has this huge inferiority complex. Believe me, that's not the only thing huge about him. He told me our romance was slated to end when the picture was finished."

"I'm falling in love with Anne Baxter, and I plan to marry her," he said.

Despite Hodiak's allegiance to Baxter at the time, he nonetheless managed to slip around and have a secret fling with Lucille. During his involvement with Alfred Hitchcock's *Lifeboat* (1944), starring Tallulah Bankhead. Lucille had sex with him, later referring to his penis (to anyone who would listen) as "a beer can." That association spread quickly through Hollywood, and Hodiak became much sought after, attracting a large coterie of gay male fans.

Right before working with Lucille, Hodiak had been Judy Garland's leading man in *The Harvey Girls* (1946).

He came into Lucille's life at a turning point. Perhaps based on both her desire and as part of her campaign "to get back at Desi," she launched affairs with her leading men in a whole series of movies during the post-war era. They included Mark Stevens, George Brent ("maybe"), George Sanders (a genuinely serious romance), and Victor Mature, despite the conflicts they'd endured from each other during the filming of their previous picture.

Missing from the list of her seductions was Bob Hope ("He's more for laughs than for sex," she claimed.)

Even more serious than her affair with Sanders was her affair with William Holden.

She confided the details of these flings to her *confidante*, Barbara Pepper, who developed a "loose tongue" in years to

Actress, activist, and politician **Melina Mercouri**, the best ambassador for the glories of (modern) Greece who ever lived.

Jules Dassin, who directed Lucille in *Two Smart People*, was later blacklisted in Hollywood and eventually moved back to Europe.

There, in 1966, he married Melina Mercouri, a sexy and mercurial Grecian goddess who became a leading spokesperson for the return of classical Greek antiquities (among them, the Elgin Marbles) to their homeland in Greece.

Anne Baxter, in her sexiest-ever publicity pose, married John Hodiak after he left Lucille's bed forever.

The granddaughter of architect Frank Lloyd Wright, the always reliable star would be immortalized in Hollywood classic films for her portrayal of Eve Harrington in *All About Eve* (1950) with Bette Davis.

come. In the early 1950s, Mike Connolly, the gossip columnist, also revealed details about these brief flings.

Two Smart People lost a quarter of a million dollars for MGM. *The New York Times* panned it: "Except for a colorful series of Mardi Gras sequences, *Two Smart People* is an otherwise boring hodgepodge about love and the confidence racket. John Hodiak and Lucille Ball are painfully defeated by the script at almost every turn. In addition to its pedestrian plot, the film suffers from a lack of competent direction."

On the last day of its shoot, Lucille departed from MGM without fanfare. "They seemed preoccupied with animal pictures, a showcase for Lassie or hung up on a deer in *The Yearling* (1946) starring Gregory Peck and Jane Wyman. I faced two questions: 'What to do with Desi after his release from the Army? And what to do with a career going nowhere?'"

***

Desi had only two weeks to stage his comeback at Ciro's in Los Angeles, a gala that brought out the elite of Hollywood, mainly because of Lucille's constant phoning of celebrities.

Amazing, he not only recruited a band but hired three back-up acts, including a comedian, Larry Storch, fresh out of the Navy and skilled at imitations. Desi also booked two beautiful female singers, a sultry Latina songbird who billed herself as "Dulcina," and a jazz artist, Amanda Lane.

During the war, Storch had served in the U.S. Navy with the bisexual actor Tony Curtis aboard the submarine tender *USS Proteus*.

Desi always claimed that he "discovered" Storch, who later made guest appearances on dozens of TV series, including *Get Smart* and *Columbo*. He was best known for his performance as the scheming Corporal Randolph Agarn in the situation comedy *F Troop* (1965-67) starring Forrest Tucker.

Storch made two dozen movies, and Curtis got Storch cast in several of his films, too. They included *Who Was That Lady?* (1960); *40 Pounds of Trouble* (1962); *Captain Newman, M.D.* (1963); *Wild and Wonderful* (1964); *Sex and the Single Girl* (1964); and *The Great Race* (1965). As late as 2003, Curtis and Storch ("buddies for life") reunited for the mu-

Although Desi claimed he was the real discoverer of the very talented **Larry Storch**, the honor really went to Tony Curtis, who served with him in the U.S. Navy.

They remained "close buddies" in the years ahead. When Curtis got him roles in more of his movies, rumors spread that the actors were having a gay old time.

That included getting Storch a small role in *Some Like It Hot* (1959), hailed by many film critics as the best film comedy ever made. In that film, Curtis (lower photo) appeared in drag as Josephine.

348

sical version of *Some Like It Hot* (1959), which Curtis had made with Marilyn Monroe Both Curtis and Jack Lemmon had disguised themselves as women in many of the movie's scenes during their escapes from the mob in Chicago.

In Hollywood, Desi recruited a twenty-two piece band to entertain at Ciro's in acts that featured Cuban music. They played drums, bongos, maracas, congas, clarinets, flutes, four violins, a guitar, a piano, and bass. He met with Ciro's owner, Herman Hover, and it was agreed that his opening would be advertised as a black tie event.

Lucille made it a point to reserve all the ringside tables at Ciro's for a parade of A-list stars: Alan Ladd, Judy Garland, Robert Taylor, Barbara Stanwyck, Orson Welles, Rita Hayworth, Ann Sheridan, Humphrey Bogart, and Lauren Bacall. Marlene Dietrich in a Jean Louis gown made the most stunning entrance.

At the opening, Lucille was seated next to Errol Flynn. As she later confessed to Barbara Pepper, "Robin Hood (aka Captain Blood) kept feeling me up under the table. In days of yore, I would have slapped his face, but this was a newly invented Lucille Ball. I let the dashing swashbuckler feel to his devilish heart's content. Why not?"

Even before the opening of the show at Ciro's, Desi admitted to Hover, "I have the hots for this Dulcina chick. What a hell of a figure!"

The premiere turned out to be one of the most successful acts at Ciro's, and, as predicted, Desi always ended with a rendition of "Babalu."

The engagement led to him being granted a contract to record for RCA Victor; a movie deal, and an extensive road tour that would begin in Manhattan at the Copacabana.

During his engagement at Ciro's, Lucille attended his show on as many nights as she could. Often, she was too tired, having risen at four in morning to arrive at the studio on time. Sometimes, they'd wave to each other

Strange but famously publicized bedfellows: **Olivia** (Melanie in *Gone With the Wind*) **de Havilland** with **Errol** (*Captain Blood*) **Flynn**.

"I came back to Hollywood after the war, hoping to become the post-war Latin lover, a newly styled Rudolph Valentino," Desi said.

"But the Latin lovers of the screen had become Ricardo Montalban and Fernando Lamas."

"My comeback picture? A quickie called **Cuban Pete** for which I was paid $10,000 lousy bucks."

as their cars passed during their respective transits back and forth from the Desilu Ranch. "Some marriage!" she said, ruefully.

"If I showed up at Ciro's, I was accused of doing so to prevent Desi from running off with one of the young beauties in the audience, no doubt a Lana Turner lookalike. If I stayed home, I was accused of sitting on my ass and doing nothing to promote my husband's career."

On nights when she wasn't his guardian, he was rumored to have conducted a series of affairs. Columnist Earl Wilson visited from New York, and he gave Desi some career advice: "If you're going to play around, go out with an unknown gal. If you take out a broad who's well-known, someone like Maria Montez, you'll be likely to end up in the gossip columns."

To that, Desi responded, "Maria looks more sultry in a sarong than Dorothy Lamour, and is the hottest piece of ass ever to come out of the Dominican Republic. Her accent is too thick, and I'm helping her with her English. In the Navy, I taught English to a bunch of illiterates. Take 'Cobra Woman' to bed, and you've entered into the most torrid pages of *Arabian Nights.* Her husband, Jean-Pierre Aumont, is one lucky fella."

[Maria Montez, star of Siren of Atlantis *(1948), went to her death from a heart attack at the age of thirty-three in 1951.]*

Before he left for New York, Desi made his first movie in three years, an hour-long "B" picture called *Cuban Pete* (1946). After being paid $10,000 for his starring role in it, half the money was seized by the IRS.

A black-and-white musical comedy, it was directed by Jean Yarborough. Desi's co-stars were Joan Fulton (the romantic interest), Don Porter, and organist Ethel Smith. The hit song of the movie was also called "Cuban Pete."

In a nutshell, Desi is recruited in Havana to come to New York with a band to perform on a weekly variety show on radio. Its oft-repeated "inside joke" involved (as part of its plot) a squeaky-voiced, addle-brained woman (the film's narrator) and her dream of becoming a big band vocalist.

Desi did not follow the advice of columnist Earl Wilson and limit his affairs to dalliances with minor-league and relatively unknown starlets. Instead, he began an affair with **Maria Montez**, the reigning queen of cinematic camp.

She's pictured above in *Cobra Woman* (1944) with **Jon Hall,** the virile but bland star of numerous swashbucklers, fairy tales, and South Sea Island adventures.

The movie was publicized with a slogan that stated: *"Desi Arnaz will have you in a whirl with his torrid samba swirl. He's the Rhumba-Rhythm King!"*

***

Lucille had made her last film for MGM, but her contract still had a few weeks before it expired. At the time of her departure, her salary had risen to $3,500 a week, "MGM wanted to drain the last drop of my blood, so they hired me out to Fox for $6,000 a week. They pocketed the difference in my salary, and my greedy agent got his cut."

She found herself cast in a *film noir* [*the term had not yet been invented*] called *The Dark Corner* (1946). It had been inspired by the success of *Laura* (1944), which had starred Gene Tierney in the title role, with Dana Andrews and Clifton Webb (cast as the prissy Waldo Lydecker) as her co-stars.

In fact, Fox liked Webb so much in the role that they instructed scriptwriters to tailor an equivalent role for him in *The Dark Corner*. In it, he would play Hardy Cathcart, the elegant and rich owner of an art gallery.

After Lucille, Webb would get star billing, even though Mark Stevens was the actual star of the picture. He played Bradford Galt, Lucille's boss with a shady past. As his secretary, Kathleen, Lucille falls in love with him. William Bendix took the third slot in the role of Stauffer, "the man in the white suit" who is stalking Bradford.

Its producer was Fred Kohlmar, whom Lucille had known since her early days in Hollywood when he was an assistant to her first boss, Samuel Goldwyn.

Henry Hathaway's reputation as a brutal director had preceded him, and Lucille was terrified of him. He had a reputation for directing tough guys like John Wayne, and he'd made seven movies with Gary Cooper, including *The Lives of a Bengal Lancer* (1935). He'd also helmed many great female stars: Mae West, Clara Bow, and Fay Wray. Marilyn Monroe lay in his directorial future.

Lucille took an instant dislike to

By the time **Lucille** teamed with **Mark Stevens** in *The Dark Corner*, she claimed to Barbara Pepper, "I had developed "leadingman-itis." *[i.e., a chronic propensity to fall in love with one's acting partner.]*

"The studios are to blame," she continued. "They kept casting me with one sexy hunk after another."

Fox attempted to turn Stevens into a leading man, but when his screen luster faded, he, like Lucille, turned to the new medium of television.

Webb, and the repulsion was mutual. In Hollywood, he was called "everyone's favorite snob."

"His nose was stuck so high in the air, it made me wonder if he'd find oxygen at that altitude," Lucille claimed. "He was so critical of everybody else, not just me but the director and his fellow cast members. On and off the screen, he could toss off witty *bon mots* and his insults had the sting of a wasp."

In the first encounter Webb had with her, he said, "I had a struggling Robert Mitchum long before you got your painted nails into all that man flesh. He cost only twenty dollars a visit. I also had his brother whenever Robert wasn't available."

"The only way you'd ever get a young Bob is to pay for it," she said with a smirk. "What man would want to go to bed with you?"

At the age of nineteen, in 1909, Webb had become a professional ballroom dancer, often appearing alongside Bonnie Glass, who eventually replaced him with Rudolph Valentino.

Webb made his Broadway debut in 1913, starring in many productions (most of them witty and musical) by Gershwin, Cole Porter, Irving Berlin, or Noël Coward.

He was in his mid-fifties when he became a movie star. Over Darryl F. Zanuck's objections, he was cast as the evil radio columnist in *Laura* (1944) by Otto Preminger. Zanuck thought he was too effeminate, always going around with his possessive mother, Mabelle. For his performance, Webb won an Oscar nomination for Best Actor in a Supporting Role. In an amazing turn of events, he was Oscar-nominated again two years later for his performance in *The Razor's Edge* (1946), starring Tyrone Power, Gene Tierney, Anne Baxter, and John Payne.

By the time he starred in the movie hit, *Sitting Pretty* (1948), the title described his status as Hollywood's most unusual male star. In it, Webb played Mr. Belvedere, a snide, know-it-all babysitter. Amazingly, this time he was Oscar nomined for Best Actor.

Mark Stevens, a native of Cleveland, was a handsome macho, five years younger than Lucille. She found him very appealing. He'd launched his career at Warner Brothers using the name Stephen Richards. The makeup de-

Long before becoming typecast as a prissy snob in feature films, **Clifton Webb** had been a dancer on Broadway.

His breakthrough role in *Laura* (1944) happened years after his early debut in films.

The first movie he ever appeared in, *Polly With a Past*, had been a silent film released way back in 1920.

A *comedienne* goes *noir.* **Lucille** in *The Dark Corner*

Cast as Kathleen Stuart, Lucille is the secretary to private eye Bradford Galt (Mark Stevens). Their relationship evolves into more than just delivering and recording dictation

partment opted to darken his red hair and straightened his curls, covering his freckles with makeup. When he went over to Fox, Zanuck changed his name to Mark Stevens.

Shortly before working with Lucille, Stevens had co-starred with Joan Fontaine in *This Day Forward* (1946). That same year, exhibitors had designated him as "Hollywood's Fifth Most Promising Star of Tomorrow."

William Bendix, a New Yorker, usually played rough, blue collar types, and he'd received a Best Supporting Oscar nod for *Wake Island* (1942). After working with Lucille, he would go on to make his best-remembered film role in *The Babe Ruth Story* (1948).

[In the early 1920s, Bendix had been a batboy for the New York Yankees and got to watch Babe Ruth hit more than a hundred home runs at Yankee Stadium.]

He told Lucille, "I was fired when I went to fetch a big order for the Babe: Four hot dogs with lots of mustard, and a super sundae. Ruth developed a belly ache and couldn't play that day. I was blamed."

Bendix would become better known as the male lead in both radio and television versions of *The Life of Riley.* The character he portrayed was a stumbling, bumbling husband of a loving wife with children.

A prop that played an important role of the storyline of *The Dark Corner* was a portrait of Cathy Downs portraying Mari Cathcart, Webb's trophy wife in the movie. *[The portrait played a role equivalent to the portrait of Laura (portrayed by Gene Tierney), the mysterious beauty and namesake of another movie starring Clifton Webb,* Laura *(1944).]*

The (evil) character played by Webb is obsessed with her, but the subject of the painting loathes him and has married him only for his money. Later, she shoots him in the back when she learns that he arranged to have her lover killed. Kurt Kreuger played her gigolo lover, Anthony Jardine. The murder is erroneously blamed on Galt (Stevens).

A former cover model for *Vogue,* Cathy Downs had arrived in Hollywood as recently as 1944. Shortly after working with Lucille, her big break arrived in the form of playing the title role in *My Darling Clementine* (1946) with Henry Fonda

Two views of starlet **Cathy Downs**, who sought stardom in the intensely competitive studios of Tinseltown.

She later claimed she was assigned an impossible role in *The Dark Corner* when cast as Mari, the wife of art dealer Hardy Cathcart (Clifton Webb).

In both *Laura* and *Dark Corner,* the Webb character worships the beauty, as manifested in portraits of Cathy Downs and Gene Tierney, respectively, to the point of ignoring the real-life women who inspired them.

For sex, the Downs character turns not to her effete husband (portrayed by Webb) but to Tony Jardine (Kurt Kreuger), with murderous consequences.

and Victor Mature.

Lucille had a reunion with Constance Collier, who had befriended her on the set of *Stage Door* (1937) which had starred one of Collier's best friends, Katharine Hepburn.

Lucille gravitated to the distinguished English actress and shared several lunches with her. In *The Dark Corner*, Collier made a memorable appearance as "Mrs. Kingsley."

Lucille complained to her that her film career was going nowhere, except perhaps to oblivion. Collier recommended that she search for the proper play, abandon movies for a while, and specialize in live theater. At first, Lucille rejected the idea, but then began to think seriously about doing just that.

From all reports, Lucille was on the verge of a breakdown during her filming of *The Dark Corner*. She had arrived on the set nervous and trembling. Her first scene in the movie called for her to be a secretary at the typewriter. The next day, an assistant showed the director what Lucille had typed and left in place under the roller of the machine:

Dear Mr. Hathaway
If you only knew how nervous I was today, you wouldn't dare shoot this movie and you'd call the whole damn thing off. LUCILLE BALL IS A SISSY!

After reading it, Hathaway inserted a message into the roller of the same typewriter. It greeted her when she came onto the set the following morning:

Dear Lucy,
Would it help to know that I'm nervous as hell myself?
Love, HH

After that temporary truce, their working relationship went downhill. That note would be the last compassion he'd show her. One day, she was so nervous, so beset with career complications and marriage vows, that she constantly flubbed her lines. "I was so unstrung, I couldn't get a word out," she said.

"God damn it, Ball, no wonder Mayer is dumping you," Hathaway charged. "I could pick up any starlet on the street, and, after fucking her all night, I'm sure she could deliver a few lines as an office secretary. You don't have to be Constance Collier to pull this off." Then he accused her of showing up drunk, which sent her running, in tears, back to her dressing room.

"I need understanding and sympathy, neither of which I'm getting from that bastard Hathaway."

Later, reflecting on her breakdown, she revealed she'd been working too hard, "worrying about money, worrying about Desi, even my own tendency to stray. I should have gone through with the divorce after all. I was also exhausted and humiliated at getting kicked out of MGM. I was a very sick girl."

354

"After I left Fox, I practically collapsed for the next three months, trying to pull myself together."

Lucille's co-star, Mark Stevens, had married Annelle Hayes in 1945 and seemed very much in love with his wife. But even the happiest of married men sometimes stray when a beautiful, sexy woman comes on to him.

In their developing liaison, Lucille was the aggressor. Although sex was involved, the real core of their burgeoning relationship was his support and compassion for her. He, too, loathed Hathaway, who was riding him just as hard as he was Lucille. These two battered egos seemed to find solace with each other in her dressing room, where Stevens virtually "camped" during the rest of filming. One day, she broke down on the set and started sobbing before running back to her dressing room.

Since Stevens wasn't needed for the rest of that afternoon, Hathaway ordered him "to go and take care of your mistress. Maybe she just needs a good fuck. I find that cures any woman."

After the film was completed, she and Stevens hugged and kissed, saying their farewells.

The New York Times defined *The Dark Corner* as "a sizzling piece of melodrama." *Newsweek* viewed it as "tough and rough talking but lacking that Sunday punch for a genuine knockout. Lucille Ball is one of the film's brightest moments."

The *Los Angeles Examiner* claimed "Lucille Ball is entitled to heavy honors. She has been given ample opportunity in this drama to display her superior ability."

For the first time, Lucille rejected the praise. "I looked just like I felt making this crapper. That look was completely bemused, with a staring, numb, fogbank look, as if I where the one being driven into *The Dark Corner*."

***

During the filming of *The Dark Corner*, Lucille befriended the Swiss-reared German

As the secretary of Bradford Galt **(Mark Stevens)** in *The Dark Corner*, Lucille's character falls desperately in love with her boss.

As director Henry Hathaway later recalled, "Lucille may not have fallen in 'real-life' love with this handsome guy, but he sure spent a hell of a lot of time in her dressing room when I didn't need them for a shoot."

Stevens later became a director, helming himself in *Cry Vengeance* (1956), whose plot evoked *The Dark Corner*.

In the lower photo, and in lighter fare, **Stevens** gets cuddly with **Joan Fontaine** in *From This Day Forward* (1946).

355

actor Kurt Kreuger. Frequently the subject of beefcake, pin-up pictures, he was the third most-requested star at Fox, topped only by Tyrone Power and John Wayne.

Born in Prussia in 1916, he'd gone to school in Switzerland and later in London and Columbia University in New York City. After he announced his intention of becoming an actor, his father, who had wanted him to study medicine, cut off his allowance.

After their movie was wrapped, when Kreuger told Lucille how much he loved the countryside and the great outdoors, she invited him for a weekend at Desilu Ranch. His visit occurred during one of the few weekends Desi was home.

In the previous three months, Desi's mood seemed to parallel her own. He'd spend most of his time by the pool, looking depressed and not wanting to be bothered by Lucille. She didn't understand why. Unlike her situation, his career in entertainment was progressing rapidly, and he and his band found it easy to line up future engagements.

"He didn't share his troubles with me," she said. "I tried to figure out what it was. If not his career, then what? Suddenly, it occurred to me: He'd fallen in love with another woman. Perhaps now, he wanted to divorce me. Sometimes, in the middle of the night, I'd vaguely hear his voice pleading on the phone in the kitchen. I'd stand outside our bedroom door trying to hear what was the matter. From the few words I could make out, he was talking to some woman. She seemed to have dumped him, and he desperately wanted her back."

In *The Dark Corner*, **Kurt Kreuger** was cast as Tony Jardine, the former business partner of Bradford Galt (Mark Stevens). His nemesis is art dealer Hardy Cathcart (Clifton Webb).

Tony is later murdered.

During its filming, Lucille grew to appreciate Kreuger as a "Prussian hunka man" and invited him to spend a weekend with Desi and her at their ranch.

She had come to believe that he'd shown some sexual interest in her, but learned—before the Sunday morning of his visit—that it was Desi he'd been after all along.

"Being on the verge of a nervous breakdown, I opted for discretion and chose not to confront him."

"When Kreuger arrived Friday night to spend the weekend, Desi didn't seem the least bit jealous, and he was a husband who often flew into fits if he thought some man was coming on to me," Lucille said.

"I soon found out why," she said. "He and Kreuger stayed up late drinking after I went to bed."

The following morning, he told her, "Kurt wanted to go skinny-dipping with me, as you Yanks call it. I knew at once that this German fellow was far more attracted to me than to you. So don't get your hopes up."

Over lunch that day, Kreuger discussed the filming of *Sahara* (1943) in the desert with Humphrey Bogart.

"In case you missed it, it was shot in the California desert about a British-American unit stranded in the path of the invading Nazi infantry. The director, Zoltán Korda, called on this actor named Tambul to jump me (I was portraying a Nazi soldier), and press my face into the sand until he suffocated me to death. Zoltán forgot to yell 'cut' and the jerk pressed harder and harder until I passed out. Finally, the crew alerted our fool director, and he yelled 'CUT!' just in time. I almost died, my head buried in the sand."

Kreuger complained that during the war, even though he detested Hitler and his Third Reich, he was often called upon to play Nazis. "Every war picture had make-believe Nazis unless they needed Japs. I was in big demand, even though I hated it. Oh, well, it's a living. I once met Darryl F. Zanuck at Fox and asked for better roles. He asked me, 'What's your hurry? With your dashing looks, you'll be good at fifty playing romantic parts.'"

"Right now, I'm getting about two hundred fan letters a week," Kreuger claimed. "They're mostly from guys, but also a lot from horny women, too. The guys request a frontal nude, and most of them ask if I'm uncut. Since I'm German, they suspect that I am, but want to make sure. I answer what mail I can. I need every fan I have. I write back that I have twelve uncut inches, and that I measure seven and a half inches around. I want to give my boys something to dream about."

"That's one way of looking at it," Desi said.

Years later, after his career as an actor had ended, Lucille encountered Kreuger at a party in Beverly Hills. "I didn't really make it as an actor, but I'm doing damn well. I don't have to play a Nazi anymore, although because of my movies I've had some trouble with my Jewish clients."

He'd become a wealthy real estate investor and invited her to visit his ski lodge in Aspen. She said that she'd love to do that, but that for the moment, her schedule wouldn't permit it.

Kreuger never married, but once falsely claimed that he had. His only known sexual liaison with a woman occurred in 1954 when he co-starred with Ingrid Bergman in *Fear*. "The Swede demanded it," he said.

Ingrid Bergman, depicted here in a publicity picture for the German-dubbed version (*Angst*)) of a film the Americans knew as *Fear* (1954).

Kurt Kreuger's name was added to the list of Bergman's lovers. They included Yul Brynner, Gary Cooper, Joseph Cotten, Bing Crosby, Leslie Howard, Gregory Peck, Anthony Quinn, and Spencer Tracy.

***

The clock had run out on Lucille's final contractual obligation to MGM. For most of the next three months, she lived in relative isolation at Desilu Ranch, "tending to their chickens, cows, and a fat sow."

Desi was often gone, and when he did come home, there were constant fights, mostly centering on his womanizing and reckless spending He eventually erected a guest house at the rear of their ranch house. Calling it "my doghouse," he retreated there following some of his more violent arguments with Lucille. "It sure as hell beats running up big hotel bills when I fled from her."

While Desi was in New York, Lucille received a visitor, Karl Frings, who arrived in a white suit on her doorstep without an appointment. "When she saw my white suit, she must have thought I was an attendant at a mental hospital come for her. There had been reports of a complete mental breakdown."

He was finally able to get inside the door after displaying whatever proof he could that Olivia de Havilland had sent him to pitch his services to her as Lucille's new agent.

As a Hollywood agent with an A-list clientele which included Edward G. Robinson, he had an unusual background for a man in his position. Born to a Jewish family in Prussia, he had once been the lightweight boxing champion of Europe. But in 1935, as the Nazis were persecuting Jews, he fled from Germany, eventually migrating to Hollywood.

His first meeting with Lucille in her living room lasted three hours. Eventually, he convinced her that she should avoid studio contracts altogether and become a freelancer in roles he could secure for her.

"Right now, I can get you the lead in a romantic comedy, *Lover Come Back* (1946) which will be released by Universal," he claimed. "Your co-star will be George Brent, who plays your husband. William Seiter has signed to direct. You had a bit part as a model in that picture he helmed, *Roberta* (1935), with Astaire and Rogers. As you know, Bill also gave you a role in *Room Service* (1938) with the Marx Brothers."

[Lucille's Lover Come Back *is not to be confused with the 1961 rom-com with the same name that had co-starred Rock Hudson and Doris Day.]*

"I'm so fucked up in my head these days, I don't think I'm able to work," she said. "I might flub my lines with this *stut-stut-stut*

Lucille, as a leggy redhead, goes global, as shown by the Italian-language promotion campaign that blanketed Rome and Milan with posters for her newest bit of light-hearted American fluff, *Lover Come Back.*

358

stutter I've developed whenever I'm nervous. I'd be impossible to work with on a picture. I'd need twenty-eight takes to get one line right."

"We've heard about that," her new agent said. "Bill is willing to work with you for a week. He's convinced that he can cure you of that stutter.'

She later recalled, "*Lover Come Back* was one of the best things to ever happen to me. Bill *[Seiter]* was wonderful, really supportive. After a week of his helping me with my speech, my confidence returned and the stutter went away. George Brent, my leading man, was wonderfully supportive, too, very loving—and I don't mean that sexually."

"I don't think George (Brent) ever got around to banging her," Seiter claimed. "But they had some heavy petting going on. I walked in on them when the horndog had his tongue down her throat."

At the time, Brent was known as a "lady killer," with a long list of seductions, a roster that included Loretta Young, Diana Barrymore, Greta Garbo, and Olivia de Havilland. His most publicized "celebrity affair" was with Bette Davis.

On the second week of the shoot, Brent astonished Lucille when he asked her to come back with him, put on boxing gloves, and join him in his home-constructed ring in his rear garden. "Greta Garbo used to come here to spar with me," he claimed.

"Count me out of that one," she answered. "I'm no Jack Dempsey. When I want to beat up on a man, no boxing gloves for me. I prefer a base-ball bat or an iron frying skillet."

When Brent and Lucille weren't scheduled for appearances before a camera, Seiter observed them sitting in a corner as he held her hand and talked to her.

He discussed his adventures as a young man growing up in Ireland, where he eventually joined the Irish War of Independence. Since he fought with the Irish Republican Army, he had to flee his native land after the British put a bounty on his head.

After appearing for a while on Broadway, he was lured to Hollywood. In time, he became a screen heartthrob at Warner Brothers. In 1930, he co-starred with Barbara Stanwyck in *So Big!* [*His future mistress, Bette Davis, had a small role in that film.*]

Before deciding on her leading man in *The Rich Are Always With Us* (1932), Ruth Chatterton watched Brent's screen test. "Where has that guy been all my life?" she asked her director. Brent not only became her co-star, he married her. [*He'd already divorced his wife from the 1920s.*]

For Brent, roles came one after another with no let-up. So did his list of star conquests: Loretta Young, Kay Francis, Margaret Lindsay, and Myrna Loy. His name on movie credits was positioned above Bette Davis' in publicity for *Housewife* (1934), and later, he was Garbo's leading man in *The Painted Veil* (also 1934).

He starred with Davis again in *Front Page Woman* (1935) and *Special Agent* that same year. It was then that he began his long-running affair with her. Davis told Hedda Hopper, "George is one of the most attractive men in Hollywood."

He reunited with Davis again in *The Golden Arrow* (1936), but their most celebrated films lay in their immediate future. He had the third lead in *Jezebel* (1938) when Davis was wooed by Henry Fonda.

Brent's greatest picture with Davis was *Dark Victory* (1939), in which she was going blind. He also made *The Old Maid* with her that same year. In that one, both Davis and Miriam Hopkins, her nemesis in private life, competed for Brent's love.

After *Honeymoon for Three* (1941), Brent's life changed. He married his co-star, Ann Sheridan, but they separated three months later. She told Hedda Hopper it was because of his sexual equipment. "Brent bent."

Before working with Lucille, he made two final pictures with Davis, *The Great Lie* (1941) with Mary Astor and *In This Life* (1942) with Olivia de Havilland.

Released in 1946, *Lover Come Back* teamed Lucille and Brent with a roster of talented supporting players, some of whom had been with her in previous movies. The cast included Charles Winniger, Carl Esmond, Wallace Ford, Louise Beavers, and Franklin Pangborn.

In *Lover Come Back,* Brent plays a war correspondent named Bill Williams, Jr. who's covering the conflicts overseas. His wife (Lucille) soon learned that he's been paying a lot of attention to other women, especially Madeleine Laslo, played by Vera Zorina, a ballerina best remembered for films choreographed by her husband, George Balanchine.

Lucille was only jealous of Zorina in the film In private, she liked her. Zorina confessed that the disappointment of her life was losing the role of Maria in the 1943 film adaptation of Ernest Hemingway's *For Whom the Bell Tolls.* "Gary Cooper wanted Ingrid Bergman instead."

In *Lover Come Back*, Brent feels it's a man's right to be a womanizer, but not the privilege

George Brent with **Bette Davis** in *Dark Victory* (1939).

He co-starred with her in more movies than any other actor, but he didn't seduce her until their filming of *Dark Victory.* Their affair lasted for two years, even though she complained about him to director Edmund Goulding:

"George is too vain, always dying his hair and getting prissy about his wardrobe. He spends a lot of time in front of the mirror."

Their romance exploded when he revealed to the press his list of the ten most glamourous women in Hollywood.

It included the most obvious choices (Marlene Dietrich and Greta Garbo), but when he subbed Joan Crawford for Bette Davis, he was never welcomed back into her boudoir.

of a wife. Lucille decides to make him jealous by being attentive to the amorous Paul Millar (Carl Esmond). Lucille had worked with Esmond before when he played another amorous "Paul" in *Without Love* co-starring Katharine Hepburn and Spencer Tracy. The plot has Charles Winniger as "Pa" Williams, the wise mentor who brings the battling Lucille and Brent characters together again in the final reel.

As Kay Williams, Lucille is a leading couturier, which meant she had to be dressed stylishly. To achieve that wardrobe, costume designer Travis Banton was hired and given a lavish budget (for the time) of $100,000. One of the most famous designers of Hollywood's Golden Age, he was better known for his long collaboration with Marlene Dietrich. But this native son of Waco, Texas also dressed Pola Negri, Clara Bow, clothes hound Kay Francis, Carole Lombard, Claudette Colbert, and Mae West, among others. "Travis clad me in satin *lamé*, beads, fur, and feathers," Lucille claimed. Later, Banton created designs for Linda Darnell, Betty Grable, Rita Hayworth, Joan Bennett, Merle Oberon, and Joan Fontaine.

"He had a big problem," Lucille said. "Although a brilliant designer, he struggled with the bottle, with the bottle winning."

Newsweek reviewed Lucille's film with: "Even if *Lover Come Back* were half as gay and amusing as it struggles to be—and it isn't by a long shot—this farce would be in dubious taste. It is a personal triumph for Lucille Ball, who from time to time rings a laugh strictly on her own."

Bosley Crowther of *The New York Times* panned it: "Miss Ball wears a wardrobe of costumes and acts as if she really has a script. The poor lady is sadly deluded, as she is completely lacking in support."

The *New York Herald Tribune* noted, "the quarreling and making up, which ostensibly is the theme of this piece, is as dull as dishwater. Our sympathy, then, to Miss Ball, who is fetching in spite of the plot's *ennui.*"

She preferred *Variety's* opinion: "This frothy little comedy may remind you customers of previous films. Miss Ball turns in one of her best comedy performances to date, mulcting every line and antic to the limit."

***

After Lucille wrapped her last picture, she had no film commitments on the horizon. The previous years had taken a severe toll on her mind and body, and she needed a vacation from Hollywood.

Desi and his band had accepted an extended engagement at New York City's Copacabana. At the time, it was the most sought-after and prominent nightclub in America. She took a train east to join him, completely aware that she would thereby cramp his love life, which was actually her intention.

He'd rented a large apartment for them at the Delmonico Hotel on Park Avenue at 59th Street.

In Manhattan, she walked along streets she'd known as a struggling model and would-be showgirl. Times were different now. She couldn't leave the hotel but what she was mobbed by eager fans, many of them teenagers, clamoring for her autograph. She felt like the Queen of Hollywood, with five of her latest films either currently showing or else scheduled to open within the month. "What star can match my record?" she asked.

Her arrival in town generated a lot of press and also invitations for appearances on radio shows, both local and national. The *Daily News* for some reason dubbed her "The Female Frank Sinatra," although she was not a singer.

The Copa booked some of the biggest names in show business, and she was happily surprised that Desi was among headliners who had recently included comedians Joe E. Lewis and Jimmy Durante, and singer Lena Horne.

Desi had arrived in town just in time to watch the closing act of songstress Jane Froman. She had survived an airplane crash in February of 1943 in the Tagus River in Lisbon. She was among fifteen survivors after the plane went down. The injuries she sustained would last a lifetime, calling for thirty-nine painful operations. She was forced to wear a leg brace and endure being hauled around in a wheelchair. Desi called her "a real trouper and survivor." Her heart-breaking story was brought to life on the screen in *With a Song In My Heart* (1952), which starred Susan Hayward.

Lucille frequently showed up in the audience at the Copa, where Desi was presenting three shows a night: at 8:30pm, at midnight, and—the loudest, most crowded, and most drunken of all—at 2:30AM.

He had told Lucille that the club was ostensibly owned by showman Monte Proser, but the real backers were Mafia syndicate gangsters Frank Costello and Lucky Luciano.

The talented comedian, Peter Lind Hayes, was Desi's opening act. Lucille had a reunion with him, since he'd starred in her film *Seven Days' Leave (1942)* in which the sexually aggressive Victor Mature was her leading man.

Frank Sinatra often showed up alone, since he knew Desi could fix him up with one of the "Copa Girls," each of them known for having "Betty Grable legs." *[The legs of that blonde movie goddess had been recently voted as "most beautiful in the world."]*

"I had a hell of a time deciding which gal to screw first," Desi told Hayes. "All of them are super gorgeous, with great tits and great everything else. All of them are skilled seducers who can really satisfy a man."

Lucille was furious at the New York gossip columnists, who actively promoted Desi as a philandering playboy and ladies' man. Publicists for the Copa hyped that image since they felt it was good for business. In her column,

The popular singer, **Jane Froman** (upper photo), was finishing her gig at The Copa. Desi caught her last act before he morphed into the newer, hotter star at that nightclub.

In 1943, after a spectacular stage and singing career, Froman bravely carried on after surviving a plane crash in Lisbon that left her confined to a wheelchair for life.

In 1952, almost a decade after Froman's debilitating accident, **Susan Hayward** brought her stunning saga to the screen in the film *With a Song in My Heart.*

Dorothy Kilgallen hinted that Desi had "auditioned" all the Copa Girls.

The club was often filled with out-of-town businessmen on vacation from their wives back in such cities as Detroit, Cleveland, St. Louis, or Chicago.

Desi's friend, Joey Adams, admitted, "Our boy Desi flirts with every good-looking doll he encounters. He'll see a hot little number shopping along Fifth Avenue and come right up to her and say, 'Hi, I'm Desi Arnaz appearing at the Copa. Would you like to go on the road with me?'"

Perhaps jealous of his success with women, a heckler in the audience at the Copa would sometimes yell at Desi on the stage. One night, a drunken millionaire from Toronto shouted out to him, "Arnaz, how many Copa Girls have you fucked?"

Proser was the first man in the club to arrive at the drunk's ringside table. He took off the man's glasses and struck at him, but hit one of the cement palm trees instead, breaking his left hand. By then, three of his security guards, two of them ex-boxers, arrived on the scene. They lifted the man from his chair and carried him onto the street, where they threw him head first into his waiting limousine.

Lucille was angry when she read about the notorious incident in a gossip column, She confronted Desi: "So did you tell the joker exactly how many Copa Girls you've had?"

"Don't tell me you believe all that crap, that cheap gossip?" he asked.

On another occasion, once again Desi expressed his feelings about marriage to a reporter from the *Daily News*. "I'm an old-fashioned and traditional son of Cuba, I was raised in the land of a double standard, one for a man, another edict for a wife. You need to marry a woman who you can trust to be faithful. A husband is allowed to fool around with a *puta,* but in no way does that affect his feelings for his wife. The bond between a husband and wife is sacred. A few peccadilloes on the part of the male doesn't mean a god damn thing."

It was in 1946, during her stay in New York, that the Associated Drama Guild of America, at their annual convention, named Danny Kaye and Lucille as the King and Queen of Comedy. Their theme that year was "The Emergence of Sophisticated Comedy on the American Scene."

Kaye had two movies being shown across America at the time, *The Wonder Man* (1945) and *The Kid from Brooklyn* (1946). He was known for his physical comedy, idiosyncratic pantomimes, and rapid-fire novelty songs.

One night at the Copa, Kaye showed up for Desi's late-late show. Desi later reported to Lucille, "Danny met with me after the show and really came on to me, finding me very sexy. He

At Desi's opening night at the Copa, Lucille had a reunion with **Peter Lind Hayes**. With Victor Mature and her, he had appeared in *Seven Days' Leave.*

At the club, he reprised the impersonations he had delivered in their film. In time, he evolved into a household name on television.

363

invited me back to his hotel room, which I declined."

Although married to Sylvia Fine in 1940, Kaye led the closeted life of a homosexual, and was said to have had a decade-long affair with Laurence Olivier.

One afternoon, Lucille accompanied Desi to the RCA Studio where he was booked to record a song. There, as a gag, she and some of the workers were making an "off the record" recording to play at private parties. They persuaded Lucille to record a falsetto and raspy interpretation of the nursery rhyme, "Peter Piper." Later, she was shocked when RCA included that on an album and identified it as a "Vocal by Lucille Ball." She sued for $100,000, and the case was settled out of court for an undisclosed sum.

Although Desi's adulterous affairs were widely visible at the time, those of Lucille were virtually unknown to her general public, although Hollywood insiders were aware of them. There had been several items in the gossip columns when she appeared with one of her leading men at such clubs as the Cocoanut Grove. It was not known at the time if Desi knew about them, but it was widely understood to Hollywood insiders that he was notoriously jealous of his wife.

When he published his memoir, *A Book,* in 1976, he revealed that he was indeed aware of his wife's cheating on him.

He admitted that Lucille had been "Outed" many times in the gossip columns, having a cozy *tête-à-téte* with the co-star of her current film. "When she was accusing me of laying

The talented comedian, **Danny Kaye**, was a closeted homosexual with an understanding wife, Sylvia Fine.

Although Samuel Goldwyn had once said, "No one wants to fuck Danny Kaye," the comedian nonetheless managed to seduce both Laurence Olivier and the French actor Louis Jourdan.

Desi claimed, "Kaye came on to me."

Regardless of the extent of his outside affairs, Kaye could always come home to "Mama," a reference to his wife.

Sylvia had met him when he was only fourteen and took his virginity, marrying him three years later.

every goddamn broad I ever worked with, she seemed to be having a ball with every co-star in her films."

She was candid once when asked about the *machismo* of Latin men who believed in the double standard. "I like to play games, too," she replied provocatively.

Also, over time, many years after appearing with her in films, her co-stars on occasion gossiped about her with "loose tongues."

Even though he was a philandering husband, and even though he knew his wife was sleeping around, Desi still claimed, "Lucy and I were very much in love, and our sexual relationship was heavenly."

As he told his comedian friend, Joe E. Lewis, "If I wasn't drained after three shows, in the pre-dawn hours, she wanted to be plowed two or three times. Once was never enough for my Lucy."

***

All things come to an end, and so did Lucille's extended stay in Manhattan with her errant husband Desi. They gave up their rented apartment when he embarked on a nation-wide tour with his band, and she landed back in Hollywood for another *film noir* with George Sanders as her leading man.

A Hunt Stromberg production, *Lured* was a brooding movie scheduled for a 1947 release by United Artists. Stromberg, its executive producer, was already a virtual legend in Hollywood. A son of Kentucky, he had churned out the ever-popular *Thin Man* series and the Jeanette Mac-Donald/Nelson Eddy musicals of the 1930s. His film, *The Great Ziegfeld,* had won the Best Picture Oscar for 1936.

He'd also produced those Jean Harlow movies and the breakthrough films of Joan Crawford. One of his achievements involved the direction of *Torrent* (1926), Greta Garbo's first American movie.

As Lucille jokingly said, "I will lie on Stromberg's casting couch any time I'm summoned."

In **Lured**, a 1947 United Artists murder mystery set in London, Lucille played Sandra Carpenter. The "Poet Killer" is on the loose, and she'd been a friend of his latest victim.

Lucille always remained glamorous, but not enough to lure post-war audiences into movie houses.

As ordered by Stromberg, Lucille reported to work in November on the picture entitled, during the early stages of its production, *Personal Column*. A murder mystery, it was a remake of the 1939 French film, *Pièges (usually translated into English as "Traps"),* which had been released a few months before the Nazis seized control of Paris. It had starred Maurice Chevalier and Erich von Stroheim.

On their first day together on the set, Lucille met her German-born director, Douglas Sirk. He had fled to Hollywood when the Nazis began persecuting his Jewish wife.

Sirk's greatest box office triumphs lay in his future, when he turned out such 1950s tear-jerkers as *Imitation of Life, All that Heaven Allows, Written on the Wind,* and *Magnificent Obsession.* These would become some of the most successful films ever for such stars as Lana Turner, Rock Hudson, Jane Wyman, and Lauren Bacall.

Lucille wasn't that much turned on by the picture, even though it was written by Leo Rosten, who had penned the script for one of her latest pictures, the *film noir, The Dark Corner.*

What she did like was her appearance on the screen. Rarely had she been photographed better and more exquisitely gowned. William Daniels, her cinematographer, had been Greta Garbo's favorite cameraman on such movies as *Mata Hari* (1931) and *Grand Hotel* (also 1931).

Lucille established a long-term relationship with dress designer Elois Jessen, who created her elegant gowns in the movie. *[Years later, in 1953, Lucille hired her to create her wardrobe for the I Love Lucy TV series. Once the show became popular, it no longer had to clothe Lucille "off the rack."]*

It was rare for her to work with such a strong and talented supporting cast: She and Sanders would each, of course, be granted star billing, but as it happened, many of their colleagues had, in their respective pasts, each been assigned featured billings of their own. They included Charles Coburn, Boris Karloff, Sir Cedric Hardwicke, Joseph Calleia, Alan Mowbray, and George Zucco.

Despite the stellar cast, Lucille, after reading the script, dismissed it as "a routine whodunit." Over the years, however, *Lured* developed a cult following.

In a nutshell, the plot focused on a taxi dancer, Sandra Carpenter (Lucille). Her friend and fellow dancer is murdered by a serial killer, notorious as the "Poet Killer" since he sends poems to taunt the police after every slaying He lures victims through ads in the personal columns of newspapers.

Scotland Yard inspector Harley Temple (Coburn) enlists Sandra's help in uncovering the psycho. She uses herself as bait, under the supervision and protection of an officer bodyguard (Zucco) hovering in the background.

Along the way, Sandra meets a dashing stage revue producer named Robert Fleming (George Sanders). She falls in love with him, even though evidence is later planted that he is the killer.

Lurking in the background is the real murderer, Julian Wilde (Hardwicke), who has developed an obsession for her.

Karloff, as Charles van Druten, is an insane dress designer. The mad couturier menaces Sandra for about six minutes of bone-chilling cinematic horror.

As Dr. Nicholas Moryani, Calleia is a mysterious figure who lures beautiful young women to South America, where he sells them as sex slaves.

Whereas she already knew many members of the cast, others were unknown to her. She admired Coburn as an actor, but

Lucille with **George Sanders** in *Lured.*

He was the husband of Zsa Zsa Gabor. In *Lured*, he's a playboy, Robert Fleming, a theatrical impresario who proposes marriage to Lucille's character.

She soon learns that Scotland Yard is investigating him as "The Poet Killer."

"I've never met any figure in Hollywood who was such a bigot." Born in Macon, Georgia, in 1877, he was a member of the White Citizens' Council, a white supremacist group opposed to racial integration.

The English actor, Boris Karloff, had friendly chats with Lucille. As Frankenstein, she had found him "terrifying on the screen," but otherwise, he was gentle and soft-spoken. He told her that as a boy growing up, "I was bow-legged and had both a stutter and a lisp. I got rid of two afflictions but kept the lisp."

When Lucille met him, Karloff had recently married his sixth wife, Evelyn Hope Helmore. "He told me that he wanted me as his wife number seven," she said. "I hope he was joking."

She found herself working once again with Alan Mowbray. He'd been cast in *Lured* as Lyle Maxwell, the murderous accomplice of the notorious Dr. Moryani. *[Mowbray had been one of the co-stars of her first-ever Hollywood movie, Roman Scandals (1933).]*

She worked again with Sir Hardwicke, who had co-starred with her in the Western, *Valley of the Sun* (1942). She also had a reunion with Calleia, who had been cast with her on their movie, *Five Came Back* (1939).

Lured grossed only $700,000 at the box office and played to mostly empty audiences.

Lucille with **Boris Karloff** in *Lured*.

Elegantly gowned, she suspects that he's menacing, and that maybe he's the "Poet Killer."

Karloff, filmdom's greatest ghoul, could look threatening even without grotesque makeup.

In *Lured*, although he appears on the screen for only about six minutes, he manages to send chills down everyone's spines.

Critic Dennis Schwartz had slight praise and a few brickbats: "This flawed movie never settles into a dark and sinister mood but succeeds only in keeping things tension-free and lighthearted with continuous breezy comical conversations. Ball does a Nancy Drew turn, sleuthing with her comic detective partner, George Zucco as gumshoe H.R. Barrett."

Film Daily wrote, "It is mystery and melodrama served up with intelligence, a mighty fine production, interesting background and performances many cuts above the ordinary."

Variety defined Lucille as having registered "her best in comic bits as a wisecracking showgirl." The *Los Angeles Times* said, "Miss Ball gives a chipper account of herself as the intrepid Lady Dick."

The *New York Herald Tribune* claimed, "Lucille Ball is quite a girl and an engaging *comedienne*."

At the end of the shoot, the director, Douglas Sirk, ironically asserted, "Lucille was supposed to fall in love with George Sanders on screen, not off the screen."

***

George Sanders, Lucille's leading man in *Lured,* was an irresistible force who collided with her. During their first week on the set, they became lovers, their romantic pairing beginning in her dressing room.

As columnist Sheilah Graham discovered but did not print, "In taking on Sanders, Lucille found herself competing with the glamourous blonde, Zsa Zsa Gabor. The blonde vs. the redhead. Not only Sanders, but both Lucille and Zsa Zsa were vying for the loving of Franchot Tone—that is, when that actor was still paying visits to his ex-wife, Joan Crawford."

The dynamic described above was first chronicled in detail in Darwin Porter's biography, *Those Glamorous Gabors, Bombshells from Budapest,* published by Blood Moon Productions to international acclaim in 2013.

An excerpt from that book is replicated here:

WOMEN WE LOVE

The "mad but brilliant and charming and *über*-glam Hungarian," **Zsa Zsa Gabor**, depicted here with **George Sanders** in 1953.

Sanders was added to her mile-long list of lovers who included Richard Burton, Sean Connery, John F. Kennedy, Frank Sinatra, Mario Lanza, Prince Aly Khan, and the notorious playboy, Porfirio Rubirosa.

At long last, Zsa Zsa's wet dream became real when she met the object of her romantic fantasy, George Sanders.

In April of 1947, the flowering trees in Manhattan's Central Park were in blossom. Zsa Zsa was at last free of her marriage to Conrad Hilton.

"I was the gay divorcée," she claimed, "and at the top of the list of any lavish party being thrown in New York. Every wolf in Manhattan was drooling at the mouth for me."

Her historic meeting of Sanders, born in 1906 to British parents in Imperial St. Petersburg, Russia, occurred inside the deluxe apartment maintained by Wall Street banker Serge Semenenko. That apartment was stylishly situated within the St. Regis Hotel, on Fifth Avenue at 55th Street in Manhattan.

When Zsa Zsa appeared in the doorway in a clinging black silk jersey dress, the creation of the then-famous designer "Alexis," all male eyes except one turned and gazed appreciatively upon her glittering entrance. Her diamonds sparkled. The only man who didn't look at her was Sanders himself, surrounded at the time with adoring women.

Because the host was too preoccupied to introduce Zsa Zsa to her idol, she walked over to him and said, "Mr. Sanders, I'm Zsa Zsa Gabor, and I'm madly in love with you."

He eyed her skeptically. "How very understandable. Very understandable indeed."

"In person, you're just as irresistible as you were on the screen when you played Charles Strickland in The Moon and Sixpence.*"*

THOSE GLAMOUROUS GABORS
BOMBSHELLS FROM BUDAPEST
as reviewed by Vincent Rafe McCabe
in the New York Journal of Books, September 10, 2013

"You will never be Ga-bored. . . . gives new meaning to the term 'compelling.'"

"Once upon a time, in the faraway kingdom of the Magyars, there lived a woman who had three daughters. This woman was very, very wise and knew well the cost of diamonds and the ways of the world. And she looked upon her daughters and her ample bosom swelled with pride.

One daughter, she saw, was a great beauty who was soon named Miss Hungary. And once more her mother was proud. A second daughter married well and became the Countess of Warsaw and told her sisters to refer to her as "Her Excellency," and again the mother was proud. The third, the youngest and blondest of the three girls, seeing that her homeland seethed with turmoil as the world prepared for war, quickly married Garbo's chiropractor and fled to the mythical land called Hollywood. And that made the mother proudest of all.

And as she boarded the Cunard liner *The Queen Mary*, the youngest and blondest of the girls suppressed a chill as she clutched tight to the gift that enveloped her, a castoff mink coat that her mother had given her along with her blessings. And the girl stood on the deck facing westward to the New World.

"I was a pauper in mink," she sighed, years later, as she remembered that day for the nice reporter sitting next to her.

Great Courtesans of the 20th Century

Given the fact that the vast majority of us have never lived in a Gabor-free world, it is hard to image what that joyless place might be like. Because despite what any number of Hiltons or Kardashians or even Real Housewives might tell you, no other family has so contributed to Western pop culture as have the Gabors, with a reach extending from the years preceding World War II to the present day.

And for that reason they are now being rewarded with the longest, most exhaustive, most salacious of family biographies, **Those Glamorous Gabors: Bombshells from Budapest,** *by Darwin Porter from Blood Moon Productions.*

"Oh, that dreary thing," he answered.

Zsa Zsa later told her friends, "My god, he was even taller than Conrad Hilton. He devoured me with those striking blue eyes. I felt he was undressing me. He was ever so good looking, a man of elegance and taste with what appeared to be the body of an Olympic athlete."

"In spite of dreadful manners and arrogance, he was a perfectly preserved male specimen at the age of forty-one," she recalled. "His face was bronzed from the California sun, and he wore Old World dinner clothes with pearl studs on his tailored black silk suit."

Without being invited, she sat down, and he joined her on the sofa. "I don't like attending parties and being surrounded by beautiful women. Actually, I don't particularly like women — they bore me."

"You're speaking about other women," she said. "I've never been boring in my life."

Before the party ended, Erich Maria Remarque had joined Zsa Zsa and Sanders. The novelist and the actor, who were friends, had arrived together at the party. When he saw her, Remarque kissed Zsa Zsa on the lips.

"I had no idea that you scandalous international figures even knew each other," Sanders said, "although I don't know why anything surprises me anymore."

When the three of them grew bored with the party at the St. Regis, Zsa Zsa suggested that they return to her penthouse apartment on Manhattan's East Side for a nightcap of vodka "with caviar, of course, dahlink."

As Zsa Zsa prepared drinks and served Beluga, the two men chatted about Remarque's latest novel, Arch of Triumph. *He reported that it was being adapted into a motion picture, starring Ingrid Bergman, Charles Boyer, and Charles Laughton. [It was eventually released in 1948.]*

"I found this pre-war novel a bit sluggish," Sanders said. As Zsa Zsa soon learned, he delivered a lot of blunt and often abrasive opinions.

By two o'clock, Sanders announced to Remarque, "Since three is a crowd, do I have to fight a duel over Zsa Zsa tonight? When I was a young man in Chile, a man challenged me to a duel. He caught me with my landlady, who just happened to be his fiancée. I wounded my opponent but didn't kill him. I was kicked out of the country."

"That won't be necessary tonight," Remarque said. "I'm meeting Marlene [Dietrich] at the Plaza for early morning cocktails."

"That means I'm staying," Sanders said.

Zsa Zsa later claimed that she was infuriated at Sander's casual announcement that he'd be sleeping over. "Who did he think he was? Did he take me for some tramp? Did he just assume that I would give in to his sexual demands?"

In spite of her private protestation, she did submit to him. After Remarque left, Sanders grabbed

Tobacco heiress **Doris Duke** proclaimed, "American men have no talent for being married to a rich woman."

Sanders was added to her list of seductions that stretched around the block, even including, on one occasion, Elvis Presley.

When not bedding General George C. Patton, she hired Hawaiian beach boys.

Hedy Lamarr, hailed as the most beautiful woman in the world, seduced Sanders, who followed others who included Charlie Chaplin, Clark Gable, Errol Flynn, and John F. Kennedy.

But did her first husband, the Austrian munitions magnate, Friedrich Mandl, really pimp her as his then-young and beautiful bride to Benito Mussolini and Adolf Hitler when she was a prominent hostess, entertaining, with her husband, some of the leaders of the Third Reich?

Rumors about that pursued her for the remainder of her life as a mega-celebrity and occasionally self-enchanted survivor.

370

her by the waist with both hands and pulled her down onto the sofa. Passionate kissing led to a trip upstairs to her boudoir.

When he woke up beside her late the next morning, he said. "'Zsa Zsa' doesn't suit you. From now on, I'll call you Cokiline. In Russian, that means 'sweet little sugar cookie.'"

Zsa Zsa confessed in a memoir that she, indeed, shared intimacies with Sanders that long ago night in Manhattan. She never went into clinical detail, but later claimed, "If I could live my entire life over again, I would spend every minute of it with George. If I live until the end of time, I'll never find another George Sanders."

Zsa Zsa and Sanders would not pledge fidelity to each other except on the day they got married, two years later. During the weeks ahead, Zsa Zsa faced a formidable arsenal of women who were also vying for the actor's affection. They included Gene Tierney, with whom Sanders had engaged in an affair since 1941 when they appeared together in the film, Sundown. Hedy Lamarr had loomed on the horizon ever since they filmed The Strange Woman together in 1946. There was also Lucille Ball, with whom he had become attached when they co-starred in Lured (1947).

Also on the scene was the Mexican beauty, Dolores Del Rio. Tobacco heiress Doris Duke was also a contender. Throughout many of these dramas, Sanders was married to actress Susan Larson, whom he had wed in 1940.

Sanders dated Zsa Zsa frequently, but often they were separated. During those times, he scheduled "reunions" with all of these other fabled women.

Zsa Zsa, however, was not sitting home alone. Although she would have preferred to date Sanders exclusively, she filled up not only her social calendar but her boudoir with an impressive array of men. Multi-millionaire Bob Topping became one of her conquests. "I broke him in for Lana Turner," Zsa Zsa later facetiously claimed. "She made the mistake of marrying Bob. I was far too savvy for that."

***

In her efforts to persuade Sanders to marry her, Zsa Zsa had to eliminate some formidable competi-

As a beauty, **Dolores Del Rio** was ranked in the same category as Greta Garbo. Her affair with George Sanders began when they co-starred in *Lancer Spy* in 1937.

Franchot Tone and **Lucille Ball** in *Her Husband's Affairs* (1947).

During their filming, the pair half-heartedly plotted to capture some "semi-pornographic" love scenes as a protest against prevailing forms of censorship.

At all times, they were fully aware that the controversial scenes would be cut from the version released to the general public.

tion. The first and most unlikely candidate was Lucille Ball. Her bandleader husband, Desi Arnaz, was frequently gone for long periods of time, performing on the road. At night in almost any city he visited, he found his own harem of willing, nubile girls.

Lucille was not an actress who liked to sleep alone. In the absence of her husband, she launched a series of affairs, including one with Peter Lawford.

Lucille became enamored of her leading men from two different pictures, *Lured* (1947), co-starring George Sanders, and *Her Husband's Affairs* (also 1947), co-starring Franchot Tone.

Complicating matters during his involvement with Lucille Ball, Zsa Zsa continued her "sometimes fling" with Tone.

"This Ball creature is moving in on my territory," Zsa Zsa claimed to friends—first with Franchot, then with George."

"I don't know what men see in her," Zsa Zsa said. "She has no breasts at all. Perhaps she fulfills some homosexual leaning in these men, who sometimes prefer a flat-chested boy. Two high-class men like Franchot and George should be ashamed of themselves for running around with this low-class hussy from hell."

Once, when Sanders was with her at her New York apartment, Zsa Zsa picked up an extension of her phone and overheard Lucille talking to him.

YOU'LL LOVE LUCY... in her funniest movie ever!

Lucille *Franchot*
BALL · TONE
in
HER HUSBAND'S
AFFAIRS
with
EDWARD EVERETT HORTON · MIKHAIL RASUMNY · GENE LOCKHART
An S. SYLVAN SIMON Production
Directed by S. SYLVAN SIMON · Produced by RAPHAEL HAKIM

"Why in the fuck are you hooked up with the Hilton woman?" Lucille asked Sanders. "What a bitch! What a gold digger! You know I love you. She's completely wrong for you."

During her eavesdropping, Zsa Zsa heard Sanders confirm a date for the following night with Lucille. She chose not to confront him about it. She was not married to him and wouldn't be for many months to come. And because he was still married to actress Susan Larson, her negotiating position was weak.

To Zsa Zsa's annoyance, Lucille and Sanders did little to conceal their involvement. In Hollywood, they were sometimes spotted dining together at a restaurant or drinking together at a nightclub.

In years to come, Lucille once discussed Sanders with Vivian Vance, her co-star in the TV series, I Love Lucy. And she made comments to other friends, too. "Desi was the only one who meant anything to me. Most men came and went in my life so fast, I hardly remembered them, except for George Sanders. What a man!"

"He had the best legs of any man in Hollywood. George told me he got his start as a chorus boy dancing on the London stage because a director 'went bat shit over my gorgeous legs.'"

Both Lucille and Zsa Zsa remembered Sanders when, tanked up on vodka, he sometimes struck them, often hard enough to knock them down on the floor. He told his best friend, actor Brian Aherne, "A woman, a dog, and a walnut tree — the more you beat them, the better they be."

Lucille admitted to Vance and others that she had once seriously considered divorcing Arnaz to marry Sanders. "But the arrogant snob never proposed to me, unlike Sammy Davis, Jr., who wanted to marry me. He told me I wouldn't know what sexual pleasure was until I'd tried a black man. In the end, Gorgeous George preferred to wrap those dynamite legs of his around that international tramp and gushing plate of goulash, Zsa Zsa Gabor. Men...who can figure them out?"

***

After it was announced that Franchot Tone would star as her leading man in Lucille's next movie, *Her Husband's Affairs* (1947), word appeared in the press that she was returning to Columbia Pictures. She had started making films for Columbia as a $75-a-week extra way back in 1934

Tone phoned her and invited her to dinner at Chasen's, ostensibly to talk about the movie. She had not worked with him since she played a showgirl in his movie, *Moulin Rouge* (1934), starring Constance Bennett.

Tone's heyday had been in the 1930s, when he was a leading man in Pre-Code movies and going on into the early 1940s when he was known for his gentlemanly, sophisticated performances. He was also in wartime movies such as *Five Graves in Cairo* (1943), where he played a soldier confronting Erich von Stroheim.

Lucille had seen two — *The Gorgeous Hussy* (1936) and *The Bride Wore Red* (1937) — of the seven movies he'd made with Joan Crawford.

In 1935, while still involved in his affair with Bette Davis, his co-star in *Dangerous,* he'd married Crawford. Divorcing her in 1939, he told the press, "Joan is like that old joke about Philadelphia: First prize is four days in Philadelphia; the second prize is eight days in Philadelphia."

In 1941, Tone remarried, this time to the blonde goddess and fashion model, Jean Wallace. But when he came together with Lucille, his marriage

LONG-DISTANCE KISSING:

Franchot Tone and **Lucille Ball**, in *Her Husband's Affairs.*

Its first cut—showing twin beds that had not been "safely' separated—provoked protests from censors.

Several scenes had to be reshot with the beds more widely separated.

That mandate was endorsed during the filming of upcoming episodes of *I Love Lucy.* Twin beds had to be separated, and occupancy of a shared bed, even by actors portraying a married man and his wife, was "unthinkable."

373

was on the rocks, eventually ending in 1948.

Since Desi was on the road, Tone invited Lucille to spend the night with him and she accepted. During the filming of *Her Husband's Affairs*, because Desi was almost always on the road, she spent many more nights with him. Whenever he wasn't with her, he was visiting Zsa Zsa Gabor for overnights. Lucille was fully aware of this second liaison.

Homosexuals who included actors Ross Alexander and William Haines had spread the word in the early 1930s that Tone was "horse hung, a real jawbreaker." His reputation spread along the Hollywood grapevine and he was sought after by both women and men.

To Barbara Pepper, Lucille confided that she found Tone "highly polished and sophisticated, with impeccable manners." He had been born to a well-to-do family and had been well educated.

"With him, I felt like a Queen Bee," Lucille said. "I was sharing this stud with that Hungarian bombshell, Zsa Zsa Gabor. He always treated me like a lady. Unlike Desi, who had a big ego, Franchot was modest about his stature in Hollywood."

"Louis B. Mayer was very frank with me," Tone asserted. "He told me I was a fine actor, but I didn't have enough charisma for super stardom like Robert Taylor or Clark Gable. He thought I lacked that 'something special' that it takes to make a real movie star."

"Mayer more or less evaluated me the same way," she confided.

When Joan Crawford heard about Tone's affair with Lucille, she said, "She must have struck it lucky. I'm sure she found Franchot a compelling lover, although he's a bit *passé* these days. His time as a leading man has gone beyond its expiration date."

One night at Ciro's, where Lucille was escorted by George Sanders, Crawford approached her table. Lucille was sitting alone, waiting for Sanders to return from a dialogue he was having at another table with director Otto Preminger. He was planning to cast Sanders as Charles II in that expensive blockbuster, *Forever Amber* (1949), starring Linda Darnell.

Crawford was candid in her discussion with Lucille about Tone: "When we broke up, it was like a scene from *A Star Is Born*. I was becoming a big star, and his career seemed to be drifting. That won't repeat itself with you and Franchot because both of you are B-picture stars. But you'd better watch out. He sometimes goes on alcoholic binges and becomes violent. He'll probably beat hell out of you."

"Thanks for the warning," Lucille said.

"There's no future in your affair with my ex," Crawford predicted. "Trust me. It will go bad, as it did for me. I got tired of barging in on him in his dressing room when he was making a picture. Time and time again, I had to pull his large penis out of some starlet's mouth. A wife gets tired of that."

[Eyewitnesses to the complicated marital life of Joan Crawford have corroborated that phraseology and her penchant for hard-hitting speech patterns like the one cited above. Within the context of her "usual" (offscreen) speech patterns, the dialogue in the paragraph above is less shocking, or pornographic, than it might otherwise seem.]

"I have no intention of seeing Franchot after our picture is wrapped," Lucille said. "It's a mere fling. I'm madly in love with my husband, but he's never home."

"At least your film is aptly titled," Crawford said. "*Her Husband's Affairs* is the story of my life with Franchot."

[*Actually, the title of* Her Husband's Affairs *was misleading. Most viewers who went to see it thought that it referred to a wife's dealing with her husband's sexual liaisons. Actually, it described her interference in his business affairs.*]

When shooting began, Lucille had a long conference with her director, S. Sylvan Simon. She had worked with him before when they had made a film starring Bud Abbott and Lou Costello.

Its original incarnation as a Broadway stage play was by the writing team of Ben Hecht and Charles Lederer. Both of them were key creators of what came to be known as "the screwball comedies" of the 1930s. Back in 1927, Hecht had won an Oscar for best screenplay for their film *Underground.*

Lucille, of course, had been a friend of Carole Lombard, who had reigned as "The Queen of Screwball Comedies." As regards her performance in *Her Husband's Affairs*, Lucille admitted that she'd been heavily influenced by Lombard's performances in *Twentieth Century* (1934) and *Nothing Sacred* (1937). Even *Life* magazine favorably compared their performances.

In *My Husband's Affairs,* Lucille, as Margaret, is married to Tone, as William Welton, who works in advertising. She is "Miss Fix-It," always interfering in his business affairs. He is promoting a "magical" hair-growing lotion, its formula the work of a crazy inventor, Mikhail Rasumny, cast as Professor Emil Glinka. His secret lotion does indeed grow hair, but in all the wrong places. In one scene, it gives a woman a thick mustache.

In the third lead was Edward Everett Horton as J.B. Cruikshank. This was Lucille's third and final picture with him. He would become the first film personality to appear on *I Love Lucy* [Episode fifteen, "Lucy Plays Cupid"].

During the course of his long career, character actor Gene Lockhart, cast as Peter Winterbottom, would appear in some 300 movies, sometimes cast as a villain. After working with Lucille, he would play the Dauphin's chief counselor in *Joan of Arc* (1948), starring Ingrid Bergman.

After *Her Husband's Affairs* was wrapped, there would be no other Lucille Ball films released in 1948.

In reference to that film, one reviewer noted that Lucille "was full of spunk in the picture, but Tone as the husband was a sexist jerk."

Although Tone and Lucille got panned by most critics, their favorite assessment appeared in the *Hollywood Reporter:* "Tone and Ball carry the ball for director Simon all the way. Tone was never better—never funnier while the ever-changing Ball is right in there with him pitching as only she can. Both parts were made to order for this team, and they really make a romp of it."

***

After he finished his successful run at the Copa in Manhattan, Desi set out "to conquer America." Lucille told friends that her husband was a familiar face in Hollywood, enjoyed a bit of a following in New York, and that he was also fairly well known on Miami Beach. "But he has to introduce himself to the good people of Chagrin Falls or Kalamazoo."

On leaving New York, Desi was in a state of panic, fearing that his type of Latin music would be a hard sell in America's Heartland. "I hear they prefer square dancing to the Conga."

His first stop was the Chicago Theater in Chicago, where he and his band were a hit, generating $65,000 for the week. They even topped the gross of the far better-known Tommy Dorsey Orchestra.

At another gig in Omaha, Nebraska, Desi's band matched the ticket sales of the Dorsey troupe.

Another profitable booking was in Las Vegas, where his band made $50,000 for the week. However, he went on a gambling binge and lost $48,000 of it, leaving Lucille to pay all the monthly bills at the Desilu Ranch.

Before working with **Bob Hope** on his radio show, Desi had heard a lot of talk about him.

"Hope is not a great comedian," Groucho Marx said. "He just translates what others write for him."

His sometimes partner, Bing Crosby, said, "He's a fast man with a squaw, but a slow man with a buck."

Desi phoned his wife every night, often very late. He told her he was getting tired of "all those one-night stands, the late hours, the seedy hotels, the lousy Midwest food at those greasy spoons, where me and my boys sometimes eat at two in the morning."

She became aware of Desi's generous and protective care of his musicians. Once, three of them, each booked into the same hotel room, contracted bad cases of the flu. Desi not only nursed them back to health but canceled three lucrative bookings until the band members recovered. "He could have left them in their sickbeds and hired three new musicians, but he was loyal to his boys, even if it meant a financial loss," Lucille said.

While she was on the road herself, touring in a stage play called *Dream Girl,* Desi and Lucille's brother Fred Ball, who was the band's manager, chartered a small plane to fly them to Detroit to see her perform in it.

After her performance, Fred and Desi planned to ride their chartered plane to their next gig in Akron, Ohio.

Desi's musicians, it was understood, would take a bus to Akron. Back in Detroit, Desi was in bed with Lucille. He'd spent most of the night making love to her. He had warned the hotel's switchboard operator, "Don't call our room under any circumstances."

Violating his command, the hotel's operator kept ringing and ringing throughout the night until, at 6AM, Desi finally picked up the receiver.

In his groggy voice, "I called her every vile name I knew. Thank God she didn't know Spanish."

She shouted back at him, "YOUR ENTIRE BAND IS IN THE HOSPITAL. DO YOU WANT TO HEAR ABOUT IT OR NOT? TWO OR THREE OF THEM MIGHT BE DYING!"

He listened to the tragic news. What followed was his heartfelt apologies to the telephone operator.

The bus that Fred Ball had rented for Desi's band had collided with a big truck on U.S. Highway 20, just outside Rolling Prairie, Indiana. Almost everyone aboard was coming from their gig in Madison, Wisconsin, heading for their next show in Akron the following night.

Ten of the sixteen members of his band were seriously injured. The worst victim was Charlie Harris, the violinist and concert master, who was seated aboard the bus in the spot usually reserved for Desi. He suffered the loss of an eye, a broken leg, and a broken arm. Almost everyone in the saxophone section was seriously injured, as well as Bobby Jones, who used to be Glenn Miller's first trumpet player.

Doris Day became the girl singer on Bob Hope's radio show. Both Hope and Desi pursued her, but she rejected both of them.

He'd heard a rumor that she preferred black men. "I'd be willing to put on black face if she'd agree to go to bed with me," Desi jokingly claimed.

After getting "patched up" in a local hospital, many of the musicians had plaster casts on their legs or bandages on their heads, but they wanted to continue with the tour. To fill in the missing slots, other bands were most generous with Desi. Tommy Dorsey sent two trombone players, Duke Ellington some saxophone players, and Xavier Cugat offered a maraca musician.

By the time Desi ended his tour and returned to California, he had his original band back, even those who had been seriously injured. No one had died.

***

His longest and most successful booking was at the Palace Theater in San Francisco. During that gig, Lucille flew up from Los Angeles to be with him. On her first visit, she met a young singer, Carole Richards, finding her talented, beautiful, and charming. She couldn't help but notice how smitten her husband was with her.

That night, they had a big fight in his suite, where she accused Desi of sleeping with her. He denied it, and then turned the accusation around, aiming it at her, and confronted her with a candid shot, replicated in a newspaper of her flirting at the Cocoanut Grove with Ken Morgan.

[Morgan was the husband of her cousin, Cleo Morgan, and often served as Lucille's escort, leading to speculation in Hollywood of an affair.]

The alleged affair between Ken and Lucille was never verified, but the rumors persisted for years. Columnist Sheilah Graham privately said,

"That Cleo cousin of Ball must be a very understanding wife."

Desi and the injured members of his band recovered enough to return as a unit for another visit to Omaha. This time, they appeared at the Orpheum. After their last show there, a phone call from Lucille came in for Desi from their ranch. During their conversation, she revealed that she had functioned as his agent.

She had made a guest appearance on Bob Hope's weekly radio show for NBC. There, she learned that his musicians, the Stan Kenton Orchestra, were leaving.

She shared lunch the next day with Hope. During their time together, she presented him with an avalanche of publicity, and evidence of the profits, generated by Desi and his band during their nationwide tour.

Hope agreed to hire him, but with the stipulation that Desi, with his band, had to be in Los Angeles within two days. Desi was so tempted with the offer that he canceled his next three bookings, the final stops of his tour. Together with Fred Ball, he chartered another plane, an antiquated DC-3, for an early-morning flight from Omaha to Los Angeles aboard a carrier that was usually confined to delivery runs for the Midwest Vegetable Company. Once aboard, they were seated in bucket seats soiled with the stains from rotted tomatoes and heads of cauliflower. Before the transport of vegetables, the plane had served in the Army during World War II for the transfer of soldiers to the battlefields of Europe.

Less than an hour after take-off, Desi was signaled to come to the front of the plane. There, the pilot told him that one of the engines had fallen off. There was nothing to do but return to Omaha with one engine operating and "a hope and a prayer" that the plane would make it there.

Back in Omaha, mechanics restored the plane and replaced the engine. The sun was high in the sky when they took off again. Somewhere over Palm Springs, the pilot signaled to Desi again, telling him, "I don't know where the Los Angeles Airport is."

Desi sat in the co-pilot's seat and took over the radio, reaching the control tower of LAX, informing them of their dilemma. One of the control tower operators was able to guide them to the airport, where they landed safely "after getting the fright of my life," Desi later told Lucille. "We even had to go into a holding pattern at a certain high altitude because other planes below us were also trying to land. Call that one a close call."

***

Desi had learned the ropes of show business from a series of masters, beginning with bandleader Xavier Cogat and going on to George Abbott and others. Even Lucille had taught him a lot about how to face the camera. Now, he'd been hired by the great showman himself, Bob Hope, whom Desi called "comedy's leading professor."

The comedian and the Cuban musician bonded on their first meeting, and Desi was hired as the musical director of Hope's NBC radio show.

Born a Londoner in 1903, and a former boxer, Hope had been a feature on radio since 1934. By the time he met Desi, he had become the master of modern American stand-up comedy. He'd also been a hit in movies, especially those "Road Comedies" starring Bing Crosby and Dorothy Lamour.

Every radio show was performed before a live audience in various cities that included New York, Los Angeles, Toledo, Philadelphia, Atlanta, Washington (DC), Detroit, Chicago, even Omaha. *[Yes, Desi dared to return again, this time on a better plane.]*

For a while, at least, Frances Langford had been Hope's regular singer, but she was fired and replaced with a different guest singer for every show. "Bob did more with most of these girls than rehearse their numbers to sing," Desi said, "if you get my drift."

One of the young singers Desi and Hope auditioned was a blonde-haired girl with a good voice named Doris Day. Off-stage, both Desi and Hope went for both her voice and her sexy figure. She rejected their overtures throughout the course of several bookings.

Desi later recalled his encounters with this soon-to-be famous future movie star. "She turned down Bob and me, and only a few other actors got lucky over the years— or so I heard, notably Tyrone Power, Ronald Reagan, and Jack Carson."

With her film career stalled, Lucille took to the stage with a touring company. Two months after *Her Husband's Affairs* was wrapped, she toured in **Dream Girl,** the play by Elmer Rice.

For six months, she played to packed houses. But once she, with her troupe, reached California, disaster set in.

"I was shocked to hear rumors over the years that she sometimes preferred black men," Desi claimed. "Romantic rumors swirled around her about a black basketball player for the LA Lakers and also about Rock Singer Sly of *Sly and the Family Stone*. Maybe the rumors rose because her German father eventually married a black woman. At any rate, I never scored, perhaps because I am brown, not black."

Ross Hunter, the producer, once said of Doris: "No one realized that under those dirndls lurked one of the hottest asses in Hollywood."

"You certainly couldn't prove that by me," Desi lamented.

In recalling his time working with Hope on his radio shows, Desi said, "Hope always came out on stage swishing from side to side and acting like a fag. I can assure you he was anything but. Jack Benny also acted like a fag, and in his case, I think it was true, although he lived deep in the closet."

"Instead of being a swish," Desi continued, "Bob Hope was the ultimate womanizer, like Frank Sinatra. They shared the favors of that blonde actress, Marilyn Maxwell. Bob was hopping her so often she became known in Hollywood as 'Mrs. Bob Hope.'"

Richard Zoglin, in his biography of Hope, wrote: "He had affairs with chorus girls, beauty queens, singers, and showbiz wannabees, even into his early eighties."

Sometimes, he was widely known to seduce a movie star, too: Rhonda Fleming, Betty Hutton, Dorothy Lamour, and Paulette Goddard.

On most occasions, Desi worked smoothly with Hope. On the few times he didn't follow his instructions, Desi was bombarded with denunciations. He heard himself called, "You dumb Cuban Spic!", "You stupid shit!", "You goddamned bastard!", "You bigtime fuck-up!", and "You sonofabitch!".

***

While Desi was touring with his band, June Havoc came to stay with Lucille at Desilu Ranch, occupying the guest house that Desi had built near the rear of their home. Lucille later wrote that she found Havoc, "Bright, warm, and fun-loving." The sister of stripper Gypsy Rose Lee provided company for her.

Born in British Columbia, Havoc was a vivacious blonde, star of stage and screen, who had emigrated to the United States.

She'd gotten her start in vaudeville. She had just finished her role in the Oscar-winning *Gentleman's Agreement* (1947) with Gregory Peck.

Her biggest Broadway hit had been in the Rodgers and Hart musical, *Pal Joey.*

Later in life, she was immortalized as the real-life model for "Baby June" in the hit musical *Gypsy.*

With no film roles offered for Lucille, Havoc found her going "stir-crazy" and suggested that she take to the stage. Havoc had heard that producer Herbert Kenwith was mounting a revival of the Elmer Rice play, *Dream Girl,* which had been a hit on Broadway in the 1945-46 season.

Rice had written it as a showcase for his actress wife, Betty Field. Havoc later took over the role.

A political activist, Rice, a New Yorker, had won the Pulitzer Prize for Drama in 1929 for *Street Scene,* a realistic play about life in the slums. In the late 1930s, he had been hailed as the "Boy Wonder" of Broadway, although not all of his plays were financially successful.

In 1942, he'd married Field, a Bostonian, who had begun her stage life at the age of fifteen. Early in her career, many Hollywood insiders had ruled her out as movie star material, claiming, "She's not pretty enough and her mouth is too large."

She got good notices, however, when she starred in the film, *Of Mice and Men* (1939). She was later cast in *Kings Row* (1942), Ronald Reagan's only "prestige film."

As it turned out, Field ended up starring in several film classics, including *The Great Gatsby* (1949) with Alan Ladd; *Picnic* (1955) with William Holden; *Bus Stop* (1956) with Marilyn Monroe; and *BUtterfield 8* (1960) for which Elizabeth Taylor carried home an Oscar.

Lucille had seen Field on Broadway in *Dream Girl* but had not viewed Havoc in the same role.

The producer of the stage version of *Dream Girl,* Herbert Kenwith, was recasting the play, and a meeting with Lucille was arranged. He had originally wanted to cast the actress Martha Scott as its female lead. She had achieved some acclaim when she'd starred in Thornton Wilder's *Our Town* in 1938, but her film career never took off. In any event, she had another commitment and was not available.

Kenwith then focused on Lucille. He found her "really terrified by the idea of going on the stage as part of a road tour." But eventually, she accepted the role. It premiered at a theater in Princeton, New Jersey to good reviews. Lucille was hailed for her portrayal of a Walter Mitty-esque female, who spends most of her time lost in a world of fantasy and daydreams.

She then embarked with it on a twenty-two city tour of the provinces, for which she was paid $2,000 a week, her fellow cast members getting much less. She played the big cities and the remote, small towns where audiences were sometimes sparse.

Lucille was not by herself on those long and sometimes lonely nights away from home. Just as Desi developed a knack for cooperative companions on the road, she found momentary comfort in the arms of a young actor from Iowa, Scott McKay.

He had immediately captured Lucille's attention. Their romance followed their first dinner together on the road. News of their liaison quickly spread and was gossiped about by other members of the cast.

As the play toured, continuing late into 1947, McKay remained married to his first wife, Margaret Spickers. After producing two sons, they divorced in 1950. In June of 1966, he married a famous movie star, Ann Sheridan, but she died in January of 1967.

McKay is almost unknown today, but during his heyday beginning in 1939, he starred in almost three dozen featured roles on Broadway. His talent ranged from light comedy to drama in such roles as Garson Kanin's *Born Yesterday* or John Van Druten's *Bell, Book, and Candle*. He also had screen appearances in such movies as *Duel in the Sun* (1946) with Gregory Peck and Jennifer Jones, and *Thirty Seconds Over Tokyo* (1944) with Spencer Tracy.

At the end of her months-long fling with McKay, Lucille, as she told Peter Lawford, kissed him with the promise heard by parting lovers around the world: "Someday we may meet again."

She recalled the tour as "one of the ordeals of my life, always on the move. You can't really be an actress until you've broken into show biz on this trail of one-night stands. I truly came to sympathize with Desi, who also ended up in towns no one had ever heard of."

Disaster set in when the cast of *The Dream Girl* got booked in Seattle over the Christmas holiday. A mysterious virus attacked a lot of the members of the cast and crew, and the show shut down.

Lucille, however, was determined to nurse the show through for its scheduled opening in Los Angeles, where she hoped that producers would see her and cast her in movies scheduled for production in 1948.

She even paid the hospital bills for some of the crew until they recovered. Most of them were able to function on opening night, January 8, 1948, at the Biltmore Theater in Los Angeles. According to Lucille, "I wanted to prove to Tinseltown what a great *comedienne* I was."

She opened to rave reviews. For the *Los Angeles Times*, Edwin Schallert wrote: "Here is a young lady of the films who could, if she would, have a dazzling footlight career. And what is more—though this may be a brash statement to make—she is, in a sense, wasting her talent in pictures. Miss Ball is a striking presence in the footlight world. She has efficiency as a comedienne. She has a special facility in dealing with sharp-edged repartée."

Regrettably, after only four performances, Lucille, too, came down with a case of the flu and was almost in a daze, struggling to get through a performance. Minutes after the curtain fell, she was rushed to the hospital.

The show soon closed because not many wanted to see the play with her understudy.

From the beginning, she knew she would probably never star in the film adaptation of *Dream Girl* (1948), since Paramount had bought the screen rights with the clear intention of starring Betty Hutton.

Months later, Lucille attended *Dream Girl* at a movie theater in Los Angeles. Then, about two weeks later, she chatted with Hutton at a party.

"*Dream Girl* was a stinker," Hutton confessed. "I was miscast. I think it's the beginning of the end of my film career. Critics said I was a dud as the poor little millionaire's daughter who goes wandering in cuckoo-land. One reporter called me 'dreadfully artificial.' You were lucky you didn't get the movie role."

Against her expectations, the applause she'd received for *Dream Girl* paid off for Lucille. Soon, CBS contacted her about making a pilot for a situation comedy on radio.

She told Havoc and others, "I'm probably on my last legs as a movie star now that I'm almost forty, but maybe I'll be a big deal on radio."

Little did she know it at the time, and it was beyond her wildest dreams, but a seed had been planted.

From that radio seed a television career would loom for herself and Desi. They were destined to become two of the most famous entertainers in the world.

CHAPTER TWELVE

THE DECLINE OF HOLLYWOOD & THE LAUNCH OF DESILU PRODUCTIONS

LES PLUS BEAUX FILMS DU MONDE
DANS LE PLUS BEAU CADRE DU MONDE

In 1946, the year after the United States and its Allies won World War II, Hollywood had its biggest financial year to that point in history. Seeking entertainment, millions of men and women returned from overseas and flooded local movie houses, perhaps as an escape from too much death and destruction. When they weren't at the movies, hundreds of thousands of ex- soldiers spent time "making babies." The birth rate increased and new generations of what were later defined as "Baby Boomers" were launched, altering the demographics of America forever.

America was rapidly reinventing itself and so was Hollywood. Stars who had been box office sensations in the 1930s faded into oblivion. Others who enjoyed acclaim during the war years experienced a decline at the box office as new stars rose to take their place.

Seismic changes were afoot. The powerful movie moguls of yesterday had either died or been ousted from their pinnacles of power. They included Louis B. Mayer, soon to be toppled from the lofty heights at Metro. At RKO, the eccentric billionaire, Howard Hughes, took over and quickly developed a reputation for cutting costs and for seducing many of its stars and starlets, both male and

It was 1946: World War II was over, but to some soothsayers in Hollywood,—as symbolized by that year's debut of the **Film Festival at Cannes**—the International Film Wars and the decline of old-time Hollywood had begun.

European stars like Brigitte Bardot and Michele Morgan were about to change the way hip Americans interpreted the movies, To some, it seemed like a death knell for the feelgood fluff that had distracted American audiences throughout the course of the war. Change was about to blow apart America's entertainment industry, and television was on its way.

Smart insiders like Lucy and Desi heard the call.

female. And in 1948, D.W. Griffith, the filmmaking giant who had directed *Birth of a Nation* (1915), died in poverty. He had once been the most famous director in Hollywood.

The changes made Lucille—who had never become the superstar she'd envisioned—even more desperate to hold onto her career. In the latter part of the tumultuous 1940s, she drifted from studio to studio, picking up gigs from United Artists, Paramount, and Columbia, her roles ranging from *film noir* to screwball comedies evocative of the ones Carole Lombard had "perfected" in the 1930s.

Desi was either on the road touring or "absent" from home much of the time.

As Lucille's youth faded and as she drifted toward middle age, she took on a series of lovers, many of whom had returned from the battlefields and were rising as leading men in film. But whereas her lovers could be "inventoried" on her ten fingers, those of her wandering and very promiscuous husband numbered in the dozens, often a different partner every night.

Within a period of only two or three years, the box office bonanza sparked by the events of 1945 faded and sputtered. Trouble was on the way. Domestic box office sales fell off by at least twenty percent. At first, the common wisdom blamed falling movie sales on the rise of television, even though it had not yet fully exploded, and America was still years away from seeing a TV set in every living room.

Post-war housing and fast-rising rates of inflation ate into every family budget, and the cost of entertainment was often the first to be cut.

In response, studios like Paramount and MGM slashed contract players from their payrolls. Many box office matinee idols of yesterday never surpassed their fame of the 1930s. Most of those who had fought overseas had had to temporarily disappear from the screen. They included James Stewart, Tyrone Power, and Robert Taylor. Betty Grable, the pin-up Queen of World, fell off in popularity, as did Veronica Lake. The love goddess, Rita Hayworth, star of that box office smash, *Gilda* (1946), disappeared from the screen during the course of her marriage (1949-1953) to Prince Aly Khan.

During the bleak years in the U.K. that followed the war, forty percent of Hollywood's profits came from American films shown in British movie houses. Then, as England struggled with massive budget deficits and no longer had millions to send west to Hollywood, the government slapped a 75 percent tax on foreign movies, something that soured Hollywood revenues even further.

Complicating matters even more, a witch hunt to punish "commies" in the film industry, had been launched in Hollywood by the House Un-American Activities Committee. Eventually, it destroyed the careers of many of its greatest actors and writers. Although Lucille would survive her half-hearted tenure as a Communist Party member in the 1930s, most others did not.

In addition to actors indelibly tainted either "red" or "pink," Hollywood also lost many of its finest directors and producers, many of whom fled abroad.

One film project after another fell through for Lucille and, to a lesser degree, for Desi. They included her failure to win a role she coveted in the film adaptation of the Broadway play, *Born Yesterday*, by Garson Kanin.

It had opened at the Lyceum Theatre on Broadway in 1946, and from what she'd heard about it, Lucille felt compelled to see it during one of her postwar trips to New York. She immediately sensed that the "adapted for film" role of Billie Dawn, would be ideal for her. Billie is the showgirl mistress of an uncouth but rich junk dealer in Washington (DC).

Knowing how dumb "my broad" is, he hires a journalist, Paul Verrall, to tutor her. The student and her teacher soon fall in love, as might have been predicted. The play starred Judy Holliday, Paul Douglas, and William Holden.

Harry Cohn bought its screen rights for Columbia, at first viewing it as a vehicle for his former box office champion, Rita Hayworth. But at this point in their (toxic) relationship, he and Hayworth were feuding, and he considered other actresses—including Gloria Grahame, Jean Arthur, Lana Turner, and Barbara Stanwyck—for the role. At one point, he even considered bringing Alice Faye out of retirement to play Billie. He finally gave the role to Holliday, who won the Best Actress Oscar for the way she'd played it.

Lucille phoned Cohn and pitched herself as the "only star in Hollywood who knew how to play Billie, even in my toenails."

He rejected her, although he did tell her that he'd liked her work

prediction:

After you've seen "Born Yesterday", your favorite new star will be Judy Holliday

COLUMBIA PICTURES

BORN YESTERDAY

starring

JUDY HOLLIDAY · WILLIAM HOLDEN · BRODERICK CRAWFORD

BROADWAY'S BIGGEST HIT...NOW A PERFECTLY SWELL MOTION PICTURE!

During the course of her long and eventful movie career, Lucille lost out on some roles she really wanted.

The one she felt she was "destined to play" was the part of Billie Dawn, the wise and very smart "dumb blonde" in *Born Yesterday*.

Instead of Lucille, **Judy Holliday** walked off with the coveted part, which netted her an Oscar in 1950.

The competition for the Best Actress Award that year was among the most fraught, tense, and memorable in the history of the Academy.

Holliday beat out Gloria Swanson in *Sunset Blvd.*, and both Bette Davis and Anne Baxter for their performances in *All About Eve*.

385

in *Her Husband's Affairs* with Franchot Tone, and that he might offer her some other comedic roles in the near future.

"I won't hold my breath," she said, sarcastically.

Already disappointed, she became depressed when *Variety* reported that the leading male roles for the film adaptation of *Born Yesterday* had been assigned to Broderick Crawford, her former lover, and to William Holden, her all-time dream man.

Before the end of 1948, Columbia did send her a script called *Pink Lady.* At first, Lucille wanted to make sure she was not going to be cast as a communist. *[Pink Lady, after all, might have been a reference to "pinko," a pejorative word for a communist. Executives at Columbia assured her that that was not the case, pink referring to the only color the heroine wore.]*

That film deal fell through.

Back on Broadway, the Shubert Brothers were considering inviting both Lucille and Desi to co-star as the leads in a musical, *Casa McClusky,* but neither of them was ever satisfied with the script rewrites.

On another front, the radio writers for Jack Benny wanted to tailor-make a possible musical for Desi and Lucille, *Hey Señorita.* It would contain comic bits for Lucille and renditions of Latin music by Desi. But that deal, too, fell apart.

The celebrated roving photographer, Robert Capa, had recently published his autobiography, and a producer thought Desi might be suitable to portray him in its film adaptation. Capa's astonished response? "Desi Arnaz? Play me? You've gotta be kidding!"

***

Although still seeking work, Lucille rejected the lead role in *Our Miss Brooks,* a radio show revolving around the misadventures of a sardonic high school English teacher. Connie Brooks, at the

As it related to **Eve Arden**, star of *Our Miss Brooks* (a gig that Lucille, to her regret, rejected), the old adage, "Men don't make passes at girls who wear glasses" never applied.

As it happened, a LOT of Americans really did want to make passes at the mythical high school teacher (Arden) who became an icon of America in the 1950s.

SGOOD CONKLIN

READY
WILLING
ABLE

Our Miss Brooks needed a fuss-budget counterpart to make the humor work. The actor the producers selected for the character of the easily frustrated high school principal of Madison High (the blustering boss that Eve Arden had to "outsmart") was Osgood Conklin (played by **Gale Gordon**).

He later became a standard fixture in Lucille's later sitcoms.

(fictional) Madison High School. In reference to her rejection, Lucille told CBS, "No one would believe me as a high school English teacher. Come on, boys."

Our Miss Brooks was a hit. As a radio series, it aired from 1948 to 1957, and as a televised spin-off (1952-1956) it became one of the most watched shows on TV.

The role of Miss Brooks went to Eve Arden, with whom Lucille had appeared in *Stage Door* (1937) and *Having Wonderful Time* (1938). Both Arden and Lucille, though rivals, maintained a casual friendship.

Our Miss Brooks featured character actor Gale Gordon, who would also become known for his appearances later on TV with Lucille.

Opposite Arden, he played the blustery, gruff, and unsympathetic principal of Madison High.

Lucille always regretted that she never got to play the role. When she heard the first radio episode, she knew she could indeed have played the high school teacher as well as Arden did. But by then, she had already committed to another radio series, *My Favorite Husband.*

***

Variety, in early January of 1948, announced that Bob Hope's next picture would be *Sorrowful Jones.* His co-star would be the beautiful redhead, Rhonda Fleming, the "Queen of Technicolor."

Hope, a then-reigning box office champ, had power over casting. He demanded Lucille for the role, having admired her talent during the times she had appeared with him on radio.

This would be her first screen appearance with him. Eventually, it evolved into such a successful blending of talent that she'd later be cast in future pictures with him.

[Sorrowful Jones *would mark Lucille's second time in a Damon Runyon story, the first having been* The Big Street *(1942) in which she had co-starred with Henry Fonda.*]

This latest version was a remake of the 1934 movie, *Little Miss Marker,* that had

Although audiences of 1946 lapped up the barely concealed references to **Lucille** as a potential matriarch, Lucille interpreted her association with motherhood as a dangerous (for an actress) sign of her advancing age.

She's depicted here with **Bob Hope** and a substitute for Shirley Temple in Paramount's "feelgood movie of the minute," *Sorrowful Jones.*

The "glue" that fed the plot line was **Mary Jane Saunders.** She closely evoked Shirley Temple in the roughly equivalent 1934 film, *Little Miss Marker.*

Lucille enjoyed working with Bob Hope in *Sorrowful Jones,* and the comedic duo would repeat their roles on radio in the popular Lux Radio Theatre in 1949.

brought major stardom to child star Shirley Temple. The film, in which she co-starred with Adolphe Menjou, was crucial in making the moppet a box office champion in the late 1930s.

Director Sidney Lanfield—well-known for helming romances and light comedies— skillfully guided Hope and Lucille through their antics. He had worked with Hope before on such pictures as *My Favorite Blonde* (1942).

The plot, based on a short story by Damon Runyon, Sorrowful Jones is a penny-pinching New York bookie who runs an illegal gambling operation. A customer leaves his four-year-old daughter with Jones as a "marker" for a bet. To everyone's consternation, he doesn't return, *[It's later revealed that he didn't run off and abandon his child, but that he was murdered.]* Hope soon finds the little girl interfering with his free-wheeling lifestyle.

Lucille was cast as Gladys O'Neill, the gambler's old flame, who becomes like a surrogate mother to the girl. In her portrayal of a nightclub singer, her singing voice was dubbed by Annette Warren.

Casting a child actress to play the abandoned girl was hard, since Paramount had to find a suitable replacement for the scene-stealing Temple. The studio conducted a six-month search, interviewing five thousand applicants before deciding on cute little Mary Jane Saunders, born in Pasadena in 1943.

[Saunders would work again with Lucille in an upcoming film, A Woman of Distinction *(1950). Her film career as a child star never really took off, and she ended up marrying athlete Jay Johnstone in 1967. A major league baseball player for nineteen seasons, he helped win the World Series for the New York Yankees in 1978 and for the Los Angeles Dodgers in 1981.]*

Rough, tough **Bruce Cabot** had immortalized himself by saving Fay Wray from the clutches of *King Kong* in 1932.

In *Sorrowful Jones*, he had a less attractive role. He plays crooked "Big Steve," who likes to rig horse races in favor of the local bookies. He also murders the father of Mary Jane Saunders.

As a hard-partying sidekick to swashbuckling Errol Flynn, Cabot was always trying to get Lucille to attend one of their orgies.

She always declined, telling him, "I prefer to have sex with just one man, alone in a bedroom, with no one watching."

The villain of the Hope film was rugged actor Bruce Cabot, a close friend of Errol Flynn. He was cast as "Big Steve," the gangster who had murdered the little girl's father.

Cabot had first flirted with Lucille in 1934 when he'd had the starring role in *Men of the Night*. On the set, he invited Lucille to join him on a trip to Palm Springs where John Wayne was having a house party. "The Duke is my good buddy ever since we made *Angel and the Badman* (1947)."

Lucille turned down his invitation but told him, "It sure sounds tempting. After all these years, I still find you very sexy."

A minor role in *Sorrowful Jones* had been assigned to the character actor

William Demarest, who had known Lucille since 1937 when they'd worked together on *Don't Tell the Wife* (1937).

Variety, in its review of *Sorrowful Jones,* wrote, "Lucille Ball was a slick choice for the female lead, interpreting Runyon's idea of a Broadway doll with considerable skill to make her entirely believable." *The New York Times* claimed, "Lucille Ball is a girl who knows her small place and keeps it as the night club singing queen."

The *New York Herald Tribune* found that she was a fine foil for Hope, "building up bits of business to a point where they are comically consequential, even though they had next to nothing to do with the plot."

"Of course I could play a damn gun moll," Lucille said after reading the reviews. "During my days with George Raft and his cronies, I *was* a gun moll."

Sorrowful Jones would be remade with its original title of *Little Miss Marker* in 1950 by Walter Matthau, Julie Andrews, and Tony Curtis. It would be remade once again in 1962 as *40 Pounds of Trouble* with Curtis as the gambler who ends up as the surrogate father to the little girl.

***

The Golden Age of Radio was nearing its end when Lucille tackled the medium, which would soon be engulfed by the newly emerged form of entertainment known as television. Happily married couples had become a standard theme for radio series, as exemplified by Jack Benny and Mary Livingston, or by Gracie Allen and George Burns.

In 1947, Hubbell Robinson had become vice president of CBS in charge of programs. He phoned Lucille's agent and set up a meeting with her in his office.

He told her that CBS Radio was considering the launching of a (radio) series called *My Favorite Husband.* It would be based on the best-selling book of 1941, *Mr. and Mrs. Cugat, the Record of a Happy Marriage,* a saga about a young bank executive and his slightly zany wife.

The author of the book it was based on, Isabel Scott Rorick, had in addition to its radio rights also sold its film rights to Paramount for a movie adaptation entitled *Are Husbands Necessary?* (1942), co-starring Ray Milland and Betty Field.

Lucille said she'd be interested in a role in the radio series but only if Desi could play her husband. Robinson rejected the idea: "Who would believe Arnaz as a bank executive? Also, who's going to believe he's married to you, a Yankee redhead?"

But I *AM* married to him," she protested. "Couldn't the plot be written to make him a Cuban bandleader?"

"No, it cannot," he said. "We've paid Rorick good money for her story, and it was a hit with the public. We've assigned Lee Bowman to star as the husband in the radio series, and we're getting ready to record a pilot. From what I hear, you and Bowman have not only appeared together on film before, but you two had an affair."

"I will neither confirm or deny that," she said.

389

Since she needed the money, she agreed to record the pilot with Bowman, and it went over with CBS executives, who agreed to turn it into a radio series.

When it came time to launch the series, Bowman had other commitments. In the aftermath of that, CBS cast actor Richard Denning as the tall, handsome blonde husband, who resembled a bank executive. Lucille was cast as his (zany) wife. At first, their characters were named George and Liz Cugat (as established in Rorick's novel). Later, to avoid associations with bandleader Xavier Cugat, their names were changed to Mr. and Mrs. Cooper.

Lucille was unfamiliar with Denning's career, but soon learned a lot about him. His father had urged him to join his family's garment business, but his son wanted to be an actor. His career was postponed after his enlistment in the U.S. Navy during World War II, during which he served in a submarine.

Lucille Ball with **Richard Denning** during a recording session of their radio program, *My Favorite Husband*.

They were billed as "Liz and George Cooper, two people who live together and like it."

Problems that arose from Liz's most recent zany idea would always be (happily) resolved before the end of each broadcast.

Before working with Lucille, he had appeared in *Unknown Island* (1948). He'd follow that in the 1950s with a string of sci-fi movies, including *Creature from the Black Lagoon* (1954). His role with Lucille would lead him to win the star part (he played it from 1952-53) in CBS's ongoing hit TV detective series, *Mr. and Mrs. North*.

Although she found him handsome, charming, and happily married, she harbored a small resentment of him since she had wanted Desi for the role.

As a happy couple, George and Liz live on 321 Bundy Drive in the fictitious town of Sheridan Falls. They were billed as "two people who live together and like it." Each episode ended with Liz saying, "Thanks, George, you're my favorite husband." The sponsors were Jello-O (that family of desserts), and she had to hawk the gelatin treat herself during advertising breaks.

As the scatter-brained wife, Lucille, without knowing it, was in rehearsal for the TV role that would immortalize her as Lucy Ricardo on *I Love Lucy*.

She and Denning would be on CBS Radio together from July 23, 1948 to March 31, 1951.

In 1942, Denning had married Evelyn Ankers, known as "The Hollywood Horror Queen," because

Bea Benaderet, playing it "zany" and defining, early, the mapcap context of what later evolved, with a different actress, into the character of Ethel Mertz.

of her roles in such pictures as *The Wolf Man, Ghost of Frankenstein,* and *Son of Dracula.*

Ankers retired from films after her marriage to Denning, which made her free to accompany him to recording sessions of his radio show with Lucille.

According to Ankers, "My husband is a gorgeous hunk of man and is highly desirable to women. Miss Ball has a reputation for sleeping with some of her leading men in films, and I want to make sure she does not exercise boudoir rights to my husband. I'm going to see that she does not get her red-painted nails wrapped around Dick's dick, if you'll forgive my vulgarity. I'm showing up for every one of the broadcasts."

In *My Favorite Husband,* George's boss at the bank was first played by Hans Conried, later by Joseph Kearns, and finally by Gale Gordon. He would later repeat the role of bank president in future comedic series with Lucille on TV.

Gordon's wife on *My Favorite Husband* was played by Bea Benaderet. She and Gordon were the Atterburys on the show. Both of them would later be given first consideration for the roles of Fred and Ethel Mertz on *I Love Lucy.* They would have signed for the roles had they not had career conflicts. Both of them would forever regret having to turn down those choice and highly profitable parts for involvement in other projects.

Lucille and Benaderet became good friends. Her acting career would span three decades, as she worked with such artists as Jack Benny or Burns and Allen. She later became a familiar face on TV, appearing in such hits as *The Beverly Hillbillies, The Flintstones,* and in the role of Kate Bradley in *Petticoat Junction.*

At Warner Brothers, she was the leading voice of female characters in its series of animated cartoons in the 1940s and early '50s. She did get to make an appearance on *I Love Lucy,* showing up in 1952 in an episode entitled "Lucy Plays Cupid," in which Benaderet was cast as Lucille's neighbor, Miss Lewis, a love-starved spinster.

The original scriptwriters for *My Favorite Husband* were Bill Davenport and Frank Fox, each of them known in radio circles for their work on the scripts of another hit TV series, *Ozzie and Harriet.*

They were later replaced by Bob Carroll Jr. and Madelyn Pugh, who had once dated before moving on to other romantic involvements.

They formed a writing team that pleased most executives at CBS, and they were later joined by Jess Oppenheimer, who also became the producer, his paycheck raised $100 a week for taking on that added burden.

Right from the beginning, Oppenheimer had been told that Lucille "might suddenly be transformed into a 'Dr. Jekyll and Mrs. Hyde' creature of rage."

When he'd presented Lucille with the first script he'd written, it was read aloud, and every now and then, she burst into laughter. However, when the final line of the script was read, she flew into hysterics. "I hate that god damn line," she shouted at him. "I won't do it!" Then she rose from her chair, ripped her copy of the script into pieces, and ran off the set.

Oppenheimer chased after her. He was finally able to subdue her with a promise that he'd rewrite the line. After that initial outburst, she apologized and, although they would have their differences in the future, it rarely exploded after that into violence or denunciations.

In fact, in a short time, she referred to him as "The Brains" of her hit TV series, *I Love Lucy*.

Before working with her, he'd been a comedy writer for Fred Astaire and a radio gag writer for Jack Benny. He'd also written the popular radio program, *Baby Snooks*. It starred Fanny Brice playing a little girl wise beyond her years who was always driving her daddy crazy. He also wrote sketches for Bing Crosby, Marlene Dietrich, Judy Garland, Bob Hope, and Ginger Rogers.

When the *I Love Lucy* TV series was greenlighted, Bob Carroll and Madelyn Pugh joined Oppenheimer as its chief writers. Pugh's writing partnership with Carroll would last for five decades, as together, they created 400 television programs and roughly 500 radio shows. As a team, they wrote for *The Steve Allen Show*. They also created a vaudeville act for Lucille and Desi to take on the road. It eventually formed the basis for the pilot episode of *I Love Lucy*.

Carroll's brother-in-law had helped him get a job at CBS, where first he worked in the publicity department before moving on to writing assignments. But it was only when teamed with Pugh that his writing career burst into bloom. The duo would still be writing for Lucille as late as 1986 in her final sitcom, *Life With Lucy*.

She claimed, "I loved working in radio. It's a great way to make a lot of money, and I don't have to memorize the script like in a feature film but can read it on air. I found out I do better in front of a live audience."

Eventually, the copyright expired on the radio episodes of *My Favorite Husband*. The series is now in the public domain.

***

In reference materials devoted to sexual liaisons in the entertainment industry, including in books written by Mart Martin, Lucille Ball is often linked to Peter Lawford.

In his biography, *Lucy and Desi*, Warren G. Harris wrote: "To get back at Desi, Lucy started going out on public dates with other men, usually younger actors from MGM like Peter Lawford and Scott McKay. Each of them at different times was seen escorting her to such popular spots as Ciro's or Cocoanut Grove."

She never spoke publicly about her affair with Lawford, although she sometimes discussed it with her longtime confidant Barbara Pepper.

"I agree with George Cukor," she confessed. "Peter is a lousy lay, strictly oral. Where is Desi when I need him?"

For an actor who allegedly was such a lousy lay, Lawford seduced a number of world class beauties and movie stars: June Allyson, Anne Baxter, Dorothy Dandridge, Ava Gardner, Judy Garland, Rita Hayworth, Rhonda Fleming, Janet Leigh, Marilyn Maxwell, Lana Turner, Kim Novak, Jane Wyman, and most definitely, Nancy Davis (later, Reagan). Davis and

Lawford were part of a *ménage à trois* with Robert Walker, once married to actress Jennifer Jones. Lawford was also a key player in the life of Marilyn Monroe, to whom he became scandalously linked, especially at the time of her murder by the mob.

To his list of Lawford's male lovers could be added Noël Coward, Tom Drake (Judy Garland's "Boy Next Door" in *Meet Me in St. Louis*), Robert Taylor, Van Johnson, Keenan Wynn, Sal Mineo, Clifton Webb, Roddy McDowall, and TV host Merv Griffin.

Martin added a postscript to his list of who managed to get "down and dirty" with Lawford: "Plus lots of college girls, starlets, beach bunnies he met while surfing, prostitutes who knew him as a $50 oral sex trick, call boys, male hustlers, young male extras at MGM, and studio messenger boys." Lawford was also known to several grips and MGM cameramen, but only the studly, good-looking ones.

Lawford's formidable, mean-spirited mother, Lady May Lawford—who aptly entitled her memoir as *Bitch*—once visited her son's boss, Louis B. Mayer, head of MGM, and asked his help in getting "treatment" for her son to "cure" him of his homosexuality. Lawford never forgave his mother for that betrayal.

At the debut of his dating relationship with Lucille, Lawford was going out with June Allyson, with whom he'd co-starred in *Good News* (1947). He was also seeing a lot of Elizabeth Taylor. *[In 1949, all three of them—Allyson, Taylor, and Lawford—would appear together in* Little Women.*]*

Lawford was close-lipped around members of the press, but rather confessional whenever he was with Lucille—especially when he realized that she thrived on insider Hollywood gossip. He told her many tantalizing tales about the private lives of many of her actor colleagues, some of whom she knew only casually.

"Many female stars went for me," Lawford later confessed. "Women like Jennifer Jones. Some of my male co-stars dug me too."

Two views of the British actor **Peter Lawford**.

In the upper photo, he co-stars with **Esther Williams** in *On an Island with You* (1948).

The lower photo shows him after his wedding in 1954 to the future president John F. Kennedy's sister, **Patricia.** The marriage lasted twelve years, produced four children, and elevated Lawford to a position close to JFK, for whom he pimped multiple sex partners including Marilyn Monroe.

Lawford's list of seductions, both male and female, was among the most random and arbitrary in Tinseltown.

He liked "beach bunnies" he met while surfing, and hustlers he paid during "quickies" in the men's toilet of local parks.

"Name names!" Lucille demanded.

"Would you believe Fred Astaire or Walter Pidgeon?"

He sometimes discussed his experiences in the late 1930s in Hollywood. A talent scout spotted him and got him cast as a minor player in *Lord Jeff* (1938) starring Freddie Bartholomew. "Freddie was hot for Judy Garland but also for me," Lawford told Lucille. "I agreed to a night with Freddie, but he spent all his time in bed sucking my toes, never going farther north than that."

She quickly learned that Lawford did not have the complete use of his right arm, a disability that he carefully concealed from cameras. When he was a teenager, he smashed it into a glass door, and a jagged shard had sliced through his forearm and hand, slitting muscles and tendons and severing an artery. He nearly bled to death.

"Some good came out of that," he claimed. "It kept me out of military service and allowed me to get good roles in the '40s that might have gone to other actors who were in the service. By 1946, I was voted most popular actor in Hollywood — imagine that."

When Lucille dated Lawford, she was married but he was not. It wasn't until 1954 that he wed Patricia Kennedy, the sister of then-Senator John F. Kennedy. By doing so, Patricia infuriated her father, Joseph Kennedy. "Don't tell me you're going to bring that Hollywood fag to our home?"

Lucille never knew if Patricia learned about her affair with her husband. In 1963, the Lawfords (Peter and Patricia) were photographed visiting Lucille on the set of *Critic's Choice,* a movie in which she co-starred with Bob Hope. Patricia would divorce Lawford in 1966.

Over the years, Lucille encountered Lawford at Hollywood parties, as she did again in 1976 when he was married to his third wife, aspiring actress Deborah Gould.

"Deborah wanted to go with me to New York, but I left her behind," he said. "Then this dreadful thing happened once I hit Manhattan. I took up with a coven of male friends. All of them turned out to be into necrophilia. I figured these guys wanted to seduce me, but if the seduction took place, they'd have to kill me first. I fled the scene."

[That revelation appeared in 1992 in James Spada's biography of Lawford.]

***

After Lucille's "homecoming" to RKO for the filming of her next picture, *Easy Living* (1949), she was disappointed to learn that her leading man once again would be "The Muscleman Actor," Victor Mature. They had feuded during the making of *Seven Days' Leave* (1942), a mid-war movie in which he played a cocky soldier.

She remembered that he carried that cockiness off-screen when he sexually assaulted her, feeling her up. Once, in a kissing scene, he bit her lip really hard. She eventually learned that he was angry that the studio hadn't cast his off-screen love interest of the moment, Rita Hayworth, into Lucille's role.

Years had passed, and much had happened in Mature's life since then.

Hayworth was now a distant memory. He had divorced his second wife, Martha Stephenson Kemp, the widow of bandleader Hal Kemp, and had married, in 1948, Dorothy Stanford Berry, shortly before working with Lucille again. But even so recent a marriage did not keep Romeo from straying at every opportunity.

RKO was not the same place she'd left years ago. It had been purchased by the aviator and business mogul, Howard Hughes, who had fired about three-fourths of the staff. Then, in a cost-cutting binge, he had dropped several pictures, not only in pre-production but some that were in the process of being filmed.

The script of Lucille's latest picture had originally been titled *Interference*, a name that was later changed to *Easy Living* before filming began in July of 1948.

It was the story of a football hero whose career is fading because of a failing heart. Its plot had been inspired by *Education of the Heart* by the noted writer, Irwin Shaw. Charles Schnee wrote the screenplay for producer Robert Sparks and director Jacques Tourneur.

Lucille was told that real-life football players from the Los Angeles Rams had been hired for verisimilitude.

Variety had first announced that the film would be made with RKO contract players, Robert Mitchum and Jane Greer, but a cast change was made shortly before shooting began.

Lucille returned to RKO to make *Easy Living* with **Victor Mature**.

She had feuded with him when they'd co-starred in Seven Days' Leave, but she found him a changed man. He was far more appealing to her in his role of the fallen football hero Pete Wilson.

"I'm in love with him in the movie, but he goes back home to his wife, played by **Lizabeth Scott** (left). She was a dyke and hated having to do love scenes with Vic."

Although at the time, Mature was under contract to Fox, he still owed RKO one final picture, which he had not made because when war broke out, he had enlisted as a member of the armed services. He had tried to join the U.S. Navy, but was rejected when a test revealed him to be color-blind. The Coast Guard, however, accepted him and as such, he spent months aboard a ship stationed off the coast of Greenland, probing coastlines and ferreting out Nazi submarines.

Back in America, he'd performed in a series of War Bond tours and acted in morale-building plays for the service-men. His final work for the Coast Guard came in May of 1945 after V-E Day in Europe. He was assigned to a transport group carrying American soldiers aboard the USS *Admiral H.T. Mayo* to the final fighting against the Japanese in the Pacific Theater.

After the war, he'd resumed his career as a movie star appearing in such hits as the John Ford Western, *My Darling Clementine* (1946). In it, he played Doc Holliday opposite Henry Fonda's Wyatt Earp.

Lucille did not like her role in *Easy Living* as a secretary, Anne, to Lloyd Nolan, the team's owner, Coach Lenahan. She and Nolan had worked smoothly together ever since filming *Two Smart People* (1946) with John Hodiak.

Mature played Pete Wilson, the star professional quarterback who has no future in football. *[His doctor had diagnosed him with a diseased heart because of a childhood bout with rheumatic fever.]*

He doesn't want to tell his scheming, money-hungry wife, Liz (Lizbeth Scott), who wants to be a big success as an interior designer, and will go far to achieve her goal, even if it means getting involved with other influential men.

Pete's best friend is Pappy McCarr (Sonny Tufts), who will eventually replace Pete as the team's star football player. As his secretary, Lucille is in love with Pete, but in the end, he returns to his errant wife, who (unconvincingly) promises to mend her ways.

Lucille met with producer Robert Sparks, who was better known as the husband of Penny Singleton, who played "Blondie Bumstead" in a number of "Blondie" movies in the late 1930s and early 1940s. He was one of the early members of the film colony urging Lucille to consider the newly emerging medium of television. In time, he would leave the movie industry al-

In the upper photo, **Lizabeth Scott,** "The Queen of *Film Noir*," co-stars with **Humphrey Bogart** in *Dead Reckoning* (1947). She played a shady dame who hooks up with him.

Bogie told the press, "She was an acceptable choice, but I would have preferred my wife, Lauren Bacall."

In the lower photo, Scott has that sultry look that made her such a feature in *film noir*. Her exposé in *Confidential* as a lesbian seriously harmed her career.

together and join CBS as a producer, developing such superhit TV series as *Gunsmoke* (1955) and *Perry Mason* (1957), among other shows.

A Parisian, Jacques Tourneur, Lucille's director, had helmed the classic film noir, *Out of the Past* (1947) with Robert Mitchum, Jane Greer, and the then-emerging Kirk Douglas. Tourneur's résumé also included the direction of such low-budget horror films as *Cat People, I Walked with a Zombie,* and *The Leopard Man.*

"Like everyone else, I skipped his French name and Anglicized it to "Jack Turner," Lucille said.

In third billing, Liza, the wife of footballer Mature, Lizabeth Scott had a far better role than Lucille's. One critic later called Scott "the most beautiful face of *film noir* to emerge from the late 1940s and early '50s." Lucille had seen only one of her movies, *The Strange Love of Martha Ivers* (1946) in which Scott had co-starred with Kirk Douglas and Barbara Stanwyck.

"Scott made me feel like a relic of the 1930s," Lucille said. "Here I was still impersonating Carole Lombard as the wise-cracking, sexy, self-actualizing type in one of her screwball types."

After the war, a lot of hard-hearted Hannahs were appearing on screens throughout the nation, including that sultry blonde, Gloria Grahame and Ida Lupino, the dime store Bette Davis. Even Lana Turner was no longer the sweet young thing: She was most convincing as the murderess of her husband in *The Postman Always Rings Twice* (1946).

Lucille concealed her jealousy of Scott and had several talks with her during the making of the film. "I'm either praised for my smoky voice or unfavorably compared to Lauren Bacall or a 'baritone babe' like Tallulah Bankhead. Bosley Crowther of *The New York Times* has it in for me," Scott confided.

"I haven't fared well with that son of a bitch either," Lucille said.

Scott had emerged scarred after her filming of *I Walk Alone* (1948), in which she played a torch singer. Crowther had written, "She has no more personality than a model in the window of a department store." She'd soon be shooting *Dark City* (1950) with Charlton Heston. Crowther called her "frighteningly grotesque. She is supposed to be a cabaret singer."

From a distance, Lucille later followed the rest of Scott's career. She was outed as a lesbian in a 1955 exposé in *Confidential,* the reigning scandal magazine of the 1950s.

In 1957, she co-starred with Elvis Presley in *Loving You,* his second movie musical. "The dyke bitch in a kissing scene with me bit my cheek, leaving a big red mark," he said. "I had to face the camera turning my other cheek. It was more than a nibble, and everybody told me she was strictly a dyke."

Scott never went looking for a husband or a male lover. Instead, she patronized a call girl service that supplied shapely starlets.

The last man she was seen in public

In *The Seven Year Itch* (1954), **Marilyn Monroe** posed for a series of iconic photographs with her skirt-blowing up, earning the ire of her husband, Joe DiMaggio.

Actor **Tom Ewell**, her co-star, looks on.

At the time, male fans of Marilyn thought he was one lucky guy. But, in his private life, he preferred male hustlers.

with involved being photographed attending an event on the arm of Michael Jackson.

As the footballer who replaced Mature on the gridiron, Sonny Tufts played Pappy McCarr with a certain gusto, although he was often ridiculed for his mediocre acting skills. A tall, handsome, well-built blonde, he was eagerly sought after by male and female members of the film colony.

He fitted well into the role of Pappy because he had been a player on Yale's football team. He flirted a lot with Lucille during the shoot, but because she was involved with Mature at the time, she did not intercept any of his passes.

Amazingly, Tufts started out in life wanting to be an opera singer before drifting to Hollywood. There, he first achieved recognition playing an affable Marine in *So Proudly We Hail* (1943), co-starring with Paulette Goddard, Veronica Lake, and, the star of the picture, Claudette Colbert. He and Goddard were rumored to have had a fling.

He was labeled the "Find of 1943."

He also starred in another wartime hit, *Here Come the Waves* (1944) with Betty Hutton and Bing Crosby.

Lucille was saddened over the years to witness his decline, as he was arrested and often sued for alleged assaults on women as his heavy drinking grew worse.

In 1977, Tom Ewell was in Key West filming the movie adaptation of Darwin Porter's classic cult novel, *Butterflies in Heat*. There, he claimed that Tuft allowed him to "service" him during their co-starring involvement in the filming of *The Seven Year Itch* (1955).

STEAM HEAT

Gay men took notice: **Sonny Tufts** (left} appears here in a locker room with **Victor Mature** in *Easy Living*.

Jack Paar on his *The Tonight Show* in 1959, interviewing then-Senator **John F. Kennedy.**

Lucille met Paar when he had the minor role of "Scoop Spooner" in *Easy Living*.

Neither of them could have imagined that in time, they'd become virtual legends in the medium of television.

As for JFK, Lucille supported him when he ran for President of the United States the following year.

Tufts never admitted that, however, claiming that off screen he "pounded " the star of the picture, Marilyn Monroe.

His career eventually drifted into oblivion, ending with a role in one of the worst movies ever made, *Cottonpickin' Chickenpickers* (1967), a film promoted at the time as a "gloriously loopy Southern fried comedy-with-music."

Paul Stewart, who had made his film debut in Orson Welles' *Citizen Kane* (1941), appeared in *Easy Living* as a reporter, Dave Argus.

Lucille also met Jack Paar, cast as Scoop Spooner. She had never liked him and was amazed at how he later rose to become a big star on television, especially during his hosting of *The Tonight Show* from 1957 to 1962.

"He was always complaining about 'fairies, dykes, and fags in the entertainment industry,'" Lucille said.

"These pansies and lezzies are also swishing around me...the boys, that is, whereas women look like they should be driving trucks," Paar said.

"I always suspected that it was Paar who was the closeted swish," Lucille said. "He protested too much."

After only a few days of working with Mature, Lucille buried the hatchet and they began spending their free time together. At this stage of his career, he seemed more modest and more self-deprecatory. "I can't help it if I've got a good set of muscles," he said. "But I want to prove I can do more than a male striptease on camera."

Ironically, during the filming of *Easy Living*, word came from Cecil B. De Mille that he wanted to cast Mature in the title role of *Samson and Delilah* (1949). At first, he told Lucille that he was tempted not to accept the role because he would have to "strip down for a muscle show as Samson... But the money is good, and I'll probably take it."

She chided him, "Think about it this way. You'll be starring opposite the face hailed as

Self-enchanted and cosmopolitan: **Hedy Lamarr** in 1941.

It was during her filming of *Ziegfeld Girl* that Lamarr became hailed as the most beautiful woman in the world. Her co-stars were Lana Turner and Judy Garland.

Lamarr's most iconic role lay in her future when she played the title role in *Samson and Delilah* (1949) with Victor Mature.

Ironically, Mature had just spent a sexy, lazy afternoon with Lucille when a phone call came in from Cecil B. De Mille, casting him in it as Samson, his most iconic role.

the world's most beautiful, that Austrian bitch, Hedy Lamarr. Surely you'll want to show this Austrian that you're a better fuck than Hitler or Mussolini."

At one point during filming, Lucille was rather shocked when Mature emerged from his dressing room stark naked. He'd had a grip place a mound of wet cement beside his doorstep, and he squatted down onto it as a durable, long-lasting showcase of his bare buttocks. To him, at least, it was a sign of protest (and contempt) for not having been asked to imprint his hands and feet outside Grauman's Chinese Theater in Hollywood, as so many other stars had already done.

Later, when Lucille went to see *Samson and Delilah,* she chatted with Groucho Marx, her former co-star in *Room Service* (1938). Smoking a cigar in the lobby, he told her, "I never like a movie where the hero's tits are bigger than the heroine's."

The De Mille's "swords and sandals" spectacular earned $12 million in its initial opening, becoming one of the most popular movies of the 1940s. It was such a hit that it ushered in a number of other Biblical epics in the 1950s. More offers of leading roles in depictions of the ancient world came to Mature, including *Androcles and the Lion* (1952), in which he was cast as an (emotionally tormented) Roman centurion.

In 1953, Mature teamed with Richard Burton to make *The Robe,* the first CinemaScope movie. It became one of the most popular films of all time. He replicated his character of Demetrius in *Demetrius and the Gladiator.* The two pictures were shot consecutively. Then, Fox cast Mature in yet another spectacle of the ancient world, *The Egyptian* (1954), a role originally intended for Marlon Brando.

Lucille confessed to her good friend, June Havoc, her sometimes guest at Desilu Ranch, "Vic and I finally made it," she said. "What's a gal to do? This hunk of male flash comes into your dressing room, tells you he'd leave his wife, Dorothy, any day if I'd agree to marry him. He takes you in those well-muscled arms of his, sticks his tongue down your throat, and he places his hand on that rising bar of iron that doesn't stop growing. Then he lures you over to the couch and says he's gotta have you or he'll kill himself."

Victor Mature with **Jean Simmons** in *Androcles and the Lion (1967).* The film was a loose adaptation of a play by George Bernard Shaw.

Meeting Lucille at a party, he said, "I was supposed to be a big box office hit, all dressed up in my Centurion drag, but the critics blasted me."

"Been there, done that," Havoc responded, revealing that she, too, had had an affair with him.

Before Mature's departure from Hollywood, his list of seductions was impressive: Wendy Barrie, Alice Faye, Betty Grable, Betty Hutton, Veronica Like, Carole Landis, K.T. Stevens, Gene Tierney, and ultimately, Lana Turner and Elizabeth Taylor.

After he seduced gossip columnist Sheilah Graham, she said, "I love Victor. He's such a crazy, attractive, friendly, son of a bitch."

At MGM, Lucille's friend, Esther Williams, was cast with Mature in *Million Dollar Mermaid* (1952), a bio pic of the swimming star, Annette Kellerman.

When Lucille met Williams for lunch one afternoon in Beverly Hills, they "dished" Mature, Williams admitting that she was having a torrid affair with him. "Best sex I ever had. Was he your best too?"

"You're assuming I had sex with Vic," Lucille said.

"C'mon, Lucy, everybody in Hollywood knows you two guys made it," Williams said. "I bet even Desi Arnaz knows. Fernando Lamas told me he hopes he measures up to Victor. You know how Desi and Fernando, as Latin lovers, like to brag about their penile measurements."

David Thomson in his *The New Biographical Dictionary of Film* delivered a critical appraisal of Mature that Lucille might have agreed with:

> *"Mature is an uninhibited creature of the naïve. Simple, crude, and heady— like ketchup or treacle— he is a diet scorned by the knowing, but obsessive if succumbed to in error. It is too easy to dismiss Mature, for he surpasses badness. He is a strong man in a land of hundred-pound weaklings, an incredible concoction of beef steak, husky voice, and brilliantine—a barely concealed sexual advertisement for soiled goods. Remarkably, he is as much himself in the cheerfully meretricious and the pretentiously serious. Such a career has no more pattern than a large ham; it slices consistently forever. The more lurid or distasteful the art the better Mature comes across."*

In *Miss Grant Takes Richmond* (1949), **Lucille** played "the world's worst secretary" to **William Holden**. Expect her to create a string of disasters.

In this publicity shot, she succeeded in fulfilling one of her longtime wishes— i.e., entrapping him in her arms.

Lucille was disappointed when *Easy Living* lost $650,000 at the box office. RKO was also slapped with a lawsuit from writers Frederick Bond and John Stone, who claimed that it had been based on their script, *Never Say Die*, which they'd submitted to that studio in 1947. RKO and author Irwin Shaw were sued for $150,000 in damages, and the case was settled out of court, the details not released.

The *Los Angeles Times* defined *Easy Living* as "moody cinema," but *The New York Times* was kind: "The film doesn't have the searing candor and impact of some of its predecessors. Neither is it a rah-rah cream puff. Its story is more complicated than the usual pigskin drama. Five important players perform their intriguing characterizations with expected finesse."

Variety wrote that "Lucille Ball's starring role is expertly done, but (it) doesn't realize the possibilities of her name and talent,"

Hollywood Citizen News found that "Lucille Ball plays that wise-cracking secretary role that she can do with one arm tied around her back."

After storming out of RKO, Lucille declared that she would not accept any more "damn secretary roles. My talent was wasted in this stinker. Some homecoming I had at RKO. I'll never appear on those sound stages ever again."

She made that declaration when she left RKO in that summer of 1948. Ironically, a decade later, she'd be right back on those same sound stages, which she now owned as part of the empire she and Desi created—Desilu Productions.

***

With movie studios in disarray as the 1940s came to an end, Lucille was delighted when Harry Cohn, her former boss at Columbia, offered her a three-picture deal at $85,000 per film. She was told that the first of the three, eventually released in 1949, would be *Miss Grant Takes Richmond*. Its title misled her into thinking that she'd play the wife of General Grant as his Union forces invade Virginia.

She was also delighted to learn that her leading man would be William Holden. She'd heard that he was having trouble in his marriage to actress Brenda Marshall, and she hoped he might be in the mood to do some "free-lancing on the side" (her words). Before they finally divorced, Holden and Marshall had many separations.

When Holden and Lucille united to make a picture, each was dissatisfied with their marriages and how their careers had been plunging.

Lucille had long told girlfriends that actor Holden was "my dreamboat of a man—handsome, intelligent, charming, sophisticated, and a hell of a hunk."

She'd known him for several years, since he and his wife lived near the Desilu Ranch. She often discussed her fascination with Holden to her friend, Barbara Pepper. "I've always tried to hide my lust for Bill, especially around Desi when we entertained him and his wife. Desi is incredibly jealous. Frankly, Bill never indicated he had the slightest sexual interest in me."

As Lucille confided to Pepper, "I'd delayed my chance to seduce that handsome hunk far too long, and I could no longer resist the temptation." What began as a seduction in her dressing room led to greater involvements in a hideaway apartment in West Hollywood that Holden shared with Glenn Ford and a recently divorced Ronald Reagan, who was having an affair at the time with both Marilyn Monroe and Doris Day.

"Bill and I laughed together, held hands, and made passionate love," Lucille said. "I

After working with Lucille, **William Holden** would be cast in the role of the gigolo to **Gloria Swanson**, in *Sunset Blvd.* (1950).

Swanson played Norma Desmond, the faded star of the silent screen, who murders him when he spurns her advances and tries to escape from her clutches.

Holden's wife, Brenda Marshall, showed up for her husband's kissing scene with the former silent screen diva. As the cameras rolled, they kissed and kissed and kissed.

When the director didn't yell "Cut!," a screech came from Holden's wife, Brenda Marshall: **"Cut, dammit, cut!"**

later became pregnant because we did not use protection. The child was never born, but, if it had been, I feared it might grow up to look like Bill instead of Desi."

"For years, Desi and I had no success at 'birthin' babies,' as Butterfly McQueen called it in *Gone With the Wind.* That's why I suspected it might be Bill's kid."

"With Bill, I forgot my cares and woes for a few stolen hours," she said. "If he had divorced his wife, and then asked me to marry him, I swear I would have divorced Desi, who was never around anyway, always traveling, always somewhere else."

"With Bill, I almost became a girl again," Lucille claimed. "The only trouble I had with him was that he was around for far too short a time. It was over before it had really begun. He told me that I'd do everything he wanted a woman to do, things that he could never persuade most of them, especially his wife, to perform."

What they couldn't possibly have imagined at the time was that each of them, going in different directions, were on the verge of worldwide stardom. Lucille would make it in television, and Holden would do so the very next year in feature films. An example occurred when he starred as the gigolo lover of Gloria Swanson in *Sunset Blvd.* (1950), and again as the teacher/romancer of Judy Holliday in *Born Yesterday* (also 1950).

Months later, when it was announced that Holden would play the second male lead in *Born Yesterday,* Lucille called him and asked him to lobby for her for the role of Billie Dawn. He promised to do so, but the producer and director had other ideas about casting.

In *Miss Grant Takes Richmond*, the on-screen Lucille faces stiff competition from **Janis Carter**, cast as Peggy Donato, a scheming heiress.

Cohn never told Lucille, but he originally wanted Rita Hayworth as Holden's leading lady in *Miss Grant Takes Richmond*. On the verge of eloping with Prince Aly Khan and retiring from Hollywood, Hayworth rejected the role,

As Holden's secretary, and operating on his behalf, Lucille has accepted and lost a $50,000 bet.

Hayworth read the script, however, and told Cohn she detested the role of the zany secretary, recommending that he offer it to Lucille instead. "She's good at that kind of thing. It's not for me."

As the plot unfolds, Holden has to pay up, even though he doesn't have the money.

Cohn took Rita's suggestion and even signed Lucille for two more pictures after *Miss Grant.*

Lucille was relieved to be working with producer S. Sylvan Simon, as she'd become his friend. He had last directed her in *Her Husband's Affairs* (1947).

[Over the course of two separate lunches, he told her he'd like to cast her in future comedies, envisioning a series of slapstick adventures. He wanted to repeat the success he'd had with Red Skelton in The Fuller Brush Man

To Lucille's fury, it soon becomes clear that the Donato dame would rather have his body as payment than the money itself.

(1948). To that effect, he suggested, "How about making a picture called The Fuller Brush Girl?*"*

"And why not?" she said. "I'm game."

Ironically, within a few years, their lunchtime daydreams actually took flight and became a reality.]

Simon assigned Lloyd Bacon to direct *Miss Grant Takes Richmond*. Over the course of his career this veteran of show business would direct such stars as Charlie Chaplin, George Raft, Humphrey Bogart, James Cagney, and Ronald Reagan in more than a hundred films between 1920 and 1955.

Bacon was aware of the age difference between Lucille and Holden, who was seven years younger. In reference to the closeups he shot of her, "I didn't want the audience to feel that Holden was young enough to play her son. It was obvious what was going on with those two. In this big come-on kissing scene, she deliberately flubbed it so that she could shoot it again and again. She couldn't get enough of Bill. I think he was giving her a hard-on."

Gloria Henry, cast as Helen White in *Miss Grant Takes Richmond*, had a minor, easily forgettable role.

A decade later, she became a familiar face throughout America for her portrayal of Alice Mitchell, the long-suffering mother of Dennis in *Dennis the Menace* (1959-63), the hit TV series.

In this photo, she reacts in horror at the latest antic from her pre-teen son, Dennis, as portrayed by **Jay North** (inset photo).

In *Miss Grant Takes Richmond*, Holden and Lucille were backed up by a strong supporting cast led by Janis Carter as Peggy Donato; James Gleason as Timothy P. Gleason; Gloria Henry as Helen White; Frank McHugh as Mr. Kilcoyne; and George Cleveland as Judge Ben Grant.

Lucille vowed she'd never play a secretary again, but here she was, cast in the role of a scatter-brained secretary, Ellen Grant, the worst student at the Woodruff Secretarial School.

As the other women in her class type furiously, Lucille's typewriter explodes, the first in a series of slapstick adventures that awaited the viewer of *Miss Grant*, even runaway bulldozers on a real estate development project.

Pretending to be a real estate agent, Holden, cast as Dick Richmond—hence the film's title (*Miss Grant Takes Richmond*)—arrives at the school with the intention of hiring a secretary. He's deliberately searching for the dumbest one in the class. [*Why? Because he wants only an "ornamental" receptionist, not a working secretary, as a legitimate-looking "prop" that would conceal his back-room activities as a bookie running an illegal gambling operation alongside his cronies Gleason and McHugh.*]

Gleason delivers his usual tough-talking, world-weary performance. McHugh would go on to appear in some 150 roles, mostly character parts, although he'd started out as a leading man. He was a close friend of James

Cagney and had starred in eleven of his films. He'd also performed with Bing Crosby in the classic *Going My Way* (1944). McHugh ended his career in the role of a comical "sea captain" opposite Elvis Presley in *Easy Come, Easy Go* (1967).

As the other woman, Janis Carter as Peggy Donato, phones Lucille, who unknowingly accepts a bet. As it turns out, that later puts Holden $50,000 in debt to the attractive temptress, who wants his body more than his money.

Fortunately, everything ends happily as Holden ends up with Lucille and "goes straight."

Over the course of her career, Carter made some thirty films for different studios, mostly B pictures. High points occurred opposite Glenn Ford in *Framed* (1948), and later with John Wayne in *Flying Leathernecks* (1951).

Gloria Henry was a damsel from New Orleans. After working with Lucille, she went on to co-star with Marlene Dietrich in *Rancho Notorious* (1952). The great German diva reportedly found her very attractive "in a wholesome sort of way."

It wasn't until 1959 that Henry, evoking domesticity and maternal warmth, landed the role on TV that would make her famous, playing Alice Mitchell, the mother of *Dennis the Menace*, the TV series that ran from 1959 to 1963. "For the rest of my life, I was typecast," she ruefully told Lucille years later.

In its review of *Miss Grant Takes Richmond*, *The New York Times* said, "Miss Ball, who substitutes her own 'do-fers' whenever the dictation gets tough, brings her skill, pantomimic as well as verbal, into play."

Variety found that "Miss Ball and Holden make a romantic team, while McHugh, as a human adding machine, and Gleason, as a worried bookie, deliver plenty of laughs."

The *Hollywood Reporter* gave this wacky comedy a good review: "Lucille Ball gives the usual first-class performance as the girl, and William Holden is at his best in the part of the bookie."

After seeing *Miss Grant Takes Richmond*, Cohn viewed it as "perhaps a laugh or two, but hardly a smash at the box office." He had maintained a friendship with Frank Sinatra, and asked him for a big favor. The singer had been booked on stage at the Capitol Theater in Manhattan. It was understood that between shows a movie would be featured, and Cohn prevailed upon the singer to force management to show *Miss Grant Takes Richmond*.

As was customary at the time, Sinatra was a hit, and the box office grossed $125,000 that week in sales. and although it wasn't completely true, Cohn ordered his publicity department to advertise that it had been Lucille's film (not Sinatra's concert) that had generated that inflow of cash during the week of its opening._

*　　　* * *

As Desi continued to tour with his band, he was often absent from the ranch at Chatsworth for weeks at a time. Lucille flew to join him whenever she could, in some cases prompting him to move out his current girlfriend before she arrived. Nonetheless, she'd often find traces of a woman within the premises of wherever he was living, discoveries that always led to fights within the ongoing drama of their marriage.

As Lucille told June Havoc, "I still love him, and I want to save our marriage such as it is. I also want to have children with him, and we have unprotected sex, but I don't get pregnant. Either something is wrong with his sperm, or else the fault is with me."

"Not all women are born to breed," Havoc said. "Perhaps you should send him to your doctor for a rather personal exam."

Night after night during phone calls from the road, Desi had expressed his own desire to father a child. Finally, she told him, "You can't become a daddy over the phone lines. It doesn't work that way."

On yet another phone call, she accused him of perhaps "fathering dozens of bastard kids from coast to coast with your latest pickup." That led to yet another fight.

On his next visit, she arranged an appointment for him with a doctor. After a thorough examination, in which "Doc juggled my balls," Desi was given a re-sealable container and instructed to provide a sperm sample.

"I'm a little too old to jerk off," Desi said. "I haven't had to do that since I was a teenager. You've got a pretty nurse. Could you let her help me out?"

"No!" the doctor said. "But there are some magazines in there that might help."

It took a while, but Desi finally managed to ejaculate into the cup.

After he got the results, he told Lucille, "Doc says my sperm is powerful enough to create an army of kids."

On his next visit, in an attempt to save his failing marriage, he asked her to symbolically repeat their marriage ceremony. This time, he wanted

At the time, scant attention was paid to the long-term detriments of smoking, as both of them would learn, years later, with agonizing consequences.

the service conducted in a Catholic Church by a priest, and not in front of a Justice of the Peace, as it had been "the last time" he married Lucille.

She agreed to marry him again, in a church, even though she wasn't Catholic. On June 19, 1949, she became Mrs. Desi Arnaz for the second time, symbolically, at Our Lady of the Valley, a lovely small church in their hometown of Chatsworth.

For the wedding, Lucille wore a well-tailored navy blue dress with a matching hat. Desi, in the Cuban tradition of his father, wore a white suit and red tie. As a novelty that surprised some guests, he also wore red shoes.

Ken Morgan, Cleo's husband, was selected as Desi's best man, even though there were rumors that he'd been having an ongoing affair with Lucille. [*Although Cleo, as noted earlier, was technically Lucille's cousin, Lucille referred to her as "my sister."*]

Desi's mother, Lolita, was matron of honor, and director Edward Sedgwick gave the bride away.

Six months after Lucille's second marriage, she announced that she was pregnant. "It is the second happiest day of my life," she told him. "The happiest day was marrying you the second time around."

Two weeks later, she awakened her husband at 3AM, screaming in pain. "I'm bleeding!" Dressing quickly, he wrapped a robe around her, grabbed a bath towel, and gently lifted her into the back seat of his car. Roaring west at eighty-five miles an hour, he was chased down by a motorcycle cop. In panic, he explained his dire situation to the cop, who then raced in front of them with his siren blaring.

Dr. Red Krone and his staff worked to save the premature baby, but it was hopeless. The news shattered Lucille, sending her into a deep depression that lasted for weeks. "I'll never be a mother," she lamented to anyone willing to lend an ear.

***

Desi still harbored a dream of becoming a Latin lover on the big screen, even though Bob Hope, with whom he worked as musical director on radio, discouraged that ambition. "You're just not funny, and a little bit silly. No one would believe you in a Rudolph Valentino role. It would come out like a burlesque. When you face the mike to say something, your speaking voice sounds like you've got a burrito stuck in it. Stick to singing. That you can do...sorta."

Instead of a *bona fide* movie star part, he was offered a role in *Jitterumba*, a fifteen-minute mu-

Every entertainer looks back on his *oeuvre* with a memory of a film, book, song, or play that, in retrospect, was an embarrassing and/or campy failure.

This **(Jitterumba)** was Desi's .

407

sical short screened in movie houses as a "filler" between other, longer, feature films. In one sequence, he appears as a college professor wearing a cap and teaching students a geography lesson. The highlight was a musical number named "Managua, Nicaragua," which became an unexpected hit.

It was not until the closing months of 1949 that Desi got his final film role of the decade. It was in *Holiday in Havana*, a musical comedy directed by Jess Marborough, who had helmed Bud Abbott and Lou Costello. *[Desi would not be seen on the screen again until 1951, when that appearance was on TV in the first installment of* I Love Lucy.*]*

Holiday in Havana ended up as just another programmer, running as one of two small features, a "sitcom-ish" bit of fluff inserted between screenings of other ("more important") feature films.

In it, his love interest was Mary Hatcher, who was made up to look like a juvenile re-interpretation of Rita Hayworth.

Desi was more or less cast as himself, a bandleader singing such songs as "Holiday in Havana," and "Arnaz Jim." His role was evocative of the character of Ricky Ricardo he later replicated for *I Love Lucy.*

Holiday in Havana soon faded into oblivion, except for the most dedicated of Desi fans.

One of his admirers wrote: "Finally, Desi can shine without being weighed down by the surprisingly untalented Lucille Ball. She could make pumpkin pie taste like a rice cake. See Desi dance! The sexy guy can rumba the night away."

***

Desi had first appeared on a television set at the then-spectacular 1939 World's Fair. *[Built on a 1,200-acre site in Queens, New York City, it was promoted for its ability to tanta-*

Two views of *Holiday in Havana.* The blonde in each of the photos above is **Mary Hatcher.**

Hatcher's dream of movie stardom was heading for oblivion, and Desi's dream of becoming Hollywood's newest Latin lover of the screen faded into hopelessness with the unfunny high jinx of *Holiday in Havana.*

lizingly showcase "The World of Tomorrow."]

He and his partner at the time, Diosa Costello, were viewed by thousands as they danced the conga.

However, with the coming of World War II, the medium of television (temporarily) faded into oblivion. Instead of manufacturing TV sets, plants across America began churning out guns, battleships, and bombers. Production of the cathode ray tube, an essential component of the then-newfangled television set, was redirected to the manufacture of high-tech components for, among other tools, radar.

Shortly after V-E Day in 1945, a Gallup Poll revealed that only one percent of Americans had even heard of television. However, by 1949, most Americans had heard of television even though they didn't own a TV set. At decade's end, two million sets had been sold to viewers who watched the tube five hours a day. By the end of 1950, 100,000 sets were being sold every week.

Television had arrived. Most screens measured ten to fifteen inches diagonally, and set into large, heavy cabinets. Color broadcasts — fierce competition to movie theaters — didn't arrive until 1954.

. As a free-lance entertainer, no longer contractually limited in her artistic and commercial choices, Lucille was free to appear on TV more or less whenever she wished. Ironically, the sponsors of the radio program (*My Favorite Husband*) in which she was appearing at the time, urged her to go on TV because of the publicity it generated for their show.

In February of 1949, she made her television debut on *The Chesterfield Supper Club,* which had originated as a radio musical variety program in 1944. *[On April 5, 1946, one of its installments was broadcast from aboard a TWA flight, 20,000 feet above the surface of the earth.]* Beginning in 1948, it was adapted into a television show hosted over the months ahead by Perry Como, Dinah Shore, and Jo Stafford, who'd been nicknamed "GI Jo" because of all the entertainment she'd brought to servicemen during the war years.

Thanks in part to her long experience before a microphone and camera, Lucille glided easily onto the TV screen.

In early December of 1949, she was invited to appear on TV once again, this time on *See the USA in a Chevrolet,* starring Peter Lind Hayes and his wife, Mary Healy. Hayes had appeared with Lucille and Victor Mature in their film, *Seven Days' Leave* (1942). In one of the TV sequences, Lucille starred as a dance hostess, with Hayes cast as a Texas oil

The husband and wife team of **Peter Lind Hayes** and his wife, **Mary Healy**, became familiar faces in American homes. They also became good friends of Lucille.

She watched their show, *See the USA in a Chevrolet,* and was saddened when the automobile company booted them and replaced them with singer Dinah Shore.

millionaire.

Meeting privately with Mary Healy, Lucille wanted to know what it was like to "always be appearing with your husband." Healy had married Hayes in 1940, beginning a fifty-year personal and professional relationship.

"Expect the inevitable tension," Healy warned. "For Peter and me, working together has cemented our love affair. Our bond has grown stronger over the years. When he comes home from work, I don't have to ask him how his day went since I lived it with him."

"In the case of you and Desi, if you're contemplating a TV show with him as your husband, you should not bring on any female guest prettier than you. You see, my dear, Desi's reputation has preceded him."

On Christmas Eve of that year, Lucille made her final 1940s appearance on television as a guest star on *The Ed Wynn Show*. It marked her first TV debut with her husband, Desi. In one skit, she had to pretend to be a Ziegfeld Girl, wearing an upside-down lampshade as a headdress.

The comedian's show was the first TV series to be filmed in Hollywood. It was also the first to be transmitted by kinescope to New York. Ed Wynn hosted the television debuts of Groucho Marx, Dinah Shore, the Three Stooges, Hattie McDaniel, and Buster Keaton.

Wynn's show ran for only one season in spite of his formidable guest list that included Gloria Swanson, Carmen Miranda, William Frawley (the future Fred Mertz), and Cesar Romero, who still harbored a gay crush on Desi.

Before Lucille and Desi were crowned King and Queen of Television, three superstars arose within the new medium:

The Ed Sullivan Show went on the air in June of 1948, enjoying a "variety program" reign that lasted until 1971. *TV Guide* named it No. 15 on its list of the fifty greatest TV shows of all time. Its viewers were treated with everything from opera and ballet to Dean Martin and Jerry Lewis. Some appearances by guest stars were legendary, notably Elvis Presley, who could be photographed only from the waist up, and The Beatles.

Comedian Milton Berle became known as "Mr. Television," emerging as the medium's first real superstar. *[Actually, he had first appeared on TV in 1929 as part of an experimental broadcast from Chicago.]*

Beginning in June of 1948, he dominated Tuesday nights on television, capturing an astonishing ninety-seven percent of the viewing public. *[One investigation in Detroit revealed that on Tuesday nights between 9 and 9:05PM, a time block usually reserved for commercials), the water levels in reservoirs across the region dropped drastically, as viewers collectively rushed to their bathrooms between TV segments.]*

"On TV, I hawked Philip Morris cigarettes, and **Arthur Godfrey** pedaled Chesterfield," Lucille said.

"If truth be known, I smoked Chesterfields in private. I got my start in show biz by being 'The Chesterfield Girl' on billboards across the country."

Arthur Godfrey, nicknamed "The Old Redhead," was the third superstar created by TV. Hawking either Chesterfield cigarettes or Lipton Tea, he reached the peak of his success in the mid-1950s. On the air, he evoked a benevolent version of "Mr. Warmth," but in time, the press outed him as volatile, egomaniacal, and controlling, revelations which led to a decline in his popularity.

Lucille had built up a higher name recognition through her radio show, *My Favorite Husband,* than she had in any of her previous feature films. Wherever she went, she was recognized and applauded, thanks to dozens of widely distributed publicity pictures. Over and over, she heard the same refrain from passersby: "Look, there's that gal who plays Liz Cooper on the radio."

In the early 1950s, big Hollywood studios did not want their contract stars appearing on televisions. In the words of Louis B. Mayer at MGM, "If they can see Lana Turner, Clark Gable, or Judy Garland for free on the tube, the public won't buy a movie ticket."

Desi was far more excited by a possible career on television than Lucille was. She told him, "You've got no more career to protect like I do. I've been warned by agents that if I star on TV, my film career is doomed."

Since the Supreme Court had ended the monopoly of big studios owning their own theaters, several big-name stars were branching out and forming their own production companies. Lucille and Desi decided to do the same, if for no other reason that to receive tax breaks.

The idea of forming their own television production company had been first presented to Lucille by Desi as he was driving her back to the Desilu Ranch. He wanted to "steal" the name of their ranch and call their new company "Desilu Productions."

They launched it in 1950. Their first project involved converting her radio show, *My Favorite Husband,* into a TV series.

"Forget Richard Denning. I want to be your husband on TV. But instead of being an executive in a bank, my character's gonna be a Cuban bandleader."

"Call that type casting," she answered.

Desi rented space at General Service Studios (now the Sunset Las Palmas Studios) at Santa Monica Boulevard and North Las Palmas Avenue. They used Stage Two, which was named Desilu Playhouse. Later, a special entrance was added at 6633 Romaine Street on the south side of the lot to allow direct access to it.

At the time they organized and established their company, they had hoped for some moderate success. Never in their wildest dreams had they ever thought they'd become the most successful pairing in the history of TV.

***

In addition to Desi and Lucille contemplating a new future in television, they also shifted to a new set of friends. *[Eve Arden still remained a favorite guest, as did June Havoc.]* New on the scene was a handsome gay actor, Farley Granger, who was getting a big build-up by Samuel Goldwyn. Lucille told him she started in films as one of the Goldwyn Girls. Granger always arrived with a different boyfriend.

Bing's brother, Bob Crosby, showed up whenever he wasn't touring with his band. Priscilla Lane and her husband, Joe Howard, were regular visitors, too.

Lucille frequently entertained a new star on the scene, handsome, studly Rory Calhoun and his wife, Lita. Although he came from a world very different from Lucille's, the two of them became very close. He'd been a former lumberjack and had even served a prison term before becoming a movie star.

He said he was discovered one night in Griffith Park by actor Alan Ladd. "He admired my physique and my other assets," Calhoun told Lucille.

"He eventually became one of "the boys"

Lucille formed an unlikely friendship with the gay actor **Farley Granger.** This candid "beefcake tease" photo of him was snapped when he was billed as "The Samuel Goldwyn Boy."

The producer had signed him to a contract right after college and starred him as the boyfriend of Anne Baxter in *The North Star* (1943).

But it would be Alfred Hitchcock, not Goldwyn, who gave Granger his most memorable role.

He was cast as a tennis player in *Stranger on a Train* (1951). There, he is trapped into a deadly alliance with Robert Walker, who played a psychotic homosexual.

412

whose career was being handled and "steered" by the gay agent Henry Willson, who was also launching the career of Rock Hudson. According to Calhoun, "My first picture, when I was still billed as Frank McCown, was *Something For the Boys* (1944). I had something for the boys all right, but I much preferred giving that something to the ladies."

There were rumors going around Hollywood that Lucille was having a clandestine affair with Calhoun. That gossip started when he was seen arriving at her ranch on some weekends without his wife and when Desi was away.

In spite of mounting evidence to the contrary, she always denied the rumor. "We're just kissin' cousins—that's all."

Eve Arden and June Havoc knew otherwise.

As it turned out, Calhoun became a ladies' man like Desi. He once confessed that his career during two decades of movie-making encompassed affairs with Susan Hayward, Betty Grable, and Marilyn Monroe.

When studly **Rory Calhoun** became a movie star, *Confidential* magazine exposed him as having previously spent time in prison.

He was friends with Lucille at the time—some say "more than just friends"—and he poured out his fears to her that his film career had been destroyed.

Such was not the case. Even Desi, years later, tried to get him cast in a TV series.

***

Lucille became more convinced than ever that she should try a career in television when she was assigned her next film role. Released by Columbia, it was only a cameo in which she would appear as herself in *A Woman of Distinction.* (1950).

The stars of the picture included Rosalind Russell cast as a nationally renowned scholar, and Ray Milland as a famous astronomer and professor. A mélange of misadventures ensue in this slapstick comedy, which *The New York Times* would define as "a custard-pie farce." Lukewarm and undistinguished, it would be the first and only pairing of these two famous stars.

Lucille's cameo with Milland occurs when she's seated next to him on an airplane. Arriving at their destination, she steals the publicity from him, despite his status as a noted British astronomer.

In Hollywood parlance, **the casting couch** usually referred to a producer seducing a female starlet in exchange for giving her a role in an upcoming movie.

The gay agent, Henry Willson, specialized in creating stars out of the pretty boys of the 1940s and 50s. He "discovered" Rock Hudson after many "auditions."

He also put the two actors depicted above , **Rory Calhoun** (left) and **Guy Madison**, not only on his casting couch, but in his bed.

413

She had long been an admirer of Russell, and had actually coveted many of her starring roles, notably *My Girl Friday* (1940), in which she had co-starred with Cary Grant.

Russell's most celebrated role would not come until 1958, when she was cast in the classic *Auntie Mame*. In it, she delivered a *tour de force* performance, uttering her most iconic line, "Life is a banquet and most poor suckers are starving to death!"

[Ironically, in 1974, Lucille would bring the flamboyant Mame to the screen once again, in her first singing and dancing role in three decades. Her reviews would range from overly excessive praise to comments that "take the skin off my ass" (Lucille's words).]

Milland had never been Lucille's favorite actor, far from it. He had a bad rap from people he had worked with. She was told that he despised minorities, "especially Hollywood fags."

Bette Davis had said, "Milland is a shit." Marlene Dietrich had deplored his hygiene. "He literally stinks," she asserted.

On Lucille's first days on the set, he asked her out to lunch. After she accepted, she found him quite amusing. He must have bathed that day because she detected no body odor.

He claimed that when he first arrived in Hollywood, he was told that he had to take a screen test. He told the assistant, "Hand me the bottle."

"I thought I had to go to the john and piss in it," Milland later confessed.

Somehow, he had found out that Lucille had had a brief fling with his co-star, Brian Donlevy, back in 1939, when they'd made *Beau Geste* together. According to Milland, "I found Donlevy annoying, and I got my revenge. In a fencing scene with him, I nicked his unpadded penis. He bled his pants. Fortunately, I didn't circumcise him as was reported."

Ray Milland with **Lucille Ball** in *A Woman of Distinction*.

According to Lucille, in reference to a very minor role and to a co-star she disliked, she later (flippantly) remembered her involvement in it like this:

"If you lingered too long at the popcorn stand, you probably missed me in this movie. The script called for me to fly in with Milland on an airplane, where reporters were waiting to interview him, a famous British astronomer."

"But the character I was playing stole his thunder by posing for provocative pinups."

414

"He seemed in working order for me," she shot back. "It must have been before you nicked him."

Once, over "more than a few" drinks, he explained to her that he was not into "golden showers."

"I did, however, indulge in a bit of water sports when I co-starred with Dorothy Lamour in *The Jungle Princess* (1936). We had this love scene in a swimming pool. As I snuggled up against her, I found the water cold, and urinated all over her."

Four years after working with Lucille, she heard that he'd become involved in a torrid affair with Grace Kelly, his co-star in *Dial M for Murder*.

"He must have bathed more frequently, because Grace was known for being very fastidious," Lucille said.

Lucille already knew many of the actors on the set. She bonded again with Eddie Buzzell, who had helmed Van Johnson and herself in *Easy to Wed* (1946).

She also spent some time with little Mary Jane Saunders, which made her want to produce a daughter of her own. She and the child star had previously co-starred with Bob Hope in *Sorrowful Jones* (1949).

One of her alltime favorite character actors was Gale Gordon, and he, too, had a small role in their film as a station clerk. A few years later, he'd be her first choice to play Fred Mertz on *I Love Lucy*.

***

Instead of immediately throwing herself into television, Lucille staged what she called "My Last Hurrah." She persuaded Desi to push ahead with movie scripts that positioned them together as a new screen team. All of these movie projects, if and when he found them, would be shot at Desilu Productions.

Both husband and wife mutually agreed that they wanted Edward Sedgwick as the director of these projected movies. He had become a kind of mentor to them.

As it turned out, Sedgwick already had a film script for them: He'd spent months working on it: *Blazing Beulah from Butte.* It was the saga of a handsome Mexican who migrates north. Eventually, although he becomes involved with a cultured lady of taste and refinement, he ends up with a brazen "blazing hussy."

Lucille's first question was, "Which role is mine? The lady or the Saturday night whore?"

Around the same time, yet another script was delivered to them, something that seemed tailor-made for their talents. *The Townsend Girl*, the namesake role of which would be portrayed by Lucille, was the story of an American woman who arrives in Havana to open a gambling casino. There, she gets involved with a local rogue and ladies' man. "For Desi, that would be type casting," she said.

Neither film, like so many other scripts in Hollywood, ever got shot.

June Havoc, Barbara Pepper, and others sensed desperation in Lucille as she fought to hold onto her marriage and her career. With them, she shared her belief that if she worked with Desi, she might stop his philandering.

"Lucille had done some screwing around on her own, especially whenever she'd been cast with screen heartthrobs that no red-blooded woman could resist," Pepper said. "But she told me she strayed only because Desi wasn't home doing his duty. Sometimes he seemed deliberately cruel to her."

To welcome the beginning of a new decade, Lucille hosted a New Year's Eve pig roast in her backyard and invited many of her friends, creating a dinner menu that focused on Desi's favorite Cuban specialties. As Pepper noted, "He did not show up until one in the morning, after all of us had sung 'Auld Lang Syne' without him."

Four years would pass before she achieved her goal of co-starring with Desi in a feature film. Complicating matters was that she still owed two pictures to Harry Cohn at Columbia.

***

Bob Hope and **Lucille Ball** doing their *schtick* in *Fancy Pants*.

"In buttons and bows, or even in buckskin, our director, George Marshall, ordered me to look sexy," Lucille said.

"I adore Bob Hope as a friend, but onscreen, when I was coming on to him, it was hard for me to be convincing."

"As a bedmate, forget it! But as a co-star, he was marvelous to work with."

Paramount was so pleased with the box office success of *Sorrowful Jones* that it teamed comedian Bob Hope with Lucille once again in *Fancy Pants* (1950), a Technicolor "rom com" directed by George Marshall. He had already helmed Lucille in a Western, *Valley of the Sun,* way back in 1942. Marshall had also directed Hope in *The Ghost Busters* (1940) and *Monsieur Beaucaire* (1946).

Paramount had acquired the rights to *Fancy Pants* in 1947 as a vehicle for Betty Hutton, who—at the time—still had a lot of box office clout. The film was then called *Lady from Lariot Loop.* Hutton rejected the role, and the project was shelved for three years.

Its storyline, in various forms, had been "kicking around" for most of the 20th Century, beginning with Harry Leon Wilson's novel, *Ruggles of Red Gap* (1915). It had been adapted for a Broadway stage as a musical the same year it was published. In 1918, it was turned into a silent film starring Taylor Holmes.

It was remade in 1923 with Edward Everett Horton, Lucille's former co-star, in the lead.

Its greatest success had come in 1935 with hefty Charles Laughton, the male lead, playing an eminently correct English manservant and "gentleman's gentleman." Laughton's employer gambles him away to his new masters, crude *nouveau riche* American millionaires portrayed by Charles Ruggles and Mary Boland. They bring the butler to Red Cap, a hick Western boom town, where he is mistaken for an aristocrat in his own right. ZaSu Pitts, as fluttery as ever, plays the butler's sweetheart.

Hope was cast as Humphrey (aka Arthur Tyler), a struggling American actor impersonating a British butler. Lucille plays Aggie, an adventurous heiress who hangs out with outlaws. At one point, she comes on to Hope dressed in buckskin, singing "Hey, Fancy Pants." Actually, her singing voice was dubbed by Annette Wareen.

As the third lead, Bruce Cabot joined Lucille once again, this time as Carl Belknap, a jealous admirer.

An uproar occurs when John Alexander, cast as Theodore Roosevelt, announces his plan to visit the town to meet the "Earl of Brinstead,"—i.e., Hope., the impersonator.

Everything gets resolved happily in the end as Aggie and Humphrey (Hope and Lucille) high tail it out of Big Squaw, where they are not very popular. But they are in love.

Filming, with music and color, of *Fancy Pants* began in the early summer of 1949. At the time, it was entitled *Where Men Are Men*. Lucille's contract called for her to be paid $8,750 per week.

She wore the most outrageous headdress of her entire career. A towering mass of blonde curls were positioned over the frame of a birdcage held in place on top of her head with an elaborate network of straps.

Cabot, who had frequently propositioned Lucille, did it once again, telling her, "This is the last time I'm going to ask. How about it tonight? I understand you're not getting that much from Arnaz."

"Why don't you go fuck Eric Blore [*one of the film's supporting players]*? I know from working with him before that he'd love it."

"Thanks, but no thanks, bitch!" Cabot snarled before stalking away. He "wreaked petty vengeance" on Lucille two days later. His horse stepped on her foot.

Hope sustained two accidents during the filming of a scene in which Lucille persuades him to practice his equestrian skills by mounting a saddle that's strapped to a mechanized barrel whose bucking and heaving emulate the movements of a wild stallion. After a minute or two, Hope lost control of both the reins and his balance and fell off the "simulated bronco," crashing six feet to the ground When it was obvious that he'd been knocked unconscious, an ambulance was summoned and, with dome lights flashing, rushed him to a hospital. He stayed there for a few days, having suffered major bruises, but no broken bones.

Another more serious accident occurred during a weekend excursion in his car. Behind the wheel of any vehicle, Hope was a speed demon, sometimes driving ninety miles an hour between his home at Toluca Lake (a suburb of Los Angeles) and Palm Springs.

One morning, he set out along Highway 60 with Fred Williams, a screenwriter. Along the way, he lost control of his Cadillac and ran it off the road. Thrown from his car, and hitting his head on a rock, he was diagnosed when it was over with a broken collarbone. Once again, he landed in a hospital, this time for a longer stay.

Since Hope was needed in nearly every scene, production on *Fancy Pants* ground to a halt. Lucille used that opening to drive south to join Desi. Eventually, she was told that he was spending sunny days in some motel at Balboa Beach, between visits to a nearby racetrack to bet on horses.

Lucille and Desi spent part of that vacation with Elliott Roosevelt, son of the former U.S. President, Franklin Delano Roosevelt, and his distinguished First Lady, Eleanor.

Desi had met FDR during

Elliott Roosevelt and his then-wife, actress and TV talk-show host **Faye Emerson**.

In gossipy Hollywood circles, a brief holiday he spent with Lucille became known as "*The Lost Weekend*," the title stolen from Ray Milland's Oscar-winning film from 1945. Lucille sailed to Catalina Island with the son of the former (1933 to 1945) U.S. President

A newsman from *The Hollywood Reporter* interviewed the manager of the hotel where they lodged in separate rooms.

"I can't tell you if they made it or not. They requested a suite with connecting doors. All Elliott had to do, if he so desired, was to open that door and he was in her bedroom."

"Did he? I don't know. Everything goes on here when that crowd from Hollywood arrives."

his presidency, and now, with Lucille, they were boating with his son, Elliott. Enlisted in the United States Army Air Force during World War II, Elliott had risen to the rank of Brigadier General.

In 1944, Elliott had married the actress and radio personality Faye Emerson in Arizona at the Grand Canyon. During this weekend with Desi and Lucille, Emerson wasn't with him, as they'd finalized their divorce in 1950.

When Desi had to break from this sojourn for a gig in Palm Springs, Lucille and Elliott sailed together, in a rented yacht with crew, to Catalina Island.

The manager of a hotel on Catalina later told the press that after Roosevelt rented a suite, a mysterious woman arrived later that evening to share it with him. That redhead was reported to have been Lucille, but that was never confirmed.

Fancy Pants eventually took in $2.6 million in ticket sales. *The New York Times* wrote, "Miss Ball is gorgeously brazen—Hope, too—in keeping this nonsense spinning." *Variety* noted that "Miss Ball is at her comedic peak, matching Hope gag for gag with uninhibited zanyisms."

Cue magazine acclaimed Lucille as "one of the finest *comediennes* in Hollywood, playing the newly rich desert heiress with gusto."

Right after the film's release, the *Hollywood Reporter* broke the news that Lucille, during its filming, had once again been confronted with the fact that she was pregnant. As such, she was anxious to finish the shoot "before my belly swelled up like a balloon."

Desi's reaction was, "Our new baby will be a gift from God. He is rewarding me for getting married like I should have in the first place, in a Catholic church, the only true religion on the planet."

Three months later, Lucille suffered through yet another miscarriage. Both of the prospective parents were devastated, and she entered into a deep depression. At the age of thirty-eight, she wondered if she'd ever have a child.

***

To fulfill the second movie of her three-picture contract with Harry Cohn at Columbia, Lucille returned to the studio to shoot *The Fuller Brush Girl* early in 1950. It was a spin-off of the Red Skelton hit, *The Fuller Brush Man*. For continuity of theme between the original and this, its "sequel," Skelton agreed to appear in it as an uncredited cameo.

Lucille's co-star was Eddie Albert, who would soon be nominated for a Best Supporting Actor Oscar for his role in *Roman Holiday* (1954) with Audrey Hepburn and Gregory Peck.

Of course, his greatest fame would come in the 1960s, when he starred as a lawyer-turned-farmer in the hit TV series, *Green Acres*. Eva Gabor portrayed his glamourous wife, whom everybody knew would rather live on Park Avenue.

For the actors gathered together on the set, it resembled a reunion of the players in *Miss Grant Takes Richmond* (1949), minus William Holden. Like before, its producer was S. Sylvan Simon,

Carmen Miranda understood that any movie star accessorized with bananas usually gets a laugh.

So did **Eddie Albert** and **Lucille Ball** in *The Fuller Brush Girl.*

with Lloyd Bacon as Lucille's director once again.

Frank Tashlin signed on again to write the screenplay for her as he had done before. He had nothing but praise for her. "She does what few female comics can do," he said. "In slapstick she can take the pratfalls like a damn good trouper, yet not sacrifice her screen beauty."

In *The Fuller Brush Girl*, Lucille was cast as Sally Elliott, a quirky, door-to-door saleswoman hawking cosmetics. Her boyfriend, Humphrey Briggs (Eddie Albert), is also employed by the Maritime Steamship Company. Neither is aware that their boss, Harvey Simpson (Jerome Cowan), is involved in illegal activities.

Rounding out the cast were Carl Benton Reid, Gale Robbins, Jeff Donnell, John Litel, and Lee Patrick.

The plot is convoluted, with lots of twists and turns, including two murders, a chase by a bunch of goons, a subplot involving a diamond-smuggling racket, a wild pursuit aboard a departing ocean line, a leaking wine barrel, and even two talking parrots giving away secrets.

In one of Lucille's best sequences, she appears in a grotesque parody as "Bubbles," a burlesque queen who evoked memories of the character she'd played in *Dance, Girl, Dance* (1933). In other words, the picture is a barrelful of comic twists and turns, never a dull moment.

At the end, as the Coast Guard moves in on the gangsters, an explosion blows up the smuggling vessel in which they're hiding. Only Lucille and Albert are saved, kissing as they stand on the only floating hunk of debris left intact.

She had several long talks with her producer, Simon, who had been tapped to film Garson Kanin's *Born Yesterday* (1950). She spoke of how she had long coveted the role of Billie Dawn more than any other part in her life. He had been named its producer. He assured her that she might have been perfect for the role, but the right of casting had been left to Harry Cohn at Columbia.

As noted before, *Born Yesterday* was eventually nominated for five Academy Awards. Judy Holliday won the Best Actress Oscar, beating out Bette Davis's performance in *All About Eve* and Gloria Swanson in her greatest role: Norma Desmond in *Sunset Blvd.*

Months after working with Simon, Lucille was shocked to learn of his sudden death at the age of forty-one on May 17, 1951. The official word was that he died of a heart attack, but Lucille, along with much of Hollywood, believed it to have been a suicide.

She and Albert also had several long talks, mainly about how they had escaped being blacklisted during the communist witch hunt of the early 1950s. He had escaped censure because of his record as a war hero. But his Mexican wife, "Margo," was not so lucky. Her career had been ruined.

"She was even spat upon in the street," Albert told Lucille. He spoke with sadness of the fate of many friends who found themselves unemployable. "Everyone was full of fear," he said. "Some took menial jobs, some committed suicide."

One week into the shoot, Lucille infuriated Cohn when he was notified that she had disappeared from the set. Frantic calls were placed, but no one could locate her. Cohn ordered her disappearance be kept out of the papers.

It was learned that she had taken off for San Francisco to "forcibly" end a torrid romance that Desi had forged with an Argentine singer. What followed was a bitter fight, as she threatened divorce action unless he mended his ways. He promised he would. But during her flight back to Los Angeles, she knew he would not keep that vow.

By the end of shooting on the set of *The Fuller Brush Girl*, Lucille claimed she had never in her entire career been called upon to perform such grueling physical stunts. Many were in partnership with Albert as their characters escaped from both the police and a gang of goons, all of whom (falsely) believe that, as a team, they'd murdered two people.

"I experienced the agonies of the damned," she said. "Migraine headaches, sprained wrists, six vertebrae displaced, an irritated sciatic nerve, and two days of blindness after talcum powder from a wind machine was blown into my eyes."

One of her most difficult scenes was when the script called for her to use her mouth to stanch a leak in a wine vat. The sound of the liquid pouring out would have alerted homicidal gangsters to their hidden location.

According to the plot, consuming a quart or so of the wine would make her drunk, thereby summoning the (false) courage and bravado to successfully fight off the goons. In lieu of wine, the props director used a "disgusting" (her word) substitute, and it later made her sick.

During the long hours filming she developed a severe cold.

Driving back to Desilu Ranch after the film was wrapped, she began coughing and suffered from a severe headache. Suddenly, she remembered that she'd made an appointment with the Los Angeles Tuberculosis Society to pose for publicity pictures. She immediately turned her car around and headed back to town.

After arriving at the headquarters of the society, a technician noted her hacking cough and offered to give her a chest X-ray. It revealed that she was suffering from pneumonia. That led to her spending the next nine days in what she termed "a themostatic pneumonia wagon."

It took her several weeks to recover from that disease and her other injuries. The only good news about her involvement with *The Fuller Brush Girl* came when the film garnered good reviews, lifting her spirits.

The Hollywood Reporter wrote: "Lucille Ball, with her wide-eyed beauty and buoyant charm, puts over her comedy with perfect timing, and just the right amount of pathos and bewilderment to arouse the viewers' sympathy while she keeps them laughing."

Variety suggested, "If ever there were any doubts as to Miss Ball's *forte*, *Fuller Brush* dispels them. In this rowdy, incoherent yarn with its Keystone Kops overtones, she garners the major laurels."

The *Los Angeles Times* decided that "Lucille Ball dominates the farce, appearing in almost every scene, and it's a good thing she does. She carries the ball for a comedy touchdown."

***

Plans at CBS-TV moved ahead to convert Lucille's hit radio series, *My Favorite Husband,* into a comedic TV series, tentatively entitled *I Love Lucy.* Her "radio husband," Richard Denning, assumed he would be designated as her husband. He was furious when he learned that Lucille, with whom he had worked so smoothly, didn't want him. She preferred her real husband, Desi Arnaz, but he ran into fierce opposition from the executives at CBS, who did not believe that the depiction of a "mixed marriage" (in this case, a Latino to an Anglo-Saxon redhead) would go over in American living rooms. One CBS memo deplored his "conga-rumba drum beat and a Babalu image" as public relations flaws that might sabotage the series' success.

It was Desi who devised a daring plan to overcome their resistance. At this point, he interpreted a co-starring role with Lucille as the "big break" he'd been working on throughout the 1940s. He suggested to Lucille, and she agreed, that they should, as a team, embark on an extended vaudeville tour of the U.S. as a test of audience reactions.

Desi drove Lucille south to San Diego to close themselves off in the Royal Suite of the Coronado Hotel. They wanted to focus exclusively on the logistics of their upcoming road show.

She borrowed a cello from his band and transformed it into a prop for what Desi later described as "one of the best comic acts she ever performed."

That trio of writers from *My Favorite Husband*—Jess Oppenheimer, Bob Carroll, Jr., and Madelyn Pugh—wrote skits for them.

Desi himself wrote lyrics for his wife to sing in the second chorus of "Cuban Pete." To end their show, he devised what he called "a crazy, go-for-broke rumba where we shook our asses off."

Heading for Manhattan, they premiered their act on familiar turf, the Roxy Theater, scene of his previous sold-out engagement. From the first night until the last, all seats were sold out, and the audiences laughed and applauded. Newspapers proclaimed them "a sensational hit," and executives at CBS took notice.

After their show closed in New York, they hit the road, visiting such cities as Chicago, Buffalo, Minneapolis, and Omaha before landing in San Francisco, where the act seemed to go over even better than it had in Manhattan.

In one of her best skits, Lucille emerges from the audience in a tattered, worn-out set of white tie and tails. She addresses Desi as "Dizzy Arnazy," and, with the cello in hand, tells him that she wants to audition for a seat in his band. When he asks to see her credentials, she covers her breasts in mock shame.

At the end of the tour, Desi told the press, "Lucy is one of the greatest pantomimists in the world. At heart, she's a clown, except at night, when she goes to bed with me, devouring my flesh." The latter part of that appraisal was not printed.

In looking back, the *schtick* that had generated some of the wildest applause was her rendition of "Sally Sweet, the Queen of Delancey Street, *chicka chicky boom."*

Many of the skits from their vaudeville gigs were later worked into episodes of *I Love Lucy.*

Within a week after the ending of their tour, Desi began another gig, this time in Palm Springs for the opening of *Chi-Chi,* promoted at the time as the resort's biggest night club. Lucille scheduled a two-week vacation so that she could join him for a much-needed rest. It was during this retreat that her husband made her pregnant.

He then managed to fit in yet another gig, hosting *Tropical Trip,* a musical quiz show whose first prize was an expense-paid trip to Latin America, the specific destination of which changed every week. His show was radio-broadcast every Sunday afternoon, and was followed later in the evening by Edgar Bergen and his dummy, Charlie McCarthy and then by Jack Benny.

After his gig in Palm Springs, Desi returned to Hollywood in November of 1950, luring fans into Ciro's night club for his late-night act.

Variety, among other news media, gave him a good review. "Maestro's showmanship, tremendously improved over the years, is flashy, even when he fluffs a line, as he does often, but he still holds the ringsiders in his palm."

Near the end of his gig at Ciro's, Lucille delivered the news: She was pregnant again. "This time," she told him, "I just know I'm not going to lose my baby."

With the new money earned, Desi began spending his days directing a team of three carpenters, adding a two-bedroom nursery to their ranch at Chatsworth.

[As a little-known fact, the original radio hit, My Favorite Husband, *was later adapted for TV, even though it was broadcast as direct competition to* I Love Lucy. *This version starred Joan Caulfield and Barry Nelson as the original Liz and George Cooper. Nelson played a well-to-do bank executive, and plots dealt with the couple's interactions with society.*

The show went on the air for the first time in September of 1953 and continued through December of 1955. In its third season, Joan Caulfield was replaced with actress Vanessa Brown.]

***

"When Gary Morton and I went to see Bette Davis in **The Star**, I realized that I had made the career mistake of my life in rejecting the role of Margaret Elliott," Lucille said. "This would have been my only chance to win an Oscar."

An advertisement hyping the movie included this banner:

THE ORCHIDS, THE FURS, THE DIAMONDS THAT WERE THE STAR'S WERE ALL GONE NOW. NOTHING REMAINED BUT THE WOMAN."

Around this time, unknown to many of her fans, Lucille was offered a film role that would perhaps have been better suited to Bette Davis or Joan Crawford.

Author Katherine Albert had once worked as an aide to Crawford. After she left her employment, she wrote a film script entitled *The Star,* which she sold to a Hollywood producer for a 1952 release.

It relayed the story of Margaret Elliott, a washed-up, self-destructive former Oscar winner who has run out of money and roles. The script opens as her furnishings, possessions, and memorabilia are being auctioned off by her creditors.

First, the script was sent to Crawford, who, interpreted it as a betrayal by Katherine Albert and a rip-off of her own life and career, and burst into a rage.

It was then sent to Claudette Colbert, another fading star. Equally furious, she rejected it with a note: "How dare you!"

For some odd reason, the producers then sent it to Lucille, who at the time, was nearing the age of forty. Although she recognized the ironies and dramatic possibilities of the part, she, too feared that Hollywood might typecast her as an aging actress desperate for movie work. She, too, rejected the role.

Staging another of her "comebacks," Bette Davis eventually accepted the role, and her portrayal of Margaret Elliott as *The Star* (1952), even though it was a commercial failure, brought her another Oscar nomination.

[Davis lost that year to Shirley Booth for her performance in Come Back, Little Sheba *(1952). In a touch of irony, Crawford herself was up for an Oscar that year for her performance in* Sudden Fear *(also 1952), co-starring with Jack Palance and Gloria Grahame.]*

***

In October of 1950, Lucille was surprised to receive a call from Cecil B. De Mille. He was in pre-production on his spectacular circus picture, *The Greatest Show on Earth.* Shot in Technicolor, the picture would be both directed and produced by him with an all-star cast. Its settings would be the arenas and backstage areas of the Ringling Brothers or the Barnum and Bailey Circus.

De Mille made it clear to Lucille that her role would not be the lead but one of the most dramatic, the "Elephant Girl" (a.k.a. "Angel"). She's a wise-cracking, red-haired

Gloria Grahame as Angel in *The Greatest Show on Earth* (1952), a role Lucille desperately wanted.

Grahame's most memorable line in that movie?

"Listen, sugar, the only way you're gonna keep me warm is to wrap me up in a marriage license."

424

beauty who drives her psychotic partner, Lyle Bettger, into jealous rages.

De Mille warned her that the role would be strenuous, calling for her to ride on an elephant's back and in one scene, for her to be curled around and be supported by the elephant's trunk. The most dangerous stunt called for her to rest her head only inches beneath an elephant's raised foot.

Because it was De Mille, Lucille accepted the role without even reading the script. "Sign me up but make sure the elephant is painted pink and has a light foot."

There was a problem: Lucille still owed Harry Cohn a third picture, for which she was to be paid $85,000. Before accepting the De Mille role, she needed him to release her from her Columbia contract. "Even though he was a vicious son of a bitch, I thought he might agree to that since he had no immediate role for me," she said.

Although Cohn adamantly refused to release her, that didn't stop her. She appeared at Paramount and began wardrobe tests as the Elephant Girl.

Not a Bed of Roses, and NOT A MAGIC CARPET EITHER

"This Arabian Nights potboiler was not only the worst film I ever made, but was the worst movie in the history of mankind," Lucille said.

"I could only pray that none of my fans went to see this stinker. Not only that, but my leading man, John Agar, turned out to be a jerk."

When Cohn heard of that, he was furious for how she'd "disobeyed his orders." He decided to get rid of her and, at the same time, skip out on having to cough up $85,000 to fulfill her contract.

With that in mind, he offered her an Arabian Nights potboiler, *The Magic Carpet*, scheduled for a 1951 release. Producer Sam Katzman sent over a screenplay he had commissioned David Matthews to write, knowing that she would reject it.

At the Desilu Ranch, she and Desi read the script, in which she would be cast as the villainous sister of a sinister caliph. She would have to wear harem pants and bejeweled breastplates.

Desi finished the script first: "Not even a dime store Maria Montez or Yvonne de Carlo would film this piece of crap. If you accept, you'll be laughed off the screen."

She surprised him: "I'm doing

Raymond Burr with **Lucille Ball** in *The Magic Carpet.*

Lucille: "I couldn't stand Agar, but I saw my friend, Mr. Burr, lusting after him, even following him to the latrine on our set."

the picture. We need that $85,000. The script is so bad, no one will go to see it. Besides, I'm pregnant. If Cohn finds out, he can use that to break my contract. Goodbye, $85,000.

"Since you're pregnant again, and I'm so happy to hear that, that also means you can't accept the De Mille role either."

"I'll think about that tomorrow. It'll only take a week to shoot that crap for Columbia. I can then fly out on my magic carpet."

Producer Sam Katzman was shocked when notified that Lucille would play Princess Narah, who spends her days lounging, eating grapes fed to her by her slaves, and inventing imaginary ailments that call for visits from the palace doctor, handsome Abdullah al Husan, summoned to her chambers. She finds him sexy, and John Agar fitted the role.

Katzman knew that Lucille's salary would eat up much of the cost of his production.

"Sam didn't make E pictures," she said. "He went down the alphabet to make F movies. Real quickies. He was also known as a deal breaker for Cohn. When he wanted to get rid of a star, he sent him or her one of Katzman's scripts, and the star would bolt and Columbia would be free."

When **John Agar** took the former child star, **Shirley Temple**, as his bride in 1946, it made headlines around the world. One of them read "JOHN AGAR ROBS THE CRADLE."

Their tumultuous marriage lasted only three years.

The former "Little Miss Lollipop" refused to have "three-ways" with the women her husband brought back to their house.

In a surprise call, a real put-on, Lucille phoned Cohn. "I'd be delighted to do *The Magic Carpet*. I can't wait to shoot it. It's really magical all right. Let's begin filming at once."

Cohn later reported, "I was dumbfounded. The bitch accepted that stinker. Lucille Ball as an Arabian princess? Get real!"

She met with Lee Landers, her director. They were well known to each other, as he'd helmed her in four previous movies, including *Twelve Crowded Hours* in 1939.

On virtually no budget, he managed to put together a talented cast for *The Magic Carpet*. In addition to leading man John Agar, the cast included Patricia Medina, George Tobias, and Raymond Burr. Landers guided the picture in on time for an October 18, 1951 release where it ran for only eighty-four minutes.

As the temptress, Princess Narah, Lucille was billed as having "lips hotter than the desert sands."

She tried to conceal her pregnancy, "but my waistline seemed to grow two inches every day of the shoot," Lucille said. "My wardrobe mistress didn't know I was pregnant and suggested that I should cool it at dinnertime. She kept letting out my harem pants. There was just so much those *lamé* pantaloons could conceal. At one point, I needed to be photographed from the waist up.

Actually, Patricia Medina was the heroine of the movie. The British actress was in the midst of divorcing another English actor, Richard Green. Medina's most famous picture, *Phantom of the Rue Morgue* (1954), lay in her future, as did her famous marriage to actor Joseph Cotten beginning in 1960.

As the rider of *The Magic Carpet*, John Agar in a dual role had the most dramatic moments in the film. He played both Dr. Ramoth, the palace doctor, and The Scarlet Falcon, a mysterious vigilante, a kind of Robin Hood of the poor. Unknown to him, he was the rightful heir to the throne of the sultan. His father, the caliph, was assassinated, and his baby boy whisked away on a magic carpet.

In time, The Scarlet Falcon would be restored to his throne, choosing Medina as his queen over Lucille in her "scheming and spoiled princess" role.

At the time Lucille met Agar, he was in the throes of divorcing his wife, Shirley Temple, the former child star. Lucille had seen him in only one film, and that was *Fort Apache* (1948). In it, in a performance opposite John Wayne and Henry Fonda, he played a Union soldier and Temple's love interest.

Agar angered Lucille on the first day of the shoot. "That cocky bastard really pissed me off. He was a handsome bastard, and he knew it. It was widely known that all through his marriage to Temple, he dated other women."

Agar approached Lucille and said, "I've heard many rumors about how you seduce your leading men — take William Holden for example. Well, let's get something straight. Don't even think of adding me to your list of conquests. I don't date mothers."

"That doesn't come as a surprise," she answered. "All the world knows you're a child molester." She was referring, of course, to his marriage to the very young Miss Temple.

George Tobias played Rashi, a friend of The Scarlet Falcon. Raymond Burr was cast as the scary-looking villain, the Grand Vizier Boreg al-Buzzar.

Like Lucille herself, in future decades, Burr would be most often associated with a TV series as attorney *Perry Mason* from 1957 to 1966.

***

When *The Magic Carpet* wrapped, the time had come for Lucille to confront De Mille and reject the role of the Elephant Girl in *The Greatest Show on Earth*.

When she revealed that it was because she was pregnant, he advised her to have an abortion. "You can have as many kids as you want in the future, but a chance to be in a really big picture that will only further your film career might not come again."

[The role Lucille had coveted went instead to the sultry and notorious blonde, Gloria Grahame.]

The picture starred Betty Hutton and Cornel Wilde as trapeze artists. Charlton Heston was cast as the circus manager. James Stewart played a supporting role as a mysterious fugitive clown who never takes off his makeup. And whereas Lucille's frothy Arabian Nights picture bombed at the box office, the De Mille spectacular grossed $36 million.

The Magic Carpet marked the end of Lucille's pre-television movie career. "I was not a failure in films, look at my record, but I didn't set Tinseltown ablaze either. In the early 1950s, a whole busload of female movie stars over forty were being loaded on a truck headed for oblivion. I was determined not to join them. I set about to reinvent myself."

When *The Magic Carpet* opened nationwide, Columbia promised "1,001 Thrills, 1,001 Delights." But the public didn't buy that hype. Making things worse, it was the first studio film to be shot in the then-novel technology known as Supercinecolor. "It was supposed to rival Technicolor," Lucille said. "All that it did was to make us look yellow."

Variety cast a dim view of it: "Lucille Ball is wasted in her role of the princess but does supply a fair amount of marquee value. John Agar, the dashing hero, is stilted."

A critic for *The Hollywood Reporter* wrote: "Lucille Ball and John Agar deliver particularly undistinguished performances—Miss Ball wouldn't, Mr. Agar couldn't."

At the premiere of *The Greatest Show on Earth,* Desi encountered De Mille, who congratulated him. "You're the only person in the world to screw Harry Cohn, Columbia Pictures, Paramount, Cecil B. De Mille, and your wife, all at the same time."

PSSSSST!! Did you get a look at **Lucille**, a hip and liberated woman who looks fabulous in *couture,* getting all dolled up and then having to HIDE behind a *chadoor* and *niqab*?

Like she said, early in her career when they were making her take OFF her clothes: "In showbiz, a girl's gotta do what a girl's gotta do."

Lucille Ball appears here with **John Agar** in what she called "the most horrible film of my career," *The Magic Carpet* (1951) .

428

CHAPTER THIRTEEN

AMERICA FALLS MADLY IN LOVE WITH LUCY

In the history of television, Lucille Ball and Desi Arnaz struck gold, the biggest load of paydirt since the Forty-Niners began digging into California soil. But they didn't know it at first.

In time, *TV Guide* would proclaim that the face of Lucille Ball would be seen by more people around the world than any other human being who ever lived.

Their panning for gold got off to a rough start. As the tumultuous war-torn 1940s ended, both Lucille and Desi faced career crises. The future looked bleak.

In 1948, as television loomed as a threat on the horizon, movie theaters across America reported a steep decline in box office receipts. In the early 1950s, more and more homes had included a television set in their living rooms.

"At the time, I was a forty-year-old broad," Lucille said. "After that dismal *The Magic Carpet* (1951), I feared there would be no more big picture offers. Perhaps only junk movies like *Devil Queen from Outer Space.*"

At thirty-four, Desi no longer oozed the sexual allure he had in the early 1940s. He was already turning gray at the temples, and his heavy drinking had made him fleshier. "The middle-age spread came early to

Lucille Ball was on the cover of *TV Guide*, including its very first issue in 1953, more than any other person in the history of television—i.e., at least 39 times, depending on the way you count them.

Later editors there defined her as the greatest TV star of all-time, and cited *I Love Lucy* as the second greatest TV show after *Seinfeld*, a statement met in some corners with strong disagreement.

me," he confessed. "I should work out more."

Fortunately, *My Favorite Husband* was earning Lucille $135,000 a year—very good pay in the 1940s. Desi was getting fewer and fewer bookings, as night clubs across the country were closing. The Big Band era of Harry James and Tommy Dorsey, even Xavier Cugat, was drawing to a close. Glenn Miller, who died in World War II, was a fading memory. When Lucille got angry at Desi, she called him "my kept boy," wounding his macho Cuban pride. But their arguments during these months were rare.

"Television might be our savior, or it could be a disaster," Lucille said. Desi tried to keep his hopes up as word leaked out that as a duo, they were shopping around for an opening on television. "At the time, I was treated like all those other Hollywood husbands, and often called 'Mr. Lucille Ball.' Those were fighting words for me, but I controlled my temper. Beverly Hills was filled with men, often failed actors, living off the incomes of their movie star wives."

Despite their career uncertainties, Lucille looked back on 1951 as "the happiest year of my life." It brought her not only the biggest career break of her life, but a daughter after all those miscarriages. It was also the most tranquil period of her life with Desi.

For the most part, in spite of several invitations for guest spots on radio or an appearance on someone's TV show, she stayed at home. She watched a lot of television shows, finding their nuances and logistics radically different from those of motion pictures. She also did a lot of knitting—first a red (Desi's favorite color) sweater for her husband, and then booties for her baby.

For the most part, she ventured out only to record episodes of her radio show, *My Favorite Husband* with Richard Denning still in place portraying her husband. When he heard that she was contemplating a TV spinoff of their series, he said, "Don't forget me when it comes to casting your TV husband. We work beautifully together." He then said, perhaps jokingly, "And if you want to try me out on the casting couch, that's OK with me."

It was those months before and after the birth of her daughter that Lucille looked back on as "the high point of my marriage to Desi."

"He was Mr. Wonderful, no more temper flare-ups, no more long disappearances. He spent more time at home than he ever did before and would ever do

New "Life-Size" Rectangular Tube
GE **BLACK-DAYLITE TELEVISION**

Critics defined many of the early models as prohibitively expensive. (The TV set illustrated above was priced at $279 in 1950 dollars—today's equivalent of more than $3,000. Reception wasn't particularly reliable, and programming by today's standards was heavily censored, primitive, simplistic, and family-friendly

But **television entertainment** forged ahead, and changed history as part of the process.

again. He was very protective of me, warning me not to overly exert myself."

"When he drove me to the radio station, he never went over fifty... how unlike his usual two-hundred miles per hour. He very much wanted to be a father and hoped for a boy to carry on the Arnaz name. At last, I was living the marriage I had dreamed about, not the one I'd lived throughout the 1940s. A faithful loving husband. My dream had come true. But like all dreams, you are forced to wake up."

Night after night, Desi talked about "how we might fit into that little box in our living room. We knew we'd have to film a pilot and shop it around, looking for a sponsor to take our bait. Lucy's being pregnant didn't exactly help. Van Johnson suggested we abort the child and any others that followed until we relaunched ourselves in show business."

"Why bring a child into the world if you can't feed it?" Johnson asked.

Many of Lucille's closest friends urged her to drop the idea of working in television, referring to the new medium as "photographed radio."

Actor Farley Granger said to Lucille, "You might end up playing *Howdy Doody.*"

Two already-established TV stars had each made feature films which had unexpectedly bombed at movie houses. Cited were Milton Berle's film, *Always Leave Them Laughing* (1949), and Danny Thomas in his remake of Al Jolson's *The Jazz Singer* (1953).

In New York, word reached William S. Paley, the chairman of CBS, that Lucille was interested in video-taping a version of *My Favorite Husband* with the belief that it would go over as a TV series. She was also telling her agent and friends that she wanted Desi to play her husband instead of Denning.

A "whistle blower" in New York leaked a private memo that Paley had sent to his executive colleagues at CBS:

"Miss Ball and Mr. Arnaz are minor B-picture types—performers, not stars, especially the Spic. At forty, Lucille is over the hill. I more or less view them as second-rate. Actually, I'd give Arnaz a far lower grade than second. Maybe tenth-rate, if that."

His memo continued with, "For TV comedy, give me Eve Arden or Ann Sothern any day. We need name actors if you make a TV series with a husband-and-wife team. I suspect that if American families tuned in to a Lucille and Desi Arnaz show, they would view it for the last time, or else turn it off after ten minutes."

Finally, after much indecision, an agreement was reached to at least make a pilot. Even Paley agreed to that. "We should at least give Ball and Arnaz a chance to show us what they can do. However, I'm not expecting much other than a flop."

In case the pilot found a sponsor, the executive had a proposal for a possible title, *The Lucille Ball Show,* based on her limited name recognition.

Back in Hollywood, however, Desi devised his own idea for a title, suggesting that it be named *The Desi Arnaz and Lucille Ball Show.* "In my native Cuba, the man's name comes first. At home, I'm the king of the castle. Why should I lose my crown when I'm at work with my wife?"

In the fourth month of her pregnancy, Lucille began to prepare for her appearance on the pilot for her show. At the time, CBS didn't know that she was pregnant, but when she met with two wardrobe mistresses, they advised that she should appear behind a piece of furniture, or in pajamas or a bathrobe, even a loose-fitting garment. She had wanted to delay shooting of the pilot, but CBS demanded that it be done at once, because if it did go over, they'd want it for their fall line-up.

"The TV thing was a big gamble," she said. "If we flopped, we might be washed up, no more chance for a movie career, certainly no more talk of a series on TV."

"Frankly, I was afraid of this new venture," she said. "Then one night, my long-time friend of yesterday, Carole Lombard, appeared to me in a dream and told me, 'Go for it, kiddo!'"

She and Desi turned immediately to the trio of writers who had come up with those zany scripts for *My Favorite Husband:* Jess Oppenheimer, Bob Carroll, Jr., and Madelyn Pugh. They seemed eager to take on the new challenge. At first, the two lead characters were named "Larry and Lucy Lopez," but that was soon changed to Lucy and Ricky Ricardo.

Oppenheimer was also the producer of the show, and he demanded that they sign a contract giving him twenty percent of the characters (Lucy and Ricky Ricardo) and five percent of future royalties with Carroll and Pugh.

He also registered the concept with the Screen Writers Guild, affording himself a kind of copyright protection.

Many differences would exist between the pilot and the eventual series, but the same theme remained prevalent for both of them.

Desi would play a Cuban bandleader living in an apartment building in Manhattan. Lucy would be his zany wife who wants a career in show business, too, and will go to great lengths to break in, even though he'd be satisfied to keep her in apron strings in his kitchen.

Martin N. Leeds, the executive in charge of representing CBS's interests during the development and launching of the *I Love Lucy* series, later exploded a myth: "Desi always claimed that he borrowed the money to film the pilot, but actually, CBS put up the dough. The total cost was $19,000. Ironically, I later came to work for Desilu."

Some of the scenes in the pilot had been ripped off from the Arnaz/Ball vaudeville tour. In one scene, Desi appears shirtless, but that later raised objections from some of the CBS brass: "He has a barrel chest," one officer maintained. "If men show their chests, they should look like Lex Barker or Johnny Weissmuller."

When he wasn't bantering with Lucy on the pilot, Desi was allowed to bang his drums and sing "Babalu."

The pilot was never meant for public viewing, but only to shop around in attempts to lure a commercial sponsor.

"In Kinescope, Lucy and I would come across looking like we were filmed through cheesecloth," Desi claimed.

Ralph Levy directed the pilot: "I had worked with them earlier on *The Ed Sullivan Show*. Lucille didn't need any direction, even though she was pregnant and tired easily. Desi needed a hell of a lot of direction." After directing them, Levy would go on to helm such hits as *Green Acres, The Beverly Hillbillies,* and *Petticoat Junction.*

On March 2, 1951, the pilot was aired on closed circuit kinescoping for the eyes of CBS executives and any would-be sponsor of the show. Lucille's agent, Don Sharpe, was asking a price tag of $26,500 for the filming of each episode of a future series.

CBS executives, including Bill Paley, interpreted the pilot as disappointing.

The next afternoon, Paley met with Oscar Hammerstein II, the composer of such hits as *Oklahoma!* and *Carousel.*

After viewing the pilot, Hammerstein told Paley, "It might work, but ditch the Cuban. Use Richard Denning, a clean-cut, good-looking guy instead. That Arnaz is one loose cannon. My friend, Lorenz Hart, told me that in the late 1930s, Arnaz was his kept boy. You don't need to hire sleaze like that for a family show. Also, stories about Desi's renting himself out as a male whore and patronizing female whores at Polly Adler's bordello might find their way into the scandal mags. And for God's sake, don't have the kid sing 'Babalu.' What crap!"

As Lucille's agent, Sharpe went from sponsor to sponsor, asking them to back the show, but weeks went by without any offers. "No sponsor, no deal," Paley warned.

"I faced one rejection after another, some of them hostile," Sharpe said.

He found some interest from Milton H. Biow. *[Recognized today as one of the pioneers of modern advertising, Biow became famous within his industry for steering Philip Morris, Pepsi-Cola, Eversharp, Anacin, Ruppert Beer, Schenley Whisky and Lady Esther Cosmetics to national prominence, usually through television ads.]*

Biow debated the idea of linking *I Love Lucy* to Philip Morris cigarettes, but with the warning that substantial creative changes would be needed.

"The pilot is weak," he asserted. "Very awkward, not enough going on and a little silly. Tell your writers to flesh out the characters a lot more. Give them more personality. Make them more lovable, and a hell of a lot funnier."

Despite his review, Biow was able to interest his client, Philip Morris, in sponsoring the series. *[At the time, Philip Morris was sponsoring the dreary* Horace Heidt Show, *a venue that featured amateur performers dreaming of higher ratings in show-biz. Its ratings at the time, according to Biow, were disastrous. "Even* I Love Lucy *might be better than this turkey."*

The cigarette company agreed to sponsor the first series but wanted to cut $5,000 off the cost of each episode. Also, whereas Desi and Lucille wanted their show to be broadcast biweekly, Phillip Morris demanded it in weekly installments.

At the time, Harry Ackerman was in charge of CBS's radio and television production. He admired Desi and had cast him as the host of *Tropical Trip,* a radio quiz show broadcast every Sunday afternoon. The winner, along with his or her companion, received a free trip to a Caribbean resort.

A young Johnny Carson had auditioned as the host of the quiz show, but Ackerman had rejected him. "This Carson kid from Nebraska, or some God forsaken place, is not TV material."

It was Ackerman who phoned Desi during a rehearsal for the next episode of *Tropical Trip*. "Philip Morris, it is! But there's one problem."

"What in hell is it?" Desi asked."

"Lucy is a known chain-smoker, and she smokes only Chesterfields. Not only that, but she was once the 'Chesterfield Girl,' plastered on billboards across the country.

"I'll try to get her to change brands, but she's pretty dedicated to those damn Chesterfields."

"Don't be an idiot," Ackerman said. "Just take a package of Chesterfields, throw them out, and replace them with Philip Morris cigarettes, and she'll never know the difference."

Horace Heidt and His Musical Knights. The German Shepherd in the lower right-hand corner was always part of his act.

Before Lucille and Desi replaced his television talent show with *I Love Lucy*, **Heidt** (first figure on the left) had known previous success. The first hit of Heidt's band was "Gone With the Wind." Released in 1937, and not associated with (or reprised in) the famous 1939 movie with the same name, it was a tame but congenial Foxtrot that swept the nation.

Heidt portrayed himself in the 1941 film, *Pot o' Gold*, starring James Stewart and Paulette Goddard. It was produced by James Roosevelt (son of the U.S. President) and directed by George Marshall (Lucille's future director).

As it so happened, Ackerman was right. Lucille, a self-described "die-hard Chesterfield devotee," became a Philip Morris addict and never knew the difference.

***

The launch of the *I Love Lucy* TV series almost collapsed during the first two weeks of negotiations. Desi demanded that it be shot at Desilu Studios in Hollywood, whereas both CBS and Philip Morris held out for filmings in New York, where nearly all major television shows were made.

In 1951, there was no coaxial cable between New York and Los Angeles. Only Kinecast was in use. It meant that a telecast, if shot in California, would appear fuzzy on TV screens in the East.

"To solve that problem," Desi boasted, "I demanded that all of our series be put on film like a regular motion picture. That meant it could be shown anywhere in the world, including China and Australia. Of course, it would cost more, but I felt it would be worth it in the long run."

Filming of *I Love Lucy* would increase the budget by $5,000 per episode.

To meet that ongoing expense, both CBS and Philip Morris each agreed to put up another $2,000, and Desi agreed that he and Lucille would accept a $1,000 reduction in their per-episode fee.

As it turned out, Desi had made a particularly lucrative "deal of a lifetime." He and his sponsors would own 50% each of the first telecast. But after it was first aired, he and Lucille would own 100%. At the time, CBS *[foolishly it was said, later]* didn't realize that millions of future dollars would be generated through re-runs.

[In that era, most filmed TV shows, after they aired, ended up in trash bins.]

During Desi's search for a suitable studio in which to tape *I Love Lucy,* he heard about General Services Studio. Eight sound stages stood on 8 ½ acres of land. In the early 1930s, at this location, child star Shirley Temple had made ten-minute shorts, each of them marketed as "child burlesque," a category that became very popular with pedophiles.

The owners, George and James Nasser, were facing bankruptcy and were eager for almost any sort of deal. Desi put up an initial $50,000 and went to work renovating the decaying sound stages, adapting them to his needs. CBS contributed $25,000 to the cost of renovations, which included the construction of a new entrance for visitors. Desi insisted that each episode of *I Love Lucy* be filmed in front of live audiences. He adopted as "standard policy" the regularly scheduled mailout of 300 invitations for every taping.

A new lighting system was installed, and the warped and splintering wood floors were replaced with concrete and covered with Masonite so that cameras could easily be rolled around. Bleachers were installed for visitors, and stages were joined together to create the Ricardos' kitchen, living room, and bedroom. Since censors at the time objected to shared beds, even for actors portraying married couples, it was outfitted with demure-looking twin beds. Another set, replicating a venue for Desi's stage productions with his *Cubano* band at the Tropicana, was also crafted.

Some scenes were shot outside the studio, depending on that episode's plot. Examples included scenes at an alligator farm, and scenarios filmed aboard the USS *Constitution.*

Desi immediately ran into a challenge from California's Health and Welfare Department as well as the local fire department: "I managed to slay all these dragons," he said, "but it took a lot of work."

As it turned out, there were no rest rooms for women within an acceptable walking distance from the sound stages. When she heard that, Lucille volunteered to have her dressing room's bathroom converted into a women's public toilet, an invasion of her privacy.

To direct the series, Marc Daniels, a native of Pittsburgh, was imported. A few years earlier, he'd been a U.S. soldier in World War II. After the war, he'd been hired by CBS to direct *Ford Theater,* the first-ever dramatic anthology series ever presented on television.

Daniels would helm the first thirty-eight episodes of *I Love Lucy.* Looking back, many years later, he recalled, "I tangled with Lucy on several occasions, both over my direction and over the scripts. Desi was much easier to get along with."

He later left the series for a better-paying job, and in time, he helmed fifteen episodes of TV's *Star Trek.*

"My walking out on *I Love Lucy* seems a stupid mistake today," he said. "But who knew we were making television history?"

In 1986, shortly before her death, Lucille would have a reunion with Daniels when they worked together on an episode of *Life With Lucy.*

She was distressed with the first script of *I Love Lucy* from her trio of writers, describing it as "a disaster." In that script, Desi would play a major-league bandleader like Harry James in the 1940s, and she would portray a "hotsy totsy" movie star always concerned with looking glamourous.

Disrupting the Ricardos' (fictional) third wedding anniversary, photographers arrived to shoot "Ricky and Lucy" for a cover story.

According to Lucille, "This is hardly a comic horror. To have photographers arrive to honor the Ricardos' anniversary and to make a big splash about it in the media isn't exactly a hardship. Viewers will judge them as damn lucky."

Then, as plot inadequacies became more obvious, Lucy demanded, "Rewrite the script. Keep Desi as a bandleader but on a modest scale, making $150 a week. Make my character not a movie star, but a klutzy housewife trying unsuccessfully to break into show biz herself. Let them live in a middle-class apartment in Manhattan. Have Desi struggling to keep Lucy on a budget."

As another (much-revised) script was being prepared, Desi began to hire a crew, knowing that much depended on the right cameraman. Lucille had fond memories of the way Karl Freund had glamorously photographed her in *Du Barry Was a Lady.*

He had been born in 1890 in the Austro-Hungarian Empire. In Europe he had become a cameraman at the age of fifteen. He eventually gravitated to Hollywood, where he became a huge success photographing love goddesses like Greta Garbo and Marlene Dietrich.

In more recent times both Lucille and Desi had been impressed by how he'd photographed *Key Largo* (1948), starring Humphrey Bogart, Lauren Bacall, and Edward G. Robinson.

Freund was hailed as "The Giotto of the Screen, "being among the first to "liberate" the camera from a sta-

Two views (one young, one middle-aged) of the Austria-born, camera-wielding aesthetic genius, **Karl Freund**.

"I started out in Hollywood photographing the love goddesses, dames like Garbo and Dietrich, and ended up with my camera focused on Lucy Ricardo."

tionery position and freely move it about, making use of cranes and dollies.

To shoot *I Love Lucy,* he created a lustrous black-and-white cinematography, inventing the "flat lighting system," still in use today. Basically, with the intention of eliminating shadows, it flooded the sets with light from many different sources and directions.

Freud is cited as the inventor of the "three-camera technique."

[Usually, that includes two "flanking" cameras shooting close-ups of the two most active characters on a set. Simultaneously, a "central camera" films a wide-angled "master shot" that records multiple characters at once and defines the layout of a room.

Multiple shots from multiple angles are thereby recorded in a single take without having to interrupt the flow and action of a scene. This is cost-effective for programs scheduled for viewing a short time after their filming, as it shortens time otherwise spent in video or film editing. As years went by, Freund's technique became widely recognized as well-suited for high-output, regularly scheduled televised soap operas.]

I Love Lucy was not the first TV series to be filmed in Los Angeles. Ralph Edwards, the host of *Truth or Consequences,* had already inaugurated a system wherein shows taped in Los Angeles in 35 millimeter were then converted *[i.e., printed down, duped down, or "double duped down"]* to 16 millimeter film.

"Papa," as Freund was called, became a familiar face on the set, going around drinking from a thermos filled with martinis made with Russian vodka.

He told Desi, "I didn't take this job because of the crappy salary you offered. I did it for the challenge. I've got all the money I need from my orange groves in the San Fernando Valley. I am doing what you want, Cuban Boy, but you've given me one tall mountain to climb."

***

The original pilot of *I Love Lucy* did not include Fred and Ethel Mertz. Jess Oppenheimer, the producer and head writer, is credited with suggesting that the Ricardos should be counterbalanced with an older couple. He said, "We could have many plot variations—couple against couple, the wives against their husbands, the haves against the have-nots."

It was decided that the newly created couple would be the landlords of the apartment building occupied by Ricky and Lucy.

What to call them? At first, the names of "Joe and Mary" were recommended, but that was soon changed to "Walter and Gloria." At least for a day, the names "Harry and Bess" were put forth, a reference to the current occupants of the White House in Washington, D.C.

It was Madelyn Pugh who came up with the names of Fred and Ethel Mertz. For inspiration, she "adopted" the names of two of her neighbors from when she lived in Indianapolis.

In her search of who to cast as Fred, Lucille immediately thought of her longtime friend, Gale Gordon. She wanted to hire her supporting players from her radio series, *My Favorite Husband.* On that show, the voice of

Gordon could be heard as Rudolph Atterbury, her husband's (Richard Denning's) short-tempered boss. Bea Benaderet was cast as Iris, the "on the air" best friend of the character portrayed by Lucille, and the "wife" of Gordon's character.

That casting combination didn't work out. Gordon, aged 45 at the time, was under contract to play the high school principal, Osgood Conklin, in the hit radio show, *Our Miss Brooks* (1948-52). He would, however, become Lucille's co-star in her future.

Likewise, Benaderet also had another commitment. At the ago of 46, she was playing Blanche Morron, the television sitcom neighbor on the *George Burns & Gracie Allen Show* (1950-1958).

As Fred Mertz, the veteran character actor, James Gleason, age 65, seemed ideal. He was available, but his salary demands eliminated him. Lucille and Desi were jointly earning $4,000 in take-home pay. Gleason demanded $3,500 per episode, pricing himself out of the running.

For a few days, at least, Marjorie Main and Percy Kilbride were suggested. They had scored a big hit when they appeared as Ma and Pa Kettle in *The Egg and I* (1947), starring Claudette Colbert and Fred MacMurray. That had led to a string of Ma and Pa Kettle spin-offs.

Desi raised the strongest objections to the casting. "Those two are country bumpkins. No one would ever believe them as landlords in a Manhattan apartment building."

No one thought of cantankerous William Frawley, a veteran character actor who was in a career slump. Balding, hawk-nosed, and 64 years old, he was nearing the end of a long career. At the time, he was working as a hot dog vendor, hawking weenies along Hollywood Boulevard and living in a rented room at the Knickerbocker Hotel with his sister. Lucille had at least a passing acquaintance with him, having met him back in the 1930s.

James Gleason was first offered the role of Fred Mertz in the *I Love Lucy* sitcom. "But he put too high a price tag on his ass," Desi claimed.

Over the course of his career, Gleason—with his long (some said "sinister") face, bald head, and suspiciously whiney voice— appeared in 100 films.

Marjorie Main and **Percy Kilbride** in *The Egg and I* (1947).

Despite its success at the box office, urban cynics reviewed it as "a hillbilly's folksy return to the Corn Belt."

According to Desi, "Hollywood has come up with some dumb casting ideas, but **Ma and Pa Kettle** as Manhattan landlords was the dumbest."

"That duo belonged down on Old MacDonald's Farm with the barnyard animals."

Frawley's only gigs in 1951 had been occasional radio spots, for which he earned fifty dollars per appearance. As Fred Mertz, he'd earn $350 a week, most of it going to pay his liquor bill.

At Lucille's urging, Desi agreed to meet with him at Nickodell's Restaurant, a hangout for cast and crew from nearby RKO and Paramount.

Desi intended to confront Frawley about his heavy drinking. He wasn't assured at the beginning of their talk when Frawley told the waiter, "Gimme a double bourbon, and keep 'em coming." Then he pointed to Desi and said, "This Cuban fella is paying."

Desi admitted, "I like a few drinks every now and then, but I don't let liquor interfere in doing my job."

Before the night ended, Desi agreed to cast Frawley, but with a

William Frawley, before anyone had heard of Fred Mertz:

"I was just as curmudgeonly as Fred Mertz. The role fitted me perfectly, and I got to make wisecracks and express comic disdain for my sitcom wife, that fat ass bitch, Vivian Vance."

warning: "If you ever show up on the set drunk, you're fired. There are hundreds of other out-of-work actors who can play Fred Mertz just as well as you."

Frawley agreed that he would not drink during the day. Instead, he delayed his liquor consumption until after work, when he rushed to join his cronies for an evening of drinking and watching TV, preferring sports programs.

As Frawley himself asserted, "I'd be perfect as Fred Mertz. I'm a typical, middle-aged American male devoted to hot dogs and hamburgers. I'm an addict for four things: bourbon, baseball, football, and boxing matches. Women come way down on my list."

Before hiring this stocky, cigar-chomping actor, Desi had to overcome objections from CBS, whose officials were aware of his addiction to the bottle. Frawley told Desi, "All of those assholes are bastards, real sons of bitches. How in hell do they know how much I drink?"

During his first days on the set, Frawley asked Desi, "Could you spare twenty bucks? I'm a bit lean of purse. You can, of course, deduct it from my first paycheck."

Frawley lived up to his promise, and during the entire run of *I Love Lucy,* he showed up every day and on time to impersonate Fred Mertz. He called Lucille "that kid" and referred to Desi as "that Cuban." He told other members of the cast, "I love that Lucy gal, but I think Desi is the living end."

Many evenings, he gravitated to Musso & Frank, a Hollywood legend since 1919, where movie stars, over the course of the years, gathered to drink and dine—Charlie Chaplin, Mae West, Clark Gable, and Carole Lombard among others.

Frawley formed a friendship with Marc Daniels, the director of *I Love Lucy*. Daniels and his wife, Emily, often dined with him at Musso and Frank.

Over time, Desi learned just who Fred Mertz was: Born in 1887 in Burlington, Iowa, Frawley as a teenager had shown an interest in the theater and got cast in local productions. His mother, Mary, a religious fanatic, had prophesied that if he went on the stage, he'd be doomed to burn in Hell's Eternal Fire.

In his 20s, he worked as a stenographer in the Omaha office of the Union Pacific Railway. Bored, he moved to Chicago, where he became a court reporter.

Frawley struggled for years trying to break into vaudeville, finally settling in Denver, where he worked as a singer in a café, helping to popularize such songs as "Carolina in the Morning" and "Melancholy Baby."

In 1914, he married another vaudeville performer, Edna Louise Broedt, with whom he toured in an act they named "Frawley and Louise." Separated in 1921, they filed for divorce in 1927. After that, he never married again.

In 1925, in New York, he landed his first role on Broadway in *Merry, Merry*. Later, he played a press agent in the original stage production (1932) of *Twentieth Century* by Ben Hecht and Charles MacArthur.

On Broadway, he became known as "difficult." In 1928, when he was appearing in *That's My Baby*, he punched its star, Clifton Webb, in the face, bloodying his nose. He later said, "The faggot deserved it."

He eventually signed a seven-year contract with Paramount, wherein he was expected to play in comedies, musicals, Westerns, and romances. His most frequently watched film, even into the 21st Century, was when he portrayed Judge Harper's political adviser in *Miracle on 34th Street* (1947), a classic that starred John Payne and Maureen O'Hara, with Kris Kringle played by Edmund Gwenn. That same year, Frawley appeared as the wedding host in Chaplin's *Monsieur Verdoux*.

***

The search for an actress to portray Ethel Mertz proved more difficult than hiring Frawley.

Several were considered: Lucille had wanted her longtime friend and confident, Barbara Pepper, but she had become an alcoholic with a reputation for unreliability and was enormously overweight.

Lucille also considered another friend, the lanky, sharp-featured Mary Wickes, but that didn't work out either. Wickes feared that working so closely with Lucille might damage their long-standing friendship.

Lucille forgot all about casting on July 17, 1951, when she was checked into the Cedars of Lebanon Hospital in Los Angeles. Doctors there determined that her unborn child would emerge feet first as a high risk "breech birth." A decision was therefore made to perform a Cesarean. From it emerged a baby girl weighing seven pounds, six ounces and measuring twenty-one inches long.

Lucille had wanted to name her Susan in honor of actress Susan Peters, but while she was still in recovery, Desi entered the name "Lucie," a variation in spelling of "Lucy," into the official record. The child's full name became Lucie Désirée Arnaz.

Lucille later told the press, "The birth of my daughter is one of the greatest moments of my life. It was a long time coming and had been preceded by miscarriages. But now she's here, and she is beautiful, my joy. I cried with happiness the first time I held her."

To celebrate her birth, Desi bought a baby blue Cadillac for the transfer of mother and daughter back to Chatsworth.

In honor of the occasion, he and his composer friend, Eddie Maxwell, composed a song. "There's a New Baby at Our House" was sung on his radio quiz show, *Tropical Trip*. It would gain even more prominence when it was reprised for the birth of his son.

During her recovery, Lucille was too busy to care for an infant. She turned the task over to the child's two grandmothers and around-the-clock nurses. When she was first put in charge of the infant, she had changed her diapers eighteen times in two hours, feeling she had to be totally dry at all times.

"There was no doubt that Lucie changed our lives," Lucille said. "We had business partners coming and going all the time as we prepared to launch *I Love Lucy* that summer. There was talk of budgets, deals, scripts, and casting, but this fragile new spark of life affected everything we thought and did."

***

Within a month, four actresses were considered for the role of Ethel Mertz. At first, the most likely candidate was Irene Ryan, who would later shoot to household fame as the grandmother ("Grannie") on the hit TV series, *The Beverly Hillbillies*.

Minor actresses such as Eileen Corb and Kathleen Freeman were recommended but rejected within a week.

An unlikely choice, but a leading contender for about ten days, was Gail Patrick. Born in Alabama in 1911, she was only two months older than Lucille. Decades before, she had come to Hollywood to play "The Panther Woman" in *Island of Lost Souls* (1932) but had then been rejected two days before shooting began. Lucille knew Patrick only slightly, having met her when they'd appeared together in RKO's, *Stage Door* (1937).

Patrick had hung around and was soon typecast in movies as "the other woman" in

Today, casting **Gail Patrick** as Ethel Mertz seems far-fetched, but at the time, the creative direction of *I Love Lucy* hadn't yet "found itself."

Here's Gail Patrick, who, for about ten eventful days, seemed like the best candidate for Ethel Mertz.

love triangles. In nearly every film in which she appeared, in the words of critics, she was "glamorously haughty."

It was Lucille herself who nixed the idea of casting Patrick. "She's supposed to be maybe fifteen years older than me, but she looks like my younger sister."

It was Marc Daniels, recently designated as director of *I Love Lucy*, who devised the idea of casting Vivian Vance. In 1947, he had helmed her in the summer stock production of *Counsellor-at-Law*, Elmer Rice's startling drama about a fabled Jewish lawyer, starring Paul Muni. Daniels later reported that the married Vance had sustained a brief fling with this talented fifty-one-year-old actor.

Daniels invited Desi and Jess Oppenheimer to journey with him to La Jolla, 120 miles south of Los Angeles. Lucille was invited, but she was still in recovery from her recent pregnancy.

Vance was performing at Mel Ferrer's theater in the John Van Druten play, *The Voice of the Turtle*. After an impressive run on Broadway, it had been filmed in 1947 with Ronald Reagan and Eleanor Parker, and with Eve Arden cast as "the sarcastic bitch."

Portraying the saucy, wise-cracking Olive Ashbrooke, Vance was far removed from any of the characteristics of Ethel Mertz.

After watching Vance's performance, Desi told Oppenheimer and Daniels, "We've found our Ethel." Both of them agreed, and as a team, they went backstage to offer the upcoming role to Vance.

Desi pitched the part to her at a salary of $350 a week. Daniels de-

Timeline of **Vivian Vance**: Top row, left, in 1913, as a four-year-old in Cherryvale, Kansas.

Top row center and right: as a jazz-age temptress in the 1930s, and

Two photos (right) **from** the 1940s, long before anyone had ever heard of Ethel Mertz

scribed the role, admitting she would need to gain twenty pounds, not wear false eyelashes, and be married to a man who had reached the age of drawing Social Security. She would also have to perform comedic stunts with Lucille and be made up to look fifteen years older than she actually was.

At first, Vance was not impressed with the role. Initially, at least, she rejected it.

It was Desi who finally persuaded her to join their team. That same year, she had appeared in the tearjerker, *The Blue Veil* (1951), star-

Left to right, **Charles Laughton, Jane Wyman, "Baby Freddy,"** and **Vivian Vance** in *The Blue Veil* (1951)

ring Jane Wyman as a war widow who loses her own child and devotes her life, ever after, to helping other children. Both Vance and her husband, Philip Ober, had supporting roles in it, and Vance got good reviews, hoping that the film would lead to other offers.

"What offers?" Desi asked.

"Well, none at the moment. Maybe some sexy siren parts."

Desi responded, "Let's face it—you're forty-two years old. Only Mae West launched a film career as a sexy vixen at the age of forty. The only roles you'll be offered are character parts."

The *Blue Veil* was more serious and morally "high-minded" than the TV series which propelled Vivian Vance to fame.

In the photo above, **Jane Wyman** (left), an emotionally unfulfilled governess who devotes her life to assisting dysfunctional families with their dysfunctional children, appears here with a young **Natalie Wood** (center) and stage and Pre-Code film actress, **Joan Blondell.**

Although insulted, Vance eventually realized that he was speaking the truth. It was Oppenheimer who raised another roadblock, warning her, "You'll have to play the wife of William Frawley."

"That old goat?"

In spite of her objections, she eventually agreed to sign for the part. Desi went ahead and booked her without Lucille's approval.

Vance would spend the rest of her life lying about her age, making herself years younger than she was.

Although unaware of it at the time, casting Vance in a possible long-running TV series was done at considerable risk. Unknown to Desi, the producer, and the director, Vance had a history of nervous breakdowns and mental illness.

In 1945, a Los Angeles policeman found her, clad in a nightgown and wandering alone along a lonely street at 3AM. She could not identify herself. Instead of arresting her, he connected her with the mental health department. It took a while before she became aware of who she was.

From that day forth, she always carried her name and address clearly stipulated in her handbag.

Even while touring with her stage production *The Voice of the Turtle,* she had a temporary nervous breakdown in a room of the hotel where the rest of the cast and crew were lodged. They could hear her running through the hallways, screaming. She later claimed, "I felt the walls of my room were closing in on me, ready to smother me." Once again, although she continued to perform onstage, mental therapy was arranged for her.

As time went by, more and more became known about her quirky past. She was born Vivian Roberta Jones in Cherryvale, Kansas, the second of six children, on July 26, 1909. As a young actress, she assumed the stage name of Vance.

From an early age, she wanted to become an actress, a venue vigorously opposed by her devoutly (some said obsessively) religious mother, who told her, "What you're telling me is that you want to grow up to be a whore."

By 1930, she was performing at the Albuquerque (New Mexico) Little Theater. One play followed another and over time, she worked with Eve Arden, Danny Kaye, and even the great Gertrude Lawrence.

At the time she signed for *I Love Lucy,* she had been married three times. In 1928, she wed Joseph Shearer Danneck, Jr., divorcing him in 1931. In 1934, she married George Koch, the union lasting until 1941.

When she joined the team of *I Love Lucy,* she was wed to actor Philip Ober, whom she'd married in 1941. Prior to that, despite their status as minor actors, the pair made scandalous headlines when Ober's then-wife accused Vance of adultery.

Press reports depicted Vance as a blonde bombshell, a "cross between Cleopatra and Mata Hari." A picture of her appeared in a newspaper looking sultry and seductive.

That negative publicity precipitated Vance's return to Albuquerque, where she was cast as a Swedish prostitute in a stage production of Eugene O'Neill's *Anna Christie.* Greta Garbo had made her film debut in the 1930 film version.

It was while she was still appearing in *The Voice of the Turtle* that Vance later admitted, "Inside my gut, I felt like a walking time bomb, ticking, ticking, just perilous seconds from exploding."

A lot of pressure came from her jealous husband, Ober, who resented the fact that her career seemed on the rise whereas he could get only minor roles, if any at all. She would later compare her marriage to him as evoking the husband-and-wife in the 1944 film, *Gaslight.* In that plot, Charles Boyer is trying to drive his wife, Ingrid Bergman, insane.

"At times, when things got really rough between Phil and me, I would literally bump my head against the bedroom wall. Actually, in spite of many problems and conflicts, my playing Ethel Mertz gave me the glue to keep my mental health and my life together."

Although Lucille and Vance later became close friends, the relationship between them in the early weeks of their emoting together was tense. "She gave me a rough time, always criticizing me," Vance said. "She would pick on me for the slightest mistake, and yell at me in front of the crew. It was ghastly. As for Desi Arnaz, I was the only female in heels he didn't proposition."

She finally came to accept Desi's vision, with high hopes for the future of the series. She told him, "I know that Ethel Mertz will be the peak of my career. I'll always detest that Frawley fart, but I guess I'll learn to love your red-headed bitch."

"Our series forever destroyed Viv's version of herself," Lucille said. "When I met her, she was dressed rather flashy and wore a lot of makeup, perhaps thinking of herself as a *femme fatale.* We downsized her and made her frumpy and dumpy, and married to an old geezer. She was closer to Marjorie Main than Lana Turner."

Pre-production of the *I Love Lucy* TV series began in April of 1951, with the actual shooting scheduled for August 15. The half-hour episode could be shot in a week, although editing would take far longer.

Lucille shared her concept of Lucy Ricardo with her trio of writers. Oppenheimer, Pugh, and Carroll. "I want her to be zany and lovable, a woman who can take a pie in the face like in one of those silent pictures. I don't have the pretensions of Lana Turner, and I can allow myself to look like a country hick with blacked-out teeth, a kind of Daisy Mae from Dogpatch."

"She is never to be mean, never to utter words from an acid tongue. I want her to be feminine regardless of the plot. I also want to convey that only she thinks she can sing and dance. I want to have her come up with crazy schemes of how to break into Desi's act at the Tropicana Club, where he and his band appear. I want Lucy Ricardo to be pathetic at times, but with her own special charm."

In contrast, she wanted the character of Ricky Ricardo to be "level-headed, unlike his wife, a good family man, a husband who always makes sense. I want him to struggle on—in a kindly, forgiving way—in support of his wife, regardless of how crazy her schemes. He is never to act violently toward her."

She wanted Ricky to have a good business sense, in marked contrast to Lucy's tendency to overspend. If he has to give her a tongue-lashing, she wanted it to be done in Spanish. "I want every script to depict that through it all, he has a deep and abiding love for his wife."

Even before shooting began, the characters of Lucy and Ricky were clearly defined. The episodes would reflect a mixture of 1950s family life with the glitter and glamour of show business. One critic would refer to them as "Yankee gumption meets Latino bravura."

Into every episode Lucille would pour her comedic skills, including her clown face, her circus-like wigs, her big blue eyes, and fair skin—all the elements of a court jester.

In contrast, Desi, with his jet-black hair pompadoured, would look somewhat akin to a gigolo at a night club in Havana. As one observer noted, "he was an amalgam of characters from the Italian theater of *commedia dell'arte.*"

Lucille referred to her writers as her "think tank." In close collaboration with them, she plotted strong characterizations and hilarious co-dependencies.

She even created an imaginary address (523 East 68th Street, in Manhattan), which—had it been real—would have been positioned under the waters of the East River. She didn't want to give a real address, based on fear of getting sued.

Everyone connected with the series agreed that the show's dynamics needed an older couple, perhaps their landlords. That had led to the creation of Fred and Ethel Mertz. Based on the math of possible combinations, situations could be created where wives could conspire with each other—in other words, ganging up in harmless battles of the sexes. If Lucy felt that Ricky was losing interest in her, she knew how "to vamp it up."

AN UNAUTHORIZED BIOGRAPHY OF
VIVIAN VANCE AND WILLIAM FRAWLEY

Meet the Mertzes

THE LIFE STORIES OF *I LOVE LUCY'S*
OTHER COUPLE

ROB EDELMAN AND AUDREY KUPFERBERG

Sociologists and reviewers of "The American Experience" have been fascinated by how, since the debut of *I Love Lucy*, **Fred and Ethel Mertz (Vivian Vance and William Frawley)** have developed almost mythic characteristics of their own.

Here's an example of an entire book devoted exclusively to their feuds, tempests, and spats, both on and off the camera.

Desi established the work schedule for filmings of *I Love Lucy* like this: Every Tuesday, cast members would be given the script for that week's episode. Rehearsals, with sets, would begin the following day. Frawley was the only actor who would not read the script. He tore out only the pages that contained his own dialogue, often without knowing what the plot was about.

Thursdays were devoted to dress rehearsals, and on Friday, two more rehearsals were squeezed in before the eight o'clock taping that night in front of a live audience. The budget for each episode was set at $21,500.

Desi defined Lucy as "a female Charlie Chaplin."

From the moment they met, Vivian Vance and William Frawley detested each other with a ferocious animosity that somehow helped to define their characters. According to Vance, "Let's face it: Millions of American women—not me, of course, but others—are disillusioned with their husbands. They go to bed with a bulging, beer-drinking gut while dreaming of a dashing Don Juan like Errol Flynn."

During the run of *I Love Lucy,* Frawley had only one (ongoing) objection: Vance as his onscreen wife. After meeting her for the first time, in a conversation with Desi, he asked, "Where in hell did you find that cunt? She has no talent. She can't sing. She can't dance. Her voice is like a barrel of shit dumped on a baked Alaska."

"You're wrong," Desi countered. "She's got talent as an actress. I'm asking only that you be her husband on camera. The deal doesn't call for you to plug her. Don't worry! You two are perfectly cast. The script calls for a minor dance number, but I'm not expecting you to become Fred and Ginger."

"I did soft shoe in vaudeville, so I guess I can teach a few steps to Fat Ass," Frawley said.

Right from the beginning, Vance had a low opinion of Frawley, and it only got worse as the series continued. She referred to him as a "grumpy old Irish boozer who has about as much sex appeal as a rotting donkey's ass. I came to dread any script that called for me to be affectionate with him. Imagine me, a fairly young and pretty woman, married to an old fart like Fred Mertz, who could be my father. Read that 'granddad.' I had hoped Desi would cast a handsome, if older, actor. I adore good-looking men."

At times on camera, Frawley would have to call her "honey-bunch." After the scene, he'd whisper to a member of the crew, "I got through that with old Fat Ass."

He really angered Vance when he told a reporter, "She came out of Kansas. I wish she'd go back there."

After two or three sessions appearing opposite Vance, Frawley said, "She has a figure like a sack of doorknobs."

***

Many members of the crew found Lucille demanding and very difficult to work with. David Connors had been hired as her assistant (really an errand boy catering to her every demand) for $35 a week. "She was a very strong-willed woman, hard to please. I got hell for the smallest thing if I didn't perform exactly like she wanted. Several times, she threatened to fire me. She had a motto: 'My way or the highway.'"

A Brooklyn-born Italian dwarf, **Johnny Roventini**, stood 47 inches tall and weighed 59 pounds.

On episodes of *I Love Lucy*, he became a "living trademark" for the show's sponsor, Philip Morris cigarettes. He was described, with *double-entendre* intended, as "an advertising giant."

Promoted as "the smallest bellboy in the world," he lived to the age of 88 and never married.

"Her instructions were to be followed to the letter," he said. "Once, she wanted this particular brand of tomato juice. The commissary didn't have it, so I brought her another brand. She raised hell."

"She seemed in command, even when 'The Man' was around," Connors claimed. "Desi was also demanding. If you didn't perform like he wanted, he'd curse you in Spanish. I survived the first season. But one night in a dimly lit club on Sunset Strip, my life changed for the better."

He met this famous director—one that he never named—who took him home for the night. The next morning, he invited him to come and live with him. "All I had to do every day was to strip naked and let him feast. For that, I got $150 a week and lots of fringe benefits: a beautiful car, a Rolex, a whole new wardrobe, and foreign travel. It sure beat working for Arnaz and that redheaded bitch."

In addition to the Ricardos and Fred and Ethel, a fifth character became famous on *I Love Lucy*. He was a four-foot midget, Johnny Roventini. Dressed in a bellhop's uniform, he introduced each episode with his inimitable cry of, "CALL FOR PHILIP MOR-REES."

In the first episode's telecast, the opening title credits depicted a cartoon version of Desi and Lucy romping in the shadow of a huge package of Philip Morris cigarettes.

***

Most business executives didn't think that Desi had what it took to become one of them. They were wrong, and as time went by, he showed them just how wrong their initial judgments were. When CBS presented him with its financial statement for the first season, he studied it overnight and found that they had made a one-million-dollar mistake. "That was money owed to Desilu."

Lucille had high praise for Desi's business sense. "He's also Nostradamus, as he seems to know what is going to happen before it takes place. He also has this incredible memory and can learn all his lines from a script in just twenty minutes,

In a hilarious scene from the premiere (October 15, 1951) of *I Love Lucy*, **Lucille** (left) and **Vivian Vance** disguise themselves as romance-starved hillbillies named "Euncy" and "Maw."

Unrecognized by their respective husbands, they're configured as the unwanted "nightclub dates" of Ricky Ricardo and Fred Mertz.

448

getting it letter perfect."

"He knows the nuts and bolts of how to run a studio. I mean, he's hip about camera angles, editing, shadowing, even shipping out episodes. Before he hires someone to do a job, he performs it himself so he knows what's entailed."

Desi even guided Karl Freund, the best cameraman in Los Angeles, about "how to take the wattles out of Lucille's neck."

He also showed what a shrewd negotiator he was, virtually creating a market for a then-unknown entity (re-runs) generated by the new medium of television.

Writers Pugh and Carroll tried out every stunt they devised before asking Lucille to replicate it. She pulled off dozens of them in the months ahead, even suffering through the placement of an enormous, two-handled "loving cup" on her head or balancing a fifteen-pound headdress evocative of the one she wore in *Du Barry Was a Lady*.

Pugh claimed: "She could imitate anything or anybody, be it an armchair or a statue standing in a town square."

During the first season, according to Carroll, so much attention was focused on Lucille that Desi got jealous of both her acclaim and her talent: "Desi had one of the biggest egos in the business and would kill anyone who called him 'Mr. Ball.' His spirits improved in January of 1952, when the *Hollywood Reporter* named him 'the most underrated performer on network TV.'"

The first episode they filmed (*Lucy Thinks Ricky Is Trying To Murder Her*) was not the first episode to be broadcast. [For technical reasons, it wouldn't be broadcast until November 5, 1951.]

Episode No. One, *The Girls Want to Go to a Nightclub*, premiered on October 15. It takes place on the occasion of the 18th wedding anniversary of the Mertzes. Although the women want to go to a night club, their husbands have already bought tickets to a boxing match. Apparently, they were planning on bringing two other women. To thwart that, Lucy and Ethel disguise themselves as hillbillies. Euncy and her "Maw," (Ethel) then show up as their dates.

Their director, Marc Daniels, invited the stars of the show to watch the premiere in his living room on Laurel Canyon. Everyone showed up except Frawley, who preferred to watch "the fights" with his Irish cronies in the bar of the Knickerbocker Hotel.

Daniels, Lucille, Vance, and Desi collectively interpreted it as a disaster, too weak to lead off the series. Their opinion was in vivid contrast to legends about how the show's first telecast was a roaring success.

The following day, Parker McComas, the head of Philip Morris, wanted to cancel the show. "It's silly, unfunny, actually boring," he complained to the director of his advertising agency, Terrence Clyde. Clyde eventually persuaded McComas to delay any final decision for at least another four episodes.

In its review of the *I Love Lucy* pilot, *The New York Times* defined the first half of the show as mildly amusing, but panned the second half, which depicted Ethel and Lucy as country yokels. "Totally unbelievable,' the critic wrote.

Variety found the episode's plot "preposterous," and asked why Desi couldn't recognize his own wife, even though she was disguised as a hill-billy with blacked-out front teeth. The *Hollywood Reporter* disagreed, labeling the show as "situation comedy at its finest," and in a later edition, reviewing it with, "Lucille Ball is America's number one *comedienne* in her own right. She is the consummate artist, born for the television. Half a step behind her comes her husband, Desi Arnaz, the perfect foil for her screwball antics and possessing comic abilities of his own. That talent is sufficient enough to make them a genuine comedy team, rather than a one-woman *tour de force.*"

In spite of some initial raves for the series, Lucille had serious doubts about its future. "I give it a year, two at the most."

Despite early objections and criticisms, *I Love Lucy*, by November, had become the 16th most-watched TV show in the country. It was on November 5 that the first episode its team had shot, "Lucy Thinks Ricky Is Trying to Murder Her," was telecast.

According to the plot, Lucy—as an avid reader of mysteries—becomes obsessed with the thriller, *The Mockingbird Murder Mystery.* Swayed by that premise, she fears Ricky is trying to bump her off. She hears him on the phone, telling someone, "I'm gonna get rid of her," and then mentions that he has a gun in a desk drawer.

As it turns out, Ricky is actually talking about getting rid of the girl singer in his band, and the gun he described turns out to be a plastic toy.

Around the time the third episode was in the can, a decision was made. Only Lucy could make fun of Desi's Cuban accent. Whenever Fred or Ethel did it, it wasn't funny.

In addition, there would be no mocking of physical defects such as a nervous twitch or "crazy people" jokes. Also forbidden was ridicule of ethnic groups, be it Jewish or black, Polish, Japanese, Chinese, or Irish.

A month after the premiere, on November 15, the viewing audience of *I Love Lucy* climbed to fourteen million—that is one out of every nine people in the country. Within a month, another two million viewers began tuning in every week.

By January of 1952, *I Love Lucy* moved up to fifth place in national ratings, with a viewing audience of 21 million fans…and growing.

At the time, there were simply not a lot of female comedians entertaining audiences. Except for Lucille Ball, Gracie Allen, Martha Raye, and Imogene Coca, comedy was a field dominated by men.

Even Desi's accent, long disdained by sponsors, was not a problem at all. Fans loved how he spoke English and mispronounced words. Thousands of immigrants, many of them viewers of this "All American" show, had arrived from outside the U.S., and they, too, were struggling with English.

By May of 1952, *I Love Lucy* had a fan base of 29 million viewers tuning in every Monday night.

***

It seemed that everyone was watching *I Love Lucy*. An item appeared in the *Detroit Free Press* that relayed how water levels in the city's reservoirs dropped drastically every Monday night between 9:30 and 9:35PM when nearly half the city got up from their sofas to urinate at the end of every episode of *I Love Lucy*. In Chicago, the city's most famous department store, Marshall Field, changed the scheduling of the only evening it was open (Mondays) to Thursday nights because on Monday, shoppers tended to be watching *I Love Lucy*.

In Manhattan, it was hard to get a taxi whenever Lucy was on the air, since most of that city's cab drivers opted to stop at their local taverns to watch *I Love Lucy* on their bar's TV set.

"There was magic in the air," Oppenheimer said. "The audience fell in love with Lucy at first sight. Once the spell was cast, laughing at our jokes wasn't enough. Fans started to laugh at the straight scenes, too."

The TV critic for *The New York Times* wrote:

> *"Miss Ball's gifts are those of the born trouper rather than the dramatic school student. First and foremost is her sense of timing; in this respect, she is the distaff equivalent of Jack Benny. Maybe it is a roll of her big eyes. Maybe it is the sublime shrug which housewives the world over will understand. Maybe it is the superb hollow laugh. Maybe it is the masterly double-take that tops the gag line. Whatever it is, it comes at the split-second instant that spell the difference between a guffaw and a smile."*

At the start of 1952, Desilu employed some 3,000 people, ranging from accountants to janitors. Lucille and Desi became so successful that they managed to persuade Eve Arden, famed as the radio star of *Our Miss Brooks,* to film its TV adaptation, *America's Most Famous Schoolteacher* at Desilu. Other TV shows would follow.

Some of the alltime favorite episodes of *I Love Lucy* emerged from its first season, telecast during the first months of 1952. They included *The Ballet*, which aired on February 18 with co-star Mary Wickes.

Wickes managed to conceal her disappointment that she hadn't been cast as Ethel Mertz. Indeed, her friendship with Lucille had survived.

A tall, gangling woman, Wickes

Character actress and close friend of Lucille, **Mary Wickes** makes her first appearance on *I Love Lucy*.

Portraying **Lucille's** ballet teacher, Madame Lamonde, she stands by helplessly as Lucy, uncomfortably wearing a *tutu*, gets her leg stuck on the *barre*.

Margot Fonteyn (and almost everyone else familiar with ballet and the fine art of self-satirization) found the episode hysterically funny.

was versatile enough to fit into almost any role—secretary, nurse, house-keeper, or nun. She was known for sarcastic remarks aimed at the lead characters of whatever movie she was in, notably in her performance as a foil to Bette Davis in *Now, Voyager* (1942).

In *The Ballet*, Wickes was cast as Lucy's ballet teacher, Madame Lam-onde. Lucy wants to join a troupe of performers at the Tropicana. To do so, she enrolls in a ballet class. Punishing her like a drill sergeant, Wickes puts her through her paces. Lucy ends up getting her left leg stuck in the *barre*. Things go downhill from there.

On a historic note, that episode also featured Lucy's first pie in the face.

On March 17, *The Moustache* was aired. In it, Ricky has grown a mus-tache, hoping to get cast as an "exotic" in a feature film. Lucy is horrified by his new look, and, in protest, glues a phony beard onto her face. A lot of laughs were generated when it couldn't be removed.

John Brown was cast as a talent scout in that episode, and it included a featured song composed by Irving Berlin: "I'll See You in C-U-B-A."

Another classic episode, *Pioneer Woman*, aired on March 31. In it, Lucy and Ethel decide to do things the way their grandmothers did and bake their own bread. In one of the most memorable scenes Lucy ever shot, a loaf of bread bursts forth from her oven, growing ten feet in just a few sec-onds and pinning her against the kitchen wall.

In its search for a loaf of bread that was big enough to inspire the laugh lines, the staff at Desilu had to scout a dozen bakeries to find one cable of producing one of suitable length.

After filming that episode, the studio audience was invited to come on stage to sample slices of the loaf with lots of butter.

In another episode, *The Freezer*, Lucille showcased her oldest and dear-est friend, Barbara Pepper, another actress, as mentioned, who had been considered for the character of Ethel Mertz.

In this segment, Lucy and Ethel buy a mammoth walk-in freezer from Ethel's uncle, who's a butcher. Thrilled with the savings they'll generate by buying food in bulk, they learn that meat will cost less than sixty-nine cents a pound if they buy it in large quantities. With that in mind, they buy two enormous sides of beef, not realizing how gigantic they'll be.

At one point, Lucy bumps into the freezer door, thereby locking herself inside. By the time she's rescued, she's turned into an Eskimo pie, her face a mass of icicles.

Another memorable episode, *Lucy Does a Commercial*, aired on May 5. The audience learns that she's the spokesperson for an energy tonic, Vita-meatavegamin, a foul-tasting liquid, 23 percent of which is pure alcohol. She tells the audience how tasty it is, but grimaces as she drinks it and later becomes hilariously intoxicated.

One television critic wrote, "Stan Laurel in his heyday in all those Lau-rel and Hardy comedies could not top Lucy in this farce."

By the spring of 1952, *I Love Lucy* had become the most-watched TV show in America. Since its first telecast, it now played to thirty million viewers. "We were the most famous couple in America," Desi boasted, "beating out Ike and Mamie."

Lucille herself noted, "we were getting more press coverage than the battles between Marilyn Monroe and Joe DiMaggio. Yes, even more than the turbulent saga of Ava Gardner and Frank Sinatra."

Unknown to viewers, Desi—who was sometimes away from Lucille for long periods of time—had resumed his extramarital affairs. Nonetheless, columnist Hedda Hopper defined them as "America's Most Ideal Couple."

Lucille complained to Barbara Pepper, "Here I am playing this childlike housewife, with Desi as my devoted husband. What a joke! Faithful? What bullshit! He's a whore-mongering bastard."

***

In the early 1950s, Joseph McCarthy, the now-notorious Senator (1947-1957) from Wisconsin, launched a witch hunt, seeking to "out" communists "concealed and conspiratorial" in both government and the entertainment industry. Careers were being destroyed.

In front of the committee in Washington, many stars and studio heads arrived to testify as friendly witnesses. They included Ronald Reagan, Gary Cooper, Louis B. Mayer, and Robert Taylor. Many others, including the distinguished screenwriter Dalton Trumbo, were "not cooperative" and sentenced to jail.

Those who weren't imprisoned (a string of stars, writers, and directors) often watched as their screen careers were trivialized and destroyed. Many went into exile in Europe or Mexico, or else worked anonymously or under assumed names.

It seemed improbable that Lucille Ball, of all people, might ever have been "fingered" as a closeted communist. However, as investigations dug into her past, it was revealed that in 1936, as "steered and pressured" by her grandfather Fred, she had registered as a member of the Los Angeles

THE ANSWER TO ALL YOUR PROBLEMS IS IN THIS LITTLE BOTTLE.

VITA-MEATA-VEGAMIN

One of the most beloved and "instantly recognizable" of the *I Love Lucy* episodes was #30, "Lucy Does a TV Commercial' (*aka* "Vitameatavegamin").

Telecast on May 5, 1952, it has a well-intentioned Lucy demonstrating the use of an alcohol-laced vitamin supplement and becoming sloppily (and adorably) incoherent.

Dialogue, some of it lampooning current news about quack medications and health supplements went like this:

LUCY, AS A TV CAMERA ROLLS: "I'm your Vitameatavegamin Girl. Are you tired, rundown, listless? Do you poop out at parties? Are you unpopular? The answer to all your problems is in this little bottle. You can spoon your way to health."

With perfect comedic timing, Lucille then demonstrates with a kind of "inspired slapstick' one of the most powerful examples ever telecast of why *We Love Lucy.*

branch of the Communist Party.

Instead of summoning her to a public hearing, a secret deal was arranged for her benefit by Andrew Hickox, the business director of Desilu. It was formatted as a private meeting between two FBI agents and Lucille at the Arnaz ranch house at Chatsworth.

In late April of 1952, the Desilu staff arranged for her to disguise herself, as part of a publicity campaign for Desi's gig at the Tropicana, as the "Maharincess of Franistan." Vance was cast as her servant girl.

After a rehearsal, Lucille drove alone from the studio to Chatsworth for her two-hour "grilling" from the FBI. The arrangements were secret, with the intention of avoiding detrimental newspaper publicity.

Under scrutiny, she admitted that she'd registered as a member of the Communist Party along with her mother, DeDe, and her brother, Fred Ball. They'd done so to appease Lucille's grandfather, Fred Hunt. An avid reader of the *Daily Worker,* he had urged them all to register.

"I let my membership drop, and I never attended a meeting," she claimed. "I was busy seven days a week, shooting films every weekday at RKO, and rehearsing every weekend for plays at the Little Theater on the studio lot. I got home before midnight and had to get up by 5AM the next morning. Politics were the last thing on my mind."

The agents seemed to believe her testimony and the next day, they filed a report stating that "Lucille Ball is politically immature. She does not appear to be a communist—not now nor in the past."

As the agents departed, a great sense of relief came over her. Yet there was a nagging feeling that this session might not be the last.

Another, more pressing issue soon consumed her.

***

On a hot May day in 1952 in Los Angeles, Lucille and Desi barged into the office of Jess Oppenheimer, their producer and chief writer. Reporting on that encounter later with the other writers, Carroll and Pugh, Oppenheimer said, "I got the shock of my life."

Entering first was Desi, trailed by Lucille, who looked rather sheepish, not with her customary take-charge face.

Desi wasted no time. "Amigo, we've got to cancel further episodes of *I Love Lucy.*"

"Are you out of your fucking mind?" Oppenheimer asked, rising to his feet, his face a mask of horror. "You guys are the top-rated TV show in America. *Lucy* is going over like gangbusters."

"We've just come from the doctor. Lucy is gonna have another baby!"

As she remembered it, "The expression on Jeff's face was like a quack doctor telling him he was going to castrate him."

At first, Oppenheimer turned on Desi, flashing anger. "You Cuban stud horse. Getting her pregnant again after only ten months or so. Tomorrow, I'm sending over a five-year supply of rubbers. What size are you?"

Desi didn't say anything, but Lucille quipped, "Make them Trojan sized."

"I have never thought so quickly in my life," Oppenheimer claimed, "But within minutes I came up with a way to save the show."

Although it seems odd seventy years from that May afternoon, the word "pregnant" could not be spoken on the "highly moralistic tube" of that era, as Lucille dubbed it.

In those days, movie studios regularly suspended pregnant actresses without pay. It was strictly forbidden for a pregnant woman to be displayed on TV, although some actresses—at least during their early stages—could get by with concealing their condition with loose clothing.

Oppenheimer warned them, "if you bow out now, you'll be finished in television. Lucille also might find her movie career doomed. I assume you've talked about an abortion, something I can arrange."

"No way!" she shouted at him. "I want this baby to go with the little girl I already have."

"In that case, we'll have to make your having a kid a part of our scripts," Oppenheimer said.

"You gotta be kidding," Desi said. "You know the rules. It can't be done."

Yet Oppenheimer detected the slightest glimmer of hope on Desi's face. "Perhaps he was thinking there was a way out of this dilemma after all."

At the time, *I Love Lucy* still boasted thirty million viewers and a Nielsen rating of 67.2 percent. In No. 2 position was *Arthur Godfrey's Talent Scouts* with 54.7 percent.

The next day, Oppenheimer had to confront both CBS and Philip Morris. They were horrified until Desi appealed to Alfred Lyons, president of Philip Morris. He fired off a memo, "Don't fuck with the Cuban."

It was ordained that future scripts would substitute the delicate French word *enceinte* for the English term "pregnant."

Lucy's unborn child was expected in January of 1953, and for both aesthetic and health reasons, Desi and Lucille's doctor didn't want her working in front of a camera until after the end of October.

That created a conflict: For scripting and production purposes, the gender of the baby would have to be defined, and the episode filmed, weeks in advance of the actual birth. Would it be a boy or a girl? *[Desi preferred a boy for the continuation of the Arnaz name.]*

During a meeting with the script writers, it was determined that it would be a boy, at least on television, and that his name would be Ricky Ricardo, Jr. The backers of *I Love Lucy* even brought in religious leaders for their approval—a rabbi, a pastor, and a priest. Each of them suggested there would be no objection, as long as the scripts were handled with good taste.

Then it was decided that instead of using the word "pregnancy," the phrase "I'm expecting," or "she's expecting" *[or, as Desi pronounced it, 'specting']* would be acceptable instead.

He warned the staff that they had to move ahead at once to film several episodes before Lucille "blew up like the Goodyear Blimp."

With the departure of Marc Daniels, William Asher came aboard as the series' new director. He became one of the most prolific directors of the early TV industry, eventually either producing or directing more than two dozen hit TV series.

When television was still in its infancy, he introduced the sitcom *Our Miss Brooks,* starring Eve Arden, and—despite that fact that it had been lifted more or less directly from Radio-land—he was soon being hailed as a *Wunderkind* of TV Land. Although it would later be challenged, he was also defined as "The Father of the Sitcom."

A New Yorker, Asher was born into a show business family. *[His sister, Betty Asher, was an MGM publicist for the then-ingénue, Judy Garland. Several biographies claim that "Betty and Judy" had a lesbian affair.]*

Asher evolved into the best director Lucille and Desi ever had, helming 110 of their series' 179 telecasts. According to Asher, "I thought at the time it was a good show, but never once did I view it as an international TV icon. I thought that once the series ended, *I Love Lucy* would become only a footnote in the history of 1950s television."

One of the first episodes that Asher directed, *Job Switching,* turned out to be the second most-remembered segment in the entire series. It was telecast for the first time on September 15, 1952.

Lucy is no good at household finances and bounces checks. Ricky chides her for what he defines as "lying around the house and playing canasta all day." Miffed and angry, she and Ethel challenge Fred and Ricky to switch jobs for a week.

As "housewives," Fred and Ricky are inept, but nothing to equal Lucy

Left to right, **Vivian Vance, Elvia Allman** (playing the supervisor) and **Lucille**, her jaws bulging with unswallowed chocolates, appear in *Job Switching*, first broadcast on September 15, 1952. The episode became one of the most iconic in the long history of *I Love Lucy.*

Ethel Mertz and Lucy have taken a job in a chocolate factory but they're no match for the fast-moving conveyor belt dispensing chocolates faster than they can wrap them. They end up stashing chocolates everywhere—and not just in their mouths.

and Ethel as factory workers.

An employment agency arranges jobs for them at a chocolate factory. Lucy becomes a candy dipper assigned to take a creamy center and gently coat it with a layer of melted chocolate.

At the assembly line, when a fly lands on the face of her co-worker, Lucy swats it. Not understanding, the worker retaliates and forcefully slaps Lucy back, splattering her face with the melted chocolate.

"I hired a real candy dipper from See's Chocolates in Los Angeles," Asher said. "She took her role a little too seriously, and almost broke Lucy's nose."

Lucy and Ethel are then assigned as assembly workers beside a conveyor belt, wrapping the chocolate nuggets in tinsel.

"The assembly line conveyor belt gag was as old as the hills, having appeared in many films," Oppenheimer said, "But Lucy made it fresh again and even memorable."

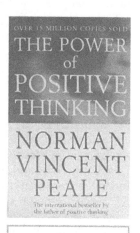

The conveyor belt moves too fast for the new, untrained workers, and Lucy stuffs the unwrapped nuggets into her chef's hat, her blouse, and even her mouth. Her antic attempts to slow it down are hopeless—she and Ethel simply can't keep up. Chaos ensues.

Returning home, Lucy finds Desi even more inept as a housewife, degrading her kitchen into a disorganized wreck.

Fred and Ricky reward their wives with boxes of chocolates.

***

For their summer vacation of 1952, Lucille and Desi flew to New York. Expecting a child, and coping fitfully with Desi's philandering, Lucille was in a nervous, agitated state as warm weather descended on the city. Pregnant and disillusioned, she survived many tormented nights. It was suggested that she turn to a psychiatrist, but instead, she chose counseling from Norman Vincent Peale, a Methodist "motivational" minister who had just published *The Power of Positive Thinking*.

She had her first meeting with him in Manhattan at the Marble Collegiate Church on Fifth Avenue. Within minutes of her entry into his study, she burst into tears, trying to unburden herself of the many fears that haunted her. Her main concern was that after all these years of struggle in the movie world, her career was going to be ripped away from her.

Although denounced as a charlatan in some quarters, **Norman Vincent Peale** hit paydirt when he wrote **The Power of Positive Thinking.**

Promoted by corporations as "required reading" for sales and marketing executives and their staffs across America, it took up residence on the bestseller list of *The New York Times.*

For years to come, Lucille would telephone the minister/author in moments of her worst despair.

457

She might have surprised him when she confessed, "If I had to make a choice between love and career, I would choose career. Ever since I walked the streets of Manhattan as a young girl, lonely and hungry, I've knocked myself out trying to make it in show business come hell or high water. I don't plan to give that up. My success in the entertainment business outranks any feeling I would have for a man, even Desi."

"The men in my life have been such disappointments. One night at a party in Hollywood, I talked with Susan Hayward. She told me that all of them should be boiled in oil. At times, I agree with her."

With Peale, she also discussed her marriage, which she defined as "on the rocks." She claimed that on the rare occasions when Desi actually came home, he was often staggeringly drunk. Once, when he couldn't make it up the stairs to a bedroom, he headed out the back door toward the guest cottage.

Unknown to him at the time, Lucille' mother, DeDe, was asleep in the bedroom there with one of her close women friends, someone in her late seventies.

During his transit to the cottage, Desi had begun to strip. By the time he reached the bedroom, he was stark naked. Then he tried to climb into bed with the two elderly ladies. When Lucille heard their screams, she raced to their rescue.

Lucille had grave concerns that she was trying to play too many roles, not only as a wife and mother, but as an actress and business executive at Desilu. "All that and trying to also have close friends—who often call on me when they're in trouble—means I can't keep up."

Peale warned her, "Don't rake up more leaves than you can fit into a wheelbarrow."

Lucille also confessed that she had not been a dedicated Christian and that she had concerns about how to bring up her children. "Should I insist they become Protestants or else give in to Desi and get them raised as Catholics?"

"I don't dare make that choice for you, as you already know my preference."

Her first session with Peale marked the beginning of a life-long friendship with him. In the years to come, she would often call him in the middle of the night for guidance.

Lucille would not be the only person affected by Peale's book, *The Power of Positive Thinking*. First published in 1952, it stayed on *The New York Times'* best-seller list for 186 consecutive weeks, selling five million copies.

She became such a devoted fan of this prolific writer that she avidly read some of his other motivational works: *The Art of Living, The Tough-Minded Optimist,* and *Inspiring Messages for Daily Living.*

Peale became a close friend of Richard Nixon, who phoned him in his deepest despair when he was being forced to give up the presidency.

As a young man, Donald Trump was forced by his Scottish mother to attend services at Peale's church. When Trump married his first wife, Ivana, he asked Peale to preside at his wedding.

***

Because of Lucille's fast-advancing pregnancy, Asher asked her to return to work early in July, cutting short her summer vacation with Desi. She was needed to shoot as many episodes as she could before she retreated to Chatsworth in November to await the birth of her second child.

An agreement was reached whereby she would shoot nine original shows. Five of them would include flashbacks to previous episodes.

Episode no. 45, *Lucy Is Enceinte,* was shot that summer, although it would not be aired until December. It was time to reveal to their vast public, a legion of fans, that Lucy was pregnant once again, and that the Ricardos were about to enlarge their family.

Scriptwriters devised a unique way to announce her pregnancy on TV. Lucy goes to hear Desi perform at the Tropicana. During his act, he is slipped an anonymous note with a request for a song, "Rock-a-Bye Baby."

It takes him a moment to get the significance of the note. He approaches Lucille at ringside, and a look in her eyes seems to alert him that he is about to become a father.

In an emotional departure from the wording of the script, Desi (not Ricky) proclaims, "It's me! I'm going to be a daddy." Tears well in his eyes. As he holds Lucille in his arms, he sings, "We're Having a Baby."

Oppenheimer recalled the night of that shoot. "Not following the script, Lucy and Desi seemed to remember their own emotions about having a child after all those miscarriages. Realizing they were soon to become parents again, they both began to cry. Desi was so emotional he could not finish his song. It was perhaps the most moving scene of all the episodes because it was real."

As part of the *schtick* associated with the on-screen shenanigans of **Lucy Goes to the Hospital** (*Episode #51, January 19, 1953*) **Desi** is dressed as a voodoo doctor, as he's scheduled to appear in a nightclub act at the Tropicana after the birth of their new baby.

As such, he terrifies the nursing staff, the local police, Fred and Ethel, and eventually, his wife.

Lucille's friend of many decades, **Barbara Pepper,** playing an alarmed nurse on *Lucy Goes to the Hospital.*

It was Pepper's fourth appearance on one of Lucy's shows.

Pepper never got over her disappointment of losing out on the Ethel Mertz role because of her heavy drinking.

459

***

Although Asher ordered that the scene be re-filmed, everyone from the cast and crew objected. That original clip, saturated with raw emotion, is the one that would be aired.

News of Lucy's second pregnancy would dominate the series' second season. It created a public debate about pregnancy, a theme that had previously been banned from the air.

In the weeks leading up to the birth of her second child, Lucille wanted Desi to stay at home with her and their little daughter Lucie. But he had other plans. "He'd split and be gone for days at a time, never telling me where he had been," Lucille complained. "Because he was so well known, I got a lot of reports that he was seeing other women,"

As Desi told Asher, "I've stopped having sex with Lucy. I mean, if you think about it, it's disgusting. I would feel like I'm screwing not only her, but our unborn son or daughter, too. Talk about being turned off."

Desi was not one to resist

The five-star Army General, **Dwight D. Eisenhower,** is seen here in an open-air convertible campaigning in Baltimore in 1952.

Famous for his service as Supreme Commander of the Allied Expeditionary Force in Europe, he had directed America to victory in World War II. He was immensely popular in the United States.

In January of 1953, his televised inauguration as the 34th President of the United States put him in competition with Desi (and Lucy) for TV viewers.

I Love Lucy beat the Inauguration in ratings. That same year, Desi also competed with Ike for the title of Best-Dressed Man in America.

temptation, and he was spotted playing golf in Palm Springs, or at the Del Mar Racetrack. He liked to sail his yacht to Catalina, often accompanied by two or three starlets, eager to do his bidding in hopes of getting cast in a TV show or in a feature film. He was also seen at the gambling tables in Las Vegas, sometimes with two or three showgirls sharing his hotel suite.

Because of her second pregnancy, Lucille and Desi had to cancel two vaudeville appearances. One at The Roxy in Manhattan, the other at the London Palladium. This cost them $200,000.

Seven episodes of *I Love Lucy* focused on her pregnancy. Vance found Lucille difficult to work with, as she was tense and nervous most of the time and quick to anger.

"Once, I had a toilet emergency and had to disappear for twenty minutes," Vance said. "When I came back on the set, she denounced me in front of the crew, like never before. She was completely out of control."

"When I couldn't take it anymore, I told her, 'I would tell you to go fuck yourself, but I see that Arnaz has already done that.'"

TV episodes derived from her pregnancy sometimes dealt with her diet. Her character's favorite foods became lobster, pickles, *éclairs*, hot fudge sundaes, and canned sardines.

Mocking the quirky nature of the foods she preferred was a mere trifle to a much larger issue. To fit in with the shooting schedule and the eventual airing of a telecast scheduled for January of 1953, the gender of the unborn child—for scriptwriting purposes—had to be clarified weeks before it was known. A boy or a girl? That was the question.

As I Love Lucy progressed, the passion of its fans for replicting aspects of **the Ricardo's apartment** and its fixtures increased.

Replicas of the furniture and accessories of their on-set kitchens and living rooms began selling briskly, a *tsunami* of enthusiasm for everything the Ricardos represented.

After hours of discussion and endless meetings, it was decided that the child would be a boy and that he'd be named Ricky Ricardo, Jr.

Lucille and Desi defined the child's birth date as January 19, 1953, with the understanding that doctors had already determined that its birth would be by Caesarian section at the Cedars of Lebanon Hospital in Los Angeles.

On Friday, November 14, 1952, weeks before Lucille actually gave birth, a child was "born" to Lucy Ricardo. In episode No. 56, *Lucy Goes to the Hospital*, she would give birth.

As the plot unfolded, Desi as Ricky rehearsed Fred and Ethel about what to do when Lucille signaled that she was ready.

When that moment arrived, they become hysterical, dashing about, gathering up what was needed. They then rushed out the door but forget to take Lucy. Of course, with brilliant comic timing, they dart back to rescue her.

Joining expectant fathers in a support group focusing on "parental pacing," Desi stands with Fred. At one point, he has to disappear into the men's toilet to put on his makeup for a later appearance that night at the Tropicana.

When he emerges from the toilet, he frightens everyone he encounters with the character he's portraying—a voodoo doctor. As a "stage grotesque," he's outfitted with a fright wig, whitened eye sockets, and flesh-eating fangs suitable for the most voracious of cannibals.

At last, the news is flashed. Ricky's dream has come true for TV audiences as he shouts, "It's a boy!"

Since Desi Jr. had not yet been born, the infant presented on TV by an actress portraying a pediatric nurse was a baby "hired" for the shoot.

[Actually, identical twins (Richard and Ronald Simmons) were used,

461

because California law dictated that an infant could appear on camera for only thirty consecutive seconds at a time. Therefore, both boys were needed to speed up the shoot. Their parents were given $50 for their joint appearance in separate scenes.

The pre-recorded episode was broadcast on January 19, 1953.

With uncanny good timing, on the day the episode was aired, Lucille, accompanied by Desi, checked into the Cedars of Lebanon Hospital. She was given a spinal anesthetic so that she'd be awake during the child's birth. She kept asking, "Is it a boy? Or girl?" She finally got the news for which she and Desi had long been waiting. "It's a boy!"

When the infant was cleaned and presented to her, she said, "His nose is so turned up, he'll drown if he's caught in the rain." She then turned onto her side and retreated into a deep, hours-long sleep.

Ironically, Desiderio Alberto Arnaz IV entered the world weighing eight pounds, nine ounces at approximately the same time as the television version of "Little Ricky" was born.

Practically every florist in the Greater Los Angeles area was emptied of flowers sent to the Cedars of Lebanon Hospital.

It was estimated that some fifty million Americans tuned in to watch *I Love Lucy*.

That was 71.1 percent of the viewing audience, as opposed to 67.6 percent who tuned in to witness, the very next day, the inauguration of the 34th President of the United States, Dwight D. Eisenhower.

Walter Winchell was the first to broadcast the news: "America had a banner week. Eisenhower became President, and Ricky and Lucy Ricardo had a baby boy."

Columnist Louella Parsons described the worldwide hysteria generated by the birth. "The miracle of the birth of Ricky Ricardo, Jr. takes second place after the birth of Jesus Christ."

Desi's recording of "There's a New Baby in Our House," released by Columbia, became one of the best-selling discs in America. Sung by Desi, it was backed up by the Paul Weston Orchestra.

On the day he received the news that he had a hit, Desi was also informed that he had been named one of the best-dressed men in

Until 1953, many of the schedules for upcoming television programs were printed in local newspapers. On April 3 of that year, three previously independent periodicals, *Television Forecast*, *Local Televiser*, and *The Television Guide*--based in Chicago, Philadelphia, and New York, respectively— merged into the first national edition of **TV Guide.**

Depicted above is the cover of the first edition of the new magazine. Its cover featured **Desi Arnaz Jr.**, the "born on TV" baby of Lucille Ball and Desi Arnaz. It's banner headline read, "Lucy's $50,000,000 Baby."

Within less than a decade, *TV Guide* became one of the most widely distributed and read magazines in the country. In 1974, it became the first magazine in history to sell a billion copies.

America. That list included Eisenhower, Harry S Truman, Danny Kaye, opera singer Ezio Pinza, and the British actor, Rex Harrison.

Years later in Palm Springs, Desi and his boy encountered Eisenhower on a golfing vacation. When they were introduced, Eisenhower said, "Is this the little fellow who knocked my Inauguration off the front pages?"

"The President didn't hold grudges," Desi Sr. said. "He invited us into the clubhouse to buy my boy a banana split."

Years later, Desi Jr. would say, "I'm about the only flesh-and-blood human being ever brought into the world on a television network."

Variety took note: "Lucille Ball and Desi Arnaz are the biggest super-stars in the entertainment industry."

One reporter asked, "Miss Ball, what about your movie career?"

"I don't give a god damn if I ever make another movie," she shot back, contradicting the confession she had transmitted to Norman Vincent Peale.

Although it had never been an issue that Desi Jr., as he grew older, would play Ricky Ricardo, Jr. on TV, a psychiatrist advised against it. "It might be harmful for your daughter. She would wonder why the boy, and not her, was chosen."

Lucille raised an objection, too: She had known a number of child stars who had turned into what she called, "monsters."

TV Guide hailed Desi Jr. as the "$50,000,000 baby" because of the spin-off of merchandise sold in the wake of his birth. He was also dubbed "America's richest baby," as the Arnazes hit the jackpot in a mountain of souvenirs sold with their endorsement. Contracts usually provided a five percent royalty on everything sold.

A fourteen-inch stuffed Ricky Ricardo, Jr. doll went over big. During a one-month period in the summer of 1953, 85,000 of them were sold in a mad rush to "get a piece of baby Ricky."

Since Philip Morris was still the show's sponsor, a cigarette lighter fea-turing a cartoon version of Lucy went over big with smokers or those who loved them.

A lot of baby-related items were hawked and sold. Merchandise in-cluded kiddie baths, a baby carriage, training chairs, insulated diaper bags—even a Lucy-inspired hobby horse.

A male and female couple could purchase matching pajamas for $6.95 each. Ricky brought the smoking jacket back into vogue, a duplicate of the one he wore on TV. It sold for $6.95.

Paper dolls of Lucy and Ricky were mass produced, and King Features ran a comic strip of the Ricardos.

Collectively, the merchandise was defined as "Desiloot."

Variety asked, "Aren't Desi Arnaz and Lucille Ball carrying their en-dorsements of merchandise too far? Their caricatures even adorn potty seats."

***

Lucille had been recovering from the ordeal of birth at Chatsworth when Desi—rare for him—returned home one day at 5PM. He hugged and kissed her. "You and I are moving tonight to a suite I've reserved at the Statler Hotel in Los Angeles."

On February 5, 1953, on a makeshift stage at that hotel, in the heart of Los Angeles, Lucille, barely recovered from her ordeal of giving birth, made her first public appearance with Desi.

TV host Art Linkletter was there to greet them and present them with two Emmy Awards. Whereas Lucille was honored as "Best TV Comedienne of the Year," Desi accepted the other Emmy for "Best Situation Comedy of the Year."

No two people in television's short history deserved these awards more.

During their drive back to Chatsworth, Desi said, "Baby, we're on top of the world. This will be our greatest year. What could go wrong?"

"Don't tempt the Gods, you crazy Cubano," she warned.

Loving (and Merchandizing) Lucy

ARE AMERICANS AS CRAZY AS THE REST OF THE WORLD IS SAYING?

An insanely diverse *tsunami* of Lucy and Ricky Ricardo **memorabilia** is available for sale on the internet.

In theory, at least, unless you're addicted or fetish-driven, everything displayed above is non-essential.

CHAPTER FOURTEEN

A REDHEAD SEES RED
AS SHE DENIES THAT SHE WAS A "COMMIE PINKO"

DESI & LUCILLE BUY RKO STUDIOS

As 1953 rolled on, and all the birth hoopla faded, some hard business decisions had to be made. On February 5, an item appeared in the *Hollywood Reporter* that in spite of its high ratings, executives at Philip Morris might not renew *I Love Lucy*.

At the cigarette company's headquarters, executive Al Lyons claimed that *I Love Lucy* had not reflected any surge in sales for their cigarettes. *Advertising Age,* in fact, reported that sales of Philip Morris cigarettes had dropped to fifth position. Lucky Strike, Camel, Chesterfield and Pall Mall had emerged as the industry leaders. *[Of course, some of that could be attributed to intensifying concerns that smoking caused lung cancer.]*

By anyone's standards, the coverage that Lucille, and to a lesser extent, Desi, received in 1953 was a smashing **press and PR success.**

Illustrations above show coverage in *Life and Look.* Even *Guideposts*—the Evangelical magazine founded by Lucille's mentor, Dr. Norman Vincent Peale—featured the Arnaz family as a moral and marital example to the rest of America.

Then an announcement emerged on February 18 from CBS that Philip Morris would remain the sponsor of *I Love Lucy*. A staggering (for the time) $8 million contract was signed with Desilu—the biggest deal in television history at that point in time. Desi immediately phoned Lucille to report the news. "Let's throw a party," he shouted into the phone. "We're the highest paid entertainers in TV history!"

Both *Look* and *Life* magazines interpreted the announcement as an item of so much interest that they featured Lucille and Desi on their covers.

The contract called for Philip Morris to sponsor 98 episodes through 1955. CBS would get four million dollars with the rest going to Desilu. The agreement called for each episode to be shot for $40,000, more than double the original per-episode budget of $19,500.

Photographers descended on Chatsworth for pictures of Desi and Lucille in scenes of domestic bliss with two young children, including a newborn. Everything was carefully staged. He was even photographed cooking in their kitchen, preparing Cuban dishes his mother had once served to his father and him in Santiago. Lucille was photographed in the living room as a loving mother with her toddlers.

MEDIA HIPSTERS AHEAD OF THEIR TIME

According to some marketing historians, Lucille was featured on the covers of various editions of *Look* magazine an astonishing nine times between 1937 and its demise in 1971.

Behind the scenes, Lucille, Desi, and/or Desilu Productions also wangled blockbuster appearances for the Ricardos on the covers of *Life, Good Housekeeping, TV Star Parade, TV Guide,* and a long list of Hollywood fan magazines.

As savvy publicists of their own media endeavors, and perhaps to thank the editors of those publications, Lucille and Desi made it a point to emphasize that the Ricardos were avid readers and to discreetly include the logos of some of those magazines within episodes of their TV series.

Displayed above are stills from *(left to right) I Love Lucy's* "Lucy Gets Ricky on the Radio", "Ricky's Life Story", "Ricky Loses His Temper," and "The Great Train Robbery."

Public recognition soared. So did magazine sales.

All this was mostly for show, as Desi had resumed his philandering, telling director Marc Daniels, "I'm not much of a homebody. It seems that every cute little secretary and would-be starlet wants my Cuban salami. Is it my sex appeal, or are they thinking I'll get them into show business?"

Jack Gould, writing in *The New York Times*, claimed that the title *I Love Lucy* was misleading: "It is not only Desi Arnaz who loves Lucy, but millions of fans love her too."

That year's final episode was filmed on November 14, 1952. After a few months' break, on April 20, 1953, Lucille began shooting yet another episode, this one for the following season. It was entitled *No Children Allowed*.

The neighbors in their apartment building are up in arms at her new baby's constant crying. The tenants sign a petition ("no children allowed") and present it to Fred and Ethel Mertz in their capacity as landlords.

The Simmons twins, both Richard and Ronald, were used again to replicate "Baby Ricky." The episode also introduced actress Elizabeth Patterson, cast as Mrs. Trumball, his babysitter. At the age of seventy-eight, Patterson, a native of Tennessee, had played supporting roles in a hundred movies, beginning in 1926 with *The Boy Friend*. She never married and lived in a room at the Roosevelt Hotel. A baby's crying was generated on cue by Jerry Hausner, who had earned his reputation as a "cry baby" on radio.

In addition to his frequent appearances as Ricky Ricardo, Desi was also running the studio, signing such stars as Danny Thomas, Ray Bolger, and Loretta Young to film TV sequences at Desilu Studios. Even Frank Sinatra approached Desi with a deal that never got launched. Entitled *Blues in the Night*, it was envisioned as a TV series about a musician and his many adventures.

During the cast and crew's summer vacation, Desi signed a deal for a feature film that would star Lucille and himself in a Technicolor romantic comedy called *The Long, Long Trailer*, scheduled for a 1954 release.

Elizabeth Patterson, a mysterious lady from the heartland of Tennessee, gravitated to Hollywood in the mid-1920s and found small roles beginning in the silent era.

She was nearing eighty years old when hired by Desi to play the babysitter for "Little Ricky."

She never married and lived in a small single room at the Roosevelt Hotel in a sort of lonely isolation.

During his involvement with *I Love Lucy*, comedian and character actor **Jerry Hausner** played at least two characters and provided the sound effects for whatever baby was misbehaving off screen.

He eventually left the show after an argument with Desi.

***

Lucille and Desi had long dreamed of co-starring in a Technicolor feature film. A surprise offer came in from MGM, a studio for which both of them had worked in previous years.

At this point in film history, studios were desperate to attract audiences back into theaters, especially consumers who had deserted them for "the little black box." Innovations were being introduced such as CinemaScope, 3-D (requiring free glasses issued within the theaters to movie goers), and stereophonic sound.

Pandro S. Berman, working now as a producer for MGM, phoned Lucille and pitched a script to her. Desi may or may not have known that he'd had a fling with her back in the late 1930s when both of them were under contract to RKO.

In 1951, Clinton Twiss had written a novel called *The Long, Long Trailer*. It was the comic saga of a married couple who had bought a large trailer home and set out on a road adventure across America. It embroiled them in one near-disaster after another, each morphing into a laugh fest.

Berman hired the widely respected husband and wife screen writing team of Albert Hackett and Florence Goodrich to adapt it for the screen. Previous successes had included their screenplay for *The Thin Man* (1934), starring William Powell and Myrna Loy as Nick and Nora Charles, stylish detectives with a knack for solving murders. *The Thin Man* was so successful that it evolved into a series. Nothing topped Hackett and Goodrich's classic, *It's a Wonderful Life* (1946), starring James Stewart and shown every year on Christmas TV. They also scripted *Father of the Bride* (1950), and later won a Pulitzer Prize for their scripting of *The Diary of Anne Frank* (1956).

Critic **Emanuel Levy** described Lucille's career status when she signed as the star of *The Long, Long Trailer:*

"When Vincente Minnelli first met Lucille, she told him she loved the idea of a big screen comeback. The big screen still held an edge over TV in *cachet*, even if not in money paid or audience size. After two decades in Hollywood, she was still a second stringer, and the public still associated her as Bob Hope's foil in mediocre Paramount movies."

"At forty, she was not young when *I Love Lucy* premiered in 1951, and the time was ripe to retry Hollywood before it was too late for her as a big screen *persona.*"

Desi and Lucille were offered a joint salary of $250,000 for their star performances. Before he signed the contract, always the gambler, Desi made a bet with Berman for $50,000. He would put up that money with the expectation that *The Long, Long Trailer* would outgross MGM's *Father of the Bride,* starring Spencer Tracy and Elizabeth Taylor.

The Tracy-Taylor pairing had been MGM's biggest box office triumph of the decade. But later, after box office receipts for *The Long, Long Trailer* were calculated, Desi won the bet, meaning that his joint salary with Lucille ended up at $300,000.

Dore Schary, who had taken over MGM from Louis B. Mayer, initially objected to making the *Trailer* movie, preferring what he called "message pictures" instead. He denounced the script as a "silly little road comedy."

But Benjamin Thau, head of casting, finally prevailed on him to move ahead, convinced as he was that it would be a hit, especially in an America where improved interstate highways and the glories of "See the U.S.A." were being touted as a postwar symbol of "the good life."

There had been an initial concern at MGM that fans of Lucille and Desi would not pay to see them in a movie, since they could watch them for free on television.

The massive trailer itself—a Redman New Moon—was nicknamed "the third star" of the film. Stretching thirty-six feet, it sold at the time for $5,400 (about $52,000 in 2021 currency). *[At the time, the average newly built home sold for $20,000.]*

Sales materials for **The Redman Corporation's "New Moon" trailer** changed forever after the release of *The Long, Long Trailer.* As shown in the upper illustration (a detail from the company's catalogue), the deluxe "New Moon" model was forever after I.D.'d as the "I Love Lucy" model.

In the lower photo, Lucy and Desi are shown happily and contentedly lounging inside one of them.

Sales of luxury motor homes, and "campers on wheels" boomed,

Coincidentally, after then-President Eisenhower authorized the fast-expanding Interstate Highway System in 1956, Americans—with or without motor homes—"hit the roads."

Towing the vehicle would be a new Mercury Monterey convertible, a favorite of American playboys.

One of the most famous (and eccentric) directors in Hollywood, Vincente Minnelli, was hired to bring the zany on-the-road adventures of Lucy and Desi to the screen. His strong supporting cast included Marjorie Main (i.e, "Ma Kettle"), Lucille's longtime friend, Keenan Wynn, Walter Baldwin, Madge Blake, and Gladys Hurlbut. Desi was cast as an Italian (not a Cuban) named Nicholas Carlos

Collini. A civil engineer, he wants to visit, with his wife Tacy (as portrayed by Lucille), some of the sites where he'll soon be working.

For filming of its opening scene, Desi returned to a sound stage at MGM, the studio where he'd filmed the wartime drama, *Bataan* (1943), eleven years before.

During their characters' celluloid cross-country trip, the most dangerous sequence was filmed as the tailer navigated its way along the Whitney Portal Road, one of the access routes to Mount Whitney in California's Sierra Nevada—a labyrinth of hairpin curves.

Minnelli recalled, "Lucy is one of the few comedic talents who can be broad and uniquely human at the same time. She can get away with things that less talented actors wouldn't even presume to handle, and she does so on television week after week, as she handles manufactured situations and passes them off for real."

Lucille expressed her own impression of Minnelli. "The poor man was a basket case, still suffering from his failed marriage to Judy Garland. He was also gay but forced to live in the closet in Hollywood after his flamboyant early years in New York. He was drinking heavily and pill popping."

Minnelli sometimes escorted his seven-year-old daughter, Liza, onto the set. He and his former wife, Judy Garland, had joint custody. Desi was charmed by her, provocatively telling the young girl, "I can't wait for you to grow up. Those eyes!"

The director cast his daughter in a short cameo, which regrettably ended up on the cutting room floor.

"He was very nervous about his daughter Liza during the times she lived with Judy," Lucille said.

At one point, with the understanding that Judy Garland sometimes showed lapses in maternal good judgment and was frequently on the road, touring, Lucille suggested that Liza come and live with her family at Chatsworth. Vincente accepted, saying, "I'm grateful."

Liza Minnelli thereby became one of Lucille's family, co-existing with the Arnaz brood for almost a year.

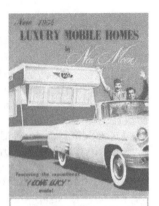

It was 1954 and the war and its dreary recovery was over. Endorsements mattered.

Fun-loving **Lucille and Desi** wave to their fans as they lend their names to trailer sales in America. After the tragic war years, Americans were buying mobile homes and heading out in them to see the U.S.A.

Two views of **Liza Minnelli:** Upper photo, with her mother, Judy Garland, on the set of *Summer Stock* (1950).

Lower photo: as a young adult with her father, director **Vincente Minnelli** at a movie premiere.

When he grew up, it would not be Desi, Sr., but Desi, Jr. that Liza heavily dated. By then, their dynamic was often interpreted as that of an older woman seducing a teenaged boy.

In reference to *The Long, Long Trailer, Film Daily* wrote, "Vincente Minnelli guides the movie along a route of frequently hilarious incidents."

The critic for the *Los Angeles Examiner* wrote: "Both Lucy and Desi rollick their way through the slapstick nonsense with a fine sense of timing, and an obvious zest that communicates itself to the audience immediately and makes for one big happy family in the zany antics." *Hollywood Reporter* claimed that "Minnelli does a good job of highlighting the slapstick and keeps the farce moving at a raucous rate."

Variety noted that both "Miss Ball and Arnaz deliver sock performances with perfect timing."

In **shameless**—some detractors labeled it as "vulgar"—**publicity**, Lucille and Desi were usually willing to lend their names for commercial promotions.

Vincente Minnelli once cracked, "Those two would even endorse toilets if asked...and paid, of course. I encouraged them to tackle these tailor-made roles in that damn trailer with their special brand of *I Love Lucy* farce."

"Actually, I viewed my direction of that trailer trash as a comedown. After all, during the course of my career, I turned out poignant melodramas such as *Some Came Running* (1958) with Frank Sinatra or that divine musical *Gigi* (also 1958) with Leslie Caron."

Not all reviews of this 96-minute film were good. One critic interpreted it as "A long, long, *I Love Lucy* movie decked out in CinemaScope."

***

It was a quiet Sunday evening, September 10, 1953, at Chatsworth. Desi was gone and Lucille had put her children to bed. She was in her study, reading a script for the next episode of *I Love Lucy*. From a few feet away, a radio was broadcasting a lineup of Sunday night shows when the newspaper gossip columnist, Walter Winchell, came on the air, addressing "Mr. and Mrs. America and all the ships at sea."

She was only half listening until her ears perked up with his proclamation: "What red-headed television comedienne has been confronted with her membership in the Communist Party?"

He did not answer his own question.

At first, as she later claimed, she didn't think Winchell was referring to her. Taking a wild guess, she thought it was a revelation about Imogene Coca, who at the time was also a reigning queen of comedy on TV.

In Del Mar, Desi was playing poker with some of his cronies after a day at the racetrack. The men also had a radio playing in the background during the broadcast of Winchell's question. Desi was paying little attention, but his ears perked up at the "outing" of Lucille. He knew at once who Winchell meant.

Within five minutes, he was in his car speeding toward Chatsworth. Amazingly, he wasn't stopped by a traffic cop. As he would later say, "The year had been going too good for us."

He rushed into the ranch house, and immediately confronted Lucille, telling her that Winchell had been referring to her. He hugged and kissed her as she began to cry.

Within the hour, Ken Morgan, their close friend and associate at Desilu, was on the scene, as he and Desi tried to decide what to do. In the next hour, Howard Strickling from MGM's publicity department also arrived at Chatsworth. MGM had invested two-million dollars in *The Long, Long Trailer*, and he was worried that this might actually incite its condemnation and boycott.

Strickling offered some bad advice, suggesting that both Desi and Lucille should ignore the broadcast and its subsequent speculation. "If you say nothing, it will fade away."

Desi challenged that, suggesting that the left-wing positions of Harry Belafonte, Judy Holliday, and Gypsy Rose Lee had virtually led to their banishment from television. He also cited careers destroyed, including those of actor Larry Parks, Will Greer, Howard Da Silva, Gale Sondergaard, and Sam Jaffe. Since his public condemnation as a socialist, screenwriter Dalton Trumbo, for years to come, would be forced to submit his scripts under a pen name.

Lucille told the men, "Here I am, the most famous woman in America and now

IS IT TRUE? WAS LUCILLE BALL A PINKO COMMUNIST?

The inset photo that's surrounded with the "polka-dot' frame shows the damning story's perpetrator, gossip columnist **Walter Winchell.**

The ironies associated with **J. Edgar Hoover**, his right-hand man (**Clyde Tolson**) and **his FBI** are not lost on the writers at Blood Moon Productions.

In 2012, we published Darwin Porter's intricately researched biography of the FBI chieftain to good reviews and what seemed like a stunned acquiescence (i.e., "no comment") from dozens of agents deeply entrenched within their ranks and unwilling to discuss the implications of their former boss's vindictive penchant for voyeurism and retribution.

I might be labeled a communist, my career destroyed."

The allegations didn't go away. That following morning, the revelation that she had joined the Communist Party in 1936 made "Second Coming" headlines across the nation. Charges against her were broadcast on both TV and radio.

One headline in Los Angeles read: SAY IT ISN'T SO. OUR BELOVED LUCY A COMMIE PINKO? The *Daily News* in New York ran the headline—REGISTERED RED IN '36: LUCILLE. The subhead blared, "Star Denies She Voted Commie."

By noon, Desi's call to J. Edgar Hoover at the F.B.I. went through. The director assured him, "My agents accepted your wife's testimony when they interviewed her at your house. There will be no charges filed against her."

The New York Journal American columnist Jack O'Brien wrote: "Lucille Ball has announced that she might retire in two years. That may come a lot sooner than she thinks."

A reporter in Baltimore weighed in. "I think Lucy's head should be

In Los Angeles, on March 19, 1936, **Lucille** had acquiesced to her socialist grandfather and went downtown, where she registered as a Communist.

"I remember feeling quite bad about the whole thing, " she later recalled. "I wasn't really a Communist--far from it. In fact, I'd become a capitalist later in life. I felt my being registered as a Communist wouldn't matter if I didn't bother to vote."

In 1952, however, she was investigated by the dreaded House Committee on Un-American Activities, which at the time was terrorizing Hollywood and destroying careers.

Influenced, perhaps, by a lot of sudden politicking with J. Edgar Hoover and her movie studio, the committee seemed to accept her explanation that she'd registered as a Communist to please her late grandfather—and that she hadn't voted in that year's presidential elections.

But 17 months later she faced renewed investigations and became the target of right-wing hatred. Desi intervened in her behalf to win back the public support, claiming, "We despise everything about Communism. Lucy is as American as Barney Baruch and Ike Eisenhower. And by the way, we both voted for Eisenhower So, ladies and gentlemen, don't judge too soon."

shaved, and her dyed red locks sent to Moscow to be exhibited at Lenin's tomb."

These revelations about a possible communist link also led to a re-evaluation of the *I Love Lucy* show. John Crosby in *The New York Times* reviewed the hit TV series itself. *"The Lucy Shows*—let's face it—are beginning to sound an awful lot alike. Miss Ball is always trying to burst out of the house. Arnaz is always trying to keep her in apron strings. The variations on that theme are infinite, but it's the same theme. I'm a mite tired of it."

Desi announced to the press that Lucille had been given a one-hundred percent clearance from the F.B.I. In the wake of Hoover's statement, the *Los Angeles Times* in a headline the next day declared—EVERYBODY STILL LOVES LUCY.

For the taping of Episode No. 68, *The Girls Go into Business*, Lucille feared appearing in front of a live audience, terrified that the crowd of 300 people might boo her. In the sketch, Ethel and Lucy decide to open a dress shop, with disastrous results.

On the night of the taping, Desi, sweating heavily, was the first to face the audience, not knowing what his reception would be.

"Ladies and gentlemen, I'm sure you've read a lot of bad headlines about my wife. I came to America from Cuba. During my early years in this country, where I served in the U.S. Army, I became an American citizen. The one thing I admire about this country is that you're considered innocent until proven guilty."

"Lucy is not a communist. She has never been a communist—not now, not ever. I was run out of Cuba by the communists. We both despise communists, and I oppose everything they stand for."

Then he glanced quickly into the wings, where Lucille appeared ready to collapse into a hysterical fit. That caused him to sweat even more under the intense lights overhead.

"Until now, you've read only what people have falsely claimed about Lucy. Now you have a chance to read our response to these false allegations in tomorrow's newspapers. Headlines will reveal our side of the story. The only thing Red about Lucy is her hair, and even that isn't real. Now, it's on with the show."

A somewhat jittery Vivian Vance and William Frawley came on next. Frawley embraced Desi, and Vance planted a kiss on him. Desi addressed the audience again. "I've been married to Lucy for thirteen years. She's as American as President Eisenhower, as J. Edgar Hoover. She is my favorite wife, the mother of my kids. I now give you the girl who plays Lucy. Lucille Ball!"

In the wings, before walking onstage, Lucille kissed her doctor, who was standing by in case she collapsed. She was met with thunderous applause as she hugged and kissed her co-stars before doing the same for Desi. She blew kisses to the audience and even to the photographers and reporters gathered, hoping for a big scoop in the morning papers.

The next day, Desi held a press conference, in the aftermath of which Dan Jenkins of *TV Guide* wrote: "I think perhaps you will agree that we owe Lucille Ball an apology."

That Sunday night in his weekly broadcast, Winchell himself went on the air, reporting that both J. Edgar Hoover and the House Un-American Activities Committee had cleared Lucille Ball of being a Red.

Privately, she told friends, "This Red witch hunt has caused me to develop sties. Not only that, but I'm suffering from bursitis and have lost fifteen pounds."

She also said, "I don't belong on any Red Channel List or whatever they're calling blacklisted stars. America was a very different place in 1936, suffering through a dangerous Depression, joblessness, hungry people standing in soup lines. Back then, being a Republican was almost worse than being labeled a communist."

Her brother, Fred Ball, told reporters, "I was never a communist. I just did what Grandpa Hunt told me to do. I didn't even know what communism was. But my membership was meaningless, and it cost me a job in a defense plant when war broke out. My membership also appeared as a roadblock when I tried to enlist in the U.S. Army."

U.S. President Dwight D. Eisenhower—Supreme Commander of the Allied Expeditionary Force in Europe during World War II, and his First Lady, **Mamie**, were said to be the only couple in America more famous than "Lucy and Desi."

In the next two weeks, mailbags of letters arrived in Hollywood from all over the country, from Alaska to Key West. Thousands of them were supportive, but a few hundred ferociously denounced her. A typical hate letter came in from Ronald Randall of Toledo, Ohio. "You're a stinking commie bitch, as Red as your hair."

The right-wing columnist, Westbrook Pegler, was critical: "The proposition that she was only twenty-four years old at the time and that her grandfather, the family tyrant, made her register as a communist, has no value at all with me."

Another letter writer from Louisville, Kentucky, mockingly suggested that the name of her TV series should be changed to *I Love Grandpa.*

Desi and Lucille nervously waited for the Nielsen ratings for their show. They were relieved to learn that in spite of the many blaring headlines, *I Love Lucy* still reached sixty percent of TV viewers. They beat out such stiff competition as singer Dennis Day on NBC. Desi said, "Dennis is a sweet little guy, but he's no Sinatra."

***

A few months later, perhaps to publicly demonstrate their "forgiveness" for the commie scare, an invitation, along with a request to perform, came in from new occupants at the White House, "Ike & Mamie."

Their performance at the White House featured a comedy skit from their vaudeville act. When it was over, Lucille and Desi joined the President and his wife, Mamie, who seemed to be a little drunk. "Next to Lucy and me, you and Mrs. Eisenhower are the second most famous couple in America," Desi quipped.

"You might be right," Ike said.

Desi also told the President, "At first, there was an objection to my Cuban accent, but it now seems to have worked in my favor."

"In my native state of Kansas, I was ridiculed when I announced that I was going to run for President. Desi, you and I beat the odds, two walking miracles. In America, a man is allowed to dream high."

***

In spite of the Red Scare, 1953 evolved into a banner year for Desilu. It produced ninety hours of television, with millions of dollars pouring in. Desi even launched a sponsored line of Lucy & Desi home furnishings that included a Lucy rug, a Lucy chair, a Lucy lamp, a Lucy double bed, and even a line of clothing marketed as a "Lucy wardrobe."

Filmed at Desilu were shows featuring Wyatt Earp, Danny Thomas, Eve Arden, and Red Skelton. On some days, Desi worked a sixteen-hour shift, assisting with production problems on shows that starred performers such as Ray Bolger or Jimmy Durante.

In the year that followed, Desi would evolve into what he called "The power behind the throne" for some 203 TV shows. He met artists he'd never encountered before, notably Tennessee Ernie Ford. In episode No. 194, Lucille "vamped" the country singer, wearing the same seductive gear she'd worn in 1949 on *The Ed Wynne Show*. Ford's appearance with Lucy helped propel him from a country singer known mainly in the South to national prominence.

Stars came and went from the *I Love Lucy* show, including Rock Hudson and Richard Widmark. In one episode, Harpo Marx appeared in three disguises—Clark Gable, Jimmy Durante, and Gary Cooper.

In February of 1954, Lucille and Desi flew to New York to promote *The Long, Long Trailer*. Arriving at Idlewild Airport at 7AM, they were met by photographers, reporters, hundreds of devoted fans, and a sixteen-member German marching band.

In a style inspired by a Hollywood premiere, a red carpet awaited them as they disembarked. They followed it into the terminal, waving to early bird fans as they moved along, blowing kisses.

Wherever they went on the streets of Manhattan, they attracted a mob of fans demanding autographs "No longer did I hear what I used to get asked: 'Miss Sothern, may I have your autograph?'"

The public relations highlight of their trip was a sold-out show at Radio City Music Hall, where their appearance was greeted with thunderous applause. "I once tried to become a Rockette, but never made it," she confessed to the audience.

Wherever they went, they were given standing ovations. One of them was unleased when they arrived at the Broadway opening of *Kind Sir*, starring Mary Martin and Charles Boyer.

"At first, I didn't know if all this applause was for Desi and me," Lucille said. "I thought Eleanor Roosevelt had walked in."

The Long, Long Trailer had fans lined up at the box office to see it. Pandro S. Berman wired from Hollywood. "At long last, you've made it, girl: a bigtime fucking movie star!"

The commie issue faded with the winter's snows, and the future for the 1954-55 season looked brighter than ever.

***

As their fame grew, so did kidnapping threats of their children. This menace had festered almost since the birth of America's celebrity system. One of the most famous cases in Hollywood history involved the real-life kidnapping of Frank Sinatra Jr.

In 1955, after Desi and Lucille's receipt of a serious kidnapping threat, they began feeling unsafe and vulnerable at Chatsworth.

The San Fernando Valley was not what it was when they'd first moved there. During the postwar boom, the population there had swelled, and traffic was much heavier. Their commutes to and from Hollywood were taking longer and longer, nearly two hours in each direction, every day.

Eventually, they made a decision to seek a home in Beverly Hills, a community with night patrols and a reputation for the most rigorous police protection in America. Sometimes, strangers walking the streets late at night were stopped and questioned.

They put their ranch house at Chatsworth on the market. Actress Jane Withers heard about it, visited the property, and bought it that same day.

Lucille had seen her in films dating from the 1930s when 20th Century Fox wanted a child actress a little feistier than its star moppet, Shirley Temple.

A wizard of a performing artist from the age of five, the Georgia-born **Jane Withers** became a child star at Fox, which already had the child actress box office champ, Shirley Temple, on their payroll.

After a successful career in films, she married a millionaire in 1947. Even though Withers didn't have to work, she became even more famous to a newer generation when she signed up to appear in those long-running commercials as Josie the Plumber, hawking Comet sink cleaners.

Darryl F. Zanuck, the studio chief, said, "We used Withers when a role called for a girl less saccharine than 'Little Miss Lollipop.'"

"I hated saying goodbye to my beloved farm animals," Lucille said, "but Jane promised to give them tender, loving care."

A realtor had showed her a modern man-

Miss Withers is shown here in a press photo from *Giant* (1956).

sion in Beverly Hills at 1001 North Roxbury at the corner of Lexington Road. She liked the house, but not enough to buy it.

As she was leaving, she spotted a home directly across the street. It was a rather spacious, two-story Georgian structure built of shingles and brick. The realtor feared that the house might not be elegant enough, but Lucille felt a strong, perhaps psychic attraction for it, even though the property was not on the market.

The elderly woman who answered the door did not have a TV set. Nor did she and her husband go to the movies, a rarity for residents of Beverly Hills. So in spite of Lucille's worldwide fame, the owner didn't know who she was. She did, however, seem to vaguely recognize her face. "Weren't you the actress exposed by the F.B.I. as a Communist? Your face looks familiar."

"No relation," Lucille responded when she came to realize that the woman had not a clue as to who she was.

As the homeowner and Lucille talked, she was told that the wife and her husband had already been discussing selling their house. Their beloved son had died. "There are just too many memories," she said to Lucille.

After a thorough inspection, Lucille offered $75,000 for the property, and they eventually settled on $85,000. Lucille bought it without Desi having even seen it. The new address of the Arnaz family became 1000 North Roxbury Drive.

It took a month for the Arnaz's to relocate and set up their new lives in Beverly Hills. The first neighbor who came to call was Jack Benny in drag, wearing the same dress and makeup he'd worn in an episode of his TV series.

"I always suspected that in private, not just on TV, you and Uncle Miltie ran around dressed as women," Lucille said, jokingly.

She and Desi eventually threw a party and invited some of their neighbors. The first arrivals were actor José Ferrer and his wife, singer Rosemary Clooney. They were followed by a drunken Oscar Levant and later by Ira Gershwin. The composer assured Lucille that his wife was on the way. "It takes her three hours to get dressed."

As the years passed, and as Lucie and Desi, Jr. became old enough for school, they bonded with the other rich kids in the neighborhood. Many were the sons and daughters of celebrities. "Dean Martin was rather prolific in providing kids to play with my kids," Lucille said. "Jeanne Crain and her husband also provided playmates for my little darlings."

With their newly acquired millions, Desi also purchased a six-bedroom house in Palm Springs, facing the fairway of the Thunderbird Country Club.

"Desi might have been an eagle flying high, but he got his wings clipped by those people at the Thunderbird," Lucille said. "Privately, they had a secret admission policy. In their bigoted language, they did not accept 'wetbacks, Spics, Jews, fairies, or niggers.'"

Desi was denied membership.

Perhaps as an act of defiance and retaliation, he built a forty-two room motel next to the Indian Wells Country Club. His hotel was discrimination

478

free. He also opened a restaurant and nightclub on the ground floor, where he employed some of the former members of his band.

***

On February 11, 1954, the Emmy Awards Ceremony was held at the Hollywood Palladium. Lucille was nominated for "Best Female Star in a Regular Series," but she lost to Eve Arden for *Our Miss Brooks*. Vivian Vance, however, won her first Emmy for "Best Supporting Actress."

In contrast, William Frawley lost to Art Carney for "Best Supporting Actor." Lucille and Desi accepted the "Best Series" Emmy.

Despite the recognition, Desi worried about the future of the series. Could *I Love Lucy* continue for another two years in its current format? His fears were heightened when he read a column by Jack Gould, a TV critic for *The New York Times*.

Gould singled out four episodes that demonstrated what he defined as "the decline of the series." One that he cited as one of its weaker episodes was "Home Movies," aired for the first time on March 1. In it, Ricky bores everyone by constantly screening home movies of their new baby. Before that, Gould was equally bored by the February 22 episode of "Ricky Loses His Temper." Lucy bets him she can refrain from the purchase of a new hat longer than he can control his temper.

According to Gould, "*I Love Lucy* was once a recognizable and hilarious farce on married life. Currently, it seems bent on succumbing to the most pedestrian and sophomoric slapstick. Perhaps *Lucy* has run its course."

In spite of that dire forecast, *I Love Lucy* remained the top-rated TV show of the 1953-54 season, with fifty-one million viewers.

Based on the success of the show, Frawley and Vance got long-delayed raises. Frawley felt confident enough to put a down payment on a Cadillac and to hire a chauffeur. *[Frawley no longer had a driver's license: the Los Angeles police had confiscated it for drunk driving.]*

One afternoon, Desi met Frawley's chauffeur. "She was a knockout, a sort of Jayne Mansfield 'busting' out all over. She could put Marilyn Monroe to shame."

"Looking at this blonde all over, I got an idea," Desi confessed to Oppenheimer. "I easily found the address of Monroe and arrived unannounced at her door, knowing she'd receive me. After all, I was Desi Arnaz, for god's sake. I heard that she slept with everything in pants and had a few lezzie flings on the side. I just knew she'd go for my Cuban salami."

When he rang the doorbell, a maid answered. She immediately recognized him and asked, "Mr. Arnaz, do you have an appointment?"

"No, but I was in the neighborhood and decided to drop by to talk to Miss Monroe about appearing on *I Love Lucy*.

After informing Desi that she'd check, the maid shut the door and was gone for about ten minutes.

When she returned, she said, "Miss Monroe is not receiving visitors today. Then the door slammed shut in his face.

He was enraged at this rejection, later referring to Monroe as "a two-bit slut. She missed out on a big thrill."

Lena Pepitone, Monroe's maid, later discussed Desi's unexpected and unannounced arrival: "At the time, Marilyn was in her bedroom with Glenn Tyler, her twenty-two-year-old stud masseur. Every time this guy came over, I would hear a lot of giggling and screeching going on in her bedroom. Her masseur always emerged exhausted, and Marilyn went to sleep for hours."

Throughout the course of 1954, in addition to regular appearances on *I Love Lucy,* Desi wore his "producer's hat." As president of Desilu, he received a one-million loan from CBS to finance pilots of new shows in development. One of them starred the veteran actor Walter Brennan; another featured Charles Coburn. There were no buyers for either of them. He did sell "Willy," starring June Havoc, to CBS, but it lasted for only one season.

His hit came when he filmed a pilot for *December Bride,* starring Spring Byington, who had been a key character in its radio version.

William Paley at CBS and others didn't want Desi to focus on Byington at all. *Confidential* and other scandal magazines were prominently flexing their muscles at the time, and there was a fear that since Byington was a lesbian, she'd be embarrassed and exposed in "these rags" as Desi called them. But he forged ahead with casting her anyway, and his judgment was rewarded when *December Bride* became one of the Top Ten TV series for four of its five seasons.

Jess Oppenheimer feared there would be too much pressure on him and his colleagues, Pugh and Carroll, during the 1954-55 season, so he hired the writing team of Robert Schiller and Robert Weiskopf.

From the beginning, "The Two Bobs," as they were called, suspected that Oppenheimer's career at Desilu might be limited. "I don't know which guy has the bigger

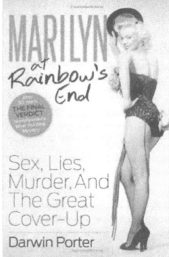

Did you know? That in 2012, Blood Moon published (lower photo) what was reviewed as "the best biography of Marilyn Monroe ever published," and that in 2020, (upper photo) it was updated and reconfigured?

It addresses everything you ever wondered about Marilyn and her murder.

It's hot, radical, thought-provoking, and available now from Amazon.com and from Blood Moon Productions.

ego, Jess or Desi," Schiller said. "They fought constantly."

Once, Schiller recalled an exasperated Lucille crying on his shoulder. In reference to Desi, she lamented, "What a beautiful man he used to be," she claimed. "What happened to him?"

***

One of the highlights of the fourth season (1954-55) of *I Love Lucy* reteamed Lucille in a TV episode with "my dreamboat" William Holden, with whom she'd had a fling when they'd co-starred in *Miss Grant Takes Richmond* (1949).

Aired on February 7, 1955, it was entitled *L.A. at Last*. In a nutshell, the Ricardos and the Mertzes have arrived in Hollywood from New York for a stay at the Beverly Palms Hotel. With the intention of confirming a possible film role, Desi leaves for the studio, and Lucy, with Ethel and Fred, head for the legendary Brown Derby Restaurant.

There, they find themselves seated in a booth next to William Holden, who is dining alone. Lucy stares so brazenly at Holden that it causes a ruckus. Embarrassed, she hastily departs, but accidently overturns a dessert tray, splattering the actor with its debris.

The plot thickens when Ricky calls, telling her he's bringing Holden with him to their hotel suite. She doesn't want to be recognized as the zany culprit at the Brown Derby, so she disguises herself with frumpy glasses, a kerchief, and a long putty nose.

As she's seated with him, her nose grows like that of Pinocchio. Holden offers to light her cigarette, but in doing so, he sets her fake proboscis on fire. She extinguishes her nose by lowering her face down into a cup of coffee.

Lucille later recalled the episode as "my favorite comic bit." Her affair with Holden had long ago been forgotten, as he had now fallen for Grace Kelly, his co-star with Bing Crosby in *The Country Girl* (1954).

***

When *I Love Lucy* was the

Lucille and William Holden "discovering" each other in *L.A. At Last*.

Lucille told her best friend, actress Barbara Pepper, "Bill is the nicest lover I ever had."

He also had a dark side, as he was a notorious alcoholic.

Once, while driving drunk in Italy, his Ferrari hit a small Fiat on the *autostrada*, and he was charged with manslaughter.

After being found guilty, Holden received an eight-month suspended jail sentence and paid the victim's widow $80,000.

#1-rated series on television, Jack Benny warned Lucille, "Being top dog is the loneliest place in the world. There's only one direction to go—and that's down."

That's exactly what happened to *I Love Lucy* in 1955 when *The $64,000 Question* and *The Ed Sullivan Show* became Numbers One and Two, respectively in terms of ratings. By December of that year, however, *I Love Lucy* was only two points below those two hits.

Change was in the air for *I Love Lucy* on March 7, 1955 For the seventh annual gathering of the ceremony for the Emmy Awards, *I Love Lucy* for the first time seemed to drop out of the race. Instead, *Make Room for Daddy* starring Danny Thomas, and *The Loretta Young Show* walked off with the top prizes.

In the supporting category, Frawley and Vance lost to Art Carney and Audrey Meadows for *The Honeymooners* which starred Jackie Gleason.

That disappointment was followed by a bombshell the following day when Philip Morris announced that it would cancel its sponsorship of *I Love Lucy* after the last episode of the season was telecast on June 27. *[Actually, that episode,* The Handcuffs, *was a re-run originally aired on October 6, 1952. In that segment, the Ricardos are stuck in a pair of antique handcuffs they cannot unlock.]*

Variety noted, "For the first time in television history, a sponsor is dropping a show that is still a top hit, although not taking home an Emmy."

New sponsors signed on almost immediately: General Foods and Proctor & Gamble. According to Lucy, "For General Foods I'll once again be hawking Jell-O, just like I did on my radio show, *My Favorite Husband.*"

William Asher, who had directed 75 episodes of *I Love Lucy,* left the show in April of 1955 for a new job with Columbia. Karl Freund, who had pioneered how the show was to be photographed, also departed that same year.

Another big departure occurred around the same time when its producer and chief writer, Jess Oppenheimer, resigned after signing a five-year contract with NBC.

Desi was rather cocky when he heard of the resignation. "Hell, he might end up working for me after all. I might buy NBC."

After leaving *I Love Lucy,* Asher worked on such shows as *Make Room for Daddy* and *The Patty Duke Show.* He also became friends with John F. Kennedy, and, along with Frank Sinatra, staged JFK's Inaugural Ceremony.

In 1963, he married actress Elizabeth Montgomery, daughter of the actor, Robert Montgomery. Asher produced and directed her hit TV series, *Bewitched,* but they divorced soon after the series was canceled in 1972.

The last time Lucille ever saw him was in Las Vegas when he was hanging out with Frank Sinatra, Peter Lawford, and Sammy Davis, Jr.

The new director of *I Love Lucy* was James V. Kern, a former attorney who became a screenwriter and later a director. One of its new writers, Bob Schiller, said, "He was a nice man but not a great director. He never learned my name, calling me Fisher instead of Kern."

At the start of the 1955-56 season, Desilu employed 3,300 workers and brought in a gross of $5 million annually.

"All business with Desi had to be concluded between 8:30 and 10:30AM, according to business manager Martin Leeds. "By noon, Desi was too deep into his gin martini hour to make much sense. He was quick to anger, especially when some person arrived and referred to him as either Ricky or Mr. Ricardo. Whenever someone did that, he would explode. However, he did tell me it was better than his name years earlier, when some people called him 'Mr. Lucille Ball.'"

On a personal level, Desi's womanizing had slowed down a bit because of his advancing middle age, weight gain, and alcohol consumption. But he was still having sexual flings at least three times a week, often not returning home.

He told his new writer, Bob Schiller, "I don't know why Lucy throws such fits when she learns about my womanizing. It's not that I'm having a romance with some broad. I only screw hookers. I leave a hundred-dollar bill on the table and say, 'See you around the block, kid.' Then I'm gone. No strings attached."

Lucille complained to Vance, "I don't know how much longer I can hold this marriage together. He's rarely at home anymore. Most of the old regulars have departed from our show, no longer able to take it. He's always drunk in the afternoon, going around clashing with everybody on the crew. He throws one temper fit after another, mostly directed at me. He thinks I'm getting too much credit for the success of the show, and that he's being ignored."

Schiller and his co-writer, Bob Weiskopf, created an episode to star John Wayne. Telecast on October 10, 1955, The Duke agreed to do it, mainly with the intention of promoting his new action film, *Blood Alley.*

In one zany segment, Lucy shatters the cement that contains the impressions of Wayne's hands and footprints in front of Grauman's Chinese Theater in Hollywood. After Wayne agrees to make another imprint, it leads to a meeting with the formidable Lucy. As expected, the episode devolves into more highjinks and more slapstick.

Although Desi ran the largest TV production company in the world at the time, many of his pilots bombed, finding no sponsor. He became fascinated with the potential of the actress Joanne Dru, a former model. She had divorced singer Dick Haymes in 1949, around the same time she' been the object of Montgomery Clift's affections in the classic Western, *Red River* (1948). She had also co-starred with Broderick Crawford, Lucille's former beau, in the Oscar-winning *All the King's Men* (1949).

Desi hired one of America's best-known pulp writers, Sidney Sheldon, to write a pilot featuring Dru, calling it *Adventures of a Model,* but it failed to find a sponsor.

By the end of 1955, *I Love Lucy* and *December Bride* were still among the Top Ten TV shows, according to the latest Nielsen rating. Desi told Lucille, "How much longer can it last? We can't go on with this crap forever without making some big changes."

"I've had it," he informed his closest associates. "I want *I Love Lucy* to end after the 1956-57 season, and I want it replaced with a more exciting show. I want to cut out this weekly shit."

He was so serious about this that he flew to New York to meet with William Paley at CBS. At first, Paley balked at canceling *I Love Lucy*, as it still had a Neilsen rating of about 42 percent. But Desi was adamant and so determined not to do it that Paley finally gave in after a bitter, three-hour argument.

Back in Hollywood, he told Lucille, "I was in no mood for compromise. You and I are now much richer."

According to the deal, *I Love Lucy* would go off the air with the final episode of its sixth season, after it aired in May of 1957. During the upcoming two seasons, reruns would be shown evenings at prime time.

After that, *I Love Lucy* would switch to daytime telecasts before going into worldwide syndication. That meant that "from here to eternity," *I Love Lucy* would be broadcast somewhere, someplace, around the world.

Their agreement with CBS, concluded on October 1, 1956, would provide Lucille and Desi with $4.5 million, spread out—for tax reasons—over a period of years. The final payment would occur in 1961. *[The sale of the re-runs for $4.5 million sounded like a fantastic deal for the Ricardos at the time, but over a period of years, CBS made $75 million from the purchase.]*

As part of the contract, Desi also sold their rights to *December Bride* for $500,000. An extra million was added to the contract to ensure that

Joanne Dru emerged from the hills of West Virginia to become a screen beauty. Her most famous role was in *All the King's Men* (1949), which brought an Oscar to its star, Broderick Crawford, Lucille's former lover.

Dru married two famous men: singer Dick Haymes (1941-1949) and actor John Ireland (1949-1956).

Desi failed to find a sponsor for his proposed sitcom starring her.

"She was a hottie, but I didn't put the make on her. I didn't want any unfavorable penile comparisons to Ireland, who was known for having the biggest dick in Hollywood."

CBS would have the TV rights to Lucille until 1971, based on a series of future "not yet developed" shows and spinoffs.

In the final deal, Desi and Lucille would produce and star in five one-hour specials for the 1957-58 season.

When news of *I Love Lucy's* upcoming cancellation hit the newspapers, CBS was bombarded with letters of protest.

When details of all this leaked to Frawley and Vance, they were "seriously pissed off," according to Frawley. "Fat Ass and I were getting only $3,500 a week," he said.

***

"I'm still on top of the mountain," Lucille said after the Eighth Annual Emmy Awards Ceremony on March 17, 1956 near the end of the 1955-56 season. Hosted by John Daly and Art Linkletter, Lucille won the Emmy for "Best Actress in a Continuing Series," her first televised win. It would also be her last Emmy until 1967.

Shortly after the ceremony, Lucille filmed one of the most iconic episodes, *Lucy's Italian Movie*. It aired on April 16, 1956. It had obviously been conceived as a spoof on the Italian film produced by Dino de Laurentiis, *Bitter Rice (Riso Amaro*; 1949) which had become an international hit during the peak years of Rome's designation as "Hollywood on the Tiber." It had starred the sultry Silvano Magnano as a postwar rice harvester in the paddies.

During a visit to Rome, Lucy is discovered by an Italian filmmaker who wants to cast her in a movie. "Vittorio Philippe," an exuberant character inspired by Fellini, praises her feet, which he likens to a large pizza. The name of this, his newest picture, is *Grapola Pungent (Bitter Grapes).*

Actually, he wants to cast Lucille as an American tourist, but she misinterprets his "easy to misinterpret" exuberance and imagines instead that he wants her to play a barefoot grape-stomper.

As a "rehearsal," and disguised as a peasant, she journeys to a small village and gets hired by a winery. She climbs into a large vat half-filled with freshly picked ripe grapes. There, she's joined by a local *paesana* who removes her shoes, lifts her skirts and begins treading the grapes alongside her. At first, all goes well until it turns into a grape fight.

Lucille later compared the episode to "stomping on eyeballs."

Her co-star, Teresa Terri, was an actual, real-life grape stomper. She seemed to take the fight for real, and Lucy, emerged from the ordeal battered, bruised, and covered with unfiltered grape juice—skins and seeds included. "I almost drowned in that vat," she lamented.

According to the plot, after her fight in the grape-stomping vat, the "Lucy We Love" is too weak to play in the movie. Making things worse, after the grape-stomping, she learns for the first time that the role

LUCY'S ITALIAN MOVIE
Feuding Paesanas
Trampling Out their Grapes of Wrath

In April of 1956, Lucille starred in her third most famous episode of *I Love Lucy.* It was episode #150, "Lucy's Italian Movie." Only "Vitameatavegamin" (episode #30) and "Job Switching," aka "The Candy Factory" (episode #36) topped it in popularity.

According to Lucille, "The bitch they hired was a real grape stomper, and she nearly beat the hell out of me."

she had signed to play was that of an American tourist, not a grape-stomper. Making things worse, the Italian director assigns the role Lucy coveted to Ethel Mertz (Vance) instead.

***

Desi would forever be bitter about the circumstances that followed the departure of Jess Oppenheimer, who later wrote an autobiography entitled *Laughs, Luck...and Lucy, How I Came to Create the Most Popular Sitcom of All Time.* As one of the founding fathers of the Ricardos and the Mertzes, he was entitled to a royalty on all episodes and their re-runs. As such, he became a millionaire.

Instead of replacing him as one of the writers, Desi—despite his over-burdened schedule—assumed his duties. Madelyn Pugh and Bob Carroll, Jr. remained on duty as the chief writers.

Desilu, with four TV series being broadcast and another dozen in development, became a very busy place.

Desi told his writers, "We need some class." To that effect, he devised the idea of hiring Orson Welles, the famous (read that "notorious") director of *Citizen Kane (1941)*, a rip-off of the life of press baron William Randolph Hearst. Welles had become widely known as the *enfant terrible* of Tinseltown.

Desi learned that he was living in Europe as a "tax exile." To entice him to return, Desi advanced him the money to settle his debt with the Internal Revenue Service. Within weeks, Welles arrived for a months-long sojourn at the home of Desi and Lucille in Beverly Hills.

He had previously (1943-1947) been married to the love goddess of the 1940s, Rita Hayworth. In 1955, he had married Paola Mori, the Countess of Girfalco, and by the time he arrived at the Arnazes, she was pregnant.

Welles didn't want to stay in a hotel, so Desi invited him and his wife to move into their guest cottage. It became a case of *The Man Who Came to Dinner* who never left.

It had been understood that his sojourn there would last for three weeks, but Welles extended it to three months. During his residency, he angered the Arnaz family and their servants, and ran up enormous expenses for long-distance phone calls, liquor, and staggering grocery deliveries, having consistently ordered lots of caviar and only the most expensive supplies. Desi later described Welles as "a gangster with money."

[It is not known if Desi ever learned that years before, his wife had sustained an affair with him.]

Both Welles and Desi envisioned scenarios for various episodes, some of them stylish adaptations of ancient Greek and Roman myths, always with a theme based on the ironies of human vanity. Desi financed a 30-minute pilot based on *The Fountain of Youth,* a story by author John Collier.

A week was allocated for the filming of its pilot, but Welles extended that allocation to six times that amount. When Desi challenged him, Welles responded, "I know what I'm doing, and haven't you heard? I'm a genius."

486

To add to the outrage of having gone spectacularly over Desi's budget, Welles spend another $10,000 hosting a lavish champagne party for cast and crew.

Ultimately, network executives rejected the proposal for the pilot, fearing that the result would be "too avant-garde and highbrow" for their audiences. Also, its quirky and deadline-averse creator, the "Glorious Gypsy," as Welles was known within the movie colony, was viewed as too unreliable for the completion of 38 difficult-to-pull-off episodes.

[Three years later, the pilot was finally telecast as an episode of NBC's Colgate Theater. Later, it won a Peabody Award, the only pilot in television history ever to be honored in that way.]

In an attempt to pay off his massive debt to Desilu, Welles agreed to be a guest on an episode of *I Love Lucy.* No. 156 in the series, it was aired on CBS on October 15, 1956 and entitled *Lucy Meets Orson Welles.*

The plot has Lucy wanting to appear in a benefit that Welles had agreed to organize at Ricky's night club. She brags about playing Juliet in high school.

He finally agrees, but she finds herself as part of his magic act on stage. She becomes a prop in a levitation trick, but when Welles angrily storms off the stage, she finds herself suspended in air, calling out, "Romeo, Romeo, get me down from here!"

***

Both Desi and Lucille were friends of Bob Hope, having worked with him before—she as a player and Desi as the band leader on some of the comedian's NBC radio broadcasts. Hope joined them for the telecast of *Lucy and Bob Hope*, aired for the first time on October 1, 1956.

According to the plot, for publicity, she wants to persuade Hope to appear at Ricky's new nightspot, Club Babalu. To that effect, and in an attempt to meet him at Yankee Stadium during a standoff between the Cleveland Indians and the New York Yankees, she disguises herself as a hot dog vendor with a fake mustache. The distraction caused by her entrance causes Hope to get

During his long-ago affair with Lucille, **Orson Welles** had wanted to co-star with her as his leading lady in a feature film. That never happened, but he did get to appear with her on television.

Shakespeare surely would be horrified at how **Lucy** and Welles made a parody of his famous play, *Romeo and Juliet.*

As part of his act, Welles levitates a hapless Lucy.

A hilarious "non-essential" scene with William Frawley and Vivian Vance had to be cut when the 30-minute episode ran overtime.

hit in the head with a baseball.

Later, disguised as a baseball player, she makes another attempt to gain an "audience" with him.

Hope finally listens to her pitch and ends up at Ricky's nightclub. There, he joins the Ricardos in a singing rendition of "Nobody Loves the Ump."

The episode with Hope is notable in that it introduced a child actor, Keith Thibodeaux, in the role of Ricky Ricardo, Jr. Desi asked him to change his stage name to "Richard Keith," and both the boy and his father acquiesced.

The Arnazes had been invited to watch the boy, billed as "The World's Tiniest Professional Drummer," on bandleader Horace Heidt's *Show Wagon* on TV. After sitting through the five-year-old's amazing performance, Lucille and Desi agreed, in a major casting decision for the series, "That's our boy!"

Privately, Desi told Bob Schiller, "The kid looks exactly like me. I don't remember being in Louisiana nine months before he was born, but I must have been."

Ten months after his birth on December 1, 1950, Keith demonstrated to his father that he had musical talent when, even before he could talk, he sat on the living room floor and, with a knife and fork, kept time to the music being broadcast over the radio.

When the child was two, his dad gave him a toy drum for Christmas, "and he beat hell out of it." It was soon replaced with a real drum. By 1954, Keith had become known for *rat-a-tat-tat* drumbeats heard all over Lafayette, Louisiana.

Robert de Grasse, whom Lucille had known since the 1930s, was signed to a seven-year contract at a salary of $491 a week to replace the by-now-departed Karl Freund. It was De Grasse who photographed Keith for his first appearance on *I Love Lucy*.

With his father's permission, Keith even lived for a while at the Arnaz home. "He was like a son to me," Lucille said.

There was no jealousy from Desi, Jr., and the two boys became best friends. The drummer taught Desi Jr. how to play the drum and a host of other things.

As he grew older, a career in show business awaited Keith.

***

With the stage name of Richard Keith, child actor and drum-playing prodigy **Keith Thibodeaux** was cast as "Little Ricky" on *I Love Lucy*.

According to Desi, "The kid looked so much like me that a rumor spread that he was my illegitimate child. I thought my real son would be jealous, but Richard and my boy became best of friends."

488

One of the biggest laugh fests ever recorded for an episode of *I Love Lucy* occurred when Lucille and Vivian Vance, as Ethel Mertz, teamed to film *Lucy Does the Tango*, aired on March 11, 1957. The Arnazes and the Mertzes have moved to the country and are trying to operate a chicken farm.

When Desi checks the accounting, he concludes that every egg one of their hens has laid costs him eighteen dollars in operating expenses. *[In two weeks, the hens have laid only six eggs.]* To rescue the enterprise, Ethel and Lucy buy five dozen eggs at the local supermarket, with the intention of placing them in the nests of the under-productive hens. Ricky, however, returns home early one day to rehearse a tango, *à la* Valentino, for an upcoming appearance at a charity show.

Just as Desi enters, Ethel and Lucy cram their eggs into their blouses, pockets, skirts, and brassieres. Then, in a tango embrace, he crushes the eggs against her body, causing her to shake and shimmy as she wiggles the crushed and slimy yolks down her legs. The laughter in the audience lasted for sixty-five seconds, the longest ever recorded during the entire series.

In one segment, Lucille accidentally fell on Desi, causing him to tear some ligaments in his back. He was in such pain, he had to be hospitalized. Doctors discovered that he also had diverticulitis, a painful inflammation of the colon. In the aftermath of that accident, he was warned that if he didn't give up drinking, he might have to have a colostomy, which would, in its aftermath, require him to evacuate his stools into a bag attached to straps around his waist. "I'd better mend my ways," he told Lucille.

***

The final episode of the *I Love Lucy*

series was entitled *The Ricardos Dedicate a Statue.* Telecast on May 6, 1957, and watched by thirty-five million viewers, it was a bit silly and not particularly funny. Writer Bob Schiller said, "That show was terrible, just terrible."

According to the plot, at Westport, Connecticut, townspeople plan to unveil a stone sculpture of a Minute Man as a celebration of the town's involvement in the Revolutionary War. Ricky was selected to deliver a dedication at the Town Square.

Immediately prior to the dedication ceremony, as the statue sits in a trailer being hauled to the site by Lucille's car, she begins a car chase for Little Ricky's runaway dog. Although she finally locates the missing pet, she piles up the car, thereby destroying the statue that's on the trailer she's hauling.

Desperate not to embarrass herself and/or ruin her husband's ceremony, she disguises herself as the Minute Man statue, but is upstaged by the dog, who turns up to lick her.

As a footnote, Lucie, not quite six years old, and Desi, Jr., then aged four, made their only appearances on the series in that episode as bystanders in the crowd with Ethel Mertz.

General Foods dropped out as a sponsor, claiming that the cost of $350,000 per episode was too high, and that the sales it generated couldn't be justified by the expenses of sponsoring the series.

One critic referred to its demise as "an occasion for national mourning."

***

The script for the film, finally entitled *Forever, Darling,* had been gathering dust since it had been written back in 1942 as a co-starring vehicle for Katharine Hepburn and Spencer Tracey or perhaps for William Powell and Myrna Loy in the aftermath of their success with those *Thin Man* movies back in the 1930s.

Its author, Helen Deutsch, had had a lot of hits, having adapted Enid Bagnold's novel, *National Velvet,* into the script that morphed Elizabeth Taylor into a movie star when she was still a teenager. Deutsch later wrote the script for *King Solomon's Mines* (1950), starring Stewart Granger, and *I'll Cry Tomorrow* (1955) featuring Susan Hayward in one of her most memorable roles. Deutsch was Oscar-nominated for her screenplay of *Lili* (1953). Her final screenplay was the screen adaption of *Valley of the Dolls* (1967) from Jacqueline Susann's controversial novel.

After five years of marriage, chemical engineer Lorenzo Xavier Vega (Desi) has been neglecting his wife, Susan (Lucille). She agrees to go with him on a camping trip to test the revolutionary new insecticide he's developed. When she wishes aloud that she had a more attentive spouse, her guardian angel appears. He is the mirror image of her favorite movie star, James Mason.

[Actually Mason was not the original choice as the guardian angel. Cary Grant had been offered the role, but he rejected it.]

Lucille heartily agreed on the casting of Mason, as she'd been thrilled by his performance in *A Star Is Born* (1955) opposite Judy Garland.

"Lucille Ball was such a brilliant *comedienne* that I always rated her as the best actress in America," Mason said. "Even so, I owed her an apology. Months later, when asked which film of mine I would like to assign to the incinerator, I came up with *Forever, Darling*. What made the film so hideous for me is that I felt I had delivered the worst performance of my career."

In addition to Mason, Desi hired a strong supporting cast. It included Louis Calhern, but that veteran actor died before the movie was released. He'd gone to Japan to star in *The Teahouse of the Autumn Moon* (1956). There, he died of a sudden heart attack. *[He was replaced with Paul Ford.]*

Another key player, the sardonically funny Nancy Kulp, would reach the peak of her career when cast as the erudite, adenoidal secretary, Jane Hathaway, in *The Beverly Hillbillies.*

John Emery, "The Poor Man's John Barrymore," was assigned a minor role as Dr. Edward R. Winter. He amused Lucille with stories of his tumultuous marriage (1937-1941) to Tallulah Bankhead.

Forever, Darling marked the swan song of Alexander Hall as a director. When it was finished, he bowed out of the movies, surviving to the age of 74 before suffering a fatal heart attack in San Francisco. *[Prior to the arrival of Desi on the scene, he had been Lucille's lover.]*

They were rich, very famous, and beloved across America.

Nonetheless, Lucille and her increasingly estranged husband felt compelled to pump ticket sales for their film, *Forever, Darling.*

Critics claimed that it was little more than a prolonged (and vaguely irritating) reprise of one of their sitcom episodes.

The photo shows **Lucille and Desi** aboard a specially outfitted train that chug-chugged its way cross country to promote it.

Despite their intentions, *Forever, Darling* ended forever their dream of re-launching themselves as a dream team in feature movies.

It didn't work...*but the times, they were a-changing.*

Its world premiere was staged in Lucille's hometown of Jamestown, New York, in February of 1956. Almost everyone in town turned out to greet its most famous former resident. She kept running into faces from her adolescence that she did not recognize, mainly because so many of them had aged badly.

Critics were harsh, *Variety* ascertaining that "the movie can't make up its mind whether it's a comedy, drama, romance, or fantasy."

The New York Herald Tribune wrote, "*Forever, Darling*" is as terrible as it sounds. The two stars devoted their best energy to the *I Love Lucy* series and tossed this one off as a quickie." Bosley Crowther of *The New York Times* defined it as "thin, overdrawn, a weak caper." *Time Out London*

491

judged it as a "fitfully amusing offering."

Unlike their first movie, *The Long, Long Trailer, Forever, Darling* flopped at the box office, making less than $3 million.

To save it, they had to go on a cross-country tour. In a railway car custom outfitted by the Santa Fe railroad, they hyped the film in such cities as Pittsburgh, Philadelphia, Detroit, Dallas, Chicago, and Cleveland.

Forever, Darling marked the end of their dream of making feature films together. As a team and as time went by, although they'd be offered other scripts, they turned them down.

Desi, at least for a while, held on to his dream of having Desilu compete with the big studios in the production of feature films.

To that effect, he considered casting Gregory Peck and James Stewart in a World War II drama. Then, as a contender within the genre of science fiction, he devoted time and money trying to launch the big-budget Europe-based project *Journey to a Star* with Dan Dailey in the lead. He also gave serious consideration to casting Mickey Rooney in the untitled saga of Johnny Longden, the famous racehorse jockey.

***

Desi was asked to be the emcee at the ninth annual Emmy Awards ceremony, broadcast over NBC on March 16, 1957 from its studio at Burbank.

I Love Lucy was not in the running, but three of its stars were nominated. *[Desi was overlooked.]*

Although each of them was nominated, Lucille, Vance, and Frawley all lost. Lucille was beat by Nanette Fabray for "Best Continuing Performance in a Series." Vance lost to Pat Carroll, and William Frawley was mowed down by Carl Reiner.

Most newspapers panned Desi as emcee, although the *Hollywood Reporter* found him "in his usual comedic form."

Desi got his wish when Desilu's program lineups for the 1957-58 season underwent major changes. First, his "masterpiece" was no longer called *I Love Lucy.* He insisted that his name be added to a new moniker, *The Lucille Ball-Desi Arnaz Show,* and that he be officially designated as its Executive Producer, with Bert Granet named as Producer and Jerry Thorpe as Director. Vance, Frawley, and Richard Keith (as Little Ricky) would remain as cast regulars.

The series' new sponsor was the Ford Motor Company, whose intention involved the promotion of its newest model, the Edsel. *[Marketed by Ford for two years beginning in 1958, it was named after Edsel Ford, the hardworking (and tragic) son of Ford's founding father, Henry Ford. Plagued with design problems and mechanical flaws, the Edsel today is viewed as a spectacularly expensive failure, a symbol of corporate bungling and marketing ineptitude.]*

To launch it, the first episode of the renamed series was *Lucy Takes a Cruise to Havana,* with guest stars Ann Sothern, Rudy Vallee, Cesar Romero, and gossip columnist Hedda Hopper.

The episode opens with Hopper interviewing the Ricardos on how their love affair began. In flashbacks, Lucille and Sothern were depicted as two New York stenographers sailing to Havana in a search of some Cuban bachelors. On board are Fred and Ethel Mertz, his "child bride from 1934." Vallee is also aboard but wants to be left alone.

After their arrival in Havana, Lucy meets Ricky Ricardo, her tour guide. She soon learns that his real wish involves emigrating to New York to become a singer. Lucy tries to cajole Vallee into hiring him for a gig on his radio show which, through a misunderstanding, leads to a public brawl. Lucy and Sothern both land in jail.

The show, envisioned as an hour-long program, ran over by fifteen minutes. Desi feared that cutting that much from its context would ruin it. In an amazing feat of negotiation and compensation, he persuaded the executives of *The U.S. Steel Hour* (1953-63) to surrender fifteen minutes allocated for one episode of their series. *[As part of the process, he more or less guaranteed that cutting that much out of one of their episodes would catalyze its highest ratings. He was right. Consequently, the premiere of the first episode of the revised* Lucy *series became the only time in CBS's history when an episode of one of their TV series ran for the "impossibly awkward" air time of 75 minutes.]*

Desi's longtime friend, Cesar Romero, was charming in his "sleek Latino way" as Desi's pal, Carlos. As Desi confessed to Lucille, "Cesar still has the hots for me after all these years."

The show did well in the Nielsen ratings, receiving 57.15

HEDDA HOPPER — RUDY VALLEE — CESAR ROMERO — ANN SOTHERN — LUCILLE BALL — DESI ARNAZ

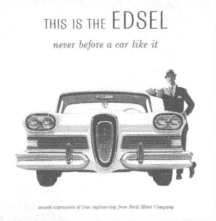

Audiences tuned in because they loved the personalities and broad humor of **Lucille Ball** and **Ann Sothern**—not because they really believed that either of them still evoked hot American secretaries ready for a romantic fling in an exotic land.

percent of viewers, but it was bashed by most critics.

From Desi and Lucy's home turf of Los Angeles, *Variety* defined it as "thin on charm." The *Hollywood Reporter* wrote, "Maybe we were expecting too much, but the show is still painfully thin as a situation comedy, with much studio laughter made over thin jokes and fancy mugging."

When asked to articulate his opinion of *Lucy Takes a Cruise to Havana*, its writer Bob Weiskopf had only one brief comment, "Rudy Vallee is a pain in the ass."

As a sign that both the original version and spinoffs of *I Love Lucy* were winding down, its longtime writers, Bob Carroll, Jr. and Madelyn Pugh wanted to resign, even though in 1956 they had signed on for another three years. During a meeting with Desi, each of them confessed that they had run out of farcical situations for Lucy.

Carroll wanted to relocate to Europe, and Pugh hoped to become a "full-time mother." Desi thanked each of them for their past services and agreed to release them from their contracts.

Although Desi was notorious for his ego, he had enough business savvy to realize that it was Lucille who had created their success. Once, she tripped over a wire and fell on the floor of the set. He rushed to her side to make sure she was all right. Helping her to her feet, he turned to the crew: "Amigos, if anything happens to our redhead, we're in the shrimp-fishing business."

At the launch of his new season, Desi kept complaining of pain. "My stomach feels like it's tied up in a knot." He had been warned before not to take on such a huge work load. "I still drink too much," he confessed, "thinking liquor would take the pain away. It does not."

On some days, he had to devote as much as eighteen hours to his rigorous duties. He complained that he had almost no time to spend with Lucie and Desi, Jr., and that he was no longer sleeping with Lucille.

"So what did I do?" Desi asked. "Instead of cutting down on the workload, and cooling it with liquor, I tripled my duties. I bought RKO."

Notorious for her outrageous humor and off-the-charts bawdiness, **Tallulah Bankhead** was the most famous woman to ever come out of Alabama.

In the 1920s, noted even then for her omnisexual scandals, she had been the Toast of London.

In the photo above, she's the focal point of the November 22, 1948 edition of *Time* magazine.

***

The second episode of the Ball-Arnaz show was labeled *The Celebrity Next Door*, and it went on the air on December 3, 1957.

As their neighbor, both Desi and Lucille wanted a world-famous actress and asked Bette Davis to star in the episode.

But when they visited her at Davis' new home in Brentwood, they discovered that she had barely recovered from an accident she'd had. Checking out the residence she wished to rent, she had opened the wrong door and had fallen down the steps onto the stone floor of the cellar. Although she had injured her back and spent weeks in recovery, she assured them she could handle the role. She also seemed to be suffering mental anguish, damaged by the fallout from her divorce from Gary Merrill, whom she'd met when they'd co-starred together in *All About Eve* (1950).

Both Lucille and Desi were put off by her haughty demands, but finally acquiesced. For her guest appearance, she wanted $20,000, more than any other performer had ever asked for an episode of their show. She also insisted on equal billing plus an air ticket from California back to her home in Maine.

At one point during filming, she was needed for a scene that required her atop a horse. Although Desi volunteered to substitute a lookalike actress in her place, Davis insisted on performing the scene herself.

The Celebrity Next Door lampooned the social pretentions of the suburban 1950s.

Ethel Mertz has been maneuvered into disguising herself as a maid for the purposes of "keeping up appearances" during **Tallulah Bankhead**'s awkward visit to Lucy's "bubble."

The horse didn't take to her and reared up on its hind legs. She fell to the ground, splintering her arm in two places and once again injuring her back.

That night, as Davis lay medicated and in agony in a hospital, Lucille and Desi decided that Tallulah Bankhead would be an ideal replacement as Lucille's "celebrity neighbor."

Ironically, but unknown to them at the time, Tallulah was also in "wretched health." When she arrived at Desilu on a late morning in September of 1957, she was obviously drunk.

She and Lucille conflicted with one another from the beginning. Bankhead was actually suffering from pneumonia at the time, and coughed at an alarming rate, sometimes splattering Lucille in the face. Once, after a bitter fight, Lucille talked to Desi, suggesting that she be replaced with Ethel Merman.

Tallulah herself later discussed her role with a reporter. "I've got not even one picayune derogatory thing to say about those wonderful people. Of course, I did have pneumonia at the time, and a hairstylist really blinded me with spray. But Lucy, she's divine to work with. And Desi is brilliant. He has temper because he's fat. I broke a tooth. Then I broke the cap they put on the tooth. I broke my nails. I suffered from triple pneumonia."

Writer Bob Schiller said, "Bankhead was drunk all the time. She would take off her panties on any occasion. Modesty was not in her character. She called Vance 'Cunty.'"

For one segment of the episode, which Desi called "a show within a show of an old Shakespearean play. I was dressed as an English lord, with a plumed hat, breeches, and stuff."

Once, during a rehearsal, Vance admired Tallulah's slacks. She pulled them off right in front of the crew and gave them to Vance. According to Desi, "There she stood in a pair of panties with a crotch that hung down to her knees."

Lucille and Desi dreaded the actual filming of *The Celebrity Next Door*, terrified that Tallulah would be combative and uncooperative. As it turned out, Tallulah gave a bravura performance, with perfect timing and spot-on deliveries. Ironically, it was Lucille who flubbed her lines, and one of her scenes had to be reshot.

In spite of its difficulties, Tallulah's appearance with the Arnazes became the highest-rated TV show of the week.

Before buying RKO, Desi managed to get a call through to its reclusive previous owner, **Howard Hughes**, the fabled aviator and movie producer.

At the time, Hughes was one of the most emotionally erratic and richest man on the planet, with a knack for seducing the most beautiful female stars (and some of the most handsome hunks) in the entertainment industry.

Here, he's seen with love goddess **Ava Gardner**. They fought frequently and abusively throughout the course of their violent relationship. During one of their arguments, he punched her in the face, dislocating her jaw.

She didn't cry out in pain: Instead, she picked up a heavy ashtray crafted from onyx and bashed it over his head, nearly killing him.

***

"I could spend my days and nights listening to deals tossed to me in my office at Desilu," its president claimed. "After all, I was the bigtime producer Desi Arnaz. Big and getting bigger…and I mean, much, much bigger. *Grande,* in fact."

At ten o'clock one Monday morning, a call came in from Daniel O'Shea, the president of RKO, with a "heads up" revelation.

Desi knew that Howard Hughes, the billionaire aviator and movie producer, had sold RKO to General Tire, and that the tire people regretted their purchase. Since taking over the fabled studio at which Lucille used to work, they had been running it at a loss.

"I found out that they wanted to dump it and all of its assets for pennies on the dollar," Desi said. "I'm talking about all their real estate, including office buildings at Culver City and elsewhere."

O'Shea told him that for $6.5 million, Desi could take possession, but time was of the essence, and Desi was warned that he had to make a decision right away. That night, he did what most people in Hollywood would find impossible: He actually got to speak to Hughes on the phone. He found him in pain and in bad shape. In a bitter (recent) fight with Ava Gardner, she had thrown a lamp at him, and he was suffering from the after-effects of a concussion.

Hughes remained on the phone for only a minute or so, telling Desi, "Buy the whole fucking lot. Even if you don't need the studios, you'll still make a huge profit. The real estate alone is extremely valuable and will become even more so in the years ahead."

Unfortunately, because of heavy taxes of that era, Desi did not have a lot of ready cash in the bank. He was delighted when he learned the next morning that General Tire wanted only $2 million as a down payment. He'd have an entire decade to pay off the full amount at a finance rate of 5 ½ percent.

By noon, he got the president of the local branch of Bank of America on the phone. "It was amazing. He said 'Okay, we'll do it. Where do you want us to send the $2 million check?"

An aerial view of **RKO** after it was acquired by Desi Arnaz and Lucille Ball as the seat of their TV production company, **Desilu**.

Lucille was informed of the acquisition (Desi had not consulted her in advance) after filming an episode of *I Love Lucy* with Tallulah Bankhead. Desi had paid more than six million dollars for both the studio and its grounds, despite the fact they had only $600,000 in the bank.

Drinking champagne to toast their purchase, she made her first request to her aides: "I want to see the gorilla dummy that was used to depict King Kong."

Her next request involved visiting the old Selznick Studio where *Gone With the Wind* (1939) had been shot. Perhaps in one of the worst miscasting ideas of all time, she had auditioned for the role of Scarlett O'Hara.

Lucille's next request involved commandeering the dressing room occupied by Ginger Rogers during her reign as "The Queen of RKO." Desi had sometimes visited her dressing room for "love in the afternoon."

To make the deal sweeter, Desi phoned William Paley at CBS, asking him if he wanted to be an equal partner. Although Paley said, "No way!" he promised to rent studio space at RKO.

Desi then phoned O'Shea to come down on his price, after much haggling. He got him to lower the cost to $6,150,000. The terms had been set, and the check from Bank of America arrived.

The first person he phoned was Lucille. He hadn't even discussed it with her yet.

"Imagine, RKO used to pay me fifty bucks a week," she said. "Now I own the whole fucking place."

497

More good news was on the way. Desi needed to release only half a million from that $2 million loan from the Bank of America. For tax reasons, General Tire wanted the cost of the sale to be paid back gradually.

That afternoon, Desi toured his new purchase, visiting thirty-five sound stages. He had concluded a real estate deal considered one of the largest land grabs in the history of Hollywood. He toured the lot where David O. Selznick had shot *Gone With the Wind* (1939) after Lucille had (unsuccessfully) auditioned for the role of Scarlett O'Hara.

Despite its willingness to sell its real estate, RKO had refused to part with its portfolio of feature films. They had almost 700 of them, many starring legends of the 1930s: Katharine Hepburn, Cary Grant, Fred Astaire, Ginger Rogers, and many others. General Tire people wanted to sell them for revivals and re-runs on television.

The scale of what Desilu had just acquired slowly began creeping up on him. It had included five acres of topnotch real estate in Culver City and Hollywood, two fully equipped film studios, and acquisition of the Motion Picture Center, a screening space whose name he changed to Desilu Cahuenga.

Lucille rode a golf cart during her tour of her new acquisition. Many elements of her former stamping grounds were, "rusty, creaky, and falling apart." Some of the sound stages hadn't sheltered a film crew in many years. RKO's heyday in the 1930s was a distant memory.

That very day, Lucille designated as her dressing room the one formerly occupied by Ginger Rogers back when she'd reigned as Queen of RKO. "The rooms looked like a bordello," Lucille told her aide. "I'll have to redecorate."

She surveyed the bed in an alcove. "This is where Ginger seduced Desi." *[Obviously, she'd learned of their long-ago affair.]* "It must have been a busy place. David Niven. James Stewart. Dick Powell. Rudy Vallee. Even Fred Astaire for one disastrous afternoon. Poor Fred."

Lucille also visited the wardrobe department where, perhaps just for the memory of a long-departed friend, she tried on some of the gowns worn by Carole Lombard in those screwball comedies of the 1930s.

"I knew that Desi and I were adored by millions of fans, but instead of all this adulation, I wanted to be home with my kids and to be with my husband—in other words, a wife and mother."

"Even on weekends, when we wanted to be alone, our ranch was overrun with business interests. Everybody, even old friends, had a script to sell and for us to produce. Even top-rated movie stars of yesteryear pounded on the door."

CHAPTER FIFTEEN

ADIOS TO RICKY & LUCY RICARDO

In 1976, Desi Arnaz appeared on Johnny Carson's *Tonight* Show to promote his autobiography, efficiently entitled *A Book.* Based on the look on Carson's face, he didn't think that was a selling title.

Desi said that the book detailed his life only up to his divorce from Lucille and the end of the *I Love Lucy* series.

"Do you have a title for a second volume?" Carson asked.

"Yeah, I do," Desi answered. "I'm calling it *Another Book."*

His story of his life was quite candid. He revealed how he had risen from "a guy who cleaned bird shit out of canary cages on Miami Beach to the pinnacle of success in television."

He spoke of his involvements in the worlds of everyone from Eleanor Roosevelt to Dwight Eisenhower, from Humphrey Bogart and Judy Garland to Doris Day and Robert Taylor.

He claimed that readers would understand his unlimited seductions of what he referred to as both "the milk girls and the Bingo Girls. Lucy didn't understand."

"The irony of it all was that our undreamed-of success, fame, and fortune turned into hell."

He concluded by saying "*I Love Lucy* was more than just a title."

***

In 1958, Desi flew to Pittsburgh, the headquarters of Westinghouse, and negotiated a $12 million sponsorship, the largest ever negotiated at the time for TV production. He winged it at just the right time as Westinghouse's sponsorship deal with *Studio One* was faltering in the Nielsen ratings.

[Studio One *was a radio anthology drama*

In his autobiography, **Desi** wrote, "The success of *I Love Lucy* is something that only happens once in a lifetime, if you are fortunate enough to have it happen at all."

"If we hadn't done anything else but bring that half hour of fun, pleasure, and relaxation to most of the world, a world in such dire need of even that short time-out from its problems and sorrows, we should be content."

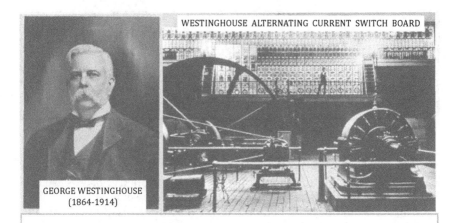

WESTINGHOUSE ALTERNATING CURRENT SWITCH BOARD

GEORGE WESTINGHOUSE
(1864-1914)

"BUT WHAT I REALLY WANTED WAS A TOASTER"

—Ethel to Lucy in Season 4, Episode 9 of I Love Lucy's, *."Ethel's Birthday."*

Did you know? That the origins of CBS—the media entity that's still involved with I Love Lucy re-runs—derived from **George Westinghouse**, one of the less famous but most influential entrepreneurs of the Industrial Revolution?

And did you know that **Westinghouse, Inc.**, his brainchild, was the orporate entity that sponsored Lucille and Desi during their early experiments with TV sitcom?

Brilliant, self-effacing, and much less famous than his cantankerous competitor, Thomas Edison, George Westinghouse was a hands-on inventor whose breakthroughs, it's argued, led to the development and expansion of the railway industry, the power grid, long-distance transport of natural gas, turbine generators (the kind that harnessed, during his lifetime, the power of Niagara Falls), and metallurgy as we know it today.

Although he died one of the richest men in America, with a reputation for not abusing his labor force, the financial panics of 1907 and beyond "confiscated" his control of the heavy industries that built his personal fortune. What remained was a scaled-down entity whose profits derived from elevators, escalators, and home appliances—especially televisions, toasters, refrigerators, stoves and vacuum cleaners—the kind favored by postwar consumers who included Ethel Mertz.

In the early 1950s, it was Westinghouse, from its base in Pittsburgh, that Desi, in one of his best business moves, got the company to sponsor the then-untested TV series, *I Love Lucy.*

Ironically, forty eventful years later, Westinghouse, Inc.'s management decided to entirely reinvent itself into a media conglomerate. In 1995, after selling off many of its original electrical businesses, it renamed itself CBS after buying the CBS television network for $5.4 billion.

What's the moral? George Westinghouse, one of the most brilliant inventors of the grimy, pollution-soaked mills and factories of America's Industrial Revolution, is distantly associated with the creative statement and spirit of two razzmatazz but overworked show-biz entrepreuneurs, **Lucille Ball and Desi Arnaz.**

series that was later adapted for TV. Every year between 1950 to 1958, it had received Emmy nominations. Annually, it created 467 episodes based on everything from TV adaptations of George Orwell's 1984 to Reginald Rose's Twelve Angry Men, later adapted into a full-length motion picture starring Henry Fonda.]

Westinghouse Electric Corporation, an American mega-corporation founded in 1886, was an early rival of Thomas Edison's Electric Company. In the 20th Century, Westinghouse registered and was granted more than 28,000 U.S. patents, the third most numerous of any company, and as such became a lynch-pin of what later became known as the "military-industrial complex." Through the development of railway equipment (including the air brake), turbine en-gines, and alternating electrical current, it became a key player in the transforma-tion of the United States into the most in-fluential techno-industrial powerhouse in human his-tory. Most American families came to recognize Westing-house for its household elec-trical products: televisions, hairdryers, electric irons, and refrigerators.

In 1958, Desi had con-vinced CBS to host the Desilu Playhouse with the promise of a bi-monthly *Lucille Ball-Desi Arnaz* TV show. It was for sponsorship of this show that Westinghouse was will-ing to shell out millions.

The new *Westinghouse Desilu Playhouse* debuted on Monday from 10 to 11pm (EST) beginning on October 6, 1958.

Desi was its host, with Betty Furness continuing as the Westinghouse spokesper-son. In addition to Lucille

Westinghouse hit its public association with Lu-cille and Desi hard, incorporating sales pitches of its appliances into TV segments in any way they thought might sell more of its products.

The middle photo is a grainy still from the closing moments of a training video intended for viewing by the Westinghouse sales staff. Lucy—supposedly hiding from Desi after ordering too many Westing-house appliances—peers out from the inside of a Westinghouse dryer at one of the company's hand-some sales directors.

And in the lower photo, Ricky and Fred, with Ethel doing most of the labor, deliver a comedy *schtick* about a Westinghouse trade-in that will swap their old refrigerator, the one that Ethel is struggling to roll onto the set, with a newer model.

What are the punch lines?

FRED, SPEAKING LOUDLY TO RICKY: *"You know Ethel, don't you? What's been in HERE (point-ing to the refrigerator) ends up HERE" (pointing to Ethel's midriff.)*

She scowled, audiences roared, and sales soared.

and Desi, Vivian Vance and William Frawley would make appearances.

At the conclusion of his meetings, during his flight back to Los Angeles, Desi felt he had made a sweetheart deal. *Variety* called it "telefilm's most costly and ambitious series to date" and was the first to report on its details.

Desilu Playhouse, sponsored by Westinghouse, agreed to produce 48 episodes of shows derived from the themes established by the *I Love Lucy* series. They would include 42 original shows, six re-runs, and four Lucille and Desi hour-long specials. Budgets for each show could rise as high as $150,000. The Lucille/Desi specials, however, were allowed to cost as much as $350,000.

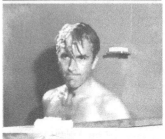

A lot depended on Desi's ability to book "top name" stars for special appearances. To his frustration, really big stars, such as Cary Grant and Humphrey Bogart, bowed out. Desi had to settle instead for well-known actors, but not major box office stars.

His roster might include such performers as George Murphy (Lucille's former co-star in the movies,), Rory Calhoun, Jean Hagen, Hugh O'Brian, Aldo Ray, or Barry Sullivan.

***

The concluding episode of Desilu's seventh season, *Lucy Goes to Sun Valley*, was telecast on April 14, 1958. It starred the famous Argentine heartthrob, Fernando Lamas.

He was no stranger to Hollywood when he co-starred with Lucille. Although they eventually became friends, Desi and Lamas had begun the late 1940s as rather tense competitors. After his stint in the U.S. Army, Desi hoped MGM would cast him as the screen's leading Latin lover, but studio executives preferred Lamas instead. They considered him "better looking, more studly, a greater physical specimen, and more of a dreamboat." In the words of starlet Nancy Davis (aka Nancy Davis Reagan), "All the starlets at the studio found Lamas alluring, and he managed to get around to most of us."

Three views of **Fernando Lamas** in *Lucy Goes to Sun Valley*. The emerging resort's tourist authorities were very cooperative.

As commentator **Bart Andrews** wrote about the (somewhat adolescent) plot: "Ricky didn't believe Lucy's stories that Fernando came on to her when he, Ricky, was away."

"Ricky, Ethel, and Fred—individually—interrupt Lamas' shower *(see above)* and ask him to 'come on' to Lucy at an afternoon skating party, just so Ricky can feign jealousy and convince Lucy that he loves her."

"Unfortunately, Latin lover Lamas goes a bit too far; Ricky loses his temper, and both men gain a black eye."

502

Even before his migration to the U.S., Lamas had already developed a formidable reputation as a seducer. A son of Buenos Aires, he had been the secret lover of that country's First Lady and co-dictator, the legendary Evita Perón.

Many of the scenes in his first American film, *The Avengers* (1950), had been shot on location in Argentina. A few of them, however, were filmed in Hollywood, the logistics of which encouraged Lamas' move to California.

Within months, he became the on- and off-screen lover of Lana Turner during their co-starring gig in the 1952 remake of *The Merry Widow*. He followed that by starring with (and seducing) Elizabeth Taylor in *The Girl Who Had Everything* (1953). He was willing to marry the violet-eyed beauty, but she had other plans.

At MGM, he was cast as the male lead opposite swimming star Esther Williams in *Dangerous When Wet* (1954). He proposed marriage to her, but she (wisely and affectionately) told him, "Come back after you've seduced half the other movie stars in Hollywood—and I know you will. Then I'll say yes."

[He took her advice and returned to her side fourteen years later. In 1969, she agreed to marry him. The union was his fourth marriage, and Williams' third.

Long before that, however, in 1954 in a bond that lasted until 1960, he wed the Titian-haired beauty of MGM, Arlene Dahl. During the course of their six-year marriage, the couple gave birth to three children, one of whom, Lorenzo Lamas (born in 1958), became a well-known actor himself.]

During the period when Lucille worked with Lamas on their TV episode, she became friends with Dahl. Lucille confessed to her, "Here we are, two hot-blooded redheads staying at home while our Latin Lovers play the field. At times, I feel like we're mothers instead of wives to these two naughty boys."

The plot for *Lucy Goes to Sun Valley* included a key role for Richard Keith as Little Ricky. Desi and Lucy make plans for a second honeymoon in Sun Valley. At the last minute, Desi has to cancel, so a dejected Lucy opts to bring Ethel with her instead. There, they meet Fernando Lamas, and Lucy comes up with a

Members of one of Hollywood's most stylish marriages, **Arlene Dahl** with **Fernando Lamas**, appear above as co-stars in *The Diamond Queen* (1953).

That marriage didn't last, but Lamas' final union with swimming star **Esther Williams** (depicted below) did.

According to Lamas, "One rumor had it that I made Esther give up her career when we got married. But she was already 'washed up' when we got married."

503

scheme to make Desi jealous. Expect the usual antics and lovers' quarrels before the episode concludes with a happy ending. Of course, Lamas and Ricky each end up with a black eye.

Lucille recalled, "It was a good thing we used a double in my ski scenes, including one where I ride piggyback down the slopes on Fernando's back. My double wound up with a broken left leg."

The telecast attracted a wide audience and got good reviews. *Variety* called it, "Good fun for the whole brood. Fernando Lamas is sensational. Miss Ball tosses off a series of comic scenes like a chef's salad."

Desi bonded with his former rival, and rumors spread that these two Latin lovers sometimes liked to take the same girl to bed at the same time. But this gossip was never really proven, except by one "ski bunny" who told a reporter, "It's all true."

In fact, Desi enjoyed working with Lamas so much that he proposed they co-star in a pilot where each of them "as real Valentino types with a string of beauties (Desi's words) would take turns starring as playboys with roving eyes."

The pilot, however, couldn't find a sponsor and never got off the drawing board.

Desi was dazzled by the beauty of Dahl and ordered his writers to create a pilot for her. It was to be a comedy series in which she would co-star with another bombshell, Zsa Zsa Gabor. Although fans of those charming beauties would certainly have found it fascinating, that pilot deal also fell through.

***

Although Desi had pulled off a major deal with Westinghouse, Martin Leeds, Desilu's Vice President, grew increasingly alarmed by Desi's heavy drinking. He had promised to wean himself off the bottle, but he had repeatedly failed.

"He had a great capacity for alcohol," said Leeds. "In time, however, drinking would severely damage his health."

Leeds was privy to Desi's private life, later revealing what was really going on with Desi after dark: Desi, according to Leeds, was a frequent patron of the notorious Hollywood Burlesque Theater in San Diego. After one of the (usually late-night) shows, Desi would select as many as five strippers to escort back to his hotel suite. Sometimes, when his own sexual powers ebbed, he amused himself by watching the girls have sex with each other. Behind his back, he was known as 'the Spic Rooster.'"

He drunkenly confessed to Leeds that Lucille had lost all sexual allure for him. "She's well on the road to fifty and looking her age. I like 'em young. Sinatra gave me some advice: He told me to keep up appearances, and that I should fuck Lucy every two weeks or so. When I told him she was a turn-off for me, he suggested that I put a paper bag over her head. That way, I could imagine she's Marilyn Monroe."

Lucille, too, expressed great concern over Desi's drinking. Police had escorted him home on three separate occasions after arresting him for drunk driving. According to her, "Instead of putting him in jail, the cops dumped him on me to sober him up." She kept a stack of money hidden in her kitchen, and always presented the Beverly Hills cops with a hundred-dollar bill for each of them.

She confided to her close friend, Marcella Rabwin, "Desi used to be the most wonderful lover in the world. I've had several leading movie stars, so I can make a judgment. But today, his boudoir skills are a distant memory to me. I'm told that he's plugging every little *puta* in every whorehouse in Hollywood."

Marcella liked Lucille, but dreaded the times her mother DeDe walked through the door. "She was a real bitch, very dogmatic, a little dictator trying to command Lucille and her kids. And DeDe certainly didn't have any control over Desi. She was also a bigot, referring to him as 'That Spic.' She also had nothing good to say about 'Jew Hollywood.' And when it came to black men, she felt the studios should hire them only as janitors, garbage collectors, and gardeners. Black women, in her opinion, should be employed only as maids or cooks, and never get cast in a picture."

Simultaneously running a major studio and acting on television left Desi little time for his young daughter and son. It was rumored that his children watched every episode of their parents on TV but found that Lucy and Ricky Ricardo had nothing in common with their actual parents, Lucille Ball and Desi Arnaz.

***

Plaza de Toros de TIJUANA

EL LUNES 6 de OCTOBRE de 1958
COLUMBIA BROADCASTING SYSTEM-TELEVISION
SENSACIONAL BULL FIGHT DEBUT
DE LA MATADORA AMERICANA LUCILLE BALL
Westinghouse presenta
LUCILLE BALL DESI ARNAZ MAURICE CHEVALIER
EN "Lucy Goes To Mexico"
EN LAS CORRIDAS EXTRAORDINARIAS DE PICADORES Y BANDERILLEROS
VIVIAN VANCE • WILLIAM FRAWLEY • RICHARD KEITH
Una Producion DESILU

There was a lot of subtle humor in the publicity associated with the technically complicated (some said "jinxed") episode called **Lucy Goes to Mexico**.

A good example is this poster advertising it for American and "south of the border" TV audiences.

Maurice Chevalier (left) and **Lucy** tip their hats to the audience. The third man in the line-up is the poorly lit **Desi** himself.

Although Maurice Chevalier isn't very well known today, he epitomized Gallic charm during the Cold War. To audiences of the 1950s, this publicity photo of an act inspired by the great days of cabaret sent thrills through Francophiles across the U.S.

As a debut for the eighth season (1958-59) of what had evolved from *I Love Lucy, Lucy Goes to Mexico* was telecast on October 6, 1958. Her co-star was the legendary French entertainer, Maurice Chevalier. Desi had long admired him and liked to refer to himself as "The Cuban Maurice Chevalier."

According to the plot, Lucy and Ethel Mertz cross the border for a visit to Tijuana. A series of misadventures, as to be expected, immediately unfold.

The highlight of the show is set in an arena, where Lucy, outfitted as a matador, is confronted with a 3,500-pound bull with foot-long horns. *[Valiantly, the writers attempted to explain how Lucy ended up as a matador.]*

She waves a handkerchief at the bull. She named its cologne *Eau de Hamburger.* For the long shots, a live but "sedated-to-the-point-of-being-comatos" bull was used.

For the closeups, a fake bull's head, mounted on a dolly and pushed by two members of the crew, raced on a track toward Lucy. Just as it came dangerously close to her, the rig jumped off its track and the entire apparatus knocked Lucy to the ground as one of the long horns of the bull's head slashed into her right arm.

In agony, she was rushed in an ambulance, with its dome lights flashing, to a hospital. There the flow of blood was stanched, she was sedated, and her wound was sutured.

After her release, she told a reporter, "All my life, I've had injuries with my arms and legs. They can snap like matchsticks."

When the episode was wrapped, Desi tossed a lavish party for Chevalier. They even sang together to amuse cast and crew. Chevalier told Lucille, "I've always wanted to sing with Desi, someone who has a worse accent than I do."

***

In association with Westinghouse's *Desilu Playhouse,* an hour-long special entitled *K.O. Kitty* was telecast on November 17, 1958.

From the beginning, its executive producer, Bert Granet, didn't like the script that Madelyn Pugh and Bob Carroll, Jr. had written before their exit from Desilu. Granet told his director, Jerry Thorpe, "Let's face it: *K.O. Kitty* is not a great script, and Lucille deserves better. It's stock and it's pat. I just don't like the idea of it.

She was pleased with her co-stars, hand-

Dance teacher Kitty Williams (**Lucy**) is delighted when she learns that she has inherited a boxer from her late Uncle Charley.

But the boxer turns out not to be a canine, but a prize fighter named Harold Tibbetts, a muscle-bound country boy, played by **Aldo Ray.**

some William Lundigan *[who had been one of Errol Flynn's boyfriends]* and sexy Aldo Ray, a former U.S. frogman turned actor.

[Lucille had thrilled to Ray as the Marine who has the hots for Rita Hayworth in Miss Sadie Thompson *(1953), the saga of a prostitute in the South Seas.]*

As "K.O. Kitty," Lucy plays an unmarried woman with an attorney boyfriend (Lundigan). Reviewers found that she looked a bit overweight in her evocation of Lucy Carmichael, the character she'd reprise again in the 1962-1968 follow-up to *I Love Lucy, The Lucy Show.*

Another critic said that with Lundigan as her co-star, viewers got a preview of what *I Love Lucy* might have been if Richard Denning, her radio broadcast co-star in *My Favorite Husband,* had evolved into her partner on TV. In other words, boring.

According to the plot, Kitty's recently deceased Uncle Charley has bequeathed her some gold and diamond jewelry and a washed-up boxer (Aldo Ray). She becomes his manager and trainer.

We won't give away what happens next, but in 1979, Barbra Streisand and Ryan O'Neal did it better in an adaptation of the episode's script, by then retitled *The Main Event.*

***

To finish off the eighth season, *Lucy's Summer Vacation*, was aired on June 8, 1959, starring Ida Lupino and Howard Duff. They were married in both the plot of the episode and in real life.

Bob Weiskopf and Bob Schiller had written its lackluster script. In it, Lucy and Ricky plan a second honeymoon at a mountain lodge in Vermont. The absent-minded owner has double booked their cabin, issuing a key to the Ricardos and another to Lupino and Duff. Making the best of a bureaucratic screw-up, the couples agree to share the lodge.

While the men go fishing, the bored housewives are left on their own. As lonely "widows," they attire themselves in elegant evening dress, hoping to arouse their husbands into more romantic behavior. When that fails, Lucy drills holes in the bottom of their rowboat. Her plan backfires when the wives are invited out onto the lake for romance under the moonlight. Even Lucy's desperate attempt to stuff bubble gum into the holes of the punctured rowboat cannot keep it afloat.

Lucy and Desi were hardly speaking to each other during filming, and Lupino and Duff were each at the ebbtide of their movie careers. *[Lupino, born in 1918 in London, had*

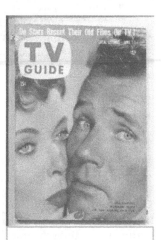

The family-friendly fame of **Ida Lupino** and **Howard Duff** (shown above on the cover of *TV Guide*) rivaled that of Lucy and Desi, so in some ways, a clash of wills might have been expected.

once been known as "the Jean Har-
low of England," a moniker risibly
outdated in the Age of Sputnik.]

Lucille had objected to casting Lupino, claiming that she had no comedic talent. "She knows how to play gun molls and bitches." But Desi and director Jerry Thorpe insisted on casting her and Duff anyway.

By the end of the season, Desi appeared tired and bloated from his excessive drinking, and Lucille, too, was eager to move on from the series. Weiskopf admitted, "It was not our finest half hour."

Tension is reflected in the grunting animosity that seemed to pervade not only the characters but the actors themselves (**Ida Lupino** and **Lucille Ball**) in this still shot from an episode of *Lucy's Summer Vacation.*

Thorpe later reported that Desi openly flirted with Lupino. "That was surprising because he was famous for digging younger stuff. Lucy became aware of Desi's intentions, and that caused a riff between her and Lupino. Behind her back, Lupino referred to her as 'Old Ball.'"

At one point, Desi went to Lupino's dressing room and proposed that they leave their spouses behind the following weekend, when they'd sail together on his yacht to Catalina. She thanked him for his "gracious offer," but rejected it anyway.

"Lucy was in one of her worst moods," Thorpe said. "She fought with me and even demanded that Desi hire another director."

"It was an awful show," Duff said, "and Ida and I had to do it for peanuts."

Its producer, Bert Granet, watched the show in his home, alongside six guests he was entertaining that night. "To cut costs, we did not use a live audience. Lucy is her best then. In this episode, she's her worst."

Lucy's Summer Vacation became one of the lowest-rated shows in the series.

***

In the summer of 1959, Lucille came up with a last-ditch effort to save her crumbling marriage to Desi. She got him to agree to travel to Europe with her and their young children, believing that it might bring all the Arnazes together again.

As a quartet, they flew to New York for a short vacation before sailing to England aboard the *S.S. Liberté,* a luxury liner with elegant suites that had attracted a gaggle of movie stars and, among others, the Woolworth heiress, Barbara Hutton. Few families ever left America with so much luggage. Collectively, they traveled with an amazing 42 suitcases and two steamer trunks.

On the voyage across sometimes rough seas, Lucille at times felt she was re-enacting scenes from an episode of *I Love Lucy*. In New York, she'd received a smallpox vaccination, and about a day later, at sea, she experienced a very bad reaction to it. On her first night aboard, her left arm became swollen. "It looked like that of a prizefighter, and I felt sick. I had to stay in our stateroom and couldn't join my family for dinner. After I recovered, I was walking on deck and stumbled over some object. I broke my big toe, the one on my left foot, and had to wear a partial cast, walking into the dining room with one crutch."

In the English port of Southampton, Lucille faced a barrage of photographers and reporters, many of them hostile, as if deliberately trying to provoke her for the sake of hot copy.

"Are you and Arnaz getting a divorce after this trip?" asked a reporter from *The Sun*. Lucille refused to answer.

"Just how old are you?" a reporter from *The Times* wanted to know. "Before you answer, let me say that movie stars are known to lie about their age."

"When I was born, my mother used to tell me to wipe the dinosaur shit off my feet before coming into the house," Lucille responded.

One female reporter grabbed little Lucie by the arm. "Is it true that your parents fight all the time? What's it like to be the richest little girl in Hollywood?"

Lucille signaled to her maid, Harriett, to rescue her daughter.

Their time in London was cut short because Desi claimed he had "urgent business" in Paris, not explaining what that meant.

"Our first night in Paris set the standard for the rest of our so-called 'family reunion' vacation," Lucille said. "Desi disappeared on our first night in Paris and on subsequent evenings, too, without telling us where he'd been."

Back in America, Lucille told Vivian Vance, "I'm sure he was servicing all the French *putas*—Desi's word for whores. I guess our kids figured it out...or not. They were so young."

While still in Paris, she accepted an invitation to visit the home of Maurice Chevalier, with whom she had co-starred in an episode of *I Love Lucy*. He welcomed her graciously and expressed his regret that Desi had been "detained." In several long conversations between Lucille and the French star, Chevalier became aware of her marital difficulties. "I've had a life of romantic troubles myself," he confessed. "One of the most painful things in life is ending a love affair. Even more painful is staying in a relationship when love has bid you *adieu*."

The family sailed back to the Port of New York aboard the famous liner, *S.S. Île de France*. It was the historic final voyage of the fabled ship, which, beginning in 1927, had hauled some of the most famous celebrities in the world to ports throughout the planet. "It was also the last voyage of my marriage," Lucille said. "Back on American soil, it was obvious that divorce was imminent."

***

During his first week back, Desi found himself with an overloaded work schedule. A lot of business decisions had been postponed while he was in Europe. "At home, we saw very little of him," Lucille said. "When he did have time off, he spent it at Del Mar racetrack or on a golf course. Our kids could only wonder what had happened to their daddy. I didn't even consider him my husband anymore."

In Los Angeles, news of Desi's heavy drinking leaked to the mainstream press for the first time.

A character actor, David McCall, filed a $100,000 lawsuit against him, alleging that Desi, while drunk, severely beat him up. The case was settled out of court. Desi agreed to pay him $25,000 plus $5,000 in medical bills and for loss of work income.

On September 19, 1959, he was a patron at a whorehouse. He had ordered five girls at once, but in his drunken condition, he had not managed to service all of them.

After settling his account, he left the bordello, wandering intoxicated down Vista Street in the La Brea neighborhood of Los Angeles. A chauffeur hired for the night was waiting for him around the corner, where he'd discreetly parked.

En route to the parked car, Desi encountered a policeman. He would probably not have been arrested, since he was not behind a wheel, but he hauled off and socked the cop in the face, bloodying his nose.

Desi was then thrown into the back of a squad car that had been summoned and taken to the main Los Angeles police station and put behind bars.

The night chief said, "Shame on you, Mr. Ricardo, for cheating on Lucy."

He was ordered to post bail, but when he reached for his wallet, he realized that it had been stolen. It had been stuffed with hundred-dollar bills.

He was locked up for an hour before an attorney from Desilu arrived to bail him out. The next day, when his case came up, Desi did not show up, thereby forfeiting bail. The fine came to twenty-one dollars, which his lawyer was only too willing to pay.

***

The next few months of 1959 completely doomed the Ball/Arnaz marriage. During the first week of October, Lucille returned home early from work. She was supposed to have reshot a scene, but because of a technical difficulty, filming was postponed until the following day.

She arrived at home before six. As she entered the ground floor of her house, she heard loud music from one of the second-floor bedrooms. She went to investigate. When she opened the door, she found Desi in bed with two prostitutes, one a redhead, the other a blonde.

She ordered the whores out of her house and screamed at Desi, who fled to the guest cottage and bolted the door.

As it turned out, the prostitutes had been sent over from a bordello that specialized in outfitting its girls as lookalikes for movie stars—for example, Marilyn Monroe, Jayne Mansfield, and/or Rita Hayworth as she'd appeared in *Gilda* (1946). By some accounts, to Lucille's horror, the redhead vaguely resembled a younger version of herself.

In his autobiography, *A Book,* Desi quoted Lucille's attack on him. "I'll tell you something, you bastard...you cheat...you drunken bum...you god damn Spic...you wetback!"

Ironically, it would be Desi who said, "Lucy, I want a divorce."

"After that night, Miss Ball and I never slept together," he claimed. "Actually, I never visited her bed in the master bedroom not once in the past year. We were husband and wife in name only. It had been almost twenty years of triumphs and failures, ecstasy and sex, jealousy and regrets, heartbreaks and laughter...and tears. The only thing we weren't able to hide was the tears."

***

As the final months of 1959 were coming to an end, so was the marriage of Desi Arnaz and Lucille Ball. Although it had been the greatest decade of their careers, both of them, although rich beyond their wildest dreams, were in poor health.

As Desi's drinking increased, Lucille to an increasing degree had to handle business decisions, as the staff turned to her during his prolonged absences. Often, without being asked, she took a strong hand in directing, ordering stars around.

Although Ann Sothern had been a longtime friend, Lucille made her uncomfortable. According to Sothern, "I was always fond of her, but she had become a real pain. She was such a perfectionist, barking orders to cast and crew. She even delivered commands to me, treating me like a newly arrived starlet. Frankly, I knew as much about how to shoot a comedy as she did."

***

Although during the course of his career Desi tried to launch many TV series, his greatest success, other than *I Love Lucy,* came with the debut of *The Untouchables,* a crime drama produced by Desilu Productions. It premiered in 1959 and flourished into 1962. Although William Paley at CBS had rejected it, Desi eventually sold it to ABC.

The series was based on the memoir of the same name by Eliot Ness, a Prohibition agent fighting crime in the Chicago of the 1920s.

When the crimefighters brought down the bootlegging empire of Al (Scarface) Capone. Ness' squad of brave men were named "The Untouchables" because of their courage and bravery, and because they could not be bribed.

As the TV series progressed, plots had to branch out to include the exploits of other legendary gangsters: Dutch Schultz, "Bugs" Moran, Ma Barker, "Mad Dog" Coll, Lucky Luciano, Legs Diamond, and, in one segment, even undercover agents of Nazi Germany.

Regrettably, Ness, nearly broke and saddled with a serious drinking problem, died suddenly in May of 1957, little knowing that within months he'd be one of the most famous television icons in America.

Ironically, before he became the executive producer of *The Untouchables*, Desi had announced to the press, "In TV shows released by Desilu, there will be no violence, no psychopaths, no dirt. There will never be any need to send the kids to bed when one of our shows is telecast."

In its time, *The Untouchables* became a landmark on TV in that no series had ever had such excessive violence and such frank depictions of drug abuse and prostitution. In reaction to that, the National Association for Better Radio and Television announced that "*The Untouchables* is not fit for the television screen."

In spite of the attacks and harsh streams of criticism, the series is today considered one of the top police TV series of all time. *The Daily News* of Lebanon, Pennsylvania wrote: "The hard-nosed approach, sharp dialogue, and a commendably crisp pace, make this series one of the few that remains fresh and vibrant. Only the monochrome presentation betrays its age. *The Untouchables* is one of the few Golden Age TV shows that deserves being called a classic."

Robert Stack, cast as Eliot Ness, had not been Desi's first choice. He had offered the role to Van Heflin, who rejected it. Then he called in Van Johnson, whom he had known since the days they had co-starred together in the 1939 Broadway version of *Too Many Girls* during Johnson's debut as a chorus boy.

Formerly labeled alongside June Allyson as one of "America's Sweethearts," Johnson's career was sliding. He told Desi that he'd be delighted to play Ness and accepted $10,000 per episode.

However, two days later, Johnson's wife, Evie, phoned Desi in Palm Springs, telling

Upper photo : a promotional banner for Desilu's **The Untouchables** TV series Its "chasing organized crime" theme aroused the ire of Italian Americans for depicting them as criminals. After wiping out Al Capone and Frank Nitti, the series continued telling the stories of other Chicago crooks.

The bottom photos, each a magazine cover, depict matinee handsome **Robert Stack** in the role of crime-busting Eliot Ness.

Until *The Untouchables*, he'd been a second-string romantic lead, swinging on the Hollywood vine since he gave Deanna Durbin her first screen kiss back in 1939.

him that her husband would not appear as Ness unless he received $20,000 per episode.

"OK, girlie," Desi said. "It's no Van. Tell him that for me."

That very afternoon, he hired Stack.

Stack was originally known for having given Deanna Durbin her first screen kiss. Handsome and possessing "a load of charm," he did more than kiss, and sustained high-profile romances with Judy Garland, Diana Barrymore, Yvonne De Carlo, Betty Grable, Lana Turner, and heiress Irene Wrightsman, plus many other (female) stars and starlets, including Lee Radziwill, sister of Jacqueline Kennedy.

In the summer of 1940, when the young, single, and charismatic John F. Kennedy showed up in Hollywood, he and Stack became close friends and lived together, bedding every night a different woman—sometimes two or three at a time. Stack referred to JFK as "My libidinous buddy."

Stack had been born into Hollywood royalty, if such a term existed. His father, an advertising executive, had crafted the famous slogan, "The Beer That Made Milwaukee Famous." His mother, a member of the wedding party at Rudolph Valentino's second marriage, was a prominent member of the upper tiers of Tinseltown society.

Stack, well-known for his "matinee idol looks," brought a commanding presence and a deep voice to TV screens. Before joining the cast of *The Untouchables*, he'd won a Best Supporting Actor Oscar for his role in *Written on the Wind* (1956), co-starring Rock Hudson, Lauren Bacall, and Dorothy Malone.

He told Desi, "I think I broke Rock's heart when I told him he couldn't have me. He got a preview of my assets, since he always managed to enter my dressing room when I was in the shower, waiting for me to emerge, sometimes wrapped in a towel. That happened on several occasions."

Over Lucille's objections, Desi hired columnist Walter Winchell to deliver the terse narration that opened the show. Winchell's distinctive New York accent became a stylistic hallmark of the series, along with the ominous theme music by Nelson Riddle.

[Lucille had detested Winchell ever since he outed her as having registered for the Communist Party in 1936, a revelation that had set fire to one of the major scandals of her life.]

Stack later claimed that during the first season of *The Untouchables*, Desi had been targeted for assassination by the Mafia for the show's depiction of Italian Americans and their association with organized crime. Many Italian organizations objected strongly to the negative stereotypes of themselves as mobsters and gangsters.

The Federation of Italian American Democratic Organizations protested at ABC's headquarters in Manhattan, urging Italian viewers to boycott Ligett & Meyers Tobacco Company. Its best-selling cigarettes, Chesterfield, were Lucille's favorites.

Sam Giancana, the Chicago mob boss, even tried, briefly, to organize the assassination of Desi through one of his henchmen, Aladena Fratianno (aka "Jimmy the Weasel"), the acting boss of the Los Angeles crime family. Desi never had a bodyguard, and always drove himself to and from work.

That made him an easy target for an assassination.

[Giancana and John F. Kennedy, during JFK's presidency, shared the same girlfriend, Judith Campbell Exner, who was suspected of carrying secret messages between them, perhaps information pertinent to the disastrous American invasion of the Bay of Pigs.]

Giancana was a friend of Frank Sinatra, and it was Sinatra who talked the mob boss out of his plan to kill Desi. He convinced him that Desi had millions of fans, who would hate Italian Americans all the more if he went through with the plan.

Although he may have saved Desi's life, Sinatra's temper flared one drunken night at the Copacabana in New York when he unexpectedly encountered Desi. Sinatra punched him in the face, bloodying his nose. Sinatra had showed up that night with a sultry blonde, Marilyn Maxwell. Later, Desi got his revenge on Sinatra by having an affair with Maxwell himself.

Eventually, Desi recognized the genuine anger behind the anti-defamation slogans and publicly committed Desilu to eliminate anti-Italian slurs from Desilu scripts. As such, he issued a three-point manifesto with the following ironclad points:

There will be no more fictional hoodlums with Italian names in future productions.

There will be more stress on the law-enforcement role of "Rico Rossi," Ness's right-hand man on the show.

There will be an emphasis on the "formidable influence" of Italian-American officials in reducing crime and an emphasis on the "great contributions" made to American culture by Americans of Italian descent.

Chicago reporter Ralph Bohning wrote, "*The Untouchables* also incurred the displeasure of the director of the F.B.I., J. Edgar Hoover, when the fictionalized scripts depicted Ness and his Treasury agents involved in operations that were actually the province of the F.B.I. The second episode of the series, for example, depicted Ness and his crew involved in the capture of the Ma Barker gang, an incident in which the real-life Ness played no part. The producers agreed to insert a spoken disclaimer on future broadcasts of the episode stating that the F.B.I. *[not the Treasury Department]* had primary responsibility for the Barker case."

Over the years, many well-known actors appeared on *The Untouchables*, a huge list that featured such stars as Luther Adler, Ed Asner, William Ben-

MAFIA BOSS
SAM GIANCANA
THE RISE AND FALL OF A CHICAGO MOBSTER

SUSAN
McNICOLL

Mob boss **Sam Giancana** always made hot copy.

Author **Tony Dark** wrote: "From movie stars like Marilyn Monroe to the President of the United States, Sam Giancana enjoyed being feared as Chicago's most infamous mob boss."

"His control over organized crime brought him power, riches, and insanity."

"The FBI spent millions over twenty years to bring the powerful man to justice. Giancana went from living a life with the stars—close friendships with Frank Sinatra and Dean Martin, and trying to influence JFK in the White House—to hiding out in a hilltop mansion in Mexico."

dix, Joan Blondell, James Caan, Mike Connors, James Coburn, Robert Du-vall, Peter Falk, Anne Francis, Telly Savalas, and Martin Landau. Even Bar-bara Stanwyck starred as the crusty, hard-bitten Lt. Agatha Stewart, head of the Missing Persons Bureau.

Neville Brand played Al Capone, appearing only in the two-hour pilot and a two-part episode.

Eventually, ratings for *The Untouchables* ranked among the Top Five TV series of all time, and Stack eventually earned $750,000 for his appear-ances.

***

During the run of *The Untouchables,* Desi began a months-long affair with a buxom blonde, Barbara Nichols, billed at the time as "a serious rival of Marilyn Monroe," which was false advertising. Nonetheless, she was a knockout, with enough charm to seduce any man she wanted.

Born in New York in 1928, she became a striptease artist when she was a late teenager. That led to a brief career in the late 1950s as a "cheesecake model," when she was cited by a gossip columnist as "the kind of blonde every *Playboy* reader wants after midnight."

She had appeared in 1952 in the Broadway revival of *Pal Joey,* and later had a small support-ing role in its 1957 film adaptation, during which she had a brief fling with its star, Frank Sinatra. *[In it, she faced on-screen competition from Rita Hay-worth and Kim Novak.]*

That same year, she had a role in *Sweet Smell of Success* where she seduced both of her co-stars, Tony Curtis and Burt Lancaster, in their dressing rooms.

In a number of films, she lent support to such stars as Clark Gable, Susan Hayward, Doris Day, and (in a contest some observers facetiously de-fined as "a battle of the bosoms") Sophia Loren.

It was *I Love Lucy* writer Bob Schiller, who in-troduced Nichols to Desi when he escorted her to a Directors' Guild dinner honoring the *I Love Lucy* series. *[Lucille had hoped her writer would come stag because she wanted to do some match-making that night, possibly hooking him up with Vivian Vance.]*

At the awards dinner, after meeting and ac-tively engaging Desi in conversation, Nichols dumped Schiller, unleashing her seductive charms not only on Desi, but at Quinn Martin, the husband of Madelyn Pugh, long the chief co-

Barbara Nichols in *Sweet Smell of Success* (1957) and (lower photo) with **Jack Warden** in *That Kind of Woman* (1959).

As one fan noted, "She wasn't just an actress, she was a Dame!"

writer of *I Love Lucy*.

Martin had started out at Desilu as a soundcutter, but soon graduated to production assistant and eventually, the producer of three Desilu Playhouse shows. Nichols was keenly aware that either of the men could help advance her career.

For Nichols, Desi, and Martin, the night ended in a bungalow at the Beverly Hills Hotel. Both men "took turns" servicing her. The "casting couch" worked, and a role was carved out for her in *The Untouchables* — in this case as a showgirl named "Brandy La France."

Desi became so smitten with Nichols that he instructed his writers to create a pilot for a TV series entitled *All About Barbara*. "Of course," Desi said, winking at his writers, "we can't tell ALL about her." [*It was Bob Carroll, Jr. and Madelyn Pugh who were assigned the task of writing it. That proved especially difficult for Pugh, who was aware that her husband, Quinn Martin, was having an affair with the woman being configured as its female lead.*]

Desi soon introduced Nichols to Fernando Lamas, whom he wanted to cast as her adventurous lover in the projected *All About Barbara*. Soon Desi, Nichols, and Lamas were involved in a three-way, too.

Lucille soon found out about Desi's involvement with Nichols. "Any time a director needed a girl to play an overripe blonde floozie, he could call on that Nichols dame. Call it typecasting!"

Ironically, the pilot for the projected series was never filmed, since no sponsor showed the slightest interest.

Years later, Nichols told a reporter, "Arnaz failed to launch that pilot with Lamas and me. I wasn't alone. He couldn't get several pilots off the ground, even with such actors as Ruth Hussey, Bobby Rydell, Darryl Hickman, Don DeFore, Eva Gabor... even one with Ginger Rogers."

Two former lovers from the 1930s, **Clark Gable** and **Loretta Young**, had a reunion when they co-starred in *Key to the City* (1950). They'd been cast as city mayors who, despite their contrasting personalities and views, find themselves attracted to one other. ("They click like keys in a lock.")

In a minor role within it, **Marilyn Maxwell** (lower photo) played a burlesque bubble dancer who arouses the jealous ire of Young.

***

516

During the final months of his marriage, Desi found time to launch a brief affair with Marilyn Maxwell, a movie star who became famous in the 1940s and 50s. She was coming to an end of her six-year marriage to writer/producer Jerry Davis.

From the cornfields of Iowa, she had arrived in Hollywood with dreams of stardom. She didn't exactly reach that goal, although during the course of her career, she was cast mostly as "window dressing" in dramas and musical comedies that called for a sultry blonde.

She took acting lessons at the Pasadena Playhouse and was later signed by MGM. One of her most notable roles was as "the other woman" opposite Kirk Douglas in his classic, hard-hitting boxing movie, *Champion* (1949). *[*Champion *won an Academy Award for Best Film Editing and five Oscar nominations, including a Best Actor nomination for Douglas. For more on this refer to Blood Moon's 2019 biography,* Kirk Douglas, More Is Never Enough.*]*

In gossipy Hollywood, Maxwell was well known for her seductions, most notably with Bob Hope. Her adulterous fling (1950-1954) with him became so widely known that she was sometimes referred to as "The 2nd Mrs. Bob Hope." Her decade-long affair with Frank Sinatra began when she was a girl singer in the late 1930s and early '40s.

Desi became involved with Maxwell when he read the script for a TV pilot for which he thought she'd be ideal as a sexy private detective. After their first night together, during the final throes of his marriage to Lucille, they began a torrid affair.

"It was one hot romance," said Danny Thomas, who at the time was discussing a possible merger of his organization with Desilu. "Whether it was true or not, Desi told me that Maxwell claimed he was better in bed than Sinatra. On the other hand, maybe she bragged to Sinatra that he was a better seducer than Desi. Who knows what a woman will say to a man in bed?"

Maxwell also had an intense friendship with Rock Hudson, although sex didn't have

Maxwell's longest-running affair was with **Bob Hope** (above). Frank Sinatra came in second.

Her fling with Desi Arnaz was brief and fleeting, but as hot as Havana in August.

At this point, **Fred Ball** (shown in this photo with his older sister, **Lucille**) was hired as Desi's road manager.

Lucille mistakenly thought the presence of her brother would make Desi cut down on his womanizing.

But whether Fred was with him or not, Desi continued to chase wine, women, and song, even gambling away his band's entire payroll during a two-week engagement in Las Vegas.

517

such a large part to play in that relationship. On March 20, 1972, Maxwell's fifteen-year-old son, Matthew, came home from school and found his mother dead in the living room. She was only fifty years old when she died of a heart attack.

At her funeral, Bob Hope, Bing Crosby, Sinatra, and Jack Benny were honorary pallbearers. After the funeral, teenaged Matthew moved in with Hudson.

***

Her energy drained, her private life in shambles, Lucille decided that the time had come for her to close down her 200-seat Desilu Playhouse, a workshop she'd established two years before as a training field for young actors and actresses.

She decided to kill it off with a production called *The Desilu Revue.* It would showcase an all-star lineup: Vivian Vance, William Frawley, gossip columnist Hedda Hopper, Ann Sothern, Hugh O'Brian, Rory Calhoun, William Demarest, George Murphy, and Spring Byington.

She labeled the revue as "Our swan song. I gave my time and money to those kids. All of them really needed a mother, but I had spread myself too thin. I didn't even have enough time for my own two kids. It was sad, but I had to tell all the students goodbye as each of them set out to try to break into show business. I could only imagine the heartbreak that awaited many of them."

Actually, she didn't tell all of the aspirant actors goodbye. During one of the workshops, she had bonded with Mildred Frances Cook, an ingénue who had migrated to Hollywood from Abilene, Texas. She became Lucille's *protégée,* and even agreed to a name change, henceforth designating herself as Carole Cook. *[Its originator, Lucille herself, borrowed it from her long-departed friend, Carole Lombard, revealing to the younger woman, "You and Carole (Lombard) have the same healthy disrespect for everything in general."]*

Cook, in time, became a regular on both *The Lucy Show* and *Here's Lucy.*

***

Upset with the impending breakup of her marriage to Desi, Lucille sometimes directed her anger toward Vivian Vance, even though they had developed a close friendship. Vance's own marriage to actor Phil Ober, her third husband, was also heading for the divorce courts.

Vance, too, was often in a foul mood. "I'm god damn tired of playing Ethel Mertz," she complained to Lucille. "It's very hard to play comedy with you and Desi anymore. The hostility between the two of you is so thick I can cut it with a knife."

Before Lucille's own divorce, Vance sued Ober, whom she had married in 1941, just prior to America's entrance into World War II.

It was an abusive relationship, and tensions were fueled by Vance's successful career and Ober's failed ambitions as an actor. If he is remembered at all today, it's for Ober's supporting role as Deborah Kerr's cold-hearted husband in *From Here to Eternity* (1953). William Frawley weighed in with his opinion of Ober: "Fat Ass had a nice husband. Okay, so she sometimes showed up on the set with a black eye for makeup to conceal. I'm sure the cow deserved it. I found the guy personable and well-spoken. But he sure didn't set the screen aglow. Ober's type is a dime a dozen in Hollywood."

[During the happier days of their marriage, Ober and Vance bought a ranch in an isolated region of New Mexico, where most of their neighbors were Mexicans and Laguna Indians.]

Vance and Ober separated in February of 1958 but didn't actually divorce until a year later. Lucille encouraged Vance to divorce him, because, like Desi, Ober had a love of the bottle.

On April 24, 1959, it was Ober who filed for the divorce before Judge Burnett Wolfson. Commenting on Vance's earning power, as opposed to that of Ober, the judge said, "If there ever was a case of killing the goose who laid the golden egg, this is it!"

As part of the settlement, Vance agreed to turn over to Ober fifty percent of their community property, which was valued at $250,000.

Each of them would marry again. Later in life, he married Jane Westmore, an NBC press agent. By 1963, he'd settled into the emerging resort of Puerto Vallarta, Mexico, where he became a town spokesperson and its unofficial mayor.

He was on hand to welcome Elizabeth Taylor and Richard Burton when they went there to shoot the film adaptation of Tennessee Williams' *The Night of the Iguana* (1964) starring Ava Gardner. In fact, it was Ober who urged the Burtons to buy a home in Puerto Vallarta, which they did. During its filming, cast and crew were saddened when news arrived from Dallas in November of 1963, reporting on the assassination of John F. Kennedy.

***

Desi constantly complained that he was being cheated out of a lot of money associated with everything to do with his series' final episodes.

"He blamed everyone," Martin Leeds, Desi's Veep, said. "He called Hollywood the most corrupt place on earth."

"Every god damn bastard is out to swindle me," Desi charged. "The producers, the agents, the sponsors."

His complaint might have been legitimate. Whereas Desilu grossed twenty million at the end of 1958, the "take home pay" for Lucille and Desi that year was "paltry in light of the sums involved" $250,000.

The dismal profit generated from a gross of $20 million led to a decision. With their lawyers as representatives and intermediaries, Lucille and Desi decided to take Desilu public on the American Stock Exchange, keeping fifty percent of the one million shares for themselves. Their combined holdings were estimated at $15 million, and an agreement was negotiated whereby they would split that in half.

***

The 1959-60 season at Desilu found the studio in decline. It was becoming harder and harder for it to compete with larger studios such as Warner Brothers, MCA's Revue, or Columbia's Screen Gems. Desilu's bright spot, at least in terms of income generated, remained *The Untouchables.*

It came as a happy surprise at Desilu when both CBS and General Foods renewed *The Ann Sothern Show.* However, in a touch of mutually self-destructive irony, Sothern's Show was telecast in the same time slot as *The Untouchables.* Viewers preferred the violence of the crimefest more than the Sothern's comedy, and the Nielsen ratings reflected their preference. The result was CBS's cancellation of Sothern.

Meanwhile, studio rentals of its sound stages and recording facilities by *The Andy Griffith Show, Miami Undercover, The Jack Benny Show,* and *My Three Sons* helped to pay Desilu's bills.

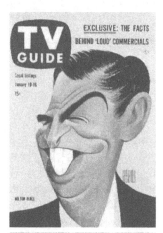

Ironically, at this point in its corporate life, Desilu's real estate had become more valuable than its television productions. Desi wanted to start selling off their acreage, but Lucille resisted, believing that its value would increase in the medium-term future, "soaring beyond belief."

During the final months of 1959, Lucille and Desi seemed to agree on nothing. She didn't mind if cast and crew knew her opinions and points of view about her husband. She was heard referring to him as "that fucking bastard."

Almost daily, she threatened him with divorce. In front of Vance, she shouted at him one afternoon, "I've got the goods on you. I'll take you to court and I'll put your ass in a sling. You'll end up begging on Hollywood Boulevard for a quarter. I'm sure you saw Ray Milland as an alcoholic in *The Lost Weekend.* If not, screen it if you want to see your future!"

She told Vance, "My kids are traumatized by our breakup. They miss their daddy. I know he still loves them very much. He just doesn't spend any time with them, as he prefers in off hours to 'audition' starlets. I hope my babies don't hear all the gossip, but I feel they know about it."

Desi was still president of Desilu, and he

Milton Berle never showed as much teeth as he did in this satirical portrait on the front cover of *TV Guide.*

Because he operated within the orbit of NBC at the time, a joint network deal had to be hammered out for him to appear on the CBS series, *I Love Lucy.*

To reciprocate, Lucille and Desi—as Lucy and Ricky Ricardo—agreed to appear on a Berle telecast. This was the first time they ever pulled that off on someone else's show and with another network.

continued to show up every day at the studio. He was bombarded with scripts for TV pilots, none of which seemed to have much potential.

From minor studios, he was still offered co-starring vehicles for Lucille and himself, but he rejected most of them.

Tailored just for them was Edmond Cheveis' *The General and the Redhead*. After a week of studying and thinking about it, he finally rejected it. Dore Schary at MGM, no great fan of Desi and Lucille, actually considered developing a co-starring vehicle for them, too, but the deal fell through.

Desi ordered that the opening frames of *I Love Lucy* episodes should have cartoon figures superimposed on a "heart-on-satin" illustration. This design, widely distributed throughout the U.S. between 1959 and 1967, was originally created for CBS's daytime network re-broadcasts. That frilly, well-upholstered image became the most famous show opener in TV history.

The *I Love Lucy* theme song was written by two-time Oscar nominee Eliot Daniel.

***

Its sixth season (1956-1957) marked the end of the series billed as *I Love Lucy*. For the seventh season (1957-1958), the title of the show was changed to *The Lucille Ball-Desi Arnaz Show*.

After that, the *I Love Lucy* series faded into television history. Yet, as syndicated re-runs, they'd continue to be shown somewhere around the world even today.

Writers Bob Schiller and Bob Weiskopf wrote the final episodes, with Bert Granet as producer and Desi as the director.

Telecast on September 25, 1959 *Milton Berle Hides Out at the Ricardos* reunited Lucille with the comedian with whom she had had a brief affair in the 1930s.

In the Berle episode, Lucy offers him her secluded home in Connecticut to escape the pressure of his business affairs so that he can finish writing a book for his publisher. She doesn't tell Ricky, but nearsighted Fred gossips

Milton Berle, in disguise, hangs out with **Lucy.**

As the plot unfolds, Ricky thinks his wife is having a romantic fling, and trouble ensues.

According to Berle (aka "Mr. TV"), "I was really impressed with Desi as a director. That Cuban boy really knew his stuff."

This picture of **Milton Berle** in drag was his all-time favorite.

"If I'd been a woman, I would have every leading man lining up to get a night with me. What a femme fatale! Absolutely gorgeous!"

521

to Ricky about some mysterious stranger spending his days with his wife.

Ricky barges into his home to confront Lucy's supposed lover, only to have Berle escape in drag.

Hoping to patch things up with both of them, Ricky pastes on a mustache and impersonates Berle's chauffeur. The episode ends happily as the trio unites for a joint appearance onstage at the local P.T.A.'s charity benefit.

Granet claimed that Lucille's motivation for firing Jerry Thorpe, her former director, was because he had favored the guest stars over her.

For another Westinghouse Desilu Playhouse Show, actor Bob Cummings was hired to co-star in *The Ricardos Go to Japan*. Little Ricky (Richard Keith) appeared in it, as well as Fred and Ethel Mertz.

Vivian Vance thought the script "stunk," and Frawley said, "Who gives a fuck? It's a paycheck, isn't it? Pays my liquor and hotel bill."

The Ricardos and the Mertzes land in Tokyo. Ricky is there on a band junket. Once they're at their hotel, Lucy learns that Cummings occupies the adjoining hotel suite.

She wants to get rid of her fake pearls and buy some real ones in Japan, where she learns that they're much cheaper. Cummings agrees to help her get that precious necklace she covets.

The Ricardos Go to Japan, broadcast in November of 1959, should have been funnier than it ended up.

It was hampered by the lack of a live audience and a sense of disbelief that Lucy and Ethel would ever pass as demure (and young) geishas. The unfunny script was based on pointless confusion about a string of souvenir pearls. At this point, Lucy Ricardo's talent for driving Ricky crazy seemed more annoying than adorable.

Making matters worse, the Arnaz family's resentments spilled over onto the sound stage, and **Lucy**, in some instances—took out her frustration on Ethel (i.e., **Vivian Vance**), who by now was bored and frustratrated by the limitations of her role.

As Burt Granet, that season's producer, phrased it, "Lucy and Desi were barely speaking to one another. The entire enterprise had begun to disentigrate. Morale hardly existed."

One mix-up follows another, as it does in every Lucy script. After some plot twists, Lucy and Ethel end up in a male-only Geisha house.

The crazy women disguise themselves as geishas and go out only to discover—guess who?—their errant husbands. After some blood-letting, all is forgiven when Fred and Ricky agree to buy their wives real pearl necklaces.

The show was not performed before a live audience, which was Lucille's preference. Critics found it "slow paced" and "clumsy."

With her hair in a stylish French twist, Vance no longer evoked Ethel Mertz.

Dedicated fans of *I Love Lucy* wrote in that in an earlier episode (No. 38), Ricky had already presented Lucy with a string of real pearls, which made the premise of *The Ricardos Go To Japan* inaccurate.

The telecast marked the last appearance of aging actress Kathryn Card, who starred in it as Lucy's mother, Mrs. McGillicuddy.

***

There was one more episode, *Lucy Meets the Mustache*, remaining to close out the 1959-1960 (i.e. ninth) season, now designated as the *Lucille Ball-Desi Arnaz Show*. Little Ricky (Richard Keith) had a role, and guest stars included comedian Ernie Kovacs and his singer wife, Edie Adams.

As an entertainer, Ricky is finding it hard to get a gig, and Lucy sets out to get him cast on Kovacs' TV show, even disguising herself as the performer's chauffeur.

After nine years, the Lucy/Desi series had played itself out and no longer appeared fresh to TV audiences. At the end of that season, *The Westinghouse/Desilu Playhouse* was canceled, ending Desi's role as its host and producer.

Variety envisioned this as the twilight of Lucille and Desi's remarkable television careers.

Its director, Bert Granet, later said, "My job was very difficult, since Lucille and Desi were not speaking to each other except on camera."

At one point during a scene, Desi, who directed it, turned to Edie and said, "Would you tell Miss Ball to move her sagging ass cheeks three feet to the right?"

Edie found Desi "brilliant as a director, but Ball was a horror, faulting everything about me, including my hairdo, subject to attack. She was taking out her marriage failure on the cast. All of us were in for it. Ball and Vivian seemed on autopilot. All of us decided we had to put up with Ball and just get through this god damn episode without tearing out every dyed-red hair of our super-charged boss. I got to sing a song that sorta summed it up. The song was called 'That's All.' When not barking orders, Ball would become quite tender. She either held back tears or burst into crying."

Richard Keith, as Little Ricky, got the bad news first: "Kid, you're now out of a job," Lucille told him. Edie watched as he burst into tears.

In the final episode **(Lucy Meets the Mustache)** of what by now had sprawled (with occasional name changes) across nine seasons, another talented husband-and-wife team, **Edie Adams** and **Ernie Kovacs**, co-starred with Lucille and Desi.

Their marriage endured until Kovacs' death in 1962, after which Adams worked valiantly to settle his enormous debt to the IRS and to fend off vindictive litigation from her former mother-in-law.

Adams said, "Desi, as director, was charming, even brilliant. Lucille, in contrast, went around raising holy hell. William Frawley and Vivian Vance were on autopilot."

"After the shoot, Ernie and I fled from the studio. We should be given an Oscar for surviving the last of the Ricardos. Good riddance, I say."

"It came as such a shock to me," Keith later said. "I thought we'd go on for a few more years, at least until I was old enough to enter junior high."

In the final scene, Lucy and Ricky Ricardo, according to the script, had to kiss. Vance, standing as a witness behind the camera, called it "their final clinch. He kissed her but it lacked his usual passion. It was like a kiss he might plant on the face of a reincarnated Himmler."

"At last it was over—their final scene," Vance said. "The last I saw of Lucy for some time was waving goodbye to her as she rushed in tears to her dressing room."

***

The very next day, March 3, 1960, Lucille, in a chauffeur-driven limousine, arrived at the Santa Monica Supreme Court.

Before getting into the vehicle, at her home, she was handed a telegram from Desi. She read it *en route* to the court: "I won't be there today to contest the divorce. So, see you around the block, kid. It's been a hell of a ride."

Arriving at the courthouse, her chauffeur went around the car and opened the door for her. She emerged from the back seat dressed almost like a widow in a black tweed suit, black hat, black veil, and black high heels.

A mob of reporters rushed to envelop her. She waved them aside with her black-gloved hand.

"The story is over, fellas," she called out.

Actually, she was wrong.

One story, indeed, was over.

BUT ANOTHER SAGA WAS ABOUT TO BEGIN.

"Sometimes, after the love, all one has is memories."

—**Lucille Ball**

DARWIN PORTER

As a precocious nine-year-old, **Darwin Porter** *began meeting entertainers through his mother, Hazel, a charismatic Southern girl whose husband had died in World War II. Migrating from the Depression-ravaged valleys of western North Carolina to Miami Beach during its most ebullient heyday, Hazel became a personal assistant to the vaudeville comedienne* **Sophie Tucker,** *the kind-hearted "Last of the Red Hot Mamas."*

Loosely supervised by his mother, Darwin was regularly dazzled by the likes of **Judy Garland, Dinah Shore, Frank Sinatra, Ronald Reagan** *(at the time near the end of his Hollywood gig), and* **Marilyn Monroe.** *Each of them made it a point, whenever they were in Miami (either on or off the record), to visit and pay their respects to "Miss Sophie."*

At the University of Miami, Darwin edited the school newspaper, raising its revenues, through advertising and public events, to unheard-of new levels. He met and interviewed **Eleanor Roosevelt** *and later invited her, as part of a sponsored event he crafted, to spend a day ("Eleanor Roosevelt Day") at the university, and to his delight, she accepted. Years later, in Manhattan, during her work as a human rights activist, he escorted her, at her request, to many public functions.*

After his graduation, Darwin, in a graceful transition from his work as editor of the University's newspaper and his sponsorship by **Wilson Hicks** *(Photo Editor and then Executive Editor of* Life *magazine) became a Bureau Chief of The Miami Herald (the youngest in that publication's history) assigned to its branch in Key West. At the time the island outpost was an avant-garde literary mecca and—thanks to the Cuban missile crisis—an flash point of the Cold War.*

Key West had been the site of Harry S Truman's "Winter White House" and Truman returned a few months before his death for a final visit. He invited young Darwin for "early morning walks" where he used the young emissary of The Miami Herald to "set the record straight."

Through Truman, Darwin was introduced and later joined the staff of **Senator George Smathers** *of Florida. His best friend was a young senator,* **John F. Kennedy.** *Through "Gorgeous George," as Smathers was known in the Senate, Darwin got to meet Jack and Jacqueline in Palm Beach. He later wrote two books about them—The Kennedys, All the Gossip Unfit to Print, and one of his all-time bestsellers, Jacqueline Kennedy Onassis—A Life Beyond Her Wildest Dreams.*

Buttressed by his status as The Miami Herald's Key West Bureau Chief, Darwin met, interviewed, and often befriended **Tennessee Williams. Ernest Hemingway, Tallulah Bankhead, Gore Vidal, Truman Capote, Carson McCullers,** *and a gaggle of other internationally famous writers and entertainers:* **Cary Grant, Rock Hudson, Marlon Brando, Montgomery Clift, Susan Hayward, Warren Beatty, Christopher Isherwood, Anne Bancroft, Angela Lansbury,** *and* **William Inge.**

Eventually transferred to Manhattan, Darwin worked for a decade in television advertising with the producer and arts-industry socialite **Stanley Mills Haggart.** *In addition to some speculative ventures associated with Marilyn Monroe, they also jointly produced TV commercials that included testimonials from* **Joan Crawford** *(then feverishly promoting Pepsi-Cola);* **Ronald Reagan** *(General Electric); and* **Debbie Reynolds** *(Singer sewing machines). Other personalities they promoted, each delivering televised sales pitches, included* **Louis Armstrong, Lena Horne, Rosalind Russell, William Holden,** *and* **Arlene Dahl,** *each of them hawking a commercial product.*

Beginning in the early 1960s, Darwin joined forces with the then-fledgling **Arthur Frommer** *organization, playing a key role in researching and writing more than 50 titles and defining the style and values that later emerged as the world's leading travel guidebooks,* ***The Frommer Guides.*** *Darwin's particular journalistic expertise on Europe, New England, California, and the Caribbean eventually propelled him into authorship of (depending on the era and whatever crises were brewing at the time), between 70 and 80% of their titles. Even during the research of his travel guides, he continued to interview show-biz celebrities, discussing their triumphs, feuds, and frustrations. At this point in their lives, many were retired and reclusive. Darwin either pursued them (sometimes though local tourist offices) or encountered them randomly as part of his extensive travels.* **Ava Gardner, Lana Turner, Hedy Lamarr, Ingrid Bergman, Ethel Merman, Andy Warhol, Elizabeth Taylor, Marlene Dietrich, Bette Davis,** **Judy Garland,** *and* **Paul Newman** *were particularly insightful.*

Porter's biographies—at this writing, they number sixty-two— have won thirty first prize or "runner-up to first prize" awards at literary festivals in cities or states which include New England, New York, Los Angeles, Hollywood, San Francisco, Florida, California, and Paris.

Darwin, also a magazine columnist, can be heard at regular intervals as a television commentator, reviewing the ironies of celebrities, pop culture, politics, and scandal.

A resident of New York City, where he spent years within the social orbit of the Queen of Off-Broadway (the eccentric and very temperamental philanthropist, **Lucille Lortel),** *Darwin is currently at work on a biography of the dysfunctionally fascinating father/daughter team of* **Henry Fonda** *and his rebellious daughter,* **Jane.**

DANFORTH PRINCE

A graduate of Hamilton College and a native of Easton and Bethlehem, Pennsylvania, he's president and founder (in 1983) of the Porter and Prince Corporation, the entity that produced the original texts and updates for dozens of key titles of **THE FROMMER GUIDES**—*travel "bibles" for millions of readers during the travel industry's go-go years in the 80s, 90s, and early millennium.*

He also founded, in 1996, the Georgia Literary Association, precursor to what morphed, in 2004, into **Blood Moon Productions**, *the corporate force behind dozens of political and Hollywood biographies.* *Its vaguely apocalyptic name was inspired by one of Darwin Porter's popular early novels,* **Blood Moon**, *a thriller about the false gods of power, wealth, and physical beauty. In 2011, Prince was named "Publisher of the Year" by a consortium of literary critics and marketers spearheaded by the J.M. Northern Media Group.*

Prince has electronically documented his stewardship of Blood Moon in at least 50 videotaped documentaries, book trailers, public speeches, and TV or radio interviews. Most of these are available on **YouTube.com** *and* **Facebook** *(keyword: "Danforth Prince"); on* **Twitter** *(#BloodyandLunar); or by clicking on* **BloodMoonProductions.com**.

Hearkening back to his days as a travel writer, Prince is also an innkeeper, maintaining and managing a historic bed & breakfast, **Magnolia House** **(www.MagnoliaHouseSaintGeorge.com)**. *Affiliated with AirBnb, and increasingly sought out by filmmakers as an evocative locale for moviemaking, it lies in St. George, at the northern tip of Staten Island, the "sometimes forgetten" Outer Borough of New York City. A landmarked building with a "formidable" historic and literary pedigree, it lies in a neighborhood closely linked to Henry James, Theodore Dreiser, the Vanderbilts, and key moments in America's colonial history.*

Set in a terraced garden with views over New York Harbor and nearby Manhattan, it's been visited by show-biz stars who have included **Tennessee Williams, Gloria Swanson, Jolie Gabor** *(mother of Zsa Zsa, Eva, and Magda),* *soap opera queen* **Ruth Warrick**, *the Viennese chanteuse* **Greta Keller,** *and many of the luminaries of Broadway. It lies within a twelve-minute walk from the ferries sailing at frequent intervals to Manhattan.*

Publicized as "a reasonably priced celebrity-centric bed & breakfast with links to the book trades," and the beneficiary of rave ("superhost") reviews (including "New York's most fascinating B&B") from hundreds of previous guests, **Magnolia House** *is loaded with furniture and memorabilia collected from around the world during his decades as a travel journalist for the Frommer Guides.* ***Since the onset of the Covid Crisis, social distancing and regular decontamination regimens have been rigorously enforced.*** *For photographs, testimonials from previous guests, and more information, click on*

www.AirBnB/H/Magnolia-House

Magnolia House is a proud, architecturally protected landmark within the St. George, Staten Island Historical District.

It's depicted here in a photo snapped by New York City's Department of Finance as part of its 1940 Tax Census.

Some visitors liken Magnolia House to a *grande dame* with a centuries-old knack for nourishing high-functioning eccentrics. Many have lived or been entertained here since New York's State Senator Howard Bayne, a transplanted Southerner, moved in with his wife, the daughter of the Surgeon General of the Confederate States of America, in the aftermath of that bloodiest of wars on North American soil, the War Between the American States.

Since then, dozens of celebrities have whispered their secrets and rehearsed their ambitions within its walls. They've included movie vamps from the silent screen, midnight cowboys, dancers from the dance, *Butterflies in Heat,* a heavyweight boxing champ, writers from every hue, faded film goddesses, playwrights who crafted blockbusters for both Marilyn (Monroe) and Elizabeth (Taylor), *ultra-avant-garde* diarists, every known variety of *prima donna* and *diva,* including some from the world of opera, and a world-class Olympic athlete.

They've also included authors Darwin Porter and Danforth Prince, who spent decades here renovating it and within its walls, producing a stream of FROMMER TRAVEL GUIDES and award-winning celebrity biographies.

Staten Island's Historic Magnolia House
(Volume I)

CELEBRITY & THE IRONIES OF FAME

A Memoir About Travel Guides, Tabloid *Exposés*,
and the Landmark Where They Were Produced

Darwin Porter & Danforth Prince

GLAMOUR, GLITZ, & GOSSIP

AT HISTORIC MAGNOLIA HOUSE

FROM THE SILVER SCREENS OF HOLLYWOOD
TO THE LIGHTS OF BROADWAY,
CELEBRITY SECRETS EXPOSED WITHIN THE WALLS
OF THIS OLD HOUSE

DARWIN PORTER & DANFORTH PRINCE

As depicted above, Volumes One and Two of Blood Moon's Magnolia House Series were conceived as affectionate testimonials to a great American monument, **MAGNOLIA HOUSE,** a nurturing and very tolerant historic home in NYC with a raft of stories to tell—some of them about how it **adapted to America's radically changing tastes, times, circumstances, and values.**

VOLUME ONE (ISBN 978-1-936003-65-5) focuses on its construction by a prominent lawyer during the booming (Northern) economy before the Civil War; its Gilded-Age purchase by the widow of the Surgeon General of the Confederate States of America; and later, its role as a branch office for dozens of travel titles during the heyday of THE FROMMER GUIDES, with detailed insights into the celebrity secrets their reporters (privately, until now) unveiled.

VOLUME TWO (ISBN 978-1-936003-73-0) is an *haute* celebrity romp through the half-century of Broadway, Hollywood, and publishing scandals swirling around Magnolia House's visitors and their frenemies...a "Reporters' Notebook" with everything that arts industry publicists didn't want fans and critics to know about at the time.

Each of these books is a celebration of the fast-disappearing PRE-COVID AMERICAN CENTURY.

And both are available now through internet purveyors worldwide.

BLOOD MOON PRODUCTIONS
Award-Winning Entertainment about America's Legends, Icons, & Celebrities

In reference to Magnolia House's status as an AirBnb, your host, handler, concierge, and problem-solver, **Danforth Prince**, says, "Come with your friends for the night and stay for breakfast.

Even with social distancing, Covid cautiousness, and a lot more 'scrub-a-dub-dubbing,' it's about healing, recuperation, razzmatazz, show-biz, Classic Hollywood, sightseeing, and conversation in the greatest city in the world.

*Stay with Us! Learn more about "Celebrity-Centric Sleepovers" at Blood Moon's **Magnolia House,** a historic and moderately priced "Airbnb" in New York City.*

 **www.AirBnB/H/Magnolia-House**

530

Judy Garland & Liza Minnelli
Too Many Damn Rainbows

Judy and Liza were the greatest, most colorful, and most tragic mother-daughter saga in show biz history. They live, laugh, and weep again in the tear-soaked pages of this remarkable biography. Darwin Porter and Danforth Prince have compiled a compelling "post-modern" spin.

According to Liza, "My mother—hailed as the world's greatest entertainer—lived eighty lives during her short time with us."

Their memorable stories unfold through eyewitness accounts of the typhoons that engulfed them. They swing across glittery landscapes of euphoria and glory, detailing the betrayals and treachery which the duo encountered almost daily. There were depressions "as deep as the Mariana Trench," suicide attempts, and obsessive identifications on deep psychological levels with roles that include Judy's Vicky Lester in *A Star is Born* (1954) and Liza's Sally Bowles in *Cabaret* (1972).

Lesser known are the jealous actress-to-actress rivalries. Fueled by klieg lights and rivers of negative publicity, they sprouted like malevolent mushrooms on steroids.

As Judy faded into the 1960s, Liza roaringly emerged as a star in her own right. "I did it my way," Liza said. She survived the whirlwinds of her mother's drug addiction with a yen for choosing all the wrong men in patterns that weirdly evoked those of Judy herself.

For millions of fans, Judy will forever remain the cheerful adolescent (Dorothy) skipping along a yellow brick road toward the other side of the rainbow. Liza followed her down that hallucinogenic path, searching for the childhood, the security, and the love that eluded her.

Judy Garland, an icon whose memory is permanently etched into the American psyche, continues to thrive as a cult goddess. Revered by thousands of die-hard fans, she's the most poignant example of both the manic and depressive (some say "schizophrenic") sides of the Hollywood myth. A recent film portrayal by Renée Zellweger helped promote and perpetuate her image.

Deep in her 70s, Liza is still with us, too, nursing memories of her former acclaim and her first visit as a little girl to her parents at MGM, the "Dream Factory," during the Golden Age of Hollywood.

Judy Garland & Liza Minnelli: Too Many Damn Rainbows
Darwin Porter & Danforth Prince
Softcover, 6" x 9", with hundreds of photos.   ISBN 9781936003693
Available Everywhere Now

Less than an hour after the discovery of Marilyn Monroe's corpse in Brentwood, a flood of theories, tainted evidence, and conflicting testimonies began pouring out into the public landscape.

Filled with rage, hysteria, and depression, "and fed up with Jack's lies, Bobby's lies," Marilyn sought revenge and mass vindication. Her revelations at an imminent press conference could have toppled political dynasties and destroyed criminal empires. Marilyn had to be stopped...

Into this steamy cauldron of deceit, Marilyn herself emerges as a most unreliable witness during the weeks leading up to her murder. Her own deceptions, vanities, and self-delusion poured toxic accelerants on an already raging fire.

MARILYN: DON'T EVEN DREAM ABOUT TOMORROW
SEX, LIES, MURDER, AND THE GREAT COVER-UP, BY DARWIN PORTER
ISBN 978-1-936003-79-2
A Revised Edition of Darwin Porter's Investigative Classic from 2012
MARILYN AT RAINBOW'S END

"Darwin Porter is fearless, honest and a great read. He minces no words. If the truth makes you wince and honesty offends your sensibility, stay away. It's been said that he deals in muck because he can't libel the dead. Well, it's about time someone started telling the truth about the dead and being honest about just what happened to get us in the mess in which we're in. If libel is lying, then Porter is so completely innocent as to deserve an award. In all of his works he speaks only to the truth, and although he is a hard teacher and task master, he's one we ignore at our peril. To quote Gore Vidal, power is not a toy we give to someone for being good. If we all don't begin to investigate where power and money really are in the here and now, we deserve what we get. Yes, Porter names names. The reader will come away from the book knowing just who killed Monroe. Porter rather brilliantly points to a number of motives, but leaves it to the reader to surmise exactly what happened at the rainbow's end, just why Marilyn was killed. And, of course, why we should be careful of getting exactly what we want. It's a very long tumble from the top."

—ALAN PETRUCELLI, Examiner.com, May 13, 2012

CARRIE FISHER & DEBBIE REYNOLDS
PRINCESS LEIA & UNSINKABLE TAMMY IN HELL

It's history's first comprehensive, unauthorized overview of the greatest mother-daughter act in showbiz history, Debbie Reynolds ("hard as nails and with more balls than any five guys I've ever known") and her talented, often traumatized daughter, Carrie Fisher ("one of the smartest, hippest chicks in Hollywood"). Evolving for decades under the unrelenting glare of public scrutiny, each became a world-class symbol of the social and cinematic tastes that prevailed during their heydays as celebrity icons in Hollywood.

It's a scandalous saga of the ferociously loyal relationship of the "boop-boop-a-doop" girl with her intergalactic STAR WARS daughter, and their iron-willed, "true grit" battles to out-race changing tastes in Hollywood.

Loaded with revelations about "who was doing what to whom" during the final gasps of Golden Age Hollywood, it's an All-American story about the price of glamour, career-related pain, family anguish, romantic betrayals, lingering guilt, and the volcanic shifts that affected a scrappy, mother-daughter team—and everyone else who ever loved the movies.

"Feeling misunderstood by the younger (female) members of your gene pool? This is the Hollywood exposé every grandmother should give to her granddaughter, a roadmap like Debbie Reynolds might have offered to Billie Lourd."

—Marnie O'Toole

"Hold onto your hats, the "bad boys" of Blood Moon Productions are back. This time, they have an exhaustively researched and highly readable account of the greatest mother-daughter act in the history of show business: Debbie Reynolds and Carrie (Princess Leia) Fisher. If celebrity gossip and inside dirt is your secret desire, check it out. This is a fabulous book that we heartily recommend. It will not disappoint. We rate it worthy of four stars."

—MAJ Glenn MacDonald, U.S. Army Reserve (Retired), © MilitaryCorruption.com

"How is a 1950s-era movie star, (TAMMY) supposed to cope with her postmodern, substance-abusing daughter (PRINCESS LEIA), the rebellious, high-octane byproduct of Rock 'n Roll, Free Love, and postwar Hollywood's most scandal-soaked marriage? Read about it here, in Blood Moon's unauthorized double exposé about how Hollywood's toughest (and savviest) mother-daughter team maneuvered their way through shifting definitions of fame, reconciliation, and fortune."

—Donna McSorley

Winner of the coveted "Best Biography" Award from the 2018
New York Book Festival

CARRIE FISHER & DEBBIE REYNOLDS,
UNSINKABLE TAMMY & PRINCESS LEIA IN HELL
Darwin Porter & Danforth Prince

630 pages Softcover with photos. Now online and in bookstores everywhere
ISBN 978-1-936003-57-0

This is What Happens When A Demented Billionaire Hits Hollywood

HOWARD HUGHES
HELL'S ANGEL
BY DARWIN PORTER

From his reckless pursuit of love as a rich teenager to his final days as a demented fossil, Howard Hughes tasted the best and worst of the century he occupied. Along the way, he changed the worlds of aviation and entertainment forever.

This biography reveals inside details about his destructive and usually scandalous associations with other Hollywood players.

'The Aviator flew both ways. Porter's biography presents new allegations about Hughes' shady dealings with some of the biggest names of the 20th century"
   —New York Daily News

"Darwin Porter's access to film industry insiders and other Hughes confidants supplied him with the resources he needed to create a portrait of Hughes that both corroborates what other Hughes biographies have divulged, and go them one better."
   —Foreword Magazine

"Thanks to this bio of Howard Hughes, we'll never be able to look at the old pinups in quite the same way again."
   —The Times (London)

Howard Hughes:
Hell's Angel

America's Notorious Bisexual Billionaire
by Darwin Porter
The Secret Life of the U.S. Emperor

Winner of a respected literary award from the Los Angeles Book Festival, this book gives an insider's perspective about what money can buy
—and what it can't.

814 pages, with photos. **Available everywhere now, online and in bookstores.**

ISBN 978-1-936003-13-6

LANA TURNER

THE SWEATER GIRL, CELLULOID VENUS, SEX NYMPH TO THE G.I.s WHO WON WORLD WAR II, AND HOLLYWOOD'S OTHER MOST NOTORIOUS BLONDE

BEAUTIFUL AND BAD, HER FULL STORY HAS NEVER BEEN TOLD. UNTIL NOW!

Lana Turner was the most scandalous, most copied, and most gossiped-about actress in Hollywood. When her abusive Mafia lover was murdered in her house, every newspaper in the Free World described the murky dramas with something approaching hysteria.

Blood Moon's salacious but empathetic new biography exposes the public and private dramas of the girl who changed the American definition of what it REALLY means to be a blonde.

Here's how CALIFORNIA BOOKWATCH and THE MIDWEST BOOK REVIEW described the mega-celebrity as revealed in this book:

"Lana Turner: Hearts and Diamonds Take All belongs on the shelves of any collection strong in movie star biographies in general and Hollywood evolution in particular, and represents no lightweight production, appearing on the 20th anniversary of Lana Turner's death to provide a weighty survey packed with new information about her life.

"One would think that just about everything to be known about The Sweater Girl would have already appeared in print, but it should be noted that Lana Turner: Hearts and Diamonds Take All offers many new revelations not just about Turner, but about the movie industry in the aftermath of World War II.

"From Lana's introduction of a new brand of covert sexuality in women's movies to her scandalous romances among the stars, her extreme promiscuity, her search for love, and her notorious flings - even her involvement in murder - are all probed in a revealing account of glamour and movie industry relationships that bring Turner and her times to life.

"Some of the greatest scandals in Hollywood history are intricately detailed on these pages, making this much more than another survey of her life and times, and a 'must have' pick for any collection strong in Hollywood history in general, gossip and scandals and the real stories behind them, and Lana Turner's tumultuous career, in particular."

Lana Turner, Hearts & Diamonds Take All
Winner of the coveted "Best Biography" Award from the San Francisco Book Festival

By Darwin Porter and Danforth Prince
Softcover, 622 pages, with photos. ISBN 978-1-936003-53-2
Available everywhere, online and in bookstores.

SCARLETT O'HARA,

Desperately in Love with Heathcliff,

Together on the Road to Hell

Damn You, Scarlett O'Hara

The Private Lives of **Vivien Leigh** and **Laurence Olivier**

by **Darwin Porter** and **Roy Moseley**

Here, for the first time, is a biography that raises the curtain on the secret lives of Lord Laurence Olivier, often cited as the finest actor in the history of England, and Vivien Leigh, who immortalized herself with her Oscar-winning portrayals of Scarlett O'Hara in Gone With the Wind, and as Blanche DuBois in Tennessee Williams' A Streetcar Named Desire.

Dashing and "impossibly handsome," Laurence Olivier was pursued by the most dazzling luminaries, male and female, of the movie and theater worlds.

Lord Olivier's beautiful and brilliant but emotionally disturbed wife (Viv to her lovers) led a tumultuous off-the-record life whose paramours ranged from the A-list celebrities to men she selected randomly off the street. But none of the brilliant roles depicted by Lord and Lady Olivier, on stage or on screen, ever matched the power and drama of personal dramas which wavered between Wagnerian opera and Greek tragedy. Damn You, Scarlett O'Hara is the definitive and most revelatory portrait ever published of the most talented and tormented actor and actress of the 20th century.

Darwin Porter is the principal author of this seminal work.

"The folks over at TMZ would have had a field day tracking Laurence Olivier and Vivien Leigh with flip cameras in hand. Damn You, Scarlett O'Hara can be a dazzling read, the prose unmannered and instantly digestible. The authors' ability to pile scandal atop scandal, seduction after seduction, can be impossible to resist."

—THE WASHINGTON TIMES

DAMN YOU, SCARLETT O'HARA

THE PRIVATE LIFES OF LAURENCE OLIVIER AND VIVIEN LEIGH

Darwin Porter and Roy Moseley

Winner of four distinguished literary awards, this is the best biography of Vivien Leigh and Laurence Olivier ever published, with hundreds of insights into the London Theatre, the role of the Oliviers in the politics of World War II, and the passion, fury, and frustration of their lives together as actors in the West End, on Broadway, and in Hollywood.

ISBN 978-1-936003-15-0   Hardcover, 708 pages, with about a hundred photos.

DONALD TRUMP
IS THE MAN WHO WOULD BE KING

This is the most famous book about our incendiary President you've probably never heard of.

Winner of three respected literary awards, and released three months before the Presidential elections of 2016, it's an entertainingly packaged, artfully salacious bombshell, a scathingly historic overview of America during its 2016 election cycle, a portrait unlike anything ever published on CANDIDATE DONALD and the climate in which he thrived and massacred his political rivals.

Its volcanic, much-suppressed release during the heat and venom of the 2016 Presidential campaign has already been heralded by the Midwestern Book Review, California Book Watch, the Seattle Gay News, the staunchly right-wing WILS-AM radio, and also by the editors at the most popular Seniors' magazine in Florida, BOOMER TIMES, which designated it as their September choice for BOOK OF THE MONTH.

TRUMPOCALYPSE: *"Donald Trump: The Man Who Would Be King* is recommended reading for all sides, no matter what political stance is being adopted: Republican, Democrat, or other.

"One of its driving forces is its ability to synthesize an unbelievable amount of information into a format and presentation which blends lively irony with outrageous observations, entertaining even as it presents eye-opening information in a format accessible to all.

"Politics dovetail with American obsessions and fascinations with trends, figureheads, drama, and sizzling news stories, but blend well with the observations of sociologists, psychologists, politicians, and others in a wide range of fields who lend their expertise and insights to create a much broader review of the Trump phenomena than a more casual book could provide.

"The result is a 'must read' for any American interested in issues of race, freedom, equality, and justice—and for any non-American who wonders just what is going on behind the scenes in this country's latest election debacle."

Diane Donovan, Senior Editor,
California Bookwatch

DONALD TRUMP, THE MAN WHO WOULD BE KING
WINNER OF "BEST BIOGRAPHY" AWARDS FROM BOOK FESTIVALS IN
NEW YORK, CALIFORNIA, AND FLORIDA
by Darwin Porter and Danforth Prince
Softcover, with 822 pages and hundreds of photos. ISBN 978-1-936003-51-8.

Available now from Ingram, Amazon.com, Barnes&Noble.com,
and other purveyors, worldwide.

LINDA LOVELACE

INSIDE LINDA LOVELACE'S DEEP THROAT
DEGRADATION, PORNO CHIC, AND THE RISE OF FEMINISM

THE MOST COMPREHENSIVE BIOGRAPHY EVER WRITTEN OF AN ADULT ENTERTAINMENT STAR, HER TORMENTED RELATIONSHIP WITH HOLLYWOOD'S UNDERBELLY, AND HOW SHE CHANGED FOREVER THE WORLD'S PERCEPTIONS ABOUT CENSORSHIP, SEXUAL BEHAVIOR PATTERNS, AND PORNOGRAPHY.

Darwin Porter, author of more than thirty critically acclaimed celebrity exposés of behind-the-scenes intrigue in the entertainment industry, was deeply involved in the Linda Lovelace saga as it unfolded in the 70s, interviewing many of the players, and raising money for the legal defense of the film's co-star, Harry Reems.

In this book, emphasizing her role as an unlikely celebrity interacting with other celebrities, he brings inside information and a never-before-published revelation to almost every page.

"This book drew me in..How could it not?" Coco Papy, Bookslut.

THE BEACH BOOK FESTIVAL'S GRAND PRIZE WINNER FOR
"BEST SUMMER READING OF 2013"

RUNNER-UP TO "BEST BIOGRAPHY OF 2013" THE LOS ANGELES BOOK FESTIVAL

Another hot and insightful commentary about major and sometimes violently controversial conflicts of the American Century, from Blood Moon Productions.

Inside Linda Lovelace's Deep Throat, by Darwin Porter
Softcover, 640 pages, 6"x9" with photos.
ISBN 978-1-936003-33-4

PINK TRIANGLE

The Feuds and Private Lives of TENNESSEE WILLIAMS, GORE VIDAL, TRUMAN CAPOTE, & Famous Members of their Entourages

Darwin Porter & Danforth Prince

This book, the only one of its kind, reveals the backlot intrigues associated with the literary and script-writing enfants terribles of America's entertainment community during the mid-20th century.

It exposes their bitchfests, their slugfests, and their relationships with the glitterati—Marilyn Monroe, Brando, the Oliviers, the Paleys, U.S. Presidents, a gaggle of other movie stars, millionaires, and international débauchés.

This is for anyone who's interested in the formerly concealed scandals of Hollywood and Broadway, and the values and pretentions of both the literary community and the entertainment industry.

"A banquet... If PINK TRIANGLE had not been written for us, we would have had to research and type it all up for ourselves...Pink Triangle is nearly seven hundred pages of the most entertaining histrionics ever sliced, spiced, heated, and serviced up to the reading public. Everything that Blood Moon has done before pales in comparison.

Given the fact that the subjects of the book themselves were nearly delusional on the subject of themselves (to say nothing of each other) it is hard to find fault. Add to this the intertwined jungle that was the relationship among Williams, Capote, and Vidal, of the times they vied for things they loved most—especially attention—and the times they enthralled each other and the world, [Pink Triangle is] the perfect antidote to the Polar Vortex."
—Vinton McCabe in the NY JOURNAL OF BOOKS

"Full disclosure: I have been a friend and follower of Blood Moon Productions' tomes for years, and always marveled at the amount of information in their books—it's staggering. The index alone to Pink Triangle runs to 21 pages—and the scale of names in it runs like a Who's Who of American social, cultural and political life through much of the 20th century."
—Perry Brass in THE HUFFINGTON POST

"We Brits are not spared the Porter/Prince silken lash either. PINK TRIANGLE's research is, quite frankly, breathtaking. PINK TRIANGLE will fascinate you for many weeks to come. Once you have made the initial titillating dip, the day will seem dull without it."
—Jeffery Tayor in THE SUNDAY EXPRESS (UK)

PINK TRIANGLE—The Feuds and Private Lives of Tennessee Williams, Gore Vidal, Truman Capote, and Famous Members of their Entourages

Darwin Porter & Danforth Prince

Softcover, 700 pages, with photos   ISBN 978-1-936003-37-2   Also Available for E-Readers

THOSE GLAMOROUS GABORS
BOMBSHELLS FROM BUDAPEST

Zsa Zsa, Eva, and Magda Gabor transferred their glittery dreams and gold-digging ambitions from the twilight of the Austro-Hungarian Empire to Hollywood. There, more effectively than any army, these Bombshells from Budapest broke hearts, amassed fortunes, lovers, and A-list husbands, and amused millions of voyeurs through the medium of television, movies, and the social registers. In this astonishing "triple-play" biography, designated "Best Biography of the Year" by the Hollywood Book Festival, Blood Moon lifts the "mink-and-diamond" curtain on this amazing trio of blood-related sisters, whose complicated intrigues have never been fully explored before.

"You will never be Ga-bored...this book gives new meaning to the term compelling. Be warned, Those Glamorous Gabors is both an epic and a pip. Not since Gone With the Wind have so many characters on the printed page been forced to run for their lives for one reason or another. And Scarlett making a dress out of the curtains is nothing compared to what a Gabor will do when she needs to scrap together an outfit for a movie premiere or late-night outing.

"For those not up to speed, Jolie Tilleman came from a family of jewelers and therefore came by her love for the shiny stones honestly, perhaps genetically. She married Vilmos Gabor somewhere around World War 1 (exact dates, especially birth dates, are always somewhat vague in order to establish plausible deniability later on) and they were soon blessed with three daughters: Magda, the oldest, whose hair, sadly, was naturally brown, although it would turn quite red in America; Zsa Zsa (born 'Sari') a natural blond who at a very young age exhibited the desire for fame with none of the talents usually associated with achievement, excepting beauty and a natural wit; and Eva, the youngest and blondest of the girls, who after seeing Grace Moore perform at the National Theater, decided that she wanted to be an actress and that she would one day move to Hollywood to become a star.

"Given that the Gabor family at that time lived in Budapest, Hungary, at the period of time between the World Wars, that Hollywood dream seemed a distant one indeed. The story—the riches to rags to riches to rags to riches again myth of survival against all odds as the four women, because of their Jewish heritage, flee Europe with only the minks on their backs and what jewels they could smuggle along with them in their decolletage, only to have to battle afresh for their places in the vicious Hollywood pecking order—gives new meaning to the term 'compelling.' The reader, as if he were witnessing a particularly gore-drenched traffic accident, is incapable of looking away."

—New York Review of Books

Those Glamorous Gabors, Bombshells from Budapest,
by Darwin Porter & Danforth Prince

Softcover, 730 pages, with hundreds of photos
ISBN 978-1-936003-35-8

BURT REYNOLDS
PUT THE PEDAL TO THE METAL
HOW A NUDE CENTERFOLD SEX SYMBOL SEDUCED HOLLYWOOD

In the 1970s and '80s, Burt Reynolds represented a new breed of movie star: Charming and relentlessly macho, he was a good old Southern boy who made hearts throb and audiences laugh. He was Burt Reynolds, a football hero and a guy you might have shared some jokes with in a redneck bar. After an impressive but tormented career, rivers of negative publicity, a self-admitted history of bad choices, and a spectacular fall from Hollywood grace, he died in Jupiter, Florida, at the age of 82 in September of 2018.

For five years, both in terms of earnings and popularity, he was the number one box office star in the world. *Smokey and the Bandit* (1977) became the biggest-grossing car-chase film of all time. As he put it, perhaps as a means of bolstering his image, "I like nothing better than making love to some of the most beautiful women in the world." Perhaps he was referring to his romantic and sexual involvements with dozens of celebrities from New Hollywood. More unusual dalliances occurred with Marilyn Monroe, whom he once picked up on his way to the Actors Studio in New York City. Love with another VIP came in the form of that "Sweetheart of the G.I.s," Dinah Shore, sparking chatter. "I appreciate older women," he once said in a moment of self-revelation. According to Sally Field, "Burt still lives in my heart." But then she expressed relief that, because of his recent death, he never read what she'd said about him in her memoir.

Men liked him too: He played poker with Frank Sinatra; shared boozy nights with John Wayne; intercepted a "pass" from closeted Spencer Tracy; talked "penis size" with Mark Wahlberg; went "wench-hunting" with Johnny Carson; and threatened to kill Marlon Brando, to whom his appearance was often compared. He also hung out with Bette Davis. ("I always had a thing for her.")

His least happy (some said "most poisonous") marriage—to Loni Anderson—was rife with dramas played out more in the tabloids than in the boudoir. According to Reynolds, "She's vain, she's a rotten mother, she sleeps around, and she spent all my money."

This biography—the first comprehensive overview of the "redneck icon" ever published—reveals the joys and sorrows of a movie star who thrived in, but who was then almost buried by the pressures and insecurities of the New Hollywood. A tribute to "truck stop" America, it's about the accelerated life of a courageous spirit who "Put His Pedal to the Metal" with humor, high jinx, and pizzazz. He predicted his own death: "Soon, I'll be racing a hotrod in Valhalla in my cowboy hat and a pair of aviators." On his tombstone, he wanted it writ: "He was not the best actor in the world, but he was the best Burt Reynolds in the world."

PETER O'TOOLE

HELLRAISER, SEXUAL OUTLAW, IRISH REBEL

At the time of its publication early in 2015, this book was widely publicized in the *Daily Mail,* the *New York Daily News,* the *New York Post,* the *Midwest Book Review, The Express (London), The Globe,* the *National Enquirer,* and in equivalent publications worldwide

One of the world's most admired (and brilliant) actors, Peter O'Toole wined and wenched his way through a labyrinth of sexual and interpersonal betrayals, sometimes with disastrous results. Away from the stage and screen, where such films as *Becket* and *Lawrence of Arabia,* made film history, his life was filled with drunken, debauched nights and edgy sexual experimentations, most of which were never openly examined in the press. A hellraiser, he shared wild times with his "best blokes" Richard Burton and Richard Harris. Peter Finch, also his close friend, once invited him to join him in sharing the pleasures of his mistress, Vivien Leigh.

"My father, a bookie, moved us to the Mick community of Leeds," O'Toole once told a reporter. "We were very poor, but I was born an Irishman, which accounts for my gift of gab, my unruly behavior, my passionate devotion to women and the bottle, and my loathing of any authority figure."

Author Robert Sellers described O'Toole's boyhood neighborhood. "Three of his playmates went on to be hanged for murder; one strangled a girl in a lovers' quarrel; one killed a man during a robbery; another cut up a warden in South Africa with a pair of shears. It was a heavy bunch."

Peter O'Toole's hell-raising life story has never been told, until now. Hot and uncensored, from a writing team which, even prior to O'Toole's death in 2013, had been collecting under-the-radar info about him for years, this book has everything you ever wanted to know about how THE LION navigated his way through the boudoirs of the Entertainment Industry IN WINTER, Spring, Summer, and a dissipated Autumn as well.

Blood Moon has ripped away the imperial robe, scepter, and crown usually associated with this quixotic problem child of the British Midlands. Provocatively uncensored, this illusion-shattering overview of Peter O'Toole's hellraising (or at least very naughty) and demented life is unique in the history of publishing.

PETER O'TOOLE
HELLRAISER, SEXUAL OUTLAW, IRISH REBEL
DARWIN PORTER & DANFORTH PRINCE
Softcover, with photos. ISBN 978-1-936003-45-7

HUMPHREY BOGART
THE MAKING OF A LEGEND

DARWIN PORTER

A "CRADLE-TO-GRAVE" HARDCOVER ABOUT THE RISE TO FAME OF AN
OBSCURE, UNLIKELY, AND FREQUENTLY UNEMPLOYED BROADWAY ACTOR

WITH STARTLING NEW INFORMATION ABOUT BOGART, THE MOVIES, &
GOLDEN AGE HOLLYWOOD

Whereas Humphrey Bogart is always at the top of any list of
the Entertainment Industry's most famous actors, very little
is known about how he clawed his way from Broadway to
Hollywood during Prohibition and the Jazz Age.

This pioneering biography begins with Bogart's origins as
the child of wealthy (morphine-addicted) parents in New
York City, then examines the love affairs, scandals, failures,
and breakthroughs that launched him as an American icon.

It includes details about behind-the-scenes dramas associated with three mysterious marriages, and films such as The
Petrified Forest, The Maltese Falcon, High Sierra, and
Casablanca. Read all about the debut and formative years of
the actor who influenced many generations of filmgoers, laying Bogie's life bare in a style you've come to expect from
Darwin Porter. Exposed with all their juicy details is what
Bogie never told his fourth wife, Lauren Bacall, herself a
screen legend.

Drawn from original interviews with friends and foes who
knew a lot about what lay beneath his trenchcoat, this exposé
covers Bogart's remarkable life as it helped define movie-
making, Hollywood's portrayal of macho, and America's evolving concept of Entertainment itself.

This revelatory book is based on dusty unpublished memoirs, letters, diaries, and often personal interviews from the women—and the men—who adored him.

There are also shocking allegations from colleagues, former friends, and jilted lovers who wanted the
screen icon to burn in hell.

All this and more, much more, in Darwin Porter's exposé of Bogie's startling secret life.

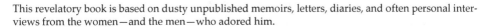

542 PAGES, WITH HUNDREDS OF PHOTOS   ISBN   978-1-936003-14-3

PAUL NEWMAN

THE MAN BEHIND THE BABY BLUES
HIS SECRET LIFE EXPOSED

Drawn from firsthand interviews with insiders who knew Paul Newman intimately, and compiled over a period of nearly a half-century, this is the world's most honest and most revelatory biography about Hollywood's pre-eminent male sex symbol.

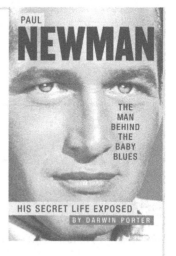

This is a respectful but candid cornucopia of once-concealed information about the sexual and emotional adventures of an affable, impossibly good-looking workaday actor, a former sailor from Shaker Heights, Ohio, who parlayed his ambisexual charm and extraordinary good looks into one of the most successful careers in Hollywood.

Whereas the situations it exposes were widely known within Hollywood's inner circles, they've never before been revealed to the general public.

But now, the full story has been published—the giddy heights and agonizing crashes of a great American star, with revelations and insights never before published in any other biography.

"Paul Newman had just as many on-location affairs as the rest of us, and he was just as bisexual as I was. But whereas I was always getting caught with my pants down, he managed to do it in the dark with not a paparazzo in sight. He might have bedded Marilyn Monroe or Elizabeth Taylor the night before, but he always managed to show up for breakfast with Joanne Woodward, with those baby blues, looking as innocent as a Botticelli angel. He never fooled me. It takes an alleycat to know another one. Did I ever tell you what really happened between Newman and me? If that doesn't grab you, what about what went on between James Dean and Newman? Let me tell you about this co-called model husband if you want to look behind those famous peepers."

—Marlon Brando

JAMES DEAN

TOMORROW NEVER COMES

HONORING THE 60TH ANNIVERSARY OF HIS VIOLENT AND EARLY DEATH

America's most enduring and legendary symbol of young, enraged rebellion, James Dean continues into the 21st Century to capture the imagination of the world.

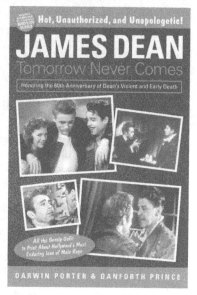

After one of his many flirtations with Death, which caught up with him when he was a celebrity-soaked 24-year-old, he said, "If a man can live after he dies, then maybe he's a great man." Today, bars from Nigeria to Patagonia are named in honor of this international, spectacularly self-destructive movie star icon.

Migrating from the dusty backroads of Indiana to center stage in the most formidable boudoirs of Hollywood, his saga is electrifying.

A strikingly handsome heart-throb, Dean is a study in contrasts: Tough but tender, brutal but remarkably sensitive; he was a reckless hellraiser badass who could revert to a little boy in bed.

A rampant bisexual, he claimed that he didn't want to go through life "with one hand tied behind my back." He demonstrated that during bedroom trysts with Marilyn Monroe, Rock Hudson, Elizabeth Taylor, Paul Newman, Natalie Wood, Shelley Winters, Marlon Brando, Steve McQueen, Ursula Andress, Montgomery Clift, Pier Angeli, Tennessee Williams, Susan Strasberg, Tallulah Bankhead, and FBI director J. Edgar Hoover.

Woolworth heiress Barbara Hutton, one of the richest and most dissipated women of her era, wanted to make him her toy boy.

Tomorrow Never Comes is the most penetrating look at James Dean to have emerged from the wreckage of his Porsche Spyder in 1955.

Before setting out on his last ride, he said, "I feel life too intensely to bear living it."

Tomorrow Never Comes presents a damaged but beautiful soul.

JAMES DEAN—TOMORROW NEVER COMES
DARWIN PORTER & DANFORTH PRINCE
Softcover, with photos. ISBN 978-1-936003-49-5

BLOOD MOON'S RESPECTFUL FAREWELL
TO A GREAT AMERICAN MOVIE STAR

KIRK DOUGLAS
MORE IS NEVER ENOUGH

OOZING MASCULINITY, A YOUNG HORNDOG SETS OUT TO CONQUER HOLLYWOOD AND TO BED ITS LEADING LADIES.

Of the many male stars of Golden Age Hollywood, Kirk Douglas became the final survivor, the last icon of a fabled, optimistic era that the world will never see again. When he celebrated his birthday in 2016, a headline read: LEGENDARY HOLLYWOOD HORNDOG TURNS 100.

He was both a charismatic actor and a man of uncommon force and vigor. His restless and volcanic spirit is reflected both in his films and through his many sexual conquests.

Douglas was the son of Russian-Jewish immigrants, his father a collector and seller of rags. After service in the Navy during World War II, he hit Hollywood, oozing masculinity and charm. Conquering Tinseltown and bedding its leading ladies, he became the personification of the American dream, moving from obscurity and (literally) rags to riches and major-league fame.

The *Who's Who* cast of characters roaring through his life included not only a daunting list of Hollywood goddesses, but the town's most colossal male talents and egos, too. They included his kindred hellraiser and best buddy Burt Lancaster, John Wayne, Henry Fonda, Billy Wilder, Laurence Olivier, Rock Hudson, and a future U.S. President, Ronald Reagan, when winning the highest office in the land was virtually unthinkable.

Over the decades, he immortalized himself in film after film, delivering, like a Trojan, one memorable performance after another. He was at home in *film noir*, as a western gunslinger, as an adventurer (in both ancient and modern sagas), as a juggler, as Tennessee Williams' "gentleman caller," as a Greek super-hero from Homer's *Odyssey*, and as roguish sailor in the Jules Verne yarn, exploring the mysteries of the ocean's depths.

En route to his status as a myth and legend, his performances reflected both his personal pain and the brutalization of the characters he played, too. In *Champion* (1949), he was beaten to a fatal bloody pulp. As the sleazy, heartless reporter in *Ace in the Hole* (1951), he was stabbed with a knife in his gut. As Van Gogh in *Lust for Life* (1956), he writhed in emotional agony and unrequited love before slicing off his ear with a razor. His World War I movie, *Paths of Glory* (1957) grows more profound over the years. He lost an eye in *The Vikings* (1958), and, as the Thracian slave leading a revolt against Roman legions in *Spartacus* (1960), he was crucified.

All of this is brought out, with photos, in this remarkable testimonial to the last hero of Hollywood's cinematic and swashbuckling Golden Age, an inspiring testimonial to the values and core beliefs of an America that's Gone With the Wind, yet lovingly remembered as a time when it, in many ways, was truly great.

KIRK DOUGLAS: MORE IS NEVER ENOUGH

Darwin Porter & Danforth Prince; ISBN 978-1-936003-61-7;   550 pages with photos.
Available everywhere now

Hugh Hefner, the most iconic Playboy in human history, was a visionary, an empire-builder, and a pajama-clad pipe-smoker with a pre-coital grin.

In 1953, he published his first edition of *Playboy* with money borrowed from his puritanical, Nebraska-born mother. Marilyn Monroe appeared on the cover, with her nude calendar inside.

Rebelling against his strict upbringing, he lost his virginity at the age of 22.

His magazine, punctuated with nudes and studded with articles by major literary figures, reached its zenith at eight million readers. As a "tasteful pornographer," Hef became a cultural warrior, fighting government censorship all the way to the U.S. Supreme Court. As the years and his notoriety progressed, he became an advocate of abortion, LGBT equality, and the legalization of pot. Eventually, he engaged in "pubic wars" with Bob Guccione, the flamboyant founder of Penthouse, which cut into Hef's sales.

Lauded by millions of avid readers, he was denounced as "the father of sex addiction," "a huckster," "a lecherous low-brow feeder of our vices," "a misogynist," and, near the end of his life, "a symbol of priapic senility."

During his heyday, some of the biggest male stars in Hollywood, including Warren Beatty, Sammy Davis, Jr., Mick Jagger, and Jack Nicholson, came to frolic behind Hef's guarded walls, stripping nude in the hot tub grotto before sampling the rotating beds upstairs. Even a future U.S. president came to call. "Donald Trump had an appreciation of Bunny tail," Hef said.

Hefner's last Viagra-fueled marriage was to a beautiful blonde, Crystal Harris, 60 years his junior. "There's nothing wrong in a man marrying a girl who could be his great-granddaughter," he was famously quoted as saying.

This ground-breaking biography, the latest in Blood Moon's string of outrageously unvarnished myth-busters, was the first published since Hefner's death at the age of 91 in 2017. It's a provocative saga, rich in tantalizing, often shocking detail. Not recommended for the sanctimonious or the faint of heart, and loaded with ironic, little-known details about the trendsetter's epic challenges, it 's available everywhere NOW.

PLAYBOY'S HUGH HEFNER
EMPIRE OF SKIN
by Darwin Porter and Danforth Prince
978-1-936003-59-4

ONE OF THE 20TH CENTURY'S MOST FASCINATING WOMAN was sired by one of its most widely heralded movie stars. As a precocious but love-starved child raised amid the bizarre abnormalities of Hollywood, Jane Fonda admitted, "I sometimes did naughty things to attract my father's attention."

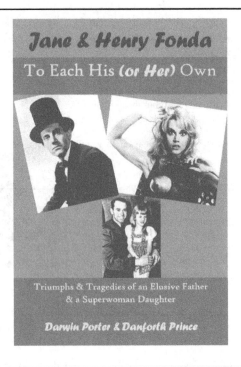

Two of Hollywood's leading biographers turn klieg lights on two emotionally intertwined Oscar winners, the lanky and boyish American hero, **Henry Fonda, and his beautiful daughter Jane,** a political activist and superstar beloved by millions despite her formerly poisonous reputation as "Hanoi Jane."

This book, unlike any other previously published, reflects the private agonies of a father and daughter engulfed by the divisions of their respective generations and the ironies of The American Experience.

JANE AND HENRY FONDA
To Each His (or Her) Own

Coming soon from Ingram and from Amazon.com, worldwide
ISBN 978-1-936003-77-8
Softcover, 450 pages, with hundreds of photos.

CPSIA information can be obtained
at www.ICGtesting.com
Printed in the USA
BVHW060948030621
608728BV00009B/208